THE LAW OF CRIMINAL INVESTIGATIONS

A College Casebook

DR. STEPHANIE LIPSON MIZRAHI
Division of Criminal Justice
California State University, Sacramento

JOSHUA DRESSLER
Michael E. Moritz College of Law
The Ohio State University
Columbus, Ohio

GEORGE C. THOMAS III
Rutgers University School of Law
Newark, New Jersey

WEST ACADEMIC PUBLISHING

444 Cedar Street, Suite 700
St. Paul, MN 55101
1-877-888-1330

Printed in the United States of America

ISBN: 978-1-68328-899-2

Preface

The study of criminal procedure examines a process: the steps that need to be taken to achieve a criminal conviction and impose punishment. This study concentrates especially on the limitations imposed on government when it seeks to subject individuals to the criminal justice system.

The process of criminal investigation, arrest, charging, adjudication, and sentencing is a balancing act (some would say a tightrope walk) between protecting individuals from criminals and protecting individuals from government. This casebook is about finding that balance, a task that is far easier said than done. The balancing point changes over time as society's values and priorities change. The events of September 11 provide a clear example of this.

While we will be seeking this balance point through the study of (mostly) United States Supreme Court cases, the goal of this casebook is not to turn students into criminal lawyers. Instead, we hope simply to introduce students to the many issues surrounding this field and to provide some of the tools needed for students—as both informed citizens and criminal justice professionals—to develop their own positions regarding the ongoing and ever-changing debates about the authority we provide to, and the limitations we place on, our criminal justice system.

This is a casebook. As such, it differs in a number of ways from a typical undergraduate textbook on criminal procedure. Most importantly, as with all casebooks, it relies on the cases themselves, rather than extensive explanatory material, to help students explore this fascinating topic. Without the cases as the main starting point, the students might lose the most important aspect of studying criminal procedure—that these are real world problems facing real world law enforcement officers, real world prosecutors, real world defense counsel, and real world defendants and victims. Cases tell stories and students love a good story. The facts of the case provide the plot or the storyline for students to grasp and use as a lens.

Focusing on the cases, and how the Court's decisions develop over time, helps students understand that the law changes with the historical, political, and cultural context in which it takes place. If there is anything we want students to take away from this work, it is that as future members of the criminal justice system (law enforcement officers, judges, attorneys, legislators, jurors, etc.) they can and will, by the decisions they make over the course of their careers, influence the paths the "law" will take in the future.

This casebook owes its existence to Joshua Dressler and George C. Thomas's Criminal Procedure: Investigating Crime. We are proud to present the college version of that book that is now in its sixth edition. While The Law of Criminal Investigations: A College Casebook maintains the best of its law school predecessor, it has been reworked to appeal to and support the unique needs of undergraduate students in such areas as criminal justice, pre-law, government, and criminology. As such, the college version does a number of things.

- It includes many of the most famous U.S. Supreme Court cases as well as important new cases covering the areas of search and seizure, police interrogation, and the right to counsel during police investigation and trial.
- The cases have been edited to reflect the needs of undergraduate students without overwhelming them with the more detailed, nuanced, and theoretical issues necessary at the law school level.
- Notes and Questions following each case provide context and additional explanations of the relevant issues, discuss related cases that expand on the issues raised in the principal case, and provide problems and hypotheticals for students to work through on their own or through classroom discussion.
- Narratives and new Notes on search incident to lawful arrest, the Katz progeny, the automobile exception, the role of reasonable suspicion and its effect on the warrant requirement, waiver of rights to counsel and silence, and other areas provide students with explanations and context not usually found in traditional law school casebooks.

This college casebook is designed to provide a much-needed balance between maintaining the challenge of the casebook method and meeting the needs of undergraduate and graduate students who may, or may not, be headed to law school.

A casebook cannot be all things to all people, but it should offer sufficient flexibility to accommodate diverse teaching goals and learning styles. We include materials that encourage students to think about constitutional interpretation, judicial decision-making, and criminal justice reform as they read cases and learn doctrine. We believe that students should learn early, and think often, about the overarching principles of the subject matter they are learning, and to critique those principles when they may no longer apply to today's society. In Chapter 1 we display both successes and failures of the criminal process as a way to get students to identify appropriate goals for a criminal process. What is a successful and ideal criminal justice system? Then we invite them to return again and again to those goals to understand, and often critique Supreme Court doctrine. For example, why does the Sixth Amendment require appointed counsel in almost every case while the Fourth Amendment receives a grudging interpretation? We believe this, and many other, interpretational issues are illuminated by considering the importance that a criminal process places on accurate outcomes, a goal that is hopefully advanced when counsel is appointed, but inevitably hindered when limitations are placed in the power of government to seek evidence.

As much as we would like the law to be neutral, we are realistic enough to know that it does not always achieve that goal. At the end of this casebook, we return students to questions of what we wish to achieve via the criminal process by looking at what happens when it goes horribly wrong (See Chapter 10). In addition, we think it important for students to realize the ways in which law fails to achieve neutrality. Thus, we do not skirt—in fact, we confront—the effects of racism and other malignant-isms in the criminal process.

There are multiple ways that professors can use this casebook. We have sought to maintain a balance among the principal cases, narratives, and the Notes and Questions that illuminate or expand on the principal cases. Professors who want to teach the cases can rely on the Notes and Questions to facilitate classroom discussion. Those who like the problem method will find Problems in conjunction with the Notes and Questions to keep a lively class discussion going. And those, who want to blend a case method with a more traditional lecture format will find the book well-suited to that approach. In addition, as with the law school casebook, this college version makes available to instructors the famously useful Teacher's Manual with suggestions for time allocation; coverage priorities; answers to the hypotheticals and Problems; and additional background and context. Also included will be access to an accompanying website that will update the casebook with relevant cases accepted by the U.S. Supreme Court in their upcoming terms and the decisions when handed down, obviating the need for printed supplements between editions.

Outside reading materials. There are many useful sources for additional reading. Among the excellent general resources are Joshua Dressler, Alan C. Michaels, & Ric Simmons, Understanding Criminal Procedure (7th ed. 2017); and Wayne R. LaFave, Jerold H. Israel, Nancy J. King & Orin S. Kerr, Criminal Procedure (6th ed. 2017). For those who want even more coverage of the Fourth Amendment, nothing can compare to Wayne R. LaFave, Search and Seizure (5th ed. 2012), a monumental six-volume treatise. We have also cited and quoted from other excellent books and articles throughout the casebook.

Editing policies. We prefer students to read judicial opinions in largely intact form. Nonetheless, deletions are necessary. Because the goal of this book is pedagogy, we have not followed all scholarly conventions in identifying omissions from the extracted materials. We have applied the following rules of thumb to extracted materials.

1. Most footnotes and citations have been omitted, always without use of ellipses to indicate their omission. Asterisks have been used, however, to indicate deletions of other textual materials.

2. Our "editors' footnotes" are designated by number.

Personal acknowledgments. Many people assisted Dressler and Thomas in producing the law school version of this casebook. We thank them all. Some are named in the Preface to the Sixth Edition of Dressler and Thomas.

Author Mizrahi thanks both her co-authors for an amazing and professionally satisfying experience and for taking a chance on an unknown and relatively inexperienced collaborator. She cannot wait to do it again. She also offers condolences to author Dressler for the Dodger's loss in last year's World Series. It was close. Wait 'till next year.

Authors Dressler and Thomas thank co-author Mizrahi for using our law school casebook, for having the idea to turn it into a college casebook, and for being the principal architect of its revision. We, too, very much enjoyed the collaboration.

Stephanie Mizrahi, J.D., Ph.D.
Division of Criminal Justice
California State University,
Sacramento

Joshua Dressler, J.D.
Michael E. Moritz College of Law
The Ohio State University
Columbus, Ohio

George C. Thomas III, M.F.A.,
J.D., LL.M., S.J.D.
Rutgers University School of Law
Newark, New Jersey

March 2018

Acknowledgments

Vivian O. Berger, *The Supreme Court and Defense Counsel: Old Roads, New Paths—A Dead End?*, 86 Columbia Law Review 9 (1986). Copyright © 1986 by the Directors of the Columbia Law Review Association. This article originally appeared at 86 Colum. L. Rev. 9 (1986). Reprinted by permission.

Craig M. Bradley, *Murray v. United States: The Bell Tolls for the Search Warrant Requirement*, 64 Indiana Law Journal 907 (1989). Copyright ©1989 by the Trustees of Indiana University. Reprinted by permission.

Gerald M. Caplan, *Questioning Miranda*, 38 Vanderbilt Law Review 1417 (1985). Copyright © 1985, Vanderbilt Law Review. Reprinted by permission.

Joshua Dresser & Alan C. Michaels, "From Probable Cause to Reasonable Suspicion: Terry Stops and the Reasonableness of Searches and Seizures, The Terry Doctrine" in Understanding Criminal Procedure (Sixth Edition 2013) (Vol 1). Reprinted from *Understanding Criminal Procedure Vol 1, 6th Ed.* with permission. Copyright 2013 Matthew Bender & Company, Inc., a member of the LexisNexis Group. All rights reserved.

Joshua Dressler & Alan C. Michaels, "Understanding Criminal Procedure" in Understanding Criminal Procedure (Fifth Edition 2010) (Vol 1, § 3.01, pp. 41–43). Reprinted from *Understanding Criminal Procedure Vol 1, 5th Ed.* with permission. Copyright 2013 Matthew Bender & Company, Inc., a member of the LexisNexis Group. All rights reserved.

James Goodman, Excerpts from Stories of Scottsboro by James Goodman. Copyright © 1994 by James E. Goodman. Used by permission of Pantheon Books, an imprint of the Knopf Doubleday Publishing Group, a division of Penguin Random House LLC. All rights reserved.

Bruce A. Green, *Lethal Fiction: The Meaning of "Counsel" in the Sixth Amendment*, 78 Iowa Law Review 433 (1993). Copyright © 1993 by the University of Iowa (Iowa Law Review) (reprinted with permission).

Gerald B. Lefcourt, *Responsibilities of a Criminal Defense Attorney*, 30 Loyola of Los Angeles Law Review (1996). Copyright © 1996, Loyola of Los Angeles Law Review. Reprinted by permission.

Tracey Maclin, *Terry v. Ohio's Fourth Amendment Legacy: Black Men and Police Discretion*, 72 St. John's Law Review 1271 (1998). Copyright © 1998, St. John's Law Review. Reprinted by permission.

John Pfaff, "A Mockery of Justice for the Poor," *New York Times*, April 29, 2016. Reprinted by permission.

Campbell Robertson, "In Louisiana, the Poor Lack Legal Defense," *New York Times*, March 16, 2016. Reprinted by permission.

George C. Thomas III, The Supreme Court on Trial: How the Supreme Court Sacrifices Innocent Defendants (Ann Arbor: The University of Michigan Press). Copyright © 2008, The University of Michigan Press. Reprinted by permission.

Summary of Contents

Table of Contents

Table of Cases

The principal cases are in bold type.

THE LAW OF CRIMINAL INVESTIGATIONS

A COLLEGE CASEBOOK

CHAPTER 1

The Criminal Process: Failures, Choices, and Legitimacy

A. FAILURES

Fear of government is fused deep within the American soul. We were born of a violent revolution against a parliament and king that the colonists viewed as powerful and hostile. When the Articles of Confederation failed, America's leaders constructed a more tightly-knit central government. But the prospect of a federal government, as opposed to a loose coalition of states, reminded many of the yoke that they had just thrown off. The president could become a king, and the Congress could become the feared English parliament. The new central government was hotly debated and barely ratified in the key states of Virginia and New York. Part of the price of ratification was the promise of a Bill of Rights that would protect Americans from government. Today, we tend to think of rights as bestowing individual liberty. While that is true enough, the founders saw the Bill of Rights primarily as a barrier to the government created in the body of the Constitution.

It is difficult for us, over two centuries later, to understand the fear of the looming central government. In colonial times, parliament issued writs of assistance that permitted customs officials to search any house, ship, or warehouse for imported goods on which excise taxes had not been paid. No judge had to be consulted and no probable cause had to be shown. As Americans became increasingly impatient with British rule, these searches were a rallying cry for the revolutionaries. With the writs of assistance and excise searches by British officials still fresh in their minds, the Anti-federalists saw potential abuses of federal power everywhere they looked. Arguing against ratification of the Constitution without a bill of rights, Patrick Henry worried that "any man may be seized, any property may be taken, in the most arbitrary manner, without any evidence or reason. Every thing the most sacred may be searched and ransacked by the strong hand of [federal] power." 3 Elliot's Debates 588 (1836) He also predicted that

> [t]he officers of Congress may come upon you now, fortified with all the terrors of paramount federal authority. Excisemen may come in multitudes; for the limitation of their numbers no man knows. They may, unless the general government be restrained by a bill of rights, or some similar restriction, go into cellars and rooms, and search, ransack, and measure, every thing you eat, drink, and wear.

Id. at 448–49. An anonymous Anti-federalist said in 1787 that excise searches by the federal government would lead "our bed-chambers to be searched by the brutal tools of power." William J. Cuddihy, The Fourth Amendment 678 (2009).

The deep-seated fear of the central government led directly to the drafting and ratification of the Bill of Rights. Early Americans viewed the Bill of Rights as a wall between themselves and the central government. It guaranteed free speech, a free press, and freedom of religion, while forbidding a national religion; it guaranteed a criminal process that is difficult to manipulate; and, in the Ninth and Tenth Amendments, it specifically reserved rights and powers to the people and the States.

> The potential tyrant has been hobbled. The citizens of the States are free to criticize the central government, to petition it, and to close their doors against its agents. Moreover, the prosecutors and judges of the central government can reach the citizens of States only through a rigorous process that includes the right to nonexcessive bail, to trial by juries drawn from the community, to assistance of counsel, and to confront accusers who might not be telling the truth. The Supreme Court comprehends that the Bill of Rights was meant to limit severely the powers of the central government, erecting a formidable wall between the citizens and the government. The Court interprets these provisions to require federal prosecutors to walk through a narrow gate in the wall. The gate is hedged with a series of requirements designed to make convictions more difficult to obtain.

See George C. Thomas III, *When Constitutional Worlds Collide: Resurrecting the Framers' Bill of Rights and Criminal Procedure*, 100 Mich. L. Rev. 145, 149 (2001).

An example of how difficult it was to obtain convictions is the Supreme Court's early intervention in the Aaron Burr case. In 1806, President Jefferson uncovered what he thought was a plot by Burr to invade Mexico, "place himself on its throne," and annex the entire Louisiana Purchase to his empire that would then be far larger than the United States. Jean Edward Smith, John Marshall: Definer of a Nation 353 (1996). Two alleged co-conspirators were arrested and held on charges of treason. The prisoners filed a writ of habeas corpus and asked the Supreme Court to rule on the legality of their detention. Several affidavits were filed in federal court alleging the details of the plot. But the Supreme Court held that the most the affidavits showed was a conspiracy to commit treason, rather than treason, and ordered the prisoners released because the government had charged treason and not conspiracy to commit treason. Ex parte Bollman & Ex parte Swartwout, 8 U.S. (4 Cranch.) 75, 2 L.Ed. 554 (1807). It is easy for us today to dismiss Burr's plans as a fantasy, but the Republic was barely twenty years old, most of North America was unsettled by Europeans, and Burr was a charismatic politician befriended by ambitious military generals. Ordering the release of two admitted conspirators was both a brave act on the part of Chief Justice Marshall's Court and a demonstration of the barrier that the Bill of Rights posed to federal power.

But the Bill of Rights did not restrain the state governments. See Barron v. Baltimore, 32 U.S. (7 Pet.) 243, 8 L.Ed. 672 (1833). As the United States careened toward the Civil War and its aftermath, state governments replaced the federal government as the principal threat to liberty and privacy. This would, of course, eventually lead to the Civil War Amendments that included the rights to due process and equal protection that directly limited state power. Initially, however, the Court interpreted the Fourteenth Amendment narrowly. See, e.g., Slaughter-House Cases, 83 U.S. (16 Wall.) 36, 21 L.Ed. 394 (1873) (holding that the privileges and immunities clause protected only rights that existed *by virtue of national citizenship*, which did not include the rights guaranteed in the Bill of Rights). This narrow compass of the Fourteenth Amendment permitted states to deny rights that existed against the federal government. These denials of liberty might be viewed as failures of state criminal processes.

BROWN V. MISSISSIPPI

Supreme Court of the United States, 1936.
297 U.S. 278, 56 S.Ct. 461, 80 L.Ed. 682.

Four catastrophic failures of state criminal processes caught the public's attention in the first decades of the twentieth century. We begin with perhaps the most outrageous failure of due process in American history.

Can you identify anything that could be consider a success with this case? Ask yourself the same question when you read *Powell v. Alabama* below.

MR. CHIEF JUSTICE HUGHES delivered the opinion of the Court [joined by JUSTICES VAN DEVANTER, MCREYNOLDS, BRANDEIS, SUTHERLAND, BUTLER, STONE, ROBERTS, AND CARDOZO].

The question in this case is whether convictions, which rest solely upon confessions shown to have been extorted by officers of the State by brutality and violence, are consistent with the due process of law required by the Fourteenth Amendment of the Constitution of the United States.

Petitioners were indicted for the murder of one Raymond Stewart, whose death occurred on March 30, 1934. They were indicted on April 4, 1934, and were then arraigned and pleaded not guilty. Counsel were appointed by the court to defend them. Trial was begun the next morning and was concluded on the following day, when they were found guilty and sentenced to death.

Aside from the confessions, there was no evidence sufficient to warrant the submission of the case to the jury. After a preliminary inquiry, testimony as to the confessions was received over the objection of defendants' counsel. Defendants then testified that the confessions were false and had been procured by physical torture. The case went to the jury with instructions, upon the request of defendants' counsel, that if the jury had reasonable doubt as to the confessions having resulted from coercion, and that they were not true, they were not to be considered as evidence. On their appeal to the Supreme Court of the State, defendants assigned as error the inadmissibility of the confessions. The judgment was affirmed.

Defendants then moved in the Supreme Court of the State to arrest the judgment and for a new trial on the ground that all the evidence against them was obtained by coercion and brutality known to the court and to the district attorney, and that defendants had been denied the benefit of counsel or opportunity to confer with counsel in a reasonable manner. The motion was supported by affidavits. At about the same time, defendants filed in the Supreme Court a "suggestion of error" explicitly challenging the proceedings of the trial, in the use of the confessions and with respect to the alleged denial of representation by counsel, as violating the due process clause of the Fourteenth Amendment of the Constitution of the United States. The state court entertained the suggestion of error, considered the federal question, and decided it against defendants' contentions. Two judges dissented. * * *

The grounds of the decision were (1) that immunity from self-incrimination is not essential to due process of law, and (2) that the failure of the trial court to exclude the confessions after the introduction of evidence showing their incompetency, in the absence of a request for such exclusion, did not deprive the defendants of life or liberty without due process of law; and that even if the trial court had erroneously overruled a motion to exclude the confessions, the ruling would have been mere error reversible on appeal, but not a violation of constitutional right.

The opinion of the state court did not set forth the evidence as to the circumstances in which the confessions were procured. That the evidence established that they were procured by coercion was not questioned. The state court said: "After the state closed its case on the merits, the appellants, for the first time, introduced evidence from which it appears that the confessions were not made voluntarily but were coerced." There is no dispute as to the facts upon this point, and as they are clearly and adequately stated in the dissenting opinion of Judge Griffith (with whom Judge Anderson concurred)—showing both the extreme brutality of the measures to extort the confessions and the participation of the state authorities—we quote this part of his opinion in full, as follows:

"The crime with which these defendants, all ignorant negroes, are charged, was discovered about one o'clock p.m. on Friday, March 30, 1934. On that night one Dial, a deputy sheriff, accompanied by others, came to the home of Ellington, one of the defendants, and requested him to accompany them to the house of the deceased, and there a number of white men were gathered, who began to accuse the defendant of the crime. Upon his denial they seized him, and with the participation of the deputy they hanged him by a rope to the limb of a tree, and having let him down, they hung him again, and when he was let down the second time, and he still protested his innocence, he was tied to a tree and whipped, and still declining to accede to the demands that he confess, he was finally released and he returned with some difficulty to his home, suffering intense pain and agony. The record of the testimony shows that the signs of the rope on his neck were plainly visible during the so-called trial. A day or two thereafter the said deputy, accompanied by another, returned to the home of the said defendant and arrested him, and departed with the prisoner towards the jail in an adjoining county, but went by a route which led into the State of Alabama; and while on the way, in that State, the deputy stopped and again severely whipped the defendant, declaring that he would continue the whipping until he confessed, and the defendant then agreed to confess to such a statement as the deputy would dictate, and he did so, after which he was delivered to jail.

"The other two defendants, Ed Brown and Henry Shields, were also arrested and taken to the same jail. On Sunday night, April 1, 1934, the same deputy, accompanied by a number of white men, one of whom was also an officer, and by the jailer, came to the jail, and the two last named defendants were made to strip and they were laid over chairs and their backs were cut to pieces with a leather strap with buckles on it, and they were likewise made by the said deputy definitely to understand that the whipping would be continued unless and until they confessed, and not only confessed, but confessed in every matter of detail as demanded by those present; and in this manner the defendants confessed the crime, and as the whippings progressed and were repeated, they changed or adjusted their confession in all particulars of detail so as to conform to the demands of their torturers. When the confessions had been obtained in the exact form and contents as desired by the mob, they left with the parting admonition and warning that, if the defendants changed their story at any time in any respect from that last stated, the perpetrators of the outrage would administer the same or equally effective treatment.

"Further details of the brutal treatment to which these helpless prisoners were subjected need not be pursued. It is sufficient to say that in pertinent respects the transcript reads more like pages torn from some medieval account, than a record made within the confines of a modern civilization which aspires to an enlightened constitutional government.

"All this having been accomplished, on the next day, that is, on Monday, April 2, when the defendants had been given time to recuperate somewhat from the tortures to which they had been subjected, the two sheriffs, one of the county where the crime was committed, and the other of the county of the jail in which the prisoners were confined, came to the jail, accompanied by eight other persons, some of them deputies, there to hear the free and voluntary confession of these miserable and abject defendants. The sheriff of the county of the crime admitted that he had heard of the whipping, but averred that he had no personal knowledge of it. He admitted that one of the defendants, when brought before him to confess, was limping and did not sit down, and that this particular defendant then and there stated that he had been strapped so severely that he could not sit down, and as already stated, the signs of the rope on the neck of another of the defendants were plainly visible to all. Nevertheless the solemn farce of hearing the free and voluntary confessions was gone through with, and these two sheriffs and one other person then present were the three witnesses used in court to establish the so-called confessions, which were received by the court and admitted in evidence over the objections of the defendants duly entered of record as each of the said three witnesses delivered their alleged testimony. There was thus enough before the court when these confessions were first offered to make known to the court that they were not, beyond all reasonable doubt, free and voluntary; and the failure of the court then to exclude the confessions is sufficient to reverse the judgment, under every rule of procedure that has heretofore been prescribed, and hence it was not necessary subsequently to renew the objections by motion or otherwise.

"The spurious confessions having been obtained—and the farce last mentioned having been gone through with on Monday, April 2d—the court, then in session, on the following day, Tuesday, April 3, 1934, ordered the grand jury to reassemble on the succeeding day, April 4, 1934, at nine o'clock, and on the morning of the day last mentioned the grand jury returned an indictment against the defendants for murder. Late that afternoon the defendants were brought from the jail in the adjoining county and arraigned, when one or more of them offered to plead guilty, which the court declined to accept, and, upon inquiry whether they had or desired counsel, they stated that they had none, and did not suppose that counsel could be of any assistance to them. The court thereupon appointed counsel, and set the case for trial for the following morning at nine o'clock, and the defendants were returned to the jail in the adjoining county about thirty miles away.

"The defendants were brought to the courthouse of the county on the following morning, April 5th, and the so-called trial was opened, and was concluded on the next day, April 6, 1934, and resulted in a pretended conviction with death sentences. The evidence upon which the conviction was obtained was the so-called confessions. Without this evidence a peremptory instruction to find for the defendants would have been inescapable. The defendants were put on the stand, and by their testimony the facts and the details thereof as to the manner by which the confessions were extorted from them were fully developed, and it is further disclosed by the record that the same deputy, Dial, under whose guiding hand and active participation the tortures to coerce the confessions were administered, was actively in the performance of the supposed duties of a court deputy in the courthouse and in the presence of the prisoners during what is denominated, in complimentary terms, the trial of these defendants. This deputy was put on the stand by the state in rebuttal, and admitted the whippings. It is interesting to note that in his testimony with reference to the whipping of the defendant Ellington, and in response to the inquiry as to how severely he was whipped, the deputy stated, 'Not too much for a negro; not as much as I would have done if it were left to me.' Two others who had participated in these whippings were introduced and admitted it—not a single witness was introduced who denied it. The facts are not only undisputed, they are admitted, and admitted to have been done by officers of the state, in conjunction with other participants, and all this was definitely well known to everybody connected with the trial, and during the trial, including the state's prosecuting attorney and the trial judge presiding." * * *

The State is free to regulate the procedure of its courts in accordance with its own conceptions of policy, unless in so doing it "offends some principle of justice so rooted in the traditions and conscience of our people as to be ranked as fundamental." The State may abolish trial by jury. It may dispense with indictment by a grand jury and substitute complaint or information. But the freedom of the State in establishing its policy is the freedom of constitutional government and is limited by the requirement of due process of law. Because a State may dispense with a jury trial, it does not follow that it may substitute trial by ordeal. The rack and torture chamber may not be substituted for the witness stand. The State may not permit an accused to be hurried to conviction under mob domination—where the whole proceeding is but a mask—without supplying corrective process. The State may not deny to the accused the aid of counsel. *Powell v. Alabama*, [p. 15]. Nor may a State, through the action of its officers, contrive a conviction through the pretense of a trial which in truth is "but used as a means of depriving a defendant of liberty through a deliberate deception of court and jury by the presentation of testimony known to be perjured." And the trial equally is a mere pretense where the state authorities have contrived a conviction resting solely upon confessions obtained by violence. The due process clause requires "that state action, whether through one agency or another, shall be consistent with the fundamental principles of liberty and justice which lie at the base of all our civil and political institutions." It would be difficult to conceive of methods more revolting to the sense of justice than those taken to procure the confessions of these petitioners, and the use of the confessions thus obtained as the basis for conviction and sentence was a clear denial of due process.

2. It is in this view that the further contention of the State must be considered. That contention rests upon the failure of counsel for the accused, who had objected to the admissibility of the confessions, to move for their exclusion after they had been introduced and the fact of coercion had been proved. It is a contention which proceeds upon a misconception of the nature of petitioners' complaint. That complaint is not of the commission of mere error, but of a wrong so fundamental that it made the whole proceeding a mere pretense of a trial and rendered the conviction and sentence wholly void. We are not concerned with a

mere question of state practice, or whether counsel assigned to petitioners were competent or mistakenly assumed that their first objections were sufficient. In an earlier case the Supreme Court of the State had recognized the duty of the court to supply corrective process where due process of law had been denied. * * * [T]he court said: "Coercing the supposed state's criminals into confessions and using such confessions so coerced from them against them in trials has been the curse of all countries. It was the chief iniquity, the crowning infamy of the Star Chamber, and the Inquisition, and other similar institutions. The constitution recognized the evils that lay behind these practices and prohibited them in this country. * * * The duty of maintaining constitutional rights of a person on trial for his life rises above mere rules of procedure and wherever the court is clearly satisfied that such violations exist, it will refuse to sanction such violations and will apply the corrective."

In the instant case, the trial court was fully advised by the undisputed evidence of the way in which the confessions had been procured. The trial court knew that there was no other evidence upon which conviction and sentence could be based. Yet it proceeded to permit conviction and to pronounce sentence. The conviction and sentence were void for want of the essential elements of due process, and the proceeding thus vitiated could be challenged in any appropriate manner. It was challenged before the Supreme Court of the State by the express invocation of the Fourteenth Amendment. That court entertained the challenge, considered the federal question thus presented, but declined to enforce petitioners' constitutional right. The court thus denied a federal right fully established and specially set up and claimed and the judgment must be

Reversed.

NOTES AND QUESTIONS

1. The Court in 1936 was loath to meddle in state criminal procedure. But how could the Court have done anything other than reverse the Mississippi courts on the outrageous facts of *Brown*? A more difficult question is how could the state supreme court have affirmed the convictions. How did the state court justify that conclusion? Does the argument seem plausible?

2. Notice that the Court drew the facts of the coercion/torture exclusively from the dissent in the Mississippi Supreme Court. Why do you think the Court did this?

3. Whenever some historical fact seems unbelievable—the deputies' conduct and the state court's opinion in Brown, for example—we should seek to recover what

might have been different about that historic period. Consider this observation about *Powell v. Alabama*, a case from the same period that we will read in a moment: "If all of this seems extraordinary to modern eyes, one must remember that for white southerners defending mob-dominated trials, the relevant comparison was to lynchings rather than to elaborate court proceedings accompanied by all the trappings of due process." Michael Klarman, *The Racial Origins of Modern Criminal Procedure*, 99 Mich. L. Rev. 48, 56 (2000). Would it be fair to say that the defendants in *Brown* should be thankful for the torture because their confessions led to a court case rather than a lynching?

4. *Brown: the rest of the story*. Are you surprised to learn that, upon remand from the United States Supreme Court, the three defendants in *Brown* accepted plea bargains rather than risk a retrial? They served from three to seven years in prison. Klarman, *supra*, at 82.

Are you surprised to learn that the prosecutor in *Brown* later served forty-two years as a United States senator? He was John Stennis, who ran for office in Mississippi thirteen times and never lost. See https://stennis.gov/senator-john-c-stennis/.

5. Racism, of course, is not limited to the South. Consider the New York City Draft Riots, which raged for five days in July of 1863. The riots were touched off by working-class hostility to the military draft, from which the affluent could purchase an exemption for a $300 fee. While rioters initially concentrated on institutions associated with the draft (the government, the elite, capitalism, and the Republican Party), the mob's rage soon expanded to New York's African-American population, which the rioters saw as competition for scarce employment. The Colored Orphan Asylum, located at Fifth Avenue and Forty-third Street, was burned and looted, although most of the children were safely evacuated. One little girl was killed after the mob found her hiding under a bed.

One newspaper reported, "A perfect reign of terror exists in the quarters of this helpless people, and if the troubles which now agitate our city continue during the week it is believed that not a single negro will remain within the metropolitan limits." New York Herald, July 15, 1863. Peter Houston, a Mohawk Indian, was mistaken for an African-American and beaten to death. Just off the Bowery, one crowd set fire to a building where African-Americans lived, waited for their victims to fall from the eaves of the rooftop, and beat them to death. Ann Derrickson, a white woman married to an African-American, was beaten by the mob as she saved her son's life. She died of her wounds. On Eighth Avenue, the mob re-strung the bodies of its African-American victims from lampposts after the authorities had come by and cut them down. Mobs also looted and burned the homes of whites who offered African-Americans safe-harbor, as well as businesses that catered to a racially mixed clientele.

The Union Army arrived from Gettysburg, where ten days earlier it had defeated Lee's Army of Northern Virginia, and put down the uprising. In the aftermath, New York's African-American population shrank by as much as a quarter. Many left for Hoboken, the outer boroughs, and the suburbs. See James McCague, The Second Rebellion: The Story of the New York City Draft Riots of 1863 (1968); see also Racial Violence in the United States, Allen D, Grimshaw, ed. (1968) at 37–42.

The state due process failure that attracted the most national attention was Powell v. Alabama, 287 U.S. 45, 53 S.Ct. 55, 77 L.Ed. 158 (1936), which occurred three years before *Brown.* Professor James Goodman wrote a book about the case. After the Goodman excerpt, you will read an edited version of *Powell.* Be warned that some of the language in the Goodman excerpt, while historically accurate, is raw and offensive.

The story of Scottsboro begins with a train from Chattanooga to Memphis that passed through northern Alabama on March 25, 1931. Nine young black men and several young white men were riding the freight train illegally. Four of the blacks were friends who had gotten on the train in Chattanooga. The black and white youths got into a fight, and the black youths "chased or threw" all but one of the whites from the train shortly after it pulled away from a station. At the next stop, Paint Rock, dozens of white men armed with pistols, rifles, and shotguns grabbed the blacks, "tied them to one another with a plow line," put them on a flatbed truck, and drove them to the jail in Scottsboro. A deputy told them they were being held on assault and attempted murder charges.

JAMES GOODMAN—STORIES OF SCOTTSBORO

(1995) 4–6, 13–16, 19, 21–23.

They were in jail for hours before they found out that there would be another charge. Not until the guards took them out of their cell and lined them up against a wall and the sheriff brought two white women by and asked them to point to the boys who had "had them" did they realize that they had been accused of rape. One of the women, Victoria Price, pointed to six of them. When the other didn't say a word, a guard said that "If those six had Miss Price, it stands to reason that the others had Miss Bates." The boys protested, insisting they hadn't touched the women, hadn't even seen them before Paint Rock, when they saw them being led away from the train. Clarence Norris called the women liars. One of the guards struck him with his bayonet, cutting to the bone the hand that Norris put up to shield his face. "Nigger," the guard hollered, "you know damn well how to talk about white women."

"I was scared before," Norris recalled years later, "but it wasn't nothing to how I felt now. I knew if a white woman accused a black man of rape, he was as good as dead. My hand was bleeding like I don't know what * * * but I didn't even think about it. All I could think was that I was going to die for something that I had not done." * * *

Without some luck they would have been dead already. The night they were arrested they were nearly lynched by several hundred "crackers" who had gathered around the old, dilapidated two-story jail as the news of the arrest spread through the hills of Scottsboro and the neighboring towns. The men leading the mob threatened to break down the doors if the sheriff wouldn't let them in or let the "niggers" out. The boys could hear their voices through the window of their cell. * * *

They were saved by the Jackson County sheriff, M. L. Wann, who, unable to disperse the crowd, called the governor of Alabama, Benjamin Meeks Miller, who, in turn, called the National Guard. But the boys had no way of knowing that the National Guardsmen, white men with guns, distinguishable only by their uniforms from the men threatening to hang them, were not part of the lynching bee. Nor in the weeks that followed that sleepless night could they ever be certain that the guardsmen would protect them from the crowds that gathered every time they were moved from one prison to another or back and forth between prison and court. Men with uniforms had beaten or threatened them in every jail they had been in. * * *

Everything white Alabamans heard or read in the next few days confirmed the story that spread from Paint Rock and Scottsboro the day the posse stopped the train. The day after the arrest, newspapers reported that Price and Bates had identified the Negroes who had attacked them and that all of the Negroes had either confessed or been implicated by the others. Editors repeated these stories in every piece they ran about the case for a week; local reporters and editors, who lived in Scottsboro, Paint Rock, Huntsville, and Decatur and worked as stringers for the Associated Press, wrote the dispatches that the wire service carried all over the South, the first drafts of the newspaper articles most people read.

On April 6, twelve days after the crime, Judge A. E. Hawkins called the Jackson County Court to order. Three days in a row Price and Bates told their story to four different juries, and to a standing-room-only audience, from which women of all ages and men under twenty-one were excluded. At recess and adjournments the audience passed the story on to the crowd outside; reporters rushed to the nearest phone or telegraph office, ensuring that highlights of the testimony made the front pages of papers published later the same day. The white audience listened to Price and Bates tell the white jurors how all nine of the defendants held knives at their throats, pinned down their legs, tore off their clothes, and raped them.

"There were six to me," Price told the jury in the first trial, "and three to her, and three of hers got away. It took three of them to hold me. One was holding my legs and the other had a knife to my throat while the other one ravished me. It took three of those negroes to hold me. It took two to hold me while one had intercourse. The one sitting behind [the] defendants' counsel took my overalls off. My step-ins were torn off. * * * This negro boy tore them off. He held me while he took them off. Six of them had intercourse with me. The one sitting there was the first one. I don't know the name of the next one. * * * I know them when I see them. I can surely point out the next one. Yonder he sits, yonder. That boy had intercourse with me. The third one was the little bit of one; yonder he is. He held my legs while this one and that one ravished me and then he took my legs again." In what seemed like two or three hours, each of them was raped six times. They begged the Negroes to quit but the men ignored them, and even after they finished they stayed in the car with them, "telling us they were going to take us north and make us their women or kill us." * * *

Writers and editors all over the region agreed that it was the most atrocious crime ever recorded in that part of the country, perhaps in the whole United States, "a wholesale debauching of society * * * so horrible in its details that all the facts could never be printed," a "heinous and unspeakable crime" that "savored of the jungle, the way back dark ages of meanest African corruption." They were revolted by the story, but not surprised. Or if surprised, surprised only by the magnitude of the crime. They expected black men to rape white women. Blacks were savages, more savage, many argued (with scientific theories to support them), than they had been as slaves. Savages with an irrepressible sex drive and an appetite for white women. They were born rapists, rapists by instinct; given the chance, they struck. Two white women swore that they had been raped. Even if all nine of the boys had denied it and told the same story it is likely they would have been convicted; accusations much less serious and less substantiated had condemned black men. Bates and Price charged rape. Most of the boys denied it.[a] There was no question in anyone's mind about whom to believe. * * *

Victoria Price and Ruby Bates knew two versions of the events on that freight train, and they told one of them to the sheriff's deputies, local reporters, solicitor, judge, and jurors. In search of work, they had traveled to Chattanooga the only way they could afford. They had no luck in Chattanooga, and much worse luck

---

[a] Two of the defendants, Wright and Patterson, testified on at least one occasion that some of the defendants (not they or their Chattanooga friends) had had intercourse with the women. Goodman, at 14–15.

on their way home, when they were brutally assaulted and repeatedly raped by nine black men. Had the posse not stopped the train in Paint Rock, the Negroes would have raped them again, or killed them, or taken them up north. "When I saw them nab those Negroes," Price told reporters, "I sure was happy. Mister, I never had a break in my life. Those Negroes have ruined me and Ruby forever. The only thing I ask is that they give them all the law allows." * * *

Price and Bates worked in the worst mills. They came from families that had been battered by underemployment and poverty in the best of times. They had meager schooling if any at all. They lived with their mothers in unpainted wooden shacks in the worst sections of town. Bates's family was the only white family on their block, and their block was in the Negro section of town.

Their lives mocked the white South's most sacred ideal. More prosperous southerners liked to boast that the color line extended from the top to the bottom of southern society, and often it did. Yet no one who looked carefully could fail to notice that by the time it reached cities like Huntsville it was frayed beyond repair. Price and Bates lived among black people, played with them as children, roamed the streets with them as teenagers, bootlegged liquor and got drunk with them as young adults. They also went out with them, slept with them, fell in and out of love with them, apparently unaware of the widespread wishful thinking that made it possible for many white southerners to call all sex between white women and black men rape. No white woman, one Mississippi editor put it, no matter how degraded or depraved, would ever willingly "bestow her favors on a black man." Price and Bates had heard the words *white supremacy*, *segregation*, and *white womanhood*, but they did not live by them. In the eyes of "respectable" southern whites, Price and Bates had sunk as low as two women with white skin could sink. Perhaps lower. One frustrated Huntsville social worker complained that the whites in the mill villages were "as bad as the niggers."

Until they were thought to have been raped. When sheriff's deputies found Price and Bates alongside the train at Paint Rock and realized they had been on it alone with the Negroes who had thrown the white boys off, their first thought was of rape. Later, no one could say for sure what came first, Price and Bates's accusation or the sheriff's interrogation. Some said that the girls had offered the charge without encouragement; others said that they had said nothing about an assault until a deputy asked if the Negroes had bothered them. Either way, Price and Bates were not deluded. They knew that the black youths had not raped them or bothered them in any way.[b] But they also knew that if they had said nothing or

---

[b] That Ruby Bates was lying when she testified that the defendants raped her is not open to serious doubt. She admitted in a letter dated January 5, 1932 that "those Negroes did not touch me or those white

no—"No, those Negroes didn't even speak to us"—the people who asked would have thought of them the way respectable white men and women had always thought of them: as the lowest of the low, vagabonds, adulterers, bootleggers, tramps. If, on the other hand, they complained or said yes, the same people would suddenly have thought of them as rape victims and treated them as white southern women, poor but virtuous, for the first time in their lives. It was a rare opportunity, and the choice was not a hard one for them to make. * * *

On the witness stand there were all sorts of things about the trip to Chattanooga and the rape that Bates could not remember. She contradicted herself when asked whether she and Price had known the white boys on the train or traveled with them the day before. And unlike Price, she couldn't say positively which of the defendants had raped her, which ones had raped Price, or in what order. But considering what she had gone through, neither juries nor spectators held her bad memory against her; she got the most important part of the story right. She remembered clearly that two of the Negroes had guns and the rest had knives and that after chasing the white boys off the train they had thrown them down in the gondola, held knives at their throats, and raped each of them six times. * * *

POWELL V. ALABAMA

Supreme Court of the United States, 1932.
287 U.S. 45, 53 S.Ct. 55, 77 L.Ed. 158.

As you read this case, ask yourself how the Alabama Supreme Court could have affirmed these convictions and how two justices on the United States Supreme Court could dissent? Note, especially, the theories underlying Justice Butler's dissent. Also ask yourself how the Court hoped its decision in *Powell* would improve Southern justice going forward?

MR. JUSTICE SUTHERLAND delivered the opinion of the Court [joined by CHIEF JUSTICE HUGHES AND JUSTICES VAN DEVANTER, BRANDEIS, STONE, ROBERTS and CARDOZO].

These cases were argued together and submitted for decision as one case.

The petitioners, hereinafter referred to as defendants, are negroes charged with the crime of rape, committed upon the persons of two white girls. The crime is said to have been committed on March 25, 1931. The indictment was returned

---

boys." Goodman, 195. Though she later recanted the letter, under police threat of one hundred days on the chain gang, *id.* at 195, she testified in a subsequent trial that "the defendants did not rape, touch, or even speak to her and Victoria." *Id.* at 132. Despite this testimony, it took the jury only moments to vote unanimously to convict (it took eleven hours to persuade one juror to vote for the death penalty). *Id.* at 145.

in a state court of first instance on March 31, and the record recites that on the same day the defendants were arraigned and entered pleas of not guilty. There is a further recital to the effect that upon the arraignment they were represented by counsel. But no counsel had been employed, and aside from a statement made by the trial judge several days later during a colloquy immediately preceding the trial, the record does not disclose when, or under what circumstances, an appointment of counsel was made, or who was appointed. During the colloquy referred to, the trial judge, in response to a question, said that he had appointed all the members of the bar for the purpose of arraigning the defendants and then of course anticipated that the members of the bar would continue to help the defendants if no counsel appeared. Upon the argument here both sides accepted that as a correct statement of the facts concerning the matter.

There was a severance upon the request of the state, and the defendants were tried in three several groups, as indicated above. As each of the three cases was called for trial, each defendant was arraigned, and, having the indictment read to him, entered a plea of not guilty. Whether the original arraignment and pleas were regarded as ineffective is not shown. Each of the three trials was completed within a single day. Under the Alabama statute the punishment for rape is to be fixed by the jury, and in its discretion may be from ten years imprisonment to death. The juries found defendants guilty and imposed the death penalty upon all. The trial court overruled motions for new trials and sentenced the defendants in accordance with the verdicts. The judgments were affirmed by the state supreme court. Chief Justice Anderson thought the defendants had not been accorded a fair trial and strongly dissented.

In this court the judgments are assailed upon the grounds that the defendants, and each of them, were denied due process of law and the equal protection of the laws, in contravention of the Fourteenth Amendment, specifically as follows: (1) they were not given a fair, impartial and deliberate trial; (2) they were denied the right of counsel, with the accustomed incidents of consultation and opportunity of preparation for trial; and (3) they were tried before juries from which qualified members of their own race were systematically excluded. These questions were properly raised and saved in the courts below.

The only one of the assignments which we shall consider is the second, in respect of the denial of counsel; and it becomes unnecessary to discuss the facts of the case or the circumstances surrounding the prosecution except in so far as they reflect light upon that question. * * *

* * * The record does not disclose [defendants'] ages, except that one of them was nineteen; but the record clearly indicates that most, if not all, of them were

youthful, and they are constantly referred to as "the boys." They were ignorant and illiterate. All of them were residents of other states, where alone members of their families or friends resided.

However guilty defendants, upon due inquiry, might prove to have been, they were, until convicted, presumed to be innocent. It was the duty of the court having their cases in charge to see that they were denied no necessary incident of a fair trial. With any error of the state court involving alleged contravention of the state statutes or constitution we, of course, have nothing to do. The sole inquiry which we are permitted to make is whether the federal Constitution was contravened; and as to that, we confine ourselves, as already suggested, to the inquiry whether the defendants were in substance denied the right of counsel, and if so, whether such denial infringes the due process clause of the Fourteenth Amendment.

First. The record shows that immediately upon the return of the indictment defendants were arraigned and pleaded not guilty. Apparently they were not asked whether they had, or were able to employ, counsel, or wished to have counsel appointed; or whether they had friends or relatives who might assist in that regard if communicated with. That it would not have been an idle ceremony to have given the defendants reasonable opportunity to communicate with their families and endeavor to obtain counsel is demonstrated by the fact that, very soon after conviction, able counsel appeared in their behalf. This was pointed out by Chief Justice Anderson in the course of his dissenting opinion. "They were nonresidents," he said, "and had little time or opportunity to get in touch with their families and friends who were scattered throughout two other states, and time has demonstrated that they could or would have been represented by able counsel had a better opportunity been given by a reasonable delay in the trial of the cases, judging from the number and activity of counsel that appeared immediately or shortly after their conviction."

It is hardly necessary to say that, the right to counsel being conceded, a defendant should be afforded a fair opportunity to secure counsel of his own choice. Not only was that not done here, but such designation of counsel as was attempted was either so indefinite or so close upon the trial as to amount to a denial of effective and substantial aid in that regard. This will be amply demonstrated by a brief review of the record.

April 6, six days after indictment, the trials began. When the first case was called, the court inquired whether the parties were ready for trial. The state's attorney replied that he was ready to proceed. No one answered for the defendants or appeared to represent or defend them. Mr. Roddy, a Tennessee lawyer not a member of the local bar, addressed the court, saying that he had not been employed, but that people who were interested had spoken to him about the case. He was asked by the court whether he intended to appear for the defendants, and answered that he would like to appear along with counsel that the court might appoint. * * *

It thus will be seen that until the very morning of the trial no lawyer had been named or definitely designated to represent the defendants. Prior to that time, the trial judge had "appointed all the members of the bar" for the limited "purpose of arraigning the defendants." Whether they would represent the defendants thereafter if no counsel appeared in their behalf, was a matter of speculation only, or, as the judge indicated, of mere anticipation on the part of the court. Such a designation, even if made for all purposes, would, in our opinion, have fallen far short of meeting, in any proper sense, a requirement for the appointment of counsel. How many lawyers were members of the bar does not appear; but, in the very nature of things, whether many or few, they would not, thus collectively named, have been given that clear appreciation of responsibility or impressed with that individual sense of duty which should and naturally would accompany the appointment of a selected member of the bar, specifically named and assigned.

That this action of the trial judge in respect of appointment of counsel was little more than an expansive gesture, imposing no substantial or definite obligation upon any one, is borne out by the fact that prior to the calling of the case for trial on April 6, a leading member of the local bar accepted employment on the side of the prosecution and actively participated in the trial. It is true that he said that before doing so he had understood Mr. Roddy would be employed as counsel for the defendants. This the lawyer in question, of his own accord, frankly stated to the court; and no doubt he acted with the utmost good faith. Probably other members of the bar had a like understanding. In any event, the circumstance lends emphasis to the conclusion that during perhaps the most critical period of the proceedings against these defendants, that is to say, from the time of their arraignment until the beginning of their trial, when consultation, thoroughgoing investigation and preparation were vitally important, the defendants did not have the aid of counsel in any real sense, although they were as much entitled to such aid during that period as at the trial itself.

Nor do we think the situation was helped by what occurred on the morning of the trial. At that time, as appears from the [record], Mr. Roddy stated to the court that he did not appear as counsel, but that he would like to appear along with counsel that the court might appoint; that he had not been given an opportunity to prepare the case; that he was not familiar with the procedure in Alabama, but merely came down as a friend of the people who were interested;

that he thought the boys would be better off if he should step entirely out of the case. Mr. Moody, a member of the local bar, expressed a willingness to help Mr. Roddy in anything he could do under the circumstances. To this the court responded, "All right, all the lawyers that will; of course I would not require a lawyer to appear if—." And Mr. Moody continued, "I am willing to do that for him as a member of the bar; I will go ahead and help do any thing I can do." With this dubious understanding, the trials immediately proceeded. The defendants, young, ignorant, illiterate, surrounded by hostile sentiment, haled back and forth under guard of soldiers, charged with an atrocious crime regarded with especial horror in the community where they were to be tried, were thus put in peril of their lives within a few moments after counsel for the first time charged with any degree of responsibility began to represent them.

It is not enough to assume that counsel thus precipitated into the case thought there was no defense, and exercised their best judgment in proceeding to trial without preparation. Neither they nor the court could say what a prompt and thoroughgoing investigation might disclose as to the facts. No attempt was made to investigate. No opportunity to do so was given. Defendants were immediately hurried to trial. Chief Justice Anderson, after disclaiming any intention to criticize harshly counsel who attempted to represent defendants at the trials, said: "* * * the record indicates that the appearance was rather *pro forma* than zealous and active * * *." Under the circumstances disclosed, we hold that defendants were not accorded the right of counsel in any substantial sense. To decide otherwise, would simply be to ignore actualities. * * *

It is true that great and inexcusable delay in the enforcement of our criminal law is one of the grave evils of our time. Continuances are frequently granted for unnecessarily long periods of time, and delays incident to the disposition of motions for new trial and hearings upon appeal have come in many cases to be a distinct reproach to the administration of justice. The prompt disposition of criminal cases is to be commended and encouraged. But in reaching that result a defendant, charged with a serious crime, must not be stripped of his right to have sufficient time to advise with counsel and prepare his defense. To do that is not to proceed promptly in the calm spirit of regulated justice but to go forward with the haste of the mob. * * *

Second. The Constitution of Alabama provides that in all criminal prosecutions the accused shall enjoy the right to have the assistance of counsel; and a state statute requires the court in a capital case, where the defendant is unable to employ counsel, to appoint counsel for him. The state supreme court held that these provisions had not been infringed, and with that holding we are powerless to interfere. The question, however, which it is our duty, and within our power, to decide, is whether the denial of the assistance of counsel contravenes the due process clause of the Fourteenth Amendment to the federal Constitution. * * *

It never has been doubted by this court, or any other so far as we know, that notice and hearing are preliminary steps essential to the passing of an enforceable judgment, and that they, together with a legally competent tribunal having jurisdiction of the case, constitute basic elements of the constitutional requirement of due process of law. The words of Webster, so often quoted, that by "the law of the land" is intended "a law which hears before it condemns," have been repeated in varying forms of expression in a multitude of decisions. * * *

What, then, does a hearing include? Historically and in practice, in our own country at least, it has always included the right to the aid of counsel when desired and provided by the party asserting the right. The right to be heard would be, in many cases, of little avail if it did not comprehend the right to be heard by counsel. Even the intelligent and educated layman has small and sometimes no skill in the science of law. If charged with crime, he is incapable, generally, of determining for himself whether the indictment is good or bad. He is unfamiliar with the rules of evidence. Left without the aid of counsel he may be put on trial without a proper charge, and convicted upon incompetent evidence, or evidence irrelevant to the issue or otherwise inadmissible. He lacks both the skill and knowledge adequately to prepare his defense, even though he have a perfect one. He requires the guiding hand of counsel at every step in the proceedings against him. Without it, though he be not guilty, he faces the danger of conviction because he does not know how to establish his innocence. If that be true of men of intelligence, how much more true is it of the ignorant and illiterate, or those of feeble intellect. If in any case, civil or criminal, a state or federal court were arbitrarily to refuse to hear a party by counsel, employed by and appearing for him, it reasonably may not be doubted that such a refusal would be a denial of a hearing, and, therefore, of due process in the constitutional sense. * * *

In the light of the facts outlined in the forepart of this opinion—the ignorance and illiteracy of the defendants, their youth, the circumstances of public hostility, the imprisonment and the close surveillance of the defendants by the military forces, the fact that their friends and families were all in other states and communication with them necessarily difficult, and above all that they stood in deadly peril of their lives—we think the failure of the trial court to give them reasonable time and opportunity to secure counsel was a clear denial of due process.

But passing that, and assuming their inability, even if opportunity had been given, to employ counsel, as the trial court evidently did assume, we are of opinion that, under the circumstances just stated, the necessity of counsel was so vital and imperative that the failure of the trial court to make an effective appointment of counsel was likewise a denial of due process within the meaning of the Fourteenth Amendment. Whether this would be so in other criminal prosecutions, or under other circumstances, we need not determine. All that it is necessary now to decide, as we do decide, is that in a capital case, where the defendant is unable to employ counsel, and is incapable adequately of making his own defense because of ignorance, feeble mindedness, illiteracy, or the like, it is the duty of the court, whether requested or not, to assign counsel for him as a necessary requisite of due process of law; and that duty is not discharged by an assignment at such a time or under such circumstances as to preclude the giving of effective aid in the preparation and trial of the case. To hold otherwise would be to ignore the fundamental postulate * * * "that there are certain immutable principles of justice which inhere in the very idea of free government which no member of the Union may disregard." * * *

The judgments must be reversed and the causes remanded for further proceedings not inconsistent with this opinion.

Judgments reversed.

MR. JUSTICE BUTLER, dissenting. * * *

If there had been any lack of opportunity for preparation, trial counsel would have applied to the court for postponement. No such application was made. There was no suggestion, at the trial or in the motion for a new trial which they made, that Mr. Roddy or Mr. Moody was denied such opportunity or that they were not in fact fully prepared. The amended motion for new trial, by counsel who succeeded them, contains the first suggestion that defendants were denied counsel or opportunity to prepare for trial. But neither Mr. Roddy nor Mr. Moody has given any support to that claim. Their silence requires a finding that the claim is groundless, for if it had any merit they would be bound to support it. And no one has come to suggest any lack of zeal or good faith on their part.

If correct, the ruling that the failure of the trial court to give petitioners time and opportunity to secure counsel was denied of due process is enough, and with this the opinion should end. But the Court goes on to declare that 'the failure of the trial court to make an effective appointment of counsel was likewise a denial of due process within the meaning of the Fourteenth Amendment.' This is an extension of federal authority into a field hitherto occupied exclusively by the several States. Nothing before the Court calls for a consideration of the point. It was not suggested below and petitioners do not ask for its decision here. The Court, without being called upon to consider it, adjudges without a hearing an important constitutional question concerning criminal procedure in state courts. * * *

MR. JUSTICE MCREYNOLDS concurs in this opinion.

NOTES AND QUESTIONS

1. In what sense did the defendants here lack a lawyer? The judge, after all, appointed all the members of the local bar.

2. *Doubts about guilt.* The excerpt about the Scottsboro defendants cannot begin to capture the richness of the account in James Goodman, Stories of Scottsboro (1995), which we highly recommend. The *Powell* Court was without Goodman's historical account strongly suggesting that no rapes took place. Even without an independent historical account, the Court could easily have been skeptical of the story told by the State, given the locale and racial dimension. If you had been on the *Powell* Court, would doubt about guilt have made you more likely to find a violation of the right to counsel? Turning the question around, would you *still* have found a violation of the right to counsel on these facts, even if the evidence of guilt had been overwhelming? If not, why not?

3. *Further proceedings not inconsistent with this opinion.* Look again at the order at the end of the majority opinion. It is a standard order when a court reverses a lower court. Alabama could then choose to dismiss the indictments or retry the defendants with effective counsel at their side. And there would be many retrials. A total of eleven trials involved the nine defendants during the 1930s. Alabama dropped charges against four of the defendants in 1937. The other five eventually received convictions that withstood appellate review; the sentences were twenty years, seventy-five years (two defendants), ninety-nine years, and death. The death sentence was commuted to life by Alabama Governor Bibb Graves. Three Scottsboro defendants were paroled in 1943, 1946, and 1950. One escaped from prison in 1948 and was arrested in Detroit in 1950. Michigan governor G. Mennen Williams refused Alabama's request for extradition, and Alabama abandoned extradition proceedings. In 1976, Governor George Wallace pardoned the last surviving Scottsboro defendant (the one who had been sentenced to death).

4. The irony of Wallace pardoning one of the Scottsboro defendants may be lost on many readers. Wallace was best known for his staunch pro-segregation views when he was governor of Alabama in the 1950s and 1960s. In 1963, he sought to block "the school house door" and prevent two black students from enrolling at the

University of Alabama. He moved out of the way when confronted by the Deputy Attorney General of the United States, federal marshals, and units of the Alabama National Guard that had been nationalized by President Kennedy. Dan T. Carter, The Politics of Rage: George Wallace, the Origins of the New Conservatism and the Transformation of American Politics 150 (1995).

Late in his life, Wallace sought reconciliation with black politicians and African-Americans in general (primarily conducted through predominantly black churches) in Alabama. As historian Dan Carter comments, "[b]lack Alabamians wanted Wallace to be forgiven." Carter, at 463. His pardon of one of the Scottsboro defendants might have been part of this effort at reconciliation.

5. *Predecessor 1 to Powell.* More than a quarter century prior to *Powell*, the Court sought to intervene in a racially-flawed Southern death penalty case. The rape of a young white woman by a black man in 1906 in Chattanooga, Tennessee unleashed a storm of fury and racism. The sheriff arrested two black men and the prosecutor chose Ed Johnson, the one the victim came closer to identifying. But at the trial, the rape victim refused to say for certain that Johnson was her attacker. She would only testify, "To the best of my knowledge and belief, he is the same man." The defense team, three white lawyers, mounted an aggressive alibi defense that put the State's case in doubt.

At one point, a member of the jury rose to his feet, "tears streaming down his face * * * and in a voice trembling with emotion, he cried: 'In God's name, Miss Taylor, tell us positively—is that the guilty negro? Can you say it—can you swear it?' "

She responded: "Listen to me. I would not take the life of an innocent man. But before God, I believe this is the guilty negro."

The jury initially voted 8–4 for conviction and the judge sent them home for the evening. When the jury returned the next day, the doubts of the four dissenting jurors had somehow been laid to rest. Ed Johnson was found guilty and sentenced to hang. The Supreme Court granted a hearing on a writ of habeas corpus to examine whether the trial met due process fairness standards. To permit the hearing to proceed, the Court granted a stay of execution and issued an order that the prisoner be kept safe. The intervention by the federal court proved too much for some in the community.

The headlines in the Chattanooga News the next day, March 20, 1906, told the whole story: " 'God Bless You All—I Am Innocent,' Ed Johnson's Last Words Before Being Shot to Death By a Mob Like a Dog, Majesty of the Law Outraged by Lynchers, Mandate of the Supreme Court of the United States Disregarded and Red Riot Rampant, Terrible and Tragic Vengeance Bows City's Head in Shame."

President Theodore Roosevelt condemned the lynching as "contemptuous of the Court." Using the bloodless language of formal judicial opinions, the Court dismissed Johnson's appeal on the ground that it was "abated by the death of the appellant." Johnson v. Tennessee, 214 U.S. 485, 29 S.Ct. 651, 53 L.Ed. 1056 (1909). But prior to dismissing the appeal, the Court did something extraordinary. It ordered a federal criminal trial that resulted in contempt convictions for the Chattanooga sheriff and several other law enforcement officers.

In 2000, a Chattanooga court granted a petition to clear Mr. Johnson of the rape. Leroy Phillips, a local lawyer, noted during the proceeding that 4,708 lynchings took place in the United States from 1882 to 1944, according to an archive at Tuskegee University in Alabama. For a fuller description of the Johnson case, the heroes and villains, and its aftermath, see Mark Curriden & Leroy Phillips, Jr., Contempt of Court (1999); George C. Thomas III, The Supreme Court on Trial: How the American Justice System Sacrifices Innocent Defendants (2008).

6. *Predecessor 2 to Powell.* A similar story of lawlessness played itself out in Georgia in 1915. The vicious murder of a young woman in Atlanta led to sensational newspaper coverage and to the arrest of Leo Frank, her employer. From the beginning, the case attracted nationwide attention, in part because Frank was Jewish and anti-Semitism was on the rise in the United States. Frank was convicted and sentenced to death based wholly on circumstantial evidence offered in a trial that took place, according to Justice Oliver Wendell Holmes, "in the presence of a hostile demonstration and seemingly dangerous crowd, thought by the presiding judge to be ready for violence unless a verdict of guilty was rendered." Leonard Dinnerstein, The Leo Frank Case 109 (1968). Despite Holmes's due process concern, the Court, 7–2, denied Frank's habeas corpus petition. Frank v. Mangum, 237 U.S. 309, 35 S.Ct. 582, 59 L.Ed. 969 (1915). Such was the reluctance of the Supreme Court in the early twentieth century to reverse the fact finding of state courts.

A petition seeking executive clemency was filed with Georgia governor John M. Slaton. Over 100,000 letters asking for commutation arrived in the offices of the governor and the Prison Commission. *Id.* at 122. The Prison Commission voted two-to-one not to recommend clemency. After holding his own hearings into the facts of the murder, Slaton commuted Frank's death sentence to life in prison. "Privately, Slaton confided to friends that he believed Frank innocent and would have granted a full pardon if he were not convinced that in a short while the truth would come out * * *." *Id.* at 129.

Many Georgians were furious at the commutation. His political career ruined, Slaton had to call out an entire battalion of state militia to keep from being lynched. *Id.* at 132. The commutation failed to save Frank. Two months later, a mob of twenty-five men stormed the prison farm, abducted Frank, and hung him. "Hordes of people made their way to the oak tree" to view Frank's body and take pictures. *Id.* at 143. Those who planned and participated in this lawless act included a "clergyman, two former Superior Court judges, and an ex-sheriff." *Id.* at 139. The Marietta Journal and Courier wrote: "We regard the hanging of Leo M. Frank in Cobb County as an act of law abiding citizens." *Id.* at 145.

7. *Trying to make sense of it all.* How could judges, law officers, and a clergyman have participated in the conduct described in Note 6? Consider these observations about the Scottsboro case:

> White Alabamians seemed genuinely puzzled at outside criticism of their handling of the Scottsboro cases. Avoiding a lynching was "a genuine step forward," and thus was deserving of commendation, not condemnation. The state supreme court lauded the speed of the Scottsboro Boys' trials as likely to instill greater respect for the law. A state member of the Commission on Interracial Cooperation thought it odd that Alabama should be criticized for delivering exactly what the [Commission] had been fighting so hard to accomplish—replacement of lynchings with trials. Several southern newspapers warned in connection with Scottsboro that if outsiders continued to assail Alabama after juries had returned guilty verdicts, then there would be little incentive to resist a lynching on future occasions.

Michael J. Klarman, *The Racial Origins of Modern Criminal Procedure*, 99 Mich. L. Rev. 48, 57 (2000).

8. *The broader effect of Powell.* Look again at Justice Butler's dissent in *Powell.* Butler is correct that federal courts, particularly in the nineteenth and early twentieth centuries, were loath to impose federal supervision over state criminal justice systems. And, as Justice Butler points out, the Court could have decided the case in favor of the defendants by finding insufficient time to prepare. Yet the Court also held that the failure to appoint counsel violated due process. Why do you think the Court went this additional step?

> Even if *Powell* did ensure better legal representation for southern black defendants, how much this affected actual case outcomes is uncertain. The [Communist International Labor Defense] criticized *Powell* because the Justices apparently had selected the least significant ground for reversing the Scottsboro Boys' convictions. Indeed, the Communists accused the Court of simply providing Alabama with instructions on how properly to lynch the defendants. Even if appointed days before trial and afforded adequate opportunity to prepare a defense, counsel generally could do little to assist clients like the Scottsboro Boys. Black lawyers, who might have been willing aggressively to pursue their clients' defense, were few and far between in the South, and in any event were distinct liabilities owing to the prejudice they aroused among white judges and juries. White lawyers, on

> the other hand, generally refrained from pressing defenses that raised broader challenges to the Jim Crow system, such as race-based exclusion from juries. In any event, even the most earnest advocacy rarely could influence case outcomes when the system was so pervasively stacked against fair adjudication of the legal claims of black defendants. The Scottsboro Boys did enjoy outstanding legal representation in their retrials, yet it made absolutely no difference to the outcomes.

Michael J. Klarman, *The Racial Origins of Modern Criminal Procedure*, 99 Mich. L. Rev. 48, 78 (2000).

9. *Relevance to today?* Given that *Brown* and *Powell* took place in the 1930s, are they simply historical relics that should be consigned to the past where they belong? Not necessarily, as our experience with the prison at Guantanamo Bay makes plain. Moreover, it is not clear that the promise of the right to counsel implicit in the *Powell* opinion has been realized in a way that would please that Court. We address this question in Chapter 9.

B. THE NORMS OF THE CRIMINAL PROCESS

By the time a case gets into court, and certainly by the time a case makes it all the way to the United States Supreme Court, it is unlikely to be solved by an easy application of a clear legal rule. There is a clear legal rule about many things—for example, the speed limit on a particular stretch of road—but disputes about clear rules rarely make it into the courts. Instead, most cases present the judge with a range of outcomes that are plausible because they fit within the precedents that she has before her. Some judges will resist this truth, at least publicly, because they want to be seen as merely applying "the law" rather than making a quasi-legislative choice, but any realistic examination of case law will make clear that judges have choices. Otherwise, how can we explain dissents?

Once we accept that most cases present judges with a range of outcomes, we must then consider what factors move judges to choose among the possible outcomes. Many factors undoubtedly are at play here, some legitimate and some illegitimate. A prior generation of legal scholars sought to unmask the power that lies in judicial choices as well as the factors that influence how this power is wielded. See, e.g., Felix Cohen, *Transcendental Nonsense and the Functional Approach*, 35 Colum. L. Rev. 809 (1935); Karl Llewellyn, *A Realistic Jurisprudence—The Next Step*, 30 Colum. L. Rev. 431 (1930). Today's scholarship about judicial choices has at least two different camps. One camp seeks to understand choices by drawing on other disciplines of knowledge—for example, law and economics, law and history, and law and philosophy. Judge *A* might think that economic principles best explain how to decide the case while Judge *B* is motivated by an historical understanding of the issue. A second camp focuses mostly on what it considers illegitimate factors and can be loosely referred to as "critical" scholarship. It seeks to show how race, sex, gender, class, and hegemony lead judges to shut the door on those who are not of the dominant political majority.

Identifying the full range of factors that move judges to make choices, and how those factors interact, is probably impossible and certainly beyond the scope of this comment. But the study of criminal procedure brings to the forefront three factors that move judges to choose one permissible outcome over another. First, American judges are citizens in a free democracy. Like every other citizen in the United States, judges bring to the task at hand a view about the importance of security and individual rights. Governments exist, in large part, to provide security from those who might harm us, but the very power of government also leads us to be fearful about how its power will be exercised when our individual rights and freedom are at stake. John Adams signed into law the Sedition Act that made it a crime to criticize the government. Richard Nixon used the Internal Revenue Service to attack his enemies. In the wake of 9/11, George W. Bush authorized wiretaps without court order. There are many possible ways to balance security and individual rights, and judges who decide criminal procedure cases will strike the balance at different points. Obviously, judges who put the balance nearer the security end of the scale will be more likely to vest discretion in police and prosecutors while judges whose tipping point is nearer the individual rights end will require more judicial supervision of those who enforce the law.

A second factor that affects criminal procedure cases is federalism. The United States has a federal government, in which states and the federal government share power in an uneasy, shifting balance. The battle over ratification of the Constitution between the Federalists and the Anti-federalists has played out in every generation since and continues to this day—think "red" states and "blue" states. The long-festering controversy over how much federal power should exist led federal judges for most of our history to be reluctant to interpose the federal Constitution in matters that might plausibly be considered "local." But where to locate the balance between too much federal supervision and not enough is also a contestable issue, one about which judges disagree.

Notice, in this regard, Justice Butler's dissent in *Powell.* He argued that the Court did not need to reach the issue of the denial of counsel, that it was enough to find a violation of due process in the failure to provide sufficient time to prepare the case. To fasten on the states some undefined obligation to provide counsel to ignorant defendants was, for Justice Butler and Justice McReynolds, "an extension of federal authority into a field hitherto occupied exclusively by the several States" that should not be done unless necessary to decide the case before the Court. This argument has, at its core, a respect for, and deference to, state actors.

Racism is a third factor that might explain the Alabama and Mississippi decisions in *Powell* and *Brown*. The range of choices that are available to judges in one state or region may be different from the acceptable range in other parts of the country. In the Mississippi Supreme Court in 1935, only two of the five judges were willing to reverse convictions obtained by torture. We will never know whether their decision was influenced by racism, but we do know that all nine members of the United States Supreme Court found the state court's decision to affirm the convictions to be an unacceptable choice. Outside the Deep South, the range of available choices was different in cases where race was a central factor.

As you read the cases in this book, you should ask yourself what range of acceptable choices the judges thought they had, how the judges came up with that range of choices, and why the judges chose one outcome over the others. You will often find the various choices best explained by the balance between security and liberty and the balance between robust and minimal federal intervention in state criminal justice. But modern judges tend to cloak their foundational views in other language—the language of (1) the accuracy of verdicts; (2) the fairness of the procedure; (3) honoring the presence of certain limitations on the power of government to find or use evidence; and (4) efficiency.

Accuracy

All systems that process and evaluate information will make errors in evaluation. If the system is indifferent to the "direction" of the error (indifferent to which party is harmed by the error), it would permit a verdict based on the slightest difference in the weight of the evidence presented by the two parties. This standard of proof, called "preponderance of the evidence," is the standard used in civil court. As a consequence, the plaintiff wins if she can show the slightest additional weight of evidence on her side of the balance; the defendant wins if the evidence is in equipoise or tilted ever so slightly in the defendant's direction.

Criminal law has adopted an "innocence-weighted" procedural approach that, in theory, protects innocent defendants. See Tom Stacy, *The Search for Truth in Constitutional Criminal Procedure*, 91 Colum. L. Rev. 1369. Blackstone put the rationale colorfully: "[T]he law holds that it is better that ten guilty persons escape than that one innocent suffer." 4 W. Blackstone's Commentaries *352 (1769). To create an "innocence-weighted" procedure, criminal law requires proof beyond a reasonable doubt.

As Professor Daniel Givelber notes, however, no one knows for certain that the reasonable-doubt standard operates to acquit a greater percentage of *innocent* defendants. It might just produce more acquittals randomly distributed among defendants generally. Daniel Givelber, *Meaningless Acquittals, Meaningful Convictions: Do We Reliably Acquit the Innocent?*, 49 Rutgers L. Rev. 1317 (1997). There are two ways in which a high standard of proof should differentially benefit innocent defendants—by encouraging more innocent defendants to stand trial rather than plea bargain, and by influencing juries to vote not guilty in cases involving innocent defendants. If more innocent defendants choose to stand trial because they have faith in the reasonable doubt standard, then even random acquittals will differentially benefit innocent defendants. But the most direct differential effect—and the one Blackstone likely meant—is that it should be more difficult to convict innocent defendants than guilty ones. This effect, however, depends crucially on whether the prosecution will have a weaker case against innocent defendants. If innocent and guilty defendants present cases of equal "strength," then the reasonable-doubt standard does not help innocent defendants any more than guilty ones. Many scholars and judges assume that our rules of procedure will permit innocent defendants to demonstrate the weakness of the prosecution case, but is it so clear?

It is not evident to Professor Givelber, who argues that our rules of adjudication "assume a guilty defendant, and focus on the task of creating a fair fight between the prosecution and the guilty defendant." For example, no current doctrine insists on "the availability of the most accurate information concerning the crime and its investigation"—such as guaranteed defense access to DNA testing. Instead, the system has "provided the defendant with a series of tactical opportunities to derail the prosecution's case." *Id.* at 1378.

Some of these opportunities to derail the State's case should, in theory, advance accurate outcomes. As we saw in Part A., providing indigent defendants with a lawyer should help avoid wrongful convictions. Other trial rights provide the lawyer with tools to test the State's case—the right to confront the prosecution witnesses, to call defense witnesses, and to have the case heard in a public trial before an impartial jury fairly soon after the events in question.

The right to confront and to call witnesses bears an obvious relationship to accuracy. The right to a speedy and public trial enhances accuracy in two ways. The sooner the trial occurs after the crime, the more accurate should be the memories of witnesses. Less obviously, the public nature of a trial should serve as a deterrent to judges who might be inclined to favor one party over another.

All of these trial rights are specifically guaranteed by the Sixth Amendment. Partly because they bear an obvious relationship to accuracy, they are much less controversial than some of the rights that are grounded more in fairness or in limited-government sentiment.

Fairness

No one denies that suspects and defendants should be treated fairly. Much debate centers, naturally, on what constitutes "fair" treatment. One famous example is Yale Kamisar's 1965 article that pre-dated the famous *Miranda* warnings requirement. Yale Kamisar, *Equal Justice in the Gatehouses and Mansions of American Criminal Procedure*, reprinted in Yale Kamisar, Police Interrogation (1980). According to Professor Kamisar, the Fifth Amendment gives everyone the right to refuse to answer police questions, but most criminal suspects do not know they have that right. Affluent suspects are able to retain counsel to advise them during interrogation. Fairness, in this context, thus meant for Kamisar that suspects should be told of their right to refuse to answer and should be provided the right to counsel during interrogation, an analysis the *Miranda* Court adopted. Fairness here implicates equality; the rich and the poor, the knowledgeable as well as the ignorant, should be able to deal with police interrogators on more or less equal terms.

Others take a different view of fairness in the interrogation room. As long as the police do not coerce a confession, one could argue that it is fair to question suspects who are under arrest, and even to take advantage of suspects who do not know of the privilege against self-incrimination. Assuming that an inconsequential number of innocent people confess when faced with non-coercive interrogation—of late, a questionable assumption—these commentators wonder why anyone cares that the police trick or encourage guilty people to confess their crimes. Moreover, to make lawyers available to all suspects, just because a very few suspects have a lawyer during interrogation, might be the wrong way to solve the inequality problem; why not ban lawyers from police interrogation, thus reaching the "equality" of zero lawyers?

To the extent equality means making all suspects as resistant to police investigation as the savvy affluent suspects, some commentators deride equality as a "sporting theory of justice"—turning the police investigation into a fox hunt where the fox must be given a fair chance. Perhaps law-abiding persons should rejoice when non-coercive police questioning causes a guilty defendant to confess.

These questions tend to divide courts and commentators because of the inherent difficulty in deciding what is fair. Of course, a procedure is not fair if it produces too many inaccurate verdicts (though defining "too many" may be difficult), but once we have identified accuracy as an independent requirement, it is much more difficult to give content to a fairness requirement. Fairness, then, is a controversial legitimacy factor precisely because fairness invites those with different views to ascribe what they please to the concept of "fairness."

Limited-Government Provisions

One could have an accurate criminal process that included the power to question defendants in court, whether or not they wished to testify, and the power to introduce evidence seized in a search later found to be too broad or too intrusive. The continental European systems typically permit the presiding judge to question the defendant at trial in front of the jury. The Canadian, European, and English systems permit evidence to be introduced even if it is seized in an unfair manner. While we may prefer our system, no one suggests that these other systems produce more inaccurate verdicts than the American system.

The reason is simple enough. Physical evidence does not need to have its accuracy tested by the adversarial process; visual examination or lab tests can disclose its true meaning. And, there is no reason to believe that a system that permits defendants to be questioned in court will be less accurate than a system that permits defendants to avoid testifying. Indeed, limitations on questioning defendants and using physical evidence found in searches make the overall set of outcomes *less* accurate. So, on balance, the Fourth Amendment and the privilege against self-incrimination are accuracy-impeding provisions.

It is more controversial to assert that a process can be *fair* when it requires defendants to submit to questioning, or uses reliable evidence that was seized wrongfully. But one could plausibly argue, as Justice Cardozo did, that the question of how police obtain physical evidence is separate from the question of whether the defendant is guilty; otherwise, "[t]he criminal is to go free because the constable has blundered." People v. Defore, 242 N.Y. 13, 150 N.E. 585 (1926). As to questioning defendants in court, one might ask why it is unfair to expect other witnesses to testify at trial but not the one witness who probably knows more about the facts of the case than anyone else—the defendant. Judge Henry Friendly even called for the Fifth Amendment privilege against self-incrimination to be repealed by constitutional amendment. Henry J. Friendly, *The Fifth Amendment Tomorrow: The Case for Constitutional Change*, 37 U. Cinn. L. Rev. 617 (1968).

However one decides the fairness question, something more than accuracy and fairness explains why the Bill of Rights includes the Fourth Amendment. Examination of the constitutional language helps here. The Fourth Amendment begins by recognizing the "right of the people to be secure in their persons, houses, papers and effects against unreasonable searches and seizures." It then establishes strict standards for issuing warrants, standards that include probable cause and a "particular[ ]" description of "the place to be searched, and the persons or things to be seized."

The Fourth Amendment is part of an overall theme in the Bill of Rights that establishes "the people" as a separate entity from the government. The First Amendment forbids a state religion and creates the right to worship freely, to speak freely, and to assemble and to petition the government. The Second Amendment provides for a militia to exist separately from the government. The Ninth and Tenth Amendments retain power in the people and the states. Viewed as part of this broad canvas, the Fourth Amendment is a statement that the government must not interfere with our daily lives (our persons, houses, papers, and effects) absent good cause. The specific requirements for warrants will keep judges from taking lightly the command that the people be "secure." The Fourth Amendment's purpose thus seems to be to limit the power of government to intrude on "the people" in this particular way.

Most of the Fifth Amendment also consists of general rights against government: it forbids re-litigating the outcome of the first trial (by forbidding double jeopardy); it forbids governmental compulsion of defendants to testify against themselves; it requires the government to obtain assent of the community through a grand jury indictment before bringing a defendant to trial; it forbids government from denying "life, liberty, or property" without due process of law, or taking private property without "just compensation." Viewed in this context, the Fifth Amendment prohibition of compelling defendants to be witnesses against themselves seems like a restriction on the power of government to invade our autonomy.

If the Fourth and Fifth Amendment rights are fundamentally to control government, rather than to enhance accuracy or fairness, it would explain why the suppression of evidence under these two provisions is more controversial than the implementation of the Sixth Amendment trial rights. Society today likely does not feel as hostile toward government as the Framers felt anti-British in 1791.

Indeed, Professor Daniel Givelber argues that these provisions actually lessen the chance that an innocent defendant can prove her innocence. "Advantages which may enhance the case of the guilty defendant such as the right to silence and to exclude relevant inculpatory evidence, work no benefit for the innocent. Instead, those advantages justify the prosecution's withholding from the accused and the factfinder evidence which might undermine the prosecution's case." Daniel Givelber, *Meaningless Acquittals, Meaningful Convictions: Do We Reliably Acquit the Innocent?*, 49 Rutgers L. Rev. 1317, 1394 (1997).

Efficiency

The political and pragmatic legitimacy of the criminal process requires a threshold level of efficiency in solving and prosecuting crime. Unfortunately police do not solve, or clear, as many crimes as society would like. Because limited-government norms are necessarily inconsistent to some degree with police efficiency, the low clearance rate has led crime control adherents to urge abolition or restriction of the limited-government provisions in the Bill of Rights. Specifically, many have urged a rethinking of the principle requiring suppression of evidence seized in violation of the Fourth Amendment, and a few scholars have suggested rethinking the *Miranda* principle requiring that suspects must be warned prior to custodial interrogation.

The criminal process following police investigation is also currently dominated by the efficiency norm. Plea bargains are much more efficient than trials, and over 90% of felony charges are bargained to guilty pleas. Most lawyers and academics contend that the system could not survive without plea bargaining. If a mere 20% of felony defendants demanded a jury trial, that would more than double the present number of trials, with the complications of choosing a jury and all the rights that attend presenting a defense. Plea bargaining, in short, is the grease that permits the wheels of justice to turn smoothly.

The Supreme Court explicitly approves of plea bargaining, and has held that prosecutors are bound by plea bargains once the defendant pleads guilty. *Santobello v. New York*, Chapter 15. These rulings have a double effect in encouraging more pleas: Judges know they can accept guilty pleas induced by plea bargains, and defendants can seek these pleas knowing that the prosecutor cannot withdraw from the bargain once the guilty plea is entered.

Efficiency is an important overlay on the legitimating norms of the American criminal process. But it must be tempered by the fairness norm and by the limited-government provisions of the Bill of Rights. How to balance these norms is always controversial. And the balance is subject to outside influences, as we witnessed in the aftermath of September 11, 2001.

The Norms Post-September 11

Larry Ellison, chief executive of Oracle Corporation, on the question of whether we should have National ID cards: "Those are political decisions that need to be made. I just think people need to ask themselves who they trust more, terrorists or the government." Robert O'Harrow Jr. & Jonathan Krim, *Is Big Brother Watching?*, The Washington Post National Weekly Edition, Dec. 24, 2001—Jan. 6, 2002, at 6, 7.

We tend to forget, when times are good, that the ultimate role of government is to protect its citizens—from crime, from anarchy, from attacks by enemies. It is particularly easy for this country to forget. From the very beginning of the Republic, we have tended to view ourselves as isolated from the political machinations in Europe and Asia. And, until Pearl Harbor, the great oceans protected us from surprise attack. But in the wake of September 11, we now know all too well that we are vulnerable. One question is how much liberty we are willing to surrender, as a society, in exchange for the hope or expectation of being made more secure.

Of course, if the relevant question when deciding how much civil liberty we should surrender is whether we trust government more than terrorists, we are likely to surrender just about all of our civil liberties. Perhaps a better way to phrase the question is how much of an intrusion is the proposed government action and how much safety will it buy, and are there any liberties or values so valuable—even sacred—that they are not susceptible to cost-benefit analysis?

A few hours after the hijacked commercial airliners struck the two World Trade Center towers and the Pentagon, the FBI was in federal court getting court orders to wiretap the phones of hundreds of persons suspected of having links with terrorist groups. Some of these phone taps produced evidence of support for the hijackers—some gave thanks to Allah for the great success of the hijackers and others gloated at the death and destruction. Did this indicate widespread conspiratorial involvement or only defiant, but lawful, speech? And we may assume that many of the phone taps produced nothing even slightly incriminating because the persons under surveillance were innocent.

Moreover, we now know that the National Security Agency soon began a two-pronged monitoring of telephone calls and e-mails, in many cases without warrants. One part included monitoring the phone calls and e-mails of people with known ties to al-Qaeda. The other aspect was described by the New York Times as mining a "vast data trove," consisting of volume and pattern phone data. Eric Lichtblau & James Risen, *Spy Agency Mined Vast Data Trove, Officials Report,*

N.Y. Times, December 24, 2005, A1. These data included who called whom, how often, and how long the calls lasted. *Id.* at A12. In 2015, Congress allowed the NSA metadata surveillance program to lapse. A separate NSA program, PRISM, still allows NSA to intercept emails and cellphone calls made by foreigners. Fred Kaplan, The State of the Surveillance State, *Slate*, June 1, 2015.

In the hours and days following September 11, we did not know whether additional attacks would occur, and whether those attacks might be nuclear, chemical, or biological. Did that risk justify the government's actions? Does it still justify mining "vast data troves"? And what about coercive interrogation methods used at our military base at Guantanamo Bay and other, secret locations overseas? The horrors of September 11, and the Government's response to it, bring into stark clarity the questions that must be asked and answered in *every* criminal investigation and prosecution. What is the optimal trade-off between liberty and privacy, on the one hand, and security against those who would destroy us, on the other hand? In the final analysis, what is the meaning of the middle word in "criminal justice system"?

NOTES AND QUESTIONS

1. *Narrow holdings and the range of permissible choices.* Lawyers and judges sometimes speak of "narrow holdings" in cases. The narrow holding is the outcome justified by the facts before the Court. Thus, the narrow holding in *Brown* is that confessions wrung from suspects by torture cannot be used. The rationale is the reasoning that supports the narrow holding. The *Brown* Court speaks of "coercion" in its reasoning, which suggests that it sees the problem of involuntary confessions extending beyond those induced by torture. But how far beyond?

Suppose, for example, that police interrogate a suspect for over forty hours, until he passes out and then the same officers interrogate him for ten hours a few days later, after which he confesses? Is this confession coerced? Or suppose the police interrogate a suspect for thirty-six hours, after which he confesses? Is either case included within the narrow holding of *Brown*? Does the rationale of *Brown* reach either case? Which hypothetical case seems more likely to be coercive? Should either or both be held to be coercive police interrogation?

What was the narrow holding in *Powell v. Alabama*? The Court stressed the role of the defense lawyer in helping achieve a more reliable outcome, but is that part of the narrow holding or the rationale? One way to ask this question is to ask whether the *holding* of *Powell* extends to a defendant who was not so young or uneducated and who was charged with a non-capital crime in a situation that did not involve racial hysteria. Another way to ask the question is to ask whether ruling against this new defendant is within the range of acceptable choices. Consider the following case.

> [T]here was no question of the commission of a robbery. The State's case consisted of evidence identifying the petitioner as the perpetrator. The defense was an alibi. Petitioner called and examined witnesses to prove that he was at another place at the time of the commission of the offense. The simple issue was the veracity of the testimony for the State and that for the defendant. * * * [T]he accused was not helpless, but was a man forty-three years old, of ordinary intelligence, and ability to take care of his own interests on the trial of that narrow issue. He had once before been in a criminal court, pleaded guilty to larceny and served a sentence and was not wholly unfamiliar with criminal procedure.

Does the narrow holding of *Powell* apply to *this* case? If not, should *Powell* be extended to cover these facts? Would denying counsel to this defendant be an acceptable outcome, given *Powell*? What if the defendant were described as "a farm hand, out of a job and on relief," "too poor to hire a lawyer," and "a man of little education"? If you were the judge, would this description make you *more* likely to provide him a lawyer? If so, you might be interested to learn that the "ordinary intelligence" description appears in a majority opinion refusing to extend *Powell* and the "little education" description is found in Justice Black's dissent, joined by Justices Douglas and Murphy. See Betts v. Brady, 316 U.S. 455, 62 S.Ct. 1252, 86 L.Ed. 1595 (1942). This tells us, of course, that both choices were permissible ways to read *Powell* and that the Court was not (yet) willing to make the choice that Black, Douglas, and Murphy supported. Black would have the final word on this issue some twenty-one years later. See Gideon v. Wainwright, 372 US 335, 83 S.Ct. 792, 9 L.Ed. 2d 799 (1963).

2. *Norms versus rules.* Another way to approach the precedential effect of *Powell* is to understand the distinction between rules and norms. Though the distinction between a norm and a rule is not always clear, it can be a useful way to classify legal argument and doctrine. Roughly, a rule requires a particular result and a norm is a way of organizing one's thinking to produce the best result in a particular case. A rule can be expressed "if X, then Y," but a norm implies a softer relationship between X and Y, sort of "if X, then we should carefully consider whether Y." It is wrong to tell a lie—a norm—suggesting that one should tell the truth. But does that mean we should tell our best friend that her husband is having an affair? Perhaps not. On the other hand if it is perjury to tell a lie under oath—a rule—then a question about the affair requires a truthful answer.

Using this admittedly oversimplified description, look again at the language from *Betts* quoted in the last Note. Can you phrase both a rule and a norm that would have governed the case?

3. *Police investigation problems.* In "solving" the following problems, do not use any constitutional doctrine that you might have learned in other courses (or think you have learned from television). Attempt to use only the norms and values we have identified in this section.

A. *Radar searches.* Suppose scientists develop a type of "radar" gun that can identify with 100% accuracy the existence of chemical compounds. This radar can be tuned so that it will *only* signal the existence of substances that cannot be legally possessed under federal law. If the police aim this machine at residences while driving up and down the streets, to provide the basis for search warrants, does this raise a fairness concern? Any other concern?

B. *The morality of torture.* Police arrested a kidnaping suspect and tried to persuade him to provide information about where the victim was located. He requested counsel, and police permitted him to call counsel. When counsel arrived, he refused to represent the kidnaper (who said the lawyer would only be paid from the ransom money). The kidnaper then insisted on meeting with the victim's father and arranging some kind of cash settlement for lawyer's fees, bail, and expenses. By the time the kidnaper led the police to where he had buried the victim in a coffin-like box in a shallow grave, she had suffocated. Should the police have acted more aggressively? Should they have attempted to coerce from the suspect the victim's location? Should they have used physical coercion? Torture? What if police knew of the victim's fate and had every reason to believe she was clinging to life? See William J. Pizzi, *The Privilege Against Self-Incrimination in a Rescue Situation*, 76 J. Crim. L. & Criminology 567 (discussing People v. Krom, 61 N.Y.2d 187, 473 N.Y.S.2d 139, 461 N.E.2d 276 (1984)).4. What is your overall impression of American criminal justice, circa 2018? Do you suppose criminal justice was better, was more fair, in the eighteenth century? Than the systems that produced *Powell* and *Brown*?

CHAPTER 1 SUMMARY

The criminal justice system in the United States processes millions of criminal cases each year. Roughly 1.5 million Americans are in prison. Any human endeavor with millions of working parts is bound to misfire and make mistakes. This chapter looked at some of the most famous and most horrific miscarriages of justice. Sometimes the system self-corrected, at least in part, as in *Powell v. Alabama* and *Brown v. Mississippi*. Other times, probably innocent defendants died (Leo Frank and Ed Johnson, to name two). The chapter examines the goals or norms of our criminal justice system. Understanding these norms will help you understand the chapters that follow. Some goals are in tension—the goal of limiting the power of government, for example, is in tension with the goal of efficiency and, to some extent, with the goal of achieving accurate outcomes. And, in all cases, the goals are simply that, goals that can never be perfectly achieved. Chapter 10 will explore in more detail the ways the system can fail innocent defendants.

CHAPTER 2

The Incorporation Story

A. THE INCORPORATION DEBATE AND THE LAW OF CRIMINAL PROCEDURE

What does it mean when we say something is unconstitutional or violates one's constitutional rights? Most of the time we are referring to rights guaranteed by the U.S. Constitution, as many of us—lay and legal—forget the sometimes more important state versions.

In the context of criminal procedure, constitutional debates center around the rights guaranteed to all U.S. citizens by the 4th, 5th, 6th, and 8th Amendments found in the now famous Bill of Rights. These include:

- prohibitions on unreasonable searches and seizures (4th)
- presentment or indictment by a grand jury (5th)
- prohibition against double jeopardy (5th)
- prohibition against compelled self-incrimination (5th)
- prohibition against taking of life, liberty, or property without due process of law (5th)
- right to a speedy and public trial by an impartial jury (6th)
- right to be informed of the nature and cause of the accusation (6th)
- right to be confronted by witnesses (6th)
- right to compel witnesses to appear (6th)
- right to assistance of counsel for defense (6th)
- prohibition against excessive bail, fines, or cruel and unusual punishment (8th).

But these original amendments, adopted in 1791, applied only to the federal government. They in no way purport to address conduct by state governments, whether we are talking about 13 states or 50. In fact, the original Bill of Rights was a compromise, designed by the Framers to placate a number of colonies who feared an overreaching federal government and were threatening to withhold ratification of the new constitution unless those rights were included. In that sense, the Bill of Rights—including the 4th, 5th, 6th, and 8th Amendments—can be seen as a way of guaranteeing states' rights, not regulating their conduct. Yet today, it is an accepted part of criminal procedure life that these rights apply in state criminal proceedings as well as federal. What changed?

Enter the 14th Amendment to the U.S. Constitution. Ratified in 1868, it is one of three Civil War amendments designed in part to address the rights and freedoms due the newly freed slaves. But its broad language has since been held to apply to all groups and classes of citizens. As a result, the 14th Amendment has been the vehicle by which those important criminal procedure rights have been applied to state as well as federal proceedings. The story of how that happened, and why it took close to a century, is the main focus of this chapter.

B. THE BILL OF RIGHTS AND THE FOURTEENTH AMENDMENT

Dating back to colonial days, criminal law and criminal justice were viewed as almost exclusively state and local matters. Federal criminal law jurisdiction was tiny; the first federal criminal code made crimes of murder, robbery, and larceny but only when committed on federal property or the high seas or against federal property. The vast bulk of criminal law and criminal prosecutions were carried out by the states as had been done when they were colonies. Thus, it is not surprising that when the Supreme Court began to "incorporate" rights from the Bill of Rights into the Due Process Clause of the Fourteenth Amendment, the criminal procedure rights were the last incorporated.

JOSHUA DRESSLER & ALAN C. MICHAELS—UNDERSTANDING CRIMINAL PROCEDURE

(5th ed. 2010), § 3.01, pp. 41–43.

The Fourteenth Amendment, adopted in 1868, imposes limits on *state* action. Section 1 of that amendment limits the state in three ways:

> No State shall [1] make or enforce any law which shall abridge the privileges or immunities of citizens of the United States; [2] *nor shall any State deprive any person of life, liberty, or property, without due process of law*

[emphasis added]; [3] nor deny to any person within its jurisdiction the equal protection of the laws.

The relationship between the Fourteenth Amendment and the Bill of Rights has been vigorously disputed. The legal battle, commonly called the "incorporation debate," centers on the second clause of section 1, namely, the Due Process Clause. The essential question is this: To what extent does the Fourteenth Amendment Due Process Clause "incorporate" (or "absorb") the Bill of Rights and, as a consequence, impose on the states the same restrictions the Bill of Rights impose on the federal government? * * * A related question is whether the Fourteenth Amendment guarantees any rights not enumerated in the Bill of Rights. * * *

The incorporation debate is important for various reasons. First, the extent to which individuals are protected from overreaching by agents of the state depends in large measure on the extent to which the Fourteenth Amendment incorporates the Bill of Rights. At one extreme, if none of the rights found in the Bill of Rights apply to the states, citizens may be subjected to, for example, warrantless invasions of the home by local police, coercive interrogation techniques, and felony trials without the assistance of counsel. On the other hand, if the Due Process Clause incorporates the Bill of Rights in its entirety, the latter charter becomes a national code of criminal procedure—federal and state action would be identically restricted.

Second, as the latter observation suggests, values of federalism are at stake in the incorporation debate. The broader the interpretation of the scope of the Fourteenth Amendment Due Process Clause, the less free are the states to develop their own rules of criminal procedure, and to adapt them to an individual state's particular social and political conditions.

Third, the incorporation debate raises important questions regarding the proper role of the judiciary in the enforcement of constitutional rights. In particular, if the Due Process Clause of the Fourteenth Amendment incorporates some, but not all, of the Bill of Rights, then judges must use some standard to decide which doctrines apply against the states and which do not, thereby increasing the risk that judges will make these determinations based on personal policy predilections rather than on a legitimate and principled constitutional basis.

NOTES AND QUESTIONS

1. *Due process.* In 1884, the Court acknowledged that the Fourteenth Amendment due process clause applied to state criminal processes, though the Court

held that the right to a grand jury indictment is not part of due process. Hurtado v. California, 110 U.S. 516, 4 S.Ct. 111, 28 L.Ed. 232 (1884). In 1900, the Court held that the right to a jury of twelve in a criminal case is not part of due process (the state constitution required a jury of eight). Maxwell v. Dow, 176 U.S. 581, 20 S.Ct. 448, 44 L.Ed. 597 (1900). Eight years later, the Court held that due process did not prohibit an instruction to the jury that it could draw a negative inference from the defendant's failure to testify, which almost certainly would have been a violation of the Fifth Amendment privilege against self-incrimination if the trial had been in federal court. Twining v. New Jersey, 211 U.S. 78, 29 S.Ct. 14, 53 L.Ed. 97 (1908).

2. *Developing standards of due process.* What test should the Supreme Court use to decide when a state trial or investigation has violated the Fourteenth Amendment due process clause? In Palko v. Connecticut, 302 U.S. 319, 58 S.Ct. 149, 82 L.Ed. 288 (1937), Justice Cardozo sought to articulate a test for what due process requires of a state criminal process.

> Our survey of the cases serves, we think, to justify the statement that the dividing line between them, if not unfaltering throughout its course, has been true for the most part to a unifying principle. On which side of the line the case made out by the appellant has appropriate location must be the next inquiry and the final one. Is that kind of double jeopardy to which the statute has subjected him a hardship so acute and shocking that our polity will not endure it? Does it violate those "fundamental principles of liberty and justice which lie at the base of all our civil and political institutions"?

The test announced by Cardozo was a restrictive one. Not many rights would qualify if the test were whether the lack of the right "subjected" the defendant to "a hardship so acute and shocking that our polity will not endure it." Nor would many rights qualify as "fundamental principles of liberty and justice which lie at the base of all our civil and political institutions." Which rights in the Bill of Rights do you think would qualify for inclusion under Cardozo's test?

3. *The theoretical debate about incorporation.* One way to read the Fourteenth Amendment, which avoids having to develop an account of due process, is Justice Hugo Black's "total" incorporation approach. In Black's view, "one of the chief objects" of the Fourteenth Amendment "was to make the Bill of Rights applicable to the states." Adamson v. California, 332 U.S. 46, 67 S.Ct. 1672, 91 L.Ed. 1903 (1947) (Black, J., dissenting). On this view, the Fourteenth Amendment simply absorbs the entire Bill of Rights—as if using the cut and paste function in a word processor—and makes each right applicable to the states. However, this approach creates no rights other than those found in the Bill of Rights, whereas this is possible with the due process approach discussed above.

An excellent example of this debate is set out in the case of Duncan v. Louisiana, 391 U.S. 145, 88 S.Ct. 1444, 20 L.Ed.2d 491 (1968). Justice Black advocates for the "total incorporation approach" in his concurring opinion with Justice Douglas while the due process approach (sometimes referred to as "selective incorporation") is addressed by Justice Harlan in his dissenting opinion with Justice Stewart.

MR. JUSTICE BLACK, with whom MR. JUSTICE DOUGLAS joins, concurring. * * *

* * * With [the Court's] holding I agree for reasons given by the Court. I also agree because of reasons given in my dissent in *Adamson v. California*, 332 U.S. 46, 68, 67 S.Ct. 1672, 1683, 91 L.Ed. 1903. In that dissent, I took the position, contrary to the holding in *Twining v. New Jersey* [p. 42, Note 1], that the Fourteenth Amendment made all of the provisions of the Bill of Rights applicable to the States. * * *

* * * [T]he dissent states that "the great words of the four clauses of the first section of the Fourteenth Amendment would have been an exceedingly peculiar way to say that 'The rights heretofore guaranteed against federal intrusion by the first eight Amendments are henceforth guaranteed against state intrusion as well.' " In response to this I can say only that the words "No State shall make or enforce any law which shall abridge the privileges or immunities of citizens of the United States" seem to me an eminently reasonable way of expressing the idea that henceforth the Bill of Rights shall apply to the States. What more precious "privilege" of American citizenship could there be than that privilege to claim the protections of our great Bill of Rights? I suggest that any reading of "privileges or immunities of citizens of the United States" which excludes the Bill of Rights' safeguards renders the words of this section of the Fourteenth Amendment meaningless. * * *

* * * [In Justice Harlan's view,] the Due Process Clause is treated as prescribing no specific and clearly ascertainable constitutional command that judges must obey in interpreting the Constitution, but rather as leaving judges free to decide at any particular time whether a particular rule or judicial formulation embodies an "immutable principl[e] of free government" or is "implicit in the concept of ordered liberty," or whether certain conduct "shocks the judge's conscience" or runs counter to some other similar, undefined and undefinable standard. Thus due process, according to my Brother Harlan, is to be a phrase with no permanent meaning, but one which is found to shift from time to time in accordance with judges' predilections and understandings of what is best for the country. If due process means this, the Fourteenth Amendment, in my

opinion, might as well have been written that "no person shall be deprived of life, liberty or property except by laws that the judges of the United States Supreme Court shall find to be consistent with the immutable principles of free government." It is impossible for me to believe that such unconfined power is given to judges in our Constitution that is a written one in order to limit governmental power.

MR. JUSTICE HARLAN, whom MR. JUSTICE STEWART joins, dissenting.

Every American jurisdiction provides for trial by jury in criminal cases. The question before us is not whether jury trial is an ancient institution, which it is; nor whether it plays a significant role in the administration of criminal justice, which it does; nor whether it will endure, which it shall. The question in this case is whether the State of Louisiana, which provides trial by jury for all felonies, is prohibited by the Constitution from trying charges of simple battery to the court alone. In my view, the answer to that question, mandated alike by our constitutional history and by the longer history of trial by jury, is clearly "no."

The States have always borne primary responsibility for operating the machinery of criminal justice within their borders, and adapting it to their particular circumstances. In exercising this responsibility, each State is compelled to conform its procedures to the requirements of the Federal Constitution. The Due Process Clause of the Fourteenth Amendment requires that those procedures be fundamentally fair in all respects. It does not, in my view, impose or encourage nationwide uniformity for its own sake; it does not command adherence to forms that happen to be old; and it does not impose on the States the rules that may be in force in the federal courts except where such rules are also found to be essential to basic fairness. * * *

I * * *

A few members of the Court have taken the position that the intention of those who drafted the first section of the Fourteenth Amendment was simply, and exclusively, to make the provisions of the first eight Amendments applicable to state action. This view has never been accepted by this Court. In my view, often expressed elsewhere, the first section of the Fourteenth Amendment was meant neither to incorporate, nor to be limited to, the specific guarantees of the first eight Amendments. * * * In short, neither history, nor sense, supports using the Fourteenth Amendment to put the States in a constitutional straitjacket with respect to their own development in the administration of criminal or civil law. * * *

* * * [The Court] has simply assumed that the question before us is whether the Jury Trial Clause of the Sixth Amendment should be incorporated into the Fourteenth, jot-for-jot and case-for-case, or ignored. Then the Court merely declares that the clause in question is "in" rather than "out."

The Court has justified neither its starting place nor its conclusion. If the problem is to discover and articulate the rules of fundamental fairness in criminal proceedings, there is no reason to assume that the whole body of rules developed in this Court constituting Sixth Amendment jury trial must be regarded as a unit. The requirement of trial by jury in federal criminal cases has given rise to numerous subsidiary questions respecting the exact scope and content of the right. It surely cannot be that every answer the Court has given, or will give, to such a question is attributable to the Founders; or even that every rule announced carries equal conviction of this Court; still less can it be that every such subprinciple is equally fundamental to ordered liberty.

Examples abound. I should suppose it obviously fundamental to fairness that a "jury" means an "impartial jury." I should think it equally obvious that the rule, imposed long ago in the federal courts, that "jury" means "jury of exactly twelve," is not fundamental to anything: there is no significance except to mystics in the number 12. Again, trial by jury has been held to require a unanimous verdict of jurors in the federal courts, although unanimity has not been found essential to liberty in Britain, where the requirement has been abandoned. * * *

Even if I could agree that the question before us is whether Sixth Amendment jury trial is totally "in" or totally "out," I can find in the Court's opinion no real reasons for concluding that it should be "in." The basis for differentiating among clauses in the Bill of Rights cannot be that only some clauses are in the Bill of Rights, or that only some are old and much praised, or that only some have played an important role in the development of federal law. These things are true of all. The Court says that some clauses are more "fundamental" than others, but it turns out to be using this word in a sense that would have astonished Mr. Justice Cardozo and which, in addition, is of no help. The word does not mean "analytically critical to procedural fairness" for no real analysis of the role of the jury in making procedures fair is even attempted. Instead, the word turns out to mean "old," "much praised," and "found in the Bill of Rights." The definition of "fundamental" thus turns out to be circular.

II * * *

I therefore see no reason why this Court should reverse the conviction of appellant, absent any suggestion that his particular trial was in fact unfair, or compel the State of Louisiana to afford jury trial in an as yet unbounded category of cases that can, without unfairness, be tried to a court. * * *

In sum, there is a wide range of views on the desirability of trial by jury, and on the ways to make it most effective when it is used; there is also considerable variation from State to State in local conditions such as the size of the criminal caseload, the ease or difficulty of summoning jurors, and other trial conditions bearing on fairness. We have before us, therefore, an almost perfect example of a situation in which the celebrated dictum of Mr. Justice Brandeis should be invoked. It is, he said,

> "one of the happy incidents of the federal system that a single courageous state may, if its citizens choose, serve as a laboratory * * *."

This Court, other courts, and the political process are available to correct any experiments in criminal procedure that prove fundamentally unfair to defendants. That is not what is being done today: instead, and quite without reason, the Court has chosen to impose upon every state one means of trying criminal cases; it is a good means, but it is not the only fair means, and it is not demonstrably better than the alternatives States might devise. * * *

4. Justices Hugo Black and John Harlan were on the Supreme Court together for sixteen years (1955–1971). As you can see from the exchange in *Duncan*, they disagreed fundamentally over how to interpret the Fourteenth Amendment. Can you articulate Justice Harlan's view of due process? Part of Black's argument in favor of total incorporation is that, otherwise, judges would be tempted "to roam at large in the broad expanses of policy and morals and to trespass, all too freely, on the legislative domain of the States as well as the Federal government" Adamson v. California, 332 U.S. 46, 67 S.Ct. 1672, 91 L.Ed. 1903 (1947) (Black, J., dissenting). Remember, Black's view of total incorporation was that the Fourteenth Amendment incorporated *all* of the Bill of Rights guarantees but otherwise created no rights against state authority. For example, he dissented in Griswold v. Connecticut, 381 U.S. 479, 85 S.Ct. 1678, 14 L.Ed.2d 510 (1965), which held that the due process clause prohibited Connecticut from enforcing its criminal law against the use of birth control. A fundamental-rights theorist could find, as the Court did, a right to privacy in the due process clause, but not an incorporationist who looked only at the relatively specific guarantees of the Bill of Rights. Can you see why?

5. Between the Harlan and Black positions in *Duncan*, which argument do you prefer? Does it matter on this issue that the Framers of the Bill of Rights considered, and rejected, an amendment that would have required states to provide jury trials?

6. *The inexorable march of incorporation.* Justice Black never persuaded a majority to accept total incorporation, but he stayed on the Court long enough (thirty-six years) to see a step-by-step "selective" incorporation that, by Black's death in 1971, was almost complete. Here is the way the Court described the status of incorporation in 1968.

> The Fourteenth Amendment denies the States the power to "deprive any person of life, liberty, or property, without due process of law." In resolving conflicting claims concerning the meaning of this spacious language, the Court has looked increasingly to the Bill of Rights for guidance; many of the rights guaranteed by the first eight Amendments to the Constitution have been held to be protected against state action by the Due Process Clause of the Fourteenth Amendment. That clause now protects the right to compensation for property taken by the State; the rights of speech, press, and religion covered by the First Amendment; the Fourth Amendment rights to be free from unreasonable searches and seizures and to have excluded from criminal trials any evidence illegally seized; the right guaranteed by the Fifth Amendment to be free of compelled self-incrimination; and the Sixth Amendment rights to counsel, to a speedy and public trial, to confrontation of opposing witnesses, and to compulsory process for obtaining witnesses.

Duncan v. Louisiana, 391 U.S. 145, 88 S.Ct. 1444, 20 L.Ed.2d 491 (1968).

7. In Donald Dripps's view, incorporation prevailed because there was not a strong advocate for the due process alternative. Donald A. Dripps, *Justice Harlan on Criminal Procedure: Two Cheers for the Legal Process School*, 3 Ohio State J. Crim. L. 125 (2005). While Justice Harlan was a brilliant justice and gifted writer, his stubborn view that criminal process questions could be left largely to the state legislatures doomed any chance that a majority of the Court would embrace his due process theory. Dripps argued that the due process clause could be read as requiring "proportionate police practices and reliable trial procedures" and that this would be a better criminal procedure world than incorporation has given us. *Id.* at 168.

8. *Don't forget state law.* The focus in criminal procedure books tends to be on the Bill of Rights provisions that now, mostly, apply to state suspects and defendants just as they do in federal cases. But don't make the mistake one of the casebook authors made. Fresh out of law school, the author was appointed to represent a defendant charged with second-degree murder based on a drunk driving accident. The police obtained a highly incriminating blood sample from the driver while he was

unconscious in the hospital. When time came to file a motion to suppress, the young lawyer decided not to bother since the Supreme Court had decided this precise issue against the defendant in Breithaupt v. Abram, 352 U.S. 432, 77 S.Ct. 408, 1 L.Ed.2d 448 (1957). An older and wiser member of the local defense bar asked why no motion to suppress was being filed. The young lawyer said, with a touch of arrogance, "The Supreme Court has already decided this issue in *Breithaupt*."

"I don't know *Breithaupt*," sputtered the wise lawyer. "But I do know the Tennessee Code Annotated."

Yes, indeed, a Tennessee statute provided that a blood sample could not be used for any purpose if taken without consent. The motion was filed and argued on state law grounds. The judge suppressed the blood sample, and a very favorable plea offer followed. (Tennessee later amended the statute so that it did not apply in homicide cases.)

C. THE FOURTH AMENDMENT, THE EXCLUSIONARY RULE, AND INCORPORATION: A CASE STUDY

The development of the exclusionary rule under Fourth Amendment law provides one of the best specific examples of the incorporation debate described above. While the Fourth Amendment will be discussed in considerable detail in the following three chapters, the development of its exclusionary rule as it relates to incorporation is worth exploring in some detail here.

After the now famous *Miranda* warnings, the exclusionary rule to the Fourth Amendment is probably one of the first things elementary school students learn about our criminal justice system. Simply put, the Fourth Amendment prohibits the government from unreasonable searches and seizures of persons or their houses, papers, and effects. The *exclusionary rule* basically states that evidence gained in violation of the Fourth Amendment cannot be used to prove a defendant guilty in a criminal trial. What surprises many students is that this rule did not apply to the states until 1961! It is now so taken for granted in our system that students often assume it has always been there—enshrined in our Constitution by the Founding Fathers. Students assume that all levels of government are required to follow this rule, well, because that's the way it has always been.

In fact, over the course of three key U.S. Supreme Court cases and fifty-four years, the exclusionary rule went through the same selective incorporation process as rights such as trial by jury or free speech.

The Birth of the Exclusionary Rule

Suppose that federal law enforcement officers, without good cause and without a search warrant, enter your home without your permission, and search it for evidence of a crime. The search is thorough: They go through every room in your house, including your bedroom, opening desk and dresser drawers, reading your personal diary, rifling through your private files, searching through closets, and opening containers. They find nothing and leave. We may assume for current purposes (with good reason) that this police conduct constitutes an unreasonable search of your home, in violation of your Fourth Amendment rights.

What is your remedy for violation of your rights? The text of the Fourth Amendment provides no answer. Perhaps you can bring a civil suit against the police, as you could have for centuries under the tort law of England and colonial America. Or, you might file a formal complaint with police authorities or seek to convince a United States Attorney to prosecute the officers for some criminal offense.

Now, suppose that the same events occur, but the federal agents *do* find evidence of a crime in your home, which they seize and seek to use against you in a criminal prosecution. The Fourth Amendment guarantees "the people"—not just those innocent of criminal activity—the right to be free from unreasonable searches and seizures. Therefore, in *this* case, what should your remedy be? The same as before? Or, should you have a right to have your property—unconstitutionally taken from your home—returned to you and, therefore, the Government denied the right to introduce it into evidence in your prosecution?

At common law, and for decades after ratification of the Fourth Amendment, your only remedy would have been a civil action against the agents. If the agents had no valid warrant, and entered and searched without your permission, they were automatically deemed trespassers and could offer no defense. As the North Carolina Supreme Court put the rule in 1814: "Every entry by one, into the dwelling-house of another, against the will of the occupant, is a trespass, unless warranted by such authority in law as will justify the entry." Gardner v. Neil, 4 N.C. 104 (1814). The most famous English search case from the colonial era was, after all, a tort case. See Entick v. Carrington, 19 How. State Trials 1029 (1765) (holding the king's messengers liable in tort to the victim of the search because even a specific warrant could not justify seizing private papers from private premises).

Does the Fourth Amendment itself offer a remedy? In Adams v. New York, 192 U.S. 585, 24 S.Ct. 372, 48 L.Ed. 575 (1904), the Supreme Court provided its initial answer. It stated that "the weight of authority" was that "testimony clearly competent as tending to establish the guilt of the accused of the offense charged" may be retained by the Government and used at a defendant's trial. According to *Adams*, "the courts do not stop to inquire as to the means by which the evidence was obtained."

Governmental misconduct, it may forcefully be argued, is a collateral matter in a criminal prosecution of one whom they have arrested. If the purpose of a trial is to determine the innocence or guilt of the accused, shouldn't the trial focus *exclusively* on *that* matter? If the evidence seized by the police serves to prove the defendant's guilt, why should a court exclude this probative evidence? Yet, as the following cases demonstrate, the Supreme Court fairly quickly turned away from the *Adams* approach and formulated a so-called "exclusionary rule." One conceptual defense of excluding evidence from a criminal trial is that if the government had obeyed the Fourth Amendment, it would never have gained possession of the evidence. Thus, the exclusionary rule simply puts the parties back in the position that would have occupied if the government had obeyed the Constitution.

The next three cases are best read as a set: a useful case study of how the Fourth Amendment and its exclusionary rule were "selectively" incorporated into the Fourteenth Amendment. In 1914, the Court establishes the exclusionary rule with regard to federal criminal trials in the case of Weeks v. United States, 232 U.S. 383, 34 S.Ct. 341, 58 L.Ed. 652 (1914). Thirty-five years later in Wolf v. Colorado, 338 U.S. 25, 69 S.Ct. 1359, 93 L.Ed. 1782 (1949), the Court makes clear that the exclusionary rule applies only to federal, not state cases. Finally, in 1961, in the famous case of Mapp v. Ohio, 367 U.S. 643, 81 S.Ct. 1684, 6 L.Ed.2d 1081 (1961), the Court overrules *Wolf* and applies the exclusionary rule to the states via the Fourteenth Amendment (the later development of the exclusionary rule is explored in chapter 7).

As you read these three cases, pay close attention to the language the Court uses to describe the purpose of the exclusionary rule, its importance, and its status, or not, as a constitutional requirement. Although the importance of the exclusionary rule in the American criminal justice system may seem assured by the end of *Mapp*, the language in all three of these cases is significantly reinterpreted when we get to the cases in chapter 7. Just when you think you have this stuff figured out . . . .

When you get to *Mapp,* you may also want to look closely at both Justice Harlan's and Justice Black's opinions. Can you see their relative views on the incorporation debate from the positions they take in *Mapp*?

WEEKS V. UNITED STATES

Supreme Court of the United States, 1914.
232 U.S. 383, 34 S.Ct. 341, 58 L.Ed. 652.

MR. JUSTICE DAY delivered the opinion of the court [joined by CHIEF JUSTICE WHITE, and JUSTICES MCKENNA, HOLMES, LURTON, HUGHES, VAN DEVANTER, LAMAR, and PITNEY].

An indictment was returned against the * * * defendant * * *. The seventh count, upon which a conviction was had, charged the use of the mails for the purpose of transporting certain coupons or tickets representing chances or shares in a lottery or gift enterprise, in violation of [federal law]. * * *

The defendant was arrested by a police officer, so far as the record shows, without warrant, at the Union Station in Kansas City, Missouri, where he was employed by an express company. Other police officers had gone to the house of the defendant and being told by a neighbor where the key was kept, found it and entered the house. They searched the defendant's room and took possession of various papers and articles found there, which were afterwards turned over to the United States Marshal. Later in the same day police officers returned with the Marshal, who thought he might find additional evidence, and, being admitted by someone in the house, probably a boarder, * * * the Marshal searched the defendant's room and carried away certain letters and envelopes found in the drawer of a chiffonier. Neither the marshal nor the police officers had a search warrant. * * *

[The defendant unsuccessfully petitioned the district court for return of the items that were seized by the local police and United States Marshal on the ground that the property was obtained in violation of the Fourth Amendment.] Among the papers retained and put in evidence were a number of lottery tickets and statements with reference to the lottery, taken at the first visit of the police to the defendant's room, and a number of letters written to the defendant in respect to the lottery, taken by the Marshal upon his search of defendant's room. * * *

The history of this Amendment is given with particularity in the opinion of Mr. Justice Bradley, speaking for the court in *Boyd v. United States*, 116 U.S. 616, 6 S.Ct. 524, 29 L.Ed. 746 (1886). As was there shown, it took its origin in the determination of the framers of the Amendments to the Federal Constitution to provide for that instrument a Bill of Rights, securing to the American people, among other things, those safeguards which had grown up in England to protect the people from unreasonable searches and seizures, such as were permitted under the general warrants issued under authority of the Government by which there had been invasions of the home and privacy of the citizens and the seizure of their private papers in support of charges, real or imaginary, made against them. Such practices had also received sanction under warrants and seizures under the so-called writs of assistance, issued in the American colonies. Resistance to these practices had established the principle which was enacted into the fundamental law in the Fourth Amendment, that a man's house was his castle and not to be invaded by any general authority to search and seize his goods and papers. * * *

In the *Boyd Case*, after citing Lord Camden's judgment in *Entick v. Carrington*, 19 Howell's State Trials 1029, Mr. Justice Bradley said:

> "The principles laid down in this opinion affect the very essence of constitutional liberty and security. They reach farther than the concrete form of the case then before the court, with its adventitious circumstances; they apply to all invasions on the part of the government and its employees of the sanctity of a man's home and the privacies of life. It is not the breaking of his doors, and the rummaging of his drawers, that constitutes the essence of the offence; but it is the invasion of his indefeasible right of personal security, personal liberty and private property, where that right has never been forfeited by his conviction of some public offence,—it is the invasion of this sacred right which underlies and constitutes the essence of Lord Camden's judgment." * * *

The effect of the Fourth Amendment is to put the courts of the United States and Federal officials, in the exercise of their power and authority, under limitations and restraints as to the exercise of such power and authority, and to forever secure the people, their persons, houses, papers and effects against all unreasonable searches and seizures under the guise of law. This protection reaches all alike, whether accused of crime or not, and the duty of giving to it force and effect is obligatory upon all entrusted under our Federal system with the enforcement of the laws. The tendency of those who execute the criminal laws of the country to obtain conviction by means of unlawful seizures and enforced confessions, the latter often obtained after subjecting accused persons to unwarranted practices destructive of rights secured by the Federal Constitution, should find no sanction in the judgments of the courts which are charged at all times with the support of the Constitution and to which people of all conditions have a right to appeal for the maintenance of such fundamental rights. * * *

* * * If letters and private documents can * * * be seized and held and used in evidence against a citizen accused of an offense, the protection of the Fourth Amendment * * * is of no value, and, so far as those thus placed are concerned, might as well be stricken from the Constitution. The efforts of the courts and their

officials to bring the guilty to punishment, praiseworthy as they are, are not to be aided by the sacrifice of those great principles established by years of endeavor and suffering which have resulted in their embodiment in the fundamental law of the land. The United States Marshal * * * acted without sanction of law, * * * and under color of his office undertook to make a seizure of private papers in direct violation of the constitutional prohibition against such action. * * * To sanction such proceedings would be to affirm by judicial decision a manifest neglect if not an open defiance of the prohibitions of the Constitution, intended for the protection of the people against such unauthorized action. * * *

We therefore reach the conclusion that the letters in question were taken from the house of the accused by an official of the United States * * * in direct violation of the constitutional rights of the defendant; that having made a seasonable application for their return, * * * the court should have restored these letters to the accused. In holding them and permitting their use upon the trial, we think prejudicial error was committed. As to the papers and property seized by the policemen, it does not appear that they acted under any claim of Federal authority such as would make the Amendment applicable to such unauthorized seizures. * * * What remedies the defendant may have against them we need not inquire, as the Fourth Amendment is not directed to individual misconduct of such officials. Its limitations reach the Federal Government and its agencies.

It results that the judgment of the court below must be reversed * * *.

NOTES AND QUESTIONS

1. Why does the Court conclude that the letters seized by the United States Marshal should be excluded from the defendant's trial? Why did the Court not treat the papers and property seized by the local police in the same manner?

2. Federal Rule of Criminal Procedure 41(g) provides that a "person aggrieved by an unlawful search and seizure of property or by the deprivation of property may move for the property's return." And, under Rule 41(h), "[a] defendant may move to suppress evidence in the court where the trial will occur * * *."

Suppose the police unlawfully search Jane's home and seize contraband, such as illegal narcotics. Should Jane be able to seek its return under the federal rule quoted above? If not, is the contraband admissible at her trial?

3. *"Silver platter" doctrine.* Because the Court in *Weeks* only applied the exclusionary rule to evidence seized under "federal authority," this seemingly left local police free to conduct unreasonable searches and seizures and then deliver the evidence to federal prosecutors "on a silver platter," to be used in federal

prosecutions. In Byars v. United States, 273 U.S. 28, 47 S.Ct. 248, 71 L.Ed. 520 (1927), however, the Court ruled that this "silver platter" doctrine did not apply to evidence obtained unlawfully during a search that "in substance and effect" was a joint state-federal venture. In *Byars*, state police conducted their search accompanied by a federal agent. And, in Gambino v. United States, 275 U.S. 310, 48 S.Ct. 137, 72 L.Ed. 293 (1927), state officers, acting alone, conducted a search solely on behalf of the federal government. In both cases, the Court applied the *Weeks* exclusionary rule to the state officers' actions.

4. *The exclusionary rule in the states.* What if state or local police officers want to use evidence in a state prosecution they obtained as a result of an unreasonable search or seizure? *Weeks* recognized an exclusionary rule in federal cases. Is there an equivalent exclusionary rule that applies in state courts through the Fourteenth Amendment due process clause? Consider the next case in this regard.

WOLF V. COLORADO

Supreme Court of the United States, 1949.
338 U.S. 25, 69 S.Ct. 1359, 93 L.Ed. 1782.

MR. JUSTICE FRANKFURTER delivered the opinion of the Court [joined by CHIEF JUSTICE VINSON, and JUSTICES REED, JACKSON, and BURTON].

The precise question for consideration is this: Does a conviction by a State court for a State offense deny the "due process of law" required by the Fourteenth Amendment, solely because evidence that was admitted at the trial was obtained under circumstances which would have rendered it inadmissible in a prosecution for violation of a federal law in a court of the United States because there deemed to be an infraction of the Fourth Amendment as applied in *Weeks v. United States*? The Supreme Court of Colorado has sustained convictions in which such evidence was admitted, and we brought the cases here.

Unlike the specific requirements and restrictions placed by the Bill of Rights (Amendments I to VIII) upon the administration of criminal justice by federal authority, the Fourteenth Amendment did not subject criminal justice in the States to specific limitations. The notion that the "due process of law" guaranteed by the Fourteenth Amendment is shorthand for the first eight amendments of the Constitution and thereby incorporates them has been rejected by this Court again and again, after impressive consideration. * * * The issue is closed.

For purposes of ascertaining the restrictions which the Due Process Clause imposed upon the States in the enforcement of their criminal law, we adhere to the views expressed in *Palko v. Connecticut*, 302 U.S. 319, 58 S.Ct. 149, 82 L.Ed. 288. * * * In rejecting the suggestion that the Due Process Clause incorporated the original Bill of Rights, Mr. Justice Cardozo reaffirmed on behalf of that Court a different but deeper and more pervasive conception of the Due Process Clause. This Clause exacts from the States for the lowliest and the most outcast all that is "implicit in the concept of ordered liberty."

Due process of law thus conveys neither formal nor fixed nor narrow requirements. It is the compendious expression for all those rights which the courts must enforce because they are basic to our free society. But basic rights do not become petrified as of any one time, even though, as a matter of human experience, some may not too rhetorically be called eternal verities. It is of the very nature of a free society to advance in its standards of what is deemed reasonable and right. Representing as it does a living principle, due process is not confined within a permanent catalogue of what may at a given time be deemed the limits or the essentials of fundamental rights.

To rely on a tidy formula for the easy determination of what is a fundamental right for purposes of legal enforcement may satisfy a longing for certainty but ignores the movements of a free society. It belittles the scale of the conception of due process. The real clue to the problem confronting the judiciary in the application of the Due Process Clause is not to ask where the line is once and for all to be drawn but to recognize that it is for the Court to draw it by the gradual and empiric process of "inclusion and exclusion." * * *

The security of one's privacy against arbitrary intrusion by the police—which is at the core of the Fourth Amendment—is basic to a free society. It is therefore implicit in "the concept of ordered liberty" and as such enforceable against the States through the Due Process Clause. The knock at the door, whether by day or by night, as a prelude to a search, without authority of law but solely on the authority of the police, did not need the commentary of recent history to be condemned as inconsistent with the conception of human rights enshrined in the history and the basic constitutional documents of English-speaking peoples.

Accordingly, we have no hesitation in saying that were a State affirmatively to sanction such police incursion into privacy it would run counter to the guaranty of the Fourteenth Amendment. But the ways of enforcing such a rule raise questions of a different order. How such arbitrary conduct should be checked, what remedies against it should be afforded, the means by which the right should be made effective, are all questions not to be so dogmatically answered as to preclude the varying solutions which spring from an allowable range of judgment on issues not susceptible to quantitative solution.

In *Weeks v. United States*, *supra*, this Court held that in a federal prosecution the Fourth Amendment barred the use of evidence secured through an illegal search and seizure. * * * It was not derived from the explicit requirements of the Fourth Amendment; it was not based on legislation expressing Congressional policy in the enforcement of the Constitution. The decision was a matter of judicial implication. Since then it has been frequently applied and we stoutly adhere to it. But the immediate question is whether the basic right to protection against arbitrary intrusion by the police demands the exclusion of logically relevant evidence obtained by an unreasonable search and seizure because, in a federal prosecution for a federal crime, it would be excluded. As a matter of inherent reason, one would suppose this to be an issue as to which men with complete devotion to the protection of the right of privacy might give different answers. When we find that in fact most of the English-speaking world does not regard as vital to such protection the exclusion of evidence thus obtained, we must hesitate to treat this remedy as an essential ingredient of the right. The contrariety of views of the States is particularly impressive in view of the careful reconsideration which they have given the problem in the light of the *Weeks* decision.

[According to the Court's survey of the law, twenty-seven states prior to *Weeks* had passed on the admissibility of evidence obtained by unlawful search or seizure. Of these, all but one state rejected an exclusionary rule. After *Weeks*, forty-seven states passed on the *Weeks* doctrine. Of this number, only sixteen adopted the *Weeks* exclusionary rule. The Court also reported that of ten jurisdictions within the United Kingdom and the British Commonwealth, none had adopted a similar doctrine. The Court concluded that, although the exclusionary rule might "be an effective way of deterring unreasonable searches, it is not for this Court to condemn as falling below the minimal standards assured by the Due Process Clause a State's reliance upon other methods which, if consistently enforced, would be equally effective."] * * *

We hold, therefore, that in a prosecution in a State court for a State crime the Fourteenth Amendment does not forbid the admission of evidence obtained by an unreasonable search and seizure. * * *

Affirmed.

[JUSTICE BLACK's concurring opinion is omitted. Also omitted are the dissenting opinions of JUSTICES DOUGLAS, MURPHY, and RUTLEDGE.]

NOTES AND QUESTIONS

1. *Wolf* represented a classic "I have good news and I have bad news" story for the defendant: "Arbitrary searches and seizures by state and local police violate the concept of ordered liberty and, therefore, violate the Fourteenth Amendment due process clause, but—sorry!—the government can still use the fruits of its agents' unconstitutional conduct in your criminal prosecution." Is there any practical value in possessing the right to be free from arbitrary or unreasonable searches and seizures if a state may use the evidence unlawfully secured in a criminal prosecution?

2. *The "Rochin" principle: the exclusionary rule in different clothing.* In Rochin v. California, 342 U.S. 165, 72 S.Ct. 205, 96 L.Ed. 183 (1952), Justice Frankfurter, author of *Wolf*, described the relevant facts in the case:

> Having "some information that [Rochin] was selling narcotics," three deputy sheriffs * * * made for the two-story dwelling house in which Rochin lived with his mother, common-law wife, brothers and sisters. Finding the outside door open, they entered and then forced open the door to Rochin's room on the second floor. Inside they found petitioner sitting partly dressed on the side of the bed, upon which his wife was lying. On a "night stand" beside the bed the deputies spied two capsules. When asked, "Whose stuff is this?" Rochin seized the capsules and put them in his mouth. A struggle ensued, in the course of which the three officers "jumped upon him" and attempted to extract the capsules. The force they applied proved unavailing against Rochin's resistance. He was handcuffed and taken to a hospital. At the direction of one of the officers a doctor forced an emetic solution through a tube into Rochin's stomach against his will. This "stomach pumping" produced vomiting. In the vomited matter were found two capsules which proved to contain morphine.

Rochin was prosecuted for possession of morphine. The chief evidence against him, admitted over defense objection, were the two capsules extracted from his stomach. Although local police conducted the search and seizure, the Supreme Court ruled that the Fourteenth Amendment due process clause prohibited admission of the capsules. Justice Frankfurter explained:

> [W]e are compelled to conclude that the proceedings by which this conviction was obtained do more than offend some fastidious squeamishness or private sentimentalism about combatting crime too energetically. This is conduct that shocks the conscience. Illegally breaking into the privacy of the petitioner, the struggle to open his mouth and remove what was there, the forcible extraction of his stomach's contents—this course of proceeding by agents of government to obtain evidence is

> bound to offend even hardened sensibilities. They are methods too close to the rack and the screw to permit of constitutional differentiation.

Is *Rochin* consistent with *Wolf*? If this had been a pre-*Weeks* federal prosecution, how would the case have been resolved?

3. *Wolf* was not the end of the story. The Court said in *Wolf* that the total incorporation theory of due process had been considered and rejected several times by eminent justices and that "[t]he issue is closed." Well, as to total incorporation, maybe, but not with respect to the Fourth Amendment. Enter Miss Mapp.

MAPP V. OHIO

Supreme Court of the United States, 1961.
367 U.S. 643, 81 S.Ct. 1684, 6 L.Ed.2d 1081.

MR. JUSTICE CLARK delivered the opinion of the Court [joined by CHIEF JUSTICE WARREN, and JUSTICES BLACK, DOUGLAS and BRENNAN].

Appellant stands convicted of knowingly having had in her possession and under her control certain lewd and lascivious books, pictures, and photographs in violation of [state law. The materials consisted of four books (Affairs of a Troubadour, Little Darlings, London Stage Affairs, Memories of a Hotel Man) and a hand-drawn obscene picture.]. * * *

On May 23, 1957, three Cleveland police officers arrived at appellant's residence in that city pursuant to information that "a person [was] hiding out in the home, who was wanted for questioning in connection with a recent bombing, and that there was a large amount of policy [gambling] paraphernalia being hidden in the home." Miss Mapp and her daughter by a former marriage lived on the top floor of the two-family dwelling. Upon their arrival at that house, the officers knocked on the door and demanded entrance but appellant, after telephoning her attorney, refused to admit them without a search warrant. They advised their headquarters of the situation and undertook a surveillance of the house.

The officers again sought entrance some three hours later when four or more additional officers arrived on the scene. When Miss Mapp did not come to the door immediately, at least one of the several doors to the house was forcibly opened" and the policemen gained admittance. Meanwhile Miss Mapp's attorney arrived, but the officers, having secured their own entry, and continuing in their defiance of the law, would permit him neither to see Miss Mapp nor to enter the house. It appears that Miss Mapp was halfway down the stairs from the upper floor to the front door when the officers, in this highhanded manner, broke into the hall. She demanded to see the search warrant. A paper, claimed to be a warrant, was held up by one of the officers. She grabbed the "warrant" and placed it in her bosom. A struggle ensued in which the officers recovered the piece of paper and as a result of which they handcuffed appellant because she had been "belligerent" in resisting their official rescue of the "warrant" from her person. Running roughshod over appellant, a policeman "grabbed" her, "twisted [her] hand," and she "yelled [and] pleaded with him" because "it was hurting." Appellant, in handcuffs, was then forcibly taken upstairs to her bedroom where the officers searched a dresser, a chest of drawers, a closet and some suitcases. They also looked into a photo album and through personal papers belonging to the appellant. The search spread to the rest of the second floor including the child's bedroom, the living room, the kitchen and a dinette. The basement of the building and a trunk found therein were also searched. The obscene materials for possession of which she was ultimately convicted were discovered in the course of that widespread search.

At the trial no search warrant was produced by the prosecution, nor was the failure to produce one explained or accounted for. At best, "There is, in the record, considerable doubt as to whether there ever was any warrant for the search of defendant's home." The Ohio Supreme Court believed a "reasonable argument" could be made that the conviction should be reversed "because the 'methods' employed to obtain the [evidence] * * * were such as to 'offend "a sense of justice," ' " but the court found determinative the fact that the evidence had not been taken "from defendant's person by the use of brutal or offensive physical force against defendant."

The State says that even if the search were made without authority, or otherwise unreasonably, it is not prevented from using the unconstitutionally seized evidence at trial, citing *Wolf v. Colorado* [p. 54], in which this Court did indeed hold "that in a prosecution in a State court for a State crime the Fourteenth Amendment does not forbid the admission of evidence obtained by an unreasonable search and seizure." On this appeal, * * * it is urged once again that we review that holding.

I. * * *

* * * [I]n the year 1914, in the *Weeks* [*v. United States*] case, this Court "for the first time" held that "in a federal prosecution the Fourth Amendment barred the use of evidence secured through an illegal search and seizure." This Court has ever since required of federal law officers a strict adherence to that command which this Court has held to be a clear, specific, and constitutionally required—even if judicially implied—deterrent safeguard without insistence upon which the Fourth Amendment would have been reduced to "a form of words." Holmes, J., *Silverthorne Lumber Co. v. United States*, 251 U.S. 385, 392, 40 S.Ct. 182, 183, 64 L.Ed.

319 (1920). It meant, quite simply, that "conviction by means of unlawful seizures and enforced confessions * * * should find no sanction in the judgments of the courts * * *," and that such evidence "shall not be used at all."

There are in the cases of this Court some passing references to the *Weeks* rule as being one of evidence. But the plain and unequivocal language of *Weeks*—and its later paraphrase in *Wolf*—to the effect that the *Weeks* rule is of constitutional origin, remains entirely undisturbed. * * *

II.

In 1949, 35 years after *Weeks* was announced, this Court, in *Wolf v. Colorado*, again for the first time, * * * decided that the *Weeks* exclusionary rule would not then be imposed upon the States as "an essential ingredient of the right." The Court's reasons for not considering essential to the right to privacy, as a curb imposed upon the States by the Due Process Clause, that which decades before had been posited as part and parcel of the Fourth Amendment's limitation upon federal encroachment of individual privacy, were bottomed on factual considerations.

While they are not basically relevant to a decision that the exclusionary rule is an essential ingredient of the Fourth Amendment as the right it embodies is vouchsafed against the States by the Due Process Clause, we will consider the current validity of the factual grounds upon which *Wolf* was based.

The Court in *Wolf* first stated that "[t]he contrariety of views of the States" on the adoption of the exclusionary rule of *Weeks* was "particularly impressive" * * *. While in 1949, prior to the *Wolf* case, almost two-thirds of the States were opposed to the use of the exclusionary rule, now, despite the *Wolf* case, more than half of those since passing upon it, by their own legislative or judicial decision, have wholly or partly adopted or adhered to the *Weeks* rule. Significantly, among those now following the rule is California, which, according to its highest court, was "compelled to reach that conclusion because other remedies have completely failed to secure compliance with the constitutional provisions * * *." *People v. Cahan*, 44 Cal.2d 434, 445, 282 P.2d 905 [1955]. In connection with this California case, we note that the second basis elaborated in *Wolf* in support of its failure to enforce the exclusionary doctrine against the States was that "other means of protection" have been afforded "the right to privacy." The experience of California that such other remedies have been worthless and futile is buttressed by the experience of other States. * * *

It, therefore, plainly appears that the factual considerations supporting the failure of the *Wolf* Court to include the *Weeks* exclusionary rule when it recognized the enforceability of the right to privacy against the States in 1949, while not basically relevant to the constitutional consideration, could not, in any analysis, now be deemed controlling.

III.

* * * Today we once again examine *Wolf's* constitutional documentation of the right to privacy free from unreasonable state intrusion, and, after its dozen years on our books, are led by it to close the only courtroom door remaining open to evidence secured by official lawlessness in flagrant abuse of that basic right, reserved to all persons as a specific guarantee against that very same unlawful conduct. We hold that all evidence obtained by searches and seizures in violation of the Constitution is, by that same authority, inadmissible in a state court.

IV.

Since the Fourth Amendment's right of privacy has been declared enforceable against the States through the Due Process Clause of the Fourteenth, it is enforceable against them by the same sanction of exclusion as is used against the Federal Government. Were it otherwise, then just as without the *Weeks* rule the assurance against unreasonable federal searches and seizures would be "a form of words," valueless and undeserving of mention in a perpetual charter of inestimable human liberties, so too, without that rule the freedom from state invasions of privacy would be so ephemeral and so neatly severed from its conceptual nexus with the freedom from all brutish means of coercing evidence as not to merit this Court's high regard as a freedom "implicit in the concept of ordered liberty." * * * Therefore, in extending the substantive protections of due process to all constitutionally unreasonable searches—state or federal—it was logically and constitutionally necessary that the exclusion doctrine—an essential part of the right to privacy—be also insisted upon as an essential ingredient of the right newly recognized by the *Wolf* case. In short, the admission of the new constitutional right by *Wolf* could not consistently tolerate denial of its most important constitutional privilege, namely, the exclusion of the evidence which an accused had been forced to give by reason of the unlawful seizure. To hold otherwise is to grant the right but in reality to withhold its privilege and enjoyment. Only last year the Court itself recognized that the purpose of the exclusionary rule "is to deter—to compel respect for the constitutional guaranty in the only effectively available way—by removing the incentive to disregard it."

* * * This Court has not hesitated to enforce as strictly against the States as it does against the Federal Government the rights of free speech and of a free press, the right to notice and to a fair, public trial, including, as it does, the right

not to be convicted by use of a coerced confession, however logically relevant it be, and without regard to its reliability. * * * The philosophy of each Amendment and of each freedom is complementary to, although not dependent upon, that of the other in its sphere of influence—the very least that together they assure in either sphere is that no man is to be convicted on unconstitutional evidence.

V.

Moreover, our holding that the exclusionary rule is an essential part of both the Fourth and Fourteenth Amendments is not only the logical dictate of prior cases, but it also makes very good sense. There is no war between the Constitution and common sense. Presently, a federal prosecutor may make no use of evidence illegally seized, but a State's attorney across the street may, although he supposedly is operating under the enforceable prohibitions of the same Amendment. Thus the State, by admitting evidence unlawfully seized, serves to encourage disobedience to the Federal Constitution which it is bound to uphold. * * *

There are those who say, as did Justice (then Judge) Cardozo, that under our constitutional exclusionary doctrine "[t]he criminal is to go free because the constable has blundered." In some cases this will undoubtedly be the result. But, * * * "there is another consideration—the imperative of judicial integrity." The criminal goes free, if he must, but it is the law that sets him free. Nothing can destroy a government more quickly than its failure to observe its own laws, or worse, its disregard of the charter of its own existence. As Mr. Justice Brandeis, dissenting, said in *Olmstead v. United States*, 277 U.S. 438, 485, 48 S.Ct. 564, 575, 72 L.Ed. 944 (1928): "Our Government is the potent, the omnipresent teacher. For good or for ill, it teaches the whole people by its example. * * * If the Government becomes a lawbreaker, it breeds contempt for law; it invites every man to become a law unto himself; it invites anarchy." Nor can it lightly be assumed that, as a practical matter, adoption of the exclusionary rule fetters law enforcement. Only last year this Court expressly considered that contention and found that "pragmatic evidence of a sort" to the contrary was not wanting. * * *

* * * Our decision, founded on reason and truth, gives to the individual no more than that which the Constitution guarantees him, to the police officer no less than that to which honest law enforcement is entitled, and, to the courts, that judicial integrity so necessary in the true administration of justice. * * *

Reversed and remanded.

MR. JUSTICE BLACK, concurring. * * *

I am still not persuaded that the Fourth Amendment, standing alone, would be enough to bar the introduction into evidence against an accused of papers and effects seized from him in violation of its commands. For the Fourth Amendment does not itself contain any provision expressly precluding the use of such evidence, and I am extremely doubtful that such a provision could properly be inferred from nothing more than the basic command against unreasonable searches and seizures. Reflection on the problem, however, in the light of cases coming before the Court since *Wolf*, has led me to conclude that when the Fourth Amendment's ban against unreasonable searches and seizures is considered together with the Fifth Amendment's ban against compelled self-incrimination, a constitutional basis emerges which not only justifies but actually requires the exclusionary rule.

The close interrelationship between the Fourth and Fifth Amendments, as they apply to this problem, has long been recognized and, indeed, was expressly made the ground for this Court's holding in *Boyd v. United States*[, 116 U.S. 616, 6 S.Ct. 524, 29 L.Ed. 746 (1886)]. There the Court fully discussed this relationship and declared itself "unable to perceive that the seizure of a man's private books and papers to be used in evidence against him is substantially different from compelling him to be a witness against himself." * * * [A]lthough I rejected the argument [in *Wolf*], its force has, for me at least, become compelling with the more thorough understanding of the problem brought on by recent cases. In the final analysis, it seems to me that the *Boyd* doctrine, though perhaps not required by the express language of the Constitution strictly construed, is amply justified from an historical standpoint, soundly based in reason, and entirely consistent with what I regard to be the proper approach to interpretation of our Bill of Rights * * *.

[JUSTICE DOUGLAS's concurring opinion is omitted. JUSTICE STEWART, who concurred in the result expressed "no view as to the merits of the constitutional issue which the Court today decides." Instead, he would have reversed the conviction on the ground that the Ohio statute punishing mere possession of obscenity violated rights of "free thought and expression assured against state action by the Fourteenth Amendment."]

MR. JUSTICE HARLAN, whom MR. JUSTICE FRANKFURTER and MR. JUSTICE WHITTAKER join, dissenting.

In overruling the *Wolf* case the Court, in my opinion, has forgotten the sense of judicial restraint which, with due regard for *stare decisis* [to stand by things decided, *i.e.*, let the precedent stand], is one element that should enter into deciding whether a past decision of this Court should be overruled. Apart from that I also believe that the *Wolf* rule represents sounder Constitutional doctrine than the new rule which now replaces it.

I.

From the Court's statement of the case one would gather that the central, if not controlling, issue on this appeal is whether illegally state-seized evidence is Constitutionally admissible in a state prosecution, an issue which would of course face us with the need for re-examining *Wolf*. However, such is not the situation. For, although that question was indeed raised here and below among appellant's subordinate points, the new and pivotal issue brought to the Court by this appeal is whether * * * the Ohio Revised Code making criminal the *mere* knowing possession or control of obscene material, and under which appellant has been convicted, is consistent with the rights of free thought and expression assured against state action by the Fourteenth Amendment. That was the principal issue which was decided by the Ohio Supreme Court, * * * and which was briefed and argued in this Court. [Indeed, Ms. Mapp's brief did not urge the overruling of *Wolf* and did not even cite the case. The brief of the American and Ohio Civil Liberties Unions, as friend of the Court did in one short concluding paragraph of its argument ask the Court to re-examine and overrule *Wolf*. Counsel for appellant on oral argument, as in his brief, did not urge that *Wolf* be overruled. Indeed, when pressed by questioning from the bench whether he was not in fact urging us to overrule *Wolf*, counsel expressly disavowed any such purpose.]

In this posture of things, I think it fair to say that five members of this Court have simply "reached out" to overrule *Wolf*. * * * I can perceive no justification for regarding this case as an appropriate occasion for re-examining *Wolf*. * * *

II.

Essential to the majority's argument against *Wolf* is the proposition that the rule of *Weeks v. United States*, excluding in federal criminal trials the use of evidence obtained in violation of the Fourth Amendment, derives not from the "supervisory power" of this Court over the federal judicial system, but from Constitutional requirement. This is so because no one, I suppose, would suggest that this Court possesses any general supervisory power over the state courts. Although I entertain considerable doubt as to the soundness of this foundational proposition of the majority, I shall assume, for present purposes, that the *Weeks* rule "is of constitutional origin."

At the heart of the majority's opinion in this case is the following syllogism: (1) the rule excluding in federal criminal trials evidence which is the product of an illegal search and seizure is "part and parcel" of the Fourth Amendment; (2) *Wolf* held that the "privacy" assured against federal action by the Fourth Amendment is also protected against state action by the Fourteenth Amendment; and (3) it is therefore "logically and constitutionally necessary" that the *Weeks* exclusionary rule should also be enforced against the States.

This reasoning ultimately rests on the unsound premise that because *Wolf* carried into the States, as part of "the concept of ordered liberty" embodied in the Fourteenth Amendment, the principle of "privacy" underlying the Fourth Amendment, it must follow that whatever configurations of the Fourth Amendment have been developed in the particularizing federal precedents are likewise to be deemed a part of "ordered liberty," and as such are enforceable against the States. For me, this does not follow at all.

It cannot be too much emphasized that what was recognized in *Wolf* was not that the Fourth Amendment as such is enforceable against the States as a facet of due process, a view of the Fourteenth Amendment which, as *Wolf* itself pointed out, has long since been discredited, but the principle of privacy "which is at the core of the Fourth Amendment." It would not be proper to expect or impose any precise equivalence, either as regards the scope of the right or the means of its implementation, between the requirements of the Fourth and Fourteenth Amendments. For the Fourth, unlike what was said in *Wolf* of the Fourteenth, does not state a general principle only; it is a particular command, having its setting in a pre-existing legal context on which both interpreting decisions and enabling statutes must at least build. * * *

I would not impose upon the States this federal exclusionary remedy. The reasons given by the majority for now suddenly turning its back on *Wolf* seem to me notably unconvincing.

First, it is said that "the factual grounds upon which *Wolf* was based" have since changed, in that more States now follow the Weeks exclusionary rule than was so at the time *Wolf* was decided. While that is true, * * * surely all this is beside the point, as the majority itself indeed seems to recognize. Our concern here, as it was in *Wolf*, is not with the desirability of that rule but only with the question whether the States are Constitutionally free to follow it or not as they may themselves determine, and the relevance of the disparity of views among the States on this point lies simply in the fact that the judgment involved is a debatable one. * * *

The preservation of a proper balance between state and federal responsibility in the administration of criminal justice demands patience on the part of those who might like to see things move faster among the States in this respect. Problems of criminal law enforcement vary widely from State to State. One State, in considering the totality of its legal picture, may conclude that the need for embracing the *Weeks* rule is pressing because other remedies are unavailable or inadequate to secure compliance with the substantive Constitutional principle involved. Another, though equally solicitous of Constitutional rights, may choose to pursue one purpose at a time, allowing all evidence relevant to guilt to be brought into a criminal trial, and dealing with Constitutional infractions by other means. Still another may consider the exclusionary rule too rough-and-ready a remedy, in that it reaches only unconstitutional intrusions which eventuate in criminal prosecution of the victims. Further, a State after experimenting with the *Weeks* rule for a time may, because of unsatisfactory experience with it, decide to revert to a non-exclusionary rule. And so on. * * * For us the question remains, as it has always been, one of state power, not one of passing judgment on the wisdom of one state course or another. In my view this Court should continue to forbear from fettering the States with an adamant rule which may embarrass them in coping with their own peculiar problems in criminal law enforcement. * * *

A state conviction comes to us as the complete product of a sovereign judicial system. Typically a case will have been tried in a trial court, tested in some final appellate court, and will go no further. In the comparatively rare instance when a conviction is reviewed by us on due process grounds we deal then with a finished product in the creation of which we are allowed no hand, and our task, far from being one of over-all supervision, is, speaking generally, restricted to a determination of whether the prosecution was Constitutionally fair. The specifics of trial procedure, which in every mature legal system will vary greatly in detail, are within the sole competence of the States. I do not see how it can be said that a trial becomes unfair simply because a State determines that evidence may be considered by the trier of fact, regardless of how it was obtained, if it is relevant to the one issue with which the trial is concerned, the guilt or innocence of the accused. Of course, a court may use its procedures as an incidental means of pursuing other ends than the correct resolution of the controversies before it. Such indeed is the Weeks rule, but if a State does not choose to use its courts in this way, I do not believe that this Court is empowered to impose this much-debated procedure on local courts, however efficacious we may consider the Weeks rule to be as a means of securing Constitutional rights. * * *

I regret that I find so unwise in principle and so inexpedient in policy a decision motivated by the high purpose of increasing respect for Constitutional rights. But in the last analysis I think this Court can increase respect for the Constitution only if it rigidly respects the limitations which the Constitution places upon it, and respects as well the principles inherent in its own processes. In the present case I think we exceed both, and that our voice becomes only a voice of power, not of reason.

NOTES AND QUESTIONS

1. So what was the progression of the exclusionary rule from the 4th Amendment via the process of incorporation through the Fourteenth Amendment to a rule that all states are required to follow? Lacking a remedy in the text of the Fourth Amendment for violations of the Amendment, the Court in *Weeks* created the exclusionary rule as a way of giving the 4th Amendment some teeth and meaning. If violations of the 4th Amendment meant cases could not be prosecuted, the thinking went, law enforcement agencies would have more incentive to obey its strictures. However, in *Wolf*, the Court held that, while the 4th Amendment applied to the States via the 14th Amendment as a fundamental part of due process, the exclusionary rule was only one way of enforcing the prohibition on unreasonable searches and seizures. States that did not like the exclusionary rule could develop their own approaches. Finally, the Court in *Mapp* found that the states had failed to do that in any effective manner and as a result, the 4th Amendment was rendered meaningless in state court proceedings, effectively denying the citizens that fundamental part of due process. Thus, the 4th Amendment's exclusionary rule was found to apply to state as well as federal actions.

This is a pretty typical example of the due process approach to incorporation. Only those rights deemed fundamental to issues of liberty and due process make the grade. Fortunately, (or unfortunately, depending on which side of the incorporation debate you fall on) almost all of the criminal procedure rights, and the rulings interpreting those rights, have been incorporated, and are now considered to apply to the states.

2. *Counting votes.* You should grow accustomed to counting the votes in Supreme Court opinions. That is, you should determine how many justices signed an opinion of the Court. (We have helped you in this casebook by listing the justices who join each opinion.) A majority opinion of five justices does not carry the same symbolic weight as a unanimous opinion and, of course, is more susceptible to erosion or outright overruling, especially as new justices join the Court. In a few cases, the Court cannot muster a majority for one opinion. In these cases, the judgment of the Court will be announced in what is known as a "plurality" opinion. The precedential value of cases without a majority opinion is tenuous.

When counting votes, it is also important to distinguish between two types of concurring opinions. Sometimes, a justice will "concur in the judgment" or "concur in the result," as Justice Stewart did in *Mapp*. In such circumstances, the concurring justice has reached the same outcome as the majority (e.g., reversal or affirmance of a lower court judgment), but does not want to attach his or her name to the main opinion, usually because the concurring justice reaches the result on different grounds.

Alternatively, concurring justices (here, Black and Douglas) may sign the Court's opinion, but still write separately. This is called a concurrence "in the opinion" of the Court. Typically, justices will write such a concurrence in order to clarify aspects of the main opinion that they believe need elucidation, or because they are unhappy with certain language in the principal opinion.

3. Do you consider Mapp an "innocent" or "guilty" person, who was subjected to police misconduct? In regard to the admissibility of the seized evidence, should such characterization matter?

4. What was the Ohio Supreme Court getting at when it stated that a "reasonable argument" could be made that the conviction should be overturned because police methods "offended a sense of justice." Why do you think it rejected that "reasonable argument"?

5. Why did Justice Harlan believe that this case was an inappropriate vehicle for overruling *Wolf*? Was he right? What should a justice who believed that *Wolf* was wrongly decided have done?

After his retirement, Justice Potter Stewart described the behind-the-scene events this way:

> At the conference following the argument, a majority of the Justices agreed that the Ohio statute violated the *first* and fourteenth amendments. Justice Tom Clark was assigned the job of writing the opinion of the Court.
>
> What transpired in the month following our conference * * * is really a matter of speculation on my part, but I have always suspected that the members of the soon-to-be *Mapp* majority had met in what I affectionately call a "rump caucus" to discuss a different basis for their decision.[1] But regardless of how they reached their decision, five Justices * * * concluded that * * * *Wolf* was to be overruled.
>
> I was shocked when Justice Clark's proposed Court opinion reached my desk. I immediately wrote him a note expressing my surprise and questioning the wisdom of overruling an important doctrine in a case in

---

1 Professor Schwartz reports that an impromptu caucus of the Mapp majority took place in an elevator at the Court immediately after the conference at which the case was discussed. [Bernard Schwartz, Super Chief: Earl Warren and His Supreme Court—A Judicial Biography 393 (1983).]

which the issue was not briefed, argued, or discussed by the state courts, by the parties' counsel, or at our conference following the oral argument.

Potter Stewart, *The Road to Mapp v. Ohio and Beyond: The Origins, Development and Future of the Exclusionary Rule in Search-and-Seizure Cases,* 83 Colum. L. Rev. 1365, 1368 (1983). For more on Justice Clark's behind-the-scenes role in *Mapp*, see Dennis D. Dorin, *Justice Tom Clark's Role in Mapp v. Ohio's Extension of the Exclusionary Rule to State Searches and Seizures*, 52 Case W. Res. L. Rev. 401 (2001).

6. Why did Justice Clark say that the "factual grounds upon which *Wolf* was based" were "basically [ir]relevant"? If so, why did he survey post-*Wolf* state law? Can it plausibly be claimed that the results of his survey actually supported the dissent?

7. *What is the purpose of an exclusionary rule?* According to the majority, why is it required in state prosecutions? How did Justice Harlan answer the majority?

8. Just as *Wolf v. Colorado* was not the end of the story thanks to *Mapp v. Ohio, Mapp* is far from the end of the story about the Fourth Amendment exclusionary rule. The exclusionary rule has evoked considerable controversy, virtually from the day *Mapp* was handed down. And, because of the misgivings of a few, and later a majority, of Supreme Court justices, the scope of the Fourth Amendment exclusionary rule has been considerably narrowed. For an excellent behind-the-scenes look at the Court's growing distaste for the exclusionary rule, see Tracey Maclin, The Supreme Court and the Fourth Amendment's Exclusionary Rule (2013).

We will wait until Chapter 7, however, to look at the significant erosion of the exclusionary rule. For now, we turn to the Fourth Amendment itself, to identify the rights "the people" hold according to the Fourth Amendment, as interpreted by the United States Supreme Court. As you study the case law set out in the next several chapters, please keep in mind that violation of a person's search-and-seizure rights has generally required, since 1914 in the federal system, and since 1961 in the state courts, exclusion of the evidence obtained unconstitutionally by the police. Put another way, whenever a defendant has sought prior to trial to demonstrate that her Fourth Amendment rights were violated, her goal has been to convince a court that—because of the alleged constitutional violation—the evidence that incriminates her should be barred from introduction at her trial.

CHAPTER 2 SUMMARY

The original criminal justice amendments to the Bill of Rights—4th, 5th, 6th, and 8th Amendments—applied only to the federal government. They in no way addressed conduct by state governments. That achievement had to wait until the passage of the 14th Amendment to the U.S. Constitution in 1868. The Due Process Clause of the 14th Amendment has been the vehicle by which all the most important criminal procedure rights have been applied to state criminal proceedings.

This has happened through a hotly-debated process known as incorporation. There are two sides to the incorporation debate. Under the "total incorporation" approach, the 14th Amendment simply absorbs the entire Bill of Rights—as if using the cut and paste function on a word processor—and makes each right applicable to the states. Under the "selective incorporation" approach, each individual criminal procedure right found in the Bill of Rights is analyzed separately; asking whether or not the right is a fundamental part of the right to a fair trial and thus vital to the concept of due process.

Despite strong and passionate arguments for those advocating the "total incorporation" approach, the U.S. Supreme Court has consistently adopted selective incorporation and considers the debate closed. While today selective incorporation has led to the application of almost all of the criminal justice provisions to the states, some of these principles—such as the right to be represented by counsel regardless of your ability to pay, and the right to have illegally obtained evidence excluded at trial—were not applied to the states until well into the 1960s. This surprises many students who grew up believing that these fundamental rights have been part of all criminal proceedings from the very beginning.

CHAPTER 3

Passing the Threshold of the Fourth Amendment

A. THE TEXT AND ITS MYSTERIES

The Fourth Amendment journey begins here. The first step in that journey, as is the case in evaluating any provision of a constitution, is to read the text being interpreted. The Fourth Amendment is just 54 words long:

> The right of the people to be secure in their persons, houses, papers, and effects, against unreasonable searches and seizures, shall not be violated, and no Warrants shall issue, but upon probable cause, supported by Oath or affirmation, and particularly describing the place to be searched, and the persons or things to be seized.

These 54 words appear to tell us a great deal, but do they? They tell us *who* is protected by the provisions of the Amendment, *i.e.*, "the people." But, who are "the people"? Only citizens of the United States? Anyone legally present in the United States? Anyone in the country, legally or not? And, are United States citizens protected when they are outside the country? These questions, always important, have grown in significance in the aftermath of terrorist attacks on the United States, the investigations of which have frequently focused on persons of foreign ancestry located in and outside the United States, as well as United States citizens.

What does the Fourth Amendment guarantee "the people"? The text tells us that the people are entitled "to be secure in their persons, houses, papers, and effects" (we will see that this phrase is not all-encompassing) "against unreasonable searches and seizures." But, what is an "unreasonable" search or seizure? For that matter, what are "searches" and "seizures"? These are matters of considerable complexity.

And notice one other oddity. The amendment, by its terms, does not *create* a right to be secure from unreasonable searches and seizures. Rather, it recognizes a *pre-existing right* that is now enshrined in the Bill of Rights. What could have been the source of that pre-existing right?

Perhaps the most controversial feature of Fourth Amendment jurisprudence relates to the relationship between the first clause (often called the "reasonableness clause" of the Fourth Amendment) and the remaining language of the text ("no Warrants shall issue, but upon probable cause * * *"), which constitutes the "warrant clause." Does the warrant clause mean that searches conducted without warrants are (at least, presumptively) unreasonable and, consequently, in violation of the reasonableness requirement? Or did the drafters of the Fourth Amendment mean only that *when* a warrant is issued it must meet the requirements of probable cause, oath or affirmation, and particularity, but that there is no warrant requirement, as such? And, however this question is answered, what does the text mean by "probable cause," and with what particularity must the warrant describe "the place to be searched, and the persons or things to be seized"?

Finally, notice what the text does *not* say. Yes, the people have a right (in their persons, houses, papers, and effects) to be free from unreasonable searches and seizures, but what is the *remedy* for violation of this right? As we saw in the last chapter, the Court staggered for decades before finally deciding that evidence seized in violation of the Fourth Amendment cannot normally be used as evidence of guilt in a criminal case, state or federal.

All of these questions suggest the aptness of Professor Anthony Amsterdam's characterization of the Fourth Amendment text as "brief, vague, general, [and] unilluminating." Anthony G. Amsterdam, *Perspectives on the Fourth Amendment*, 58 Minn. L. Rev. 349, 353–54 (1974). The judiciary, in particular the United States Supreme Court, has endeavored to illuminate the text. Justice Felix Frankfurter observed in 1961, however, that "[t]he course of true law pertaining to [the Fourth Amendment] * * * has not * * * run smooth." Chapman v. United States, 365 U.S. 610, 81 S.Ct. 776, 5 L.Ed.2d 828 (1961) (concurring opinion). Indeed, although the text of the Amendment has not changed over the years, the personnel of the Supreme Court and its interpretation of the Constitution, *have* changed. As a consequence, the path you will be following in your Fourth Amendment journey includes many significant turns, including some U-turns, as well as zigs and zags. At the conclusion of your voyage, you will have a basis for determining whether Professor Akhil Amar overstated the situation when he equated Fourth Amendment case law to "a sinking ocean liner—rudderless and badly off course." Akhil Reed Amar, *Fourth Amendment First Principles*, 107 Harv. L. Rev. 757, 759 (1994).

B. THE REACH OF THE FOURTH AMENDMENT

How far does the Fourth Amendment reach? Two issues relating to the Amendment's scope—one relating to the category of persons who are searched and seized, and the other regarding the nature of persons who do the searching and seizing—deserve attention.

Consider, first, the criminal investigations that occurred in the aftermath of the September 11 attacks on the United States. Apparently all nineteen hijackers of the four airplanes were of Middle Eastern descent. After the events, the federal government investigated hundreds of persons in order to try to identify possible co-conspirators in the crimes and to identify persons who might be planning future attacks. Initial reports suggested that these investigations primarily focused on four categories of individuals: (a) American citizens of Middle Eastern descent living in the United States; (b) citizens of other countries *lawfully* in the United States on student (or other) visas; (c) citizens of other countries *unlawfully* in this country (persons who came lawfully but whose visas had expired, as well as those who illegally entered the country); and (d) non-U.S. citizens residing in other countries suspected of planning criminal activities in the United States or against U.S. interests on foreign land. Obviously, category (a) individuals are covered by the Fourth Amendment, but what rights do the other classes of suspects possess? May federal law enforcement agents conduct unlimited surveillance of such persons? May their homes be searched and their property seized with impunity? Remarkably, the Supreme Court has rarely spoken on the subject.

The Fourth Amendment provides that "the people" should "be secure in their persons, houses, papers, and effects, against unreasonable searches and seizures." It turns out, however, that the term "people" is not all-inclusive. In United States v. Verdugo-Urquidez, 494 U.S. 259, 110 S.Ct. 1056, 108 L.Ed.2d 222 (1990), Verdugo-Urquidez, a Mexican resident, was arrested on drug charges and brought to the United States for trial. While he was in a San Diego federal correctional facility, United States Drug Enforcement Agency (DEA) agents entered and seized property from defendant's Mexican residences without a search warrant. The issue presented to the Supreme Court was "whether the Fourth Amendment applies to the search and seizure by United States agents of property that is owned by a non-resident alien and located in a foreign country."

A seriously splintered Court held that Verdugo-Urquidez could not object to the DEA action on Fourth Amendment grounds, because he was not among "the people" the Framers intended to protect from unreasonable searches and seizures. Specifically, a search or seizure of property located in a foreign country, which is owned by a nonresident who is only briefly on U.S. soil, is not covered by the Amendment, even if the search is conducted by U.S. law enforcement agents. According to Chief Justice Rehnquist writing for the majority, the words "the people" found in the Fourth Amendment (and elsewhere in the Constitution) "refer[ ] to a class of persons who are part of a national community or who have otherwise developed sufficient connection with this country to be considered part of that community." The defendant's connection to the United States—"lawful but involuntary [presence]—is not of the sort to indicate any substantial connection with our country."

The justices left a great deal open for future resolution in category (b) and (c) cases, including whether the Fourth Amendment applies if a non-citizen's involuntary "stay in the United States were to be prolonged—by a prison sentence, for example." Also undecided—and certainly of greater significance—is whether, and to what extent, the Fourth Amendment protects a person *voluntarily* but *unlawfully* living in this country, i.e., one who has "presumably * * * accepted some societal obligations," such as paying taxes, who is subjected to a search or seizure on U.S. land. Indeed, *Verdugo-Urquidez* even leaves open the issue of the scope of rights of non-U.S. citizens *lawfully* in this country temporarily or with the intention of becoming citizens. (Obviously, category (d) individuals are not protected by the Fourth Amendment.)

The second coverage issue relates to the *searching*, not the searched, party. In *Verdugo-Urquidez*, the contested searches were conducted by law enforcement agents. But, what if a search or seizure occurs in the United States, of a United States citizen, by a *private* party? Suppose that Burglar John breaks into Jane's home while she is at work, and is arrested while fleeing the crime scene. In an effort to avoid prosecution, John hands over to the police a large quantity of illegal drugs he discovered in Jane's home. May Jane object to the Government's use of these drugs against her in a drug prosecution? Or suppose that a private detective, hired by Jack to discover evidence of wife Jill's adulterous behavior, searches through Jill's belongings and, to his surprise, discovers evidence linking Jill to a murder. If the private detective furnishes the evidence to the police, may Jill object on Fourth Amendment grounds?

The answer in both cases is "no." The Supreme Court ruled in Burdeau v. McDowell, 256 U.S. 465, 41 S.Ct. 574, 65 L.Ed. 1048 (1921), that the Fourth

Amendment limits only governmental action. It does not reach private searches or seizures. Consequently, the Fourth Amendment is not violated if a landlord searches her tenant's possessions, or an airline employee searches luggage, or a private company monitors telephone calls of its employees without their knowledge. On the other hand, the Amendment is implicated if the police instigate or participate in the search or seizure, such as when an officer requests a landlord to search through her tenant's belongings or assists in the process.

But notice: This amendment does not prohibit *all* unreasonable law enforcement practices. As far as the Fourth Amendment is concerned, *a police officer may act as arbitrarily or unreasonably as she wants*, as long as she does not conduct a "search" or "seizure"; and, even searches and seizures are unregulated by the Fourth Amendment unless the police search or seize a "person," "house," "paper," or "effect."

The remainder of this chapter, therefore, considers the threshold of the Fourth Amendment. It focuses on the following question, the first step in a checklist if you will: What governmental conduct constitutes a *search* or *seizure* of a *person, house, paper, or effect* and, therefore, triggers Fourth Amendment protection?

C. WHAT IS A "SEARCH"?

Whether one views the Fourth Amendment as two related clauses or one requirement, it may be helpful to view the Fourth Amendment through the lens of a checklist: a step-by-step process to be followed when undertaking an analysis of when and how the Fourth Amendment might apply in a given situation. Since the Amendment only applies to *unreasonable* searches and seizures, we must first ask if there was a search or seizure at all. If not, the Fourth Amendment does not apply and that is the end of the inquiry. If there is a search or seizure, then and only then do we ask if it was reasonable. A search might be reasonable because there was a valid warrant. Or, it might be reasonable because a warrant was not necessary or practical; creating an exception to the normal and preferred requirement of a warrant. By the same token, a search might be unreasonable because there was no warrant, no valid exception, or the warrant itself was invalid for some reason.

So what might our checklist look like?:

- ☑ Is there a search? *If no, Fourth Amendment does not apply.*
- ☑ If yes, was the search reasonable?
    - ☑ Was there a valid warrant? *If yes, the search is reasonable.*

- ☑ If no valid warrant, was there an exception to the warrant requirement? *If yes, the search is still reasonable.*

☑ If no valid warrant and no exception, the search is unreasonable and thus prohibited by the Fourth Amendment.

Admittedly, this checklist is a bit simplified given the intricacies of Fourth Amendment law—and we haven't even mentioned "seizures" yet—but it should serve as a useful starting point for the analysis of most of the Fourth Amendment cases you will come across.

With this checklist in mind, the remainder of this chapter focuses on the first step—determining if government conduct was a search. Chapter 4 will examine the second step by looking at what makes a warrant valid, including the all-important requirement of probable cause. Chapters 5 and 6 then take us to step three by first looking at exceptions to the warrant requirement that still require probable cause, and then at exceptions that allow searches (and seizures) without a warrant and with something less than probable cause.

1. General Principles: From Trespass to Privacy

Fourth Amendment "search" analysis can be seen as two historical periods. In the first period, the justices treated Fourth Amendment search issues exclusively as a property-focused inquiry. This follows naturally from the language of the amendment protecting "persons, houses, papers and effects" and also from the common law tort of trespass that had historically been the protector of private property.

Boyd v. United States [116 U.S. 616, 6 S.Ct. 524, 29 L.Ed. 746 (1886)] was the Court's first major exposition of a property-rights interpretation of the Fourth Amendment. The Court quoted extensively from the "memorable discussion" in *Entick v. Carrington* [19 Howell St. Tr. 1029, 1066 (1765) (Eng.)], in which Lord Camden stated that "every invasion of private property, be it ever so minute, is a trespass."

Boyd further quoted Lord Camden's property analysis: "The great end for which men entered into society was to secure their property. That right is preserved sacred and incommunicable in all instances where it has not been taken away . . . by some public law for the good of the whole."[1]

---

1 These three paragraphs are drawn, and include some quotes, from Joshua Dressler, Alan C. Michaels, Understanding Criminal Procedure (Vol. 1: Investigation) (6th ed. 2013), at 68–69. Authors of this casebook made substantial changes and did not indicate quoted by authors of casebook.

The so-called "trespass" approach to "search" law provided that there was no violation of the Fourth Amendment law in the absence of a trespass to private property. The second period of "search" law commenced eighty years after *Boyd* with the next case.

KATZ V. UNITED STATES

Supreme Court of the United States, 1967.
389 U.S. 347, 88 S.Ct. 507, 19 L.Ed.2d 576.

The *Katz* case presented here is one of the seminal cases in Fourth Amendment law for determining if governmental conduct is a search, and thus whether the Fourth Amendment applies at all. As noted in the three paragraphs above, search law prior to *Katz* was governed by the trespass test—government agents had to physically enter or trespass onto property or interfere with one's possession of tangible, material items. *Katz* opens up a whole new world of Fourth Amendment law that takes into account people's assumptions about what is and what is not private, and the steps they take based on those assumptions.

Justice Stewart's opinion gave us several additions to the lexicon of famous U.S. Supreme Court quotes. However, it is Justice Harlan's *Katz* concurrence that had the strongest impact on Fourth Amendment search law—one that still resonates today. In fact, the test for determining when government conduct is a search is often referred to either as "the *Katz* test" or "Harlan's two-pronged test". After reading Justice Harlan's concurrence, see if you can identify the two separate prongs. Each prong will be discussed further in the Notes and Questions following *Katz*.

Justice Black dissented in this case. Since there is no wording in the Fourth Amendment specifically addressing "privacy," Justice Black argues that the Court cannot read the Fourth Amendment to protect privacy in order to make the amendment fit the times. According to Justice Black, if the Framers wanted to include protections for something as intangible as eavesdropping on a conversation, they would have said so.

Note, too, the relationship between Justice Black's dissent in *Katz* and his advocacy of the total incorporation approach to the Fourteenth Amendment (as discussed in Chapter 2). Selective incorporation that retains a place for fundamental fairness allows for the broadening of rights implicit in the idea of "due process"—such as privacy. The total incorporation approach is inconsistent with finding new rights in the Due Process Clause.

MR. JUSTICE STEWART delivered the opinion of the Court [joined by CHIEF JUSTICE WARREN, and JUSTICES BRENNAN, DOUGLAS, FORTAS, HARLAN, and WHITE].

The petitioner was convicted * * * under an eight-count indictment charging him with transmitting wagering information by telephone from Los Angeles to Miami and Boston, in violation of a federal statute. At trial the Government was permitted, over the petitioner's objection, to introduce evidence of the petitioner's end of telephone conversations, overheard by FBI agents who had attached an electronic listening and recording device to the outside of the public telephone booth from which he had placed his calls. In affirming his conviction, the Court of Appeals rejected the contention that the recordings had been obtained in violation of the Fourth Amendment, because "[t]here was no physical entrance into the area occupied by [the petitioner]." We granted certiorari in order to consider the constitutional questions thus presented.

The petitioner has phrased those questions as follows:

A. Whether a public telephone booth is a constitutionally protected area so that evidence obtained by attaching an electronic listening recording device to the top of such a booth is obtained in violation of the right to privacy of the user of the booth.

B. Whether physical penetration of a constitutionally protected area is necessary before a search and seizure can be said to be violative of the Fourth Amendment to the United States Constitution."

We decline to adopt this formulation of the issues. In the first place, the correct solution of Fourth Amendment problems is not necessarily promoted by incantation of the phrase "constitutionally protected area." Secondly, the Fourth Amendment cannot be translated into a general constitutional "right to privacy." That Amendment protects individual privacy against certain kinds of governmental intrusion, but its protections go further, and often have nothing to do with privacy at all. Other provisions of the Constitution protect personal privacy from other forms of governmental invasion. But the protection of a person's *general* right to privacy—his right to be let alone by other people—is, like the protection of his property and of his very life, left largely to the law of the individual States.

Because of the misleading way the issues have been formulated, the parties have attached great significance to the characterization of the telephone booth from which the petitioner placed his calls. The petitioner has strenuously argued that the booth was a "constitutionally protected area." The Government has maintained with equal vigor that it was not. But this effort to decide whether or not a given "area," viewed in the abstract, is "constitutionally protected" deflects attention from the problem presented by this case. For the Fourth Amendment protects people, not places. What a person knowingly exposes to the public, even in his own home or office, is not a subject of Fourth Amendment protection. But what he seeks to preserve as private, even in an area accessible to the public, may be constitutionally protected.

The Government stresses the fact that the telephone booth from which the petitioner made his calls was constructed partly of glass, so that he was as visible after he entered it as he would have been if he had remained outside. But what he sought to exclude when he entered the booth was not the intruding eye—it was the uninvited ear. He did not shed his right to do so simply because he made his calls from a place where he might be seen. No less than an individual in a business office, in a friend's apartment, or in a taxicab, a person in a telephone booth may rely upon the protection of the Fourth Amendment. One who occupies it, shuts the door behind him, and pays the toll that permits him to place a call is surely entitled to assume that the words he utters into the mouthpiece will not be broadcast to the world. To read the Constitution more narrowly is to ignore the vital role that the public telephone has come to play in private communication.

The Government contends, however, that the activities of its agents in this case should not be tested by Fourth Amendment requirements, for the surveillance technique they employed involved no physical penetration of the telephone booth from which the petitioner placed his calls. It is true that the absence of such penetration was at one time thought to foreclose further Fourth Amendment inquiry, *Olmstead v. United States*, 277 U.S. 438, 457, 464, 466, 48 S.Ct. 564, 565, 567, 568, 72 L.Ed. 944 [(1928)]; *Goldman v. United States*, 316 U.S. 129, 134–136, 62 S.Ct. 993, 995–97, 86 L.Ed. 1322 [(1942)], for that Amendment was thought to limit only searches and seizures of tangible property. But "[t]he premise that property interests control the right of the Government to search and seize has been discredited." Thus, although a closely divided Court supposed in *Olmstead* that surveillance without any trespass and without the seizure of any material object fell outside the ambit of the Constitution, we have since departed from the narrow view on which that decision rested. Indeed, we have expressly held that the Fourth Amendment governs not only the seizure of tangible items, but extends as well to the recording of oral statements, overheard without any "technical trespass under * * * local property law." *Silverman v. United States*, 365 U.S. 505, 511, 81 S.Ct. 679, 682, 5 L.Ed.2d 734 [(1961)]. Once this much is acknowledged, and once it is recognized that the Fourth Amendment protects people—and not simply "areas"—against unreasonable searches and seizures, it becomes clear that the reach of that Amendment cannot turn upon the presence or absence of a physical intrusion into any given enclosure.

We conclude that the underpinnings of *Olmstead* and *Goldman* have been so eroded by our subsequent decisions that the "trespass" doctrine there enunciated can no longer be regarded as controlling. The Government's activities in electronically listening to and recording the petitioner's words violated the privacy upon which he justifiably relied while using the telephone booth and thus constituted a "search and seizure" within the meaning of the Fourth Amendment. The fact that the electronic device employed to achieve that end did not happen to penetrate the wall of the booth can have no constitutional significance.

The question remaining for decision, then, is whether the search and seizure conducted in this case complied with constitutional standards. [The Court went on to hold that they did not, as explained more fully in Note 5, *infra*.] Since the page numbers and even note numbers will change, for references like this, I have gone ahead and put in a place maker 'x' as a reminder to go back and put in the correct page and note numbers when we have them.

[JUSTICE DOUGLAS's concurring opinion, with whom JUSTICE BRENNAN joined, is omitted. MR. JUSTICE MARSHALL took no part in the consideration or decision of this case.]

MR. JUSTICE HARLAN, concurring.

I join the opinion of the Court, which I read to hold only (a) that an enclosed telephone booth is an area where, like a home, and unlike a field, a person has a constitutionally protected reasonable expectation of privacy; (b) that electronic as well as physical intrusion into a place that is in this sense private may constitute a violation of the Fourth Amendment; and (c) that the invasion of a constitutionally protected area by federal authorities is, as the Court has long held, presumptively unreasonable in the absence of a search warrant.

As the Court's opinion states, "the Fourth Amendment protects people, not places." The question, however, is what protection it affords to those people. Generally, as here, the answer to that question requires reference to a "place." My understanding of the rule that has emerged from prior decisions is that there is a twofold requirement, first that a person have exhibited an actual (subjective) expectation of privacy and, second, that the expectation be one that society is prepared to recognize as "reasonable." Thus a man's home is, for most purposes, a place where he expects privacy, but objects, activities, or statements that he exposes to the "plain view" of outsiders are not "protected" because no intention to keep them to himself has been exhibited. On the other hand, conversations in the open would not be protected against being overheard, for the expectation of privacy under the circumstances would be unreasonable.

The critical fact in this case is that "[o]ne who occupies it [a telephone booth], shuts the door behind him, and pays the toll that permits him to place a call is surely entitled to assume" that his conversation is not being intercepted. The point is not that the booth is "accessible to the public" at other times, but that it is a temporarily private place whose momentary occupants' expectations of freedom from intrusion are recognized as reasonable.

In *Silverman v. United States*, we held that eavesdropping accomplished by means of an electronic device that penetrated the premises occupied by petitioner was a violation of the Fourth Amendment. That case established that interception of conversations reasonably intended to be private could constitute a "search and seizure," and that the examination or taking of physical property was not required. * * * In *Silverman* we found it unnecessary to re-examine *Goldman v. United States*, which had held that electronic surveillance accomplished without the physical penetration of petitioner's premises by a tangible object did not violate the Fourth Amendment. This case requires us to reconsider *Goldman*, and I agree that it should now be overruled. Its limitation on Fourth Amendment protection is, in the present day, bad physics as well as bad law, for reasonable expectations of privacy may be defeated by electronic as well as physical invasion. * * *

[*JUSTICE WHITE's concurring opinion is omitted.*]

MR. JUSTICE BLACK, dissenting.

If I could agree with the Court that eavesdropping carried on by electronic means (equivalent to wiretapping) constitutes a "search" or "seizure," I would be happy to join the Court's opinion. * * *

My basic objection is twofold: (1) I do not believe that the words of the Amendment will bear the meaning given them by today's decision, and (2) I do not believe that it is the proper role of this Court to rewrite the Amendment in order "to bring it into harmony with the times" and thus reach a result that many people believe to be desirable.

While I realize that an argument based on the meaning of words lacks the scope, and no doubt the appeal, of broad policy discussions and philosophical discourses on such nebulous subjects as privacy, for me the language of the Amendment is the crucial place to look in construing a written document such as our Constitution. * * * The first clause protects "persons, houses, papers, and effects, against unreasonable searches and seizures * * *." These words connote the idea of tangible things with size, form, and weight, things capable of being searched, seized, or both. The second clause of the Amendment still further establishes its Framers' purpose to limit its protection to tangible things by providing that no warrants shall issue but those "particularly describing the place to be searched, and the persons or things to be seized." A conversation overheard by eavesdropping, whether by plain snooping or wiretapping, is not tangible and, under the normally accepted meanings of the words, can neither be searched nor seized. In addition the language of the second clause indicates that the Amendment refers not only to something tangible so it can be seized but to something already in existence so it can be described. Yet the Court's interpretation would have the Amendment apply to overhearing future conversations which by their very nature are nonexistent until they take place. How can one "describe" a future conversation, and, if one cannot, how can a magistrate issue a warrant to eavesdrop one in the future? * * * Rather than using language in a completely artificial way, I must conclude that the Fourth Amendment simply does not apply to eavesdropping.

Tapping telephone wires, of course, was an unknown possibility at the time the Fourth Amendment was adopted. But eavesdropping (and wiretapping is nothing more than eavesdropping by telephone) was * * * "an ancient practice which at common law was condemned as a nuisance. 4 Blackstone, Commentaries 168. In those days the eavesdropper listened by naked ear under the eaves of houses or their windows, or beyond their walls seeking out private discourse." There can be no doubt that the Framers were aware of this practice, and if they had desired to outlaw or restrict the use of evidence obtained by eavesdropping, I believe that they would have used the appropriate language to do so in the Fourth Amendment. They certainly would not have left such a task to the ingenuity of language-stretching judges. * * *

Since I see no way in which the words of the Fourth Amendment can be construed to apply to eavesdropping, that closes the matter for me. In interpreting the Bill of Rights, I willingly go as far as a liberal construction of the language takes me, but I simply cannot in good conscience give a meaning to words which they have never before been thought to have and which they certainly do not have in common ordinary usage. I will not distort the words of the Amendment in order to "keep the Constitution up to date" or "to bring it into harmony with the times." It was never meant that this Court have such power, which in effect would make us a continuously functioning constitutional convention.

With this decision the Court has completed, I hope, its rewriting of the Fourth Amendment, which started only recently when the Court began referring incessantly to the Fourth Amendment not so much as a law against *unreasonable* searches and seizures as one to protect an individual's privacy. * * *

The Fourth Amendment protects privacy only to the extent that it prohibits unreasonable searches and seizures of "persons, houses, papers, and effects." No general right is created by the Amendment so as to give this Court the unlimited power to hold unconstitutional everything which affects privacy. Certainly the Framers, well acquainted as they were with the excesses of governmental power, did not intend to grant this Court such omnipotent lawmaking authority as that. The history of governments proves that it is dangerous to freedom to repose such powers in courts.

For these reasons I respectfully dissent.

NOTES AND QUESTIONS

1. *Variations on the theme.* Telephone booths are an endangered species—have you ever seen one?—in the era of smartphones and other new methods of technological communication. One observer at the time of *Katz*, perhaps thinking the question was merely rhetorical, asked, "Would the case have been different if the pay phone has not been surrounded by a booth?" Edmund W. Kitch, *Katz v. United States: The Limits of the Fourth Amendment*, 1968 Sup. Ct. Rev. 133, 140. Well, how would Justice Stewart have answered his question?

Or, suppose that the FBI, rather than conducting electronic surveillance, had positioned a lip reader immediately outside the telephone booth, who observed Katz's lips and recorded his words on paper? Would Justice Stewart consider *this* conduct a "search"?

2. Is a telephone booth a "person, house, paper, or effect"? If not, why does the Fourth Amendment apply to *Katz's* conversations there? Does the majority provide a suitable answer to Justice Black's textual argument that electronic surveillance falls outside the coverage of the Fourth Amendment?

3. *The subjective prong in Justice Harlan's test: things to think about.* As the cases that follow will show, the two-prong formula set out in Justice Harlan's concurring opinion has become the primary standard for determining whether police conduct constitutes a search.

Do you see any problems with Harlan's subjective prong? Do *you* have an expectation of privacy in your home? Do you have an expectation of privacy in your belongings at the airport? Do you have an expectation of privacy regarding the web sites you have visited on your computer, or the e-mails you have written? Have your answers to any of these questions changed in recent years in light of what you know about technology and news accounts of government surveillance? Why might the answers to these questions have motivated one scholar to write that "[a]n actual, subjective expectation of privacy obviously has no place * * * in a theory of what the fourth amendment protects." Anthony G. Amsterdam, *Perspectives on the Fourth Amendment*, 58 Minn. L. Rev. 349, 384 (1974).

4. *The objective prong in Justice Harlan's test: things to think about.* How should a court apply the second prong of Justice Harlan's test? Should it consider whether the American people, in general, expect privacy in certain circumstances? If so, should a court consider public opinion polls and other reliable evidence of public attitudes in this regard? *E.g.*, Christopher Slobogin & Joseph E. Schumacher, *Reasonable Expectations of Privacy and Autonomy in Fourth Amendment Cases: An Empirical Look at "Understandings Recognized and Permitted by Society*," 42 Duke L.J. 727 (1993) (surveying public attitudes regarding privacy, and concluding that "the Supreme Court's conclusions about the scope of the Fourth Amendment are often not in tune with commonly held attitudes about police investigative techniques"). And, what if public expectations of privacy change over time—what then? Or, is Justice Harlan suggesting that courts should conduct a normative inquiry to determine what privacy rights people living in a democracy are entitled to possess?

All of these questions assume that a judge will determine what constitutes a "reasonable expectation of privacy" in a particular situation. But, is it desirable to permit judges to answer this question? Would it be better to leave this question to the jury, perhaps to re-litigate at the trial, if the judge first determines that the Fourth Amendment is not implicated? See Meghan J. Ryan, *Juries and the Criminal Constitution*, 65 Ala. L. Rev. 849 (2014).

5. *If electronic surveillance is a search, what then*? Please keep in mind that in the excerpt of the *Katz* opinion set out above, the issue considered was whether the wiretapping constituted a Fourth Amendment "search," *i.e.*, whether the restrictions of the Fourth Amendment applied to the electronic surveillance. Having answered this question affirmatively, the Court next had to consider whether the FBI agents' actions complied with the Fourth Amendment.

The *Katz* Court, quoting prior case law, observed that the Fourth Amendment generally "requires adherence to judicial processes." Justice Stewart, using oft-quoted language, stated the rule that "searches conducted outside the judicial process, without prior approval by judge or magistrate [*i.e.*, in the form of a search warrant] are *per se* unreasonable under the Fourth Amendment—subject only to a few specifically established well-delineated exceptions." The Court proceeded:

> Accepting * * * the Government's [account of its] actions as accurate, it is clear that this surveillance was so narrowly circumscribed that a duly authorized magistrate, properly notified of the need for such investigation,

> specifically informed of the basis on which it was to proceed, and clearly apprised of the precise intrusion it would entail, could constitutionally have authorized, with appropriate safeguards, the very limited search and seizure that the Government asserts in fact took place.

All would have been well, in other words, had the FBI obtained a judicially authorized warrant to conduct the surveillance. Because no warrant was secured, however, the Court ruled that the Fourth Amendment was violated.

6. *Obtaining a search warrant to conduct electronic surveillance: special problems.* Search warrants are considered in detail in the next chapter, but it is worth noting here that the search warrant process in electronic surveillance cases creates special constitutional issues. Notice that if the police want to search a suspect's home for a tangible object, let's say a stolen painting, they can tell the magistrate, with particularity, what it is they are looking for (the painting) and where they expect to find it. Once they seize the object, the search ends. But, in an electronic surveillance case, the police must request permission to "search" and "seize" something that is not only intangible but does not even exist at the time of the warrant request, namely, a future conversation.

The Court in *Katz* assumed that the search of the conversation would have been constitutionally permissible had the FBI secured a search warrant. And one year after *Katz*, Congress enacted legislation, the 1968 Omnibus Crime Control and Safe Streets Act, that includes warrant procedures for electronic surveillance. It is thus clear today that a search warrant to surveil future conversations is constitutional if it complies with the 1968 statute.

7. *"So, do I really want to be a police officer?"* The police suspect a person of rape. The suspect denies his guilt but refuses to provide a DNA sample to the police. Later, an officer observes the suspect spit on a public sidewalk. The officer retrieves the saliva for DNA testing. Search? See Commonwealth v. Cabral, 69 Mass.App.Ct. 68, 866 N.E.2d 429 (2007).

8. A student once asked one of the casebook authors how the police knew which telephone booth to wiretap. The answer is that they didn't precisely know, but they were aware that Katz regularly used one of two phone booths, so they obtained permission from the phone company to put one of the booths out of order, and then they installed the listening devices in the other booth! According to the attorney who argued Katz's case before the United States Supreme Court, when he informed his client "of the historic decision that now bears his name, his first response was not one of thanks or gratitude. Rather, he wanted to know if he could sue the telephone company for permitting the FBI agents to put the one telephone booth out of order." Harvey A. Schneider, *Katz v. United States: The Untold Story*, 40 McGeorge L. Rev. 13, 23 (2009).

2. The *Katz* Doctrine: What Does Privacy Mean?

UNITED STATES V. WHITE

Supreme Court of the United States, 1971.
401 U.S. 745, 91 S.Ct. 1122, 28 L.Ed.2d 453.

The next case, *United States v. White*, as well as the cases that follow, are sometimes referred to as the *Katz* progeny, applying *Katz* to different sets of facts. These cases form a history of *Katz* from its ruling in 1967 to the present. As you read *White, Smith v. Maryland*, and all the cases in the Notes and Questions that follow, observe how long it took—after the government conduct was found to be a search in *Katz*—for the Court to find one again.

White is also a good example of how court cases often represent small incremental decisions. For all its length, *White* is not a particularly earth-shattering change in Fourth Amendment law. Going into *White*, we already knew based on the previous case of Hoffa v. United States, 385 US 293, 87 S.Ct. 408, 17 L.Ed. 2d 374 (1966), that the Fourth Amendment does not protect a defendant who confides in an accomplice/informant who then confides in the police. All *White* does is apply *Hoffa* to an informant who was transmitting or recording the conversation. Does the fact that the conversation was recorded help the defendant at all? As you will see, the primary opinion in *White* answers no. All we have is a more accurate record of the conversation. In neither situation has a search been conducted. The Court declined to recognize an expectation of privacy in a defendant's tendency to blab to the wrong person.

Note that *White* is considered a plurality opinion. Only four Justices (Justice White, the author, Chief Justice Burger and Justices Stewart, and Blackmun) joined the main opinion, one short of a majority. However, defendant White was still out of luck, as Justices Brennan and Black concurred in the result—that there was no search—but for different reasons. That meant there were six votes to affirm defendant White's conviction.

Justices Marshall, Douglas, and Harlan dissented. The dissents of both Justice Douglas and Harlan are useful to keep in mind as you read the remaining cases in this chapter. In both dissents we start to see a concern raised about technological changes that seem to be overtaking established law, and questions about just how much privacy we lose when we disclose

information to a third-party. What do you think Justice Harlan and Justice Douglas would say if they were alive today? Perhaps, "we told you so."

As you read the dissenting opinions in *White*, keep in mind that there is no dispute among any of the Justices regarding the facts of the case. Yet they come to very different conclusions, both stemming from perfectly reasonable perspectives. So does the chance of a defendant winning his or her Fourth Amendment case depend on which lawyer provides the more persuasive argument to a jury? To a judge? To a set of particular judges? Or does it depend more on the judge's intuition about the right balance between the individual's right to be left alone and the government's need to uncover crime?

Finally, timing also matters. It is always important to keep in mind the year in which the case was decided. *White* takes place only four years after *Katz* but it is an important four years. Chief Justice Warren retired in 1969 and was replaced by Warren E. Burger. The Burger Court, which lasted until 1986, was much more conservative and law enforcement oriented. Harlan's test originally set out in *Katz* was used in *White* but Harlan is now in the dissent. Stewart, who wrote *Katz*, joined the plurality opinion.

MR. JUSTICE WHITE announced the judgment of the Court and an opinion in which THE CHIEF JUSTICE, MR. JUSTICE STEWART, and MR. JUSTICE BLACKMUN join.

In 1966, respondent James A. White was tried and convicted under two consolidated indictments charging various illegal transactions in narcotics * * *. * * * The issue before us is whether the Fourth Amendment bars from evidence the testimony of governmental agents who related certain conversations which had occurred between defendant White and a government informant, Harvey Jackson, and which the agents overheard by monitoring the frequency of a radio transmitter carried by Jackson and concealed on his person. On four occasions the conversations took place in Jackson's home; each of these conversations was overheard by an agent concealed in a kitchen closet with Jackson's consent and by a second agent outside the house using a radio receiver. Four other conversations—one in respondent's home, one in a restaurant, and two in Jackson's car—were overheard by the use of radio equipment. The prosecution was unable to locate and produce Jackson at the trial and the trial court overruled objections to the testimony of the agents who conducted the electronic surveillance. The jury returned a guilty verdict and defendant appealed. * * *

I * * *

Katz v. United States * * * finally swept away doctrines that electronic eavesdropping is permissible under the Fourth Amendment unless physical invasion of a constitutionally protected area produced the challenged evidence. In that case government agents, without petitioner's consent or knowledge, attached a listening device to the outside of a public telephone booth and recorded the defendant's end of his telephone conversations. In declaring the recordings inadmissible in evidence in the absence of a warrant authorizing the surveillance, the Court overruled Olmstead [v. United States, 277 U.S. 438, 48 S.Ct. 564, 72 L.Ed. 944 (1928)] and Goldman [v. United States, 316 U.S. 129, 62 S.Ct. 993, 86 L.Ed. 1322 (1942)] and held that the absence of physical intrusion into the telephone booth did not justify using electronic devices in listening to and recording Katz' words, thereby violating the privacy on which he justifiably relied while using the telephone in those circumstances.

The Court of Appeals understood *Katz* to render inadmissible against White the agents' testimony concerning conversations that Jackson broadcast to them. We cannot agree. *Katz* involved no revelation to the Government by a party to conversations with the defendant nor did the Court indicate in any way that a defendant has a justifiable and constitutionally protected expectation that a person with whom he is conversing will not then or later reveal the conversation to the police.

Hoffa v. United States, 385 U.S. 293, 87 S.Ct. 408, 17 L.Ed.2d 374 (1966), which was left undisturbed by *Katz*, held that however strongly a defendant may trust an apparent colleague, his expectations in this respect are not protected by the Fourth Amendment when it turns out that the colleague is a government agent regularly communicating with the authorities. In these circumstances, "no interest legitimately protected by the Fourth Amendment is involved," for that Amendment affords no protection to "a wrongdoer's misplaced belief that a person to whom he voluntarily confides his wrongdoing will not reveal it." No warrant to "search and seize" is required in such circumstances, nor is it when the Government sends to defendant's home a secret agent who conceals his identity and makes a purchase of narcotics from the accused, *Lewis v. United States*, 385 U.S. 206, 87 S.Ct. 424, 17 L.Ed.2d 312 (1966), or when the same agent, unbeknown to the defendant, carries electronic equipment to record the defendant's words and the evidence so gathered is later offered in evidence. *Lopez v. United States*, 373 U.S. 427, 83 S.Ct. 1381, 10 L.Ed.2d 462 (1963).

Conceding that *Hoffa*, *Lewis*, and *Lopez* remained unaffected by *Katz*, the Court of Appeals nevertheless read both *Katz* and the Fourth Amendment to require a different result if the agent not only records his conversations with the defendant but instantaneously transmits them electronically to other agents equipped with radio receivers. Where this occurs, the Court of Appeals held, the Fourth Amendment is violated and the testimony of the listening agents must be excluded from evidence.

To reach this result it was necessary for the Court of Appeals to hold that *On Lee v. United States* [343 U.S. 747, 72 S.Ct. 967, 96 L.Ed. 1270 (1952)] was no longer good law. In that case, which involved facts very similar to the case before us, the Court first rejected claims of a Fourth Amendment violation because the informer had not trespassed when he entered the defendant's premises and conversed with him. To this extent the Court's rationale cannot survive *Katz*. But the Court announced a second and independent ground for its decision; for it went on to say that overruling *Olmstead* and *Goldman* would be of no aid to On Lee since he "was talking confidentially and indiscreetly with one he trusted, and he was overheard. * * * It would be a dubious service to the genuine liberties protected by the Fourth Amendment to make them bedfellows with spurious liberties improvised by farfetched analogies which would liken eavesdropping on a conversation, with the connivance of one of the parties, to an unreasonable search or seizure. We find no violation of the Fourth Amendment here." We see no indication in *Katz* that the Court meant to disturb that understanding of the Fourth Amendment or to disturb the result reached in the *On Lee* case, nor are we now inclined to overturn this view of the Fourth Amendment.

Concededly a police agent who conceals his police connections may write down for official use his conversations with a defendant and testify concerning them, without a warrant authorizing his encounters with the defendant and without otherwise violating the latter's Fourth Amendment rights. *Hoffa v. United States*. For constitutional purposes, no different result is required if the agent instead of immediately reporting and transcribing his conversations with defendant, either (1) simultaneously records them with electronic equipment which he is carrying on his person, *Lopez v. United States*; (2) or carries radio equipment which simultaneously transmits the conversations either to recording equipment located elsewhere or to other agents monitoring the transmitting frequency. *On Lee v. United States*. If the conduct and revelations of an agent operating without electronic equipment do not invade the defendant's constitutionally justifiable expectations of privacy, neither does a simultaneous recording of the same conversations made by the agent or by others from transmissions received from the agent to whom the defendant is talking and whose trustworthiness the defendant necessarily risks.

Our problem is not what the privacy expectations of particular defendants in particular situations may be or the extent to which they may in fact have relied on the discretion of their companions. Very probably, individual defendants neither know nor suspect that their colleagues have gone or will go to the police or are carrying recorders or transmitters. Otherwise, conversation would cease and our problem with these encounters would be nonexistent or far different from those now before us. Our problem, in terms of the principles announced in *Katz*, is what expectations of privacy are constitutionally "justifiable"—what expectations the Fourth Amendment will protect in the absence of a warrant. So far, the law permits the frustration of actual expectations of privacy by permitting authorities to use the testimony of those associates who for one reason or another have determined to turn to the police, as well as by authorizing the use of informants in the manner exemplified by *Hoffa* and *Lewis*. If the law gives no protection to the wrongdoer whose trusted accomplice is or becomes a police agent, neither should it protect him when that same agent has recorded or transmitted the conversations which are later offered in evidence to prove the State's case.

Inescapably, one contemplating illegal activities must realize and risk that his companions may be reporting to the police. If he sufficiently doubts their trustworthiness, the association will very probably end or never materialize. But if he has no doubts, or allays them, or risks what doubt he has, the risk is his. In terms of what his course will be, what he will or will not do or say, we are unpersuaded that he would distinguish between probable informers on the one hand and probable informers with transmitters on the other. Given the possibility or probability that one of his colleagues is cooperating with the police, it is only speculation to assert that the defendant's utterances would be substantially different or his sense of security any less if he also thought it possible that the suspected colleague is wired for sound. At least there is no persuasive evidence that the difference in this respect between the electronically equipped and the unequipped agent is substantial enough to require discrete constitutional recognition, particularly under the Fourth Amendment which is ruled by fluid concepts of "reasonableness."

Nor should we be too ready to erect constitutional barriers to relevant and probative evidence which is also accurate and reliable. An electronic recording will many times produce a more reliable rendition of what a defendant has said than will the unaided memory of a police agent. It may also be that with the recording in existence it is less likely that the informant will change his mind, less chance that threat or injury will suppress unfavorable evidence and less chance that cross-examination will confound the testimony. Considerations like these obviously do not favor the defendant, but we are not prepared to hold that a defendant who has no constitutional right to exclude the informer's unaided testimony nevertheless has a Fourth Amendment privilege against a more accurate version of the events in question. * * *

The judgment of the Court of Appeals is * * * reversed.

[JUSTICE BLACK concurred in the Court's judgment for the reasons set forth in his dissent in Katz. JUSTICE BRENNAN's concurrence in the result is omitted.]

MR. JUSTICE DOUGLAS, dissenting. * * *

The issue in this case is clouded and concealed by the very discussion of it in legalistic terms. What the ancients knew as "eavesdropping," we now call "electronic surveillance"; but to equate the two is to treat man's first gunpowder on the same level as the nuclear bomb. Electronic surveillance is the greatest leveler of human privacy ever known. * * * [T]he concepts of privacy which the Founders enshrined in the Fourth Amendment vanish completely when we slavishly allow an all-powerful government, proclaiming law and order, efficiency, and other benign purposes, to penetrate all the walls and doors which men need to shield them from the pressures of a turbulent life around them and give them the health and strength to carry on. * * *

Today no one perhaps notices because only a small, obscure criminal is the victim. But every person is the victim, for the technology we exalt today is everyman's master. * * *

It is urged by the Department of Justice that *On Lee* be established as the controlling decision in this field. I would stand by * * * *Katz* and reaffirm the need for judicial supervision under the Fourth Amendment of the use of electronic surveillance which, uncontrolled, promises to lead us into a police state. * * *

MR. JUSTICE HARLAN, dissenting. * * *

I

Before turning to matters of precedent and policy, several preliminary observations should be made. We deal here with the constitutional validity of instantaneous third-party electronic eavesdropping, conducted by federal law enforcement officers, without any prior judicial approval of the technique utilized, but with the consent and cooperation of a participant in the conversation * * *. The magnitude of the issue at hand is evidenced not simply by the obvious doctrinal difficulty of weighing such activity in the Fourth Amendment balance, but also, and more importantly, by the prevalence of police utilization of this technique. Professor Westin has documented in careful detail the numerous devices that make technologically feasible the Orwellian Big Brother. Of immediate relevance is his observation that " 'participant recording,' in which one participant in a conversation or meeting, either a police officer or a cooperating party, wears a concealed device that records the conversation or broadcasts it to others nearby * * * is used tens of thousands of times each year throughout the country, particularly in cases involving extortion, conspiracy, narcotics, gambling, prostitution, corruption by police officials * * * and similar crimes * * *.

II * * *

A

On Lee involved circumstances virtually identical to those now before us. There, Government agents enlisted the services of Chin Poy, a former friend of Lee, who was suspected of engaging in illegal narcotics traffic. Poy was equipped with a "minifon" transmitting device which enabled outside Government agents to monitor Poy's conversations with Lee. In the privacy of his laundry, Lee made damaging admissions to Poy which were overheard by the agents and later related at trial. Poy did not testify. Mr. Justice Jackson, writing for five Justices, held the testimony admissible. Without reaching the question of whether a conversation could be the subject of a "seizure" for Fourth Amendment purposes, as yet an unanswered if not completely open question, the Court concluded that in the absence of a trespass, no constitutional violation had occurred.

The validity of the trespass rationale was questionable even at the time the decision was rendered. In this respect *On Lee* rested on common-law notions and looked to a waning era of Fourth Amendment jurisprudence. * * *

III

A

That the foundations of *On Lee* have been destroyed does not, of course, mean that its result can no longer stand. Indeed, the plurality opinion today fastens upon our decisions in *Lopez*, *Lewis v. United States*, and *Hoffa v. United States*, to resist the undercurrents of more recent cases emphasizing the warrant procedure as a safeguard to privacy. But this category provides insufficient support. In each of these cases the risk the general populace faced was different from that surfaced by the instant case. No surreptitious third ear was present, and in each opinion that fact was carefully noted. * * *

The plurality opinion seeks to erase the crucial distinction between the facts before us and these holdings by the following reasoning: if A can relay verbally what is revealed to him by B (as in *Lewis* and *Hoffa*), or record and later divulge it (as in *Lopez*), what difference does it make if A conspires with another to betray B by contemporaneously transmitting to the other all that is said? The contention is, in essence, an argument that the distinction between third-party monitoring and other undercover techniques is one of form and not substance. The force of the contention depends on the evaluation of two separable but intertwined assumptions: first, that there is no greater invasion of privacy in the third-party situation, and, second, that uncontrolled consensual surveillance in an electronic age is a tolerable technique of law enforcement, given the values and goals of our political system.

The first of these assumptions takes as a point of departure the so-called "risk analysis" approach of *Lewis*, and *Lopez*, and to a lesser extent *On Lee*, or the expectations approach of *Katz*. While these formulations represent an advance over the unsophisticated trespass analysis of the common law, they too have their limitations and can, ultimately, lead to the substitution of words for analysis. The analysis must, in my view, transcend the search for subjective expectations or legal attribution of assumptions of risk. Our expectations, and the risks we assume, are in large part reflections of laws that translate into rules the customs and values of the past and present.

Since it is the task of the law to form and project, as well as mirror and reflect, we should not, as judges, merely recite the expectations and risks without examining the desirability of saddling them upon society. The critical question, therefore, is whether under our system of government, as reflected in the Constitution, we should impose on our citizens the risks of the electronic listener or observer without at least the protection of a warrant requirement.

This question must, in my view, be answered by assessing the nature of a particular practice and the likely extent of its impact on the individual's sense of security balanced against the utility of the conduct as a technique of law enforcement. For those more extensive intrusions that significantly jeopardize the sense of security which is the paramount concern of Fourth Amendment liberties, I am of the view that more than self-restraint by law enforcement officials is required and at the least warrants should be necessary.

B

The impact of the practice of third-party bugging, must, I think, be considered such as to undermine that confidence and sense of security in dealing with one another that is characteristic of individual relationships between citizens in a free society. It goes beyond the impact on privacy occasioned by the ordinary type of "informer" investigation upheld in *Lewis* and *Hoffa*. The argument of the plurality opinion, to the effect that it is irrelevant whether secrets are revealed by the mere tattletale or the transistor, ignores the differences occasioned by third-party monitoring and recording which insures full and accurate disclosure of all that is said, free of the possibility of error and oversight that inheres in human reporting.

Authority is hardly required to support the proposition that words would be measured a good deal more carefully and communication inhibited if one suspected his conversations were being transmitted and transcribed. Were third-party bugging a prevalent practice, it might well smother that spontaneity—reflected in frivolous, impetuous, sacrilegious, and defiant discourse—that liberates daily life. Much off-hand exchange is easily forgotten and one may count on the obscurity of his remarks, protected by the very fact of a limited audience, and the likelihood that the listener will either overlook or forget what is said, as well as the listener's inability to reformulate a conversation without having to contend with a documented record. All these values are sacrificed by a rule of law that permits official monitoring of private discourse limited only by the need to locate a willing assistant. * * *

Finally, it is too easy to forget—and, hence, too often forgotten—that the issue here is whether to interpose a search warrant procedure between law enforcement agencies engaging in electronic eavesdropping and the public generally. By casting its "risk analysis" solely in terms of the expectations and risks that "wrongdoers" or "one contemplating illegal activities" ought to bear, the plurality opinion, I think, misses the mark entirely. *On Lee* does not simply mandate that criminals must daily run the risk of unknown eavesdroppers prying into their private affairs; it subjects each and every law-abiding member of society to that risk. The very purpose of interposing the Fourth Amendment warrant requirement is to redistribute the privacy risks throughout society in a way that produces the results the plurality opinion ascribes to the *On Lee* rule. Abolition of *On Lee* would not end electronic eavesdropping. It would prevent public officials from engaging in that practice unless they first had probable cause to suspect an individual of involvement in illegal activities and had tested their version of the facts before a detached judicial officer. * * *

The Fourth Amendment does, of course, leave room for the employment of modern technology in criminal law enforcement, but in the stream of current developments in Fourth Amendment law I think it must be held that third-party electronic monitoring, subject only to the self-restraint of law enforcement officials, has no place in our society.

IV * * *

What this means is that the burden of guarding privacy in a free society should not be on its citizens; it is the Government that must justify its need to electronically eavesdrop. * * *

I would hold that *On Lee* is no longer good law and affirm the judgment below.

[*JUSTICE MARSHALL's dissent is omitted.*]

NOTES AND QUESTIONS

1. In *Katz*, the Supreme Court held that the electronic surveillance of Katz's conversations with others constituted a search and, therefore, was regulated by the Fourth Amendment. In *White*, however, the Court held that the Government's use of an informant "wired" with a transmitter fell outside the scope of the Fourth Amendment. As one scholar has observed:

> The law treats secret surveillance of speech or other behavior largely according to whether the surveilling agent is visible or invisible to the subject. An agent, visibly present though masquerading [as a confidant], is thought to gather evidence in a fundamentally different manner than a concealed agent or a hidden electronic device. The theory is that the contents of the mind, deliberately revealed to another person, are willingly shared, while the secret eye or ear, possibly electronically enhanced, bypasses constitutional concern to spirit the evidence away.

H. Richard Uviller, *Evidence from the Mind of the Criminal Suspect: A Reconsideration of the Current Rules of Access and Restraint*, 87 Colum. L. Rev. 1137, 1151 (1987).

2. *False friends, false friends with tape recorders, and "wired" false friends.* Notice that there are various ways the Government listens to conversations of persons suspected of crime. First, it may surreptitiously eavesdrop on a conversation between A and B, as in *Katz*. Second, the Government may participate in the conversation itself, as when A talks to B, who turns out to be an undercover police officer or friend-turned-government-agent, as in *Hoffa*. In this latter case we may characterize B as a "false friend." Third, it is possible that false friend B will tape record the conversation (*Lopez*) or be "wired" with a transmitter (*On Lee, White*).

Consider first the pure false friend, *Hoffa*, situation. Should such a case fall outside the protection of the Fourth Amendment? Consider:

> [T]he Court [has] viewed betrayal as an expected (if reprehensible) behavior among human beings * * *. Nosy neighbors and pretend friends are not unheard-of phenomena. We trust such people at our own risk. * * *
>
> By allowing the police to send out pretend friends, however, the Court does more than simply mimic the sorts of betrayals that would inevitably occur from time to time in the real world of friendship. By planting moles in our midst, the government deliberately manipulates reality to create relationships for the sole purpose of betrayal. * * * By utilizing such spies, the government therefore adds a level of unusual risk to our private lives. Even for those of us who trust our own judgment in detecting pretend friends, the government-issue friend is peculiar enough to be more like the recording device on Katz's telephone booth than like a friend in the real world who fails to keep a secret. Such creatures are more difficult to discover (since they are not naturally occurring) and could therefore chill even the savvy individual, otherwise insulated by a sixth sense, from trusting other people.

Sherry F. Colb, *What Is a Search? Two Conceptual Flaws in Fourth Amendment Doctrine and Some Hints of a Remedy*, 55 Stan. L. Rev. 119, 141–43 (2002).

Do you agree with Professor Colb's observations? If so, are you prepared to set up constitutional obstacles to the use of undercover police agents in criminal investigations?

However you feel about *Hoffa* and false friends, is there something even worse about false friend B tape recording his conversations with A or transmitting them live to agents away from the scene, as in *White*? Do you think, for example, that if persons in the Nixon White House had known that their Watergate conversations were being taped by the president, that they would have been more careful with their words? Do you think you would be more cautious in *your* conversations if you knew that the government was listening? If so, is this a valid reason to provide Fourth Amendment protection to such conversations? In this regard, notice that some states make criminal the recording of a conversation unless all parties consent to it being recorded. See, e.g., Cal. Penal Code § 632 (violations punishable by a fine not exceeding $2,500 *per violation*, or imprisonment for up to one year, or by both fine and imprisonment).

3. *The objective prong of Harlan's "search" test.* Reconsider p. 84, Note 4. Based on his dissent here, how would Justice Harlan answer the questions raised in that Note?

In relation to the objective prong of the Harlan "search" test, Professor Anthony Amsterdam would phrase the issue this way:

> The ultimate question, plainly, is a value judgment. It is whether, if the particular form of surveillance practiced by the police is permitted to go

> unregulated by constitutional restraints, the amount of privacy and freedom remaining to citizens would be diminished to a compass inconsistent with the aims of a free and open society.

Anthony G. Amsterdam, *Perspectives on the Fourth Amendment*, 58 Minn. L. Rev. 349, 403 (1974). How would you decide *White* according to this standard?

4. *Historical tidbit.* Timing sometimes matters a great deal. Consider: In 1938, Earl Warren's father was murdered in Bakersfield, California. The police had no leads until a San Quentin prisoner came under suspicion. The Bakersfield Chief of Police wanted to put a "stool pigeon" in the cell with the suspect and record their conversations. However, Warren, then District Attorney in Alameda County, rejected the use of the recorder, on the ground that he considered eavesdropping an inappropriate law enforcement technique. Therefore, no taping occurred, and the murder was never solved. Bernard Schwartz, Super Chief: Earl Warren and His Supreme Court—A Judicial Biography 11–12 (1983).

Warren joined the Supreme Court in 1953 upon the death of Chief Justice Fred Vinson, one year after the Court ruled, 5–4 (with Vinson joining the majority), in *On Lee v. United States, supra*, that use of a secret microphone by an undercover agent to transmit conversations to a third party did not implicate Fourth Amendment interests. Had the case come to the Court after Warren had joined the Court, the outcome might have been different. Had *On Lee* been decided differently, it is intriguing to consider how the law, culminating in *White*, might have evolved.

For a fuller examination of Chief Justice Warren's law enforcement background and its likely influence on his criminal justice opinions, see Yale Kamisar, *How Earl Warren's Twenty-Two Years in Law Enforcement Affected His Work as Chief Justice*, 3 Ohio St. J. Crim. L. 11 (2005).

5. *Justice Harlan and Big Brother.* Justice Harlan expressed his concern that the plurality's approach to the Fourth Amendment "might well smother that spontaneity—reflected in frivolous, impetuous, sacrilegious, and defiant discourse—that liberates daily life." He also pointed to the risks of "Orwellian Big Brother" technology that can be "used to unearth 'political' crimes."

One person's "political" crimes and free speech is another person's incipient terrorism. One post-September 11 commentator observed: "How the times have changed. Today the talk is of more, rather than less, surveillance. Instead of 'Big Brother is watching you,' we hear 'Big Brother is watching out for you.' " Editors, *Here's Looking at You*, Scientific American, Dec. 2001, at 8. Do you believe that the Supreme Court in *White* set the proper balance between security from crime and individual liberty?

6. The *White* plurality relied in part on *Lewis v. United States*, a 1966 "consent" case, in which a federal agent, "misrepresenting his identity and stating his willingness to purchase narcotics, was invited into petitioner's home where an unlawful narcotics transaction was consummated." The Court found no violation in this conduct. It made the following observation about the use of undercover agents:

> Were we to hold the deceptions of the agent in this case constitutionally prohibited, we would come near to a rule that the use of undercover agents in any manner is virtually unconstitutional per se. Such a rule would * * * severely hamper the Government in ferreting out those organized criminal activities that are characterized by covert dealings with victims who either cannot or do not protest.

Does this represent a valid reason to uphold the *Hoffa-White* approach to false friends?

7. *The slow march of common law precedent.* Notice that *White* is distinguishable on its facts from *Katz*. White's case is, however, not distinguishable from *On Lee*. Thus, the doctrine of *stare decisis* or precedent required the Court to reject White's argument unless it was willing to overrule *On Lee*. The common law methodology strongly disfavors overruling precedent. So White lost.

8. *Problem.* Undercover police officer Alice seeks to negotiate a drug sale with Barbara. Barbara informs Alice that she will only discuss the matter in a specified spot in a public park at 2:00 a.m., because "nobody is ever there at that hour." Alice agrees to meet her there. In the meantime, with Alice's knowledge, the police install a hidden transmitter in a tree near the meeting place, so that another officer can listen to the conversation. Is it a "search" when the officer listens to Alice's and Barbara's conversations via the transmitter? Put another way, is this *Katz* or *White*? What if agent Alice is herself unaware of the transmitter?

Suppose that the police leave the device in the tree and listen to other conversations in the park by passersby. Is the Fourth Amendment implicated by this surveillance?

SMITH V. MARYLAND

Supreme Court of the United States, 1979.
442 U.S. 735, 99 S.Ct. 2577, 61 L.Ed.2d. 220.

The analysis of Harlan's two-prong test from *Katz* continues in this next case. Pay particular attention to Justice Marshall's dissent. He asks an important question: If we give information to a third-party for a specific purpose, do we lose all expectation of privacy in that information, or, is it

perhaps a matter of degree? Does the purpose for which we released the information in the first place matter?

If the facts in *Smith*, a 1979 case, seem hauntingly familiar, think of the NSA data mining program after 9/11 for which *Smith v. Maryland* was often cited in support of the program's legality.[2]

The Notes and Questions following *Smith* present an overview of how *Katz* has been applied to a myriad of government conduct. This includes dog sniffs, open fields , the curtilage of a house , aerial surveillance over a home , and garbage left on a sidewalk for pick-up . In which of these situations, if any, do you think a search has occurred?

In addition, the Notes raise an important question about Harlan's subjective prong. How does our understanding of technology (say, a pen register) affect our actual expectation of privacy? As first suggested by the Notes after *Katz*, does, for example, an increased understanding of information technology or cybersecurity after taking a college class result in a decreased expectation of privacy in online activities compared to a person who knows little about computers other than how to turn one on? Remember, under the *Katz/Harlan* test, if there is no actual expectation of privacy, whether or not that expectation is reasonable does not matter. The issues that start here arise with even more relevance in later cases as the tools used to "search" become more and more technologically advanced.

MR. JUSTICE BLACKMUN delivered the opinion of the Court [joined by CHIEF JUSTICE BURGER, and JUSTICES WHITE, REHNQUIST, and STEVENS].

This case presents the question whether the installation and use of a pen register constitutes a "search" within the meaning of the Fourth Amendment, made applicable to the States through the Fourteenth Amendment.

[Footnote 1 of the majority opinion described a pen register as follows: "A pen register is a mechanical device that records the numbers dialed on a telephone by monitoring the electrical impulses caused when the dial on the telephone is released. It does not overhear oral communications and does not indicate whether calls are actually completed. A pen register is 'usually installed at a central telephone facility [and] records on a paper tape all numbers dialed from [the] line' to which it is attached."]

---

[2] For more discussion on the application of *Smith v. Maryland* to the data mining program, see John Yoo. *NSA Surveillance: Issues of Security, Privacy, and Civil Liberty*, 10 IS: A Journal of Law 301 (2014); Mark Rapisarda. *Privacy, Technology, and Surveillance: NSA Bulk Collection and the End of the Smith v. Maryland Era*, 51 Gonzaga L. R. 121 (2015–2016).

I

On March 5, 1976, in Baltimore, Md., Patricia McDonough was robbed. She gave the police a description of the robber and of a 1975 Monte Carlo automobile she had observed near the scene of the crime. After the robbery, McDonough began receiving threatening and obscene phone calls from a man identifying himself as the robber. On one occasion, the caller asked that she step out on her front porch; she did so, and saw the 1975 Monte Carlo she had earlier described to police moving slowly past her home. On March 16, police spotted a man who met McDonough's description driving a 1975 Monte Carlo in her neighborhood. By tracing the license plate number, police learned that the car was registered in the name of petitioner, Michael Lee Smith.

The next day, the telephone company, at police request, installed a pen register at its central offices to record the numbers dialed from the telephone at petitioner's home. The police did not get a warrant or court order before having the pen register installed. The register revealed that on March 17 a call was placed from petitioner's home to McDonough's phone. On the basis of this and other evidence, the police obtained a warrant to search petitioner's residence. The search revealed that a page in petitioner's phone book was turned down to the name and number of Patricia McDonough; the phone book was seized. * * *

Petitioner was indicted in the Criminal Court of Baltimore for robbery. By pretrial motion, he sought to suppress "all fruits derived from the pen register" on the ground that the police had failed to secure a warrant prior to its installation. The trial court denied the suppression motion, holding that the warrantless installation of the pen register did not violate the Fourth Amendment. * * * The pen register tape (evidencing the fact that a phone call had been made from petitioner's phone to McDonough's phone) and the phone book seized in the search of petitioner's residence were admitted into evidence against him. Petitioner was convicted, and was sentenced to six years. * * *

II

A

* * * In determining whether a particular form of government-initiated electronic surveillance is a "search" within the meaning of the Fourth Amendment, our lodestar is *Katz v. United States*. In *Katz*, * * * [the] Court rejected the argument that a "search" can occur only when there has been a "physical intrusion" into a "constitutionally protected area," noting that the Fourth Amendment "protects people, not places." Because the Government's monitoring of Katz' conversation "violated the privacy upon which he justifiably

relied while using the telephone booth," the Court held that it "constituted a 'search and seizure' within the meaning of the Fourth Amendment."

Consistently with *Katz*, this Court uniformly has held that the application of the Fourth Amendment depends on whether the person invoking its protection can claim a "justifiable," a "reasonable," or a "legitimate expectation of privacy" that has been invaded by government action. This inquiry, as Mr. Justice Harlan aptly noted in his *Katz* concurrence, normally embraces two discrete questions. The first is whether the individual, by his conduct, has "exhibited an actual (subjective) expectation of privacy"—whether, in the words of the *Katz* majority, the individual has shown that "he seeks to preserve [something] as private." The second question is whether the individual's subjective expectation of privacy is "one that society is prepared to recognize as 'reasonable' "—whether, in the words of the *Katz* majority, the individual's expectation, viewed objectively, is "justifiable" under the circumstances.

B

In applying the *Katz* analysis to this case, it is important to begin by specifying precisely the nature of the state activity that is challenged. The activity here took the form of installing and using a pen register. Since the pen register was installed on telephone company property at the telephone company's central offices, petitioner obviously cannot claim that his "property" was invaded or that police intruded into a "constitutionally protected area." Petitioner's claim, rather, is that, notwithstanding the absence of a trespass, the State, as did the Government in *Katz*, infringed a "legitimate expectation of privacy" that petitioner held. Yet a pen register differs significantly from the listening device employed in *Katz*, for pen registers do not acquire the contents of communications. This Court recently noted:

> "Indeed, a law enforcement official could not even determine from the use of a pen register whether a communication existed. These devices do not hear sound. They disclose only the telephone numbers that have been dialed—a means of establishing communication. Neither the purport of any communication between the caller and the recipient of the call, their identities, nor whether the call was even completed is disclosed by pen registers."

Given a pen register's limited capabilities, therefore, petitioner's argument that its installation and use constituted a "search" necessarily rests upon a claim that he had a "legitimate expectation of privacy" regarding the numbers he dialed on his phone.

This claim must be rejected. First, we doubt that people in general entertain any actual expectation of privacy in the numbers they dial. All telephone users realize that they must "convey" phone numbers to the telephone company, since it is through telephone company switching equipment that their calls are completed. All subscribers realize, moreover, that the phone company has facilities for making permanent records of the numbers they dial, for they see a list of their long-distance (toll) calls on their monthly bills. In fact, pen registers and similar devices are routinely used by telephone companies "for the purposes of checking billing operations, detecting fraud, and preventing violations of law." * * * Although most people may be oblivious to a pen register's esoteric functions, they presumably have some awareness of one common use: to aid in the identification of persons making annoying or obscene calls. Most phone books tell subscribers, on a page entitled "Consumer Information," that the company "can frequently help in identifying to the authorities the origin of unwelcome and troublesome calls." Telephone users, in sum, typically know that they must convey numerical information to the phone company; that the phone company has facilities for recording this information; and that the phone company does in fact record this information for a variety of legitimate business purposes. Although subjective expectations cannot be scientifically gauged, it is too much to believe that telephone subscribers, under these circumstances, harbor any general expectation that the numbers they dial will remain secret.

Petitioner argues, however, that, whatever the expectations of telephone users in general, he demonstrated an expectation of privacy by his own conduct here, since he "us[ed] the telephone *in his house* to the exclusion of all others." But the site of the call is immaterial for purposes of analysis in this case. Although petitioner's conduct may have been calculated to keep the *contents* of his conversation private, his conduct was not and could not have been calculated to preserve the privacy of the number he dialed. Regardless of his location, petitioner had to convey that number to the telephone company in precisely the same way if he wished to complete his call. The fact that he dialed the number on his home phone rather than on some other phone could make no conceivable difference, nor could any subscriber rationally think that it would.

Second, even if petitioner did harbor some subjective expectation that the phone numbers he dialed would remain private, this expectation is not "one that society is prepared to recognize as 'reasonable.' " This Court consistently has held that a person has no legitimate expectation of privacy in information he voluntarily turns over to third parties. *E.g., United States v. Miller*, 425 U.S. [435, 442–444, 96 S.Ct. 1619, 1623–24, 48 L.Ed.2d 71 (1976)]; *United States v. White*, [p. 86]. In Miller, for example, the Court held that a bank depositor has no "legitimate 'expectation of privacy' " in financial information "voluntarily conveyed to * * * banks and exposed to their employees in the ordinary course of business." The Court explained:

> "The depositor takes the risk, in revealing his affairs to another, that the information will be conveyed by that person to the Government. * * * This Court has held repeatedly that the Fourth Amendment does not prohibit the obtaining of information revealed to a third party and conveyed by him to Government authorities, even if the information is revealed on the assumption that it will be used only for a limited purpose and the confidence placed in the third party will not be betrayed."

Because the depositor "assumed the risk" of disclosure, the Court held that it would be unreasonable for him to expect his financial records to remain private.

This analysis dictates that petitioner can claim no legitimate expectation of privacy here. When he used his phone, petitioner voluntarily conveyed numerical information to the telephone company and "exposed" that information to its equipment in the ordinary course of business. In so doing, petitioner assumed the risk that the company would reveal to police the numbers he dialed. The switching equipment that processed those numbers is merely the modern counterpart of the operator who, in an earlier day, personally completed calls for the subscriber. * * * We are not inclined to hold that a different constitutional result is required because the telephone company has decided to automate. * * *

We therefore conclude that petitioner in all probability entertained no actual expectation of privacy in the phone numbers he dialed, and that, even if he did, his expectation was not "legitimate." The installation and use of a pen register, consequently, was not a "search," and no warrant was required. * * *

[MR. JUSTICE POWELL took no part in the consideration or decision of this case.]

MR. JUSTICE STEWART, with whom MR. JUSTICE BRENNAN joins, dissenting. * * *

I think that the numbers dialed from a private telephone—like the conversations that occur during a call—are within the constitutional protection recognized in *Katz*. * * * The information captured by such surveillance emanates from private conduct within a person's home or office—locations that without question are entitled to Fourth and Fourteenth Amendment protection. * * *

The numbers dialed from a private telephone—although certainly more prosaic than the conversation itself—are not without "content." Most private telephone subscribers may have their own numbers listed in a publicly distributed directory, but I doubt there are any who would be happy to have broadcast to the world a list of the local or long distance numbers they have called. This is not because such a list might in some sense be incriminating, but because it easily could reveal the identities of the persons and the places called, and thus reveal the most intimate details of a person's life. * * *

MR. JUSTICE MARSHALL, with whom MR. JUSTICE BRENNAN joins, dissenting. * * *

Applying the standards set forth in *Katz v. United States*, the Court first determines that telephone subscribers have no subjective expectations of privacy concerning the numbers they dial. To reach this conclusion, the Court posits that individuals somehow infer from the long-distance listings on their phone bills, and from the cryptic assurances of "help" in tracing obscene calls included in "most" phone books, that pen registers are regularly used for recording local calls. But even assuming, as I do not, that individuals "typically know" that a phone company monitors calls for internal reasons, it does not follow that they expect this information to be made available to the public in general or the government in particular. Privacy is not a discrete commodity, possessed absolutely or not at all. Those who disclose certain facts to a bank or phone company for a limited business purpose need not assume that this information will be released to other persons for other purposes.

The crux of the Court's holding, however, is that whatever expectation of privacy petitioner may in fact have entertained regarding his calls, it is not one "society is prepared to recognize as 'reasonable.' " In so ruling, the Court determines that individuals who convey information to third parties have "assumed the risk" of disclosure to the government. This analysis is misconceived in two critical respects.

Implicit in the concept of assumption of risk is some notion of choice. At least in the third-party consensual surveillance cases, which first incorporated risk analysis into Fourth Amendment doctrine, the defendant presumably had exercised some discretion in deciding who should enjoy his confidential communications. See, *e.g.*, [*United States v. White, supra*]. By contrast here, unless a person is prepared to forgo use of what for many has become a personal or professional necessity, he cannot help but accept the risk of surveillance. It is idle to speak of "assuming" risks in contexts where, as a practical matter, individuals have no realistic alternative.

More fundamentally, to make risk analysis dispositive in assessing the reasonableness of privacy expectations would allow the government to define the scope of Fourth Amendment protections. For example, law enforcement officials, simply by announcing their intent to monitor the content of random samples of first-class mail or private phone conversations, could put the public on notice of the risks they would thereafter assume in such communications. Yet, although acknowledging this implication of its analysis, the Court is willing to concede only that, in some circumstances, a further "normative inquiry would be proper." No meaningful effort is made to explain what those circumstances might be, or why this case is not among them.

In my view, whether privacy expectations are legitimate within the meaning of *Katz* depends not on the risks an individual can be presumed to accept when imparting information to third parties, but on the risks he should be forced to assume in a free and open society. By its terms, the constitutional prohibition of unreasonable searches and seizures assigns to the judiciary some prescriptive responsibility. As Mr. Justice Harlan, who formulated the standard the Court applies today, himself recognized: "[s]ince it is the task of the law to form and project, as well as mirror and reflect, we should not * * * merely recite * * * risks without examining the desirability of saddling them upon society." *United States v. White, supra* (dissenting opinion). In making this assessment, courts must evaluate the "intrinsic character" of investigative practices with reference to the basic values underlying the Fourth Amendment. And for those "extensive intrusions that significantly jeopardize [individuals'] sense of security * * *, more than self-restraint by law enforcement officials is required."

The use of pen registers, I believe, constitutes such an extensive intrusion. To hold otherwise ignores the vital role telephonic communication plays in our personal and professional relationships, as well as the First and Fourth Amendment interests implicated by unfettered official surveillance. Privacy in placing calls is of value not only to those engaged in criminal activity. The prospect of unregulated governmental monitoring will undoubtedly prove disturbing even to those with nothing illicit to hide. Many individuals, including members of unpopular political organizations or journalists with confidential sources, may legitimately wish to avoid disclosure of their personal contacts. Permitting governmental access to telephone records on less than probable cause may thus impede certain forms of political affiliation and journalistic endeavor that are the hallmark of a truly free society. * * * I am unwilling to insulate use of pen registers from independent judicial review.

Just as one who enters a public telephone booth is "entitled to assume that the words he utters into the mouthpiece will not be broadcast to the world," *Katz v. United States, supra*, so too, he should be entitled to assume that the numbers he dials in the privacy of his home will be recorded, if at all, solely for the phone company's business purposes. Accordingly, I would require law enforcement officials to obtain a warrant before they enlist telephone companies to secure information otherwise beyond the government's reach.

NOTES AND QUESTIONS

1. Is *Smith* consistent with *Katz*? Justice Stewart, author of *Katz*, dissented. Do you find the dissents more persuasive than the majority opinion?

2. Justice Stewart announced in *Katz* that what a "person knowingly exposes to the public" is unprotected by the Fourth Amendment. Is the implication of *Smith* that when a person exposes private information to one person or entity that she thereby altogether loses Fourth Amendment protection in that information? In this regard, consider:

> A person going on vacation * * * might give a neighbor the key to her house and ask him to water her plants while she is gone. The neighbor now has explicit permission to observe what would otherwise be hidden from view * * *. By granting this permission that vacationer has forfeited a measure of privacy and has thus knowingly exposed part of her home to her neighbor. Still, if the neighbor were to invite his friends * * * into the apartment to see the vacationer's personal items, even just those things visible from where the plants are located, that act would go beyond the scope of the vacationer's permission and therefore represent an invasion of her privacy. There are degrees of privacy and, accordingly, degrees of exposure, and one might choose to forfeit some of her freedom of exposure without thereby forfeiting all of it.

Sherry F. Colb, *What Is a Search? Two Conceptual Flaws in Fourth Amendment Doctrine and Some Hints of a Remedy*, 55 Stan. L. Rev. 119, 122–23 (2002).

Do you agree? If so, how would you have the Court define "the public" in Justice Stewart's rule? Note also how Justice Blackmun addressed the purely subjective expectation of privacy in *Smith* in footnote 5 of the majority opinion:

> Situations can be imagined, of course, in which *Katz*' two-pronged inquiry would provide an inadequate index of Fourth Amendment protection. For example, if the Government were to suddenly announce on nationwide television that all homes henceforth would be subject to

> warrantless entry, individuals thereafter might not in fact entertain any actual expectation of privacy regarding their homes, papers, and effects. Similarly, if a refugee from a totalitarian country, unaware of this Nation's traditions, erroneously assumed that police were continuously monitoring his telephone conversations, a subjective expectation of privacy regarding the content of his calls might be lacking as well. In such circumstances, where an individual's subjective expectations had been "conditioned" by influences alien to well-recognized Fourth Amendment freedoms, those subjective expectations obviously could play no meaningful role in ascertaining what the scope of Fourth Amendment protection was. In determining whether a "legitimate expectation of privacy" existed in such cases, a normative inquiry would be proper.

3. In a footnote to his scathing dissent, Justice Marshall had this to say about people's understanding of what phone companies do with phone numbers dialed:

> Lacking the Court's apparently exhaustive knowledge of the Nation's telephone books and the reading habits of telephone subscribers, I decline to assume general public awareness of how obscene phone calls are traced. Nor am I persuaded that the scope of the Fourth Amendment protection should turn on the concededly "esoteric functions" of pen registers in corporate billing, functions with which subscribers are unlikely to have intimate familiarity.

4. *What the Court taketh away, Congress can giveth back. Smith* placed the installation and use of pen registers outside the scope of the Fourth Amendment. In 1986, however, Congress placed statutory limits on use of pen registers in law enforcement. See 18 U.S.C. §§ 3121–3126 (2008) (generally barring installation or use of pen registers without a court order).

5. *"Dog sniffs."* You will remember that the *Smith* Court's analysis of pen registers relied in part on the "limited capabilities" of the device (it does not acquire the contents of communications). The Court has repeated this theme elsewhere. In United States v. Place, 462 U.S. 696, 103 S.Ct. 2637, 77 L.Ed.2d 110 (1983), federal drug authorities at LaGuardia Airport in New York subjected a passenger's luggage to a "sniff test" by a dog trained to identify narcotics by smell. One issue in the case was whether the dog sniff constituted a Fourth Amendment search:

> A "canine sniff" by a well-trained narcotics detection dog * * * does not require opening the luggage. It does not expose noncontraband items that otherwise would remain hidden from public view, as does, for example, an officer's rummaging through the contents of the luggage. Thus, the manner in which information is obtained through this investigative technique is much less intrusive than a typical search. Moreover, the sniff discloses only

> the presence or absence of narcotics, a contraband item. Thus, despite the fact that the sniff tells the authorities something about the contents of the luggage, the information obtained is limited. This limited disclosure also ensures that the owner of the property is not subjected to the embarrassment and inconvenience entailed in less discriminate and more intrusive investigative methods.
>
> In these respects, the canine sniff is *sui generis*. We are aware of no other investigative procedure that is so limited both in the manner in which the information is obtained and in the content of the information revealed by the procedure. Therefore, we conclude that the particular course of investigation that the agents intended to pursue here—exposure of respondent's luggage, which was located in a public place, to a trained canine—did not constitute a "search" within the meaning of the Fourth Amendment.

The Supreme Court reaffirmed *Place* and explained it further in Illinois v. Caballes, 543 U.S. 405, 125 S.Ct. 834, 160 L.Ed.2d 842 (2005). In *Caballes*, police officers used a "well-trained narcotics-detection dog" to sniff the exterior of the trunk of an automobile, which was lawfully stopped on the highway for a traffic ticket. The Court, 6–2, per Justice John Stevens, wrote:

> Official conduct that does not "compromise any legitimate interest in privacy" is not a search subject to the Fourth Amendment. [*United States v.*] *Jacobsen*, 466 U.S. [109,] at 123, 104 S.Ct. 1652, 80 L.Ed.2d 85 [(1984)]. We have held [in *Jacobsen*] that any interest in possessing contraband cannot be deemed "legitimate," and thus, governmental conduct that *only* reveals the possession of contraband "compromises no legitimate privacy interest." This is because the expectation "that certain facts will not come to the attention of the authorities" is not the same as an interest in "privacy that society is prepared to consider reasonable." * * *
>
> Accordingly, the use of a well-trained narcotics-detection dog—one that "does not expose noncontraband items that otherwise would remain hidden from public view"—during a lawful traffic stop, generally does not implicate legitimate privacy interests. In this case, * * * [a]ny intrusion on respondent's privacy expectations does not rise to the level of a constitutionally cognizable infringement.

Justice Souter dissented:

> I would hold that using the dog for the purposes of determining the presence of marijuana in the car's trunk was a search * * *. * * *

> At the heart both of *Place* and the Court's opinion today is the proposition that sniffs by a trained dog are *sui generis* because a reaction by the dog in going alert is a response to nothing but the presence of contraband. Hence, the argument goes, because the sniff can only reveal the presence of items devoid of any legal use, the sniff "does not implicate legitimate privacy interests" and is not to be treated as a search.
>
> The infallible dog, however, is a creature of legal fiction. * * * [T]heir supposed infallibility is belied by judicial opinions describing well-trained animals sniffing and alerting with less than perfect accuracy, whether owing to errors by their handlers, the limitations of the dogs themselves, or even the pervasive contamination of currency by cocaine. Indeed, a study cited by Illinois in this case for the proposition that dog sniffs are "generally reliable" shows that dogs in artificial testing situations return false positives anywhere from 12.5 to 60% of the time, depending on the length of the search. In practical terms, the evidence is clear that the dog that alerts hundreds of times will be wrong dozens of times.
>
> Once the dog's fallibility is recognized, * * * that ends the justification claimed in *Place* for treating the sniff as sui generis under the Fourth Amendment: the sniff alert does not necessarily signal hidden contraband * * *. * * *
>
> It makes sense, then, to treat a sniff as the search that it amounts to in practice, and to rely on the body of our Fourth Amendment cases * * * in determining whether such a search is reasonable.

What if the police use a narcotics-detection dog to sniff at the front door of a person's home? Should that be treated differently? The Supreme Court has now answered this question, but it is premature to disclose the result. (Trust us, we will get there in due time.)

6. *Open fields.* In Hester v. United States, 265 U.S. 57, 44 S.Ct. 445, 68 L.Ed. 898 (1924), the Supreme Court first enunciated the so-called "open fields" doctrine, which provides that police entry of an open field does not implicate the Fourth Amendment. In Oliver v. United States, 466 U.S. 170, 104 S.Ct. 1735, 80 L.Ed.2d 214 (1984), the Court held that this doctrine remains good law after *Katz*.

What is an "open field"? According to *Oliver*, it "may include any unoccupied or undeveloped area outside of the curtilage [area in proximity to a home; see next Note]. An open field need be neither 'open' nor a 'field' as those terms are used in common speech. For example, * * * a thickly wooded area nonetheless may be an open field as that term is used in construing the Fourth Amendment."

In *Oliver* and a companion case, law enforcement officers, without a warrant or probable cause, trespassed on defendants' rural property, even ignoring "No Trespassing" signs, and discovered fields of marijuana. In an opinion written by Justice Lewis Powell, the Court ruled, 6–3, that an open field does not constitute a "person, house, paper, or effect":

> The rule announced in *Hester v. United States* was founded upon the explicit language of the Fourth Amendment. That Amendment indicates with some precision the places and things encompassed by its protections. As Justice Holmes explained for the Court in his characteristically laconic style: "[T]he special protection accorded by the Fourth Amendment to the people in their 'persons, houses, papers, and effects,' is not extended to the open fields. The distinction between the latter and the house is as old as the common law." deleted footnote here, since not coming from a main case anyway.
>
> Nor are the open fields "effects" within the meaning of the Fourth Amendment. In this respect, it is suggestive that James Madison's proposed draft of what became the Fourth Amendment preserves "[t]he rights of the people to be secured in their persons, their houses, their papers, and their other property, from all unreasonable searches and seizures * * *." Although Congress' revisions of Madison's proposal broadened the scope of the Amendment in some respects, the term "effects" is less inclusive than "property" and cannot be said to encompass open fields. We conclude * * * that the government's intrusion upon the open fields is not one of those "unreasonable searches" proscribed by the text of the Fourth Amendment.

The Court could have stopped at this point, relying on the plain meaning of the Fourth Amendment text, but it did not. Five justices also concluded that entry of an open field does not constitute a "search" within the post-*Katz* meaning of that concept:

> [A]n individual may not legitimately demand privacy for activities conducted out of doors in fields, except in the area immediately surrounding the home. This rule is true to the conception of the right to privacy embodied in the Fourth Amendment. The Amendment reflects the recognition of the Framers that certain enclaves should be free from arbitrary government interference. For example, the Court since the enactment of the Fourth Amendment has stressed "the overriding respect for the sanctity of the home that has been embedded in our traditions since the origins of the Republic." *Payton v. New York*, [p. 185].

> In contrast, open fields do not provide the setting for those intimate activities that the Amendment is intended to shelter from government interference or surveillance. There is no societal interest in protecting the privacy of those activities, such as the cultivation of crops, that occur in open fields. Moreover, as a practical matter these lands usually are accessible to the public and the police in ways that a home, an office, or commercial structure would not be. It is not generally true that fences or "No Trespassing" signs effectively bar the public from viewing open fields in rural areas. And both petitioner Oliver and respondent Thornton concede that the public and police lawfully may survey lands from the air. For these reasons, the asserted expectation of privacy in open fields is not an expectation that "society recognizes as reasonable."
>
> The historical underpinnings of the open fields doctrine also demonstrate that the doctrine is consistent with respect for "reasonable expectations of privacy." As Justice Holmes, writing for the Court, observed in *Hester*, the common law distinguished "open fields" from the "curtilage," the land immediately surrounding and associated with the home. The distinction implies that only the curtilage, not the neighboring open fields, warrants the Fourth Amendment protections that attach to the home. At common law, the curtilage is the area to which extends the intimate activity associated with the "sanctity of a man's home and the privacies of life," and therefore has been considered part of the home itself for Fourth Amendment purposes. Thus, courts have extended Fourth Amendment protection to the curtilage; and they have defined the curtilage, as did the common law, by reference to the factors that determine whether an individual reasonably may expect that an area immediately adjacent to the home will remain private. Conversely, the common law implies, as we reaffirm today, that no expectation of privacy legitimately attaches to open fields.

Justice Marshall, writing also for Justices Brennan and Stevens, rejected the majority's "search" analysis:

> If a person has not marked the boundaries of his fields or woods in a way that informs passersby that they are not welcome, he cannot object if members of the public enter onto the property. There is no reason why he should have any greater rights as against government officials. * * *
>
> A very different case is presented when the owner of undeveloped land has taken precautions to exclude the public. * * * [A] deliberate entry by a private citizen onto private property marked with "No Trespassing" signs will expose him to criminal liability. I see no reason why a government

official should not be obliged to respect such unequivocal and universally understood manifestations of a landowner's desire for privacy.

7. *Curtilage: what is it?* In *Oliver* (Note 6), Justice Powell defined and distinguished the curtilage of a house from an open field. In United States v. Dunn, 480 U.S. 294, 107 S.Ct. 1134, 94 L.Ed.2d 326 (1987), the Court explained the curtilage concept further. It stated that "curtilage questions should be resolved with reference to four factors: the proximity of the area claimed to be curtilage to the home, whether the area is included within an enclosure surrounding the home, the nature of the uses to which the area is put, and the steps taken by the resident to protect the area from observation by people passing by."

Dunn warned that the four factors do not produce a "fine tuned formula that, when mechanically applied, yields a 'correct' answer to all extent-of-curtilage questions. Rather, these factors are useful analytical tools only to the degree that, in any given case, they bear upon the centrally relevant consideration—whether the area in question is so intimately tied to the home itself that it should be placed under the home's 'umbrella' of Fourth Amendment protection."

In view of the four "curtilage" factors set out in *Dunn*, how would you characterize the area inspected by the police in that case? Here are the relevant facts:

> [Dunn]'s ranch comprised approximately 198 acres and was completely encircled by a perimeter fence. The property also contained several interior fences, constructed mainly of posts and multiple strands of barbed wire. The ranch residence was situated ½ miles from a public road. A fence encircled the residence and a nearby small greenhouse. Two barns were located approximately 50 yards from this fence. The front of the larger of the two barns was enclosed by a wooden fence and had an open overhang. Locked, waist-high gates barred entry into the barn proper, and netting material stretched from the ceiling to the top of the wooden gates.
>
> * * *[L]aw enforcement officials made a warrantless entry onto respondent's ranch property. A DEA agent accompanied by an officer from the Houston Police Department crossed over the perimeter fence and one interior fence. Standing approximately midway between the residence and the barns, the DEA agent smelled what he believed to be phenylacetic acid, the odor coming from the direction of the barns. The officers approached the smaller of the barns—crossing over a barbed wire fence—and, looking into the barn, observed only empty boxes. The officers then proceeded to the larger barn, crossing another barbed wire fence as well as a wooden fence that enclosed the front portion of the barn. The officers walked under the barn's overhang to the locked wooden gates and, shining a flashlight through the netting on top of the gates, peered into the barn.

Were the police standing in the "curtilage" or in an "open field"? What if the government agents had actually entered the barn? How might that change the Fourth Amendment analysis?

8. *Aerial surveillance of a curtilage (part 1).* It does not follow from the fact that an area is identified as a curtilage that police surveillance of it inevitably constitutes a Fourth Amendment search. That lesson is learned from two cases of aerial surveillance of curtilages. Consider the first case, California v. Ciraolo, 476 U.S. 207, 106 S.Ct. 1809, 90 L.Ed.2d 210 (1986):

> On September 2, 1982, Santa Clara Police received an anonymous telephone tip that marijuana was growing in respondent's backyard. Police were unable to observe the contents of respondent's yard from ground level because of a 6-foot outer fence and a 10-foot inner fence completely enclosing the yard. Later that day, Officer Shutz, who was assigned to investigate, secured a private plane and flew over respondent's house at an altitude of 1,000 feet, within navigable airspace; he was accompanied by Officer Rodriguez. Both officers were trained in marijuana identification. From the overflight, the officers readily identified marijuana plants 8 feet to 10 feet in height growing in a 15- by 25-foot plot in respondent's yard; they photographed the area with a standard 35mm camera.

Based on this surveillance, the police obtained a warrant to search the premises. The issue was whether the information secured from the aerial surveillance properly was used to secure the warrant. That, in turn, raised the question of whether the surveillance was, itself, a search that may have required a warrant. The Court, per Chief Justice Burger, declared, 5–4, that the surveillance of the curtilage of Ciraolo's home was not a search and, therefore, fell outside the protections of the Fourth Amendment. The Court dealt briefly with the subjective prong of Harlan's "search" test before turning to the critical objective prong:

> Clearly—and understandably—respondent has met the test of manifesting his own subjective intent and desire to maintain privacy as to his unlawful agricultural pursuits. * * * It can reasonably be assumed that the 10-foot fence was placed to conceal the marijuana crop from at least street-level views. * * *
>
> Yet a 10-foot fence might not shield these plants from the eyes of a citizen or a policeman perched on the top of a truck or a two-level bus. Whether respondent therefore manifested a subjective expectation of privacy from all observations of his backyard, or whether instead he manifested merely a hope that no one would observe his unlawful gardening pursuits, is not entirely clear in these circumstances. * * *

> We turn * * * to the second inquiry under *Katz*, i.e., whether that expectation is reasonable. * * *
>
> That the area is within the curtilage does not itself bar all police observation. The Fourth Amendment protection of the home has never been extended to require law enforcement officers to shield their eyes when passing by a home on public thoroughfares. Nor does the mere fact that an individual has taken measures to restrict some views of his activities preclude an officer's observations from a public vantage point where he has a right to be and which renders the activities clearly visible. "What a person knowingly exposes to the public, even in his own home or office, is not a subject of Fourth Amendment protection." *Katz, supra.*
>
> The observations by Officers Shutz and Rodriguez in this case took place within public navigable airspace, in a physically nonintrusive manner; from this point they were able to observe plants readily discernible to the naked eye as marijuana. That the observation from aircraft was directed at identifying the plants and the officers were trained to recognize marijuana is irrelevant. * * * Any member of the public flying in this airspace who glanced down could have seen everything that these officers observed. On this record, we readily conclude that respondent's expectation that his garden was protected from such observation is unreasonable and is not an expectation that society is prepared to honor. * * *
>
> * * * In an age where private and commercial flight in the public airways is routine, it is unreasonable for respondent to expect that his marijuana plants were constitutionally protected from being observed with the naked eye from an altitude of 1,000 feet. The Fourth Amendment simply does not require the police traveling in the public airways at this altitude to obtain a warrant in order to observe what is visible to the naked eye.

Are you persuaded? Four justices were not. Justice Powell, who wrote the open-fields *Oliver* decision, explained their disagreement:

> As the decision in *Katz* held, and dissenting opinions written by Justices of this Court prior to *Katz* recognized, a standard that defines a Fourth Amendment "search" by reference to whether police have physically invaded a "constitutionally protected area" provides no real protection against surveillance techniques made possible through technology. Technological advances have enabled police to see people's activities and associations, and to hear their conversations, without being in physical proximity. Moreover, the capability now exists for police to conduct intrusive surveillance without any physical penetration of the walls

of homes or other structures that citizens may believe shelters their privacy. Looking to the Fourth Amendment for protection against such "broad and unsuspected governmental incursions" into the "cherished privacy of law-abiding citizens," the Court in *Katz* abandoned its inquiry into whether police had committed a physical trespass. * * *

This case involves surveillance of a home, for as we stated in *Oliver v. United States*, the curtilage "has been considered part of the home itself for Fourth Amendment purposes." * * *

* * * [R]espondent's yard unquestionably was within the curtilage. Since Officer Shutz could not see into this private family area from the street, the Court certainly would agree that he would have conducted an unreasonable search had he climbed over the fence, or used a ladder to peer into the yard without first securing a warrant.

The Court concludes, nevertheless, that Shutz could use an airplane—a product of modern technology—to intrude visually into respondent's yard. * * * It * * * relies on the fact that the surveillance was not accompanied by a physical invasion of the curtilage. Reliance on the manner of surveillance is directly contrary to the standard of *Katz*, which identifies a constitutionally protected privacy right by focusing on the interests of the individual and of a free society. Since *Katz*, we have consistently held that the presence or absence of physical trespass by police is constitutionally irrelevant to the question whether society is prepared to recognize an asserted privacy interest as reasonable.

The Court's holding, therefore, must rest solely on the fact that members of the public fly in planes and may look down at homes as they fly over them. * * *

This line of reasoning is flawed. First, the actual risk to privacy from commercial or pleasure aircraft is virtually nonexistent. Travelers on commercial flights, as well as private planes used for business or personal reasons, normally obtain at most a fleeting, anonymous, and nondiscriminating glimpse of the landscape and buildings over which they pass. The risk that a passenger on such a plane might observe private activities, and might connect those activities with particular people, is simply too trivial to protect against. It is no accident that, as a matter of common experience, many people build fences around their residential areas, but few build roofs over their backyards. Therefore, contrary to the Court's suggestion, people do not " 'knowingly expos[e]' " their residential yards " 'to the public' " merely by failing to build barriers that prevent aerial surveillance. * * * [T]he Court fails to acknowledge the qualitative

> difference between police surveillance and other uses made of the airspace. Members of the public use the airspace for travel, business, or pleasure, not for the purpose of observing activities taking place within residential yards. Here, police conducted an overflight at low altitude solely for the purpose of discovering evidence of crime within a private enclave into which they were constitutionally forbidden to intrude at ground level without a warrant. It is not easy to believe that our society is prepared to force individuals to bear the risk of this type of warrantless police intrusion into their residential areas.

Notice that Justice Powell stated that "[r]eliance on the *manner* of surveillance is directly contrary to the standard of *Katz*." Is it?

Justice Powell also was critical of the majority for failing "to acknowledge the qualitative difference between police surveillance and other uses made of the airspace." *Should* courts draw such a distinction? That is, even if we generally do not have reason to expect freedom from private invasions of our privacy, should the issue in Fourth Amendment cases be whether a person has a reasonable expectation of privacy from purposeful *governmental* surveillance?

9. *Aerial surveillance of a curtilage (part 2). Ciraolo* is not the Supreme Court's only effort to wrestle with the problems of aerial surveillance. In Florida v. Riley, 488 U.S. 445, 109 S.Ct. 693, 102 L.Ed.2d 835 (1989), a police officer observed the interior of a partially covered greenhouse in Riley's backyard, while circling 400 feet above the greenhouse in a police helicopter. Justice White, in an opinion joined only by Chief Justice Rehnquist and Justices Scalia and Kennedy, concluded that *Ciraolo* controlled the case:

> Under the holding in *Ciraolo*, Riley could not reasonably have expected the contents of his greenhouse to be immune from examination by an officer seated in a fixed-wing aircraft flying in navigable airspace at an altitude of 1,000 feet or * * * at an altitude of 500 feet, the lower limit of the navigable airspace for such an aircraft. * * *
>
> Nor on the facts before us, does it make a difference for Fourth Amendment purposes that the helicopter was flying at 400 feet when the officer saw what was growing in the greenhouse through the partially open roof and sides of the structure. We would have a different case if flying at that altitude had been contrary to law or regulation. But helicopters are not bound by the lower limits of the navigable airspace allowed to other aircraft.

In dictum, the plurality suggested some additional limitations on aerial surveillance:

> This is not to say that an inspection of the curtilage of a house from an aircraft will always pass muster under the Fourth Amendment simply because the plane is within the navigable airspace specified by law. But it is of obvious importance that the helicopter in this case was *not* violating the law * * *. Neither is there any intimation here that the helicopter interfered with respondent's normal use of the greenhouse or of other parts of the curtilage. As far as this record reveals, no intimate details connected with the use of the home or curtilage were observed, and there was no undue noise, and no wind, dust, or threat of injury. In these circumstances, there was no violation of the Fourth Amendment.

What does Justice White mean by these limitations? For example, suppose that the surveillance of Riley's greenhouse had been conducted by *airplane* at 400 feet. Because an airplane should not ordinarily be at such a low altitude, has a search occurred, although the same surveillance by helicopter is permissible? Does such a distinction make sense?

Does Justice White also mean that if an officer in a helicopter simultaneously observes marijuana in a greenhouse and sexually intimate acts occurring in the same curtilage, the surveillance constitutes a search as to the latter, but not as to the former, sighting? Does such a distinction make sense? And, why is it a Fourth Amendment concern whether a helicopter is noisy or blows dust in a person's backyard?

Justice O'Connor concurred in the judgment in *Riley*, thus adding a fifth vote:

> In my view, the defendant must bear the burden of proving that his expectation of privacy was a reasonable one, and thus that a "search" within the meaning of the Fourth Amendment even took place.
>
> Because there is reason to believe that there is considerable public use of airspace at altitudes of 400 feet and above, and because Riley introduced no evidence to the contrary * * *, I conclude that Riley's expectation that his curtilage was protected from naked-eye aerial observation from that altitude was not a reasonable one. However, public use of altitudes lower than that—particularly public observations from helicopters circling over the curtilage of a home—may be sufficiently rare that police surveillance from such altitudes would violate reasonable expectations of privacy, despite compliance with F.A.A. safety regulations.

10. *Rifling through garbage: surveillance outside the curtilage, near a house, but not in an open field.* In California v. Greenwood, 486 U.S. 35, 108 S.Ct. 1625, 100 L.Ed.2d 30 (1988), officers searched through plastic garbage bags left on the curb in front of a house for trash pickup. The Court ruled that a person does not have a reasonable expectation of privacy in garbage left outside the curtilage of a home for trash

removal. Justice White explained that the objective prong of *Katz* is not satisfied in such circumstances:

> It is common knowledge that plastic garbage bags left on or at the side of a public street are readily accessible to animals, children, scavengers, snoops, and other members of the public. Moreover, respondents placed their refuse at the curb for the express purpose of conveying it to a third party, the trash collector, who might himself have sorted through respondents' trash or permitted others, such as the police, to do so. * * *
>
> Furthermore, as we have held, the police cannot reasonably be expected to avert their eyes from evidence of criminal activity that could have been observed by any member of the public. Hence, "[w]hat a person knowingly exposes to the public, even in his own home or office, is not a subject of Fourth Amendment protection." *Katz v. United States.* We held in *Smith v. Maryland* [p. 98], for example, that * * * [a]n individual has no legitimate expectation of privacy in the numbers dialed on his telephone * * * because he voluntarily conveys those numbers to the telephone company when he uses the telephone.

If you represented Greenwood, how would you try to distinguish the holding in *Smith* and the *Katz* "knowingly exposes" language from the circumstances here?

11. After all of the Supreme Court "no search" decisions, it is worth noting one that went the other way. In Bond v. United States, 529 U.S. 334, 120 S.Ct. 1462, 146 L.Ed.2d 365 (2000), Border Patrol agents walked through a Greyhound bus that was stopped at a checkpoint. They routinely squeezed the soft luggage that passengers had placed in the overhead storage bins. In Bond's case, an agent felt a brick-like object. Bond then allowed the agents to open his luggage, at which point illegal drugs were discovered. At issue was the agent's pre-consent act of squeezing the luggage. Chief Justice Rehnquist, writing for seven members of the Court, held that this constituted a "search":

> [T]he Government asserts that by exposing his bag to the public, petitioner lost a reasonable expectation that his bag would not be physically manipulated. The Government relies on our decisions in *California v. Ciraolo* and *Florida v. Riley* [Notes 8 & 9] for the proposition that matters open to public observation are not protected by the Fourth Amendment. * * * But *Ciraolo* and *Riley* are different from this case because they involved only visual, as opposed to tactile, observation. Physically invasive inspection is simply more intrusive than purely visual inspection.

The Chief Justice went on to observe further that:

> When a bus passenger places a bag in an overhead bin, he expects that other passengers or bus employees may move it for one reason or another. Thus, a bus passenger clearly expects that his bag may be handled. He does not expect that other passengers or bus employees will, as a matter of course, feel the bag in an exploratory manner. But this is exactly what the agent did here. We therefore hold that the agent's physical manipulation of petitioner's bag violated the Fourth Amendment.

3. *Katz* and the New Technology: Back to the Future?

KYLLO V. UNITED STATES

Supreme Court of the United States, 2001.
533 U.S. 27, 121 S.Ct. 2038, 150 L.Ed.2d 94.

In his opinion in the following case, Justice Scalia writes that "it would be foolish to contend that the degree of privacy secured to citizens by the 4th Amendment has been entirely unaffected by the advance of technology."

This 2001 quote could not be more prescient, or today more accurately descriptive of Fourth Amendment law. The future of the development of the law of search and seizure may well be the story of the dichotomy between the fast-pace of technology and the slow-pace of the court system. For example, the Court in *Kyllo* noted in its search analysis that the technology was not one that was in general public use. How does that standard change our expectation of privacy? Put another way; how useful is the expectation-of-privacy prong in our fast-paced digital world? This is the essence of Justice Stevens' dissenting opinion in this case.

SCALIA delivered the opinion of the Court [joined by JUSTICES SOUTER, THOMAS, GINSBERG, and BREYER].

This case presents the question whether the use of a thermal-imaging device aimed at a private home from a public street to detect relative amounts of heat within the home constitutes a "search" within the meaning of the Fourth Amendment.

I

In 1991 Agent William Elliott of the United States Department of the Interior came to suspect that marijuana was being grown in the home belonging to petitioner Danny Kyllo * * *. Indoor marijuana growth typically requires high-intensity lamps. In order to determine whether an amount of heat was emanating from petitioner's home consistent with the use of such lamps, at 3:20 a.m. on January 16, 1992, Agent Elliott and Dan Haas used an Agema Thermovision 210 thermal imager to scan the triplex. Thermal imagers detect infrared radiation, which virtually all objects emit but which is not visible to the naked eye. The imager converts radiation into images based on relative warmth—black is cool, white is hot, shades of gray connote relative differences; in that respect, it operates somewhat like a video camera showing heat images. The scan of Kyllo's home took only a few minutes and was performed from the passenger seat of Agent Elliott's vehicle across the street from the front of the house and also from the street in back of the house. The scan showed that the roof over the garage and a side wall of petitioner's home were relatively hot compared to the rest of the home and substantially warmer than neighboring homes * * *. Agent Elliott concluded that petitioner was using halide lights to grow marijuana in his house, which indeed he was. Based on tips from informants, utility bills, and the thermal imaging, a Federal Magistrate Judge issued a warrant authorizing a search of petitioner's home, and the agents found an indoor growing operation involving more than 100 plants. Petitioner * * * unsuccessfully moved to suppress the evidence seized from his home * * *. * * *

II

* * * "At the very core" of the Fourth Amendment "stands the right of a man to retreat into his own home and there be free from unreasonable governmental intrusion." With few exceptions, the question whether a warrantless search of a home is reasonable and hence constitutional must be answered no.

On the other hand, the antecedent question of whether or not a Fourth Amendment "search" has occurred is not so simple under our precedent. The permissibility of ordinary visual surveillance of a home used to be clear because, well into the 20th century, our Fourth Amendment jurisprudence was tied to common-law trespass. Visual surveillance was unquestionably lawful because " 'the eye cannot by the laws of England be guilty of a trespass.' " *Boyd v. United States*, 116 U.S. 616, 628 (1886) (quoting *Entick v. Carrington*, 19 How. St. Tr. 1029, 95 Eng. Rep. 807 (K. B. 1765)). We have since decoupled violation of a person's Fourth Amendment rights from trespassory violation of his property, but the lawfulness of warrantless visual surveillance of a home has still been preserved. As we observed in *California v. Ciraolo*, [p. 113, Note 8], "[t]he Fourth Amendment protection of the home has never been extended to require law enforcement officers to shield their eyes when passing by a home on public thoroughfares."

One might think that the new validating rationale would be that examining the portion of a house that is in plain public view, while it is a "search despite the absence of trespass, is not an "unreasonable" one under the Fourth Amendment. But in fact we have held that visual observation is no "search" at all * * *. In assessing when a search is not a search, we have applied somewhat in reverse the principle first enunciated in *Katz v. United States*. *Katz* involved eavesdropping by means of an electronic listening device placed on the outside of a telephone booth—a location not within the catalog ("persons, houses, papers, and effects") that the Fourth Amendment protects against unreasonable searches. We held that the Fourth Amendment nonetheless protected *Katz* from the warrantless eavesdropping because he "justifiably relied" upon the privacy of the telephone booth. As Justice Harlan's oft-quoted concurrence described it, a Fourth Amendment search occurs when the government violates a subjective expectation of privacy that society recognizes as reasonable. * * * We have applied this test in holding that it is not a search for the police to use a pen register at the phone company to determine what numbers were dialed in a private home, *Smith v. Maryland*, [p. 98], and we have applied the test on two different occasions in holding that aerial surveillance of private homes and surrounding areas does not constitute a search, *Ciraolo, supra*; *Florida v. Riley*, [p. 116, Note 9].

The present case involves officers on a public street engaged in more than naked-eye surveillance of a home. We have previously reserved judgment as to how much technological enhancement of ordinary perception from such a vantage point, if any, is too much. While we upheld enhanced aerial photography of an industrial complex in *Dow Chemical* [*v. United States*, 476 U.S. 227, 106 S.Ct. 1819, 90 L.Ed.2d 226 (1986)] we noted that we found "it important that this is not an area immediately adjacent to a private home, where privacy expectations are most heightened."

III

It would be foolish to contend that the degree of privacy secured to citizens by the Fourth Amendment has been entirely unaffected by the advance of technology. For example, as the cases discussed above make clear, the technology enabling human flight has exposed to public view (and hence, we have said, to official observation) uncovered portions of the house and its curtilage that once were private. The question we confront today is what limits there are upon this power of technology to shrink the realm of guaranteed privacy.

The *Katz* test—whether the individual has an expectation of privacy that society is prepared to recognize as reasonable—has often been criticized as circular, and hence subjective and unpredictable. While it may be difficult to refine *Katz* when the search of areas such as telephone booths, automobiles, or even the curtilage and uncovered portions of residences are at issue, in the case of the search of the interior of homes—the prototypical and hence most commonly litigated area of protected privacy—there is a ready criterion, with roots deep in the common law, of the minimal expectation of privacy that *exists*, and that is acknowledged to be *reasonable*. To withdraw protection of this minimum expectation would be to permit police technology to erode the privacy guaranteed by the Fourth Amendment. We think that obtaining by sense-enhancing technology any information regarding the interior of the home that could not otherwise have been obtained without physical "intrusion into a constitutionally protected area" constitutes a search—at least where (as here) the technology in question is not in general public use. This assures preservation of that degree of privacy against government that existed when the Fourth Amendment was adopted. On the basis of this criterion, the information obtained by the thermal imager in this case was the product of a search.

The Government maintains, however, that the thermal imaging must be upheld because it detected "only heat radiating from the external surface of the house." The dissent makes this its leading point, contending that there is a fundamental difference between what it calls "off-the-wall" observations and "through-the-wall surveillance." But just as a thermal imager captures only heat emanating from a house, so also a powerful directional microphone picks up only sound emanating from a house—and a satellite capable of scanning from many miles away would pick up only visible light emanating from a house. We rejected such a mechanical interpretation of the Fourth Amendment in *Katz*, where the eavesdropping device picked up only sound waves that reached the exterior of the phone booth. Reversing that approach would leave the homeowner at the mercy of advancing technology—including imaging technology that could discern all human activity in the home. While the technology used in the present case was relatively crude, the rule we adopt must take account of more sophisticated systems that are already in use or in development. * * *

The Government also contends that the thermal imaging was constitutional because it did not "detect private activities occurring in private areas." * * * The Fourth Amendment's protection of the home has never been tied to measurement of the quality or quantity of information obtained. * * * In the home, our cases show, *all* details are intimate details, because the entire area is held safe from prying government eyes. Thus, in [*United States v.*] *Karo*, [summarized in p. 130, Note 6], the only thing detected was a can of ether in the home; and in *Arizona v. Hicks*, [p. 296], the only thing detected by a physical search that went beyond what officers lawfully present could observe in "plain view" was the registration number of a phonograph turntable. These were intimate details because they were details of the home, just as was the detail of how warm—or even how relatively warm—Kyllo was heating his residence.

Limiting the prohibition of thermal imaging to "intimate details" would not only be wrong in principle; it would be impractical in application, failing to provide "a workable accommodation between the needs of law enforcement and the interests protected by the Fourth Amendment." To begin with, there is no necessary connection between the sophistication of the surveillance equipment and the "intimacy" of the details that it observes—which means that one cannot say (and the police cannot be assured) that use of the relatively crude equipment at issue here will always be lawful. The Agema Thermovision 210 might disclose, for example, at what hour each night the lady of the house takes her daily sauna and bath—a detail that many would consider "intimate"; and a much more sophisticated system might detect nothing more intimate than the fact that someone left a closet light on. We * * * would have to develop a jurisprudence specifying which home activities are "intimate" and which are not. And even when (if ever) that jurisprudence were fully developed, no police officer would be able to know in advance whether his through-the-wall surveillance picks up "intimate" details—and thus would be unable to know *in advance* whether it is constitutional.

The dissent's proposed standard—whether the technology offers the "functional equivalent of actual presence in the area being searched"—would seem quite similar to our own at first blush. The dissent concludes that *Katz* was such a case, but then inexplicably asserts that if the same listening device only revealed the volume of the conversation, the surveillance would be permissible. Yet, if without technology, the police could not discern volume without being actually present in the phone booth, Justice Stevens should conclude a search has occurred. * * * Thus the driving force of the dissent, despite its recitation of the above standard, appears to be a distinction among different types of information—whether the "homeowner would even care if anybody noticed." The dissent offers no practical guidance for the application of this standard, and for reasons already discussed, we believe there can be none. The people in their houses, as well as the police, deserve more precision.

We have said that the Fourth Amendment draws "a firm line at the entrance to the house." That line, we think, must be not only firm but also bright—which requires clear specification of those methods of surveillance that require a warrant. While it is certainly possible to conclude from the videotape of the thermal imaging that occurred in this case that no "significant" compromise of the homeowner's privacy has occurred, we must take the long view, from the original meaning of the Fourth Amendment forward. * * * Where, as here, the

Government uses a device that is not in general public use, to explore details of the home that would previously have been unknowable without physical intrusion, the surveillance is a "search" and is presumptively unreasonable without a warrant. * * *

JUSTICE STEVENS, with whom CHIEF JUSTICE REHNQUIST, JUSTICE O'CONNOR, and JUSTICE KENNEDY join, dissenting. * * *

While the Court "take[s] the long view" and decides this case based largely on the potential of yet-to-be-developed technology that might allow "through-the-wall surveillance," this case involves nothing more than off-the-wall surveillance by law enforcement officers to gather information exposed to the general public from the outside of petitioner's home. All that the infrared camera did in this case was passively measure heat emitted from the exterior surfaces of petitioner's home; all that those measurements showed were relative differences in emission levels, vaguely indicating that some areas of the roof and outside walls were warmer than others. * * * [N]o details regarding the interior of petitioner's home were revealed. Unlike an x-ray scan, or other possible "through-the-wall" techniques, the detection of infrared radiation emanating from the home did not accomplish "an unauthorized physical penetration into the premises," nor did it "obtain information that it could not have obtained by observation from outside the curtilage of the house."

Indeed, the ordinary use of the senses might enable a neighbor or passerby to notice the heat emanating from a building, particularly if it is vented, as was the case here. Additionally, any member of the public might notice that one part of a house is warmer than another part or a nearby building if, for example, rainwater evaporates or snow melts at different rates across its surfaces. * * * [An] observation [similarly does not] become an unreasonable search if made from a distance with the aid of a device that merely discloses that the exterior of one house, or one area of the house, is much warmer than another. Nothing more occurred in this case.

Thus, the notion that heat emissions from the outside of a dwelling is a private matter implicating the protections of the Fourth Amendment * * * is not only unprecedented but also quite difficult to take seriously. Heat waves, like aromas that are generated in a kitchen, or in a laboratory or opium den, enter the public domain if and when they leave a building. A subjective expectation that they would remain private is not only implausible but also surely not "one that society is prepared to recognize as 'reasonable.' " * * *

* * * Just as "the police cannot reasonably be expected to avert their eyes from evidence of criminal activity that could have been observed by any member of the public," so too public officials should not have to avert their senses or their equipment from detecting emissions in the public domain such as excessive heat, traces of smoke, suspicious odors, odorless gases, airborne particulates, or radioactive emissions, any of which could identify hazards to the community. In my judgment, monitoring such emissions with "sense-enhancing technology," and drawing useful conclusions from such monitoring, is an entirely reasonable public service.

On the other hand, the countervailing privacy interest is at best trivial. After all, homes generally are insulated to keep heat in, rather than to prevent the detection of heat going out, and it does not seem to me that society will suffer from a rule requiring the rare homeowner who both intends to engage in uncommon activities that produce extraordinary amounts of heat, and wishes to conceal that production from outsiders, to make sure that the surrounding area is well insulated. * * *

Since what was involved in this case was nothing more than drawing inferences from off-the-wall surveillance, rather than any "through-the-wall" surveillance, the officers' conduct did not amount to a search and was perfectly reasonable.

II

* * * [T]he Court has fashioned a rule that is intended to provide essential guidance for the day when "more sophisticated systems" gain the "ability to 'see' through walls and other opaque barriers." The newly minted rule encompasses "obtaining [1] by sense-enhancing technology [2] any information regarding the interior of the home [3] that could not otherwise have been obtained without physical intrusion into a constitutionally protected area * * * [4] at least where (as here) the technology in question is not in general public use." In my judgment, the Court's new rule is at once too broad and too narrow, and is not justified by the Court's explanation for its adoption. * * *

Despite the Court's attempt to draw a line that is "not only firm but also bright," the contours of its new rule are uncertain because its protection apparently dissipates as soon as the relevant technology is "in general public use." Yet how much use is general public use is not even hinted at by the Court's opinion, which makes the somewhat doubtful assumption that the thermal imager used in this case does not satisfy that criterion. In any event, putting aside its lack of clarity, this criterion is somewhat perverse because it seems likely that the threat to privacy will grow, rather than recede, as the use of intrusive equipment becomes more readily available.

It is clear, however, that the category of "sense-enhancing technology" covered by the new rule is far too broad. It would, for example, embrace potential mechanical substitutes for dogs trained to react when they sniff narcotics. But in *United States v. Place*, [p. 107, Note 5], we held that a dog sniff that "discloses only the presence or absence of narcotics" does "not constitute a 'search' within the meaning of the Fourth Amendment," and it must follow that sense-enhancing equipment that identifies nothing but illegal activity is not a search either. Nevertheless, the use of such a device would be unconstitutional under the Court's rule, as would the use of other new devices that might detect the odor of deadly bacteria or chemicals for making a new type of high explosive, even if the devices (like the dog sniffs) are "so limited in both the manner in which" they obtain information and "in the content of the information" they reveal. * * *

Because the new rule applies to information regarding the "interior" of the home, it is too narrow as well as too broad. Clearly, a rule that is designed to protect individuals from the overly intrusive use of sense-enhancing equipment should not be limited to a home. If such equipment did provide its user with the functional equivalent of access to a private place—such as, for example, the telephone booth involved in *Katz*, or an office building—then the rule should apply to such an area as well as to a home. See *Katz* ("[T]he Fourth Amendment protects people, not places"). * * *

The * * * reasons advanced by the Court as justifications for the adoption of its new rule are * * * unpersuasive. [T]he Court suggests that its rule is compelled by our holding in *Katz*, because in that case, as in this, the surveillance consisted of nothing more than the monitoring of waves emanating from a private area into the public domain. Yet there are critical differences between the cases. In *Katz*, the electronic listening device attached to the outside of the phone booth allowed the officers to pick up the content of the conversation inside the booth, making them the functional equivalent of intruders * * *. By contrast, the thermal imager here disclosed only the relative amounts of heat radiating from the house; it would be as if, in *Katz*, the listening device disclosed only the relative volume of sound leaving the booth, which presumably was discernible in the public domain * * * It is pure hyperbole for the Court to suggest that refusing to extend the holding of *Katz* to this case would leave the homeowner at the mercy of "technology that could discern all human activity in the home." * * *

III

* * * Instead of concentrating on the rather mundane issue that is actually presented by the case before it, the Court has endeavored to craft an all-encompassing rule for the future. It would be far wiser to give legislators an unimpeded opportunity to grapple with these emerging issues rather than to shackle them with prematurely devised constitutional constraints. * * *

NOTES AND QUESTIONS

1. As a matter of public policy, whom do you believe has the better side of the argument, Scalia or Stevens? Or, do you agree with Professor Wayne LaFave, who suggested that "after reading both opinions * * * I feel as if I have witnessed a sword fight in which both sides drew blood"? Wayne R. LaFave, *The Fourth Amendment as a "Big Time" TV Fad*, 53 Hastings L.J. 265, 277 (2001).

In terms of privacy from governmental intrusion, what should matter more in Fourth Amendment analysis: (1) where the government surveilling agent is physically located; or (2) where the private information is physically situated? Do you agree with Justice Scalia that in regard to the home "*all* details are intimate details" that should be "held safe from prying government eyes"?

2. Which opinion—the majority or the dissent—seems more faithful to the principles of *Katz*? To post-*Katz* case law?

3. In footnote 3 in *Kyllo*, the majority described the state of the technology at issue as follows:

> The ability to "see" through walls and other opaque barriers is a clear and scientifically feasible, goal of law enforcement research and development. The National Law Enforcement and Corrections Technology Center, a program within the United States Department of Justice, features on its Internet Website projects that include a "Radar-Based Through-the-Wall Surveillance System," "Handheld Ultrasound Through the Wall Surveillance, and a "Radar Flashlight" that "will enable law officers to detect individuals through interior building walls." Some devices may emit low levels of radiation that travel "through-the-wall," but others, such as more sophisticated thermal imaging devices, are entirely passive, or "off-the-wall" as the dissent puts it.

4. According to *Kyllo*, is it a "search" for the police to use a Geiger counter on public streets to locate plutonium (used in nuclear bomb-making) cached in someone's home?

What if some enterprising business tomorrow begins selling "pocket-thermal-imagers-'n'-toenail-clippers" on cable television for $10.99 (but you get a second one free if you call within twenty minutes)? Would police use of a thermal imager *now* constitute a Fourth Amendment search? See John P. Elwood, *What Were They Thinking: The Supreme Court in Revue, October Term 2000*, 4 Green Bag 2d 365, 371 (2001).

5. Do you sense that if he had the votes, Justice Scalia would seek to overrule some of the pre-*Kyllo* "search" cases? If so, which ones would seem to be on his potential "hit list"?

In regard to *Katz* itself, Justice Scalia previously observed in Minnesota v. Carter, 525 U.S. 83, 119 S.Ct. 469, 142 L.Ed.2d 373 (1998) (concurring opinion):

> In my view, the only thing the past three decades have established about the *Katz* test (which has come to mean the test enunciated by Justice Harlan's separate concurrence in *Katz*) is that, unsurprisingly, those "actual (subjective) expectation[s] of privacy" "that society is prepared to recognize as 'reasonable,' " bear an uncanny resemblance to those expectations of privacy that this Court considers reasonable. When that self-indulgent test is employed * * * to determine whether a "search or seizure" within the meaning of the Constitution has occurred (as opposed to whether that "search or seizure" is an "unreasonable" one), it has no plausible foundation in the text of the Fourth Amendment.

What does Scalia say about *Katz* in *Kyllo*?

6. *Primitive technology: the "beeper" cases.* In *Smith v. Maryland* (p. 98), the Supreme Court justified use of a technological device, the pen register, installed outside the defendant's home, in order to obtain information regarding an activity (telephone calls made) occurring *inside* his residence. But, technology can also assist law enforcement agents to determine the location of a suspect and/or to follow the suspect's movements. The Supreme Court has been called upon more than once to determine whether technologically-enhanced surveillance constitutes a search or seizure. (The "seizure" issues are considered in Section B. of this chapter.)

In the 1980s, "modern" surveillance technology included the use of a "beeper": In United States v. Knotts, 460 U.S. 276, 103 S.Ct. 1081, 75 L.Ed.2d 55 (1983), as part of an investigation of the manufacture of illicit drugs, federal agents installed a radio transmitter, which emitted periodic signals ("beeps"), in a five-gallon container of chloroform later purchased by defendant Petschen (presumably for use in the production of illicit drugs). By use of the beeper, the police monitored the suspect's movements from the point of purchase in Minneapolis, Minnesota along public roads to a secluded cabin in Wisconsin belonging to co-defendant Knotts. As is turned out, the police ended visual surveillance of the Petschen car when he made evasive maneuvers, but they picked up the signals from the beeper by helicopter, where the drum had been left outside the Knotts cabin. Based on this information, the police secured a warrant to search the cabin.

Defendants Petschen and Knotts sought to suppress evidence found in the cabin, on the ground that the surveillance, conducted without a warrant, was unconstitutional. The Court concluded that the surveillance did not constitute a Fourth Amendment search:

> A person traveling in an automobile on public thoroughfares has no reasonable expectation of privacy in his movements from one place to another. When Petschen traveled over the public streets he voluntarily conveyed to anyone who wanted to look the fact that he was traveling over particular roads in a particular direction, the fact of whatever stops he made, and the fact of his final destination when he exited from public roads onto private property. * * *
>
> Visual surveillance from public places along Petschen's route or adjoining Knotts' premises would have sufficed to reveal all of these facts to the police. The fact that the officers in this case relied not only on visual surveillance, but also on the use of the beeper to signal the presence of Petschen's automobile to the police receiver, does not alter the situation. Nothing in the Fourth Amendment prohibited the police from augmenting the sensory faculties bestowed upon them at birth with such enhancement as science and technology afforded them in this case. * * *
>
> Respondent does not actually quarrel with this analysis, though he expresses the generalized view that the result of the holding sought by the Government would be that "twenty-four hour surveillance of any citizen of this country will be possible, without judicial knowledge or supervision." * * * [I]f such dragnet-type law enforcement practices as respondent envisions should eventually occur, there will be time enough then to determine whether different constitutional principles may be applicable. Insofar as respondent's complaint appears to be simply that scientific devices such as the beeper enabled the police to be more effective in detecting crime, it simply has no constitutional foundation. We have never equated police efficiency with unconstitutionality, and we decline to do so now. * * *
>
> We think that respondent's contentions * * * to some extent lose sight of the limited use which the government made of the signals from this particular beeper. As we have noted, nothing in this record indicates that the beeper signal was received or relied upon after it had indicated that the drum containing the chloroform had ended its automotive journey at rest

> on respondent's premises in rural Wisconsin. * * * [T]here is no indication that the beeper was used in any way to reveal information as to the movement of the drum within the cabin, or in any way that would not have been visible to the naked eye from outside the cabin.

Notice the Court's observation in the last sentence. Didn't the pen register in *Smith v. Maryland* reveal information regarding activities inside a residence that was otherwise "hidden"? In any case, the *Knotts* Court's observation proved critical in a second "beeper" case, United States v. Karo, 468 U.S. 705, 104 S.Ct. 3296, 82 L.Ed.2d 530 (1984). In *Karo*, Karo ordered 50 gallons of ether from a government informant, to be used in drug offenses. With the permission of the informant, federal agents substituted their own ether can containing a beeper for one of those sold to Karo. They then monitored Karo's movements over public roads, as in *Knotts*, but also monitored the tracking device in Karo's home, as well as in two other houses. The Court held that the warrantless "monitoring of a beeper in a private residence, a location not open to visual surveillance, violates the Fourth Amendment rights of those who have a justifiable interest in the privacy of the residence." More specifically:

> In this case, had a DEA agent thought it useful to enter the * * * residence to verify that the ether was actually in the house and had he done so surreptitiously and without a warrant, there is little doubt that he would have engaged in an unreasonable search within the meaning of the Fourth Amendment. For purposes of the Amendment, the result is the same where * * * the Government surreptitiously employs an electronic device to obtain information that it could not have obtained by observation from outside the curtilage of the house. * * *
>
> * * * The case is thus not like *Knotts*, for there the beeper told the authorities nothing about the interior of *Knotts'* cabin. The information obtained in *Knotts* was "voluntarily conveyed to anyone who wanted to look * * *"; here, as we have said, the monitoring indicated that the beeper was inside the house, a fact that could not have been visually verified.

Is *Karo* Consistent with *Smith v. Maryland*? With *Kyllo*?

UNITED STATES V. JONES

Supreme Court of the United States, 2012.
565 U.S. 400, 132 S.Ct. 945, 181 L.Ed.2d 911.

At the beginning of this chapter, we situated the *Katz* case at the beginning of the era when the analysis of "what is a search" moved from the trespass approach to the privacy approach. At the beginning of this section, we situated *Kyllo* at the start of a series of cases (*Kyllo, Knotts,*

Karo) that struggled to apply the *Katz* test to new technological developments.

The 1980s "beeper" seems almost primitive by today's technological standards, particularly in view of the advent of Global Positioning System (GPS) tracking devices. Indeed, it is the latter technological "advance" that has required the Supreme Court to determine whether its interpretations of the Fourth Amendment announced in *Knotts* and *Karo*—and, for that matter, in *Katz*—adequately deal with the world in which we now live. Thus, we turn to: *United States v. Jones.*

The *Jones* case simultaneously forces us to take another step forward into the world of ever expanding technological developments while, at the same time, sends us back to the past for an analytical framework that may or may not (your choice) help us make sense of it all; ye olde trespass doctrine. In *Jones*, the government placed a GPS locator on a vehicle and then argued that the owner of the vehicle had no expectation of privacy on the location of a vehicle on public roads and while parked in public spaces.

Ironically, the Government had a warrant for the placement of the GPS locator but failed to follow its provisions; the locator was attached after the warrant had expired and outside of the warrant's jurisdiction. Having lost its ability to rely on the warrant, the Government fell back on a *Katz* argument that, based on *Karo* and *Knotts*, probably seemed like a sure thing. Oops.

The majority opinion in *Jones* never reached the *Katz* argument. Instead, as you will see, they held that *Katz* was never meant to apply when the State committed a trespass—a tangible, physical, interference with a piece of property owned by the defendant. In terms of reinstating the trespass doctrine, this is a 5–4 decision. In terms of finding a search, it was unanimous. Four Justices found a search via the trespass doctrine, one (Justice Sotomayor) found a search via both trespass and *Katz*, and four would have found a search strictly via *Katz*.

Perhaps the most intriguing and prophetic opinion in *Jones* comes from Justice Sotomayor's concurrence. After applying both the trespass doctrine and the *Katz* test—and finding a search—Justice Sotomayor goes on to raise important questions about ways the *Katz* test may need to be reconsidered in the digital age. Specifically, she questions the idea in *Smith v. Maryland* (our pen register case) that once information is provided to a third-party—any third-party—we lose all expectations of privacy in that

information for all purposes. In doing so, she harkens back to Justice Marshall's dissent in *Smith*, suggesting that distribution of information to third-parties can and should be for limited purposes and that expectations of privacy—especially from government intrusion—remain.

The question for the Court going forward is: where do we draw those lines? Is *Katz* even viable in cases involving the digital world? Is that perhaps why five of the Justices returned to the trespass doctrine in search of a simpler line to draw? At the same time, *Jones* involved a truck. Can one trespass on the internet? Keep these questions in mind as you read *Jones* and the thought-provoking Notes that follow.

JUSTICE SCALIA delivered the opinion of the Court [joined by CHIEF JUSTICE ROBERTS, and JUSTICES KENNEDY, THOMAS, and SOTOMAYOR].

We decide whether the attachment of a Global-Positioning-System (GPS) tracking device to an individual's vehicle, and subsequent use of that device to monitor the vehicle's movements on public streets, constitutes a search or seizure within the meaning of the Fourth Amendment.

I

In 2004 respondent Antoine Jones, owner and operator of a nightclub in the District of Columbia, came under suspicion of trafficking in narcotics and was made the target of an investigation by a joint FBI and Metropolitan Police Department task force. Officers employed various investigative techniques, including visual surveillance of the nightclub, installation of a camera focused on the front door of the club, and a pen register and wiretap covering Jones's cellular phone.

Based in part on information gathered from these sources, in 2005 the Government applied * * * for a warrant authorizing the use of an electronic tracking device on the Jeep Grand Cherokee registered to Jones's wife. A warrant issued, authorizing installation of the device in the District of Columbia and within 10 days.

On the 11th day, and not in the District of Columbia but in Maryland agents installed a GPS tracking device on the undercarriage of the Jeep while it was parked in a public parking lot. Over the next 28 days, the Government used the device to track the vehicle's movements, and once had to replace the device's battery when the vehicle was parked in a different public lot in Maryland. By means of signals from multiple satellites, the device established the vehicle's location within 50 to 100 feet, and communicated that location by cellular phone to a Government computer. It relayed more than 2,000 pages of data over the 4-week period.

The Government ultimately obtained a multiple-count indictment charging Jones and several alleged co-conspirators with, as relevant here, conspiracy to distribute and possess with intent to distribute five kilograms or more of cocaine and 50 grams or more of cocaine base, in violation of [federal law]. Before trial, Jones filed a motion to suppress evidence obtained through the GPS device. The District Court granted the motion only in part, suppressing the data obtained while the vehicle was parked in the garage adjoining Jones's residence. It held the remaining data admissible, because " '[a] person traveling in an automobile on public thoroughfares has no reasonable expectation of privacy in his movements from one place to another.' " ([Q]uoting *United States v. Knotts*, [p. 128, Note 6]). * * *

* * * The jury returned a guilty verdict, and the District Court sentenced Jones to life imprisonment.

The United States Court of Appeals for the District of Columbia Circuit reversed the conviction because of admission of the evidence obtained by warrantless use of the GPS device which, it said, violated the Fourth Amendment. * * *

II

A

The Fourth Amendment provides in relevant part that "[t]he right of the people to be secure in their persons, houses, papers, and effects, against unreasonable searches and seizures, shall not be violated." It is beyond dispute that a vehicle is an "effect" as that term is used in the Amendment. We hold that the Government's installation of a GPS device on a target's vehicle, and its use of that device to monitor the vehicle's movements, constitutes a "search."

It is important to be clear about what occurred in this case: The Government physically occupied private property for the purpose of obtaining information. We have no doubt that such a physical intrusion would have been considered a "search" within the meaning of the Fourth Amendment when it was adopted. *Entick v. Carrington*, 95 Eng. Rep. 807 (C. P. 1765), is a "case we have described as a 'monument of English freedom' 'undoubtedly familiar' to 'every American statesman' at the time the Constitution was adopted, and considered to be 'the true and ultimate expression of constitutional law' " with regard to search and seizure. In that case, Lord Camden expressed in plain terms the significance of property rights in search-and-seizure analysis:

> "[O]ur law holds the property of every man so sacred, that no man can set his foot upon his neighbour's close without his leave; if he does he is a trespasser, though he does no damage at all; if he will tread upon his neighbour's ground, he must justify it by law."

The text of the Fourth Amendment reflects its close connection to property, since otherwise it would have referred simply to "the right of the people to be secure against unreasonable searches and seizures"; the phrase "in their persons, houses, papers, and effects" would have been superfluous.

Consistent with this understanding, our Fourth Amendment jurisprudence was tied to common-law trespass, at least until the latter half of the 20th century. * * *

Our later cases, of course, have deviated from that exclusively property-based approach. In *Katz v. United States*, [p. 77], we said that "the Fourth Amendment protects people, not places," and found a violation in attachment of an eavesdropping device to a public telephone booth. Our later cases have applied the analysis of Justice Harlan's concurrence in that case, which said that a violation occurs when government officers violate a person's "reasonable expectation of privacy."

The Government contends that the Harlan standard shows that no search occurred here, since Jones had no "reasonable expectation of privacy" in the area of the Jeep accessed by Government agents (its underbody) and in the locations of the Jeep on the public roads, which were visible to all. But we need not address the Government's contentions, because Jones's Fourth Amendment rights do not rise or fall with the *Katz* formulation. At bottom, we must "assur[e] preservation of that degree of privacy against government that existed when the Fourth Amendment was adopted." As explained, for most of our history the Fourth Amendment was understood to embody a particular concern for government trespass upon the areas ("persons, houses, papers, and effects") it enumerates. *Katz* did not repudiate that understanding. * * *

More recently, in *Soldal v. Cook County*, 506 U. S. 56, 113 S.Ct. 538, 121 L.Ed.2d 450 (1992), * * * [we] established that "property rights are not the sole measure of Fourth Amendment violations," but [that *Katz*] did not "snuf[f] out the previously recognized protection for property." * * * We have embodied that preservation of past rights in our very definition of "reasonable expectation of privacy" which we have said to be an expectation "that has a source outside of the Fourth Amendment, either by reference to concepts of real or personal property law or to understandings that are recognized and permitted by society." *Katz* did not narrow the Fourth Amendment's scope.

The Government contends that several of our post-*Katz* cases foreclose the conclusion that what occurred here constituted a search. It relies principally on two cases in which we rejected Fourth Amendment challenges to "beepers," electronic tracking devices that represent another form of electronic monitoring. The first case, *Knotts*, upheld against Fourth Amendment challenge the use of a "beeper" that had been placed in a container of chloroform, allowing law enforcement to monitor the location of the container. We said that there had been no infringement of *Knotts'* reasonable expectation of privacy since the information obtained—the location of the automobile carrying the container on public roads, and the location of the off-loaded container in open fields near *Knotts'* cabin—had been voluntarily conveyed to the public. But as we have discussed, the *Katz* reasonable-expectation-of-privacy test has been added to, not substituted for, the common-law trespassory test. The holding in *Knotts* addressed only the former, since the latter was not at issue. The beeper had been placed in the container before it came into Knotts' possession, with the consent of the then-owner. Knotts did not challenge that installation, and we specifically declined to consider its effect on the Fourth Amendment analysis. *Knotts* would be relevant, perhaps, if the Government were making the argument that what would otherwise be an unconstitutional search is not such where it produces only public information. The Government does not make that argument, and we know of no case that would support it.

The second "beeper" case, *United States v. Karo*, does not suggest a different conclusion. There we addressed the question left open by *Knotts*, whether the installation of a beeper in a container amounted to a search or seizure. As in *Knotts*, at the time the beeper was installed the container belonged to a third party, and it did not come into possession of the defendant until later. Thus, the specific question we considered was whether the installation "*with the consent of the original owner* constitute[d] a search or seizure * * * when the container is delivered to a buyer having no knowledge of the presence of the beeper." We held not. The Government, we said, came into physical contact with the container only before it belonged to the defendant Karo; and the transfer of the container with the unmonitored beeper inside did not convey any information and thus did not invade Karo's privacy. That conclusion is perfectly consistent with the one we reach here. Karo accepted the container as it came to him, beeper and all, and was therefore not entitled to object to the beeper's presence, even though it was used to monitor the container's location. Jones, who possessed the Jeep at the time the

Government trespassorily inserted the information-gathering device, is on much different footing. * * *

Finally, the Government's position gains little support from our conclusion in *Oliver v. United States*, [p. 109, Note 6], that officers' information-gathering intrusion on an "open field" did not constitute a Fourth Amendment search even though it was a trespass at common law. Quite simply, an open field, unlike the curtilage of a home, is not one of those protected areas enumerated in the Fourth Amendment. The Government's physical intrusion on such an area—unlike its intrusion on the "effect" at issue here—is of no Fourth Amendment significance.

B

The concurrence begins by accusing us of applying "18th-century tort law." That is a distortion. What we apply is an 18th-century guarantee against unreasonable searches, which we believe must provide *at a minimum* the degree of protection it afforded when it was adopted. The concurrence does not share that belief. It would apply *exclusively Katz's* reasonable-expectation-of-privacy test, even when that eliminates rights that previously existed.

The concurrence faults our approach for "present[ing] particularly vexing problems" in cases that do not involve physical contact, such as those that involve the transmission of electronic signals. We entirely fail to understand that point. For unlike the concurrence, which would make *Katz* the exclusive test, we do not make trespass the exclusive test. Situations involving merely the transmission of electronic signals without trespass would remain subject to *Katz* analysis.

In fact, it is the concurrence's insistence on the exclusivity of the *Katz* test that needlessly leads us into "particularly vexing problems" in the present case. This Court has to date not deviated from the understanding that mere visual observation does not constitute a search. * * * Thus, even assuming that the concurrence is correct to say that "[t]raditional surveillance" of Jones for a 4-week period "would have required a large team of agents, multiple vehicles, and perhaps aerial assistance," our cases suggest that such visual observation is constitutionally permissible. It may be that achieving the same result through electronic means, without an accompanying trespass, is an unconstitutional invasion of privacy, but the present case does not require us to answer that question.

And answering it affirmatively leads us needlessly into additional thorny problems. The concurrence posits that "relatively short-term monitoring of a person's movements on public streets" is okay, but that "the use of longer term GPS monitoring in investigations *of most offenses*" is no good. That introduces yet another novelty into our jurisprudence. There is no precedent for the proposition that whether a search has occurred depends on the nature of the crime being investigated. And even accepting that novelty, it remains unexplained why a 4-week investigation is "surely" too long and why a drug-trafficking conspiracy involving substantial amounts of cash and narcotics is not an "extraordinary offens[e]" which may permit longer observation. * * * We may have to grapple with these "vexing problems" in some future case where a classic trespassory search is not involved and resort must be had to *Katz* analysis; but there is no reason for rushing forward to resolve them here.

III

The Government argues in the alternative that even if the attachment and use of the device was a search, it was reasonable—and thus lawful—under the Fourth Amendment because "officers had reasonable suspicion, and indeed probable cause, to believe that [Jones] was a leader in a large-scale cocaine distribution conspiracy." We have no occasion to consider this argument. The Government did not raise it below, and the D. C. Circuit therefore did not address it. We consider the argument forfeited.

* * *

The judgment of the Court of Appeals for the D. C. Circuit is affirmed. * * *

JUSTICE SOTOMAYOR, concurring.

I join the Court's opinion because I agree that a search within the meaning of the Fourth Amendment occurs, at a minimum, "[w]here, as here, the Government obtains information by physically intruding on a constitutionally protected area." * * * The Government usurped Jones' property for the purpose of conducting surveillance on him, thereby invading privacy interests long afforded, and undoubtedly entitled to, Fourth Amendment protection.

Of course, the Fourth Amendment is not concerned only with trespassory intrusions on property. Rather, even in the absence of a trespass, "a Fourth Amendment search occurs when the government violates a subjective expectation of privacy that society recognizes as reasonable." In *Katz*, this Court enlarged its then-prevailing focus on property rights by announcing that the reach of the Fourth Amendment does not "turn upon the presence or absence of a physical intrusion." As the majority's opinion makes clear, however, *Katz's* reasonable-expectation-of-privacy test augmented, but did not displace or diminish, the common-law trespassory test that preceded it. * * * Justice Alito's approach, which discounts altogether the constitutional relevance of the Government's physical intrusion on Jones' Jeep, erodes that longstanding protection for privacy expectations inherent in items of property that people possess or control. By contrast, the trespassory test applied in the majority's opinion reflects an irreducible constitutional minimum: When the Government physically invades personal property to gather information, a search occurs. The reaffirmation of that principle suffices to decide this case.

Nonetheless, as Justice Alito notes, physical intrusion is now unnecessary to many forms of surveillance. With increasing regularity, the Government will be capable of duplicating the monitoring undertaken in this case by enlisting factory- or owner-installed vehicle tracking devices or GPS-enabled smartphones. In cases of electronic or other novel modes of surveillance that do not depend upon a physical invasion on property, the majority opinion's trespassory test may provide little guidance. * * * As Justice Alito incisively observes, the same technological advances that have made possible nontrespassory surveillance techniques will also affect the *Katz* test by shaping the evolution of societal privacy expectations. Under that rubric, I agree with Justice Alito that, at the very least, "longer term GPS monitoring in investigations of most offenses impinges on expectations of privacy."

In cases involving even short-term monitoring, some unique attributes of GPS surveillance relevant to the *Katz* analysis will require particular attention. GPS monitoring generates a precise, comprehensive record of a person's public movements that reflects a wealth of detail about her familial, political, professional, religious, and sexual associations. See, *e.g., People v. Weaver*, 12 N. Y. 3d 433, 441–442, 909 N. E. 2d 1195, 1199 (2009) ("Disclosed in [GPS] data . . . will be trips the indisputably private nature of which takes little imagination to conjure: trips to the psychiatrist, the plastic surgeon, the abortion clinic, the AIDS treatment center, the strip club, the criminal defense attorney, the by-the-hour motel, the union meeting, the mosque, synagogue or church, the gay bar and on and on"). The Government can store such records and efficiently mine them for information years into the future. And because GPS monitoring is cheap in comparison to conventional surveillance techniques and, by design, proceeds surreptitiously, it evades the ordinary checks that constrain abusive law enforcement practices: "limited police resources and community hostility."

Awareness that the Government may be watching chills associational and expressive freedoms. And the Government's unrestrained power to assemble data that reveal private aspects of identity is susceptible to abuse. The net result is that GPS monitoring—by making available at a relatively low cost such a substantial quantum of intimate information about any person whom the Government, in its unfettered discretion, chooses to track—may "alter the relationship between citizen and government in a way that is inimical to democratic society."

I would take these attributes of GPS monitoring into account when considering the existence of a reasonable societal expectation of privacy in the sum of one's public movements. I would ask whether people reasonably expect that their movements will be recorded and aggregated in a manner that enables the Government to ascertain, more or less at will, their political and religious beliefs, sexual habits, and so on. I do not regard as dispositive the fact that the Government might obtain the fruits of GPS monitoring through lawful conventional surveillance techniques. I would also consider the appropriateness of entrusting to the Executive, in the absence of any oversight from a coordinate branch, a tool so amenable to misuse, especially in light of the Fourth Amendment's goal to curb arbitrary exercises of police power to and prevent "a too permeating police surveillance.

More fundamentally, it may be necessary to reconsider the premise that an individual has no reasonable expectation of privacy in information voluntarily disclosed to third parties. E.g., *Smith* [*v. Maryland*, p. 98]; *United States v. Miller*. This approach is ill suited to the digital age, in which people reveal a great deal of information about themselves to third parties in the course of carrying out mundane tasks. People disclose the phone numbers that they dial or text to their cellular providers; the URLs that they visit and the e-mail addresses with which they correspond to their Internet service providers; and the books, groceries, and medications they purchase to online retailers. Perhaps, as Justice Alito notes, some people may find the "tradeoff" of privacy for convenience "worthwhile," or come to accept this "diminution of privacy" as "inevitable," and perhaps not. I for one doubt that people would accept without complaint the warrantless disclosure to the Government of a list of every Web site they had visited in the last week, or month, or year. But whatever the societal expectations, they can attain constitutionally protected status only if our Fourth Amendment jurisprudence ceases to treat secrecy as a prerequisite for privacy. I would not assume that all information voluntarily disclosed to some member of the public for a limited purpose is, for that reason alone, disentitled to Fourth Amendment protection. See *Smith* (Marshall, J., dissenting) ("Privacy is not a discrete commodity, possessed absolutely or not at all. * * *"); see also *Katz* ("[W]hat [a person] seeks to preserve as private, even in an area accessible to the public, may be constitutionally protected").

Resolution of these difficult questions in this case is unnecessary, however, because the Government's physical intrusion on Jones' Jeep supplies a narrower basis for decision. I therefore join the majority's opinion.

JUSTICE ALITO, with whom JUSTICE GINSBURG, JUSTICE BREYER, and JUSTICE KAGAN join, concurring in the judgment.

This case requires us to apply the Fourth Amendment's prohibition of unreasonable searches and seizures to a 21st-century surveillance technique * * *. Ironically, the Court has chosen to decide this case based on 18th-century tort law. By attaching a small GPS device to the underside of the vehicle that respondent drove, the law enforcement officers in this case engaged in conduct that might have provided grounds in 1791 for a suit for trespass to chattels. And for this reason, the Court concludes, the installation and use of the GPS device constituted a search.

This holding, in my judgment, is unwise. It strains the language of the Fourth Amendment; it has little if any support in current Fourth Amendment case law; and it is highly artificial.

I would analyze the question presented in this case by asking whether respondent's reasonable expectations of privacy were violated by the long-term monitoring of the movements of the vehicle he drove.

I

A

The Fourth Amendment prohibits "unreasonable searches and seizures," and the Court makes very little effort to explain how the attachment or use of the GPS device fits within these terms. * * *

The Court does claim that the installation and use of the GPS constituted a search, but this conclusion is dependent on the questionable proposition that these two procedures cannot be separated for purposes of Fourth Amendment analysis. If these two procedures are analyzed separately, it is not at all clear from the Court's opinion why either should be regarded as a search. It is clear that the attachment of the GPS device was not itself a search; if the device had not functioned or if the officers had not used it, no information would have been obtained. And the Court does not contend that the use of the device constituted a search either. On the contrary, the Court accepts the holding in *United States v. Knotts* that the use of a surreptitiously planted electronic device to monitor a vehicle's movements on public roads did not amount to a search.

The Court argues—and I agree—that "we must 'assur[e] preservation of that degree of privacy against government that existed when the Fourth Amendment was adopted.' " But it is almost impossible to think of late-18th-century situations that are analogous to what took place in this case. (Is it possible to imagine a case in which a constable secreted himself somewhere in a coach and remained there for a period of time in order to monitor the movements of the coach's owner?) [In footnote 3 of his concurrence, Justice Alito added this comment: "The Court suggests that something like this might have occurred in 1791, but this would have required either a gigantic coach, a very tiny constable, or both—not to mention a constable with incredible fortitude and patience."] The Court's theory seems to be that the concept of a search, as originally understood, comprehended any technical trespass that led to the gathering of evidence, but we know that this is incorrect. At common law, any unauthorized intrusion on private property was actionable, but a trespass on open fields, as opposed to the "curtilage" of a home, does not fall within the scope of the Fourth Amendment because private property outside the curtilage is not part of a "hous[e]" within the meaning of the Fourth Amendment.

B

The Court's reasoning in this case is very similar to that in the Court's early decisions involving wiretapping and electronic eavesdropping, namely, that a technical trespass followed by the gathering of evidence constitutes a search. * * *

This trespass-based rule was repeatedly criticized. * * *

Katz v. United States finally did away with the old approach, holding that a trespass was not required for a Fourth Amendment violation. * * * [T]he *Katz* Court, "repudiate[ed]" the old doctrine and held that "[t]he fact that the electronic device employed * * * did not happen to penetrate the wall of the booth can have no constitutional significance." What mattered, the Court now held, was whether the conduct at issue "violated the privacy upon which [the defendant] justifiably relied while using the telephone booth."

Under this approach, as the Court later put it when addressing the relevance of a technical trespass, "an actual trespass is neither necessary nor sufficient to establish a constitutional violation." * * *

III

Disharmony with a substantial body of existing case law is only one of the problems with the Court's approach in this case.

I will briefly note * * * others. First, the Court's reasoning largely disregards what is really important (the use of a GPS for the purpose of long-term tracking) and instead attaches great significance to something that most would view as relatively minor (attaching to the bottom of a car a small, light object that does not interfere in any way with the car's operation). Attaching such an object is generally regarded as so trivial that it does not provide a basis for recovery under modern tort law. But under the Court's reasoning, this conduct may violate the Fourth Amendment. By contrast, if long-term monitoring can be accomplished without committing a technical trespass—suppose, for example, that the Federal Government required or persuaded auto manufacturers to include a GPS tracking device in every car—the Court's theory would provide no protection.

Second, the Court's approach leads to incongruous results. If the police attach a GPS device to a car and use the device to follow the car for even a brief time, under the Court's theory, the Fourth Amendment applies. But if the police follow the same car for a much longer period using unmarked cars and aerial assistance, this tracking is not subject to any Fourth Amendment constraints. * * *

[Third], the Court's reliance on the law of trespass will present particularly vexing problems in cases involving surveillance that is carried out by making electronic, as opposed to physical, contact with the item to be tracked. For example, suppose that the officers in the present case had followed respondent by surreptitiously activating a stolen vehicle detection system that came with the car when it was purchased. Would the sending of a radio signal to activate this system constitute a trespass to chattels? Trespass to chattels has traditionally required a physical touching of the property. In recent years, courts have wrestled with the application of this old tort in cases involving unwanted electronic contact with computer systems, and some have held that even the transmission of electrons that occurs when a communication is sent from one computer to another is enough. But may such decisions be followed in applying the Court's trespass theory? Assuming that what matters under the Court's theory is the law of trespass as it existed at the time of the adoption of the Fourth Amendment, do these recent decisions represent a change in the law or simply the application of the old tort to new situations?

IV

A

The *Katz* expectation-of-privacy test avoids the problems and complications noted above, but it is not without its own difficulties. * * * [J]udges are apt to confuse their own expectations of privacy with those of the hypothetical reasonable person to which the Katz test looks. In addition, the *Katz* test rests on the assumption that this hypothetical reasonable person has a well-developed and stable set of privacy expectations. But technology can change those expectations. Dramatic technological change may lead to periods in which popular expectations are in flux and may ultimately produce significant changes in popular attitudes.

New technology may provide increased convenience or security at the expense of privacy, and many people may find the tradeoff worthwhile. And even if the public does not welcome the diminution of privacy that new technology entails, they may eventually reconcile themselves to this development as inevitable.

On the other hand, concern about new intrusions on privacy may spur the enactment of legislation to protect against these intrusions. This is what ultimately happened with respect to wiretapping. After *Katz*, Congress did not leave it to the courts to develop a body of Fourth Amendment case law governing that complex subject. Instead, Congress promptly enacted a comprehensive statute, and since that time, the regulation of wiretapping has been governed primarily by statute and not by case law. * * *

B

Recent years have seen the emergence of many new devices that permit the monitoring of a person's movements. In some locales, closed-circuit television video monitoring is becoming ubiquitous. On toll roads, automatic toll collection systems create a precise record of the movements of motorists who choose to make use of that convenience. Many motorists purchase cars that are equipped with devices that permit a central station to ascertain the car's location at any time so that roadside assistance may be provided if needed and the car may be found if it is stolen.

Perhaps most significant, cell phones and other wireless devices now permit wireless carriers to track and record the location of users—and as of June 2011, it has been reported, there were more than 322 million wireless devices in use in the United States. For older phones, the accuracy of the location information depends on the density of the tower network, but new "smart phones," which are equipped with a GPS device, permit more precise tracking. * * * Similarly, phone-location-tracking services are offered as "social" tools, allowing consumers to find (or to avoid) others who enroll in these services. The availability and use of these and other new devices will continue to shape the average person's expectations about the privacy of his or her daily movements.

V

In the pre-computer age, the greatest protections of privacy were neither constitutional nor statutory, but practical. Traditional surveillance for any extended period of time was difficult and costly and therefore rarely undertaken. The surveillance at issue in this case—constant monitoring of the location of a vehicle for four weeks—would have required a large team of agents, multiple vehicles, and perhaps aerial assistance. Only an investigation of unusual importance could have justified such an expenditure of law enforcement resources. Devices like the one used in the present case, however, make long-term monitoring relatively easy and cheap. In circumstances involving dramatic technological change, the best solution to privacy concerns may be legislative. A legislative body is well situated to gauge changing public attitudes, to draw detailed lines, and to balance privacy and public safety in a comprehensive way.

To date, however, Congress and most States have not enacted statutes regulating the use of GPS tracking technology for law enforcement purposes. The best that we can do in this case is to apply existing Fourth Amendment doctrine and to ask whether the use of GPS tracking in a particular case involved a degree of intrusion that a reasonable person would not have anticipated.

Under this approach, relatively short-term monitoring of a person's movements on public streets accords with expectations of privacy that our society has recognized as reasonable. But the use of longer term GPS monitoring in investigations of most offenses impinges on expectations of privacy. For such offenses, society's expectation has been that law enforcement agents and others would not—and indeed, in the main, simply could not—secretly monitor and catalogue every single movement of an individual's car for a very long period. * * * We need not identify with precision the point at which the tracking of this vehicle became a search, for the line was surely crossed before the 4-week mark. Other cases may present more difficult questions. But where uncertainty exists with respect to whether a certain period of GPS surveillance is long enough to constitute a Fourth Amendment search, the police may always seek a warrant. We also need not consider whether prolonged GPS monitoring in the context of investigations involving extraordinary offenses would similarly intrude on a constitutionally protected sphere of privacy. In such cases, long-term tracking might have been mounted using previously available techniques.

* * *

For these reasons, I conclude that the lengthy monitoring that occurred in this case constituted a search under the Fourth Amendment. I therefore agree with the majority that the decision of the Court of Appeals must be affirmed.

NOTES AND QUESTIONS

1. Which opinion—Justice Scalia's or Justice Alito's—provides a broader interpretation of the Fourth Amendment? Which opinion do you find more faithful to stare decisis? As a matter of public policy, which of the three opinions (including that of Justice Sotomayor), do you prefer?

2. Julia Angwin, FBI Turns Off Thousands of GPS Devices After Supreme Court Ruling, Wall Street Journal, Feb. 25, 2012:

> The Supreme Court's recent ruling overturning the warrantless use of GPS tracking devices has caused a "sea change" inside the U.S. Justice Department, according to FBI General Counsel Andrew Weissmann.
>
> Mr. Weissmann, speaking at a University of San Francisco conference called "Big Brother in the 21st Century" on Friday, said that the court ruling prompted the FBI to turn off about 3,000 GPS tracking devices that were in use. * * *
>
> After the ruling, the FBI had a problem collecting the devices that it had turned off, Mr. Weissmann said. In some cases, he said, the FBI sought court orders to obtain permission to turn the devices on briefly—only in order to locate and retrieve them.

3. The most recent generation of "smart phones" have a GPS transponder that sends signals about location periodically even when the phone is turned off. Those GPS units can thus be monitored without a trespass. How do you think the Court should ultimately resolve that issue? Recently, the New Jersey Supreme Court observed that "no one buys a cell phone to share detailed information about their whereabouts with the police." Therefore, applying the state constitution, the court held that police monitoring of a person's movements by means of an individual's smart phone GPS transponder constitutes a search. State v. Earls, 70 A.3d 630 (N.J. 2013).

4. What if a State wants to subject a recidivist sex-offender to nonconsensual, life-long satellite-based monitoring (SBM), by affixing a bracelet to the offender's ankle? SBM provides continuous tracking of the geographic location of the offender and reports violations of location requirements. Is *that* a search? The North Carolina Supreme Court thought it was not a search because *Jones* "considered the propriety of a search in the context of a motion to suppress evidence," rather than monitoring in a civil context.

In Grady v. North Carolina, 575 U.S. ___, 135 S.Ct. 1368, 191 L.Ed.2d 459 (2015) (*per curiam*), the Court unanimously reversed the North Carolina courts' opinion, The Court reaffirmed earlier decisions that Fourth Amendment protections extend beyond the sphere of criminal investigations. And, therefore, "it follows that a State also conducts a search when it attaches a device to a person's body, without consent, for the purpose of tracking that individual's movements."

The Court remanded the case to the State to decide the ultimate question of constitutionality: whether the SBM constitutes an unreasonable search.

FLORIDA V. JARDINES

Supreme Court of the United States, 2013.
569 U.S. 1, 133 S.Ct. 1409, 185 L.Ed.2d 495.

The Supreme Court—and lower courts and lawyers—now have two ways to argue that particular police conduct is a Fourth Amendment "search." Earlier in this chapter (p. 107, Note 5) we saw that the Supreme Court, applying *Katz*-ian privacy analysis, ruled that police use of a dog trained to identify narcotics does not constitute a "search" when the dog sniffs a person's luggage at an airport, or smells the exterior of an automobile stopped on the highway. But, what if the trained canine comes to the front door of your home to smell for possible narcotics? The next case demonstrates the Court's post-*Jones* approach to this question.

JUSTICE SCALIA delivered the opinion of the Court [joined by JUSTICES THOMAS, GINSBURG, SOTOMAYOR, and KAGAN].

We consider whether using a drug-sniffing dog on a homeowner's porch to investigate the contents of the home is a search within the meaning of the Fourth Amendment.

I

In 2006, Detective William Pedraja of the Miami-Dade Police Department received an unverified tip that marijuana was being grown in the home of respondent Joelis Jardines. One month later, the Department and the Drug Enforcement Administration sent a joint surveillance team to Jardines' home. Detective Pedraja was part of that team. He watched the home for fifteen minutes and saw no vehicles in the driveway or activity around the home, and could not see inside because the blinds were drawn. Detective Pedraja then approached Jardines' home accompanied by Detective Douglas Bartelt, a trained canine handler who had just arrived at the scene with his drug-sniffing dog. The dog was trained to detect the scent of marijuana, cocaine, heroin, and several other drugs, indicating the presence of any of these substances through particular behavioral changes recognizable by his handler.

Detective Bartelt had the dog on a six-foot leash, owing in part to the dog's "wild" nature, and tendency to dart around erratically while searching. As the dog approached Jardines' front porch, he apparently sensed one of the odors he had been trained to detect, and "began energetically exploring the area for the strongest point source of that odor. As Detective Bartelt explained, the dog began tracking that airborne odor by * * * tracking back and forth," engaging in what is called "bracketing," "back and forth, back and forth." Detective Bartelt gave the dog "the full six feet of the leash plus whatever safe distance [he could] give him" to do this—he testified that he needed to give the dog "as much distance as I can." And Detective Pedraja stood back while this was occurring, so that he would not get knocked over when the dog was "spinning around trying to find" the source.

After sniffing the base of the front door, the dog sat, which is the trained behavior upon discovering the odor's strongest point. Detective Bartelt then pulled the dog away from the door and returned to his vehicle. He left the scene after informing Detective Pedraja that there had been a positive alert for narcotics.

On the basis of what he had learned at the home, Detective Pedraja applied for and received a warrant to search the residence. When the warrant was executed later that day, * * * the search revealed marijuana plants, and he was charged with trafficking in cannabis.

At trial, Jardines moved to suppress the marijuana plants on the ground that the canine investigation was an unreasonable search. * * *

We granted certiorari, limited to the question of whether the officers' behavior was a search within the meaning of the Fourth Amendment.

II

The Fourth Amendment * * * establishes a simple baseline, one that for much of our history formed the exclusive basis for its protections: When "the Government obtains information by physically intruding" on persons, houses, papers, or effects, "a 'search' within the original meaning of the Fourth Amendment" has "undoubtedly occurred." *United States v. Jones*, [p. 130]. By reason of our decision in *Katz v. United States*, [p. 77], property rights "are not the sole measure of Fourth Amendment violations,"—but though *Katz* may add to the baseline, it does not subtract anything from the Amendment's protections "when the Government does engage in [a] physical intrusion of a constitutionally protected area."

That principle renders this case a straightforward one. The officers were gathering information in an area belonging to Jardines and immediately surrounding his house in the curtilage of the house, which we have held enjoys protection as part of the home itself. And they gathered that information by physically entering and occupying the area to engage in conduct not explicitly or implicitly permitted by the homeowner.

A

The Fourth Amendment "indicates with some precision the places and things encompassed by its protections": persons, houses, papers, and effects. The Fourth Amendment does not, therefore, prevent all investigations conducted on private property; for example, an officer may (subject to *Katz*) gather information in what we have called "open fields"—even if those fields are privately owned because such fields are not enumerated in the Amendment's text. [*Oliver*, p. 109, Note 6.]

But when it comes to the Fourth Amendment, the home is first among equals. At the Amendment's "very core" stands "the right of a man to retreat into his own home and there be free from unreasonable governmental intrusion." This right would be of little practical value if the State's agents could stand in a home's porch or side garden and trawl for evidence with impunity; the right to retreat would be significantly diminished if the police could enter a man's property to observe his repose from just outside the front window.

We therefore regard the area "immediately surrounding and associated with the home"—what our cases call the curtilage—as "part of the home itself for Fourth Amendment purposes." That principle has ancient and durable roots. Just as the distinction between the home and the open fields is as old "as the common law," so too is the identity of home and what Blackstone called the "curtilage or homestall," for the "house protects and privileges all its branches and appurtenants." This area around the home is "intimately linked to the home, both physically and psychologically," and is where "privacy expectations are most heightened."

* * * Here there is no doubt that the officers entered it: The front porch is the classic exemplar of an area adjacent to the home and "to which the activity of home life extends."

B

Since the officers' investigation took place in a constitutionally protected area, we turn to the question of whether it was accomplished through an unlicensed physical intrusion. While law enforcement officers need not "shield their eyes" when passing by the home "on public thoroughfares," an officer's leave to gather information is sharply circumscribed when he steps off those thoroughfares and enters the Fourth Amendment's protected areas. In permitting, for example, visual observation of the home from "public navigable airspace," we were careful to note that it was done "in a physically nonintrusive manner." *Entick v. Carrington*, 2 Wils. K.B. 275, 95 Eng. Rep. 807 (K.B.1765), a case "undoubtedly familiar" to "every American statesman" at the time of the Founding, states the general rule clearly: "[O]ur law holds the property of every man so sacred, that no man can set his foot upon his neighbour's close without his leave." As it is undisputed that the detectives had all four of their feet and all four of their companion's firmly planted on the constitutionally protected extension of Jardines' home, the only question is whether he had given his leave (even implicitly) for them to do so. He had not.

"A license may be implied from the habits of the country," notwithstanding the "strict rule of the English common law as to entry upon a close." We have accordingly recognized that "the knocker on the front door is treated as an invitation or license to attempt an entry, justifying ingress to the home by solicitors, hawkers and peddlers of all kinds." This implicit license typically permits the visitor to approach the home by the front path, knock promptly, wait briefly to be received, and then (absent invitation to linger longer) leave. Complying with the terms of that traditional invitation does not require fine-grained legal knowledge; it is generally managed without incident by the Nation's Girl Scouts and trick-or-treaters. Thus, a police officer not armed with a warrant may approach a home and knock, precisely because that is "no more than any private citizen might do."

But introducing a trained police dog to explore the area around the home in hopes of discovering incriminating evidence is something else. There is no customary invitation to do that. An invitation to engage in canine forensic investigation assuredly does not inhere in the very act of hanging a knocker. To find a visitor knocking on the door is routine (even if sometimes unwelcome); to spot that same visitor exploring the front path with a metal detector, or marching his bloodhound into the garden before saying hello and asking permission, would inspire most of us to—well, call the police. The scope of a license—express or implied—is limited not only to a particular area but also to a specific purpose. * * * Here, the background social norms that invite a visitor to the front door do not invite him there to conduct a search.

* * *III

The State argues that investigation by a forensic narcotics dog by definition cannot implicate any legitimate privacy interest. The State cites for authority our decisions in *United States v. Place*, and *Illinois v. Caballes*, [p. 107, Note 5], which held, respectively, that canine inspection of luggage in an airport, * * * and canine inspection of an automobile during a lawful traffic stop, do not violate the reasonable expectation of privacy described in *Katz*.

Just last Term [in *Jones*], we considered an argument much like this. *Jones* held that tracking an automobile's whereabouts using a physically-mounted GPS receiver is a Fourth Amendment search. The Government argued that the *Katz* standard "show[ed] that no search occurred," as the defendant had "no 'reasonable expectation of privacy' " in his whereabouts on the public roads * * *. But because the GPS receiver had been physically mounted on the defendant's automobile (thus intruding on his "effects"), we held that tracking the vehicle's movements was a search: a person's "Fourth Amendment rights do not rise or fall with the *Katz* formulation." The *Katz* reasonable-expectations test "has been *added to*, not *substituted for*," the traditional property-based understanding of the Fourth Amendment, and so is unnecessary to consider when the government gains evidence by physically intruding on constitutionally protected areas.

Thus, we need not decide whether the officers' investigation of Jardines' home violated his expectation of privacy under *Katz*. One virtue of the Fourth Amendment's property-rights baseline is that it keeps easy cases easy. That the officers learned what they learned only by physically intruding on Jardines' property to gather evidence is enough to establish that a search occurred. * * *

* * *

The government's use of trained police dogs to investigate the home and its immediate surroundings is a "search" within the meaning of the Fourth Amendment. The judgment of the Supreme Court of Florida is therefore affirmed.

JUSTICE KAGAN, with whom JUSTICE GINSBURG and JUSTICE SOTOMAYOR join, concurring.

For me, a simple analogy clinches this case—and does so on privacy as well as property grounds. A stranger comes to the front door of your home carrying super-high-powered binoculars. He doesn't knock or say hello. Instead, he stands on the porch and uses the binoculars to peer through your windows, into your home's furthest corners. It doesn't take long (the binoculars are really very fine): In just a couple of minutes, his uncommon behavior allows him to learn details of your life you disclose to no one. Has your "visitor" trespassed on your property, exceeding the license you have granted to members of the public to, say, drop off the mail or distribute campaign flyers? Yes, he has. And has he also invaded your "reasonable expectation of privacy," by nosing into intimacies you sensibly thought protected from disclosure? Yes, of course, he has done that too.

That case is this case in every way that matters. Here, police officers came to Joelis Jardines' door with a super-sensitive instrument, which they deployed to detect things inside that they could not perceive unassisted. The equipment they used was animal, not mineral. But contra the dissent, that is of no significance in determining whether a search occurred. Detective Bartelt's dog was not your neighbor's pet, come to your porch on a leisurely stroll. * * * [D]rug-detection dogs are highly trained tools of law enforcement, geared to respond in distinctive ways to specific scents so as to convey clear and reliable information to their human partners. They are to the poodle down the street as high-powered binoculars are to a piece of plain glass. Like the binoculars, a drug-detection dog is a specialized device for discovering objects not in plain view (or plain smell). And as in the hypothetical above, that device was aimed here at a home—the most private and inviolate (or so we expect) of all the places and things the Fourth Amendment protects. Was this activity a trespass? Yes, as the Court holds today. Was it also an invasion of privacy? Yes, that as well.

The Court today treats this case under a property rubric; I write separately to note that I could just as happily have decided it by looking to Jardines' privacy interests. A decision along those lines would have looked . . . well, much like this one. It would have talked about " 'the right of a man to retreat into his own home and there be free from unreasonable governmental intrusion.' " It would have insisted on maintaining the "practical value" of that right by preventing police officers from standing in an adjacent space and "trawl[ing]" for evidence with impunity. It would have explained that " 'privacy expectations are most heightened' " in the home and the surrounding area. And it would have determined that police officers invade those shared expectations when they use trained canine assistants to reveal within the confines of a home what they could not otherwise have found there

It is not surprising that in a case involving a search of a home, property concepts and privacy concepts should so align. The law of property "naturally enough influence[s]" our "shared social expectations" of what places should be free from governmental incursions. And so the sentiment "my home is my own," while originating in property law, now also denotes a common understanding—extending even beyond that law's formal protections—about an especially private sphere. Jardines' home was his property; it was also his most intimate and familiar space. The analysis proceeding from each of those facts, as today's decision reveals, runs mostly along the same path.

I can think of only one divergence: If we had decided this case on privacy grounds, we would have realized that *Kyllo v. United States* already resolved it. The *Kyllo* Court held that police officers conducted a search when they used a thermal-imaging device to detect heat emanating from a private home, even though they committed no trespass. Highlighting our intention to draw both a "firm" and a "bright" line at "the entrance to the house," we announced the following rule:

> "Where, as here, the Government uses a device that is not in general public use, to explore details of the home that would previously have been unknowable without physical intrusion, the surveillance is a 'search' and is presumptively unreasonable without a warrant."

That "firm" and "bright" rule governs this case: The police officers here conducted a search because they used a "device * * * not in general public use (a trained drug-detection dog) to explore details of the home" (the presence of certain substances) that they would not otherwise have discovered without entering the premises.

And again, the dissent's argument that the device is just a dog cannot change the equation. As *Kyllo* made clear, the "sense-enhancing" tool at issue may be "crude" or "sophisticated," may be old or new (drug-detection dogs actually go back * * * only a few decades), may be either smaller or bigger than a breadbox; still, "at least where (as here)" the device is not "in general public use," training it on a home violates our "minimal expectation of privacy"—an expectation "that *exists*, and that is acknowledged to be *reasonable*. That does not mean the device is off-limits, as the dissent implies, it just means police officers cannot use it to examine a home without a warrant or exigent circumstance.

With these further thoughts, suggesting that a focus on Jardines' privacy interests would make an "easy cas[e] easy" twice over, I join the Court's opinion in full.

JUSTICE ALITO, with whom THE CHIEF JUSTICE [ROBERTS], JUSTICE KENNEDY, and JUSTICE BREYER join, dissenting.

The Court's decision in this important Fourth Amendment case is based on a putative rule of trespass law that is nowhere to be found in the annals of Anglo-American jurisprudence.

The law of trespass generally gives members of the public a license to use a walkway to approach the front door of a house and to remain there for a brief time. This license is not limited to persons who intend to speak to an occupant or who actually do so. (Mail carriers and persons delivering packages and flyers are examples of individuals who may lawfully approach a front door without intending to converse.) Nor is the license restricted to categories of visitors whom an occupant of the dwelling is likely to welcome; as the Court acknowledges, this license applies even to "solicitors, hawkers and peddlers of all kinds." And the license even extends to police officers who wish to gather evidence against an occupant (by asking potentially incriminating questions).

According to the Court, however, the police officer in this case, Detective Bartelt, committed a trespass because he was accompanied during his otherwise lawful visit to the front door of respondent's house by his dog, Franky. Where is the authority evidencing such a rule? Dogs have been domesticated for about 12,000 years; they were ubiquitous in both this country and Britain at the time of the adoption of the Fourth Amendment; and their acute sense of smell has been used in law enforcement for centuries. Yet the Court has been unable to find a single case—from the United States or any other common-law nation—that supports the rule on which its decision is based. Thus, trespass law provides no support for the Court's holding today.

The Court's decision is also inconsistent with the reasonable-expectations-of-privacy test that the Court adopted in *Katz*. A reasonable person understands that odors emanating from a house may be detected from locations that are open to the public, and a reasonable person will not count on the strength of those odors remaining within the range that, while detectible by a dog, cannot be smelled by a human.

For these reasons, I would hold that no search within the meaning of the Fourth Amendment took place in this case, and I would reverse the decision below.

* * *

II

The Court concludes that the conduct in this case was a search because Detective Bartelt exceeded the boundaries of the license to approach the house that is recognized by the law of trespass, but the Court's interpretation of the scope of that license is unfounded.

* * *

B

Detective Bartelt did not exceed the scope of the license to approach respondent's front door. He adhered to the customary path; he did not approach in the middle of the night; and he remained at the front door for only a very short period (less than a minute or two).

The Court concludes that Detective Bartelt went too far because he had the "*objectiv*[*e*] * * * *purpose* to conduct a search." What this means, I take it, is that anyone aware of what Detective Bartelt did would infer that his subjective purpose was to gather evidence. But if this is the Court's point, then * * * most * * * police visits would likewise constitute searches. With the exception of visits to serve warrants or civil process, police almost always approach homes with a purpose of discovering information. * * *

What the Court must fall back on, then, is the particular instrument that Detective Bartelt used to detect the odor of marijuana, namely, his dog. But in the entire body of common-law decisions, the Court has not found a single case holding that a visitor to the front door of a home commits a trespass if the visitor is accompanied by a dog on a leash. On the contrary, the common law allowed even unleashed dogs to wander on private property without committing a trespass.

The Court responds that "[i]t is not the dog that is the problem, but the behavior that here involved use of the dog." But where is the support in the law of trespass for this proposition? Dogs' keen sense of smell has been used in law enforcement for centuries. The antiquity of this practice is evidenced by a Scottish law from 1318 that made it a crime to "disturb a tracking dog or the men coming with it for pursuing thieves or seizing malefactors." * * *

For these reasons, the real law of trespass provides no support for the Court's holding today. While the Court claims that its reasoning has "ancient and durable roots," its trespass rule is really a newly struck counterfeit.

III

The concurring opinion attempts to provide an alternative ground for today's decision, namely, that Detective Bartelt's conduct violated respondent's reasonable expectations of privacy. * * * I see no basis for concluding that the occupants of a dwelling have a reasonable expectation of privacy in odors that emanate from the dwelling and reach spots where members of the public may lawfully stand.

It is clear that the occupant of a house has no reasonable expectation of privacy with respect to odors that can be smelled by human beings who are standing in such places. And, I would not draw a line between odors that can be smelled by humans and those that are detectible only by dogs.

Consider the situation from the point of view of the occupant of a building in which marijuana is grown or methamphetamine is manufactured. Would such an occupant reason as follows? "I know that odors may emanate from my building and that atmospheric conditions, such as the force and direction of the wind, may affect the strength of those odors when they reach a spot where members of the public may lawfully stand. I also know that some people have a much more acute sense of smell than others, and I have no idea who might be standing in one of the spots in question when the odors from my house reach that location. In addition, I know that odors coming from my building, when they reach these locations, may be strong enough to be detected by a dog. But I am confident that they will be so faint that they cannot be smelled by any human being." Such a finely tuned expectation would be entirely unrealistic, and I see no evidence that society is prepared to recognize it as reasonable.

In an attempt to show that respondent had a reasonable expectation of privacy in the odor of marijuana wafting from his house, the concurrence argues that this case is just like *Kyllo v. United States*, which held that police officers conducted a search when they used a thermal imaging device to detect heat emanating from a house. This Court, however, has already rejected the argument that the use of a drug-sniffing dog is the same as the use of a thermal imaging device. * * *

Contrary to the interpretation propounded by the concurrence, *Kyllo* is best understood as a decision about the use of new technology. The *Kyllo* Court focused on the fact that the thermal imaging device was a form of "sense-enhancing technology" that was "not in general public use," and it expressed concern that citizens would be "at the mercy of advancing technology" if its use was not restricted. A dog, however, is not a new form of "technology" or a "device." And, as noted, the use of dogs' acute sense of smell in law enforcement dates back many centuries. * * *

The concurrence's *Kyllo*-based approach would have a much wider reach. When the police used the thermal imaging device in *Kyllo*, they were on a public street, and "committed no trespass." Therefore, if a dog's nose is just like a thermal imaging device for Fourth Amendment purposes, a search would occur if a dog alerted while on a public sidewalk or in the corridor of an apartment building. And the same would be true if the dog was trained to sniff, not for marijuana, but for more dangerous quarry, such as explosives or for a violent fugitive or kidnaped child. I see no ground for hampering legitimate law enforcement in this way.

IV

The conduct of the police officer in this case did not constitute a trespass and did not violate respondent's reasonable expectations of privacy. I would hold that this conduct was not a search, and I therefore respectfully dissent.

NOTES AND QUESTIONS

1. Does this case make you more, or less, inclined to favor the direction Justice Scalia took in Jones in returning the Court's "search" analysis to pre-*Katz* trespass analysis? As a matter of *Katz* analysis exclusively, how do you believe this case should have been resolved?

2. In light of *Jardines*, would the police have conducted a search if they had used Franky to walk through the second floor of an apartment building sniffing for the odor of marijuana? See State v. Nguyen, 841 N.W. 676 (N.D. 2013).

What if Franky had placed his paws on a vehicle (without the car driver's consent) and alerted the officer to a hidden cache of marijuana in the car trunk? See United States v. Thomas, 726 F.3d 1086 (9th Cir. 2013).

D. WHAT IS A SEARCH AFTER *JARDINES*?

Now that we have chased Franky off Mr. Jardines' property, what do we do next? A good place to start is to look back at where we have been.

We started this chapter with a Fourth Amendment checklist of sorts:

- ☑ Is there a search? *If no, Fourth Amendment does not apply.*
- ☑ If yes, was the search reasonable?
    - ☑ Was there a valid warrant? *If yes, the search is reasonable.*
    - ☑ If no valid warrant, was there an exception to the warrant requirement? *If yes, the search is still reasonable.*
- ☑ If no valid warrant and no exception, the search is unreasonable and thus prohibited by the Fourth Amendment.

We then focused in this chapter on the first box to be checked: Was there a search?

Prior to the case of *Katz v. United States* [p. 77], this question was answered by determining whether or not the government trespassed on to one's property by physically entering on to the property or interfering with the possession of a tangible, material item. By the time *Katz* came along, strict adherence to trespass as the only determining factor had become problematic. What about non-tangible things that people still might want to keep to themselves and the government out of, such as phone conversations?

Thus, in *Katz*, the Court moved to a focus on a person's conduct rather than the location where that conduct took place. Remember Justice Stewart's famous quote in *Katz*:

> "What a person knowingly exposes to the public, even in his own home or office, is not a subject of Fourth Amendment protection. But what he seeks to preserve as private, even in an area accessible to the public, may be constitutionally protected."

Thus we can refine our checklist after *Katz* to look something like this:

- ☑ Is there a search?
  - ☑ Is there an actual expectation of privacy? *If no, the Fourth Amendment does not apply.*
  - ☑ If yes, is that expectation one that society views as reasonable? *If no, the Fourth Amendment does not apply.*
- ☑ If there was a search, was the search reasonable?
  - ☑ Was there a valid warrant? *If yes, the search is reasonable.*
  - ☑ If no valid warrant, was there an exception to the warrant requirement? *If yes, the search is still reasonable*
- ☑ If no valid warrant and no exception, the search is unreasonable and thus prohibited by the Fourth Amendment.

We have spent most of this chapter applying the *Katz* test to a wide variety of government conduct. If we map out those cases on a chart, based on whether or not a search was found, it might look something like this:

CASE NAME	DATE	PG. NO.	DESCRIPTION	TEST USED	SEARCH
Katz v. U.S.	1967		listening device placed on phone booth	Katz	Yes
U.S. v. White	1971		recording of informant's conversation with defendant	Katz	No
Smith v. Maryland	1979		review of pen register on defendant's phone	Katz	No
U.S. v. Place	1983		dog sniff of passenger's luggage at airport	Katz	No

CASE NAME	DATE	PG. NO.	DESCRIPTION	TEST USED	SEARCH
U.S. v. Knotts	1983		monitoring of a beeper placed on a container located in a car	Katz	No
U.S. v. Karo	1984		monitoring of a beeper placed on a container to learn beeper located in a house.	Katz	Yes
Oliver v. U.S.	1984		open field	Katz and Fourth Amendment text	No
California v. Ciralo	1986		aerial surveillance of marijuana in backyard	Katz	No
U.S. v. Dunn	1987		observation of outside of barn in open field	Katz and Fourth Amendment text	No
California v. Greenwood	1988		trash left on sidewalk in front of house for pickup	Katz	No
Florida v. Riley	1989		helicopter surveillance of partially covered greenhouse	Katz	No
Bond v. U.S.	2000		physical manipulation of luggage on bus stopped at checkpoint	Katz	Yes
Kyllo v. U.S.	2001		thermal imaging device directed at interior of home from the street	Katz	Yes
Illinois v. Caballes	2005		dog sniff of trunk of automobile	Katz	No

CASE NAME	DATE	PG. NO.	DESCRIPTION	TEST USED	SEARCH
U.S. v. Jones	2012		GPS located on a car and monitored for 28 days	Trespass: 4 Justices; Katz and Trespass: 1 Justice; Katz only: 4 Justices	Yes
Florida v. Jardines	2013		dog sniff of porch and front door of home	Trespass: 5 Justices; Katz and Trespass: 3 Justices (4 Justices dissenting).	Yes

Of the sixteen cases listed in the chart, the Court failed to find a search in over 60% of them. Thus the Fourth Amendment did not apply and the government was free to do what it wished with the evidence gathered. From 1967 to 2000, there was only a single case applying *Katz* that found the government conduct was a search. Why did it take so long for defendants to begin winning the question of whether the government conduct was a search?

Changes in the make-up of the Court is always one possibility. The U.S. Supreme Court of the twenty-first century is more conservative and more law-enforcement oriented, certainly compared to the Warren Court. But there is also an interesting, if subtle, pattern to the cases where a search was found. They all involve either interferences with tangible property (a clear trespass)—where you do not need *Katz*—or advancing technology where the use of *Katz*, especially its subjective prong, could lead to "Big Brother" results that would have made the Court uncomfortable. Do we really want police driving up and down streets aiming Agema Thermovision 210 devices at all our homes?

So now our checklist may look something like this:

- ☑ Is there a search?
  - ☑ Is there a trespass? *If yes, then there is a search. If no, continue:*
  - ☑ Is there an actual expectation of privacy? *If no, the Fourth Amendment does not apply. If yes, continue:*
  - ☑ If yes, is that expectation one that society views as reasonable? *If no, the Fourth Amendment does not apply. If yes, there is a search.*
- ☑ If there was a search, was the search reasonable?
  - ☑ Was there a valid warrant? *If yes, the search is reasonable.*

☑ If no valid warrant, was there an exception to the warrant requirement? *If yes, the search is still reasonable.*

☑ If no valid warrant and no exception, the search is unreasonable and thus prohibited by the Fourth Amendment.

From here we take our checklist into the next chapter. Assuming we have a search, is the search reasonable? One of the easiest ways to demonstrate the reasonableness of a search is with a valid warrant. What makes a valid warrant? Turn the page to find out.

CHAPTER 3 SUMMARY

The Fourth Amendment to the U.S. Constitution bars "unreasonable searches and seizures" of "persons, houses, papers, and effects". In this chapter, we dealt with searches; a later chapter will concern seizures. The Amendment does not bar reasonable searches and it does not bar government conduct that is not a search at all. Thus, any Fourth Amendment analysis must begin with the question asked in this chapter: *Was there a search?* If there is no search, the Fourth Amendment does not even apply.

Prior to the case of *Katz v. United States* (p. 77) this question was answered by determining whether the government trespassed on one's property by physically entering on to the property or interfering with the possession of a tangible, material item. By the time *Katz* came along, strict adherence to trespass as the only determining factor had weakened, at least in part because of new surveillance methods that allowed government to invade non-tangible things that people might want to keep private from government, such as phone conversations. *Katz* established a test (sometimes called Harlan's two-pronged test) for determining when there was a search. It required government conduct to meet two criteria: 1) did the conduct violate an actual expectation of privacy; 2) and was that expectation one that society was prepared to view as reasonable? For the remainder of the 20th century, and the first part of the 21st, this was the sole test for determining the existence (or not) of a search. In the course of this chapter, we have seen the *Katz* test applied to a dizzying array of situations, including conversations with co-conspirators; agents recording conversations with co-conspirators; open fields; aerial surveillance over houses; garbage left on the sidewalk for pickup; dog sniffs of luggage; dog sniffs of property; electronic beepers placed on chemical containers; thermal imagers; and GPS locators on trucks. Of sixteen cases examined between 1967 and 2013, the Court failed to find a search in over 60% of them. Thus the Fourth Amendment did not apply and the government was free to engage in the conduct that produced the evidence it used against the defendant.

In cases where the Court has found a search, there seem to be two recurring themes: concerns over the rise of a digital and technologically based society and concerns about the amount of information we are now expected to provide to third parties in order to function in an online world. These concerns were raised by some of the Justices as early as 1971, but have accelerated with the onset of such developments as cell phones and GPS locators. Where fast-paced technological developments were at the heart of government conduct, the Court has sought to subject that conduct to the Fourth Amendment, even if it meant returning to the former trespass test seemingly once overruled by *Katz*—but apparently not.

Much of the challenge in today's search law is rooted in how technology affects what expectations of privacy are reasonable. Moreover, are actual expectations of privacy (Harlan's first prong) affected by individual understanding of technology? For example, would an increased understanding of information technology and cybersecurity after taking a college class result in a decreased expectation of privacy in online activities compared to a person who knows little about computers other than how to turn one on? Indeed, the Court may have returned to the trespass doctrine as an option in search cases (along with the *Katz* test) because it provides a simpler definition of privacy in an era where our expectations of privacy may fluctuate year-to-year and person to person.

Even as this book is going to publication, the Court is considering two cases concerning the use of cell phones. As these decisions are handed down, the authors will update this discussion via the website that accompanies this book. Stay tuned. The end of this chapter has yet to be written.

CHAPTER 4

The Substance of the Fourth Amendment: Probable Cause and Warrants

A. PROBABLE CAUSE

Introductory Comment

The Fourth Amendment prohibits *unreasonable* searches and seizures. Very generally speaking, this means that searches and seizures must be supported by probable cause. Put differently, a search or seizure conducted *in the absence* of probable cause ordinarily is considered an *unreasonable one*. As the Court has put it, "probable cause" is the "traditional standard" of the Fourth Amendment. Arizona v. Hicks, 480 U.S. 321, 107 S.Ct. 1149, 94 L.Ed.2d 347 (1987). The standard, of course, comes from the second clause of the amendment, which requires probable cause for a warrant to be constitutional.

It is easier to state the definition of "probable cause" than it is to determine whether it exists in a particular case. Probable cause to arrest "exists where 'the facts and circumstances within [the officers'] knowledge and of which they [have] reasonably trustworthy information [are] sufficient in themselves to warrant a man of reasonable caution in the belief that' *an offense has been or is being committed*" by the person to be arrested. Brinegar v. United States, 338 U.S. 160, 69 S.Ct. 1302, 93 L.Ed. 1879 (1949) (quoting Carroll v. United States, 267 U.S. 132, 45 S.Ct. 280, 69 L.Ed. 543 (1925)) (emphasis added). The same definition applies to "probable cause to search," except that the italicized language is replaced with "evidence subject to seizure will be found in the place to be searched."

Procedurally, the issue of probable cause typically arises in one of two circumstances. First, the police may apply to a magistrate for an arrest or search warrant. Warrants constitutionally may only be issued if there is probable cause to make the arrest or conduct the search. Therefore, the police must set out for the magistrate, under oath, the information in their possession that they believe justifies issuance of the warrant, *i.e.,* the facts that constitute probable cause for the arrest or search.

Alternatively, the police may conduct an arrest or search without a warrant. Assuming that it results in seizure of criminal evidence, the defendant may seek to have this evidence excluded from the trial at a suppression hearing. The defendant may argue that the police acted in violation of the Fourth Amendment because they did not obtain a warrant (an issue to which we will turn shortly), or she may argue that, warrant issues aside, the police lacked probable cause. In the latter case, the judge must decide whether the police had adequate evidence—probable cause—*before* they conducted the warrantless search or arrest. She must ask herself, in essence, "If the police *had* sought a warrant, would it properly have been granted?"

In some cases, police need neither a warrant nor probable cause. We cover those doctrines in Chapter 6.

ILLINOIS V. GATES

Supreme Court of the United States, 1983.
462 U.S. 213, 103 S.Ct. 2317, 76 L.Ed.2d 527.

As you can see from the introduction above, probable cause is not an easy legal concept to define. The definition in *Brinegar* does not necessarily explain when information is reasonably trustworthy, which facts and circumstances are relevant to any given probable cause determination, or how we even know when someone is a person of 'reasonable caution'.

To aid in determinations such as these, the Court typically comes up with a test—think Harlan's two-pronged test from *Katz*—designed to tell us whether a set of facts fit within certain criteria or not. In the case of probable cause, there have been two key tests developed by the Court. The first, known as the *Aguilar-Spinelli* test, is described in *Gates* below. The Court in *Gates* then goes on to overrule *Aguilar-Spinelli* in favor of a new test: the *totality of the circumstances test.* By the end of the case, see if you can identify the elements of each test. Ask yourself if you would have decided *Gates* differently under one test or the other.

One of the goals of the Court in *Gates* might have been to ease what the justices saw as overly rigid restrictions on the ability of law enforcement officers to get warrants; all things being equal, having a warrant is always better than not having one. The Court in *Gates*, therefore, sought to create a test that would "usefully illuminate the common sense practical question

regarding the existence of probable cause". In addition, the Court did not want to diminish the use of informants in police work and had come to believe that the *Aguilar-Spinelli* test discouraged the use of a valuable investigative tool. When reading the *Gates* case, ask yourself how well you think the decision achieved these two goals.

Also note Justice White's concurrence. Using the exact same set of facts, Justice White comes to the same conclusion as the majority, but does so using the old test. We saw the same phenomena in *Florida v. Jardines.* In fact, this can happen fairly often. What does that say about the utility of different tests? Do the tests themselves matter, or as human beings, do almost of our decisions come down to an instinctive sense of what is "common sense" and what is not.

Finally, as noted by the Court in *Gates*, informants are an often used as valuable investigative tool. But what happens if your informant is a dog? For all you dog-lovers out there, enjoy Note 10 after *Gates*.

JUSTICE REHNQUIST delivered the opinion of the Court [joined by CHIEF JUSTICE BURGER, and JUSTICES BLACKMUN, POWELL, and O'CONNOR]. * * *

II

* * * Bloomingdale, Ill., is a suburb of Chicago located in Du Page County. On May 3, 1978, the Bloomingdale Police Department received by mail an anonymous handwritten letter which read as follows:

> "This letter is to inform you that you have a couple in your town who strictly make their living on selling drugs. They are Sue and Lance Gates, they live on Greenway, off Bloomingdale Rd. in the condominiums. Most of their buys are done in Florida. Sue his wife drives their car to Florida, where she leaves it to be loaded up with drugs, then Lance flys down and drives it back. Sue flys back after she drops the car off in Florida. May 3 she is driving down there again and Lance will be flying down in a few days to drive it back. At the time Lance drives the car back he has the trunk loaded with over $100,000.00 in drugs. Presently they have over $100,000.00 worth of drugs in their basement.
>
> "They brag about the fact they never have to work, and make their entire living on pushers.

"I guarantee if you watch them carefully you will make a big catch. They are friends with some big drugs dealers, who visit their house often.

"Lance & Susan Gates

"Greenway

"in Condominiums"

The letter was referred by the Chief of Police of the Bloomingdale Police Department to Detective Mader, who decided to pursue the tip. Mader learned, from the office of the Illinois Secretary of State, that an Illinois driver's license had been issued to one Lance Gates, residing at a stated address in Bloomingdale. He contacted a confidential informant, whose examination of certain financial records revealed a more recent address for the Gateses, and he also learned from a police officer assigned to O'Hare Airport that "L. Gates" had made a reservation on Eastern Airlines Flight 245 to West Palm Beach, Fla., scheduled to depart from Chicago on May 5 at 4:15 p.m.

Mader then made arrangements with an agent of the Drug Enforcement Administration for surveillance of the May 5 Eastern Airlines flight. The agent later reported to Mader that Gates had boarded the flight, and that federal agents in Florida had observed him arrive in West Palm Beach and take a taxi to the nearby Holiday Inn. They also reported that Gates went to a room registered to one Susan Gates and that, at 7 o'clock the next morning, Gates and an unidentified woman left the motel in a Mercury bearing Illinois license plates and drove northbound on an interstate highway frequently used by travelers to the Chicago area. In addition, the DEA agent informed Mader that the license plate number on the Mercury was registered to a Hornet station wagon owned by Gates. The agent also advised Mader that the driving time between West Palm Beach and Bloomingdale was approximately 22 to 24 hours.

Mader signed an affidavit setting forth the foregoing facts, and submitted it to a judge of the Circuit Court of Du Page County, together with a copy of the anonymous letter. The judge of that court thereupon issued a search warrant for the Gateses' residence and for their automobile. * * *

At 5:15 a.m. on March 7, only 36 hours after he had flown out of Chicago, Lance Gates, and his wife, returned to their home in Bloomingdale, driving the car in which they had left West Palm Beach some 22 hours earlier. The Bloomingdale police were awaiting them, searched the trunk of the Mercury, and uncovered approximately 350 pounds of marihuana. A search of the Gateses' home revealed marihuana, weapons, and other contraband. * * *

The Illinois Supreme Court concluded—and we are inclined to agree—that, standing alone, the anonymous letter sent to the Bloomingdale Police Department would not provide the basis for a magistrate's determination that there was probable cause to believe contraband would be found in the Gateses' car and home. The letter provides virtually nothing from which one might conclude that its author is either honest or his information reliable; likewise, the letter gives absolutely no indication of the basis for the writer's predictions regarding the Gateses' criminal activities. Something more was required, then, before a magistrate could conclude that there was probable cause to believe that contraband would be found in the Gateses' home and car. See *Aguilar v. Texas*, 378 U.S. [108, 109 n. 1, 84 S.Ct. 1509, 1511 n. 1, 12 L.Ed.2d 723 (1964)]; *Nathanson v. United States*, 290 U.S. 41, 54 S.Ct. 11, 78 L.Ed. 159 (1933).

The Illinois Supreme Court also properly recognized that Detective Mader's affidavit might be capable of supplementing the anonymous letter with information sufficient to permit a determination of probable cause. In holding that the affidavit in fact did not contain sufficient additional information to sustain a determination of probable cause, the Illinois court applied a "two-pronged test," derived from our decision in *Spinelli v. United States*. The Illinois Supreme Court, like some others, apparently understood *Spinelli* as requiring that the anonymous letter satisfy each of two independent requirements before it could be relied on. According to this view, the letter, as supplemented by Mader's affidavit, first had to adequately reveal the "basis of knowledge" of the letterwriter—the particular means by which he came by the information given in his report. Second, it had to provide facts sufficiently establishing either the "veracity" of the affiant's informant, or, alternatively, the "reliability" of the informant's report in this particular case.

The Illinois court, alluding to an elaborate set of legal rules that have developed among various lower courts to enforce the "two-pronged test," found that the test had not been satisfied. First, the "veracity" prong was not satisfied because, "[t]here was simply no basis [for] conclud[ing] that the anonymous person [who wrote the letter to the Bloomingdale Police Department] was credible." The court indicated that corroboration by police of details contained in the letter might never satisfy the "veracity" prong, and in any event, could not do so if, as in the present case, only "innocent" details are corroborated. In addition, the letter gave no indication of the basis of its writer's knowledge of the Gateses' activities. * * *

We agree with the Illinois Supreme Court that an informant's "veracity," "reliability," and "basis of knowledge" are all highly relevant in determining the value of his report. We do not agree, however, that these elements should be understood as entirely separate and independent requirements to be rigidly exacted in every case, which the opinion of the Supreme Court of Illinois would imply. Rather, as detailed below, they should be understood simply as closely intertwined issues that may usefully illuminate the commonsense, practical question whether there is "probable cause" to believe that contraband or evidence is located in a particular place.

III

This totality-of-the-circumstances approach is far more consistent with our prior treatment of probable cause than is any rigid demand that specific "tests" be satisfied by every informant's tip. Perhaps the central teaching of our decisions bearing on the probable-cause standard is that it is a "practical, nontechnical conception." "In dealing with probable cause, * * * as the very name implies, we deal with probabilities. These are not technical; they are the factual and practical considerations of everyday life on which reasonable and prudent men, not legal technicians, act." * * *

As these comments illustrate, probable cause is a fluid concept—turning on the assessment of probabilities in particular factual contexts—not readily, or even usefully, reduced to a neat set of legal rules. Informants' tips doubtless come in many shapes and sizes from many different types of persons. * * * Rigid legal rules are ill-suited to an area of such diversity. * * *

Moreover, the "two-pronged test" directs analysis into two largely independent channels—the informant's "veracity" or "reliability" and his "basis of knowledge." There are persuasive arguments against according these two elements such independent status. Instead, they are better understood as relevant considerations in the totality-of-the-circumstances analysis that traditionally has guided probable-cause determinations: a deficiency in one may be compensated for, in determining the overall reliability of a tip, by a strong showing as to the other, or by some other indicia of reliability.

If, for example, a particular informant is known for the unusual reliability of his predictions of certain types of criminal activities in a locality, his failure, in a particular case, to thoroughly set forth the basis of his knowledge surely should not serve as an absolute bar to a finding of probable cause based on his tip. Likewise, if an unquestionably honest citizen comes forward with a report of criminal activity—which if fabricated would subject him to criminal liability—we have found rigorous scrutiny of the basis of his knowledge unnecessary. Conversely, even if we entertain some doubt as to an informant's motives, his explicit and detailed description of alleged wrongdoing, along with a statement that the event was observed firsthand, entitles his tip to greater weight than might otherwise be the case. Unlike a totality-of-the-circumstances analysis, which permits a balanced assessment of the relative weights of all the various indicia of reliability (and unreliability) attending an informant's tip, the "two-pronged test" has encouraged an excessively technical dissection of informants' tips, with undue attention being focused on isolated issues that cannot sensibly be divorced from the other facts presented to the magistrate.

As early as *Locke v. United States*, 7 Cranch 339, 348, 3 L.Ed. 364 (1813), Chief Justice Marshall observed, in a closely related context: "[T]he term 'probable cause,' according to its usual acceptation, means less than evidence which would justify condemnation * * *. It imports a seizure made under circumstances which warrant suspicion." More recently, we stated that "the *quanta* * * * of proof" appropriate in ordinary judicial proceedings are inapplicable to the decision to issue a warrant. Finely tuned standards such as proof beyond a reasonable doubt or by a preponderance of the evidence, useful in formal trials, have no place in the magistrate's decision. While an effort to fix some general, numerically precise degree of certainty corresponding to "probable cause" may not be helpful, it is clear that "only the probability, and not a prima facie showing, of criminal activity is the standard of probable cause."

We also have recognized that affidavits "are normally drafted by nonlawyers in the midst and haste of a criminal investigation. Technical requirements of elaborate specificity once exacted under common law pleadings have no proper place in this area." Likewise, search and arrest warrants long have been issued by persons who are neither lawyers nor judges, and who certainly do not remain abreast of each judicial refinement of the nature of "probable cause." The rigorous inquiry into the *Spinelli* prongs and the complex superstructure of evidentiary and analytical rules that some have seen implicit in our *Spinelli* decision, cannot be reconciled with the fact that many warrants are—quite properly—issued on the basis of nontechnical, common-sense judgments of laymen applying a standard less demanding than those used in more formal legal proceedings. Likewise, given the informal, often hurried context in which it must be applied, the "built-in subtleties" of the "two-pronged test" are particularly unlikely to assist magistrates in determining probable cause.

Similarly, we have repeatedly said that after-the-fact scrutiny by courts of the sufficiency of an affidavit should not take the form of *de novo* review. A magistrate's "determination of probable cause should be paid great deference by reviewing courts." *Spinelli, supra.* "A grudging or negative attitude by reviewing courts toward warrants" is inconsistent with the Fourth Amendment's strong preference for searches conducted pursuant to a warrant; "courts should not invalidate warrant[s] by interpreting affidavit[s] in a hypertechnical, rather than a commonsense, manner."

If the affidavits submitted by police officers are subjected to the type of scrutiny some courts have deemed appropriate, police might well resort to warrantless searches, with the hope of relying on consent or some other exception to the Warrant Clause that might develop at the time of the search. In addition, the possession of a warrant by officers conducting an arrest or search greatly reduces the perception of unlawful or intrusive police conduct, by assuring "the individual whose property is searched or seized of the lawful authority of the executing officer, his need to search, and the limits of his power to search." Reflecting this preference for the warrant process, the traditional standard for review of an issuing magistrate's probable-cause determination has been that so long as the magistrate had a "substantial basis for * * * conclud[ing]" that a search would uncover evidence of wrongdoing, the Fourth Amendment requires no more. We think reaffirmation of this standard better serves the purpose of encouraging recourse to the warrant procedure and is more consistent with our traditional deference to the probable-cause determinations of magistrates than is the "two-pronged test."

Finally, the direction taken by decisions following *Spinelli* poorly serves "[t]he most basic function of any government": "to provide for the security of the individual and of his property." The strictures that inevitably accompany the "two-pronged test" cannot avoid seriously impeding the task of law enforcement. If, as the Illinois Supreme Court apparently thought, that test must be rigorously applied in every case, anonymous tips would be of greatly diminished value in police work. * * * Yet, such tips, particularly when supplemented by independent police investigation, frequently contribute to the solution of otherwise "perfect crimes." While a conscientious assessment of the basis for crediting such tips is required by the Fourth Amendment, a standard that leaves virtually no place for anonymous citizen informants is not.

For all these reasons, we conclude that it is wiser to abandon the "two-pronged test" established by our decisions in *Aguilar* and *Spinelli*. In its place we reaffirm the totality-of-the-circumstances analysis that traditionally has informed probable-cause determinations. The task of the issuing magistrate is simply to make a practical, common-sense decision whether, given all the circumstances set forth in the affidavit before him, including the "veracity" and "basis of knowledge" of persons supplying hearsay information, there is a fair probability that contraband or evidence of a crime will be found in a particular place. And the duty of a reviewing court is simply to ensure that the magistrate had a "substantial basis for * * * conclud[ing]" that probable cause existed. We are convinced that this flexible, easily applied standard will better achieve the accommodation of public and private interests that the Fourth Amendment requires than does the approach that has developed from *Aguilar* and *Spinelli*.

Our earlier cases illustrate the limits beyond which a magistrate may not venture in issuing a warrant. A sworn statement of an affiant that "he has cause to suspect and does believe" that liquor illegally brought into the United States is located on certain premises will not do. *Nathanson v. United States*. An affidavit must provide the magistrate with a substantial basis for determining the existence of probable cause, and the wholly conclusory statement at issue in *Nathanson* failed to meet this requirement. * * * Sufficient information must be presented to the magistrate to allow that official to determine probable cause; his action cannot be a mere ratification of the bare conclusions of others. In order to ensure that such an abdication of the magistrate's duty does not occur, courts must continue to conscientiously review the sufficiency of affidavits on which warrants are issued. But when we move beyond the "bare bones" affidavits present in cases such as *Nathanson* and *Aguilar*, this area simply does not lend itself to a prescribed set of rules, like that which had developed from *Spinelli*. Instead, the flexible, common-sense standard * * * better serves the purposes of the Fourth Amendment's probable-cause requirement. * * *

IV

Our decisions applying the totality-of-the-circumstances analysis outlined above have consistently recognized the value of corroboration of details of an informant's tip by independent police work. * * *

Our decision in *Draper v. United States* [358 U.S. 307, 79 S.Ct. 329, 3 L.Ed.2d 327 (1959)] * * * is the classic case on the value of corroborative efforts of police officials. [In *Draper*, an informant provided police "with minute particularity" information about the upcoming train travel of the defendant. In addition, the informant described what Draper would be wearing, including the type of bag (allegedly carrying illegal drugs) he would be carrying. Before arresting Draper, the officer was able to observe the defendant arriving at the specified time, dressed precisely as described, with the bag in hand]. * * *

The showing of probable cause in the present case was fully as compelling as that in *Draper*. Even standing alone, the facts obtained through the independent investigation of Mader and the DEA at least suggested that the Gateses were involved in drug trafficking. In addition to being a popular vacation site, Florida is well known as a source of narcotics and other illegal drugs. Lance Gates' flight to West Palm Beach, his brief, overnight stay in a motel, and apparent immediate return north to Chicago in the family car, conveniently awaiting him in West Palm Beach, is as suggestive of a prearranged drug run, as it is of an ordinary vacation trip.

In addition, the judge could rely on the anonymous letter, which had been corroborated in major part by Mader's efforts—just as had occurred in *Draper*. The Supreme Court of Illinois reasoned that *Draper* involved an informant who had given reliable information on previous occasions, while the honesty and reliability of the anonymous informant in this case were unknown to the Bloomingdale police. While this distinction might be an apt one at the time the Police Department received the anonymous letter, it became far less significant after Mader's independent investigative work occurred. The corroboration of the letter's predictions that the Gateses' car would be in Florida, that Lance Gates would fly to Florida in the next day or so, and that he would drive the car north toward Bloomingdale all indicated, albeit not with certainty, that the informant's other assertions also were true. "[B]ecause an informant is right about some things, he is more probably right about other facts," *Spinelli* (White, J., concurring)—including the claim regarding the Gateses' illegal activity. This may well not be the type of "reliability" or "veracity" necessary to satisfy some views of the "veracity prong" of *Spinelli*, but we think it suffices for the practical, common-sense judgment called for in making a probable-cause determination. It is enough, for purposes of assessing probable cause, that "[c]orroboration through other sources of information reduced the chances of a reckless or prevaricating tale," thus providing "a substantial basis for crediting the hearsay."

Finally, the anonymous letter contained a range of details relating not just to easily obtained facts and conditions existing at the time of the tip, but to future actions of third parties ordinarily not easily predicted. The letterwriter's accurate information as to the travel plans of each of the Gateses was of a character likely obtained only from the Gateses themselves, or from someone familiar with their not entirely ordinary travel plans. If the informant had access to accurate information of this type a magistrate could properly conclude that it was not unlikely that he also had access to reliable information of the Gateses' alleged illegal activities. Of course, the Gateses' travel plans might have been learned from a talkative neighbor or travel agent; under the "two-pronged test" developed from *Spinelli*, the character of the details in the anonymous letter might well not permit a sufficiently clear inference regarding the letterwriter's "basis of knowledge." But, as discussed previously, probable cause does not demand the certainty we associate with formal trials. It is enough that there was a fair probability that the writer of the anonymous letter had obtained his entire story either from the Gates or someone they trusted. And corroboration of major portions of the letter's predictions provides just this probability. * * *

Reversed.

JUSTICE WHITE, concurring in the judgment. * * *

III

* * * Abandoning the "two-pronged test" of *Aguilar v. Texas* and *Spinelli v. United States*, the Court upholds the validity of the warrant under a new "totality of the circumstances" approach. Although I agree that the warrant should be upheld, I reach this conclusion in accordance with the *Aguilar-Spinelli* framework.

A * * *

In the present case, it is undisputed that the anonymous tip, by itself, did not furnish probable cause. The question is whether those portions of the affidavit describing the results of the police investigation of the respondents, when considered in light of the tip, "would permit the suspicions engendered by the informant's report to ripen into a judgment that a crime was probably being committed." *Spinelli*, *supra*. The Illinois Supreme Court concluded that the corroboration was insufficient to permit such a ripening. * * *

In my view, the lower court's characterization of the Gateses' activity here as totally "innocent" is dubious. In fact, the behavior was quite suspicious. I agree with the Court that Lance Gates' flight to West Palm Beach, an area known to be a source of narcotics, the brief overnight stay in a motel, and apparent immediate return north, suggest a pattern that trained law enforcement officers have recognized as indicative of illicit drug-dealing activity.

Even, however, had the corroboration related only to completely innocuous activities, this fact alone would not preclude the issuance of a valid warrant. The critical issue is not whether the activities observed by the police are innocent or suspicious. Instead, the proper focus should be on whether the actions of the suspects, whatever their nature, give rise to an inference that the informant is credible and that he obtained his information in a reliable manner. * * *

As in *Draper*, the police investigation in the present case satisfactorily demonstrated that the informant's tip was as trustworthy as one that would alone satisfy the *Aguilar* tests. The tip predicted that Sue Gates would drive to Florida, that Lance Gates would fly there a few days after May 3, and that Lance would then drive the car back. After the police corroborated these facts, the judge could reasonably have inferred, as he apparently did, that the informant, who had specific knowledge of these unusual travel plans, did not make up his story and that he obtained his information in a reliable way. It is theoretically possible, as respondents insist, that the tip could have been supplied by a "vindictive travel agent" and that the Gateses' activities, although unusual, might not have been unlawful. But *Aguilar* and *Spinelli*, like our other cases, do not require that certain guilt be established before a warrant may properly be issued. * * * I therefore conclude that the judgment of the Illinois Supreme Court invalidating the warrant must be reversed.

B

The Court agrees that the warrant was valid, but, in the process of reaching this conclusion, it overrules the *Aguilar-Spinelli* tests and replaces them with a "totality of the circumstances" standard. As shown above, it is not at all necessary to overrule *Aguilar-Spinelli* in order to reverse the judgment below. Therefore, because I am inclined to believe that, when applied properly, the *Aguilar-Spinelli* rules play an appropriate role in probable-cause determinations, and because the Court's holding may foretell an evisceration of the probable-cause standard, I do not join the Court's holding.

The Court reasons that the "veracity" and "basis of knowledge" tests are not independent, and that a deficiency as to one can be compensated for by a strong showing as to the other. Thus, a finding of probable cause may be based on a tip from an informant "known for the unusual reliability of his predictions" or from "an unquestionably honest citizen," even if the report fails thoroughly to set forth the basis upon which the information was obtained. If this is so, then it must follow *a fortiori* that "the affidavit of an officer, known by the magistrate to be honest and experienced, stating that [contraband] is located in a certain building" must be acceptable. It would be "quixotic" if a similar statement from an honest informant, but not one from an honest officer, could furnish probable cause. But we have repeatedly held that the unsupported assertion or belief of an officer does not satisfy the probable-cause requirement. Thus, this portion of today's holding can be read as implicitly rejecting the teachings of these prior holdings.

The Court may not intend so drastic a result. Indeed, the Court expressly reaffirms the validity of cases such as *Nathanson* that have held that, no matter how reliable the affiant-officer may be, a warrant should not be issued unless the affidavit discloses supporting facts and circumstances. The Court limits these cases to situations involving affidavits containing only "bare conclusions" and holds that, if an affidavit contains anything more, it should be left to the issuing magistrate to decide, based solely on "practical[ity]" and "common sense," whether there is a fair probability that contraband will be found in a particular place.

Thus, as I read the majority opinion, it appears that the question whether the probable-cause standard is to be diluted is left to the common-sense judgments of issuing magistrates. I am reluctant to approve any standard that does not expressly require, as a prerequisite to issuance of a warrant, some showing of facts from which an inference may be drawn that the informant is credible and that his information was obtained in a reliable way. * * * Hence, I do not join the Court's opinion rejecting the *Aguilar-Spinelli* rules.

JUSTICE BRENNAN, with whom JUSTICE MARSHALL joins, dissenting. * * *

I * * *

In recognition of the judiciary's role as the only effective guardian of Fourth Amendment rights, this Court has developed over the last half century a set of coherent rules governing a magistrate's consideration of a warrant application and the showings that are necessary to support a finding of probable cause. We start with the proposition that a neutral and detached magistrate, and not the police, should determine whether there is probable cause to support the issuance of a warrant. * * *

In order to emphasize the magistrate's role as an independent arbiter of probable cause and to insure that searches or seizures are not effected on less than probable cause, the Court has insisted that police officers provide magistrates with the underlying facts and circumstances that support the officers' conclusions. * * *

Although the rules drawn from the cases * * * are cast in procedural terms, they advance an important underlying substantive value: Findings of probable cause, and attendant intrusions, should not be authorized unless there is some assurance that the information on which they are based has been obtained in a reliable way by an honest or credible person. As applied to police officers, the rules focus on the way in which the information was acquired. As applied to informants, the rules focus both on the honesty or credibility of the informant and on the reliability of the way in which the information was acquired. Insofar as it is more complicated, an evaluation of affidavits based on hearsay involves a more difficult inquiry. This suggests a need to structure the inquiry in an effort to insure greater accuracy. The standards announced in *Aguilar*, as refined by *Spinelli*, fulfill that need. * * *

II * * *

At the heart of the Court's decision to abandon *Aguilar* and *Spinelli* appears to be its belief that "the direction taken by decisions following *Spinelli* poorly serves '[t]he most basic function of any government': 'to provide for the security of the individual and of his property.' " This conclusion rests on the judgment that *Aguilar* and *Spinelli* "seriously imped[e] the task of law enforcement," and render anonymous tips valueless in police work. Surely, the Court overstates its case. But of particular concern to all Americans must be that the Court gives virtually no consideration to the value of insuring that findings of probable cause are based on information that a magistrate can reasonably say has been obtained in a reliable way by an honest or credible person. I share Justice White's fear that the Court's rejection of *Aguilar* and *Spinelli* and its adoption of a new totality-of-the-circumstances test, "may foretell an evisceration of the probable-cause standard * * *." * * *

JUSTICE STEVENS, with whom JUSTICE BRENNAN joins, dissenting.

The fact that Lance and Sue Gates made a 22-hour nonstop drive from West Palm Beach, Florida, to Bloomingdale, Illinois, only a few hours after Lance had flown to Florida provided persuasive evidence that they were engaged in illicit activity. That fact, however, was not known to the judge when he issued the warrant to search their home.

What the judge did know at that time was that the anonymous informant had not been completely accurate in his or her predictions. The informant had indicated that "Sue * * * drives their car to Florida *where she leaves it to be loaded up with drugs * * *. Sue fl[ies] back after she drops the car off in Florida.*" Yet Detective Mader's affidavit reported that she " 'left the West Palm Beach area driving the Mercury northbound.' "

The discrepancy between the informant's predictions and the facts known to Detective Mader is significant for three reasons. First, it cast doubt on the informant's hypothesis that the Gates already had " 'over [$100,000] worth of drugs in their basement.' " The informant had predicted an itinerary that always kept one spouse in Bloomingdale, suggesting that the Gates did not want to leave their home unguarded because something valuable was hidden within. That inference obviously could not be drawn when it was known that the pair was actually together over a thousand miles from home.

Second, the discrepancy made the Gates' conduct seem substantially less unusual than the informant had predicted it would be. It would have been odd if, as predicted, Sue had driven down to Florida on Wednesday, left the car, and flown right back to Illinois. But the mere facts that Sue was in West Palm Beach with the car, that she was joined by her husband at the Holiday Inn on Friday, and that the couple drove north together the next morning are neither unusual nor probative of criminal activity.

Third, the fact that the anonymous letter contained a material mistake undermines the reasonableness of relying on it as a basis for making a forcible entry into a private home.

Of course, the activities in this case did not stop when the judge issued the warrant. The Gates drove all night to Bloomingdale, the officers searched the car and found 400 pounds of marihuana, and then they searched the house. However, none of these subsequent events may be considered in evaluating the warrant, and the search of the house was legal only if the warrant was valid. I cannot accept the Court's casual conclusion that, *before the Gates arrived in Bloomingdale*, there was probable cause to justify a valid entry and search of a private home. * * * I must surmise that the Court's evaluation of the warrant's validity has been colored by subsequent events. * * *

NOTES AND QUESTIONS

1. Suppose that your professor announced in class that the Dean of your college "has cocaine in her office, which she uses every morning." Based exclusively on this statement, would you believe your professor's claim? If not, why not? If you were a magistrate, and you were told this under oath by your professor, would you issue a warrant to search the dean's office? If not, what more information would you demand? Are the facts you considered in making a judgment in your dean's case similar to those set out by the Supreme Court in *Gates*? In *Aguilar-Spinelli*?

2. *A bit more on Sue and Lance Gates and the anonymous informant.* According to Professor Thomas Davies, the anonymous informant was Sue Gates's beautician, who was infuriated at her client's frequent boasts about not working. Davies reports that "the hairdresser called the police after the case made the Chicago papers, and said that she would have signed the letter if she knew how much trouble she was causing!" (E-mail correspondence from Davies to author Dressler, January 24, 2001.)

Susan and Lance Gates pleaded guilty to the drug charges. "[N]ot exactly a Bonnie & Clyde operation," according to Professor Davies, and neither Sue nor Lance has reportedly been prosecuted in the intervening years.

3. Is the *Gates* case an example of good law enforcement? The anonymous informant stated "I guarantee *if you watch them carefully* you will make a big catch. They are friends with some big drug *dealers, who visit their house often*." According to one

scholar, "[o]ut of the mouths of babes and anonymous informants sometimes comes wisdom." Yale Kamisar, Gates*, "Probable Cause," "Good Faith," and Beyond*, 69 Iowa L. Rev. 551, 576 (1984). Professor Kamisar reasons that if the police had been more patient they would have satisfied the two-pronged standard and, perhaps more importantly, have apprehended "big drug dealers."

4. Suppose a friend you have known for years and who has proven to be a truthful individual alleges illegal behavior by another individual whom you do not know. Notice: here the veracity prong is satisfied, but the basis-of-knowledge prong has not been proven. Would you still believe your friend's allegations?

What if a stranger tells you he personally observed criminal behavior by another individual (whom you also do not know), even setting out very specific details of what he observed. Here, the basis-of-knowledge is provided, but the veracity prong is not satisfied. Would you believe the stranger?

Do your answers suggest the *Gates* Court was right to abandon the strict two-pronged test of *Aguilar-Spinelli*?

5. The police often use informants to obtain critical information in criminal investigations. In one study in the San Diego Judicial District, for example, 63.9% of search warrant affidavits contained information provided by informants. Laurence A. Benner & Charles T. Samarkos, *Searching for Narcotics in San Diego: Preliminary Findings from the San Diego Search Warrant Project*, 36 Cal. Western L. Rev. 221, 239 (2000). However, in half of the cases the affiant did not personally know the informant. That is, "the officer simply related information given him by another officer who did not join in signing the affidavit. Thus, Officer A swears under oath that Officer B told him that there was [a confidential informant] who gave him certain information." *Id.* at 241. Thus, the magistrate was receiving double hearsay. What problems do you see in this?

6. *The "confidential informant": How confidential is he?* The police rarely disclose the identity of their informants—many of whom provide information on a regular basis—to magistrates in warrant applications. In McCray v. Illinois, 386 U.S. 300, 87 S.Ct. 1056, 18 L.Ed.2d 62 (1967), the Supreme Court ruled that the due process clause does not require a judge in every probable cause or evidence-suppression hearing to compel disclosure of the informant's identity. In reaching this conclusion the Court quoted the following reasoning of the New Jersey Supreme Court in State v. Burnett, 42 N.J. 377, 201 A.2d 39 (1964):

> If a defendant may insist upon disclosure of the informant in order to test the truth of the officer's statement that there is an informant or as to what the informant related or as to the informant's reliability, we can be sure that every defendant will demand disclosure. He has nothing to lose

> and the prize may be the suppression of damaging evidence if the State cannot afford to reveal its source, as is so often the case. * * *
>
> The Fourth Amendment is served if a judicial mind passes upon the existence of probable cause. Where the issue is submitted upon an application for a warrant, the magistrate is trusted to evaluate the credibility of the affiant in an *ex parte* proceeding. * * * If the magistrate doubts the credibility of the affiant, he may require that the informant be identified or even produced.

7. *The "oath and affirmation" requirement of the Fourth Amendment.* A police officer-affiant is ordinarily considered reliable because she provides her information under oath. But, suppose that the defendant fears that the officer lied under oath to the judge who issued a search warrant? Perhaps the defense believes that the affiant lied to the judge as to what she personally observed, or made up the existence of an informant, or lied as to a real informant's reliability, or knew or should have known that the informant's claims were false. What may the defendant do to attack a warrant in such circumstances?

The Fourth Amendment provides that warrants, founded on probable cause, must be "supported by Oath or affirmation." The Supreme Court held in Franks v. Delaware, 438 U.S. 154, 98 S.Ct. 2674, 57 L.Ed.2d 667 (1978), that in view of this requirement, a defendant may challenge the truthfulness of statements made under oath in an affidavit supporting a warrant under limited circumstances. *Franks* explains the procedure:

> [W]here the defendant makes a substantial preliminary showing that a false statement knowing and intentionally, or with reckless disregard for the truth, was included by the affiant in the warrant affidavit, the Fourth Amendment requires that a hearing be held at the defendant's request. In the event that at that hearing the allegation of perjury or reckless disregard is established * * * by a preponderance of the evidence, and, with the affidavit's false material set to one side, the affidavit's remaining content is insufficient to establish probable cause, the search warrant must be voided and the fruits of the search excluded to the same extent as if probable cause was lacking on the face of the affidavit.

Franks does not authorize a special hearing if a defendant claims that the *informant* lied to an *innocent* affiant. Do you see why this is so?

8. *Preference for the warrant process.* As noted in *Gates*, the constitutionally preferable arbiter of probable cause is a "neutral and detached magistrate," rather than a police officer "engaged in the often competitive enterprise of ferreting out crime." Johnson v. United States, 333 U.S. 10, 68 S.Ct. 367, 92 L.Ed. 436 (1948). In order to

provide the police with an incentive to seek warrants, the Supreme Court has stated that "the resolution of doubtful or marginal cases [of probable cause] * * * should be largely determined by the preference to be accorded to warrants." United States v. Ventresca, 380 U.S. 102, 85 S.Ct. 741, 13 L.Ed.2d 684 (1965). In other words, in close cases, a search pursuant to a warrant may be upheld where, without one, it would not be.

9. *How probable is "probable cause"? Gates* eschewed the quantification of any "precise degree of certainty corresponding to 'probable cause'." The Court has stated, however, that the standard does *not* "demand any showing that such a belief be * * * more likely true than false." Texas v. Brown, 460 U.S. 730, 103 S.Ct. 1535, 75 L.Ed.2d 502 (1983). As Professor Sherry Colb has put it:

> We do not know exactly what the phrase "probable cause" means, in strict numerical terms. We do, however, know what it does *not* mean: "probably." That is, probable cause does not—in the context of Fourth Amendment law—mean that the police must have evidence sufficient to conclude that a suspect is *probably* guilty or that she *probably* has evidence of a crime inside her home.

Sherry F. Colb, *Probabilities in Probable Cause and Beyond: Statistical Versus Concrete Harms*, 73 Law & Contemp. Probs. 69, 71 (2010).

Should this be the rule? What if the police have extremely solid evidence, amounting to near certainty, that one (but only one) of two identical twins committed a particular offense? (For real-life examples of this, see Jess Bidgood, *New DNA Test Sought in Identical Twin's Rape Case*, New York Times, Sept. 16, 2014; and Marc Lacey, *Identical Twins, One Charged in a Fatal Shooting, Create Confusion for the Police*, New York Times (National Edition), August 9, 2011.) In light of *Brown*, *supra*, should the police arrest *both* of the twins, even though they know one of them is innocent? If not, should they flip a coin and arrest the unlucky one? What if we are dealing with triplets? In this regard consider this true case recounted to the authors of this casebook by Professor Neil Cohen:

> A few years ago I got a call from a judge who had this case. Very late at night on a rural dark road a police officer spotted a car driving erratically. The officer * * * pulled over the car. * * * When the officer shined his flashlight in the car, he found three young men "asleep" in the back seat. No one was in the front seat. He "awakened" them and all said the same thing: They had been at a party, drank too much, and fell asleep in the back seat of the car. Each denied knowing who the driver was. The officer had kept the car in eyesight the entire time and was confident that no one had gotten out of it. All three of the young men were drunk.

Was there probable cause to charge anyone with driving the vehicle under the influence of alcohol? What *should* the answer be? Do you believe, as one commentator has written about a one-in-ten, rather than one-in-three, situation, "[t]he question is whether one may reasonably expect—indeed, require—each suspect to sacrifice some liberty or privacy in order to unmask the offender. I think we can. In constitutional language, I would say that probable cause exists to arrest or search each suspect." Joseph D. Grano, *Probable Cause and Common Sense: A Reply to the Critics of* Illinois v. Gates, 17 U. Mich. J.L. Reform 465, 497 (1984).

Now consider Maryland v. Pringle, 540 U.S. 366, 124 S.Ct. 795, 157 L.Ed.2d 769 (2003). In *Pringle*, an officer lawfully stopped a speeding vehicle occupied by three men. As a result of a lawful search, the officer discovered a large amount of rolled-up money in the glove compartment, and five baggies of cocaine hidden in the back-seat armrest and elsewhere in the back seat. The officer questioned the men about the ownership of the drugs and warned them that if they did not answer he would arrest all three of them for possession of the cocaine, which he did when nobody admitted ownership. The Supreme Court unanimously upheld Pringle's arrest:

> We think it an entirely reasonable inference from [the] facts of the case that any or all three of the occupants had knowledge of, and exercised dominion and control over, the cocaine. [Under state law, "possession" of property exists if one or more persons has "actual or constructive dominion or control" over the property—Eds.] Thus a reasonable officer could conclude that there was probable cause to believe Pringle committed the crime of possession of cocaine, either solely or jointly.

Does this case resolve the triplet hypothetical or the three-drunks-in-the-back-seat case?

Finally, consider the common law role of magistrates in issuing warrants. There is evidence that no fixed standards governed the magistrates' decision whether to issue a warrant. Lord Hale put the mater thusly: "It is convenient, tho not always necessary, to take an information upon oath of the person that desires the warrant, that a felony was committed, that he doth suspect or know [who is] the felon; and if suspected, then to set down the causes of his suspicion." 1 Matthew Hale, Please of the Crown (1736). Hale's language, replicated in many early colonial form books and manuals, suggests that the magistrate's decision was final and unreviewable. See Fabio Arcila, Jr., *In the Trenches: Searches and the Misunderstood Common-Law History of Suspicion and Probable Cause*, 10 U. Pa. J. Const. L. 1 (2007).

10. *Bobo, a police officer's friendly four-legged informant.* In United States v. Florez, 871 F.Supp. 1411 (D.N.M. 1994), a police officer's dog, Bobo, sniffed luggage in a train station and alerted the officer to the supposed presence of a controlled substance

inside certain suitcases. The police seized the luggage, opened it, and discovered large quantities of cocaine.

Bobo got it right, but dogs, like humans, are imperfect. As Justice Souter stated in his dissent in Illinois v. Caballes, 543 U.S. 405, 125 S.Ct. 834, 160 L.Ed.2d 842 (2005), "the infallible dog * * * is a creature of legal fiction." As a dog trainer testified in *Florez, supra*, "dogs are not unlike humans, dogs can have good and bad days just like we can." Indeed, reconsider the data on "dog sniffing" recounted by Justice Souter in *Caballes* (p. 108, Note 5). And note the observation of the Seventh Circuit in a recent case regarding canine Lex: "Lex is lucky the Canine Training Institute doesn't calculate class rank. If it did, Lex would have been at the bottom of the class." United States v. Bentley, 795 F.3d 630 (7th Cir. 2015). So how *should* a court go about evaluating the reliability of the Bobos and Lexes of this world?

The United States Supreme Court recently spoke to this issue, albeit in regard to one Aldo, rather than Bobo or Lex. In Florida v. Harris, 568 U.S. 237, 133 S.Ct. 1050, 185 L.Ed.2d 61 (2013), the state supreme court stated that the fact that a dog "has been trained and certified is simply not enough to establish probable cause." It ruled that the government is such a case must present evidence of the "dogs training and certification records, * * * field performance records (including any unverified alerts) and evidence concerning the experience and training of the officer handling the dog."

The Supreme Court, per Justice Kagan, unanimously reversed the Florida court. According to the Court, "evidence of a dog's satisfactory performance in a certification or training program can itself provide sufficient reason to trust his alert." Indeed, Justice Kagan observed that evidence of certification of successful training is apt to be more useful information than records of a dog's field performance:

> Errors abound in such records. If a dog on patrol fails to alert to a car containing drugs, the mistake will usually go undetected because the officer will not initiate a search. Field data thus may not capture a dog's false negatives. Conversely, * * * if the dog alerts to a car in which the officer finds no narcotics, the dog may not have made a mistake at all. The dog may have detected substances that were too well hidden or present in quantities too small for the officer to locate. Or the dog may have smelled the residual odor of drugs previously in the vehicle or on the driver's person.

Justice Kagan stated that, "[i]n short, a probable-cause hearing focusing on a dog's alert should proceed like any other."

11. *A "sliding scale" of probable cause?* In Schmerber v. California, 384 U.S. 757, 86 S.Ct. 1826, 16 L.Ed.2d 908 (1966), the Supreme Court observed that the taking of a blood sample from a motorist arrested for drunk driving, because it involves an

intrusion into a human body, is a more offensive type of search than the ordinary type and, therefore, requires "a clear indication that in fact such evidence [of intoxication] will be found." One can interpret this latter language as, perhaps, requiring "probable cause plus," i.e., a heightened degree of likelihood of discovering evidence when the police wish to conduct such a hyper-intrusive search. And, indeed, in Winston v. Lee, 470 U.S. 753, 105 S.Ct. 1611, 84 L.Ed.2d 662 (1985), a case in which the police sought a warrant to compel a surgical intrusion into a suspect's body in order to seize a bullet that might incriminate him, the Court stated that "when the State seeks to intrude upon an area in which our society recognizes a significantly heightened privacy interest, a more substantial justification is required" to authorize such a search. That standard was not met in *Winston* and the State was unable to force the suspect to undergo surgery to remove the bullet.

Does this suggest, therefore, a sliding scale of "probable cause"? And, if so, one may expect that the sliding scale could work in both directions. Might there be cases in which "probable cause" requires *less* than the ordinary degree of proof?

Consider this scenario: The police have a credible report that an atomic bomb, smaller than a suitcase, has been smuggled into New York City. The bomb, if detonated, will kill thousands of persons and make the city uninhabitable for generations. The report is confirmed by use of radiation sensors, which determine that the bomb is hidden in one of 100 homes. Therefore, Homeland Security officials search all 100 homes simultaneously. Ronald M. Gould & Simon Stern, *Catastrophic Threats and the Fourth Amendment*, 77 S. Cal. L. Rev. 777, 779 (2004). Did the government act with "probable cause"? Would your answer be the same if police instead searched the same houses for a small stash of cocaine, based on the same likelihood of success?

Does your response to these hypotheticals suggest that the Court is right in suggesting that "probable cause" should be a fluid concept—that there should be a sliding scale of probable cause? Can you suggest a plausible Fourth Amendment textual argument for such a distinction?

12. *Probable cause as an objective concept.* According to the Supreme Court, "evenhanded law enforcement is best achieved by the application of objective standards of conduct, rather than standards that depend upon the subjective state of mind of the [police] officer." Horton v. California, 496 U.S. 128, 110 S.Ct. 2301, 110 L.Ed.2d 112 (1990). Therefore, as will be developed more fully later, the Supreme Court has stated that an officer's "state of mind (except for the facts that he knows) is irrelevant to the existence of probable cause." Devenpeck v. Alford, 543 U.S. 146, 125 S.Ct. 588, 160 L.Ed.2d 537 (2004). As the Court held in *Devenpeck,* an arrest is lawful, even if an officer incorrectly believes he has probable cause to arrest a person

for Crime A (and, therefore, makes such an arrest), if based on the facts known to the arresting officer, probable cause objectively exists to arrest for Crime B.

13. *Self-proving probable cause.* Notice that probable cause issues are litigated in criminal cases only when the search or arrest produces evidence of a crime. The search of the car and home of Lance and Sue Gates uncovered hundreds of pounds of marijuana, other contraband, and weapons. This is bound to have at least a little influence on judges who hear motions to suppress. To remove that self-proving effect, here are some problems in which you do not know whether the police action produced evidence.

A. A mother reported to the police that her three-year-old son told her that *S*, an adult, had sexually touched him on his penis ("he touched my pee-pee"). Is this sufficient grounds to arrest *S* for child sexual abuse? United States v. Shaw, 464 F.3d 615 (6th Cir. 2006).

B. Ready for a little 1940s *film noir*? Here is how Chief Justice Roberts described the facts in Pennsylvania v. Dunlap, 555 U.S. 964, 129 S.Ct. 448, 172 L.Ed.2d 321 (2008) (dissenting from denial of certiorari):

> North Philly, May 4, 2001. Officer Sean Devlin, Narcotics Strike Force, was working the morning shift. Undercover surveillance. The neighborhood? Tough as a three-dollar steak. Devlin knew. Five years on the beat, nine months with the Strike Force. He'd made fifteen, twenty drug busts in the neighborhood. Devlin spotted him: a lone man on the corner. Another approached. Quick exchange of words. Cash handed over; small objects handed back. Each man then quickly on his own way. Devlin knew the guy wasn't buying bus tokens. He radioed a description and Officer Stein picked up the buyer. Sure enough: three bags of crack in the guy's pocket. Head downtown and book him. Just another day at the office.

Do these facts support a finding of probable cause to arrest the man (who handed over cash) for the offense of possession of illegal drugs, although Officer Devlin did not see any drugs transferred?

C. Two adult men accused *B*, an Episcopal priest and former chaplain of a boarding school, of sexual abuse sixteen years earlier when they were teenagers. The police sought a warrant to search *B*'s home (a different home) for a footlocker that the complainants stated had, by their observation at the time of the crimes, contained pornographic material, photographs of sodomy performed on them, and sexual aids used on them in the sexual abuse. Probable cause? Behrel v. State, 151 Md.App. 64, 823 A.2d 696 (2003).

B. ARREST WARRANTS

PAYTON V. NEW YORK

Supreme Court of the United States, 1980.
445 U.S. 573, 100 S.Ct. 1371, 63 L.Ed.2d 639.

We know from our readings about the Fourth Amendment that one's home holds a special consideration when determining whether or not a search violates one's privacy. But what about an arrest—a seizure of one's person. After all, the Fourth Amendment prohibits *unreasonable* searches *and* seizures. The short answer laid out in our next case: similar rules apply. By the time of *Payton*, it is well-settled law that an arrest can be made of a suspect in a public place without a warrant, assuming there is probable cause to believe the suspect has committed a crime. But what if, absent exigent circumstances (discussed in the next chapter), an officer wants to arrest the suspect inside *his or her* home (for what happens when the suspect is in someone else's home, see Note 6). Can the officer do so without an arrest warrant? What if the officer has a search warrant to search the home for the suspect, but does not have an arrest warrant. The answer is: . . . well, see for yourself.

MR. JUSTICE STEVENS delivered the opinion of the Court [joined by JUSTICES BRENNAN, STEWART, MARSHALL, BLACKMUN, and POWELL].

These appeals challenge the constitutionality of New York statutes that authorize police officers to enter a private residence without a warrant and with force, if necessary, to make a routine felony arrest.

The important constitutional question presented by this challenge has been expressly left open in a number of our prior opinions. In *United States v. Watson*, 423 U.S. 411, 96 S.Ct. 820, 46 L.Ed.2d 598 [1976], we upheld a warrantless "midday public arrest," expressly noting that the case did not pose "the still unsettled question * * * 'whether and under what circumstances an officer may enter a suspect's home to make a warrantless arrest.' " * * *

I

On January 14, 1970, after two days of intensive investigation, New York detectives had assembled evidence sufficient to establish probable cause to believe that Theodore Payton had murdered the manager of a gas station two days earlier. At about 7:30 a.m. on January 15, six officers went to Payton's apartment in the Bronx, intending to arrest him. They had not obtained a warrant. Although light and music emanated from the apartment, there was no response to their knock on the metal door. They summoned emergency assistance and, about 30 minutes later, used crowbars to break open the door and enter the apartment. No one was there. In plain view, however, was a .30-caliber shell casing that was seized and later admitted into evidence at Payton's murder trial.

In due course Payton surrendered to the police, was indicted for murder, and moved to suppress the evidence taken from his apartment. The trial judge held that the warrantless and forcible entry was authorized by the New York Code of Criminal Procedure, and that the evidence in plain view was properly seized. * * *

On March 14, 1974, Obie Riddick was arrested for the commission of two armed robberies that had occurred in 1971. He had been identified by the victims in June 1973, and in January 1974 the police had learned his address. They did not obtain a warrant for his arrest. At about noon on March 14, a detective, accompanied by three other officers, knocked on the door of the Queens house where Riddick was living. When his young son opened the door, they could see Riddick sitting in bed covered by a sheet. They entered the house and placed him under arrest. Before permitting him to dress, they opened a chest of drawers two feet from the bed in search of weapons and found narcotics and related paraphernalia. Riddick was subsequently indicted on narcotics charges. At a suppression hearing, the trial judge held that the warrantless entry into his home was authorized by the revised New York statute, and that the search of the immediate area [as an incident of the arrest] was reasonable under *Chimel v. California*, 395 U.S. 752, 89 S.Ct. 2034, 23 L.Ed.2d 685. * * *

Before addressing the narrow question presented by these appeals, we put to one side other related problems that are *not* presented today. Although it is arguable that the warrantless entry to effect Payton's arrest might have been justified by exigent circumstances, none of the New York courts relied on any such justification. * * * Accordingly, we have no occasion to consider the sort of emergency or dangerous situation, described in our cases as "exigent circumstances," that would justify a warrantless entry into a home for the purpose of either arrest or search.

Nor do these cases raise any question concerning the authority of the police, without either a search or arrest warrant, to enter a third party's home to arrest a suspect. The police broke into Payton's apartment intending to arrest Payton, and they arrested Riddick in his own dwelling. We also note that in neither case is it argued that the police lacked probable cause to believe that the suspect was at home when they entered. Finally, in both cases we are dealing with entries into homes made without the consent of any occupant. In *Payton*, the police used crowbars to break down the door and in *Riddick*, although his 3-year-old son answered the door, the police entered before Riddick had an opportunity either to object or to consent.

II

It is familiar history that indiscriminate searches and seizures conducted under the authority of "general warrants" were the immediate evils that motivated the framing and adoption of the Fourth Amendment. Indeed, as originally proposed in the House of Representatives, the draft contained only one clause, which directly imposed limitations on the issuance of warrants, but imposed no express restrictions on warrantless searches or seizures. As it was ultimately adopted, however, the Amendment contained two separate clauses, the first protecting the basic right to be free from unreasonable searches and seizures and the second requiring that warrants be particular and supported by probable cause. * * *

It is thus perfectly clear that the evil the Amendment was designed to prevent was broader than the abuse of a general warrant. Unreasonable searches or seizures conducted without any warrant at all are condemned by the plain language of the first clause of the Amendment. Almost a century ago the Court stated in resounding terms that the principles reflected in the Amendment "reached farther than the concrete form" of the specific cases that gave it birth, and "apply to all invasions on the part of the government and its employees of the sanctity of a man's home and the privacies of life." *Boyd v. United States*, 116 U.S. 616, 630, 6 S.Ct. 524, 532, 29 L.Ed. 746. * * *

It is a "basic principle of Fourth Amendment law" that searches and seizures inside a home without a warrant are presumptively unreasonable. Yet it is also well settled that objects such as weapons or contraband found in a public place may be seized by the police without a warrant. The seizure of property in plain view involves no invasion of privacy and is presumptively reasonable, assuming that there is probable cause to associate the property with criminal activity. The distinction between a warrantless seizure in an open area and such a seizure on private premises was plainly stated in *G. M. Leasing Corp. v. United States*, 429 U.S. 338, 354, 97 S.Ct. 619, 629, 50 L.Ed.2d 530:

> "It is one thing to seize without a warrant property resting in an open area or seizable by levy without an intrusion into privacy, and it is quite another thing to effect a warrantless seizure of property, even that owned by a corporation, situated on private premises to which access is not otherwise available for the seizing officer."

As the late Judge Leventhal recognized, this distinction has equal force when the seizure of a person is involved. Writing on the constitutional issue now before us for the United States Court of Appeals for the District of Columbia Circuit sitting en banc, *Dorman v. United States*, 140 U.S.App.D.C. 313, 435 F.2d 385 (1970), Judge Leventhal first noted the settled rule that warrantless arrests in public places are valid. He immediately recognized, however, that

> "[a] greater burden is placed * * * on officials who enter a home or dwelling without consent. Freedom from intrusion into the home or dwelling is the archetype of the privacy protection secured by the Fourth Amendment."

His analysis of this question then focused on the long-settled premise that, absent exigent circumstances, a warrantless entry to search for weapons or contraband is unconstitutional even when a felony has been committed and there is probable cause to believe that incriminating evidence will be found within. He reasoned that the constitutional protection afforded to the individual's interest in the privacy of his own home is equally applicable to a warrantless entry for the purpose of arresting a resident of the house; for it is inherent in such an entry that a search for the suspect may be required before he can be apprehended. Judge Leventhal concluded that an entry to arrest and an entry to search for and to seize property implicate the same interest in preserving the privacy and the sanctity of the home, and justify the same level of constitutional protection.

* * * We find this reasoning to be persuasive and in accord with this Court's Fourth Amendment decisions.

The majority of the New York Court of Appeals, however, suggested that there is a substantial difference in the relative intrusiveness of an entry to search for property and an entry to search for a person. It is true that the area that may legally be searched is broader when executing a search warrant than when executing an arrest warrant in the home. This difference may be more theoretical than real, however, because the police may need to check the entire premises for safety reasons, and sometimes they ignore the restrictions on searches incident to arrest.

But the critical point is that any differences in the intrusiveness of entries to search and entries to arrest are merely ones of degree rather than kind. The two intrusions share this fundamental characteristic: the breach of the entrance to an individual's home. The Fourth Amendment protects the individual's privacy in a variety of settings. In none is the zone of privacy more clearly defined than when bounded by the unambiguous physical dimensions of an individual's home—a zone that finds its roots in clear and specific constitutional terms: "The right of the people to be secure in their * * * houses * * * shall not be violated." That language unequivocally establishes the proposition that "[a]t the very core [of the Fourth Amendment] stands the right of a man to retreat into his own home and there be free from unreasonable governmental intrusion." In terms that apply equally to seizures of property and to seizures of persons, the Fourth Amendment has drawn a firm line at the entrance to the house. Absent exigent circumstances, that threshold may not reasonably be crossed without a warrant. * * *

IV

The parties have argued at some length about the practical consequences of a warrant requirement as a precondition to a felony arrest in the home. In the absence of any evidence that effective law enforcement has suffered in those States that already have such a requirement, we are inclined to view such arguments with skepticism. More fundamentally, however, such arguments of policy must give way to a constitutional command that we consider to be unequivocal. * * *

Because no arrest warrant was obtained in either of these cases, the judgments must be reversed and the cases remanded to the New York Court of Appeals for further proceedings not inconsistent with this opinion. * * *

[JUSTICE BLACKMUN's concurring opinion is omitted.]

MR. JUSTICE WHITE, with whom THE CHIEF JUSTICE BURGER and MR. JUSTICE REHNQUIST join, dissenting. * * *

I * * *

B

The history of the Fourth Amendment does not support the rule announced today. At the time that Amendment was adopted the constable possessed broad inherent powers to arrest. The limitations on those powers derived, not from a warrant "requirement," but from the generally ministerial nature of the constable's office at common law. Far from restricting the constable's arrest power, the institution of the warrant was used to expand that authority by giving the constable delegated powers of a superior officer such as a justice of the peace. Hence at the time of the Bill of Rights, the warrant functioned as a powerful tool of law enforcement rather than as a protection for the rights of criminal suspects.

In fact, it was the abusive use of the warrant power, rather than any excessive zeal in the discharge of peace officers' inherent authority, that precipitated the Fourth Amendment. * * *

* * * [T]he background, text, and legislative history of the Fourth Amendment demonstrate that the purpose was to restrict the abuses that had developed with respect to warrants; the Amendment preserved common-law rules of arrest. Because it was not considered generally unreasonable at common law for officers to break doors to effect a warrantless felony arrest, I do not believe that the Fourth Amendment was intended to outlaw the types of police conduct at issue in the present cases. * * *

II

A

Today's decision rests, in large measure, on the premise that warrantless arrest entries constitute a particularly severe invasion of personal privacy. I do not dispute that the home is generally a very private area or that the common law displayed a special "reverence * * * for the individual's right of privacy in his house." However, the Fourth Amendment is concerned with protecting people, not places, and no talismanic significance is given to the fact that an arrest occurs in the home rather than elsewhere. * * * The inquiry in the present case, therefore, is whether the incremental intrusiveness that results from an arrest's being made *in the dwelling* is enough to support an inflexible constitutional rule requiring warrants for such arrests whenever exigent circumstances are not present.

Today's decision ignores the carefully crafted restrictions on the common-law power of arrest entry and thereby overestimates the dangers inherent in that practice. At common law, absent exigent circumstances, entries to arrest could be made only for felony. Even in cases of felony, the officers were required to announce their presence, demand admission, and be refused entry before they were entitled to break doors. Further, it seems generally accepted that entries could be made only during daylight hours. And, in my view, the officer entering to arrest must have reasonable grounds to believe, not only that the arrestee has committed a crime, but also that the person suspected is present in the house at the time of the entry.

These four restrictions on home arrests—felony, knock and announce, daytime, and stringent probable cause—constitute powerful and complementary protections for the privacy interests associated with the home. The felony requirement guards against abusive or arbitrary enforcement and ensures that invasions of the home occur only in case of the most serious crimes. The knock-and-announce and daytime requirements protect individuals against the fear, humiliation, and embarrassment of being roused from their beds in states of partial or complete undress. And these requirements allow the arrestee to surrender at his front door, thereby maintaining his dignity and preventing the officers from entering other rooms of the dwelling. The stringent probable-cause requirement would help ensure against the possibility that the police would enter when the suspect was not home, and, in searching for him, frighten members of the family or ransack parts of the house, seizing items in plain view. In short, these requirements, taken together, permit an individual suspected of a serious crime to surrender at the front door of his dwelling and thereby avoid most of the humiliation and indignity that the Court seems to believe necessarily accompany a house arrest entry. Such a front-door arrest, in my view, is no more intrusive on personal privacy than the public warrantless arrests which we found to pass constitutional muster in *Watson*.

* * * The Court substitutes, in one sweeping decision, a rigid constitutional rule in place of the common-law approach, evolved over hundreds of years, which achieved a flexible accommodation between the demands of personal privacy and the legitimate needs of law enforcement. * * *

B

While exaggerating the invasion of personal privacy involved in home arrests, the Court fails to account for the danger that its rule will "severely hamper effective law enforcement." * * *

* * * [P]olice officers will often face the difficult task of deciding whether the circumstances are sufficiently exigent to justify their entry to arrest without a warrant. This is a decision that must be made quickly in the most trying of circumstances. If the officers mistakenly decide that the circumstances are exigent, the arrest will be invalid and any evidence seized incident to the arrest or in plain view will be excluded at trial. On the other hand, if the officers mistakenly determine that exigent circumstances are lacking, they may refrain from making the arrest, thus creating the possibility that a dangerous criminal will escape into the community. The police could reduce the likelihood of escape by staking out all possible exits until the circumstances become clearly exigent or a warrant is obtained. But the costs of such a stakeout seem excessive in an era of rising crime and scarce police resources.

The uncertainty inherent in the exigent-circumstances determination burdens the judicial system as well. * * * Under today's decision, whenever the police have made a warrantless home arrest there will be the possibility of "endless litigation with respect to the existence of exigent circumstances, whether it was practicable to get a warrant, whether the suspect was about to flee, and the like," *United States v. Watson, supra.* * * *

[*Justice Rehnquist's dissenting opinion is omitted.*]

NOTES AND QUESTIONS

1. What interest is served by the arrest warrant requirement? Does *Payton* protect the arrestee's *person* from unlawful seizure or, instead, the resident's interest in freedom from *unlawful invasion of privacy in the dwelling*?

2. Warrant issues aside, *all* arrests, whether conducted in a public place (*Watson*) or made in a private residence (*Payton*), *must* be supported by probable cause. What is the Fourth Amendment textual basis for this rule?

3. Though the colonial historical evidence is murky, it probably supports Justice White's dissent. Does this matter? Should it matter?

4. *Exceptions to the Payton rule.* In Minnesota v. Olson, 495 U.S. 91, 110 S.Ct. 1684, 109 L.Ed.2d 85 (1990), two men robbed a gas station and killed the attendant. The gunman was quickly arrested and the murder weapon retrieved. His accomplice, however, escaped. The next day, the police learned that the second man was hiding with two women in the upper unit of a duplex. Hours later, the police surrounded the dwelling and, without permission or a warrant, entered the upper unit and arrested the suspect. The State sought to justify the warrantless entry on exigency grounds. Justice White, for seven justices, disagreed:

> In *Payton v. New York*, the Court had no occasion to "consider the sort of emergency or dangerous situation, described in our cases as 'exigent circumstances,' that would justify a warrantless entry into a home for the purpose of either arrest or search." This case requires us to determine whether the Minnesota Supreme Court was correct in holding that there were no exigent circumstances that justified the warrantless entry into the house to make the arrest.
>
> The Minnesota Supreme Court applied essentially the correct standard in determining whether exigent circumstances existed. The court observed that "a warrantless intrusion may be justified by hot pursuit of a fleeing felon, or imminent destruction of evidence, or the need to prevent a suspect's escape, or the risk of danger to the police or to other persons inside or outside the dwelling." The court also apparently thought that in the absence of hot pursuit there must be at least probable cause to believe that one or more of the other factors justifying the entry were present and that in assessing the risk of danger, the gravity of the crime and likelihood

> that the suspect is armed should be considered. Applying this standard, the state court determined that exigent circumstances did not exist.
>
> We are not inclined to disagree with this fact-specific application of the proper legal standard. The court pointed out that although a grave crime was involved, respondent "was known not to be the murderer but thought to be the driver of the getaway car," and that the police had already recovered the murder weapon. "The police knew that [two women] were with the suspect in the upstairs duplex with no suggestion of danger to them. Three or four Minneapolis police squads surrounded the house. The time was 3 p.m., Sunday. * * * It was evident the suspect was going nowhere. If he came out of the house he would have been promptly apprehended." We do not disturb the state court's judgment that these facts do not add up to exigent circumstances.

5. *Getting around Payton?* In *Payton*, suppose that Riddick, rather than his 3-year-old son, had come to the door. If the officers had said, "You are under arrest," would this warrantless arrest have been valid? What if they asked him to come outside, he complied, and *then* they arrested him?

Suppose that police surround an individual's residence and, with a bullhorn, order him out of the house, at which point they arrest him (again, without a warrant). Is *Payton* violated?

6. *Arrests in a third person's residence: the Steagald principle.* In Steagald v. United States, 451 U.S. 204, 101 S.Ct. 1642, 68 L.Ed.2d 38 (1981), the police secured a valid warrant to arrest Ricky Lyons, a fugitive, on drug charges. Based on information that Lyons could be found "during the next 24 hours" at the residence of acquaintance Gary Steagald, twelve officers proceeded to the house and entered without consent. They did not find Lyons, but they did observe cocaine belonging to Steagald. Steagald was later indicted on drug charges and sought to suppress the evidence discovered in the search on the ground that the officers entered the premises without a *search* warrant. The Court, per Justice Marshall, agreed:

> The question before us is a narrow one. The search at issue here took place in the absence of consent or exigent circumstances. Except in such special situations, we have consistently held that the entry into a home to conduct a search or make an arrest is unreasonable under the Fourth Amendment unless done pursuant to a warrant. * * * Here, of course, the agents had a warrant—one authorizing the arrest of Ricky Lyons. However, the Fourth Amendment claim here is not being raised by Ricky Lyons. Instead, the challenge to the search is asserted by a person not named in the warrant who was convicted on the basis of evidence uncovered during a search of his residence for Ricky Lyons. Thus, the narrow issue before us

is whether an arrest warrant—as opposed to a search warrant—is adequate to protect the Fourth Amendment interests of persons not named in the warrant, when their homes are searched without their consent and in the absence of exigent circumstances.

* * * [W]hile an arrest warrant and a search warrant both serve to subject the probable-cause determination of the police to judicial review, the interests protected by the two warrants differ. An arrest warrant is issued by a magistrate upon a showing that probable cause exists to believe that the subject of the warrant has committed an offense and thus the warrant primarily serves to protect an individual from an unreasonable seizure. A search warrant, in contrast, is issued upon a showing of probable cause to believe that the legitimate object of a search is located in a particular place, and therefore safeguards an individual's interest in the privacy of his home and possessions against the unjustified intrusion of the police.

Thus, whether the arrest warrant issued in this case adequately safeguarded the interests protected by the Fourth Amendment depends upon what the warrant authorized the agents to do. To be sure, the warrant embodied a judicial finding that there was probable cause to believe that Ricky Lyons had committed a felony, and the warrant therefore authorized the officers to seize Lyons. However, the agents sought to do more than use the warrant to arrest Lyons in a public place or in his home; instead, they relied on the warrant as legal authority to enter the home of a third person based on their belief that Ricky Lyons might be a guest there. Regardless of how reasonable this belief might have been, it was never subjected to the detached scrutiny of a judicial officer. Thus, while the warrant in this case may have protected Lyons from an unreasonable seizure, it did absolutely nothing to protect petitioner's privacy interest in being free from an unreasonable invasion and search of his home. * * * In the absence of exigent circumstances, we have consistently held that such judicially untested determinations are not reliable enough to justify * * * a search of a home for objects in the absence of a search warrant. We see no reason to depart from this settled course when the search of a home is for a person rather than an object.

7. *Problem: Payton versus Watson.* Police officers have probable cause to arrest Alice for a drug-related offense. The officers drive to Alice's residence without a warrant. Upon arrival in their police van, they observe Alice standing directly in the doorway ("one step forward would have put her outside, one step backward would have put her in the vestibule of her residence"). The officers get out of the van, guns

drawn, shouting "police." Alice retreats into her residence. The officers follow her inside through the open door and arrest her. Inside, the police discover drugs in plain view. Should evidence of these drugs be excluded from her trial? See United States v. Santana, 427 U.S. 38, 96 S.Ct. 2406, 49 L.Ed.2d 300 (1976).

Executing an Arrest: Use of Force

Recent events in cities around the United States (e.g., Chicago, Illinois; Ferguson, Missouri; Cleveland, Ohio; and Charleston, South Carolina), in which unarmed citizens (frequently young African-American males) have been shot by law enforcement officers, have increased attention to the question of what level of force is justifiable in law enforcement, in particular, to make arrests. A 2008 Police Public Contact Survey conducted by the federal Bureau of Justice Statistics reported that, among persons who had contact with police, 1.4% "had force used or threatened against them during the most recent contact," that "men were more likely than females to have force used or threatened, * * * and blacks were more likely than whites or Hispanics to experience use or threat of force." Of those who had force used or threatened, 74% felt that the officer's actions were excessive in view of the circumstances. http://www.bjs.gov/index.cfm?ty=tp&tid=703. An April, 2016 Police Accountability Task Force report in Chicago similarly reported that its "own data gives validity to the widely held belief the police have no regard for the sanctity of life when it comes to people of color." https://chicagopatf.org/wp-content/uploads/2016/04/PATF_Final_Report_4_13_16-1.pdf. (at p. 7).

Of course, that a suspect *believed* the force used was excessive does not make it so, but the Justice Department has determined that some police departments (*e.g.*, Albuquerque, New Mexico and Cleveland, Ohio) have been guilty of a pattern of use of excessive force. http://www.justice.gov/sites/default/files/crt/legacy/2014/04/10/apd_findings_4-10-14.pdf (April 10, 2014 letter from Jocelyn Samuels, Acting Assistant Attorney General, Department of Justice, Civil Rights Division, to Albuquerque Mayor Richard J. Berry); https://www.justice.gov/opa/pr/justice-department-reaches-agreement-city-cleveland-reform-cleveland-division-police (Justice Department Office of Public Affairs announcement that "Justice Department Reaches Agreement with City of Cleveland to Reform Division of Police Following Finding of a Pattern or Practice of Excessive Force").

The Fourth Amendment is relevant in this regard. After all, an arrest constitutes a seizure of the person, and the Fourth Amendment prohibits unreasonable seizures. This means that an arrest is constitutionally unreasonable, even if an arrest is based on probable cause, if it is executed in an excessive manner. But, what constitutes excessive force from a Fourth Amendment perspective?

The Supreme Court initially spoke to the issue in Tennessee v. Garner, 471 U.S. 1, 105 S.Ct. 1694, 85 L.Ed.2d 1 (1985), when it held that an officer's use of deadly force against a fleeing "young, slight, unarmed" burglary suspect violated the Fourth Amendment. As Justice White put it for the Court, "[i]t is not better that all felony suspects die than that they escape. Where the suspect poses no immediate threat to the officer and no threat to others, the harm resulting from failing to apprehend him does not justify the use of deadly force to do so."

More recent Supreme Court opinions have backed away from *Garner.* In Scott v. Harris, 550 U.S. 372, 127 S.Ct. 1769, 167 L.Ed.2d 686 (2007), the Court stated that the issue of what constitutes excessive force and, thus, what constitutes an unreasonable seizure of a person, is not susceptible to "an easy-to-apply legal test." Instead, "in the end we must still slosh through the factbound morass of 'reasonableness.' 'The Court noted that "*Garner* does not establish a magical on/off switch that triggers rigid preconditions whenever an officer's actions constitute 'deadly force.' " Thus, the *Scott* Court held that a deputy sheriff did not use unreasonable force when he rammed a motorist's car from behind to end a long "public endangering" car chase that began when the deputy sought to pull over the motorist for driving 73 miles-per-hour in a 55-mile zone. The deputy's action caused the speeding car to go off the roadway, turn over, crash, and leave its driver a quadriplegic. The Court reasoned that the fleeing driver posed a "substantial" and "immediate" risk of serious injury to innocent persons on the road, rendering the officer's action—seizure—reasonable.

As the Court put it in Graham v. Connor, 490 U.S. 386, 109 S.Ct. 1865, 104 L.Ed.2d 443 (1989), "what was implicit in *Garner*'s analysis" is "that *all* claims that law enforcement officers have used excessive force—deadly or not—in the course of an arrest, investigatory stop, or other 'seizure' of a free citizen should be analyzed under the Fourth Amendment * * * 'reasonableness' standard."

C. SEARCH WARRANTS: THE CHECKLIST CONTINUED

Let us return to the checklist we set out at the end of Chapter 3.

- ☑ Is there a search?
  - ☑ Is there a trespass? *If yes, then there is a search. If no, continue:*
  - ☑ Is there an actual expectation of privacy? *If no, the Fourth Amendment does not apply. If yes, continue:*

- ☑ If yes, is that expectation one that society views as reasonable? *If no, the Fourth Amendment does not apply. If yes, there is a search.*

☑ If there was a search, was the search reasonable?

- ☑ Was there a valid warrant? *If yes, the search is reasonable.*
- ☑ If no valid warrant, was there an exception to the warrant requirement? *If yes, the search is still reasonable.*

☑ If no valid warrant and no exception, the search is unreasonable and thus prohibited by the Fourth Amendment.

In this section we are now focused on whether there was a valid warrant. In the next two chapters, we will look at when warrants are or are not required. For purposes of this section, assume that a warrant is required. In order for a warrant to be valid, two things must happen. First, the warrant must contain all required information. As set out in the text of the Fourth Amendment, this means that the warrant "must be supported by Oath or affirmation," based on probable cause, and that it must particularly describe "the place to be searched and the persons or things to be seized." Second, the warrant must be executed correctly. As we saw in *United States v. Jones*, the benefits of a perfectly valid warrant were lost because the warrant was not executed at the time and in the place specified in the warrant. The first case in this section examines in more detail the question of what the warrant must contain. The second case addresses how warrants are executed in the context of the "knock and announce" requirement.

Why are warrants important? Consider first Justice Jackson's observations for the Court in Johnson v. United States, 333 U.S. 10, 68 S.Ct. 367, 92 L.Ed. 436 (1948):

> The point of the Fourth Amendment, which often is not grasped by zealous officers, is not that it denies law enforcement the support of the usual inferences which reasonable men draw from evidence. Its protection consists in requiring that those inferences be drawn by a neutral and detached magistrate instead of being judged by the officer engaged in the often competitive enterprise of ferreting out crime. * * *
>
> There are exceptional circumstances in which, on balancing the need for effective law enforcement against the right of privacy, it may be contended that a magistrate's warrant for search may be dispensed with. But * * * [n]o reason is offered [in this case] for not obtaining a search warrant except the inconvenience to the officers and some slight delay necessary to prepare papers and present the evidence to a

magistrate. These are never very convincing reasons and, in these circumstances, certainly are not enough to by-pass the constitutional requirement.

Johnson represents the traditional position that the Fourth Amendment is better served if police officers apply for warrants, rather than act on the basis of their own probable cause determinations. *Johnson*'s reasoning has led courts often to say that there is a "search warrant requirement" in the Fourth Amendment. As Justice Jackson noted above, there may be times when the benefit of a judicial determination is outweighed by other law enforcement concerns, but convenience will never be one of them.

In truth, though, we do have to ask ourselves a tough question with regard to the warrant process. If it *is* better for magistrates, rather than "officers engaged in the often competitive enterprise of ferreting out crime," to make probable cause determinations, d*oes* the warrant application process serve its intended purpose? *Do* magistrates give warrant applications careful attention?

Perhaps not. In the most thorough national study of search warrant procedures ever conducted, the National Center for State Courts reported that in one city studied, the average length of magisterial review was a mere two minutes and forty-eight seconds; ten percent of the warrant applications were approved in less than one minute. Richard Van Duizend et al., The Search Warrant Process: Preconceptions, Perceptions, and Practices 31 (1984). In a more recent study in San Diego, only a few judges handled the great majority of warrant applications because of magistrate-shopping by the police. As a "veteran officer" candidly admitted, "some judges were known for being liberal in granting search warrants." Laurence A. Benner & Charles T. Samarkos, *Searching for Narcotics in San Diego: Preliminary Findings from the San Diego Search Warrant Project*, 36 Cal. West. L. Rev. 221, 227–228 (2000). As one scholar has put it, "warrants [are] commonly issu[ed] upon something more akin to 'possible cause' rather than 'probable cause.' " Fabio Arcila, Jr., *In the Trenches: Searches and the Misunderstood Common-Law History of Suspicion and Probable Cause*, 10 U. Pa. J. Const. L. 1, 58 (2007) (also suggesting that this approach does not appreciably differ from the Framers' era).

1. Elements of a Valid Search Warrant

Warrants must meet constitutional specifications. They must be based on probable cause and supported by oath or affirmation, matters considered in Part A of this chapter. Two other required features are considered here.

LO-JI SALES, INC. V. NEW YORK

Supreme Court of the United States, 1979.
442 U.S. 319, 99 S.Ct. 2319, 60 L.Ed.2d 920.

The idea of a judicial determination of probable cause for a warrant is based on the assumption that the magistrate making the determination is "neutral and detached." The magistrate issuing the warrant in this case was anything but. In fact, Justice Burger referred to him as less a judicial officer than an "adjunct law enforcement officer." What problems do you think this might present? This question is explored in more detail in the Notes and Questions after the case.

MR. CHIEF JUSTICE BURGER delivered the opinion of the Court [joined by JUSTICES BRENNAN, STEWART, WHITE, MARSHALL, BLACKMUN, POWELL, REHNQUIST, and STEVENS]. * * *

I

On June 20, 1976, an investigator for the New York State Police purchased two reels of film from petitioner's so-called "adult" bookstore. Upon viewing them, he concluded the films violated New York's obscenity laws. On June 25, he took them to a Town Justice for a determination whether there was reasonable cause to believe the films violated the state obscenity laws so as to justify a warrant to search the seller's store. The Town Justice viewed both films in their entirety, and he apparently concluded they were obscene. Based upon an affidavit of the investigator subscribed before the Town Justice after this viewing, a warrant issued authorizing the search of petitioner's store and the seizure of other copies of the two films exhibited to the Town Justice.

The investigator's affidavit also contained an assertion that "similar" films and printed matter portraying similar activities could be found on the premises, and a statement of the affiant's belief that the items were possessed in violation of the obscenity laws. The warrant application requested that the Town Justice accompany the investigator to petitioner's store for the execution of the search warrant. The stated purpose was to allow the Town Justice to determine independently if any other items at the store were possessed in violation of law and subject to seizure. The Town Justice agreed. Accordingly, the warrant also contained a recital that authorized the seizure of "[t]he following items that the Court independently [on examination] has determined to be possessed in violation of Article 235 of the Penal Law * * *." However, at the time the Town Justice signed the warrant there were no items listed or described following this statement. As noted earlier, the only "things to be seized" that were described in the warrant were copies of the two films the state investigator had purchased. * * *

The Town Justice and the investigator enlisted three other State Police investigators, three uniformed State Police officers, and three members of the local prosecutor's office—a total of 11—and the search party converged on the bookstore. * * *

The search began in an area of the store which contained booths in which silent films were shown by coin-operated projectors. The clerk adjusted the machines so that the films could be viewed by the Town Justice without coins; it is disputed whether he volunteered or did so under compulsion * * *. The Town Justice viewed 23 films for two to three minutes each and, satisfied there was probable cause to believe they were obscene, then ordered the films and the projectors seized.

The Town Justice next focused on another area containing four coin-operated projectors showing both soundless and sound films. After viewing each film for two to five minutes, again without paying, he ordered them seized along with their projectors.

The search party then moved to an area in which books and magazines were on display. The magazines were encased in clear plastic or cellophane wrappers which the Town Justice had two police officers remove prior to his examination of the books. Choosing only magazines that did not contain significant amounts of written material, he spent not less than 10 seconds nor more than a minute looking through each one. When he was satisfied that probable cause existed, he immediately ordered the copy which he had reviewed, along with other copies of the same or "similar" magazines, seized. An investigator wrote down the titles of the items seized. All told, 397 magazines were taken.

The final area searched was one in which petitioner displayed films and other items for sale behind a glass enclosed case. When it was announced that each box of film would be opened, the clerk advised that a picture on the outside of the box was representative of what the film showed. Therefore, if satisfied from the picture that there was probable cause to believe the film in the box was obscene, the Town Justice ordered the seizure of all copies of that film. As with the magazines, an investigator wrote down the titles of the films seized, a total of 431 reels. * * *

After the search and seizure was completed, the seized items were taken to a State Police barracks where they were inventoried. Each item was then listed on the search warrant, and late the same night the completed warrant was given to the Town Justice. The warrant, which had consisted of 2 pages when he signed it before the search, by late in the day contained 16 pages. It is clear, therefore, that the particular description of "things to be seized" was entered in the document after the seizure and impoundment of the books and other articles. * * *

II

This search warrant and what followed the entry on petitioner's premises are reminiscent of the general warrant or writ of assistance of the 18th century against which the Fourth Amendment was intended to protect. Except for the specification of copies of the two films previously purchased, the warrant did not purport to "particularly describ[e] * * * the * * * things to be seized." Based on the conclusory statement of the police investigator that other similarly obscene materials would be found at the store, the warrant left it entirely to the discretion of the officials conducting the search to decide what items were likely obscene and to accomplish their seizure. The Fourth Amendment does not permit such action. Nor does the Fourth Amendment countenance open-ended warrants, to be completed while a search is being conducted and items seized or after the seizure has been carried out.

This search began when the local justice and his party entered the premises. But at that time there was not sufficient probable cause to pursue a search beyond looking for additional copies of the two specified films, assuming the validity of searching even for those. And the record is clear that the search began and progressed pursuant to the sweeping open-ended authorization in the warrant. It was not limited at the outset as a search for other copies of the two "sample" films; it expanded into a more extensive search because other items were found that the local justice deemed illegal. * * *

III

We have repeatedly said that a warrant authorized by a neutral and detached judicial officer is "a more reliable safeguard against improper searches than the hurried judgment of a law enforcement officer 'engaged in the often competitive enterprise of ferreting out crime.' " * * *

The Town Justice did not manifest that neutrality and detachment demanded of a judicial officer when presented with a warrant application for a search and seizure. We need not question the subjective belief of the Town Justice in the propriety of his actions, but the objective facts of record manifest an erosion of whatever neutral and detached posture existed at the outset. He allowed himself to become a member, if not the leader, of the search party which was essentially a police operation. Once in the store, he conducted a generalized search under authority of an invalid warrant; he was not acting as a judicial officer but as an adjunct law enforcement officer. When he ordered an item seized because he believed it was obscene, he instructed the police officers to seize all "similar" items as well, leaving determination of what was "similar" to the officer's discretion. Indeed, he yielded to the State Police even the completion of the general provision of the warrant. * * *

IV * * *

* * * Our society is better able to tolerate the admittedly pornographic business of petitioner than a return to the general warrant era; violations of law must be dealt with within the framework of constitutional guarantees. * * *

NOTES AND QUESTIONS

1. *"Neutral and detached magistrate" requirement.* What is it, precisely, that the Town Justice did wrong in *Lo-Ji Sales*? Is it that he left his regular office to make himself available to law enforcement personnel? What if he had sat in his office and added items to the warrant as they were described to him via email or telephone and then had an officer deliver the 16 page warrant to the officers on the scene to execute? Would that violate the Fourth Amendment?

Should a search warrant be invalidated (and if so, why) in the following circumstances: (a) it is issued by the State Attorney General, see Coolidge v. New Hampshire, 403 U.S. 443, 91 S.Ct. 2022, 29 L.Ed.2d 564 (1971); (b) the magistrate is paid a fee for issuing a warrant, but is not paid if she denies an application for a warrant, see Connally v. Georgia, 429 U.S. 245, 97 S.Ct. 546, 50 L.Ed.2d 444 (1977); (c) the magistrate fails to read the warrant that she signs, see United States v. Decker, 956 F.2d 773 (8th Cir. 1992); or (d) she spends only 2 minutes, 48 seconds considering the warrant application (see p. 198)?

2. *The warrant particularity requirement.* This requirement is intended to prevent general searches, the immediate evil "that motivated the framing and adoption of the Fourth Amendment," *Payton v. New York*, and to prevent "the seizure of one thing under a warrant describing another." Andresen v. Maryland, 427 U.S. 463, 96 S.Ct. 2737, 49 L.Ed.2d 627 (1976).

Andresen also teaches that a court should read a search warrant in fair context. For example, in *Andresen*, a warrant authorized the police to seize a long list of specific items relating to a specific incident of false pretenses, "together with other fruits, instrumentalities, and evidence of crime at this [time] unknown." Although Andresen argued that the latter phrase permitted the search and seizure of *any* evidence of *any* crime—clearly a violation of the particularity requirement—the Court concluded that the challenged phrase, coming as part of the same sentence that included the long list of specific items, "must be read as authorizing only the search for and seizure of evidence relating to" the particular crime under investigation.

3. *Particularity by incorporation?* Suppose a search warrant fails to properly specify the property to be seized. May this constitutional failing be cured if the *application* for the warrant particularizes the items to be seized? In Groh v. Ramirez, 540 U.S. 551, 124 S.Ct. 1284, 157 L.Ed.2d 1068 (2004), the Supreme Court answered this way:

> The fact that the *application* adequately described "the things to be seized" does not save the *warrant* from its facial invalidity. The Fourth Amendment by its terms requires particularity in the warrant, not in the supporting documents. * * * We do not say that the Fourth Amendment forbids a warrant from cross-referencing other documents. Indeed, most Courts of Appeals have held that a court may construe a warrant with reference to a supporting application or affidavit if the warrant uses appropriate words of incorporation, and if the supporting document accompanies the warrant. But in this case the warrant did not incorporate other documents by reference, nor did either the affidavit or the application * * * accompany the warrant. Hence, we need not further explore the matter of incorporation.

2. Execution of a Search Warrant

Introductory Comment

Consider these facts: An informant reported to Atlanta police officers that he purchased two bags of crack cocaine from a man at a house the address of which he provided to the police. Based on this information, the officers obtained a warrant to search the residence. Armed with the warrant, eight members of the Atlanta police department went to the home where, in a military-type raid, broke into the house without warning—they did not knock at the door, nor did they announce their identity and purpose before breaking in. Inside the house was one person, Kathryn Johnston, a 92-year-old woman living alone.

Assume for current purposes (there is more to the story, which will be disclosed later) that the information the police received justified the search warrant. Thus, the police had a valid search warrant. And, surely the fact that the information proved wrong—this was not a house where drugs were sold—does not render the warrant invalid. Warrants are based on probable cause, not certainty. However, was the *means* of execution of the warrant unconstitutional? Specifically, does it violate the Fourth Amendment for agents of the government to enter a person's home forcibly, rather than giving the occupant(s) notice of their presence and allowing the resident(s) an opportunity to comply with the officers' demand for entry?

In Wilson v. Arkansas, 514 U.S. 927, 115 S.Ct. 1914, 131 L.Ed.2d 976 (1995), the Supreme Court, per Justice Clarence Thomas, ruled unanimously that the Fourth Amendment prohibition on unreasonable searches and seizures contains an implicit knock-and-announce rule previously embedded in the common law. However, the Court warned that "[t]his is not to say, of course, that every entry must be preceded by an announcement. The Fourth Amendment's flexible requirement of reasonableness should not be read to mandate a rigid rule of announcement that ignores countervailing law enforcement interests." Without "attempt[ing] a comprehensive catalog" of exceptions to the requirement, Justice Thomas suggested in dictum that the knock-and-announce principle does not apply

> under circumstances presenting a threat of physical violence. Similarly, courts [have] held that an officer may dispense with announcement in cases where a prisoner escapes from him and retreats to his dwelling. Proof of "demand and refusal" was deemed unnecessary in such cases because it would be a "senseless ceremony" to require an officer in pursuit of a recently escaped arrestee to make an announcement prior to breaking the door to retake him. Finally, courts have indicated that unannounced entry may be justified where police officers have reason to believe that evidence would likely be destroyed if advance notice were given.

Soon after *Wilson*, the Supreme Court considered the exceptions to the knock-and-announce principle more fully.

RICHARDS V. WISCONSIN

Supreme Court of the United States, 1997.
520 U.S. 385, 117 S.Ct. 1416, 137 L.Ed.2d 615.

In this case, the State of Wisconsin asked the U.S. Supreme Court to uphold a blanket rule that in *all* felony drug investigations for which law enforcement agents have a warrant, the "knock and announce" rule is not required. Wisconsin's argument was that, given the drug culture of the day (the 1990s), weapons and the risk of the destruction of the drugs were always going to be present. The Court said no.

However, there are two parts to this case. While the Court refused to set out a blanket list of crimes where "knock and announce" does not apply, the justices unanimously upheld the search in *Richards* on the basis

that, in the given circumstances, the officers had a *reasonable suspicion* that the defendant might destroy the evidence if he had the chance to do so. Blanket exception aside, it is hard to imagine a drug case where that would not apply.

The standard of *reasonable suspicion* is much easier for law enforcement officers to meet than that of the *probable cause* we have been dealing with so far. In Chapter 7, we will look more at how the *reasonable suspicion* standard for searches came to be and how it differs from *probable cause.*

Ironically, although the Court in *Richards* upheld the "knock and announce" requirement as part of the reasonableness of a search, the requirement may no longer have much meaning. In *Hudson v. Michigan*, as we will see in Chapter 8, evidence gained in violation of the "knock and announce" rule is no longer subject to the exclusionary rule. Stay tuned.

JUSTICE STEVENS delivered the opinion of the Court [joined by CHIEF JUSTICE REHNQUIST, and JUSTICES O'CONNOR, SCALIA, KENNEDY, SOUTER, THOMAS, GINSBURG, and BREYER]. * * *

In this case, the Wisconsin Supreme Court concluded that police officers are *never* required to knock and announce their presence when executing a search warrant in a felony drug investigation. In so doing, it * * * concluded that *Wilson* [*v. Arkansas*, Introductory Note] did not preclude this *per se* rule. We disagree with the court's conclusion that the Fourth Amendment permits a blanket exception to the knock-and-announce requirement for this entire category of criminal activity. * * *

I

On December 31, 1991, police officers in Madison, Wisconsin obtained a warrant to search Steiney Richards' hotel room for drugs and related paraphernalia. The search warrant was the culmination of an investigation that had uncovered substantial evidence that Richards was one of several individuals dealing drugs out of hotel rooms in Madison. The police requested a warrant that would have given advance authorization for a "no-knock" entry into the hotel room, but the magistrate explicitly deleted those portions of the warrant.

The officers arrived at the hotel room at 3:40 a.m. Officer Pharo, dressed as a maintenance man, led the team. With him were several plainclothes officers and at least one man in uniform. Officer Pharo knocked on Richards' door and, responding to the query from inside the room, stated that he was a maintenance man. With the chain still on the door, Richards cracked it open. Although there is some dispute as to what occurred next, Richards acknowledges that when he opened the door he saw the man in uniform standing behind Officer Pharo. He quickly slammed the door closed and, after waiting two or three seconds, the officers began kicking and ramming the door to gain entry to the locked room. At trial, the officers testified that they identified themselves as police while they were kicking the door in. When they finally did break into the room, the officers caught Richards trying to escape through the window. They also found cash and cocaine hidden in plastic bags above the bathroom ceiling tiles.

Richards sought to have the evidence from his hotel room suppressed on the ground that the officers had failed to knock and announce their presence prior to forcing entry into the room. The trial court denied the motion, concluding that the officers could gather from Richards' strange behavior when they first sought entry that he knew they were police officers and that he might try to destroy evidence or to escape. * * * Richards appealed the decision to the Wisconsin Supreme Court and that court affirmed.

The Wisconsin Supreme Court did not delve into the events underlying Richards' arrest in any detail, but accepted the following facts: "[O]n December 31, 1991, police executed a search warrant for the motel room of the defendant seeking evidence of the felonious crime of Possession with Intent to Deliver a Controlled Substance in violation of [state law]. They did not knock and announce prior to their entry. Drugs were seized."

Assuming these facts, the court * * * held that "when the police have a search warrant, supported by probable cause, to search a residence for evidence of delivery of drugs or evidence of possession with intent to deliver drugs, they necessarily have reasonable cause to believe exigent circumstances exist" to justify a no-knock entry. The court concluded that nothing in *Wilson*'s acknowledgment that the knock-and-announce rule was an element of the Fourth Amendment "reasonableness" requirement would prohibit application of a *per se* exception to that rule in a category of cases.

In reaching this conclusion, the Wisconsin court found it reasonable—after considering criminal conduct surveys, newspaper articles, and other judicial opinions—to assume that all felony drug crimes will involve "an extremely high risk of serious if not deadly injury to the police as well as the potential for the disposal of drugs by the occupants prior to entry by the police." Notwithstanding its acknowledgment that in "some cases, police officers will undoubtedly decide that their safety, the safety of others, and the effective execution of the warrant dictate that they knock and announce," the court concluded that exigent circumstances justifying a no-knock entry are always present in felony drug cases.

* * * Accordingly, the court determined that police in Wisconsin do not need specific information about dangerousness, or the possible destruction of drugs in a particular case, in order to dispense with the knock-and-announce requirement in felony drug cases. * * *

II

We recognized in *Wilson* that the knock-and-announce requirement could give way "under circumstances presenting a threat of physical violence," or "where police officers have reason to believe that evidence would likely be destroyed if advance notice were given." It is indisputable that felony drug investigations may frequently involve both of these circumstances. The question we must resolve is whether this fact justifies dispensing with case-by-case evaluation of the manner in which a search was executed.

The Wisconsin court explained its blanket exception as necessitated by the special circumstances of today's drug culture, and the State asserted at oral argument that the blanket exception was reasonable in "felony drug cases because of the convergence in a violent and dangerous form of commerce of weapons and the destruction of drugs." But creating exceptions to the knock-and-announce rule based on the "culture" surrounding a general category of criminal behavior presents at least two serious concerns.

First, the exception contains considerable overgeneralization. For example, while drug investigation frequently does pose special risks to officer safety and the preservation of evidence, not every drug investigation will pose these risks to a substantial degree. For example, a search could be conducted at a time when the only individuals present in a residence have no connection with the drug activity and thus will be unlikely to threaten officers or destroy evidence. Or the police could know that the drugs being searched for were of a type or in a location that made them impossible to destroy quickly. In those situations, the asserted governmental interests in preserving evidence and maintaining safety may not outweigh the individual privacy interests intruded upon by a no-knock entry. Wisconsin's blanket rule impermissibly insulates these cases from judicial review.

A second difficulty with permitting a criminal-category exception to the knock-and-announce requirement is that the reasons for creating an exception in one category can, relatively easily, be applied to others. Armed bank robbers, for example, are, by definition, likely to have weapons, and the fruits of their crime may be destroyed without too much difficulty. If a *per se* exception were allowed for each category of criminal investigation that included a considerable—albeit hypothetical—risk of danger to officers or destruction of evidence, the knock-

and-announce element of the Fourth Amendment's reasonableness requirement would be meaningless.

Thus, the fact that felony drug investigations may frequently present circumstances warranting a no-knock entry cannot remove from the neutral scrutiny of a reviewing court the reasonableness of the police decision not to knock and announce in a particular case. Instead, in each case, it is the duty of a court confronted with the question to determine whether the facts and circumstances of the particular entry justified dispensing with the knock-and-announce requirement.

In order to justify a "no-knock" entry, the police must have a reasonable suspicion that knocking and announcing their presence, under the particular circumstances, would be dangerous or futile, or that it would inhibit the effective investigation of the crime by, for example, allowing the destruction of evidence. This standard—as opposed to a probable cause requirement—strikes the appropriate balance between the legitimate law enforcement concerns at issue in the execution of search warrants and the individual privacy interests affected by no-knock entries. This showing is not high, but the police should be required to make it whenever the reasonableness of a no-knock entry is challenged.

III

Although we reject the Wisconsin court's blanket exception to the knock-and-announce requirement, we conclude that the officers' no-knock entry into Richards' hotel room did not violate the Fourth Amendment. We agree with the trial court * * * that the circumstances in this case show that the officers had a reasonable suspicion that Richards might destroy evidence if given further opportunity to do so.

The judge who heard testimony at Richards' suppression hearing concluded that it was reasonable for the officers executing the warrant to believe that Richards knew, after opening the door to his hotel room the first time, that the men seeking entry to his room were the police. Once the officers reasonably believed that Richards knew who they were, the court concluded, it was reasonable for them to force entry immediately given the disposable nature of the drugs. * * *

Accordingly, although we reject the blanket exception to the knock-and-announce requirement for felony drug investigations, the judgment of the Wisconsin Supreme Court is affirmed.

NOTES AND QUESTIONS

1. The facts are a bit odd. Why go to the trouble to dress an officer as a hotel maintenance man if a uniformed officer stands beside him when the door is opened?

As a practical matter, who are the big winners in this case, the police or home dwellers? Is it fair to assert that in virtually every drug-dealer case the police will possess reasonable suspicion that persons inside are armed or that contraband will likely be destroyed if they announce their presence and intention?

Why does the *Richards* Court permit the police to apply a less demanding standard than probable cause in determining whether an exception to the knock-and-announce requirement exists? Does Justice Stevens offer an explanation? As you will see in Chapter 7, to satisfy the "reasonable suspicion" standard, an officer must be able to articulate something more than an "inchoate and unparticularized suspicion or 'hunch.' " *Terry v. Ohio.* There must exist "some minimal level of objective justification" for the police conduct. This is a less demanding standard than "probable cause." See generally, *Alabama v. White.*

2. What interests are served by the knock-and-announce rule? Here is what the Court said in a footnote in *Richards*:

> The State asserts that the intrusion on individual interests effectuated by a no-knock entry is minimal because the execution of the warrant itself constitutes the primary intrusion on individual privacy and that the individual privacy interest cannot outweigh the generalized governmental interest in effective and safe law enforcement. While it is true that a no-knock entry is less intrusive than, for example, a warrantless search, the individual interests implicated by an unannounced, forcible entry should not be unduly minimized. As we observed in *Wilson* v. *Arkansas,* the common law recognized that individuals should be provided the opportunity to comply with the law and to avoid the destruction of property occasioned by a forcible entry. These interests are not inconsequential.
>
> Additionally, when police enter a residence without announcing their presence, the residents are not given any opportunity to prepare themselves for such an entry. The State pointed out at oral argument that, in Wisconsin, most search warrants are executed during the late night and early morning hours. The brief interlude between announcement and entry with a warrant may be the opportunity that an individual has to pull on clothes or get out of bed.

3. *The rest of the Atlanta story.* We promised you more to the story of the Atlanta police officers who entered a "drug house" only to find a 92-year-old woman inside. The story is more sordid than we suggested, and tragic. As it turned out, the informant

lied to the police about purchasing drugs at that home. He had never been there and, it seems, picked that address at random. The police, in turn, lied to the magistrate when they applied for the warrant: an officer under oath falsely claimed that he had personally purchased drugs at that address in his undercover status. He further perjured himself by stating that he had seen surveillance cameras in the house. (Based on these false statements, *was* the warrant valid? What case or doctrine would come into play with this new information?

The sordid story now turns tragic. The elderly and infirm Kathryn Johnston, fearful of intruders, apparently kept a gun with her, which she fired at them when the intruders entered her small house. The outcome was inevitable: She was shot to death in the ensuing hail of police bullets. And, then to finish the ugly events, one or more of the officers planted a small quantity of drugs on the premises to try to justify their actions.

The family of the deceased has sued the city. Two police officers were charged with murder and pleaded guilty to manslaughter and federal civil rights violations. A third officer, who had been stationed at the rear of the house, was charged with violating his oath of office (acquitted), falsely imprisoning Johnston (acquitted), and lying in an official investigation (convicted). See, *e.g.*, Shaila Dewan & Brenda Goodman, *Atlanta Officers Suspended In Inquiry on Killing in Raid*, New York Times, Nov. 28, 2006, at A16; Steve Visser, *Officer in Fatal '06 Raid Guilty of One Charge*, The Atlanta Journal-Constitution, May 21, 2008, at 1A; *Former Atlanta Cop Gets 4½ Years*, Atlanta Journal-Constitution, May 23, 2008, at 16; and Christian Boone & Marcus K. Garner, *Family Offers to Settle in Notorious Raid*, Atlanta Journal-Constitution, July 18, 2008, at 5H.

4. After knocking and announcing their presence, how long must the police wait before they forcibly enter a residence and execute a warrant to search for cocaine? In United States v. Banks, 540 U.S. 31, 124 S.Ct. 521, 157 L.Ed.2d 343 (2003), officers armed with a warrant to search Banks's two-bedroom apartment for cocaine, knocked loudly, announced their purpose, and waited fifteen to twenty seconds for a response. When nobody came to the door, the police broke open the door with a battering ram, entered, and executed their warrant. As it turned out, Banks was in the shower and had not heard the police knock.

The Court unanimously held that although the "call is a close one, * * * we think that after 15 or 20 seconds without a response, police could fairly suspect that cocaine would be gone if they were reticent any longer." In short, an exigency justified the forcible entry. The fact that Banks was in the shower was irrelevant: "[I]t is enough to say that the facts known to the police are what count in judging reasonable waiting time."

Does it matter to the analysis that the police entry required them to damage the property? The Court explained that where, as here, an exigency justifies immediate forcible entry, the police "may damage premises so far as necessary for a no-knock entrance without demonstrating the suspected risk in any more detail than the law demands for an unannounced intrusion simply by lifting the latch." However, the Court suggested that in some circumstances damage to property *could* be relevant to the reasonableness of an entry to execute a search warrant. Specifically, when immediate entry is *not* required as a result of an exigency, "the reasonable wait time" before causing damage to enter "may well be longer" than if the door to the house is open and they can enter without damaging the residence:

> Suffice it to say that the need to damage property in the course of getting in is a good reason to require more patience than it would be reasonable to expect if the door were open. Police seeking a stolen piano may be able to spend more time to make sure they really need the battering ram.

5. *In anticipation of a warrant.* What, if anything, may the police do *before* they execute a warrant—indeed, before they even have a warrant—to ensure that criminal evidence they expect to find during the search will not be destroyed or moved while they apply for the warrant? For example, in Illinois v. McArthur, 531 U.S. 326, 121 S.Ct. 946, 148 L.Ed.2d 838 (2001), police officers who were already lawfully at McArthur's home, developed probable cause at the scene to believe that he had hidden marijuana in his trailer home. Two officers asked McArthur for permission to search the premises for marijuana, but he refused. As a consequence, one officer left to apply for a search warrant. The second officer informed McArthur, who by this time was standing on the porch, that he could not reenter his trailer unless accompanied by an officer. McArthur reentered his home two or three times, to make phone calls and get cigarettes, and each time the officer stood just inside the door to observe McArthur. The first officer returned two hours later with a search warrant, which was promptly executed.

The Supreme Court, 8–1, approved the police action, although it conceded that by preventing McArthur or others from entering the trailer home, the police had effectively seized the premises without a warrant. Justice Breyer explained:

> We conclude that the restriction at issue was reasonable, and hence lawful, in light of the following circumstances, which we consider in combination. First, the police had probable cause to believe that McArthur's trailer home contained evidence of a crime and contraband, namely, unlawful drugs. * * *
>
> Second, the police had good reason to fear that, unless restrained, McArthur would destroy the drugs before they could return with a warrant. * * * They reasonably could have concluded that McArthur, * * *

suspecting an imminent search, would, if given the chance, get rid of the drugs fast.

Third, the police made reasonable efforts to reconcile their law enforcement needs with the demands of personal privacy. They neither searched the trailer nor arrested McArthur before obtaining a warrant. Rather, they imposed a significantly less restrictive restraint, preventing McArthur only from entering the trailer unaccompanied. They left his home and his belongings intact—until a neutral Magistrate, finding probable cause, issued a warrant.

Fourth, the police imposed the restraint for a limited period of time, namely, two hours. As far as the record reveals, this time period was no longer than reasonably necessary for the police, acting with diligence, to obtain the warrant. Given the nature of the intrusion and the law enforcement interest at stake, this brief seizure of the premises was permissible.

6. *Executing a warrant after entry: The scope of the search of the premises.* Once officers are lawfully on premises to execute a warrant, various search principles apply. First, the police may search containers large enough to hold the criminal evidence for which they are searching. For example, if a warrant authorizes a search of a suspect's bedroom for a stolen ring, the officer may, pursuant to the warrant, open dresser drawers, jewelry boxes, and other containers in the bedroom that could hold the ring. In contrast, if they are searching a bedroom for a stolen 60-inch television set, the police would not be authorized to open drawers or to open boxes smaller than the television.

Second, while officers execute a search warrant, they may seize an object *not* described in the warrant, if they have probable cause to believe it is a seizable item (contraband, or a fruit, instrumentality or evidence of a crime).

Third, as Maryland v. Garrison, 480 U.S. 79, 107 S.Ct. 1013, 94 L.Ed.2d 72 (1987), teaches, information that becomes available to officers immediately before or during the execution of a warrant may require them to cease or narrow their search, notwithstanding the dictates of the warrant. In *Garrison*, the officers obtained a warrant to search "the premises known as 2036 Park Avenue third floor apartment" belonging to one Lawrence McWebb. What the officers did not know when they sought the warrant, or even as they entered the third floor "apartment," was that the third floor was divided into *two* apartments, one occupied by McWebb, and a second by petitioner Garrison. The officers erroneously entered Garrison's premises; only after they discovered contraband there did they realize the mistake. They immediately ceased the search of Garrison's premises. However, the State sought to prosecute him on the basis of the evidence they found before they discovered their error. The Court upheld the validity of the erroneous warrant and its execution:

> If the officers had known, or should have known, that the third floor contained two apartments before they entered the living quarters on the third floor, and thus had been aware of the error in the warrant, they would have been obligated to limit their search to McWebb's apartment. Moreover, as the officers recognized, they were required to discontinue the search of respondent's apartment as soon as they discovered that there were two separate units on the third floor and therefore were put on notice of the risk that they might be in a unit erroneously included within the terms of the warrant. The officers' conduct and the limits of the search were based on the information available as the search proceeded. While the purposes justifying a police search strictly limit the permissible extent of the search, the Court has also recognized the need to allow some latitude for honest mistakes that are made by officers in the dangerous and difficult process of making arrests and executing search warrants.

What is the essence of the Fourth Amendment lesson of *Garrison*?

7. *Searching persons during the execution of a warrant.* A warrant may authorize the search of a person, but it should be explicit. A warrant to search a home or other premises does not provide implicit authority to search persons found at the scene, even if the criminal evidence for which the police are looking might be on them.

For example, in Ybarra v. Illinois, 444 U.S. 85, 100 S.Ct. 338, 62 L.Ed.2d 238 (1979), the police obtained a valid warrant to search a tavern and "Greg," the bartender, for "evidence of the offense of possession of a controlled substance." Seven or eight officers proceeded to the tavern in the late afternoon. While most of the officers searched the premises and bartender Greg, one officer conducted cursory searches of a dozen or so customers present and, in the case of Ventura Ybarra, conducted a more extensive search. The latter search turned up a cigarette pack, inside which were six tinfoil packets containing a brown powdery substance that later turned out to be heroin. The Court held that the warrant did not authorize the Ybarra search.

Ybarra does *not* stand for the proposition that police officers may *never* search persons coincidentally at the scene during a warranted search. However, the police must have independent probable cause to search the person ("a person's mere propinquity to others independently suspected of criminal activity does not, without more, give rise to probable cause to search that person"), as well as some justification for conducting the search without a warrant, *i.e.*, they must be able to point to an exception to the "warrant requirement."

8. *Seizure of persons during warranted searches.* Although the police may not automatically *search* persons present at the scene during the execution of a search warrant (Note 7), the Supreme Court announced a bright-line rule in Michigan v. Summers, 452 U.S. 692, 101 S.Ct. 2587, 69 L.Ed.2d 340 (1981), regarding *seizure* of persons in such circumstances: "[A] warrant to search [a residence] for contraband founded on probable cause implicitly carries with it the limited authority to detain the occupants of the premises while a proper search is conducted."

The right of detention pursuant to *Summers* is automatic: it "does not require law enforcement to have particular suspicion that an individual [seized under the rule] is involved in criminal activity or poses a specific danger to the officers." Bailey v. United States, 568 U.S. 186, 133 S.Ct. 1031, 185 L.Ed.2d 19 (2013). Moreover, the right of the police under *Summers* to detain an occupant during a warranted search of a residence necessarily includes the right to use reasonable force to secure and maintain detention of the occupant. Muehler v. Mena, 544 U.S. 93, 125 S.Ct. 1465, 161 L.Ed.2d 299 (2005). Mena was asleep in her bed when a SWAT team entered the premises. She was placed in handcuffs at gunpoint, moved to a garage, and detained there in that condition for two to three hours while the premises were searched pursuant to the warrant. The Court held that this was reasonable force.

On the other hand, because the right of detention is automatic and can result in a relatively lengthy detention while the search is conducted, the *Summers* rule is limited to the detention of occupants of the residence at the time of the search, and persons discovered "immediately outside a residence at the moment the police officers execute[ ] the search warrant." However, "[o]nce an individual has left the immediate vicinity of the premises to be searched," the bright-line *Summers* rule no longer applies. *Bailey, supra.*

In *Bailey*, the police observed *B* leave the residence that they intended to search pursuant to a warrant, but he was not detained until he was approximately a mile away from the premises. Because this detention was beyond "any reasonable understanding" of the term "immediate vicinity" of the residence, the Court held, 6–3, that *B*'s seizure fell outside the scope of *Summers.*

Justice Scalia, joined by Justices Ginsburg and Kagan, joined the Court's opinion, but added:

> It bears repeating that the "general rule" is "that Fourth Amendment seizures are 'reasonable' only if based on probable cause." *Summers* embodies a categorical judgment that *in one narrow circumstance*—the presence of occupants during the execution of a search warrant—seizures are reasonable despite the absence of probable cause. * * *

> *Summers*' clear rule simplifies the task of officers who encounter occupants during a search. * * * But having received the advantage of *Summers*' categorical authorization to detain occupants incident to a search, the Government must take the bitter with the sweet: Beyond *Summers*' spatial bounds, seizures must comport with ordinary Fourth Amendment principles.

Justice Breyer, joined by Justices Thomas and Alito, dissented, contending that the majority had "substituted a line based on indeterminate geography for a line based on realistic considerations related to basic Fourth Amendment concerns such as privacy, safety, evidence destruction, and flight."

CHAPTER 4 SUMMARY

In Chapter 3 we examined the question of what is a search or seizure. Here in Chapter 4, we began the discussion of whether or not a particular search or seizure is reasonable. For purposes of this chapter, a search or seizure is reasonable if it is supported by probable cause and a warrant (we will discuss exceptions to this rule in Chapters 5 and 6).

As noted at the beginning of this chapter, probable cause to arrest "exists where 'the facts and circumstances within the officers' knowledge and of which they have reasonably trustworthy information are sufficient in themselves to warrant a man of reasonable caution in the belief that *an offense has been or is being committed by the person to be arrested*." Probable cause to search "exists where the facts and circumstances within the officers' knowledge and of which they have reasonably trustworthy information are sufficient in themselves to warrant a man of reasonable caution in the belief that *evidence subject to seizure will be found in the place to be searched*." As demonstrated in the cases and readings, this standard is much easier to state than to apply. In *Illinois v. Gates*, the Court has adopted a "totality of the circumstances" approach to determine whether probable cause exists. This test requires a judge to consider all circumstances and facts known to the officers at the time—including the detail of the information, how the information was obtained, and the credibility and track record of any sources. The Court itself has refused to try to quantify any standard of probable cause and has moved away from overly rigid checklists. Indeed, some scholars have suggested the existence of a "sliding scale" of probable cause: the more intrusive the search, the more substantial the justification needed; the more serious the crime at issue, the less justification needed.

Search warrants provide for the search and seizure of evidence, but what about the seizure of persons? While a warrantless arrest can be made of a suspect in a public place, arresting a suspect in his or her home requires an arrest warrant—a search warrant will not do. Whether a search warrant or an arrest warrant is at issue, several requirements normally need to be met. First, the warrant must be supported by the probable cause discussed above and specifically describe the place to be searched or the evidence or person to be seized. This determination must be made by a "neutral and detached" magistrate. See *Lo Ji Sales v. New York* for what not to do in this regard. Second, warrants must be executed properly. At the very least, the instructions in the warrant as to time and place of execution must be honored. See *U.S. v. Jones* for how to forfeit a perfectly valid warrant by ignoring this requirement.

CHAPTER 5

Valid Warrantless Searches, Part I: Probable Cause (Mostly) Required

In Chapter 4 we examined what a warrant is required to contain, and when and how it needs to be executed. In this chapter, we begin our look at when warrants are required, or more specifically, when they are not. As we often learn in early childhood, to every rule there is an exception, and sometimes even lots of exceptions!

According to Katz v. United States, 389 U.S. 347, 88 S.Ct. 507, 19 L.Ed.2d 576 (1967), "searches conducted outside the judicial process, without prior approval by judge or magistrate, are *per se* unreasonable under the Fourth Amendment—subject only to a few specifically established and well-delineated exceptions." Yet sometimes the exceptions can come close to swallowing the rule. In 1991, Justice Scalia complained, in his concurring opinion in California v. Acevedo, 500 U.S.565, 111 S.Ct. 1982, 114 L.Ed.2d 619 (1991), that the "warrant requirement" had become so riddled with exceptions that it was basically unrecognizable.

In this chapter, we will examine several long-standing exceptions to the need for a search warrant: including exigent circumstances, search incident to lawful arrest (SILA), the automobile exception, and plain view. There is an important constant in all of these exceptions. They are mainly exceptions to the warrant requirement; the need for an officer to run down to the courthouse, get a magistrate to sign that pesky piece of paper, and come back to the scene to conduct the search or seizure. In most of the situations in this chapter, probable cause of some type is still needed to search or seize persons or property. For example, exigent circumstances requires probable cause to believe the suspect is committing or has committed a crime (and that evidence could be destroyed or public safety threatened); SILA requires probable cause to arrest; the automobile exception requires probable cause to believe that weapons or evidence of a crime will be found in the car; and plain view is often derived from one of the above exceptions, with the probable cause that goes along with it. Throughout this chapter, our starting point is still the same: *is there probable cause to search or seize?*

A. EXIGENT CIRCUMSTANCES

WARDEN V. HAYDEN

Supreme Court of the United States, 1967.
387 U.S. 294, 87 S.Ct. 1642, 18 L.Ed.2d 782.

MR. JUSTICE BRENNAN delivered the opinion of the Court. * * *

I

About 8 a.m. on March 17, 1962, an armed robber entered the business premises of the Diamond Cab Company in Baltimore, Maryland. He took some $363 and ran. Two cab drivers in the vicinity, attracted by shouts of "Holdup," followed the man to 2111 Cocoa Lane. One driver notified the company dispatcher by radio that the man was a Negro about 5'8" tall, wearing a light cap and dark jacket, and that he had entered the house on Cocoa Lane. The dispatcher relayed the information to police who were proceeding to the scene of the robbery. Within minutes, police arrived at the house in a number of patrol cars. An officer knocked and announced their presence. Mrs. Hayden answered, and the officers told her they believed that a robber had entered the house, and asked to search the house. She offered no objection.

The officers spread out through the first and second floors and the cellar in search of the robber. Hayden was found in an upstairs bedroom feigning sleep. He was arrested when the officers on the first floor and in the cellar reported that no other man was in the house. Meanwhile an officer was attracted to an adjoining bathroom by the noise of running water, and discovered a shotgun and a pistol in a flush tank; another officer who, according to the District Court, "was searching the cellar for a man or the money" found in a washing machine a jacket and trousers of the type the fleeing man was said to have worn. A clip of ammunition for the pistol and a cap were found under the mattress of Hayden's bed, and ammunition for the shotgun was found in a bureau drawer in Hayden's room. All these items of evidence were introduced against respondent at his trial.

II

We agree with the Court of Appeals that neither the entry without warrant to search for the robber, nor the search for him without warrant was invalid. Under the circumstances of this case, "the exigencies of the situation made that course imperative." The police were informed that an armed robbery had taken place, and that the suspect had entered 2111 Cocoa Lane less than five minutes before they reached it. They acted reasonably when they entered the house and began to search for a man of the description they had been given and for weapons which he had used in the robbery or might use against them. The Fourth Amendment does not require police officers to delay in the course of an investigation if to do so would gravely endanger their lives or the lives of others. Speed here was essential, and only a thorough search of the house for persons and weapons could have insured that Hayden was the only man present and that the police had control of all weapons which could be used against them or to effect an escape. * * *

It is argued that, while the weapons, ammunition, and cap may have been seized in the course of a search for weapons, the officer who seized the clothing was searching neither for the suspect nor for weapons when he looked into the washing machine in which he found the clothing. But even if we assume, although we do not decide, that the exigent circumstances in this case made lawful a search without warrant only for the suspect or his weapons, it cannot be said on this record that the officer who found the clothes in the washing machine was not searching for weapons. He testified that he was searching for the man or the money, but his failure to state explicitly that he was searching for weapons, in the absence of a specific question to that effect, can hardly be accorded controlling weight. He knew that the robber was armed and he did not know that some weapons had been found at the time he opened the machine. In these circumstances the inference that he was in fact also looking for weapons is fully justified. * * *

[*The concurring opinion of JUSTICE FORTAS, with whom CHIEF JUSTICE WARREN concurred, is omitted. JUSTICE DOUGLAS dissented on unrelated grounds.*]

NOTES AND QUESTIONS

1. The officer who looked in the washing machine testified that he was searching for the suspect or the money taken in the robbery. Yet, in upholding the search, the Court only went so far as to say that exigent circumstances justified a search for the robbery suspect *and for weapons*. Obviously, the officer was not looking in the washing machine for Hayden, so that leaves his testimony that he was searching for money (as distinguished from weapons). How did Justice Brennan get around this problem? What is arguably wrong with his solution?

2. Suppose that Mrs. Hayden had objected to the officers' entry of her home? Would the result have been different?

3. *Warrantless entry of a home (part 1).* Various exigencies, not just those specified in *Hayden,* may justify a warrantless entry of a home. In Minnesota v. Olson, 495 U.S. 91, 110 S.Ct. 1684, 109 L.Ed.2d 85 (1990), the Supreme Court considered the exigencies that might justify a warrantless entry of a home to make an arrest or conduct a search. It stated:

> The Minnesota Supreme Court [in this case] applied essentially the correct standard in determining whether exigent circumstances [to enter a residence] existed. The court observed that "a warrantless intrusion may be justified by hot pursuit of a fleeing felon, or imminent destruction of evidence, or the need to prevent a suspect's escape, or the risk of danger to the police or to other persons inside or outside the dwelling." The court also apparently thought that in the absence of hot pursuit there must be at least probable cause to believe that one or more of the other factors justifying the entry were present and that in assessing the risk of danger, the gravity of the crime and likelihood that the suspect is armed should be considered.

Notwithstanding these exceptions, the Supreme Court has hesitated to give the police free rein to enter a home without a warrant. For example, in Welsh v. Wisconsin, 466 U.S. 740, 104 S.Ct. 2091, 80 L.Ed.2d 732 (1984), the police received information that *W* had been driving his vehicle in a manner that suggested either that he was inebriated or very sick. The police immediately proceeded to *W*'s nearby home and entered without consent or, despite *Payton v. New York* an arrest warrant. Inside they discovered *W* in bed. They placed him under arrest for operating a motor vehicle under the influence of an intoxicant, a noncriminal offense that could result in a monetary fine and subject *W* to civil forfeiture of his automobile. The Supreme Court held, however, that the warrantless entry of *W*'s house was unlawful:

> It is axiomatic that the "physical entry of the home is the chief evil against which the wording of the Fourth Amendment is directed." And a principal protection against unnecessary intrusions into private dwellings is the warrant requirement imposed by the Fourth Amendment on agents of the government who seek to enter the home for purposes of search or arrest. It is not surprising, therefore, that the Court has recognized, as "a 'basic principle of Fourth Amendment law[,]' that searches and seizures inside a home without a warrant are presumptively unreasonable." * * *
>
> Consistently with these long-recognized principles, the Court decided in *Payton v. New York* that warrantless felony arrests in the home are prohibited by the Fourth Amendment, absent probable cause and exigent circumstances. * * *

> Our hesitation in finding exigent circumstances, especially when warrantless arrests in the home are at issue, is particularly appropriate when the underlying offense for which there is probable cause to arrest is relatively minor. Before agents of the government may invade the sanctity of the home, the burden is on the government to demonstrate exigent circumstances that overcome the presumption of unreasonableness that attaches to all warrantless home entries. When the government's interest is only to arrest for a minor offense, that presumption of unreasonableness is difficult to rebut, and the government usually should be allowed to make such arrests only with a warrant issued upon probable cause by a neutral and detached magistrate.
>
> * * *[T]he only potential exigency claimed by the State was the need to ascertain the petitioner's blood-alcohol level.
>
> Even assuming, however, that the underlying facts would support a finding of this exigent circumstance * * *, [t]he State of Wisconsin has chosen to classify the first offense for driving while intoxicated as a noncriminal, civil forfeiture offense for which no imprisonment is possible. This is the best indication of the State's interest in precipitating the arrest * * *. Given this expression of the State's interest, a warrantless home arrest cannot be upheld simply because evidence of the petitioner's blood-alcohol level might have dissipated while the police obtained a warrant.

The rule in *Welsh* was addressed many years later in Stanton v. Sims, 571 U.S. 3, 134 S.Ct. 3, 187 L.Ed.2d 341 (2013). In *Stanton*, a civil case, the Court held unanimously that a warrantless hot pursuit entry into a residence can be constitutional, even if it is only based on the belief that a minor crime had been committed. The Court said that *Welsh* does not "lay down a categorical rule [requiring warrants to enter a home] for all cases involving minor offenses." It observed that *Welsh* said "only that a warrant is 'usually' required." It also observed that, unlike the facts in *Stanton*, *Welsh* did not involve a warrantless entry of a home in hot pursuit: "there was no immediate or continuous pursuit of [Welsh] from the scene of the crime [into the home]." Although the Court was not called upon in *Stanton* to announce a firm rule on the subject, it noted that "despite our emphasis in *Welsh* on the fact that the crime at issue was minor * * *[,] nothing in the opinion establishes that the seriousness of the crime is equally important *in cases of hot pursuit*."

4. *Warrantless entry of a home (part 2): the "murder scene" non-exception.* In Mincey v. Arizona, 437 U.S. 385, 98 S.Ct. 2408, 57 L.Ed.2d 290 (1978), the Supreme Court rejected a "murder scene warrant exception" to the Fourth Amendment that the Arizona Supreme Court had recognized. However, it is essential to draw a distinction between this *non*-exception to the warrant requirement and a true emergency:

After the shooting, the narcotics agents, thinking that other persons in the apartment might have been injured, looked about quickly for other victims. They found a young woman wounded in the bedroom closet and Mincey apparently unconscious in the bedroom, as well as Mincey's three acquaintances (one of whom had been wounded in the head) in the living room. Emergency assistance was requested, and some medical aid was administered to Officer Headricks. But the agents refrained from further investigation, pursuant to a Tucson Police Department directive that police officers should not investigate incidents in which they are involved. They neither searched further nor seized any evidence; they merely guarded the suspects and the premises.

Within 10 minutes, however, homicide detectives who had heard a radio report of the shooting arrived and took charge of the investigation. They supervised the removal of Officer Headricks and the suspects, trying to make sure that the scene was disturbed as little as possible, and then proceeded to gather evidence. Their search lasted four days, during which period the entire apartment was searched, photographed, and diagrammed. The officers opened drawers, closets, and cupboards, and inspected their contents; they emptied clothing pockets; they dug bullet fragments out of the walls and floors; they pulled up sections of the carpet and removed them for examination. Every item in the apartment was closely examined and inventoried, and 200 to 300 objects were seized. In short, Mincey's apartment was subjected to an exhaustive and intrusive search. No warrant was ever obtained. * * *

The State's * * * argument in support of its categorical exception to the warrant requirement is that a possible homicide presents an emergency situation demanding immediate action. We do not question the right of the police to respond to emergency situations. Numerous state and federal cases have recognized that the Fourth Amendment does not bar police officers from making warrantless entries and searches when they reasonably believe that a person within is in need of immediate aid. Similarly, when the police come upon the scene of a homicide they may make a prompt warrantless search of the area to see if there are other victims or if a killer is still on the premises. * * * And the police may seize any evidence that is in plain view during the course of their legitimate emergency activities.

But a warrantless search must be "strictly circumscribed by the exigencies which justify its initiation," and it simply cannot be contended that this search was justified by any emergency threatening life or limb. All the persons in Mincey's apartment had been located before the investigating

> homicide officers arrived there and began their search. And a four-day search that included opening dresser drawers and ripping up carpets can hardly be rationalized in terms of the legitimate concerns that justify an emergency search.

5. *Warrantless Entry into a Home, Part 3: May Officers Create Exigent Circumstances?* *Hayden* is a relatively uncontroversial application of the exigency exception to the "search warrant requirement." After all, the officers had probable cause to believe the robber was in the home they entered, and time was of the essence in this so-called "hot pursuit" situation. But, now, consider the case of Kentucky v. King, 563 U.S. 452, 131 S.Ct. 1849, 179 L.Ed.2d 865 (2011).

In *King*, the Court considered the role of the exigent circumstances exception when police, by knocking on the door and announcing their presence, might have caused the occupants to attempt to destroy evidence. Police set up a controlled buy of crack cocaine outside an apartment complex in Lexington, Kentucky. Officers then followed a drug suspect into the breezeway of the building. "Just as they entered the breezeway, they heard a door shut and detected a very strong odor of marijuana", but they did not observe which apartment the suspect had entered. "Because they smelled marijuana smoke emanating from the apartment on the left, they approached the door of that apartment."

> Officer Steven Cobb, one of the uniformed officers who approached the door, testified that the officers banged on the left apartment door "as loud as [they] could" and announced, " 'This is the police' " or " 'Police, police, police.' " Cobb said that "[a]s soon as [the officers] started banging on the door," they "could hear people inside moving," and "[i]t sounded as [though] things were being moved inside the apartment." These noises, Cobb testified, led the officers to believe that drug-related evidence was about to be destroyed.
>
> At that point, the officers announced that they "were going to make entry inside the apartment." Cobb then kicked in the door, the officers entered the apartment, and they found three people in the front room: respondent Hollis King, respondent's girlfriend, and a guest who was smoking marijuana. * * * [T]hey saw marijuana and powder cocaine in plain view. In a subsequent search, they also discovered crack cocaine, cash, and drug paraphernalia.
>
> Police eventually entered the apartment on the right. Inside, they found the suspected drug dealer who was the initial target of their investigation.

By the time of the *King* case, a number of lower courts had developed rules that barred police from using the exigent circumstances exception if they themselves created the exigent circumstances. The Court in *King*, with Justice Alito writing for the majority, rejected this distinction as overly subtle and subjective and held that "the exigent circumstances rule applies when the police do not gain entry to premises by means of an actual or threatened violation of the Fourth Amendment."

Applying their ruling to the facts of *King*, the Court found no evidence "that the officers either violated the Fourth Amendment or threatened to do so prior to the point when they entered the apartment * * * (for example, by announcing that they would break down the door if the occupants did not open the door voluntarily)." Dissenting, Justice Ginsburg argued that:

> The Court today arms the police with a way routinely to dishonor the Fourth Amendment's warrant requirement in drug cases. In lieu of presenting their evidence to a neutral magistrate, police officers may now knock, listen, then break the door down, never mind that they had ample time to obtain a warrant. * * * The urgency must exist, I would rule, when the police come on the scene, not subsequent to their arrival, prompted by their own conduct.

Notice: Although the police did not obtain a pre-search determination of probable cause by a magistrate, i.e., a warrant, the search would have been valid if police had probable cause that evidence was being destroyed. As noted in the introduction to this chapter and worth repeating here: An exception to the warrant requirement does *not* necessarily (or, even usually) dispense with the probable cause requirement.

Do you believe the police acted reasonably here? Why, or why not? If your answer is yes, and since the Fourth Amendment only prohibits unreasonable searches and seizures, isn't the Court correct in its ruling?

Let's look further. Suppose a police officer believes she has probable cause to search a suspect's house for drugs, but she is lazy and does not want to go to the effort of seeking a warrant. Or, maybe she just doesn't care about the Fourth Amendment, so she decides to act on her own. Therefore, she goes to the suspect's house and, just as in *King*, she bangs on the door as loud as possible, and announces, "This is the police," or "Police, police, police." The officer hears the sound of what may be drugs being flushed down the toilet. So, she breaks in without a warrant. Under *King*, is *her* warrantless entry constitutional? *Should* it be?

If *Katz* (p. 77) is right that warrantless searches "are *per se* unreasonable * * * subject to a few * * * well-delineated exceptions"—that is, if the default position truly is that police officers should almost always get warrants rather than act on their own belief that they have sufficient grounds for the search—and if it is true that "physical entry of the home is the chief evil against which the wording of the Fourth Amendment is directed," *Payton* (p. 185) then is Justice Ginsburg right that this case improperly reduces the force of the Fourth Amendment?

The Supreme Court remanded the *King* case for the state courts to determine whether in fact an exigency existed (the case had been litigated on the assumption that the noises inside the apartment created exigent circumstances). On remand, the Kentucky Supreme Court held that the State had failed to prove that the officers had probable cause that evidence was being destroyed. King v. Commonwealth, 386 S.W.3d 119 (Ky. 2012). The court noted that "the sounds as described at the suppression hearing were indistinguishable from ordinary household sounds, and were consistent with the natural and reasonable result of a knock on the door. Nothing in the record suggests that the sounds officers heard were anything more than the occupants preparing to answer the door."

6. *Warrantless entry of a home (part 4): the "community caretaking" emergency doctrine.* Sometimes the police act in a "community caretaking" function. For example, suppose the police look through a window and see a person apparently having a heart attack. Under what circumstances may officers enter a home without a warrant (which, after all, is a document intended to be used in criminal investigations), in order to deal with such an emergency? What if the emergency has criminal law implications, as well? Consider the unanimous opinion of Chief Justice Roberts in Brigham City, Utah v. Stuart, 547 U.S. 398, 126 S.Ct. 1943, 164 L.Ed.2d 650 (2006):

> At about 3 a.m., four police officers responded to a call regarding a loud party at a residence. Upon arriving at the house, * * * they observed two juveniles drinking beer in the backyard. They entered the backyard, and saw—through a screen door and windows—an altercation taking place in the kitchen of the home. * * * [F]our adults were attempting, with some difficulty, to restrain a juvenile. The juvenile eventually "broke free, swung a fist and struck one of the adults in the face." The officer testified that he observed the victim of the blow spitting blood into a nearby sink. The other adults continued to try to restrain the juvenile, pressing him up against a refrigerator with such force that the refrigerator began moving across the floor. At this point, an officer opened the screen door and announced the officers' presence. Amid the tumult, nobody noticed. The officer entered the kitchen and again cried out, and as the occupants slowly became aware that the police were on the scene, the altercation ceased.
>
> The officers subsequently arrested respondents and charged them with contributing to the delinquency of a minor, disorderly conduct, and intoxication. In the trial court, respondents filed a motion to suppress all

evidence obtained after the officers entered the home, arguing that the warrantless entry violated the Fourth Amendment. * * *

It is a " 'basic principle of Fourth Amendment law that searches and seizures inside a home without a warrant are presumptively unreasonable.' " Nevertheless, because the ultimate touchstone of the Fourth Amendment is "reasonableness," the warrant requirement is subject to certain exceptions. * * *

One exigency obviating the requirement of a warrant is the need to assist persons who are seriously injured or threatened with such injury. * * * [L]aw enforcement officers may enter a home without a warrant to render emergency assistance to an injured occupant or to protect an occupant from imminent injury. * * *

Respondents * * * contend that their conduct was not serious enough to justify the officers' intrusion into the home. They rely on *Welsh* v. *Wisconsin* [Note 3 *supra*], in which we held that "an important factor to be considered when determining whether any exigency exists is the gravity of the underlying offense for which the arrest is being made." This contention, too, is misplaced. *Welsh* involved a warrantless entry by officers to arrest a suspect for driving while intoxicated. There, the "only potential emergency" confronting the officers was the need to preserve evidence (*i.e.*, the suspect's blood-alcohol level)—an exigency that we held insufficient under the circumstances to justify entry into the suspect's home. Here, the officers were confronted with *ongoing* violence occurring *within* the home. *Welsh* did not address such a situation.

We think the officers' entry here was plainly reasonable under the circumstances. * * * [T]hey could see that a fracas was taking place inside the kitchen. A juvenile, fists clenched, was being held back by several adults. As the officers watch, he breaks free and strikes one of the adults in the face, sending the adult to the sink spitting blood.

In these circumstances, the officers had an objectively reasonable basis for believing both that the injured adult might need help and that the violence in the kitchen was just beginning. Nothing in the Fourth Amendment required them to wait until another blow rendered someone "unconscious" or "semi-conscious" or worse before entering. The role of a peace officer includes preventing violence and restoring order, not simply rendering first aid to casualties; an officer is not like a boxing (or hockey) referee, poised to stop a bout only if it becomes too one-sided.

> The manner of the officers' entry was also reasonable. After witnessing the punch, one of the officers opened the screen door and "yelled in police." When nobody heard him, he stepped into the kitchen and announced himself again. Only then did the tumult subside. The officer's announcement of his presence was at least equivalent to a knock on the screen door. Indeed, it was probably the only option that had even a chance of rising above the din. Under these circumstances, there was no violation of the Fourth Amendment's knock-and-announce rule. Furthermore, once the announcement was made, the officers were free to enter; it would serve no purpose to require them to stand dumbly at the door awaiting a response while those within brawled on, oblivious to their presence.

7. *Problem.* A police officer drove to *C*'s residence in order to talk to him about a noise complaint. When he arrived, he smelled the aroma of burnt marijuana coming from *C*'s apartment. The officer testified that, at that moment, "he knew he lacked authority to enter." Therefore, to increase the chances *C* would open the door, he covered the front door peephole, moved to the side to ensure that he could not be seen through a nearby window, and knocked. *C* partially opened the front door to see who was there. The officer could see that *C* was holding a handgun (although not aimed at him). When *C* saw the officer, he shut the door. Now, perceiving *C* to be a threat, the officer shoved the door open and entered. Fourth Amendment violation? State v. Campbell, 300 P.3d 72 (Kan. 2013).

B. SEARCHES INCIDENT TO A LAWFUL ARREST

1. General Principles

CHIMEL V. CALIFORNIA

Supreme Court of the United States, 1969.
395 U.S. 752, 89 S.Ct. 2034, 23 L.Ed.2d 685.

The "search incident to a lawful arrest" exception (hereinafter SILA) is just that: the basis for the exception is a valid arrest. The exception *only* arises if there is probable cause to make an arrest—or even better, an arrest warrant—*and an actual arrest is made.* There are two aspects to the SILA exception, both of which are at play in *Chimel.* First, the search of the *person* being arrested. Second, the search of the place where the arrest took *place.*

The former follows fairly well-settled law. Indeed, though the precise origins of the right to search the person of the arrestee are obscure, it is mentioned in the 1764 and 1788 editions of *Conductor Generalis*, a manual for justices of the peace that was widely used in the eighteenth century. The need to search arrestees also follows well-settled notions of common sense. If an officer is going to handcuff a suspect and transport that suspect in the back of a patrol car, the officer, at minimum, is going to need to make sure the suspect does not have access to a weapon with which he can threaten the officer or anyone else. In addition, it also makes sense to ensure that the suspect cannot destroy the evidence of the crime on the way to the police station.

***Chimel's* home is a little more problematic. Absent a situation such as that in *Warden v. Hayden*—where there was reason to believe that weapons and other dangerous persons could be hiding in the house—*Chimel* stands for the proposition that officers, once they have conducted a valid arrest and searched the person of the arrestee, are not free then to rummage through the remainder of the house in search of whatever they may find. There are limits. According to the Court in *Chimel*, those limits are bounded by "the person and the area within his immediate control."**

Now, of course, the fun begins. How does one define "area within immediate control"? As you read *Chimel*, ask yourself what aspects of the search went beyond the scope of the exception. Where would you draw the line?

MR. JUSTICE STEWART delivered the opinion of the Court [joined by CHIEF JUSTICE WARREN, and JUSTICES DOUGLAS, HARLAN, BRENNAN, FORTAS, and MARSHALL]. * * *

The relevant facts are essentially undisputed. Late in the afternoon of September 13, 1965, three police officers arrived at the Santa Ana, California, home of the petitioner with a warrant authorizing his arrest for the burglary of a coin shop. The officers knocked on the door, identified themselves to the petitioner's wife, and asked if they might come inside. She ushered them into the house, where they waited 10 or 15 minutes until the petitioner returned home from work. When the petitioner entered the house, one of the officers handed him the arrest warrant and asked for permission to "look around." The petitioner objected, but was advised that "on the basis of the lawful arrest," the officers would nonetheless conduct a search. No search warrant had been issued.

Accompanied by the petitioner's wife, the officers then looked through the entire three-bedroom house, including the attic, the garage, and a small workshop. In some rooms the search was relatively cursory. In the master bedroom and sewing room, however, the officers directed the petitioner's wife to open drawers and "to physically move contents of the drawers from side to side so that [they] might view any items that would have come from [the] burglary." After completing the search, they seized numerous items—primarily coins, but also several medals, tokens, and a few other objects. The entire search took between 45 minutes and an hour.

At the petitioner's subsequent state trial on two charges of burglary, the items taken from his house were admitted into evidence against him, over his objection that they had been unconstitutionally seized. * * * [T]he appellate courts went on to hold that the search of the petitioner's home had been justified, despite the absence of a search warrant, on the ground that it had been incident to a valid arrest. * * *

Without deciding the question, we proceed on the hypothesis that the California courts were correct in holding that the arrest of the petitioner was valid under the Constitution. This brings us directly to the question whether the warrantless search of the petitioner's entire house can be constitutionally justified as incident to that arrest. The decisions of this Court bearing upon that question have been far from consistent, as even the most cursory review makes evident.

Approval of a warrantless search incident to a lawful arrest seems first to have been articulated by the Court in 1914 as dictum in *Weeks v. United States*, [p. 51], in which the Court stated:

> "What then is the present case? Before answering that inquiry specifically, it may be well by a process of exclusion to state what it is not. It is not an assertion of the right on the part of the Government, always recognized under English and American law, to search the person of the accused when legally arrested to discover and seize the fruits or evidences of crime."

That statement made no reference to any right to search the *place* where an arrest occurs, but was limited to a right to search the "person." Eleven years later the case of *Carroll v. United States*, 267 U.S. 132, 45 S.Ct. 280, 69 L.Ed. 543, brought the following embellishment of the *Weeks* statement:

> "When a man is legally arrested for an offense, whatever is found upon his person *or in his control* which it is unlawful for him to have and which

> may be used to prove the offense may be seized and held as evidence in the prosecution." (Emphasis added.)

Still, that assertion too was far from a claim that the "place" where one is arrested may be searched so long as the arrest is valid. Without explanation, however, the principle emerged in expanded form a few months later in *Agnello v. United States*, 269 U.S. 20, 46 S.Ct. 4, 70 L.Ed. 145—although still by way of dictum:

> "The right without a search warrant contemporaneously to search persons lawfully arrested while committing crime and to search the place where the arrest is made in order to find and seize things connected with the crime as its fruits or as the means by which it was committed, as well as weapons and other things to effect an escape from custody, is not to be doubted."

[The Court then proceeded to summarize a long line of cases, including Harris v. United States, 331 U.S. 145, 67 S.Ct. 1098, 91 L.Ed. 1399 (1947) and Trupiano v. United States, 334 U.S. 699, 68 S.Ct. 1229, 92 L.Ed. 1663 (1948), in which the justices veered back and forth between an expansive and then narrow interpretation of the *Agnello* dictum (which subsequently became a holding) that police may, incident to an arrest, conduct a warrantless search of "the place where the arrest is made."]

In 1950 * * * came *United States v. Rabinowitz*, 339 U.S. 56, 70 S.Ct. 430, 94 L.Ed. 653, the decision upon which California primarily relies in the case now before us. In *Rabinowitz*, federal authorities had been informed that the defendant was dealing in stamps bearing forged overprints. On the basis of that information they secured a warrant for his arrest, which they executed at his one-room business office. At the time of the arrest, the officers "searched the desk, safe, and file cabinets in the office for about an hour and a half," and seized 573 stamps with forged overprints. The stamps were admitted into evidence at the defendant's trial, and this Court affirmed his conviction, rejecting the contention that the warrantless search had been unlawful. The Court held that the search in its entirety fell within the principle giving law enforcement authorities "[t]he right 'to search the place where the arrest is made in order to find and seize things connected with the crime * * *.' " * * * The opinion rejected the rule of *Trupiano* that "in seizing goods and articles, law enforcement agents must secure and use search warrants wherever reasonably practicable." The test, said the Court, "is not whether it is reasonable to procure a search warrant, but whether the search was reasonable."

Rabinowitz has come to stand for the proposition, *inter alia*, that a warrantless search "incident to a lawful arrest" may generally extend to the area that is considered to be in the "possession" or under the "control" of the person arrested. And it was on the basis of that proposition that the California courts upheld the search of the petitioner's entire house in this case. That doctrine, however, at least in the broad sense in which it was applied by the California courts in this case, can withstand neither historical nor rational analysis.

Even limited to its own facts, the *Rabinowitz* decision was, as we have seen, hardly founded on an unimpeachable line of authority. * * *

Nor is the rationale by which the State seeks here to sustain the search of the petitioner's house supported by a reasoned view of the background and purpose of the Fourth Amendment. Mr. Justice Frankfurter wisely pointed out in his *Rabinowitz* dissent that the Amendment's proscription of "unreasonable searches and seizures" must be read in light of "the history that gave rise to the words"—a history of "abuses so deeply felt by the Colonies as to be one of the potent causes of the Revolution * * *." The Amendment was in large part a reaction to the general warrants and warrantless searches that had so alienated the colonists and had helped speed the movement for independence. In the scheme of the Amendment, therefore, the requirement that "no Warrants shall issue, but upon probable cause," plays a crucial part. * * *

* * * Clearly, the general requirement that a search warrant be obtained is not lightly to be dispensed with, and "the burden is on those seeking [an] exemption [from the requirement] to show the need for it * * *." * * *

* * * When an arrest is made, it is reasonable for the arresting officer to search the person arrested in order to remove any weapons that the latter might seek to use in order to resist arrest or effect his escape. Otherwise, the officer's safety might well be endangered, and the arrest itself frustrated. In addition, it is entirely reasonable for the arresting officer to search for and seize any evidence on the arrestee's person in order to prevent its concealment or destruction. And the area into which an arrestee might reach in order to grab a weapon or evidentiary items must, of course, be governed by a like rule. A gun on a table or in a drawer in front of one who is arrested can be as dangerous to the arresting officer as one concealed in the clothing of the person arrested. There is ample justification, therefore, for a search of the arrestee's person and the area "within his immediate control"—construing that phrase to mean the area from within which he might gain possession of a weapon or destructible evidence.

There is no comparable justification, however, for routinely searching any room other than that in which an arrest occurs—or, for that matter, for searching through all the desk drawers or other closed or concealed areas in that room itself.

Such searches, in the absence of well-recognized exceptions, may be made only under the authority of a search warrant. The "adherence to judicial processes" mandated by the Fourth Amendment requires no less. * * *

It is argued in the present case that it is "reasonable" to search a man's house when he is arrested in it. But that argument is founded on little more than a subjective view regarding the acceptability of certain sorts of police conduct, and not on considerations relevant to Fourth Amendment interests. Under such an unconfined analysis, Fourth Amendment protection in this area would approach the evaporation point. It is not easy to explain why, for instance, it is less subjectively "reasonable" to search a man's house when he is arrested on his front lawn—or just down the street—than it is when he happens to be in the house at the time of arrest. As Mr. Justice Frankfurter put it:

> "To say that the search must be reasonable is to require some criterion of reason. It is no guide at all either for a jury or for district judges or the police to say that an 'unreasonable search' is forbidden—that the search must be reasonable. What is the test of reason which makes a search reasonable? The test is the reason underlying and expressed by the Fourth Amendment: the history and the experience which it embodies and the safeguards afforded by it against the evils to which it was a response." * * *

It would be possible, of course, to draw a line between *Rabinowitz* and *Harris* on the one hand, and this case on the other. For *Rabinowitz* involved a single room, and *Harris* a four-room apartment, while in the case before us an entire house was searched. But such a distinction would be highly artificial. The rationale that allowed the searches and seizures in *Rabinowitz* and *Harris* would allow the searches and seizures in this case. No consideration relevant to the Fourth Amendment suggests any point of rational limitation, once the search is allowed to go beyond the area from which the person arrested might obtain weapons or evidentiary items. The only reasoned distinction is one between a search of the person arrested and the area within his reach on the one hand, and more extensive searches on the other.

The petitioner correctly points out that one result of decisions such as *Rabinowitz* and *Harris* is to give law enforcement officials the opportunity to engage in searches not justified by probable cause, by the simple expedient of arranging to arrest suspects at home rather than elsewhere. We do not suggest that the petitioner is necessarily correct in his assertion that such a strategy was utilized here, but the fact remains that had he been arrested earlier in the day, at his place of employment rather than at home, no search of his house could have been made without a search warrant. In any event, even apart from the possibility of such police tactics, the general point so forcefully made by Judge Learned Hand in *United States v. Kirschenblatt*, 2 Cir., 16 F.2d 202, 51 A.L.R. 416, remains:

> "After arresting a man in his house, to rummage at will among his papers in search of whatever will convict him, appears to us to be indistinguishable from what might be done under a general warrant; indeed, the warrant would give more protection, for presumably it must be issued by a magistrate. True, by hypothesis the power would not exist, if the supposed offender were not found on the premises; but it is small consolation to know that one's papers are safe only so long as one is not at home."

Rabinowitz and *Harris* * * * are no longer to be followed.

Application of sound Fourth Amendment principles to the facts of this case produces a clear result. The search here went far beyond the petitioner's person and the area from within which he might have obtained either a weapon or something that could have been used as evidence against him. There was no constitutional justification, in the absence of a search warrant, for extending the search beyond that area. The scope of the search was, therefore, "unreasonable" under the Fourth and Fourteenth Amendments, and the petitioner's conviction cannot stand.

[*JUSTICE HARLAN'S concurring opinion is omitted.*]

MR. JUSTICE WHITE, with whom MR. JUSTICE BLACK joins, dissenting.

Few areas of the law have been as subject to shifting constitutional standards over the last 50 years as that of the search "incident to an arrest." There has been a remarkable instability in this whole area, which has seen at least four major shifts in emphasis. Today's opinion makes an untimely fifth. In my view, the Court should not now abandon the old rule. * * *

II

The rule which has prevailed, but for very brief or doubtful periods of aberration, is that a search incident to an arrest may extend to those areas under the control of the defendant and where items subject to constitutional seizure may be found. The justification for this rule must, under the language of the Fourth Amendment, lie in the reasonableness of the rule. * * * [T]he Court must decide whether a given search is reasonable. The Amendment does not proscribe "warrantless searches" but instead it proscribes "unreasonable searches" and this

Court has never held nor does the majority today assert that warrantless searches are necessarily unreasonable.

Applying this reasonableness test to the area of searches incident to arrests, one thing is clear at the outset. Search of an arrested man and of the items within his immediate reach must in almost every case be reasonable. There is always a danger that the suspect will try to escape, seizing concealed weapons with which to overpower and injure the arresting officers, and there is a danger that he may destroy evidence vital to the prosecution. Circumstances in which these justifications would not apply are sufficiently rare that inquiry is not made into searches of this scope, which have been considered reasonable throughout.

The justifications which make such a search reasonable obviously do not apply to the search of areas to which the accused does not have ready physical access. This is not enough, however, to prove such searches unconstitutional. The Court has always held, and does not today deny, that when there is probable cause to search and it is "impracticable" for one reason or another to get a search warrant, then a warrantless search may be reasonable. This is the case whether an arrest was made at the time of the search or not.

This is not to say that a search can be reasonable without regard to the probable cause to believe that seizable items are on the premises. But when there are exigent circumstances, and probable cause, then the search may be made without a warrant, reasonably. An arrest itself may often create an emergency situation making it impracticable to obtain a warrant before embarking on a related search. Again assuming that there is probable cause to search premises at the spot where a suspect is arrested, it seems to me unreasonable to require the police to leave the scene in order to obtain a search warrant when they are already legally there to make a valid arrest, and when there must almost always be a strong possibility that confederates of the arrested man will in the meanwhile remove the items for which the police have probable cause to search. This must so often be the case that it seems to me as unreasonable to require a warrant for a search of the premises as to require a warrant for search of the person and his very immediate surroundings.

This case provides a good illustration of my point that it is unreasonable to require police to leave the scene of an arrest in order to obtain a search warrant when they already have probable cause to search and there is a clear danger that the items for which they may reasonably search will be removed before they return with a warrant. * * * There was doubtless probable cause not only to arrest petitioner, but also to search his house. He had obliquely admitted, both to a neighbor and to the owner of the burglarized store, that he had committed the burglary. In light of this, and the fact that the neighbor had seen other admittedly stolen property in petitioner's house, there was surely probable cause on which a warrant could have issued to search the house for the stolen coins. Moreover, had the police simply arrested petitioner, taken him off to the station house, and later returned with a warrant it seems very likely that petitioner's wife, who in view of petitioner's generally garrulous nature must have known of the robbery, would have removed the coins. For the police to search the house while the evidence they had probable cause to search out and seize was still there cannot be considered unreasonable. * * *

IV

* * * Like the majority, I would permit the police to search the person of a suspect and the area under his immediate control either to assure the safety of the officers or to prevent the destruction of evidence. And like the majority, I see nothing in the arrest alone furnishing probable cause for a search of any broader scope. However, where as here the existence of probable cause is independently established and would justify a warrant for a broader search for evidence, I would follow past cases and permit such a search to be carried out without a warrant, since the fact of arrest supplies an exigent circumstance justifying police action before the evidence can be removed, and also alerts the suspect to the fact of the search so that he can immediately seek judicial determination of probable cause in an adversary proceeding, and appropriate redress.

This view, consistent with past cases, would not authorize the general search against which the Fourth Amendment was meant to guard, nor would it broaden or render uncertain in any way whatsoever the scope of searches permitted under the Fourth Amendment. The issue in this case is not the breadth of the search, since there was clearly probable cause for the search which was carried out. No broader search than if the officers had a warrant would be permitted. The only issue is whether a search warrant was required as a precondition to that search. It is agreed that such a warrant would be required absent exigent circumstances. I would hold that the fact of arrest supplies such an exigent circumstance, since the police had lawfully gained entry to the premises to effect the arrest and since delaying the search to secure a warrant would have involved the risk of not recovering the fruits of the crime. * * *

NOTES AND QUESTIONS

1. Who has the better side of the argument, Justice Stewart or Justice White? In his dissent, Justice White included the following footnote:

There were three officers at the scene of the arrest, one from the city where the coin burglary had occurred, and two from the city where the arrest was made. Assuming that one policeman from each city would be needed to bring the petitioner in and obtain a search warrant, one policeman could have been left to guard the house. However, if he not only could have remained in the house against petitioner's wife's will, but followed her about to assure that no evidence was being tampered with, the invasion of her privacy would be almost as great as that accompanying an actual search. Moreover, had the wife summoned an accomplice, one officer could not have watched them both. Applying the majority's approach, what should the police have done about Chimel's wife?

2. According to Justice Stewart, what is the scope of a proper warrantless search incident to a lawful arrest (that is, *where* may the police search, and for *what* may they search)? Must the police have probable cause to search the permissible areas? Answer the same questions according to the dissent.

3. *"Principle of particular justification."* The majority opinion in *Chimel* applied what may be described as the "principle of particular justification" (James B. White, *The Fourth Amendment as a Way of Talking About People: A Study of Robinson and Matlock*, 1974 Sup. Ct. Rev. 165, 190). According to this principle, "the police must, whenever practicable, obtain advance judicial approval of searches and seizures through the warrant procedure," and "[t]he scope of [a] search must be 'strictly tied to and justified by' the circumstances which rendered its initiation permissible." Terry v. Ohio, 392 U.S. 1, 88 S.Ct. 1868, 20 L.Ed.2d 889 (1968).

Applying this doctrine, we start from the proposition—in computer terms, the "default" position—that warrantless searches are unreasonable and, therefore, unconstitutional. If the police seek to justify a warrantless search, the burden is on them to demonstrate the existence of a justification for dispensing with the warrant requirement. Assuming that a justification exists, the scope of the permissible warrantless search must be no broader than the justification for the warrantless conduct compels. Once the circumstances that justify the warrantless conduct no longer exist, or once the police go beyond the legitimate scope of the warrantless search, the original obtain-a-warrant default position returns.

Can you articulate how the principle of particular justification applies in *Chimel*?

4. *Bright versus fuzzy lines.* A recurring issue in criminal jurisprudence is whether the Supreme Court, in devising rules of criminal procedure, should announce bright-line rules or rules that are "fuzzy" in nature that require case-by-case adjudication. In *Chimel*, did the Court announce a bright-line rule? If Justice White had prevailed, would the search-incident-to-lawful-arrest rule have been brighter?

5. *Problem.* Officers Gonzalez and Rogers believe they have probable cause to arrest Donald for murder. They come to Donald's home to arrest him, but nobody is home. They return to their car across the street, and await Donald's arrival. Ninety minutes later, Donald arrives and enters his house. Fifteen minutes later, the officers come to the door, knock, and arrest Donald at the doorway when he opens the door. Donald is now shoeless but otherwise fully dressed. The police handcuff Donald at the door and move him into the living room, twelve feet from an open closet. The police search Donald, but they find nothing. Officer Gonzales, hoping to find the murder weapon, goes to the closet, pats down trousers on closet hangers, and shakes pairs of shoes. In one pair, the officer discovers a gun, later determined to be the murder weapon. Prior to trial, Donald moves to suppress the gun from evidence. Should the motion be granted? (The officers had neither an arrest nor a search warrant in the foregoing facts.)

6. The Supreme Court has expanded the lawful scope of a warrantless search incident to an arrest in a home. See *Maryland v. Buie*, p. 391.

2. Search Incident to Arrest: There and Back Again

The forty-year story of the search incident to arrest exception (SILA), from *Chimel* in 1969, to the case of *Arizona v. Gant* in 2009, is the story of a swinging pendulum. The pendulum starts tethered to the basis of the holding in *Chimel*—that the search incident to a lawful arrest exception is designed to protect the safety of the officers and others, and to preserve evidence of the crime for which the defendant is being arrested. This tether comes undone as soon as we get into a series of cars, and drive away with defendants Robinson (1973), Belton (1981), and Thornton (2004). By the time Mr. Thornton seeks to challenge the search incident to his arrest, the exception has become almost an automatic one; any search of a car regardless of scope is valid simply by virtue of an arrest taking place; no further explanation needed. The Court makes little effort to slam on the brakes until we end up in a driveway with Mr. Gant, at which point the Court grabs hold of our wildly swinging pendulum, and once again tethers it to the original basis for the exception laid out forty years before.

The important thing to remember about *Chimel* is that there were indeed limitations to the search officers could constitutionally conduct when arresting Mr. Chimel (with a valid arrest warrant)—especially in his own home. While the police were justified in searching Chimel's person, and the area in his immediate control (broadly defined) where he could conceivably grab a weapon or criminal evidence, they had no similar justification for searching the rest of the house. Once Chimel was under arrest and in the officers' control, there was no valid concern that items in other parts of the house could pose a threat to officer safety or that evidence related to the robbery of the coin shop could be destroyed. There was, therefore, no reason that the officers could not take the time to obtain a warrant before searching the rest of the house. Notice the similarity in the reasoning in *Chimel*, regarding a search incident to a lawful arrest, with the basis for the exigent circumstances exception set out in *Warden* and *Welsh*. They both reflect the same concerns regarding safety and preservation of evidence that justify not requiring an officer to leave the scene to go get that all-important piece of paper. Once those concerns are alleviated, a warrant is once again required.

The actual language of the case of United States v. Robinson, 414 U.S. 218, 94 S.Ct. 467, 38 L.Ed.2d. 427 (1973), did not do much to change the underlying premise of *Chimel*, but it did provide what ended up being an unintended consequence of a fairly straightforward case. In *Robinson*, the defendant was pulled over when Officer Jenks had probable cause to believe that Robinson was driving on a suspended license (DWLS). Jenks arrested Robinson for DWLS, patted him down for weapons (perfectly valid), and found heroin in a cigarette packet in his coat pocket. The Court upheld the search, noting that "the validity of the search of a person incident to a lawful arrest has been regarded as settled since its first enunciation, and has remained virtually unchallenged until the present case."

The Court used *Robinson* not only to once again confirm the rule, but to make it an automatic, bright-line one. The Court made clear in *Robinson* that an arrest is an arrest, and anything on the person of the arrestee is fair game. What makes *Robinson* particularly interesting was that the facts of the case alleviated any significant concerns about safety or evidence. A simple check with the relevant Department of Motor Vehicles provides all the evidence needed for a DWLS charge, and given the nature of the charge, there was no reason for Officer Jenks to believe Robinson was violent. Indeed, Officer Jenks testified that while he did not know what the cigarette package might be at first, he did not believe it was a weapon. The bright-line rule enunciated in *Robinson* stems from the nature of an arrest itself, regardless of the crime. Any time an officer handcuffs and prepares to transport a suspect, there is a risk to officers and others by not searching the defendant. As the Court noted in *Robinson*:

> The authority to search the person incident to a lawful custodial arrest, while based upon the need to disarm and to discover evidence, does not depend on what a court later may decide was the probability in a particular arrest situation that weapons or evidence would in fact be found upon the person of the suspect.

The language and holding of *Robinson* was meant to apply to the search of a person, and the law would have been clear if thus limited to search of a person. It is when the language of *Robinson* begins to be applied to searches of the areas in which the defendant is found—in particular, the passenger compartments of automobiles—that our pendulum becomes untethered from the moorings of *Chimel* and starts to swing wildly.

In New York v. Belton, 453 U.S. 454, 101 S.Ct. 2860, 69 L.Ed.2d. 768 (1981), Officer Nicot pulled over a speeding vehicle containing four passengers, none of whom turned out to be the owner of the car. While talking with the driver, Officer Nicot smelled burnt marijuana and observed a package with the word "Supergold" (often associated with marijuana) on the floor of the car. Officer Nicot removed the passengers from the car, placed them under arrest, and moved them away from the car into separate parts of the Thruway and at a distance where they could not physically touch each other or quickly enter the vehicle. After confirming that the package held marijuana, Officer Nicot then read them their *Miranda* rights, and searched each arrestee. He then searched the car and found cocaine in a zippered pocket of a jacket belonging to defendant Belton.

Showing its attachment to bright-line rules, the Court upheld the search of the vehicle, citing specifically the language and holding in *Robinson.* Referring to the rule in *Robinson* as "straightforward, easily applied, and predictably enforced," the Court held that the same reasoning applied to the search of Belton's jacket in the automobile, with no further justification needed. The precise holding in *Belton* was "when a policeman has made a lawful custodial arrest of the occupant of an automobile, he may, as a contemporaneous incident of that arrest, search the passenger compartment of that automobile."

However, it is important to keep in mind that the language from *Robinson* being cited in *Belton* referred to the search of a person. In *Belton,* the search was of the passenger compartment of the car, and was conducted after the passengers had been removed from the car, arrested, and presumably moved to an area where the passenger compartment was no longer within their immediate control (think *Chimel* and the rest of his house). Citing the importance of police knowing clearly the scope of their authority in any arrest situation, the Court expanded *Robinson* to include searching the passenger compartment the suspect was traveling in, as well as the suspect himself.

The Court linked this expanded scope of authority back to *Chimel* by holding that "[o]ur reading of the cases suggests the generalization that articles inside the relatively narrow compass of the passenger compartment of an automobile are in fact, generally, if not inevitably, within the area into which an arrestee might reach."

The assumption after *Belton* is that if one is arrested while traveling in a vehicle, not only the person of the arrestee but the entire passenger compartment of the car including any containers in the passenger compartment (jackets, purses, glove compartments, bags, boxes, etc.) can be searched without a warrant and with no further consideration of issues of safety or preservation of evidence. The simple fact of an arrest, even for the most innocuous of offenses, destroys, or at least severely limits, any expectation of privacy in one's person or in the car in which they are traveling. This bright-line rule applies even if the defendant was arrested after exiting a parked car and the car was searched after the defendant was handcuffed and placed in the back of a patrol car.

This was the case in Thornton v. United States, 541 U.S. 615, 124 S.Ct. 2127, 158 L.Ed.2d 905 (2004). Thornton was observed driving a car whose registration tags did not match the type of car he was driving. Before the officer could pull him over, Thornton parked and exited the car. After a brief contact with Thornton, Officer Nichols asked and received consent to conduct a pat-down search. When the search revealed that Thornton was in possession of marijuana and crack cocaine, he was lawfully arrested for possession of illegal drugs, searched, handcuffed, and placed in the back of the patrol car. Only then, did the officer search the passenger compartment of the car, finding a handgun under the front seat.

On appeal, Thornton argued that *Belton* only applied when officers initiated contact with an arrestee while he was in a car. Thornton lost. The Court upheld the search, expanding *Belton* to include recent occupants of a vehicle, such as Thornton.

Even as they agreed with the search in the case of *Thornton*, however, concurring Justices Scalia and Ginsberg noted the shaky foundation on which cases such as *Belton* and *Thornton* now stood. Given that by 2004, the practice of handcuffing a suspect and placing the suspect in the patrol car before searching the car was "legion," it becomes hard to argue—as in *Belton*—that the passenger compartment is still generally within the arrestee's immediate control. If a passenger compartment can no longer be viewed as generally in an area of immediate control, then the language set out in *Belton,* and used in *Thornton*, is nothing more than a legal fiction designed to justify an otherwise unreasonable search.

In searching for a bright-line rule for searches incident to a lawful arrest, the Court may have created a warrant exception that could be easily abused by officers, or at least overused. This can be seen if one looks at how the Court resolved two other cases. In Knowles v. Iowa, 525 U.S. 113, 119 S.Ct. 484, 142

L.Ed.2d. 492 (1998), the Supreme Court held that the SILA warrant exception does *not* apply to a search of a car if the officer only issues a traffic citation to the driver, rather than takes the person into custody. But, then, in Atwater v. City of Lago Vista, 532 U.S. 318, 121 S.Ct. 1536, 149 L.Ed.2d. 549 (2001), the Court ruled that if an officer has the option of either issuing a ticket or taking the person into custody, and the officer chooses to make a custodial arrest, the full authority to search incident to that arrest applies (even if the arrest is for a misdemeanor infraction that can only result in a fine). In today's modern and statutory-based society, the number of misdemeanor provisions where an officer has the discretion to either arrest or cite-and-release are too numerous to count. Just because an officer may have probable cause to make a custodial arrest, does not mean he or she has to do so. So, under *Knowles* and *Atwater*, what is to prevent an officer from arresting a person (assuming probable cause to arrest) simply to gain the ability to conduct a warrantless search, even if nine times out of ten the officer would cite-and-release for the same violation? Answer: nothing.

In fact, Justice O'Connor, dissenting in *Atwater*, noted this very concern.

> Although the Fourth Amendment expressly requires that the latter course [arrest and search incident to] be a reasonable and proportional response to the circumstances of the offense, the majority gives officers unfettered discretion to choose that course without articulating a single reason why such action is appropriate. . . . Such unbounded discretion carries with it grave potential for abuse. [A] relatively minor traffic infraction may often serve as an excuse for stopping and harassing an individual.

What 'types' of individuals might be most vulnerable to such harassment? What do you think is Justice O'Connor's real concern here?

Here is why the search incident to arrest exception is a good example of the inherent difficulties in choosing between bright-line rules and a case-by-case analysis. Bright-line rules can be a double-edged sword. Too restrictive and they limit the ability of officers to use their experience and judgment to best address the specific situation they face. Too broad, however, and we open the door to abuses of that discretion based not on experienced judgment, but on biases, stereotypes, and even personal vendettas that can poison the relationship between the police and the communities they are trying to serve, often at the risk of their own lives.

By 2009, forty-years after *Chimel*, the Court had finally had enough and sought to regain control of the SILA pendulum. Membership in the Court had changed over time and some of the strongest proponents of the bright-line reasoning in cases like *Belton* and *Thornton* were no longer on the bench. And so, we reach the evening where Mr. Gant pulls into a driveway and ends up in the wrong place at the wrong time. Note the response the officers gave when asked why they conducted the search of Mr. Gant's vehicle. *Because the law says we can do it.*

ARIZONA V. GANT

Supreme Court of the United States, 2009.
556 U.S. 332, 129 S.Ct. 1710, 173 L.Ed.2d 485.

The fact that *Gant* involves a charge of Driving With License Suspended (DWLS) makes this a particularly good set of facts under which to reconsider *Belton* and *Thornton*. While we hesitate to label any criminal prosecution a formality, the elements of the crime of DWLS are ridiculously easy to prove. Assuming there was probable cause to stop and contact the driver, most cases go something like this:

- **Prosecutor puts arresting officer on the stand.**
- **PROSECUTOR: Did you observe the defendant driving?**
- **OFFICER: Yes.**
- **Prosecutor establishes reason for stop and contact with driver.**
- **PROSECUTOR: Did you run the defendant's driver's license through the state DMV records?**
- **OFFICER: Yes**
- **PROSECUTOR: Was the defendant's license suspended?**
- **OFFICER: Yes.**
- **PROSECUTOR: Your Honor, no more questions.**
- **A defense attorney, if present, may or may not cross-examine the officer.**
- **PROSECUTOR: Your Honor, the State rests.**

You can see why charges of DWLS rarely go to trial.

It is difficult, if not impossible, to argue that the charge of DWLS alone involves any concern regarding weapons or violence, and there is no evidence to look for in the passenger compartment of the car. As a result,

once the Court returns to the rationale for the *Chimel* exception, applying it to the facts in *Gant* becomes rather straightforward.

Justice Alito's dissent nicely lists the five factors that typically must be present for the Court to overrule one of its own decisions. Although Justice Stevens denies that the Court is overruling *Belton*, it is true that *Gant* rejects the long-accepted view of *Belton* in the lower courts. Do you agree with Justice Stevens or Justice Alito as to whether the broad reading of *Belton* should have been rejected?

JUSTICE STEVENS delivered the opinion of the Court [joined by JUSTICES SCALIA, SOUTER, THOMAS, and GINSBURG].

After Rodney Gant was arrested for driving with a suspended license, handcuffed, and locked in the back of a patrol car, police officers searched his car and discovered cocaine in the pocket of a jacket on the backseat. Because Gant could not have accessed his car to retrieve weapons or evidence at the time of the search, the Arizona Supreme Court held that the search-incident-to-arrest exception to the Fourth Amendments warrant requirement, as defined in *Chimel* v. *California*, [p. 227] and applied to vehicle searches in *New York* v. *Belton*, , did not justify the search in this case. We agree with that conclusion.

Under *Chimel*, police may search incident to arrest only the space within an arrestee's immediate control, meaning the area from within which he might gain possession of a weapon or destructible evidence. The safety and evidentiary justifications underlying *Chimel*'s reaching-distance rule determine *Belton*'s scope. Accordingly, we hold that *Belton* does not authorize a vehicle search incident to a recent occupant's arrest after the arrestee has been secured and cannot access the interior of the vehicle. Consistent with the holding in *Thornton* v. *United States*,, and following the suggestion in Justice Scalia's opinion concurring in the judgment in that case, we also conclude that circumstances unique to the automobile context justify a search incident to arrest when it is reasonable to believe that evidence of the offense of arrest might be found in the vehicle.

I

[The police had reliable information that there was an outstanding warrant for the arrest of Rodney Gant for driving with a suspended license. Officers proceeded to the house where they expected to find Gant. Shortly thereafter, Gant drove into the driveway. He was arrested after he got out of his car. Gant was handcuffed and placed in a locked patrol car. Two officers then searched his vehicle and discovered a gun, as well as a bag of cocaine in the pocket of a jacket on the backseat.]

Gant was charged with two offenses—possession of a narcotic drug for sale and possession of drug paraphernalia (*i.e.*, the plastic bag in which the cocaine was found). He moved to suppress the evidence seized from his car on the ground that the warrantless search violated the Fourth Amendment. * * * Gant argued that *Belton* did not authorize the search of his vehicle because he posed no threat to the officers after he was handcuffed in the patrol car and because he was arrested for a traffic offense for which no evidence could be found in his vehicle. When asked at the suppression hearing why the search was conducted, Officer Griffith responded: "Because the law says we can do it."

The trial court * * * denied the motion to suppress. * * *

After protracted state-court proceedings, the Arizona Supreme Court concluded that the search of Gant's car was unreasonable within the meaning of the Fourth Amendment. The court's opinion discussed at length our decision in *Belton* * * *. The court distinguished *Belton* as a case concerning the permissible scope of a vehicle search incident to arrest and concluded that it did not answer "the threshold question whether the police may conduct a search incident to arrest at all once the scene is secure." Relying on our earlier decision in *Chimel*, the court observed that the search-incident-to-arrest exception to the warrant requirement is justified by interests in officer safety and evidence preservation. When "the justifications underlying *Chimel* no longer exist because the scene is secure and the arrestee is handcuffed, secured in the back of a patrol car, and under the supervision of an officer," the court concluded, a "warrantless search of the arrestee's car cannot be justified as necessary to protect the officers at the scene or prevent the destruction of evidence." Accordingly, the court held that the search of Gant's car was unreasonable. * * *

The chorus that has called for us to revisit *Belton* includes courts, scholars, and Members of this Court who have questioned that decision's clarity and its fidelity to Fourth Amendment principles. We therefore granted the State's petition for certiorari.

II

Consistent with our precedent, our analysis begins, as it should in every case addressing the reasonableness of a warrantless search, with the basic rule that "searches conducted outside the judicial process, without prior approval by judge or magistrate, are *per se* unreasonable under the Fourth Amendment—subject only to a few specifically established and well-delineated exceptions." Among the exceptions to the warrant requirement is a search incident to a lawful arrest. * * *

In *Chimel*, we held that a search incident to arrest may only include "the arrestee's person and the area 'within his immediate control'—construing that phrase to mean the area from within which he might gain possession of a weapon or destructible evidence." That limitation, which continues to define the boundaries of the exception, ensures that the scope of a search incident to arrest is commensurate with its purposes of protecting arresting officers and safeguarding any evidence of the offense of arrest that an arrestee might conceal or destroy. If there is no possibility that an arrestee could reach into the area that law enforcement officers seek to search, both justifications for the search-incident-to-arrest exception are absent and the rule does not apply.

In *Belton*, we considered *Chimel*'s application to the automobile context. * * *

* * * [W]e held that when an officer lawfully arrests "the occupant of an automobile, he may, as a contemporaneous incident of that arrest, search the passenger compartment of the automobile" and any containers therein. That holding was based in large part on our assumption "that articles inside the relatively narrow compass of the passenger compartment of an automobile are in fact generally, even if not inevitably, within 'the area into which an arrestee might reach.' "

The Arizona Supreme Court read our decision in *Belton* as merely delineating "the proper scope of a search of the interior of an automobile" incident to an arrest. That is, *when* the passenger compartment is within an arrestee's reaching distance, *Belton* supplies the generalization that the entire compartment and any containers therein may be reached. On that view of *Belton*, the state court concluded that the search of Gant's car was unreasonable because Gant clearly could not have accessed his car at the time of the search. * * *

Gant now urges us to adopt the reading of *Belton* followed by the Arizona Supreme Court.

III

Despite the textual and evidentiary support for the Arizona Supreme Court's reading of *Belton*, our opinion has been widely understood to allow a vehicle search incident to the arrest of a recent occupant even if there is no possibility the arrestee could gain access to the vehicle at the time of the search. This reading may be attributable to Justice Brennan's dissent in *Belton*, in which he characterized the Court's holding as resting on the "fiction * * * that the interior of a car is *always* within the immediate control of an arrestee who has recently been in the car." * * *

* * * As Justice O'Connor observed [in *Thornton*], "lower court decisions seem now to treat the ability to search a vehicle incident to the arrest of a recent occupant as a police entitlement rather than as an exception justified by the twin rationales of *Chimel*." Justice Scalia has similarly noted that, although it is improbable that an arrestee could gain access to weapons stored in his vehicle after he has been handcuffed and secured in the backseat of a patrol car, cases allowing a search in "this precise factual scenario * * * are legion." * * *

Under this broad reading of *Belton*, a vehicle search would be authorized incident to every arrest of a recent occupant notwithstanding that in most cases the vehicle's passenger compartment will not be within the arrestee's reach at the time of the search. To read *Belton* as authorizing a vehicle search incident to every recent occupant's arrest would thus untether the rule from the justifications underlying the *Chimel* exception * * *. Accordingly, we reject this reading of *Belton* and hold that the *Chimel* rationale authorizes police to search a vehicle incident to a recent occupant's arrest only when the arrestee is unsecured and within reaching distance of the passenger compartment at the time of the search.

Although it does not follow from *Chimel*, we also conclude that circumstances unique to the vehicle context justify a search incident to a lawful arrest when it is "reasonable to believe evidence relevant to the crime of arrest might be found in the vehicle." In many cases, as when a recent occupant is arrested for a traffic violation, there will be no reasonable basis to believe the vehicle contains relevant evidence. But in others, including *Belton* and *Thornton*, the offense of arrest will supply a basis for searching the passenger compartment of an arrestee's vehicle and any containers therein.

Neither the possibility of access nor the likelihood of discovering offense-related evidence authorized the search in this case. * * * Because police could not reasonably have believed either that Gant could have accessed his car at the time of the search or that evidence of the offense [of driving with a suspended license] for which he was arrested might have been found therein, the search in this case was unreasonable.

IV

The State * * * asks us to uphold the search of his vehicle under the broad reading of *Belton* discussed above. The State argues that *Belton* searches are reasonable regardless of the possibility of access in a given case because that expansive rule correctly balances law enforcement interests, including the interest in a bright-line rule, with an arrestee's limited privacy interest in his vehicle.

For several reasons, we reject the State's argument. First, the State seriously undervalues the privacy interests at stake. * * * It is particularly significant that *Belton* searches authorize police officers to search not just the passenger compartment but every purse, briefcase, or other container within that space. A rule that gives police the power to conduct such a search whenever an individual is caught committing a traffic offense, when there is no basis for believing evidence of the offense might be found in the vehicle, creates a serious and recurring threat to the privacy of countless individuals. Indeed, the character of that threat implicates the central concern underlying the Fourth Amendment—the concern about giving police officers unbridled discretion to rummage at will among a person's private effects.

At the same time as it undervalues these privacy concerns, the State exaggerates the clarity that its reading of *Belton* provides. Courts that have read *Belton* expansively are at odds regarding how close in time to the arrest and how proximate to the arrestee's vehicle an officer's first contact with the arrestee must be to bring the encounter within *Belton*'s purview and whether a search is reasonable when it commences or continues after the arrestee has been removed from the scene. The rule has thus generated a great deal of uncertainty, particularly for a rule touted as providing a "bright line." * * *

* * * Construing *Belton* broadly to allow vehicle searches incident to any arrest would serve no purpose except to provide a police entitlement, and it is anathema to the Fourth Amendment to permit a warrantless search on that basis. * * *

V

Our dissenting colleagues argue that the doctrine of *stare decisis* requires adherence to a broad reading of *Belton* even though the justifications for searching a vehicle incident to arrest are in most cases absent. The doctrine of *stare decisis* is of course "essential to the respect accorded to the judgments of the Court and to the stability of the law," but it does not compel us to follow a past decision when its rationale no longer withstands "careful analysis."

* * * The safety and evidentiary interests that supported the search in *Belton* simply are not present in this case. Indeed, it is hard to imagine two cases that are factually more distinct, as *Belton* involved one officer confronted by four unsecured arrestees suspected of committing a drug offense and this case involves several officers confronted with a securely detained arrestee apprehended for driving with a suspended license. This case is also distinguishable from *Thornton*, in which the petitioner was arrested for a drug offense. It is thus unsurprising that

Members of this Court who concurred in the judgments in *Belton* and *Thornton* also concur in the decision in this case.

We do not agree with the contention in Justice Alito's dissent * * * that consideration of police reliance interests requires a different result. Although it appears that the State's reading of *Belton* has been widely taught in police academies and that law enforcement officers have relied on the rule in conducting vehicle searches during the past 28 years, many of these searches were not justified by the reasons underlying the *Chimel* exception. Countless individuals guilty of nothing more serious than a traffic violation have had their constitutional right to the security of their private effects violated as a result. The fact that the law enforcement community may view the State's version of the *Belton* rule as an entitlement does not establish the sort of reliance interest that could outweigh the countervailing interest that all individuals share in having their constitutional rights fully protected. * * *

The experience of the 28 years since we decided *Belton* has shown that the generalization underpinning the broad reading of that decision is unfounded. We now know that articles inside the passenger compartment are rarely "within 'the area into which an arrestee might reach,' " and blind adherence to *Belton*'s faulty assumption would authorize myriad unconstitutional searches. The doctrine of *stare decisis* does not require us to approve routine constitutional violations.

VI

Police may search a vehicle incident to a recent occupant's arrest only if the arrestee is within reaching distance of the passenger compartment at the time of the search or it is reasonable to believe the vehicle contains evidence of the offense of arrest. When these justifications are absent, a search of an arrestee's vehicle will be unreasonable unless police obtain a warrant or show that another exception to the warrant requirement applies. * * * Accordingly, the judgment of the State Supreme Court is affirmed.

[*JUSTICE SCALIA'S concurring opinion omitted.*]

[*JUSTICE BREYER'S dissenting opinion omitted.*]

JUSTICE ALITO, with whom THE CHIEF JUSTICE [ROBERTS] and JUSTICE KENNEDY join, and with whom JUSTICE BREYER joins except as to Part II-E, dissenting.

* * * Today's decision effectively overrules [*Belton* and *Thornton*], even though respondent Gant has not asked us to do so.

To take the place of the overruled precedents, the Court adopts a new two-part rule under which a police officer who arrests a vehicle occupant or recent occupant may search the passenger compartment if (1) the arrestee is within reaching distance of the vehicle at the time of the search or (2) the officer has reason to believe that the vehicle contains evidence of the offense of arrest. The first part of this new rule may endanger arresting officers and is truly endorsed by only four Justices; Justice Scalia joins solely for the purpose of avoiding a "4-to-1-to-4 opinion." The second part of the new rule is taken from Justice Scalia's separate opinion in *Thornton* * * *. * * * I would follow *Belton*, and I therefore respectfully dissent.

I

Although the Court refuses to acknowledge that it is overruling *Belton* and *Thornton*, there can be no doubt that it does so. * * *

The precise holding in *Belton* could not be clearer. The Court stated unequivocally: " '[W]e hold that when a policeman has made a lawful custodial arrest of the occupant of an automobile, he may, as a contemporaneous incident of that arrest, search the passenger compartment of that automobile."

Despite this explicit statement, the opinion of the Court in the present case curiously suggests that *Belton* may reasonably be read as adopting a holding that is narrower than the one explicitly set out in the *Belton* opinion, namely, that an officer arresting a vehicle occupant may search the passenger compartment "*when* the passenger compartment is within an arrestee's reaching distance." According to the Court, the broader reading of *Belton* that has gained wide acceptance may be attributable to Justice Brennan's dissent."

Contrary to the Court's suggestion, however, Justice Brennan's *Belton* dissent did not mischaracterize the Court's holding in that case or cause that holding to be misinterpreted. As noted, the *Belton* Court explicitly stated precisely what it held. * * * [The *Belton*] "bright-line rule" has now been interred.

II

Because the Court has substantially overruled *Belton* and *Thornton,* the Court must explain why its departure from the usual rule of *stare decisis* is justified. I recognize that stare decisis is not an "inexorable command," and applies less rigidly in constitutional cases. But the Court has said that a constitutional precedent should be followed unless there is a " 'special justification' " for its abandonment. Relevant factors identified in prior cases include whether the precedent has engendered reliance, whether there has been an important change in circumstances in the outside world, whether the precedent has proved to be unworkable, whether the precedent has been undermined by later decisions, and whether the decision was badly reasoned. These factors weigh in favor of retaining the rule established in *Belton*.

A

Reliance. * * *

* * * [T]here certainly is substantial reliance here. The *Belton* rule has been taught to police officers for more than a quarter century. Many searches—almost certainly including more than a few that figure in cases now on appeal—were conducted in scrupulous reliance on that precedent. It is likely that, on the very day when this opinion is announced, numerous vehicle searches will be conducted in good faith by police officers who were taught the *Belton* rule.

The opinion of the Court recognizes [this] * * *. But for the Court, this seemingly counts for nothing. * * *

B

Changed circumstances. Abandonment of the *Belton* rule cannot be justified on the ground that the dangers surrounding the arrest of a vehicle occupant are different today than they were 28 years ago. * * * [S]urely it was well known in 1981 that a person who is taken from a vehicle, handcuffed, and placed in the back of a patrol car is unlikely to make it back into his own car to retrieve a weapon or destroy evidence.

C

Workability. The *Belton* rule has not proved to be unworkable. On the contrary, the rule was adopted for the express purpose of providing a test that would be relatively easy for police officers and judges to apply. The Court correctly notes that even the *Belton* rule is not perfectly clear in all situations. Specifically, it is sometimes debatable whether a search is or is not contemporaneous with an arrest, but that problem is small in comparison with the problems that the Court's new two-part rule will produce. * * *

D

Consistency with later cases. The *Belton* bright-line rule has not been undermined by subsequent cases. On the contrary, that rule was reaffirmed and extended just five years ago in *Thornton*.

E

Bad reasoning. The Court is harshly critical of *Belton*'s reasoning, but the problem that the Court perceives cannot be remedied simply by overruling *Belton*.

Belton represented only a modest—and quite defensible—extension of *Chimel*, as I understand that decision. * * *

* * * *Chimel* did not say whether "the area from within which [an arrestee] might gain possession of a weapon or destructible evidence" is to be measured at the time of the arrest or at the time of the search, but unless the *Chimel* rule was meant to be a specialty rule, applicable to only a few unusual cases, the Court must have intended for this area to be measured at the time of arrest.

This is so because the Court can hardly have failed to appreciate the following two facts. First, in the great majority of cases, an officer making an arrest is able to handcuff the arrestee and remove him to a secure place before conducting a search incident to the arrest. Second, because it is safer for an arresting officer to secure an arrestee before searching, it is likely that this is what arresting officers do in the great majority of cases. * * * Thus, if the area within an arrestee's reach were assessed, not at the time of arrest, but at the time of the search, the *Chimel* rule would rarely come into play. * * *

I do not think that this is what the *Chimel* Court intended. Handcuffs were in use in 1969. The ability of arresting officers to secure arrestees before conducting a search—and their incentive to do so—are facts that can hardly have escaped the Court's attention. I therefore believe that the *Chimel* Court intended that its new rule apply in cases in which the arrestee is handcuffed before the search is conducted.

The *Belton* Court, in my view, proceeded on the basis of this interpretation of *Chimel*. * * * Viewing *Chimel* as having focused on the time of arrest, *Belton*'s only new step was to eliminate the need to decide on a case-by-case basis whether a particular person seated in a car actually could have reached the part of the passenger compartment where a weapon or evidence was hidden. For this reason, if we are going to reexamine *Belton*, we should also reexamine the reasoning in *Chimel* on which *Belton* rests.

F

The Court, however, does not reexamine *Chimel* and thus leaves the law relating to searches incident to arrest in a confused and unstable state. The first part of the Court's new two-part rule—which permits an arresting officer to search the area within an arrestee's reach at the time of the search—applies, at least for now, only to vehicle occupants and recent occupants, but there is no logical reason why the same rule should not apply to all arrestees.

The second part of the Court's new rule, which the Court takes uncritically from Justice Scalia's separate opinion in *Thornton,* raises doctrinal and practical problems that the Court makes no effort to address. Why, for example, is the standard for this type of evidence-gathering search "reason to believe" rather than probable cause? And why is this type of search restricted to evidence of the offense of arrest? It is true that an arrestee's vehicle is probably more likely to contain evidence of the crime of arrest than of some other crime, but if reason-to-believe is the governing standard for an evidence-gathering search incident to arrest, it is not easy to see why an officer should not be able to search when the officer has reason to believe that the vehicle in question possesses evidence of a crime other than the crime of arrest.

Nor is it easy to see why an evidence-gathering search incident to arrest should be restricted to the passenger compartment. The *Belton* rule was limited in this way because the passenger compartment was considered to be the area that vehicle occupants can generally reach, but since the second part of the new rule is not based on officer safety or the preservation of evidence, the ground for this limitation is obscure.

III

Respondent in this case has not asked us to overrule *Belton*, much less *Chimel*. Respondent's argument rests entirely on an interpretation of *Belton* that is plainly incorrect, an interpretation that disregards *Belton*'s explicit delineation of its holding. I would therefore leave any reexamination of our prior precedents for another day, if such a reexamination is to be undertaken at all. In this case, I would simply apply *Belton* and reverse the judgment below.

NOTES AND QUESTIONS

1. *Problem.* In view of *Gant*, would a warrantless search of the passenger compartment of a vehicle be permissible to search for illegal weapons, after the driver of the vehicle (now handcuffed and in the police vehicle) is arrested for possession of a prohibited weapon? See United States v. Vinton, 594 F.3d 14 (D.C. Cir. 2010). What if the person is arrested for driving under the influence of alcohol: would it permissible to search the car for open containers of alcohol? United States v. Taylor, 49 A.3d 818 (D.C. Ct. of App. 2012).

2. *Arrest inventories: another warrant "exception."* Reconsider *United States v. Robinson* (search incident to arrest for DWLS). After Robinson was taken into custody, he had to be transported to the police station for booking, an administrative process that includes photographing and fingerprinting the arrestee (and, as we will see in Chapter 6), sometimes taking a DNA sample). But there is more: any person who will be incarcerated, even temporarily, undergoes a second search: an "arrest inventory."

This inventory search, which occurs without a warrant and in the absence of probable cause, is constitutionally justified on various grounds: to protect the arrestee from theft of her valuables while in jail; to reduce the risk of false claims of theft by the arrestee; and to ensure that contraband and dangerous instrumentalities that might have been missed by the police in the initial search incident to the arrest are not smuggled into the jail. Illinois v. Lafayette, 462 U.S. 640, 103 S.Ct. 2605, 77 L.Ed.2d 65 (1983). To be valid, the inventory must follow procedures standardized in that jurisdiction.

Notice the significance of this warrant exception: Even if Officer Jenks had not searched Robinson's clothing at the scene and discovered the crumpled up cigarette package, it presumably would have been discovered in a routine inventory search. Although inventory operating procedures of police departments vary, the police typically open containers found on arrestees, such as wallets or, as here, cigarette packages. Therefore, as a practical matter, once Robinson's custodial arrest was made, his fate was virtually sealed: If one warrant exception didn't justify the search of his person, another would!

3. Search Incident to Arrest: The Pendulum Re-Tethered.

RILEY V. CALIFORNIA

Supreme Court of the United States, 2014.
573 U.S. ___, 134 S.Ct. 2473, 189 L.Ed.2d 430.

It is important to remember that search incident to a lawful arrest is *not* an automobile-based exception to the warrant requirement (we will be reviewing the actual automobile exception shortly). Indeed, this entire journey through the SILA exception started in Mr. Chimel's home.

Mr. Riley, like Mr. Chimel, was not a passenger in a car. So, given that so much of the language in *Gant* was related to automobile occupants, does the exception remain re-tethered to *Chimel* once cars are no longer involved? The answer in *Riley* is: so far. The Court in *Riley* also returns us to discussions in *Robinson* regarding the allowable scope of a search of the *person* of an arrestee. This time, however, the question centers around the search not only of a person, but of a person's digital information. Having become utterly ubiquitous in our daily lives, smart phones have finally found their way to the U.S. Supreme Court.

In reading *Riley*, note the discussion of the amount of personal data available on smartphones. We saw a similar discussion in Justice Sotomayor's concurrence in *Jones* when she compared the placement of a beeper with that of a GPS locator. The question still remains, though: "do

we have a legitimate expectation of privacy in our digital data"? Since the existence of a search in *Riley* was assumed, the Court does not provide an answer to this question. It is likely, however, that the Court will have to at some point. Given that *Riley* is a 9–0 decision, how do you think the Court will rule when that time comes?

CHIEF JUSTICE ROBERTS delivered the opinion of the Court [joined by JUSTICES SCALIA, KENNEDY, THOMAS, GINSBURG, BREYER, SOTOMAYOR, KAGAN, and in part by JUSTICE ALITO].

These two cases raise a common question: whether the police may, without a warrant, search digital information on a cell phone seized from an individual who has been arrested.

I

A

In the first case, petitioner David Riley * * * was arrested for possession of concealed and loaded firearms * * *.

An officer searched Riley incident to the arrest and found items associated with the "Bloods" street gang. He also seized a cell phone from Riley's pants pocket. According to Riley's uncontradicted assertion, the phone was a "smart phone," a cell phone with a broad range of other functions based on advanced computing capability, large storage capacity, and Internet connectivity. The officer accessed information on the phone and noticed that some words (presumably in text messages or a contacts list) were preceded by the letters "CK"—a label that, he believed, stood for "Crip Killers," a slang term for members of the Bloods gang.

At the police station about two hours after the arrest, a detective specializing in gangs further examined the contents of the phone. The detective testified that he "went through" Riley's phone "looking for evidence, because * * * gang members will often video themselves with guns or take pictures of themselves with the guns." Although there was "a lot of stuff" on the phone, particular files that "caught [the detective's] eye" included videos of young men sparring while someone yelled encouragement using the moniker "Blood." The police also found photographs of Riley standing in front of a car they suspected had been involved in a shooting a few weeks earlier.

Riley was ultimately charged, in connection with that earlier shooting. * * *. * * * Prior to trial, Riley moved to suppress all evidence that the police had obtained from his cell phone. He contended that the searches of his phone violated the Fourth Amendment, because they had been performed without a warrant and were not otherwise justified by exigent circumstances. The trial court rejected that argument. * * * Riley was convicted * * *. * * *

B

In the second case, a police officer performing routine surveillance observed respondent Brima Wurie make an apparent drug sale from a car. Officers subsequently arrested Wurie and took him to the police station. At the station, the officers seized two cell phones from Wurie's person. The one at issue here was a "flip phone," a kind of phone that is flipped open for use and that generally has a smaller range of features than a smart phone. Five to ten minutes after arriving at the station, the officers noticed that the phone was repeatedly receiving calls from a source identified as "my house" on the phone's external screen. A few minutes later, they opened the phone and saw a photograph of a woman and a baby set as the phone's wallpaper. They pressed one button on the phone to access its call log, then another button to determine the phone number associated with the "my house" label. They next used an online phone directory to trace that phone number to an apartment building.

When the officers went to the building, they saw Wurie's name on a mailbox and observed through a window a woman who resembled the woman in the photograph on Wurie's phone. They secured the apartment while obtaining a search warrant and, upon later executing the warrant, found and seized 215 grams of crack cocaine, marijuana, drug paraphernalia, a firearm and ammunition, and cash.

Wurie * * * moved to suppress the evidence obtained from the search of the apartment, arguing that it was the fruit of an unconstitutional search of his cell phone. The District Court denied the motion. Wurie was convicted * * *. * * *

II * * *

As the [Fourth Amendment] text makes clear, "the ultimate touchstone of the Fourth Amendment is 'reasonableness.' " Our cases have determined that "[w]here a search is undertaken by law enforcement officials to discover evidence of criminal wrongdoing, * * * reasonableness generally requires the obtaining of a judicial warrant." Such a warrant ensures that the inferences to support a search are "drawn by a neutral and detached magistrate instead of being judged by the officer engaged in the often competitive enterprise of ferreting out crime." In the absence of a warrant, a search is reasonable only if it falls within a specific exception to the warrant requirement.

The two cases before us concern the reasonableness of a warrantless search incident to a lawful arrest. [The Court then proceeded to review "search incident to lawful arrest" case law, focusing in particular on *Chimel v. California* (p. 227), *United States v. Robinson*, and *Arizona v. Gant* (p. 242), a case involving the scope of a warrantless search of an automobile as an incident of the lawful arrest of a car occupant.]

III

These cases require us to decide how the search incident to arrest doctrine applies to modern cell phones, which are now such a pervasive and insistent part of daily life that the proverbial visitor from Mars might conclude they were an important feature of human anatomy. A smart phone of the sort taken from Riley was unheard of ten years ago; a significant majority of American adults now own such phones. Even less sophisticated phones like Wurie's, which have already faded in popularity since Wurie was arrested in 2007, have been around for less than 15 years. Both phones are based on technology nearly inconceivable just a few decades ago, when *Chimel* and *Robinson* were decided.

Absent more precise guidance from the founding era, we generally determine whether to exempt a given type of search from the warrant requirement "by assessing, on the one hand, the degree to which it intrudes upon an individual's privacy and, on the other, the degree to which it is needed for the promotion of legitimate governmental interests." Such a balancing of interests supported the search incident to arrest exception in *Robinson*, and a mechanical application of *Robinson* might well support the warrantless searches at issue here.

But while *Robinson*'s categorical rule [permitting an arresting officer to search containers discovered on an arrestee's person] strikes the appropriate balance in the context of physical objects, neither of its rationales has much force with respect to digital content on cell phones. On the government interest side, *Robinson* concluded that the two risks identified in *Chimel*—harm to officers and destruction of evidence—are present in all custodial arrests. There are no comparable risks when the search is of digital data. In addition, *Robinson* regarded any privacy interests retained by an individual after arrest as significantly diminished by the fact of the arrest itself. Cell phones, however, place vast quantities of personal information literally in the hands of individuals. A search of the information on a cell phone bears little resemblance to the type of brief physical search considered in *Robinson*.

We therefore decline to extend *Robinson* to searches of data on cell phones, and hold instead that officers must generally secure a warrant before conducting such a search.

A

We first consider each *Chimel* concern in turn. In doing so, we do not overlook *Robinson*'s admonition that searches of a person incident to arrest * * * are reasonable regardless of "the probability in a particular arrest situation that weapons or evidence would in fact be found." Rather than requiring the "case-by-case adjudication" that *Robinson* rejected, we ask instead whether application of the search incident to arrest doctrine to this particular category of effects would "untether the rule from the justifications underlying the *Chimel* exception."

1

Digital data stored on a cell phone cannot itself be used as a weapon to harm an arresting officer or to effectuate the arrestee's escape. Law enforcement officers remain free to examine the physical aspects of a phone to ensure that it will not be used as a weapon—say, to determine whether there is a razor blade hidden between the phone and its case. Once an officer has secured a phone and eliminated any potential physical threats, however, data on the phone can endanger no one.

Perhaps the same might have been said of the cigarette pack seized from Robinson's pocket. Once an officer gained control of the pack, it was unlikely that Robinson could have accessed the pack's contents. But unknown physical objects may always pose risks, no matter how slight, during the tense atmosphere of a custodial arrest. The officer in *Robinson* testified that he could not identify the objects in the cigarette pack but knew they were not cigarettes. Given that, a further search was a reasonable protective measure. No such unknowns exist with respect to digital data. * * *

The United States and California both suggest that a search of cell phone data might help ensure officer safety in more indirect ways, for example by alerting officers that confederates of the arrestee are headed to the scene. There is undoubtedly a strong government interest in warning officers about such possibilities, but neither the United States nor California offers evidence to suggest that their concerns are based on actual experience. The proposed consideration would also represent a broadening of *Chimel*'s concern that an *arrestee himself* might grab a weapon and use it against an officer "to resist arrest or effect his escape." And any such threats from outside the arrest scene do not "lurk[ ] in all custodial arrests." Accordingly, the interest in protecting officer safety does not justify dispensing with the warrant requirement across the board. To the extent dangers to arresting officers may be implicated in a particular way in a particular case, they are better addressed through consideration of case-specific exceptions to the warrant requirement, such as the one for exigent circumstances.

2

The United States and California focus primarily on the second *Chimel* rationale: preventing the destruction of evidence.

Both Riley and Wurie concede that officers could have seized and secured their cell phones to prevent destruction of evidence while seeking a warrant. That is a sensible concession. And once law enforcement officers have secured a cell phone, there is no longer any risk that the arrestee himself will be able to delete incriminating data from the phone.

The United States and California argue that information on a cell phone may nevertheless be vulnerable to two types of evidence destruction unique to digital data—remote wiping and data encryption. Remote wiping occurs when a phone, connected to a wireless network, receives a signal that erases stored data. This can happen when a third party sends a remote signal or when a phone is preprogrammed to delete data upon entering or leaving certain geographic areas (so-called "geofencing"). Encryption is a security feature that some modern cell phones use in addition to password protection. When such phones lock, data becomes protected by sophisticated encryption that renders a phone all but "unbreakable" unless police know the password.

As an initial matter, these broader concerns about the loss of evidence are distinct from *Chimel*'s focus on a defendant who responds to arrest by trying to conceal or destroy evidence within his reach. With respect to remote wiping, the Government's primary concern turns on the actions of third parties who are not present at the scene of arrest. And data encryption is even further afield. There, the Government focuses on the ordinary operation of a phone's security features, apart from *any* active attempt by a defendant or his associates to conceal or destroy evidence upon arrest.

We have also been given little reason to believe that either problem is prevalent. The briefing reveals only a couple of anecdotal examples of remote wiping triggered by an arrest. Similarly, the opportunities for officers to search a password-protected phone before data becomes encrypted are quite limited. Law enforcement officers are very unlikely to come upon such a phone in an unlocked state because most phones lock at the touch of a button or, as a default, after some very short period of inactivity. * * *

Moreover, in situations in which an arrest might trigger a remote-wipe attempt or an officer discovers an unlocked phone, it is not clear that the ability to conduct a warrantless search would make much of a difference. The need to effect the arrest, secure the scene, and tend to other pressing matters means that law enforcement officers may well not be able to turn their attention to a cell phone right away. * * *

In any event, as to remote wiping, law enforcement is not without specific means to address the threat. Remote wiping can be fully prevented by disconnecting a phone from the network. There are at least two simple ways to do this: First, law enforcement officers can turn the phone off or remove its battery. Second, if they are concerned about encryption or other potential problems, they can leave a phone powered on and place it in an enclosure that isolates the phone from radio waves. Such devices are commonly called "Faraday bags," after the English scientist Michael Faraday. They are essentially sandwich bags made of aluminum foil: cheap, lightweight, and easy to use. They may not be a complete answer to the problem, but at least for now they provide a reasonable response. In fact, a number of law enforcement agencies around the country already encourage the use of Faraday bags.

* * * If "the police are truly confronted with a 'now or never' situation,"—for example, circumstances suggesting that a defendant's phone will be the target of an imminent remote-wipe attempt—they may be able to rely on exigent circumstances to search the phone immediately. Or, if officers happen to seize a phone in an unlocked state, they may be able to disable a phone's automatic-lock feature in order to prevent the phone from locking and encrypting data. * * * Such a preventive measure could be analyzed under the principles set forth in our decision in [*Illinois v.*] *McArthur*, [p. 211] which approved officers' reasonable steps to secure a scene to preserve evidence while they awaited a warrant.

B

The search incident to arrest exception rests not only on the heightened government interests at stake in a volatile arrest situation, but also on an arrestee's reduced privacy interests upon being taken into police custody. * * * Put simply, a patdown of Robinson's clothing and an inspection of the cigarette pack found in his pocket constituted only minor additional intrusions compared to the substantial government authority exercised in taking Robinson into custody.

The fact that an arrestee has diminished privacy interests does not mean that the Fourth Amendment falls out of the picture entirely. Not every search "is acceptable solely because a person is in custody." To the contrary, when "privacy-related concerns are weighty enough" a "search may require a warrant, notwithstanding the diminished expectations of privacy of the arrestee." One such example, of course, is *Chimel*. *Chimel* refused to "characteriz[e] the invasion of privacy that results from a top-to-bottom search of a man's house as 'minor.'" Because a search of the arrestee's entire house was a substantial invasion beyond the arrest itself, the Court concluded that a warrant was required.

Robinson is the only decision from this Court applying *Chimel* to a search of the contents of an item found on an arrestee's person. * * *

The United States asserts that a search of all data stored on a cell phone is "materially indistinguishable" from searches of these sorts of physical items. That is like saying a ride on horseback is materially indistinguishable from a flight to the moon. Both are ways of getting from point A to point B, but little else justifies lumping them together. * * * A conclusion that inspecting the contents of an arrestee's pockets works no substantial additional intrusion on privacy beyond the arrest itself may make sense as applied to physical items, but any extension of that reasoning to digital data has to rest on its own bottom.

1

Cell phones differ in both a quantitative and a qualitative sense from other objects that might be kept on an arrestee's person. The term "cell phone" is itself misleading shorthand; many of these devices are in fact minicomputers that also happen to have the capacity to be used as a telephone. They could just as easily be called cameras, video players, rolodexes, calendars, tape recorders, libraries, diaries, albums, televisions, maps, or newspapers.

One of the most notable distinguishing features of modern cell phones is their immense storage capacity. Before cell phones, a search of a person was limited by physical realities and tended as a general matter to constitute only a narrow intrusion on privacy. Most people cannot lug around every piece of mail they have received for the past several months, every picture they have taken, or every book or article they have read—nor would they have any reason to attempt to do so. And if they did, they would have to drag behind them a trunk * * *, rather than a container the size of the cigarette package in *Robinson*.

But the possible intrusion on privacy is not physically limited in the same way when it comes to cell phones. The current top-selling smart phone has a standard capacity of 16 gigabytes (and is available with up to 64 gigabytes). Sixteen gigabytes translates to millions of pages of text, thousands of pictures, or hundreds of videos. Cell phones couple that capacity with the ability to store many different types of information: Even the most basic phones * * * might hold photographs, picture messages, text messages, Internet browsing history, a calendar, a thousand-entry phone book, and so on. We expect that the gulf between physical practicability and digital capacity will only continue to widen in the future. * * *

Finally, there is an element of pervasiveness that characterizes cell phones but not physical records. Prior to the digital age, people did not typically carry a cache of sensitive personal information with them as they went about their day. Now it is the person who is not carrying a cell phone, with all that it contains, who is the exception. According to one poll, nearly three-quarters of smart phone users report being within five feet of their phones most of the time, with 12% admitting that they even use their phones in the shower. A decade ago police officers searching an arrestee might have occasionally stumbled across a highly personal item such as a diary. But those discoveries were likely to be few and far between. Today, by contrast, it is no exaggeration to say that many of the more than 90% of American adults who own a cell phone keep on their person a digital record of nearly every aspect of their lives—from the mundane to the intimate. Allowing the police to scrutinize such records on a routine basis is quite different from allowing them to search a personal item or two in the occasional case.

Although the data stored on a cell phone is distinguished from physical records by quantity alone, certain types of data are also qualitatively different. An Internet search and browsing history, for example, can be found on an Internet-enabled phone and could reveal an individual's private interests or concerns—perhaps a search for certain symptoms of disease, coupled with frequent visits to WebMD. Data on a cell phone can also reveal where a person has been. Historic location information is a standard feature on many smart phones and can reconstruct someone's specific movements down to the minute, not only around town but also within a particular building. * * *

In 1926, Learned Hand observed (in an opinion later quoted in *Chimel*) that it is "a totally different thing to search a man's pockets and use against him what they contain, from ransacking his house for everything which may incriminate him." If his pockets contain a cell phone, however, that is no longer true. Indeed, a cell phone search would typically expose to the government far *more* than the most exhaustive search of a house: A phone not only contains in digital form many sensitive records previously found in the home; it also contains a broad array of private information never found in a home in any form—unless the phone is.

2

To further complicate the scope of the privacy interests at stake, the data a user views on many modern cell phones may not in fact be stored on the device itself. Treating a cell phone as a container whose contents may be searched incident to an arrest is a bit strained as an initial matter. But the analogy crumbles entirely when a cell phone is used to access data located elsewhere, at the tap of a screen. That is what cell phones, with increasing frequency, are designed to do by taking advantage of "cloud computing." * * *

The United States concedes that the search incident to arrest exception may not be stretched to cover a search of files accessed remotely—that is, a search of files stored in the cloud. Such a search would be like finding a key in a suspect's pocket and arguing that it allowed law enforcement to unlock and search a house. But officers searching a phone's data would not typically know whether the information they are viewing was stored locally at the time of the arrest or has been pulled from the cloud. * * *

C

Apart from their arguments for a direct extension of *Robinson*, the United States and California offer various fallback options for permitting warrantless cell phone searches under certain circumstances. Each of the proposals is flawed and contravenes our general preference to provide clear guidance to law enforcement through categorical rules. * * *

The United States first proposes that * * * a warrantless search of an arrestee's cell phone [be permitted] whenever it is reasonable to believe that the phone contains evidence of the crime of arrest. * * *

* * * [This] standard would prove no practical limit at all when it comes to cell phone searches. * * * In the cell phone context, * * * it is reasonable to expect that incriminating information will be found on a phone regardless of when the crime occurred. * * * It would be a particularly inexperienced or unimaginative law enforcement officer who could not come up with several reasons to suppose evidence of just about any crime could be found on a cell phone. * * *

The United States also proposes a rule that would restrict the scope of a cell phone search to those areas of the phone where an officer reasonably believes that information relevant to the crime, the arrestee's identity, or officer safety will be discovered. This approach would again impose few meaningful constraints on officers. The proposed categories would sweep in a great deal of information, and officers would not always be able to discern in advance what information would be found where.

We also reject the United States' final suggestion that officers should always be able to search a phone's call log, as they did in Wurie's case. The Government relies on *Smith* v. *Maryland*, [p. 98], which held that no warrant was required to use a pen register at telephone company premises to identify numbers dialed by a particular caller. The Court in that case, however, concluded that the use of a pen register was not a "search" at all under the Fourth Amendment. There is no dispute here that the officers engaged in a search of Wurie's cell phone. Moreover, call logs typically contain more than just phone numbers; they include any identifying information that an individual might add, such as the label "my house" in Wurie's case. * * *

IV

We cannot deny that our decision today will have an impact on the ability of law enforcement to combat crime. Cell phones have become important tools in facilitating coordination and communication among members of criminal enterprises, and can provide valuable incriminating information about dangerous criminals. Privacy comes at a cost.

Our holding, of course, is not that the information on a cell phone is immune from search; it is instead that a warrant is generally required before such a search, even when a cell phone is seized incident to arrest. Our cases have historically recognized that the warrant requirement is "an important working part of our machinery of government," not merely "an inconvenience to be somehow 'weighed' against the claims of police efficiency." Recent technological advances similar to those discussed here have, in addition, made the process of obtaining a warrant itself more efficient.

Moreover, even though the search incident to arrest exception does not apply to cell phones, other case-specific exceptions may still justify a warrantless search of a particular phone. * * *

In light of the availability of the exigent circumstances exception, there is no reason to believe that law enforcement officers will not be able to address some of the more extreme hypotheticals that have been suggested: a suspect texting an accomplice who, it is feared, is preparing to detonate a bomb, or a child abductor who may have information about the child's location on his cell phone. The defendants here recognize * * * that such fact-specific threats may justify a warrantless search of cell phone data. The critical point is that, unlike the search incident to arrest exception, the exigent circumstances exception requires a court to examine whether an emergency justified a warrantless search in each particular case.

* * *

Our cases have recognized that the Fourth Amendment was the founding generation's response to the reviled "general warrants" and "writs of assistance" of the colonial era, which allowed British officers to rummage through homes in an unrestrained search for evidence of criminal activity. Opposition to such searches was in fact one of the driving forces behind the Revolution itself. In 1761, the patriot James Otis delivered a speech in Boston denouncing the use of writs of assistance. A young John Adams was there, and he would later write that "[e]very man of a crowded audience appeared to me to go away, as I did, ready to take arms against writs of assistance." According to Adams, Otis's speech was "the first scene of the first act of opposition to the arbitrary claims of Great Britain. Then and there the child Independence was born."

Modern cell phones are not just another technological convenience. With all they contain and all they may reveal, they hold for many Americans "the privacies of life." The fact that technology now allows an individual to carry such information in his hand does not make the information any less worthy of the protection for which the Founders fought. Our answer to the question of what police must do before searching a cell phone seized incident to an arrest is accordingly simple—get a warrant. * * *

JUSTICE ALITO concurring in part and concurring in the judgment.

I agree with the Court that law enforcement officers, in conducting a lawful search incident to arrest, must generally obtain a warrant before searching information stored or accessible on a cell phone. I write separately to address two points.

I

A

First, I am not convinced at this time that the ancient rule on searches incident to arrest is based exclusively (or even primarily) on the need to protect the safety of arresting officers and the need to prevent the destruction of evidence. * * *

* * * For example, an 1839 case stated that "it is clear, and beyond doubt, that * * * constables * * * are entitled, upon a lawful arrest by them of one charged with treason or felony, to take and detain property found in his possession which will form material evidence in his prosecution for that crime." The court noted that the origins of that rule "deriv[e] from the interest which the State has in a person guilty (or reasonably believed to be guilty) of a crime being brought to

justice, and in a prosecution, once commenced, being determined in due course of law." * * *

The idea that officer safety and the preservation of evidence are the sole reasons for allowing a warrantless search incident to arrest appears to derive from the Court's reasoning in *Chimel* v. *California*, a case that involved the lawfulness of a search of the scene of an arrest, not the person of an arrestee. * * * *Chimel*'s reasoning is questionable, and I think it is a mistake to allow that reasoning to affect cases like these that concern the search of the person of arrestees.

B

Despite my view on the point discussed above, I agree that we should not mechanically apply the rule used in the predigital era to the search of a cell phone. Many cell phones now in use are capable of storing and accessing a quantity of information, some highly personal, that no person would ever have had on his person in hard-copy form. This calls for a new balancing of law enforcement and privacy interests.

The Court strikes this balance in favor of privacy interests with respect to all cell phones and all information found in them, and this approach leads to anomalies. For example, the Court's broad holding favors information in digital form over information in hard-copy form. Suppose that two suspects are arrested. Suspect number one has in his pocket a monthly bill for his land-line phone, and the bill lists an incriminating call to a long-distance number. He also has in his a wallet a few snapshots, and one of these is incriminating. Suspect number two has in his pocket a cell phone, the call log of which shows a call to the same incriminating number. In addition, a number of photos are stored in the memory of the cell phone, and one of these is incriminating. Under established law, the police may seize and examine the phone bill and the snapshots in the wallet without obtaining a warrant, but under the Court's holding today, the information stored in the cell phone is out.

While the Court's approach leads to anomalies, I do not see a workable alternative. Law enforcement officers need clear rules regarding searches incident to arrest, and it would take many cases and many years for the courts to develop more nuanced rules. And during that time, the nature of the electronic devices that ordinary Americans carry on their persons would continue to change.

II

This brings me to my second point. While I agree with the holding of the Court, I would reconsider the question presented here if either Congress or state legislatures, after assessing the legitimate needs of law enforcement and the privacy interests of cell phone owners, enact legislation that draws reasonable distinctions based on categories of information or perhaps other variables. * * *

NOTES AND QUESTIONS

1. Are you persuaded by the Chief Justice's efforts to distinguish *Robinson*? If not, which case was wrongly decided, *Robinson* or *Riley*?

2. Rather than require a search warrant, should the Court have "permitted the police to conduct a [warrantless] brief field search of a cell phone incident to arrest, * * * when there is reason to believe that the phone contains useful evidence of the crime of arrest," as long as "the police limit their search to the places where such evidence might realistically be found"? Richard H. McAdams, Riley*'s Less Obvious Tradeoff: Forgoing Scope-Limited Searches*, 48 Tex. Tech. L. Rev. 97, 131 (2015).

3. *Drunk driving and search-incident law.* In Birchfield v. North Dakota, 579 U.S. ___, 136 S.Ct. 2160, 195 L.Ed.2d 560 (2016), the Supreme Court for the first time considered the following question: may the police, who have arrested a motorist suspected of drunk driving, compel the motorist to submit to the taking of a blood sample or to a breath test as an incident of the arrest.

But, you might ask: why not simply justify such a warrantless search under the "exigent circumstances" warrant exception? Indeed, the Court has held that the natural dissipation of alcohol from the blood stream sometimes, *but does not always*, constitute an exigency justifying the warrantless taking of a blood sample. The constitutionality of such testing must be determined, as with all exigency cases, on a case-by-case, totality-of-the-factual-circumstances basis, sometimes justifying the warrantless search, *e.g.*, Schmerber v. California, 384 U.S. 757, 86 S.Ct. 1826, 16 L.Ed.2d 908 (1966), and sometimes not. Missouri v. McNeely, 569 U.S. 141, 133 S.Ct. 1552, 185 L.Ed.2d 696 (2013).

As we have seen, however, in contrast to the exigency exception, the search-incident warrant exception eschews the case-by-case approach in regard to searches of an arrestee: warrantless searches of the person are either allowed in all cases or they are barred in all cases. In *Riley*, the Court barred warrantless searches of cell phones discovered on the person of the arrestee.

In *Birchfield*, the search-incident exception issue arose in the context of drunk-driving investigations. In order to secure greater cooperation from drivers stopped on the highway, some states have recently enacted laws making it a criminal offense for the driver to refuse to undergo a breath test or the taking of a blood sample. In three cases consolidated on appeal, the *Birchfield* Court considered the constitutionality of two warrantless, nonconsensual blood tests and one similar breath test conducted after the drivers were arrested *for their refusal.*

Justice Alito, writing for five justices, held that warrantless breath tests, incident to a lawful arrest, are per se constitutional. (The arrests themselves were lawful: "it follows that a State may criminalize the refusal to comply with a demand to submit to the required testing, just as a State may make it a crime for a person to obstruct the execution of a valid search warrant.") As in *Riley*, the Court balanced the privacy interest of the individual against the interest of the government in combatting drunk driving.

Justice Alito, citing prior cases, noted that breath tests "do not 'implicate significant privacy concerns.' " The physical intrusion is "almost negligible." Although the testing requires the insertion of a mouthpiece connected to a machine into the individual's mouth, "there is nothing painful or strange about this requirement." The Court analogized this to use of a straw to drink beverages, "a common practice and one to which few object." Nor do people "assert a possessory interest in or any emotional attachment to *any* of the air in their lungs." Finally, the testing process does not result in "any great enhancement in the embarrassment that is inherent in any arrest."

Weighed against the minimal privacy interest of the arrestee is the government's " 'paramount interest * * * in preserving the safety of * * * public highways.' " The Court noted that "[d]runk drivers take a grisly toll on the Nation's roads, claiming thousands of lives, injuring many more victims, and inflicting billions of dollars in property damage every year." Therefore, a warrantless breath test, as an incident to a lawful arrest in a drunk-driving case, is constitutional.

The Court majority, however, held that warrantless *blood* tests are *not* justifiable as an incident to a lawful arrest. "Blood tests are a different matter," Justice Alito wrote. They require piercing of the arrestee's skin as well as extraction of a part of the subject's body. Unlike air, which human exhale "many times per minute, humans do not continually shed blood." It is not a process people "relish." Moreover, "a blood test, unlike a breath test, places in the hands of law enforcement authorities a sample that can be preserved and from which it is possible to extract information beyond" the driver's blood alcohol content. The reasonableness of this more intrusive testing process "must be judged in light of the availability of the less invasive alternative of a breath test." The States here "offered no satisfactory justification for demanding the more intrusive alternative without a warrant."

Justices Sotomayor and Ginsburg, concurring and dissenting in part, would require warrants in both circumstances in search-incident cases: "no governmental interest categorically makes it impractical for an officer to obtain a warrant before measuring a driver's alcohol level * * * unless exigent circumstances exist in a particular case." If an exigency exists, of course the latter exception to the warrant requirement would apply.

Justice Thomas also concurred and dissented in part. He accused the majority of "contort[ing] the search-incident-to-arrest exception." He would apply the exigency exception, but he would adopt a bright-line rule justifying both warrantless breath and blood testing under *that* exception.

Notice: it can matter which warrant exception is asserted in a given case. Although a warrantless blood test is not justified as a search incident to an arrest, the prosecutor, with the proper facts, may still win a case by invoking a different warrant exception (*e.g.*, exigency). One exception might work when another doesn't. Keep this in mind as you learn about other exceptions to the warrant requirement.

C. PRETEXTUAL STOPS AND ARRESTS (PARTICULARLY IN AUTOMOBILES)

WHREN V. UNITED STATES

Supreme Court of the United States, 1996.
517 U.S. 806, 116 S.Ct. 1769, 135 L.Ed.2d 89.

Consider for a moment State v. Ladson, 138 Wash.2d 343, 979 P.2d 833 (1999):

> **On October 5, 1995 City of Lacey police officer Jim Mack and Thurston County sheriff's detective Cliff Ziesmer were on proactive gang patrol. The officers explained they do not make routine traffic stops while on proactive gang patrol although they use traffic infractions as a means to pull over people in order to initiate contact and questioning. * * ***
>
> **On the day in question Richard Fogle attracted the attention of officers Mack and Ziesmer as he drove by. Fogle and his passenger Thomas Ladson are both African-American. Although the officers had never seen Ladson before, they recognized Fogle from an unsubstantiated street rumor that Fogle was involved with drugs. * * ***
>
> **The officers tailed the Fogle vehicle looking for a legal justification to stop the car. They shadowed the vehicle while it refueled at a local filling station and then finally pulled Fogle over several blocks later on the grounds that Fogle's license plate tabs had expired five days earlier. The officers do not deny the stop was pretextual.**
>
> **The police then discovered Fogle's driver's license was suspended and arrested him on the spot. After securing Fogle in**

> handcuffs in the squad car, the police conducted a full search of the car "incident to Fogle's arrest." [The police proceeded to order passenger Ladson out of the vehicle, patted him down for weapons, and found a handgun resulting in his arrest and subsequent search. A search of his person turned up baggies of marijuana.]

Notice that this entire process began with an unsubstantiated rumor that could not justify the arrest or search of Fogle, his car, or Ladson. The police strategy, therefore, was to find lawful grounds to stop the vehicle. A traffic violation was the pretext. It gave the officers the opportunity to have forced contact with Fogle, visually peer inside the car in the hope of finding incriminating evidence of drugs, and perhaps find a way to "negotiate" consent to search the car. More conveniently in this case, the expired driver's license provided police with apparent authority to take Fogle into custody and use "search incident to lawful arrest" law to conduct a nonconsensual warrantless search of him and (in the pre-*Gant* era) his car, and then to turn their attention to Ladson. The police had the authority, that is, unless the pretextual aspects of the case affects the analysis.

The *Ladson* scenario is not rare. It is played out often on the sidewalks and highways of the United States. Sometimes the scenario even lacks the unsubstantiated rumor that triggered the car stop in *Ladson.* A person's race, ethnicity, or national origin may motivate the police conduct. The term "DWB"—Driving While Black—describes the phenomenon in which officers target persons based on race for traffic (or other) detentions in order to follow up on hunches of criminal behavior.

So, this brings us to the question: *Does* the Fourth Amendment bar pretextual police conduct? The next case considers this question.

JUSTICE SCALIA delivered the opinion of the Court [joined by CHIEF JUSTICE REHNQUIST, and JUSTICES STEVENS, O'CONNOR, KENNEDY, SOUTER, THOMAS, GINSBURG, and BREYER].

In this case we decide whether the temporary detention of a motorist who the police have probable cause to believe has committed a civil traffic violation is inconsistent with the Fourth Amendment's prohibition against unreasonable seizures unless a reasonable officer would have been motivated to stop the car by a desire to enforce the traffic laws.

I

On the evening of June 10, 1993, plainclothes vice-squad officers of the District of Columbia Metropolitan Police Department were patrolling a "high drug area" of the city in an unmarked car. Their suspicions were aroused when they passed a dark Pathfinder truck with temporary license plates and youthful occupants waiting at a stop sign, the driver looking down into the lap of the passenger at his right. The truck remained stopped at the intersection for what seemed an unusually long time—more than 20 seconds. When the police car executed a U-turn in order to head back toward the truck, the Pathfinder turned suddenly to its right, without signaling, and sped off at an "unreasonable" speed. The policemen followed, and in a short while overtook the Pathfinder when it stopped behind other traffic at a red light. They pulled up alongside, and Officer Ephraim Soto stepped out and approached the driver's door, identifying himself as a police officer and directing the driver, petitioner Brown, to put the vehicle in park. When Soto drew up to the driver's window, he immediately observed two large plastic bags of what appeared to be crack cocaine in petitioner Whren's hands. Petitioners were arrested, and quantities of several types of illegal drugs were retrieved from the vehicle.

Petitioners were charged in a four-count indictment with violating various federal drug laws * * *. At a pretrial suppression hearing, they challenged the legality of the stop and the resulting seizure of the drugs. They argued that the stop had not been justified by probable cause to believe, or even reasonable suspicion, that petitioners were engaged in illegal drug-dealing activity; and that Officer Soto's asserted ground for approaching the vehicle—to give the driver a warning concerning traffic violations—was pretextual. The District Court denied the suppression motion, concluding that "the facts of the stop were not controverted," and "[t]here was nothing to really demonstrate that the actions of the officers were contrary to a normal traffic stop."

Petitioners were convicted of the counts at issue here. The Court of Appeals affirmed the convictions, holding with respect to the suppression issue that, "regardless of whether a police officer subjectively believes that the occupants of an automobile may be engaging in some other illegal behavior, a traffic stop is permissible as long as a reasonable officer in the same circumstances *could have* stopped the car for the suspected traffic violation." * * *

II * * *

Petitioners accept that Officer Soto had probable cause to believe that various provisions of the District of Columbia traffic code had been violated. See

18 D. C. Mun. Regs. §§ 2213.4 (1995) ("An operator shall * * * give full time and attention to the operation of the vehicle"); 2204.3 ("No person shall turn any vehicle * * * without giving an appropriate signal"); 2200.3 ("No person shall drive a vehicle * * * at a speed greater than is reasonable and prudent under the conditions"). They argue, however, that "in the unique context of civil traffic regulations" probable cause is not enough. Since, they contend, the use of automobiles is so heavily and minutely regulated that total compliance with traffic and safety rules is nearly impossible, a police officer will almost invariably be able to catch any given motorist in a technical violation. This creates the temptation to use traffic stops as a means of investigating other law violations, as to which no probable cause or even articulable suspicion exists. Petitioners, who are both black, further contend that police officers might decide which motorists to stop based on decidedly impermissible factors, such as the race of the car's occupants. To avoid this danger, they say, the Fourth Amendment test for traffic stops should be, not the normal one (applied by the Court of Appeals) of whether probable cause existed to justify the stop; but rather, whether a police officer, acting reasonably, would have made the stop for the reason given.

A

Petitioners contend that the standard they propose is consistent with our past cases' disapproval of police attempts to use valid bases of action against citizens as pretexts for pursuing other investigatory agendas. We are reminded that in *Florida v. Wells*, 495 U.S. 1, 4, 110 S.Ct. 1632, 1635, 109 L.Ed.2d 1 (1990), we stated that "an inventory search must not be used as a ruse for a general rummaging in order to discover incriminating evidence"; that in *Colorado v. Bertine*, 479 U.S. 367, 372, 107 S.Ct. 738, 741, 93 L.Ed.2d 739 (1987), in approving an inventory search, we apparently thought it significant that there had been "no showing that the police, who were following standard procedures, acted in bad faith or for the sole purpose of investigation"; and that in *New York v. Burger*, 482 U.S. 691, 716–717, n. 27, 107 S Ct. 2636, 2651, n. 27, 96 L.Ed.2d 601 (1987), we observed, in upholding the constitutionality of a warrantless administrative inspection, that the search did not appear to be "a 'pretext' for obtaining evidence of * * * violation of * * * penal laws." But only an undiscerning reader would regard these cases as endorsing the principle that ulterior motives can invalidate police conduct that is justifiable on the basis of probable cause to believe that a violation of law has occurred. In each case we were addressing the validity of a search conducted in the *absence* of probable cause. Our quoted statements simply explain that the exemption from the need for probable cause (and warrant), which is accorded to searches made for the purpose of inventory or administrative regulation, is not accorded to searches that are *not* made for those purposes.

Petitioners also rely upon *Colorado v. Bannister*, 449 U.S. 1, 101 S.Ct. 42, 66 L Ed.2d 1 (1980) (*per curiam*), a case which, like this one, involved a traffic stop as the prelude to a plain-view sighting and arrest on charges wholly unrelated to the basis for the stop. Petitioners point to our statement that "there was no evidence whatsoever that the officer's presence to issue a traffic citation was a pretext to confirm any other previous suspicion about the occupants" of the car. That dictum *at most* demonstrates that the Court in *Bannister* found no need to inquire into the question now under discussion; not that it was certain of the answer. And it may demonstrate even less than that: if by "pretext" the Court meant that the officer really had not seen the car speeding, the statement would mean only that there was no reason to doubt probable cause for the traffic stop.

It would, moreover, be anomalous, to say the least, to treat a statement in a footnote in the *per curiam Bannister* opinion as indicating a reversal of our prior law. Petitioners' difficulty is not simply a lack of affirmative support for their position. Not only have we never held, outside the context of inventory search or administrative inspection (discussed above), that an officer's motive invalidates objectively justifiable behavior under the Fourth Amendment; but we have repeatedly held and asserted the contrary. In *United States v. Villamonte-Marquez*, 462 U.S. 579, 584, n. 3, 103 S.Ct. 2573, 2577, n. 3, 77 L.Ed.2d 22 (1983), we held that an otherwise valid warrantless boarding of a vessel by customs officials was not rendered invalid "because the customs officers were accompanied by a Louisiana state policeman, and were following an informant's tip that a vessel in the ship channel was thought to be carrying marihuana." We flatly dismissed the idea that an ulterior motive might serve to strip the agents of their legal justification. In *United States v. Robinson* we held that a traffic-violation arrest (of the sort here) would not be rendered invalid by the fact that it was "a mere pretext for a narcotics search"; and that a lawful postarrest search of the person would not be rendered invalid by the fact that it was not motivated by the officer-safety concern that justifies such searches. And in *Scott v. United States*, 436 U.S. 128, 138, 98 S.Ct. 1717, 1723, 56 L.Ed.2d 168 (1978), in rejecting the contention that wiretap evidence was subject to exclusion because the agents conducting the tap had failed to make any effort to comply with the statutory requirement that unauthorized acquisitions be minimized, we said that "[s]ubjective intent alone * * * does not make otherwise lawful conduct illegal or unconstitutional." We described *Robinson* as having established that "the fact that the officer does not have the state of mind which is hypothecated by the reasons which provide the legal justification for the officer's action does not invalidate the action taken as long as the circumstances, viewed objectively, justify that action."

We think these cases foreclose any argument that the constitutional reasonableness of traffic stops depends on the actual motivations of the individual officers involved. We of course agree with petitioners that the Constitution prohibits selective enforcement of the law based on considerations such as race. But the constitutional basis for objecting to intentionally discriminatory application of laws is the Equal Protection Clause, not the Fourth Amendment. Subjective intentions play no role in ordinary, probable-cause Fourth Amendment analysis.

* * *

III

In what would appear to be an elaboration on the "reasonable officer" test, petitioners argue that the balancing inherent in any Fourth Amendment inquiry requires us to weigh the governmental and individual interests implicated in a traffic stop such as we have here. That balancing, petitioners claim, does not support investigation of minor traffic infractions by plainclothes police in unmarked vehicles; such investigation only minimally advances the government's interest in traffic safety, and may indeed retard it by producing motorist confusion and alarm—a view said to be supported by the Metropolitan Police Department's own regulations generally prohibiting this practice. And as for the Fourth Amendment interests of the individuals concerned, petitioners point out that our cases acknowledge that even ordinary traffic stops entail "a possibly unsettling show of authority"; that they at best "interfere with freedom of movement, are inconvenient, and consume time" and at worst "may create substantial anxiety." That anxiety is likely to be even more pronounced when the stop is conducted by plainclothes officers in unmarked cars.

It is of course true that in principle every Fourth Amendment case, since it turns upon a "reasonableness" determination, involves a balancing of all relevant factors. With rare exceptions not applicable here, however, the result of that balancing is not in doubt where the search or seizure is based upon probable cause. * * *

Where probable cause has existed, the only cases in which we have found it necessary actually to perform the "balancing" analysis involved searches or seizures conducted in an extraordinary manner, unusually harmful to an individual's privacy or even physical interests—such as, for example, seizure by means of deadly force, see *Tennessee v. Garner*, 471 U.S. 1, 105 S.Ct. 1694, 85

L.Ed.2d 1 (1985), unannounced entry into a home, see *Wilson v. Arkansas*, 514 U.S. 927, 115 S.Ct. 1914, 131 L.Ed.2d 976 (1995), * * * or physical penetration of the body, see *Winston v. Lee*, 470 U.S. 753, 105 S.Ct. 1611, 84 L.Ed.2d 662 (1985). The making of a traffic stop out-of-uniform does not remotely qualify as such an extreme practice, and so is governed by the usual rule that probable cause to believe the law has been broken "outbalances" private interest in avoiding police contact. * * *

For the run-of-the-mine case, which this surely is, we think there is no realistic alternative to the traditional common-law rule that probable cause justifies a search and seizure. * * *

Here the District Court found that the officers had probable cause to believe that petitioners had violated the traffic code. That rendered the stop reasonable under the Fourth Amendment, the evidence thereby discovered admissible, and the upholding of the convictions by the Court of Appeals for the District of Columbia Circuit correct.

NOTES AND QUESTIONS

1. Note the discussion of *Ladson* above. The State of Washington disallowed the pretext stop even though under *Whren*, the U.S. Supreme Court would have allowed it. *Ladson* is a good reminder that the U.S. Constitution provides a minimum standard to which states, via the Fourteenth Amendment, must adhere. Nothing prevents a state from enacting stronger civil liberty protections for its citizens than the federal Constitution requires. One of the authors of this text, who practiced briefly in Washington State, actually had a case that challenged a traffic stop under *Ladson*. In that case, however, the officer was a patrol officer in the city of Kettle Falls, and unlike the officers in *Ladson* or *Whren,* enforcement of traffic laws within the city limits was part of his normal duties. The stop and the conviction were upheld and the defendant then pled guilty.

2. *The "pervasive police practice" of pretextual stops and arrests (with race added in).* A police officer explains why he will pull over a car on the road: "I have what you might call a profile. I pull up alongside a car with black males in it. Something don't [sic] match—maybe the style of the car with the guys in it. * * * We go from there." Jeffrey Goldberg, *What Cops Talk About When They Talk About Race*, New York Times Magazine, June 20, 1999, at 51.

Race may explain why Peter Lawson Jones, an African-American lawyer was pulled over in his new Mercury Sable in a white neighborhood by a police officer for allegedly running a stop sign. When the officer learned that Jones was not only an attorney but a state legislator, no ticket was issued. Hope Viner Samborn, *Profiled and Pulled Over*, American Bar Association Journal, October, 1999, at 18.

Or consider Robert Wilkins, an African-American Harvard Law School graduate who was pulled over for speeding as he was returning home from a family funeral. Instead of issuing a speeding citation at that time, the officer sought consent to search the car. When Wilkins refused, he was held for thirty minutes until a drug-sniffing dog could be brought to the scene. Only when nothing was discovered did the officer get around to issuing a speeding citation. David Cole, No Equal Justice 34–35 (1999).

Statistical evidence seemingly reinforces these anecdotes. A survey conducted by the Justice Department of contacts between the police and the public in 2008 provided this data: (1) the most common reason for contact with the police was a traffic stop (44.1%); (2) whites (8.4%), African-Americans (8.8%), and Hispanics (9.1%) were stopped by police at statistically similar rates; but (3) African-American drivers were three times as likely as white drivers, and about twice as likely as Hispanic drivers, to be searched during a traffic stop. Bureau of Justice Statistics, Special Report, Contacts between Police and the Public, 2008 (NCJ 234599, Oct. 2011).

In a subsequent study, more African-American drivers were pulled over in a traffic stop (13%) than whites and Hispanics (10%); and, among those stopped, Hispanics (6.6%) and African-Americans (6.4%) had their person or vehicle searched more often than whites (2.3%). Bureau of Justice Statistics, Police Behavior During Traffic and Street Stops, 2011 (NCJ 242937, Sept. 2013). The classic study on this police practice is David A. Harris, *"Driving While Black" and All Other Traffic Offenses: The Supreme Court and Pretextual Traffic Stops*, 87 J. Crim. L. & Criminology 544 (1997).

3. The Supreme Court rarely rules unanimously on any controversial legal issue. Why do you think the justices were united on this subject?

4. *Subjective versus objective standards.* If you dislike the outcome in *Whren*, can you suggest a workable standard for adjudicating allegations of pretextual searches and seizures? The petitioners in *Whren* suggested an objective standard, *i.e.*, would a reasonable police officer have stopped and issued a ticket for the traffic violation in question. Why did the Court reject this standard? Is this a suitable standard?

Some critics eschew an exclusively objective standard. They favor a test that permits courts to consider whether the particular officer subjectively acted as the result of illegitimate motives. According to Professor Morgan Cloud, a "test that denies [judges] the power to examine important elements of the encounter—like the subjective motives of the actors—is misguided." Morgan Cloud, *Judges, "Testifying," and the Constitution*, 69 S. Cal. L. Rev. 1341, 1386 (1996). Thoughts?

Would it be appropriate for a court to hold that an officer's deviation from usual police practices in the jurisdiction constitutes prima facie evidence of an improper motive which, in the absence of a proven justification, renders a traffic stop constitutionally unreasonable?

D. THE AUTOMOBILE EXCEPTION

1. General Principles

CALIFORNIA V. CARNEY

Supreme Court of the United States, 1985.
471 U.S. 386, 105 S.Ct. 2066, 85 L.Ed.2d 406.

The automobile exception to the warrant requirement was set out in the cases of Carroll v. United States, 267 U.S. 132, 45 S.Ct. 280, 69 L.Ed. 543 (1925), Chambers v. Maroney, 399 U.S. 42, 90 S.Ct. 1975, 26 L.Ed.2d 419 (1970), and Coolidge v. New Hampshire, 403 U.S. 443, 91 S.Ct. 2022, 29 L.Ed.2d 564 (1971). The exception is described again in our next case and in a Note after the case. See if you can identify the two justifications for the existence of the warrant exception. They are slightly different from the public safety emphasis we saw under exigent circumstances and search incident to a lawful arrest. Keep the justifications in mind as we work our way through the rest of the materials on the automobile exception. How closely do you think the Court adheres to the justifications in the cases that follow *Carney*? Does the pendulum swing as wildly as it did with search incident to lawful arrest? Why or why not?

CHIEF JUSTICE BURGER delivered the opinion of the Court [joined by JUSTICES WHITE, BLACKMUN, POWELL, REHNQUIST, and O'CONNOR].

We granted certiorari to decide whether law enforcement agents violated the Fourth Amendment when they conducted a warrantless search, based on probable cause, of a fully mobile "motor home" located in a public place.

I

On May 31, 1979, Drug Enforcement Agency Agent Robert Williams watched respondent, Charles Carney, approach a youth in downtown San Diego. The youth accompanied Carney to a Dodge Mini Motor Home parked in a nearby lot. Carney and the youth closed the window shades in the motor home, including one across the front window. Agent Williams had previously received uncorroborated information that the same motor home was used by another person who was exchanging marihuana for sex. Williams, with assistance from other agents, kept the motor home under surveillance for the entire one and one-quarter hours that Carney and the youth remained inside. When the youth left the motor home, the agents followed and stopped him. The youth told the agents that he had received marihuana in return for allowing Carney sexual contacts.

At the agents' request, the youth returned to the motor home and knocked on its door; Carney stepped out. The agents identified themselves as law enforcement officers. Without a warrant or consent, one agent entered the motor home and observed marihuana, plastic bags, and a scale of the kind used in weighing drugs on a table. Agent Williams took Carney into custody and took possession of the motor home. A subsequent search of the motor home at the police station revealed additional marihuana in the cupboards and refrigerator.

Respondent was charged with possession of marihuana for sale. At a preliminary hearing, he moved to suppress the evidence discovered in the motor home. The Magistrate denied the motion * * *.

Respondent * * * pleaded *nolo contendere* to the charges against him, and was placed on probation for three years. * * *

II

* * * There are, of course, exceptions to the general rule that a warrant must be secured before a search is undertaken; one is the so-called "automobile exception" at issue in this case. This exception to the warrant requirement was first set forth by the Court 60 years ago in *Carroll v. United States*, 267 U.S. 132, 45 S.Ct. 280, 69 L.Ed. 543 (1925). There, the Court recognized that the privacy interests in an automobile are constitutionally protected; however, it held that the ready mobility of the automobile justifies a lesser degree of protection of those interests. The Court rested this exception on a long-recognized distinction between stationary structures and vehicles * * *.

The capacity to be "quickly moved" was clearly the basis of the holding in *Carroll*, and our cases have consistently recognized ready mobility as one of the principal bases of the automobile exception. * * *

However, although ready mobility alone was perhaps the original justification for the vehicle exception, our later cases have made clear that ready mobility is not the only basis for the exception. The reasons for the vehicle exception, we have said, are twofold. "Besides the element of mobility, less rigorous warrant requirements govern because the expectation of privacy with respect to one's automobile is significantly less than that relating to one's home or office." [*South Dakota v. Opperman*, 428 U.S. 364, 96 S.Ct. 3092, 49 L.Ed.2d 1000 (1976).] * * *

These reduced expectations of privacy derive not from the fact that the area to be searched is in plain view, but from the pervasive regulation of vehicles capable of traveling on the public highways. As we explained in *South Dakota v. Opperman*, an inventory search case:

> "Automobiles, unlike homes, are subjected to pervasive and continuing governmental regulation and controls, including periodic inspection and licensing requirements. As an everyday occurrence, police stop and examine vehicles when license plates or inspection stickers have expired, or if other violations, such as exhaust fumes or excessive noise, are noted, or if headlights or other safety equipment are not in proper working order."

The public is fully aware that it is accorded less privacy in its automobiles because of this compelling governmental need for regulation. * * * In short, the pervasive schemes of regulation, which necessarily lead to reduced expectations of privacy, and the exigencies attendant to ready mobility justify searches without prior recourse to the authority of a magistrate so long as the overriding standard of probable cause is met.

When a vehicle is being used on the highways, or if it is readily capable of such use and is found stationary in a place not regularly used for residential purposes—temporary or otherwise—the two justifications for the vehicle exception come into play. First, the vehicle is obviously readily mobile by the turn of an ignition key, if not actually moving. Second, there is a reduced expectation of privacy stemming from its use as a licensed motor vehicle subject to a range of police regulation inapplicable to a fixed dwelling. At least in these circumstances, the overriding societal interests in effective law enforcement justify an immediate search before the vehicle and its occupants become unavailable.

While it is true that respondent's vehicle possessed some, if not many of the attributes of a home, it is equally clear that the vehicle falls clearly within the scope of the exception laid down in *Carroll* and applied in succeeding cases. Like the automobile in *Carroll*, respondent's motor home was readily mobile. Absent the prompt search and seizure, it could readily have been moved beyond the reach of the police. Furthermore, the vehicle was licensed to "operate on public streets; [was] serviced in public places; * * * and [was] subject to extensive regulation and inspection." And the vehicle was so situated that an objective observer would conclude that it was being used not as a residence, but as a vehicle.

Respondent urges us to distinguish his vehicle from other vehicles within the exception because it was *capable of functioning as a home.* In our increasingly mobile society, many vehicles used for transportation can be and are being used not only for transportation but for shelter, *i.e.,* as a "home" or "residence." To distinguish between respondent's motor home and an ordinary sedan for purposes of the vehicle exception would require that we apply the exception depending upon the size of the vehicle and the quality of its appointments. Moreover, to fail to apply the exception to vehicles such as a motor home ignores the fact that a motor home lends itself easily to use as an instrument of illicit drug traffic and other illegal activity. * * * We decline today to distinguish between "worthy" and "unworthy" vehicles which are either on the public roads and highways, or situated such that it is reasonable to conclude that the vehicle is not being used as a residence.

Our application of the vehicle exception has never turned on the other uses to which a vehicle might be put. The exception has historically turned on the ready mobility of the vehicle, and on the presence of the vehicle in a setting that objectively indicates that the vehicle is being used for transportation. * * *

JUSTICE STEVENS, with whom JUSTICE BRENNAN and JUSTICE MARSHALL join, dissenting. * * *

The hybrid character of the motor home places it at the crossroads between the privacy interests that generally forbid warrantless invasions of the home, and the law enforcement interests that support the exception for warrantless searches of automobiles based on probable cause. By choosing to follow the latter route, the Court * * * has accorded priority to an exception rather than to the general rule, and * * * has abandoned the limits on the exception imposed by prior cases. * * *

II * * *

In *United States v. Ross*, [456 U.S. 798, 102 S.Ct. 2157, 72 L.Ed.2d 572 (1982),] the Court reaffirmed the primary importance of the general rule condemning warrantless searches, and emphasized that the exception permitting the search of automobiles without a warrant is a narrow one. * * * Given this warning and the presumption of regularity that attaches to a warrant, it is hardly unrealistic to expect experienced law enforcement officers to obtain a search warrant when one can easily be secured.

* * * If the motor home were parked in the exact middle of the intersection between the general rule and the exception for automobiles, priority should be given to the rule rather than the exception.

III

The motor home, however, was not parked in the middle of that intersection. Our prior cases teach us that inherent mobility is not a sufficient justification for the fashioning of an exception to the warrant requirement, especially in the face of heightened expectations of privacy in the location searched. Motor homes, by their common use and construction, afford their owners a substantial and legitimate expectation of privacy when they dwell within. When a motor home is parked in a location that is removed from the public highway, I believe that society is prepared to recognize that the expectations of privacy within it are not unlike the expectations one has in a fixed dwelling. As a general rule, such places may only be searched with a warrant based upon probable cause. Warrantless searches of motor homes are only reasonable when the motor home is traveling on the public streets or highways, or when exigent circumstances otherwise require an immediate search without the expenditure of time necessary to obtain a warrant. * * *

In this case, the motor home was parked in an off-the-street lot only a few blocks from the courthouse in downtown San Diego where dozens of magistrates were available to entertain a warrant application. The officers clearly had the element of surprise with them, and with curtains covering the windshield, the motor home offered no indication of any imminent departure. The officers plainly had probable cause to arrest the respondent and search the motor home, and on this record, it is inexplicable why they eschewed the safe harbor of a warrant. * * *

Unlike a brick bungalow or a frame Victorian, a motor home seldom serves as a permanent lifetime abode. The motor home in this case, however, was designed to accommodate a breadth of ordinary everyday living. Photographs in the record indicate that its height, length, and beam provided substantial living space inside: stuffed chairs surround a table; cupboards provide room for storage of personal effects; bunk beds provide sleeping space; and a refrigerator provides ample space for food and beverages. Moreover, curtains and large opaque walls inhibit viewing the activities inside from the exterior of the vehicle. The interior configuration of the motor home establishes that the vehicle's size, shape, and mode of construction should have indicated to the officers that it was a vehicle containing mobile living quarters. * * *

In my opinion, searches of places that regularly accommodate a wide range of private human activity are fundamentally different from searches of automobiles which primarily serve a public transportation function. Although it may not be a castle, a motor home is usually the functional equivalent of a hotel room, a vacation and retirement home, or a hunting and fishing cabin. These places may be as spartan as a humble cottage when compared to the most majestic mansion, but the highest and most legitimate expectations of privacy associated with these temporary abodes should command the respect of this Court. In my opinion, a warrantless search of living quarters in a motor home is "presumptively unreasonable absent exigent circumstances."

NOTES AND QUESTIONS

1. *The reduced-expectation-of-privacy rationale.* Is the Court correct that we have a reduced expectation of privacy in our automobiles because of pervasive governmental regulation of them?

Are there other grounds for claiming that we have a lesser expectation of privacy in our cars than we do in our homes? Yes, according to Cardwell v. Lewis, 417 U.S. 583, 94 S.Ct. 2464, 41 L.Ed.2d 325 (1974):

> One has a lesser expectation of privacy in a motor vehicle because its function is transportation and it seldom serves as one's residence or as the repository of personal effects. A car has little capacity for escaping public scrutiny. It travels public thoroughfares where both its occupants and its contents are in plain view.

Do these arguments withstand scrutiny? Why, or why not?

2. *What if a motor home really is a "home"?* In a footnote to his opinion in *Carney*, Justice Burger described a situation where a motor home such as Mr. Carney was driving could be a home subject to increased privacy concerns:

> We need not pass on the application of the vehicle exception to a motor home that is situated in a way or place that objectively indicates that it is being used as a residence. Among the factors that might be relevant in determining whether a warrant would be required in such a circumstance is its location, whether the vehicle is readily mobile or instead, for instance, elevated on blocks, whether the vehicle is licensed, whether it is connected to utilities, and whether it has convenient access to a public road.

However, since that situation was not at issue in *Carney*, the question was left open.

3. *The origin of the vehicle exception to the warrant requirement.* In Carroll v. United States, 267 U.S. 132, 45 S.Ct. 280, 69 L.Ed. 543 (1925), the Court considered a search of a car (an Oldsmobile Roadster, circa 1920; look it up on the internet) stopped on the open road and searched without a warrant. The Court found that the warrantless search of a vehicle, based on probable cause, was authorized by a section of the National Prohibition Act. The Court also found that the congressional authorization of a warrantless probable cause search of a vehicle did not violate the Fourth Amendment. By the time we get to Chambers v. Maroney, 399 U.S. 42, 90 S.Ct. 1975, 26 L.Ed.2d 419 (1970), the Court read the Fourth Amendment itself as authorizing a

warrantless search of a vehicle stopped on the open road as long as the police had probable cause to search it; congressional authorization was no longer required.

4. *Automobile inventories: another warrant "exception."* A warrantless search of a car may be permissible on various grounds. First, if the police have probable cause to search a car, the "automobile exception" comes into play. Second, if an occupant (or recent occupant) of an automobile is arrested, the police may sometimes conduct, as an incident of the arrest, a contemporaneous search of the passenger compartment of the vehicle, even without probable cause to search.

A third basis for a car search is the "automobile inventory" warrant exception. In South Dakota v. Opperman, 428 U.S. 364, 96 S.Ct. 3092, 49 L.Ed.2d 1000 (1976), *O*'s automobile was towed to a city impound lot, as permitted by local ordinance, after it was ticketed twice for being parked in a restricted zone. Pursuant to standard operating procedures, officers unlocked the vehicle and, using a standard inventory form, inventoried the contents of the car. In the glove compartment, the police discovered marijuana. *O* was prosecuted for possession of the marijuana discovered during the warrantless, suspicionless search.

The Court determined that the probable cause and warrant requirements of the Fourth Amendment do not apply to routine inventory searches:

> The standard of probable cause is peculiarly related to criminal investigations, not routine, non-criminal procedures. The probable-cause approach is unhelpful when analysis centers upon the reasonableness of routine administrative caretaking functions, particularly when no claim is made that the protective procedures are a subterfuge for criminal investigations.
>
> In view of the noncriminal context of inventory searches, and the inapplicability in such a setting of the requirement of probable cause, courts have held—and quite correctly—that search warrants are not required, linked as the warrant requirement textually is to the probable-cause concept. We have frequently observed that the warrant requirement assures that legal inferences and conclusions as to probable cause will be drawn by a neutral magistrate unrelated to the criminal investigative-enforcement process. With respect to noninvestigative police inventories of automobiles lawfully within governmental custody, however, the policies underlying the warrant requirement * * * are inapplicable.

With the warrant clause eliminated from analysis, the Court focused exclusively on the reasonableness requirement of the Fourth Amendment. In this regard, the Court balanced the competing interests. From the car owner's perspective there is his lesser expectation of privacy in the contents of the automobile. The Court then considered the government's side of the equation:

> When vehicles are impounded, local police departments generally follow a routine practice of securing and inventorying the automobiles' contents. These procedures developed in response to three distinct needs: the protection of the owner's property while it remains in police custody; the protection of the police against claims or disputes over lost or stolen property; and the protection of the police from potential danger. The practice has been viewed as essential to respond to incidents of theft or vandalism. In addition, police frequently attempt to determine whether a vehicle has been stolen and thereafter abandoned.

Balancing the competing interests, the Court concluded that routine inventory searches are reasonable. Essential to this reasoning, however, is the requirement that the police follow standard procedures, *i.e.*, that they do not exceed the scope of their own rules. The police should not have unfettered discretion in conducting an inventory, in part to ensure that the inventory is "routine," rather than "a pretext concealing an investigatory police motive." *Id.*

For example, in Florida v. Wells, 495 U.S. 1, 110 S.Ct. 1632, 109 L.Ed.2d 1 (1990), the Court unanimously held that highway patrol officers were not permitted to open a locked suitcase they discovered during an inventory search because "the Florida Highway Patrol had no policy whatever with respect to the opening of closed containers encountered during an inventory search." A five-justice majority stated in dictum, however, that

> in forbidding uncanalized discretion to police officers conducting inventory searches, there is no reason to insist that they be conducted in a totally mechanical "all or nothing" fashion. * * * A police officer may be allowed sufficient latitude to determine whether a particular container should or should not be opened in light of the nature of the search and characteristics of the container itself. Thus, while policies of opening all containers or of opening no containers are unquestionably permissible, it would be equally permissible, for example, to allow the opening of closed containers whose contents officers determine they are unable to ascertain from examining the containers' exteriors. The allowance of the exercise of judgment based on concerns related to the purposes of an inventory search does not violate the Fourth Amendment.

2. Cars and Containers: Chasing the Probable Cause

In *Chambers* the police discovered criminal evidence concealed in a compartment of the vehicle they searched. In *Coolidge*, the police found particles of gun powder, apparently on the car upholstery or floor. In *Carney*, drugs and related paraphernalia were in plain view on a table inside the motor home. That is, in each of these cases, the criminal evidence inside the car was in the open. Now suppose, in an otherwise valid car search, the police discover a closed container, such as a briefcase, an envelope, or paper bag. May the police open the container as part of the car search, or must they seize it, take it to the police station, and there hold it while they apply for a search warrant?

This is the question raised in a myriad of cases referred to as "container-in-car" cases. Keep in mind that in legal terms, a "container" can be *any* object that can hold another object. The term is not limited to the idea most of us have of a receptacle with some sort of cover on it. A "container" in these cases can be a suitcase, a footlocker, a paper bag, a glove compartment, a jacket pocket, an envelope, a lunch box, a bottle, a cooler . . . well, you get the idea. A container can also be open, closed, or locked.

"Container-in-car" cases usually come up in one of two ways: 1) a container that coincidentally ends up in a car; or 2) a car that coincidentally contains a container. Clear as mud, right? In the first case, law enforcement has probable cause to believe that a certain container holds evidence of a crime. At some point during the surveillance of the container, but before it is seized, the container is placed in an automobile. There is no reason to believe that the car itself is part of any criminal activity. Can an officer search the container? The car?

In the second case, law enforcement has probable cause to believe that an automobile is being used for criminal activity. Based on the probable cause, they stop and search the vehicle. Inside the vehicle they find a container, but perhaps have no reason to believe the container itself holds evidence of a crime. Can an officer search the container? The key to both of these situations is to *always* follow the probable cause. Does the probable cause to search attach to the container or the car? As with most of the exceptions in this chapter, note once again that probable cause is still required to search. The exception applies only to the need for a warrant.

Let us now look at several examples.

In United States v. Chadwick, 433 U.S. 1, 97 U.S. 2476, 53 L.Ed.2d 538 (1977), two suspects with a large footlocker aroused the suspicions of Amtrak officials in San Diego who believed, based on their observations, that the footlocker contained marijuana. Amtrak officials in San Diego relayed their concerns to their counterparts in Boston along with a detailed description of the suspects, Machado, and Leary, and the footlocker. Two days later, federal narcotics agents, armed with a canine trained to sniff for narcotics, watched Machado and Leary as they exited the train in Boston and retrieved the footlocker from the baggage cart and sat down on it to wait.

> The agents then released the dog near the footlocker. Without alerting respondents, the dog signaled the presence of a controlled substance inside. Respondent Chadwick then joined Machado and Leary, and they engaged an attendant to move the footlocker outside to Chadwick's waiting automobile. Machado, Chadwick, and the attendant together lifted the 200-pound footlocker into the trunk of the car, while Leary waited in the front seat. At that point, while the trunk of the car was still open and before the car engine had been started, the officers arrested all three. A search disclosed no weapons, but the keys to the footlocker were apparently taken from Machado.

The suspects and the footlocker were transported to the federal building where the footlocker was searched without a search warrant 90 minutes after the arrest.

The question for the Court was whether or not the presence of the footlocker in the trunk of the car obviated the need for a warrant under the automobile exception. After all, being in the trunk of the car increased the mobility of the footlocker, argued the government, and if Chadwick has a decreased expectation of privacy in his highly-regulated automobile, the same can certainly be said of the expectation of privacy Machado and Leary have in Chadwick's car.

Here the Court said no; the automobile exception does not apply to the search of the footlocker without a warrant. Writing for the Court, Chief Justice Burger noted that the probable cause attached to the footlocker, not to Chadwick's car. There was no diminished expectation of privacy in a container just because it ends up in a car; the connection between the footlocker and the car was merely "coincidental." There was no risk of any destruction of evidence or suspect access to the container, once the container was seized, and no indication of explosives or other dangerous materials inside.

Here also, the nature of the container seemed to play a role. The Court noted in some detail that luggage, such as a footlocker, was not meant for transportation, but as a "repository for personal effects". Nor is luggage subject to the same regulations and inspections as automobiles. "In sum, a person's expectations of privacy in personal luggage are substantially greater than in an automobile". Also influencing the Court's refusal to apply the automobile exception to these facts was the ease with which authorities could have obtained a warrant once the footlocker was secured:

> Here the search was conducted more than an hour after federal agents had secured had gained exclusive control of the footlocker and long after respondents were securely in custody; the search therefore cannot be viewed as incidental to the arrest or as justified by any other exigency. Even though on this record the issuance of a warrant by a judicial officer was reasonably predictable, a line must be drawn * * * [T]he Warrant Clause places the line at the point where the property to be searched comes under the dominion of police authority. Respondents were therefore entitled to the protections of the Warrant Clause with the evaluation of a neutral magistrate before their privacy interests in the contents of the footlocker were invaded. * * *

Two years later, we come across another container that happens to end up in a car. This time the container is a suitcase and the car is moving *before* the suitcase is seized. In Arkansas v. Sanders, 442 U.S. 753, 99 S.Ct. 2586, 61 L.Ed.2d 235 (1979), the police had probable cause to believe that Sanders would arrive at the airport with a green suitcase filled with marijuana. The officers put the airport under surveillance. They observed Sanders, and later a second man, place a closed but unlocked green suitcase into a taxicab trunk and, shortly thereafter, drive away. The officers stopped the taxi within a few blocks, opened the taxi trunk, took out the suitcase, and opened it, all without a search warrant. At a subsequent trial, Sanders and his partner sought to exclude the marijuana found inside.

Notice that *Sanders* involves a container coincidentally in a car when it was seized. That is, as in *Chadwick*, the police in *Sanders* had probable cause to search a particular container before it was placed in an automobile. But here, unlike in *Chadwick*, the police did not confront the suspects until the vehicle was on the highway. As a consequence, unlike in *Chadwick*, the government in *Sanders* argued to the Supreme Court that the search was justifiable under the "automobile search" exception to the warrant requirement. As Justice Powell put it for the Court, "we thus are presented with the task of determining whether the warrantless search of respondent's suitcase falls on the *Chadwick* or the *Chambers/Carroll* side of the Fourth Amendment line." The majority concluded that it fell on the *Chadwick* side:

> [A] suitcase taken from an automobile stopped on the highway is not necessarily attended by any lesser expectation of privacy than is associated with luggage taken from other locations. One is not less inclined to place private, personal possessions in a suitcase merely

> because the suitcase is to be carried in an automobile rather than transported by other means or temporarily checked or stored. Indeed, the very purpose of a suitcase is to serve as a repository for personal items when one wishes to transport them. Accordingly, the reasons for not requiring a warrant for the search of an automobile do not apply to searches of personal luggage taken by police from automobiles. We therefore find no justification for the extension of *Carroll* and its progeny to the warrantless search of one's personal luggage merely because it was located in an automobile lawfully stopped by the police.

The fact that the car was moving did not change the analysis in *Chadwick*.

In both *Chadwick* and *Sanders*, the probable cause interest was in the containers that were then placed in an automobile. In United States v. Ross, 456 U.S. 798, 102 S.Ct. 2157, 72 L.Ed.2d 572 (1982), however, the probable cause interest was in the defendant's car itself. In *Ross*, the police had probable cause to believe that a particular individual was selling drugs from the trunk of his car at a specified location. When the police discovered the car and suspect, now on the road, they stopped the automobile and searched the car trunk. Inside, they found a closed brown paper bag, which they opened and in which they discovered heroin.

The police stopped the car in *Ross* under the automobile exception. But did the automobile exception extend to containers in the car—in this case the brown paper bag in the trunk? Justice Stevens, writing for the Court, said yes. Stevens pointed out that a warrant to search a home provides the police with implicit authority to open any container—for example, a dresser drawer, a jewelry box, a briefcase—that might contain the criminal evidence for which they are searching. Likewise, "[a] warrant to search a vehicle would support a search of every part of the vehicle"—including containers therein—"that might contain the object of the search." Because the vehicle exception to the warrant requirement substituted for a warrant, a car search should be treated as if the police had a search warrant. When the police have probable cause to search a car without a warrant under the *Carroll-Chambers-Carney* line of cases, they may also search any container found during the car search that is large enough to hold the evidence for which they are looking.

Thus, immediately after *Ross*, an uneasy—and complicated—car/container distinction existed. If the police had probable cause to search a car, they could search fixed parts thereof (*e.g.*, glove compartments, trunks) as well as movable containers carried within it (assuming they could conceal the object of the search). But, if the police had probable cause to search a specific container, which coincidentally was found in a car, they could search the car on the highway (or tow it to the police station, per *Chambers v. Maroney*), without a warrant in order to find and seize the container, but they needed a warrant to open the container.

As you might guess, this resulted in quite a few arguments and motions at trial over the admissibility of containers, as police would often jump through some very oddly shaped hoops in order to attach the probable cause to the car and not the container. A district attorney told us that in the *Chadwick-Sanders* era, he instructed his police officers to avoid learning from informants where in a vehicle the contraband was located, thus permitting a *Ross* search of the entire vehicle. Any doctrine that prompted such an odd approach to police investigation was not likely to last very long.

And it did not.

CALIFORNIA V. ACEVEDO

Supreme Court of the United States, 1991.
500 U.S. 565, 111 S.Ct. 1982, 114 L.Ed.2d 619.

By the time Mr. Acevedo comes along, the Court has had enough of the complicated and time-consuming distinctions between cars and containers. Note the way Justice Blackmun, in writing the *Acevedo* opinion, describes some of the problems with the law as it stood in 1991.

- **"By attempting to distinguish between a container for which the police are specifically searching and a container which they come across in a car, we have provided only minimal protection for privacy and have impeded effective law enforcement."**
- **"The line between probable cause to search a vehicle and probable cause to search a package in that vehicle is not always clear, and separate rules that govern the two objects to be searched may enable police to broaden their power to make warrantless searches and disserve privacy interests."**

For those of you who are Lord of the Rings fans, think of *Acevedo* as the one case to rule them all.

JUSTICE BLACKMUN delivered the opinion of the Court [joined by CHIEF JUSTICE REHNQUIST, and JUSTICES O'CONNOR, KENNEDY, and SOUTER]. * * *

I

[Jamie Daza picked up a package from a Federal Express office, sent from Hawaii, that the police knew from prior inspection contained marijuana. Officers observed Daza take the package to his home. They kept the Daza residence under surveillance, while another officer left to obtain a warrant to search the Daza residence. Before a warrant could be obtained, the following events ensued.]

* * * [R]espondent Charles Steven Acevedo arrived. He entered Daza's apartment, stayed for about 10 minutes, and reappeared carrying a brown paper bag that looked full. The officers noticed that the bag was the size of one of the wrapped marijuana packages sent from Hawaii. Acevedo walked to a silver Honda in the parking lot. He placed the bag in the trunk of the car and started to drive away. Fearing the loss of evidence, officers in a marked police car stopped him. They opened the trunk and the bag, and found marijuana. * * *

The California Court of Appeal * * * concluded that the marijuana found in the paper bag in the car's trunk should have been suppressed. The court concluded that the officers had probable cause to believe that the paper bag contained drugs but lacked probable cause to suspect that Acevedo's car, itself, otherwise contained contraband. Because the officers' probable cause was directed specifically at the bag, the court held that the case was controlled by *United States v. Chadwick*, [p. 284] rather than by *United States v. Ross* [p. 287]. Although the court agreed that the officers could seize the paper bag, it held that, under *Chadwick*, they could not open the bag without first obtaining a warrant for that purpose. * * *

We granted certiorari to reexamine the law applicable to a closed container in an automobile, a subject that has troubled courts and law enforcement officers since it was first considered in *Chadwick*. * * *

III * * *

This Court in *Ross* * * * recognized that it was arguable that the same exigent circumstances that permit a warrantless search of an automobile would justify the warrantless search of a movable container. In deference to the rule of *Chadwick* and *[Arkansas v.] Sanders* [p. 286], however, the Court put that question to one side. * * * We now must decide the question deferred in *Ross*: whether the Fourth Amendment requires the police to obtain a warrant to open the sack in a movable vehicle simply because they lack probable cause to search the entire car. We conclude that it does not.

IV

Dissenters in *Ross* asked why the suitcase in *Sanders* was "more private, less difficult for police to seize and store, or in any other relevant respect more properly subject to the warrant requirement, than a container that police discover in a probable-cause search of an entire automobile?" We now agree that a container found after a general search of the automobile and a container found in a car after a limited search for the container are equally easy for the police to store and for the suspect to hide or destroy. In fact, we see no principled distinction in terms of either the privacy expectation or the exigent circumstances between the paper bag found by the police in *Ross* and the paper bag found by the police here. Furthermore, by attempting to distinguish between a container for which the police are specifically searching and a container which they come across in a car, we have provided only minimal protection for privacy and have impeded effective law enforcement.

The line between probable cause to search a vehicle and probable cause to search a package in that vehicle is not always clear, and separate rules that govern the two objects to be searched may enable the police to broaden their power to make warrantless searches and disserve privacy interests. * * * At the moment when officers stop an automobile, it may be less than clear whether they suspect with a high degree of certainty that the vehicle contains drugs in a bag or simply contains drugs. If the police know that they may open a bag only if they are actually searching the entire car, they may search more extensively than they otherwise would in order to establish the general probable cause required by *Ross*. * * *

To the extent that the *Chadwick-Sanders* rule protects privacy, its protection is minimal. Law enforcement officers may seize a container and hold it until they obtain a search warrant. *Chadwick*. "Since the police, by hypothesis, have probable cause to seize the property, we can assume that a warrant will be routinely forthcoming in the overwhelming majority of cases." *Sanders* (dissenting opinion). And the police often will be able to search containers without a warrant, despite the *Chadwick-Sanders* rule, as a search incident to a lawful arrest. * * *

Finally, the search of a paper bag intrudes far less on individual privacy than does the incursion sanctioned long ago in *Carroll*. In that case, prohibition agents slashed the upholstery of the automobile. This Court nonetheless found their search to be reasonable under the Fourth Amendment. If destroying the interior of an automobile is not unreasonable, we cannot conclude that looking inside a closed container is. In light of the minimal protection to privacy afforded by the *Chadwick-Sanders* rule, and our serious doubt whether that rule substantially serves privacy interests, we now hold that the Fourth Amendment does not compel separate treatment for an automobile search that extends only to a container within the vehicle.

V

The *Chadwick-Sanders* rule not only has failed to protect privacy but also has confused courts and police officers and impeded effective law enforcement. * * *

The discrepancy between the two rules has led to confusion for law enforcement officers. For example, when an officer, who has developed probable cause to believe that a vehicle contains drugs, begins to search the vehicle and immediately discovers a closed container, which rule applies? The defendant will argue that the fact that the officer first chose to search the container indicates that his probable cause extended only to the container and that *Chadwick* and *Sanders* therefore require a warrant. On the other hand, the fact that the officer first chose to search in the most obvious location should not restrict the propriety of the search. The *Chadwick* rule, as applied in *Sanders*, has devolved into an anomaly such that the more likely the police are to discover drugs in a container, the less authority they have to search it. We have noted the virtue of providing " ' "clear and unequivocal" guidelines to the law enforcement profession.' " The *Chadwick-Sanders* rule is the antithesis of a " 'clear and unequivocal' guideline." * * *

* * * We conclude that it is better to adopt one clear-cut rule to govern automobile searches and eliminate the warrant requirement for closed containers set forth in *Sanders*.

VI

The interpretation of the *Carroll* doctrine set forth in *Ross* now applies to all searches of containers found in an automobile. In other words, the police may search without a warrant if their search is supported by probable cause. The Court in *Ross* * * * went on to note: "Probable cause to believe that a container placed in the trunk of a taxi contains contraband or evidence does not justify a search of the entire cab." We reaffirm that principle. In the case before us, the police had probable cause to believe that the paper bag in the automobile's trunk contained marijuana. That probable cause now allows a warrantless search of the paper bag. The facts in the record reveal that the police did not have probable cause to believe that contraband was hidden in any other part of the automobile and a search of the entire vehicle would have been without probable cause and unreasonable under the Fourth Amendment.

Our holding today neither extends the *Carroll* doctrine nor broadens the scope of the permissible automobile search delineated in *Carroll*, *Chambers*, and *Ross*. It remains a "cardinal principle that 'searches conducted outside the judicial process, without prior approval by judge or magistrate, are *per se* unreasonable under the Fourth Amendment—subject only to a few specifically established and well-delineated exceptions.' " * * *

Until today, this Court has drawn a curious line between the search of an automobile that coincidentally turns up a container and the search of a container that coincidentally turns up in an automobile. The protections of the Fourth Amendment must not turn on such coincidences. We therefore interpret *Carroll* as providing one rule to govern all automobile searches. The police may search an automobile and the containers within it where they have probable cause to believe contraband or evidence is contained.

[*JUSTICE SCALIA's opinion concurring in the judgment is omitted.*]

[*JUSTICE WHITE'S dissent is omitted.*]

JUSTICE STEVENS, with whom JUSTICE MARSHALL joins, dissenting.

At the end of its opinion, the Court pays lipservice to the proposition that should provide the basis for a correct analysis of the legal question presented by this case: It is " 'a cardinal principle that "searches conducted outside the judicial process, without prior approval by judge or magistrate, are *per se* unreasonable under the Fourth Amendment—subject only to a few specifically established and well-delineated exceptions." ' "

Relying on arguments that conservative judges have repeatedly rejected in past cases, the Court today—despite its disclaimer to the contrary—enlarges the scope of the automobile exception to this "cardinal principle," which undergirded our Fourth Amendment jurisprudence * * *. * * *

II

In its opinion today, the Court recognizes that the police did not have probable cause to search respondent's vehicle and that a search of anything but the paper bag that respondent had carried from Daza's apartment and placed in the trunk of his car would have been unconstitutional. Moreover, as I read the opinion, the Court assumes that the police could not have made a warrantless inspection of the bag before it was placed in the car. Finally, the Court also does not question the fact that, under our prior cases, it would have been lawful for the police to seize the container and detain it (and respondent) until they obtained a search warrant. Thus, all of the relevant facts that governed our decisions in *Chadwick* and *Sanders* are present here whereas the relevant fact that justified the vehicle search in *Ross* is not present.

The Court does not attempt to identify any exigent circumstances that would justify its refusal to apply the general rule against warrantless searches. Instead, it advances these three arguments: First, the rules identified in the foregoing cases are confusing and anomalous. Second, the rules do not protect any significant interest in privacy. And, third, the rules impede effective law enforcement. None of these arguments withstands scrutiny.

The "Confusion" * * *

The Court summarizes the alleged "anomaly" created by the coexistence of *Ross*, *Chadwick*, and *Sanders* with the statement that "the more likely the police are to discover drugs in a container, the less authority they have to search it." This juxtaposition is only anomalous, however, if one accepts the flawed premise that the degree to which the police are likely to discover contraband is correlated with their authority to search *without a warrant.* Yet, even proof beyond a reasonable doubt will not justify a warrantless search that is not supported by one of the exceptions to the warrant requirement. And, even when the police have a warrant or an exception applies, once the police possess probable cause, the extent to which they are more or less certain of the contents of a container has no bearing on their authority to search it.

To the extent there was any "anomaly" in our prior jurisprudence, the Court has "cured" it at the expense of creating a more serious paradox. For surely it is anomalous to prohibit a search of a briefcase while the owner is carrying it exposed on a public street yet to permit a search once the owner has placed the briefcase in the locked trunk of his car. One's privacy interest in one's luggage can certainly not be diminished by one's removing it from a public thoroughfare and placing it—out of sight—in a privately owned vehicle. Nor is the danger that evidence will escape increased if the luggage is in a car rather than on the street. In either location, if the police have probable cause, they are authorized to seize the luggage and to detain it until they obtain judicial approval for a search. Any line demarking an exception to the warrant requirement will appear blurred at the edges, but the Court has certainly erred if it believes that, by erasing one line and drawing another, it has drawn a clearer boundary.

The Privacy Argument

The Court's statement that *Chadwick* and *Sanders* provide only "minimal protection to privacy" is also unpersuasive. Every citizen clearly has an interest in the privacy of the contents of his or her luggage, briefcase, handbag or any other container that conceals private papers and effects from public scrutiny. That privacy interest has been recognized repeatedly in cases spanning more than a century.

Under the Court's holding today, the privacy interest that protects the contents of a suitcase or a briefcase from a warrantless search when it is in public view simply vanishes when its owner climbs into a taxicab. Unquestionably the rejection of the *Sanders* line of cases by today's decision will result in a significant loss of individual privacy.

To support its argument that today's holding works only a minimal intrusion on privacy, the Court suggests that "[i]f the police know that they may open a bag only if they are actually searching the entire car, they may search more extensively than they otherwise would in order to establish the general probable cause required by *Ross*." * * * [T]his fear is unexplained and inexplicable. Neither evidence uncovered in the course of a search nor the scope of the search conducted can be used to provide *post hoc* justification for a search unsupported by probable cause at its inception. * * *

The Burden on Law Enforcement

The Court's suggestion that *Chadwick* and *Sanders* have created a significant burden on effective law enforcement is unsupported, inaccurate, and, in any event, an insufficient reason for creating a new exception to the warrant requirement. * * *

Even if the warrant requirement does inconvenience the police to some extent, that fact does not distinguish this constitutional requirement from any other procedural protection secured by the Bill of Rights. It is merely a part of the price that our society must pay in order to preserve its freedom. * * *

NOTES AND QUESTIONS

1. *Acevedo* overruled *Sanders*. Did it overrule *Chadwick*? If not, why not? If not, what is left of the *Chadwick* doctrine?

2. *Problem.* Would the following warrantless search variations on *Acevedo* be permissible?

A. The police in *Acevedo* open the trunk, immediately spot the paper bag, open it, and find marijuana. The police proceed to search the remainder of the trunk. They find and seize transparent bags of cocaine hidden under a blanket. They search the passenger compartment. Under the front seat, they find a small quantity of marijuana.

B. The same as A., except that when the police open the paper bag in the trunk they discover that it contains non-contraband lawful items. They proceed to search the remainder of the trunk, as in A.

C. The police open the trunk, and do not immediately see the paper bag. They hunt through the trunk. They do not find the paper bag, but they do discover a briefcase. They open it, find the brown paper bag inside, and open it.

D. The police stop Acevedo, but do not arrest him, before he enters the car. They seize and open the paper bag.

E. The police stop Acevedo before he enters the car. They arrest him for possession of marijuana, seize the paper bag, and open it.

3. What if, during an otherwise valid warrantless car search, the police come upon a smart phone. If they have probable cause to believe it contains incriminating evidence, may they turn the phone on and, for example, search the phone log? (Assume nobody in the vehicle is under arrest.) See United States v. Camou, 773 F.3d 932 (9th Cir. 2014).

4. *Containers belonging to passengers.* Does probable cause to search a car entitle the police to open containers they have reason to know belong to an occupant whom they lack probable cause to arrest? In Wyoming v. Houghton, 526 U.S. 295, 119 S.Ct. 1297, 143 L.Ed.2d 408 (1999), the police lawfully stopped a vehicle containing a male driver and two female front seat passengers. The police uncontestedly obtained probable cause to search the car for drugs after they lawfully seized an illegal syringe from the driver, who admitted that he used it to take drugs. During the car search, the police discovered a purse in the back seat that one of the passengers, Houghton, claimed belonged to her. At the time, the officers did *not* have probable cause to suspect her of drug use, nor was the driver under arrest.

The Supreme Court, 6–3, per Justice Scalia, announced that "police officers with probable cause to search a car may inspect [any] passengers' belongings found in the car that are capable of concealing the object of the search." According to Scalia, "[p]assengers, no less than drivers, possess a reduced expectation of privacy with regard to the property that they transport in cars * * *." Moreover, "the degree of intrusiveness upon personal privacy and indeed even personal dignity" of a property search is less than the intrusiveness of a search of one's person. The Court concluded that the Government's legitimate interest in effective law enforcement justified a search of all car containers that might hold drugs, and not simply those containers apparently belonging to the driver.

E. PLAIN VIEW (AND TOUCH) DOCTRINES

ARIZONA V. HICKS

Supreme Court of the United States, 1987.
480 U.S. 321, 107 S.Ct. 1149, 94 L.Ed.2d 347.

Various features of Justice Scalia's opinion in *Hicks* are noteworthy. First, he seems to be a strong advocate here of the concept of probable cause, particularly in contrast to the lesser standard of reasonable suspicion (which we will be studying in the next chapter), presumably because the former concept is found in the Constitution, and the latter is not. Second, we see that Justice Scalia is inclined toward bright-line rules, given his unwillingness to accept the "cursory inspection" approach. Third, Scalia reminds us that the "Constitution sometimes insulates the criminality of a few in order to protect the privacy of us all"—a slightly different way of stating the premise inherent in our judicial system that it "is better that 10 guilty men go free than that one innocent man is convicted."

The important thing to remember about the plain view exception set out in *Hicks* is that is a "derivative" exception. It derives from, or exists, only because, and only when, law enforcement officers already have a valid reason to be at the location and "looking around." What was the reason the officers had for being in, and searching, Mr. Hick's apartment?

Also remember that like other exceptions in this chapter, the plain view exception still requires probable cause. In this case, once the officer noticed the stereo equipment in the defendant's apartment, he still needed probable cause to engage with the equipment in the manner he did. Did the Court find that all important probable cause in this case?

JUSTICE SCALIA delivered the opinion of the Court [joined by JUSTICES BRENNAN, WHITE, MARSHALL, BLACKMUN, and STEVENS]. * * *

I

On April 18, 1984, a bullet was fired through the floor of respondent's apartment, striking and injuring a man in the apartment below. Police officers arrived and entered respondent's apartment to search for the shooter, for other victims, and for weapons. They found and seized three weapons, including a sawed-off rifle, and in the course of their search also discovered a stocking-cap mask.

One of the policemen, Officer Nelson, noticed two sets of expensive stereo components, which seemed out of place in the squalid and otherwise ill-appointed four-room apartment. Suspecting that they were stolen, he read and recorded their serial numbers—moving some of the components, including a Bang and Olufsen turntable, in order to do so—which he then reported by phone to his headquarters. On being advised that the turntable had been taken in an armed robbery, he seized it immediately. It was later determined that some of the other serial numbers matched those on other stereo equipment taken in the same armed robbery, and a warrant was obtained and executed to seize that equipment as well. Respondent was subsequently indicted for the robbery. * * *

II

As an initial matter, the State argues that Officer Nelson's actions constituted neither a "search" nor a "seizure" within the meaning of the Fourth Amendment. We agree that the mere recording of the serial numbers did not constitute a seizure. To be sure, that was the first step in a process by which respondent was eventually deprived of the stereo equipment. In and of itself, however, it did not "meaningfully interfere" with respondent's possessory interest in either the serial numbers or the equipment, and therefore did not amount to a seizure.

Officer Nelson's moving of the equipment, however, did constitute a "search" separate and apart from the search for the shooter, victims, and weapons that was the lawful objective of his entry into the apartment. Merely inspecting those parts of the turntable that came into view during the latter search would not have constituted an independent search, because it would have produced no additional invasion of respondent's privacy interest. But taking action, unrelated to the objectives of the authorized intrusion, which exposed to view concealed portions of the apartment or its contents, did produce a new invasion of respondent's privacy unjustified by the exigent circumstance that validated the entry. This is why, contrary to Justice Powell's suggestion [in dissent], the "distinction between 'looking' at a suspicious object in plain view and 'moving' it even a few inches" is much more than trivial for purposes of the Fourth Amendment. It matters not that the search uncovered nothing of any great personal value to respondent—serial numbers rather than (what might conceivably have been hidden behind or under the equipment) letters or photographs. A search is a search, even if it happens to disclose nothing but the bottom of a turntable.

III

The remaining question is whether the search was "reasonable" under the Fourth Amendment. * * *

* * * "It is well established that under certain circumstances the police may *seize* evidence in plain view without a warrant," *Coolidge v. New Hampshire* (emphasis added). * * * It would be absurd to say that an object could lawfully be seized and taken from the premises, but could not be moved for closer examination. It is clear, therefore, that the search here was valid if the "plain view" doctrine would have sustained a seizure of the equipment.

There is no doubt it would have done so if Officer Nelson had probable cause to believe that the equipment was stolen. The State has conceded, however, that he had only a "reasonable suspicion," by which it means something less than probable cause. We have not ruled on the question whether probable cause is required in order to invoke the "plain view" doctrine. * * *

We now hold that probable cause is required. To say otherwise would be to cut the "plain view" doctrine loose from its theoretical and practical moorings. The theory of that doctrine consists of extending to nonpublic places such as the home, where searches and seizures without a warrant are presumptively unreasonable, the police's longstanding authority to make warrantless seizures in public places of such objects as weapons and contraband. And the practical justification for that extension is the desirability of sparing police, whose viewing of the object in the course of a lawful search is as legitimate as it would have been in a public place, the inconvenience and the risk—to themselves or to preservation of the evidence—of going to obtain a warrant. Dispensing with the need for a warrant is worlds apart from permitting a lesser standard of *cause* for the seizure than a warrant would require, *i.e.*, the standard of probable cause. No reason is apparent why an object should routinely be seizable on lesser grounds, during an unrelated search and seizure, than would have been needed to obtain a warrant for that same object if it had been known to be on the premises.

We do not say, of course, that a seizure can never be justified on less than probable cause. We have held that it can—where, for example, the seizure is minimally intrusive and operational necessities render it the only practicable means of detecting certain types of crime. No special operational necessities are relied on here, however—but rather the mere fact that the items in question came lawfully within the officer's plain view. That alone cannot supplant the requirement of probable cause.

The same considerations preclude us from holding that, even though probable cause would have been necessary for a *seizure*, the *search* of objects in plain view that occurred here could be sustained on lesser grounds. A dwelling-place search, no less than a dwelling-place seizure, requires probable cause, and there is no reason in theory or practicality why application of the "plain view" doctrine would supplant that requirement. Although the interest protected by the Fourth Amendment injunction against unreasonable searches is quite different from that protected by its injunction against unreasonable seizures, neither the one nor the other is of inferior worth or necessarily requires only lesser protection. We have not elsewhere drawn a categorical distinction between the two insofar as concerns the degree of justification needed to establish the reasonableness of police action, and we see no reason for a distinction in the particular circumstances before us here. Indeed, to treat searches more liberally would especially erode the plurality's warning in *Coolidge* that "the 'plain view' doctrine may not be used to extend a general exploratory search from one object to another until something incriminating at last emerges." In short, whether legal authority to move the equipment could be found only as an inevitable concomitant of the authority to seize it, or also as a consequence of some independent power to search certain objects in plain view, probable cause to believe the equipment was stolen was required.

Justice O'Connor's dissent suggests that we uphold the action here on the ground that it was a "cursory inspection" rather than a "full-blown search," and could therefore be justified by reasonable suspicion instead of probable cause. As already noted, a truly cursory inspection—one that involves merely looking at what is already exposed to view, without disturbing it—is not a "search" for Fourth Amendment purposes, and therefore does not even require reasonable suspicion. We are unwilling to send police and judges into a new thicket of Fourth Amendment law, to seek a creature of uncertain description that is neither a "plain view" inspection nor yet a "full-blown search." Nothing in the prior opinions of this Court supports such a distinction * * *.

Justice Powell's dissent reasonably asks what it is we would have had Officer Nelson do in these circumstances. The answer depends, of course, upon whether he had probable cause to conduct a search * * *. If he had, then he should have done precisely what he did. If not, then he should have followed up his suspicions, if possible, by means other than a search—just as he would have had to do if, while walking along the street, he had noticed the same suspicious stereo equipment sitting inside a house a few feet away from him, beneath an open window. It may well be that, in such circumstances, no effective means short of a search exist. But there is nothing new in the realization that the Constitution sometimes insulates the criminality of a few in order to protect the privacy of us all. Our disagreement with the dissenters pertains to where the proper balance should be struck; we choose to adhere to the textual and traditional standard of probable cause. * * *

[*JUSTICE WHITE'S concurring opinion is omitted.*]

JUSTICE POWELL, with whom THE CHIEF JUSTICE [REHNQUIST] and JUSTICE O'CONNOR join, dissenting. * * *

It is fair to ask what Officer Nelson should have done in these circumstances. Accepting the State's concession that he lacked probable cause, he could not have obtained a warrant to seize the stereo components. Neither could he have remained on the premises and forcibly prevented their removal. * * *

The Court holds that there was an unlawful search of the turntable. It agrees that the "mere recording of the serial numbers did not constitute a seizure." Thus, if the computer had identified as stolen property a component with a visible serial number, the evidence would have been admissible. But the Court further holds that "Officer Nelson's moving of the equipment * * * did constitute a 'search' * * *." It perceives a constitutional distinction between reading a serial number on an object and moving or picking up an identical object to see its serial number. * * * With all respect, this distinction between "looking" at a suspicious object in plain view and "moving" it even a few inches trivializes the Fourth Amendment. The Court's new rule will cause uncertainty, and could deter conscientious police officers from lawfully obtaining evidence necessary to convict guilty persons. * * * Accordingly, I dissent.

JUSTICE O'CONNOR, with whom THE CHIEF JUSTICE [REHNQUIST] and JUSTICE POWELL join, dissenting.

The Court today gives the right answer to the wrong question. The Court asks whether the police must have probable cause before either seizing an object in plain view or conducting a full-blown search of that object, and concludes that they must. I agree. In my view, however, this case presents a different question: whether police must have probable cause before conducting a cursory inspection of an item in plain view. Because I conclude that such an inspection is reasonable if the police are aware of facts or circumstances that justify a reasonable suspicion that the item is evidence of a crime, I would reverse the judgment of the Arizona Court of Appeals, and therefore dissent.

* * * [T]he dispute in this case focuses on the application of the "immediately apparent" requirement; at issue is whether a police officer's reasonable suspicion is adequate to justify a cursory examination of an item in plain view.

The purpose of the "immediately apparent" requirement is to prevent "general, exploratory rummaging in a person's belongings." If an officer could indiscriminately search every item in plain view, a search justified by a limited purpose—such as exigent circumstances—could be used to eviscerate the protections of the Fourth Amendment. In order to prevent such a general search, therefore, we require that the relevance of the item be "immediately apparent." * * *

Thus, I agree with the Court that even under the plain-view doctrine, probable cause is required before the police seize an item, or conduct a full-blown search of evidence in plain view. Such a requirement of probable cause will prevent the plain-view doctrine from authorizing general searches. This is not to say, however, that even a mere inspection of a suspicious item must be supported by probable cause. When a police officer makes a cursory inspection of a suspicious item in plain view in order to determine whether it is indeed evidence of a crime, there is no "exploratory rummaging." Only those items that the police officer "reasonably suspects" as evidence of a crime may be inspected, and perhaps more importantly, the scope of such an inspection is quite limited. In short, if police officers have a reasonable, articulable suspicion that an object they come across during the course of a lawful search is evidence of crime, in my view they may make a cursory examination of the object to verify their suspicion. If the officers wish to go beyond such a cursory examination of the object, however, they must have probable cause. * * *

This distinction between searches based on their relative intrusiveness * * * is entirely consistent with our Fourth Amendment jurisprudence. We have long recognized that searches can vary in intrusiveness, and that some brief searches "may be so minimally intrusive of Fourth Amendment interests that strong countervailing governmental interests will justify a [search] based only on specific articulable facts" that the item in question is contraband or evidence of a crime. * * *

In my view, the balance of the governmental and privacy interests strongly supports a reasonable-suspicion standard for the cursory examination of items in plain view. * * *

Unfortunately, in its desire to establish a "bright-line" test, the Court has taken a step that ignores a substantial body of precedent and that places serious roadblocks to reasonable law enforcement practices. * * *

NOTES AND QUESTIONS

1. *Making sense of Hicks.* What appear to be the elements that must be met in order for the plain-view doctrine to apply? According to Justice Scalia, what element of "plain view" was not proven by the Government? Suppose that Officer Nelson had feared that a gun was hidden behind a closed curtain in the Hicks residence. Could

he lawfully have opened the curtain, without a warrant, in the absence of probable cause?

In dictum, Justice Scalia stated that if Officer Nelson had had probable cause to believe that the stereo equipment was stolen, "he should have done precisely what he did." Does that seem correct? Why or why not?

2. *Plain touch.* The Supreme Court announced for the first time in Minnesota v. Dickerson, 508 U.S. 366, 113 S.Ct. 2130, 124 L.Ed.2d 334 (1993), that there is a comparable plain-*touch* doctrine:

> We think that [the plain-view] doctrine has an obvious application by analogy to cases in which an officer discovers contraband through the sense of touch during an otherwise lawful search. * * * If a police officer lawfully pats down a suspect's outer clothing [for weapons] and feels an object whose contour or mass makes its identity immediately apparent, there has been no invasion of the suspect's privacy beyond that already authorized by the officer's search for weapons; if the object is contraband, its warrantless seizure would be justified by the same practical considerations that inhere in the plain view context. * * *

3. *Problem.* A police officer obtained a warrant to search *F*'s home and computer for marijuana and documents and computer files pertaining to marijuana sales. When the officer found the computer, he turned it on, went to the "Documents" sub-menu of the "Start" menu, and there discovered a list of recently opened files. He opened the first file and, to his surprise, it was a child pornography image. He then opened two or three more documents on the list, and they also contained child pornography. Does the plain-view doctrine justify the warrantless seizure of these photographs? Frasier v. State, 794 N.E.2d 449 (Ind. App. 2003).

4. *Problem.* A police officer, with consent, entered *H*'s residence to investigate an allegation of an abandoned minor at the residence. Inside, the officer observed a pipe sitting on a table that, based on his experience and training was "predominantly used to smoke marijuana." The officer picked it up and smelled the odor of marijuana. The officer seized the pipe and arrested *H* for possession of drug paraphernalia. Did the officer's actions violate *Hicks*? Commonwealth v. Hatcher, 199 S.W.3d 124 (Ky. 2006).

CHAPTER 5 SUMMARY

In Chapter 4 we examined what a warrant is required to contain, and when and how it needs to be executed. In this chapter, we began our look at when warrants are required, or more specifically, when they are not. As we often learn in early childhood, to every rule there is an exception, and sometimes even lots of exceptions! In this case, some legal scholars have argued that the exceptions have come close to swallowing the rule.

In this chapter, we examined several long-standing exceptions to the need for a search warrant: including exigent circumstances, search incident to lawful arrest (SILA), the automobile exception, and plain view. There is an important constant in all of these exceptions. They are mainly exceptions to the warrant requirement; the need for an officer to run down to the courthouse, get a magistrate to sign that pesky piece of paper, and come back to the scene to conduct the search or seizure. In *most* of the situations in this chapter, *some* probable cause is still needed to search or seize persons or property. For example, exigent circumstances requires probable cause to believe the suspect is committing or has committed a crime (and that evidence could be destroyed or public safety threatened); a SILA requires probable cause to arrest; the automobile exception requires probable cause to believe that weapons or evidence of a crime will be found in the car; and plain view is often derived from one of the above exceptions, with the probable cause that goes along with it. Throughout this chapter, our starting point is still the same: *is there probable cause to search or seize?*

Exigent circumstances and SILA share a common theme of ensuring officer and public safety and preventing the destruction of evidence. By contrast, while the automobile exception is designed in part to prevent the loss of evidence while a warrant is being sought, its basis lies in the belief that we have a lesser expectation of privacy in vehicles than in other possessions and that their inherent mobility creates unique circumstances whereby a warrant requirement could defeat legitimate law enforcement efforts.

Exigent circumstances (your typical hot pursuit case) does not provide officers with *carte blanche* to claim an emergency. The less serious the crime at issue, the more likely it is that the exigent circumstances justification must be stronger, especially when the entry into a home is involved.

It is also important for students to remember that the SILA exception and the automobile exception are not interchangeable. While many searches incident to lawful arrests take place with the occupants of automobiles, it is the arrest that provides the justification for the search, not the fact that an automobile was involved. By contrast, if an officer has probable cause to search an automobile, she can do so regardless of whether an arrest is made.

CHAPTER 6

Valid Warrantless Searches, Part II: The Diminishing Role of Probable Cause

The theme of the previous chapter was that while that pesky piece of paper signed by a neutral magistrate—a warrant—was not required in certain specific circumstances, probable cause still often was. In other words, in most cases, both probable cause and an established exception to the warrant requirement had to be present for the search under discussion to be reasonable. In this chapter, that is no longer the case. The exceptions discussed here—consent, *Terry* stops, and administrative/special needs searches—require neither a warrant nor the traditional requirement for probable cause.

How can a search without a warrant or probable cause be reasonable? In some cases, it is because there is nothing in the Fourth Amendment that prevents law enforcement officers from simply asking if they can conduct a search, and nothing that prevents us from saying yes. In other cases, the Court has recognized that there may be instances of contact between the police and the public that may implicate police and public safety, requiring split-second decisions on the part of an officer that necessitates an initial intrusion on someone's privacy based on something more than a hunch, but less than probable cause. Finally, there are some searches where conduct is heavily regulated and the level of intrusion deemed minor enough that the full protections of the Fourth Amendment do not apply.

Look once again at the wording of the Fourth Amendment:

> *The right of the people to be secure in their persons, houses, papers, and effects, against unreasonable searches and seizures, shall not be violated, and no Warrants shall issue, but upon probable cause, supported by Oath or affirmation, and particularly describing the place to be searched, and the persons or things to be seized.*

The checklist we have been using to determine when and how we apply the Fourth Amendment to particular government conduct (see Chapters 3, 4 and 5) looked at the Fourth Amendment as a whole. A search is reasonable if there is probable cause and a warrant or an exception to the warrant requirement. However, for the searches discussed in this chapter, it is sometimes helpful to view the Fourth Amendment as containing two separate parts or clauses: the Reasonableness Clause and the Warrant Clause.

1. *The right of the people to be secure in their persons, houses, papers, and effects, against unreasonable searches and seizures, shall not be violated* (Reasonableness Clause);

2. *[N]o Warrants shall issue, but upon probable cause, supported by Oath or affirmation, and particularly describing the place to be searched, and the persons or things to be seized* (Warrant Clause).

Notice that, although we used a semi-colon to separate the two clauses in the Amendment in the numbered list above, the actual text uses commas. Can you draw any inference from this punctuation? Specifically, should the two clauses be read in conjunction? The traditional position taken by the courts is that the Fourth Amendment is better served if police officers apply for warrants, rather than act on the basis of their own determinations. This position is represented in the well-known passage from *Katz* (p. 77) that we have seen cited in so many of the search and seizure cases we have read so far: "Searches conducted outside the judicial process, without prior approval by judge or magistrate [a warrant], are *per se* unreasonable under the Fourth Amendment—subject to only a few established and well-delineated exceptions."

The competing view is that the Fourth Amendment test "is not whether it is reasonable [or practicable] to procure a search warrant, but whether the search was reasonable." United States v. Rabinowitz, 339 U.S. 56, 70 S.Ct. 430, 94 L.Ed. 653 (1950). After all, the argument goes, the text of the Amendment bars unreasonable searches and seizures. Nowhere does it state that warrants are required, only that when warrants *are* sought they must meet certain requirements (i.e.: specificity, supported by probable cause). This view is bolstered by the fact that since *Katz*, the number of 'established and well-delineated' exceptions have proliferated to the point where one wonders if the warrant requirement—even if one does still exist—has any teeth left.

This leaves us with two ways to analyze the cases in this chapter. The first approach is to view these as exceptions to both the 'requirement' for a warrant and as an exception to the requirement that police have probable cause to search.

The second approach is to simply ask if given the circumstances of the search, the government's conduct is reasonable or not; questions about warrants and probable cause found in the second clause of the Amendment are not even part of the equation. The main focus of the cases then becomes what in these particular circumstances—consent, *Terry* stops, administrative searches—qualifies as reasonable?

As you read the cases in this chapter, consider what you have learned about the Fourth Amendment so far. Ask yourself if the warrant requirement still means anything and if the Fourth Amendment itself still has the force envisioned by the Warren Court?

A. CONSENT

SCHNECKLOTH V. BUSTAMONTE

Supreme Court of the United States, 1973.
412 U.S. 218, 93 S.Ct. 2041, 36 L.Ed.2d 854.

"It is * well settled that one of the specifically established exceptions to the requirements of both a warrant and probable cause is a search that is conducted pursuant to consent."** ***Schneckloth*** **starts by putting this statement front and center. But what is 'consent'?**

The main focus of ***Schneckloth*** **is to help us determine when one's consent has been properly sought and given. The simple answer is that consent is valid when given voluntarily. But how do we know when a consent is voluntary. As set out in** ***Schneckloth*****, that determination is made by looking at the** ***totality of the circumstances. Schneckloth*** **also discusses a number of factors that might be relevant. See how many you can identify.**

The important thing to keep in mind is that in considering the totality of the circumstances, no one factor is key; including whether or not the defendant knew of their right to refuse consent. Put another way, there is no requirement that officers inform a suspect of their right to say ***no*** **to a search. Whether or not one knows they can refuse is simply one factor among many to be considered. Pay close attention as to why the Court chose not to require such a warning and compare the majority's reasoning with that of Justice Marshall in his dissent. Which side to you agree with?**

Also, note the emphasis placed by the Court on the importance of consent searches to law enforcement. Like many of the decisions during the Burger Court, the focus was on broadening the tools and discretion law

enforcement officers have to investigate crime. Justice Marshall, on the other hand, does not favor this type of search; hence his dissent.

The Notes following the case explore more of the factors considered when determining the voluntariness of consent; including to what extent, if any, can considerations of culture and race play a role.

MR. JUSTICE STEWART delivered the opinion of the Court [joined by CHIEF JUSTICE BURGER, and JUSTICES WHITE, BLACKMUN, POWELL, and REHNQUIST].

It is well settled under the Fourth and Fourteenth Amendments that a search conducted without a warrant issued upon probable cause is "*per se* unreasonable * * * subject only to a few specifically established and well-delineated exceptions." It is equally well settled that one of the specifically established exceptions to the requirements of both a warrant and probable cause is a search that is conducted pursuant to consent. The constitutional question in the present case concerns the definition of "consent" in this Fourth and Fourteenth Amendment context.

I

[While on routine patrol at 2:40 a.m., a police officer stopped a car containing six persons because he observed that one headlight and the car's license plate light were burned out. The driver could not produce a license. The officer requested the occupants to get out of the car, and the officer requested permission from Joe Alcala, who claimed to be the brother of the car owner, to search the vehicle. Alcala purportedly replied, "Sure, go ahead." Two reinforcement officers arrived at the scene. According to the officer's uncontradicted testimony, nobody was threatened with arrest prior to this time; it "was all very congenial." Wadded up under the left rear seat, the police discovered three stolen checks, later linked to one of the passengers, Bustamonte, who was prosecuted for theft. The trial court denied the defendant's pretrial motion to suppress the evidence, after which he was convicted at trial.]

II

* * * The respondent concedes that a search conducted pursuant to a valid consent is constitutionally permissible. * * * And similarly the State concedes that "[w]hen a prosecutor seeks to rely upon consent to justify the lawfulness of a search, he has the burden of proving that the consent was, in fact, freely and voluntarily given."

The precise question in this case, then, is what must the prosecution prove to demonstrate that a consent was "voluntarily" given. * * * The Court of Appeals for the Ninth Circuit concluded that it is an essential part of the State's initial burden to prove that a person knows he has a right to refuse consent. The California courts have followed the rule that voluntariness is a question of fact to be determined from the totality of all the circumstances, and that the state of a defendant's knowledge is only one factor to be taken into account in assessing the voluntariness of a consent.

A

The most extensive judicial exposition of the meaning of "voluntariness" has been developed in those cases in which the Court has had to determine the "voluntariness" of a defendant's confession for purposes of the Fourteenth Amendment. * * * It is to that body of case law to which we turn for initial guidance on the meaning of "voluntariness" in the present context. * * *

In determining whether a defendant's will was overborne in a particular case, the Court has assessed the totality of all the surrounding circumstances—both the characteristics of the accused and the details of the interrogation. * * *

The significant fact about all of these decisions is that none of them turned on the presence or absence of a single controlling criterion; each reflected a careful scrutiny of all the surrounding circumstances. * * *

B

Similar considerations lead us to agree with the courts of California that the question whether a consent to a search was in fact "voluntary" or was the product of duress or coercion, express or implied, is a question of fact to be determined from the totality of all the circumstances. While knowledge of the right to refuse consent is one factor to be taken into account, the government need not establish such knowledge as the *sine qua non* of an effective consent. As with police questioning, two competing concerns must be accommodated in determining the meaning of a "voluntary" consent—the legitimate need for such searches and the equally important requirement of assuring the absence of coercion.

In situations where the police have some evidence of illicit activity, but lack probable cause to arrest or search, a search authorized by a valid consent may be the only means of obtaining important and reliable evidence. In the present case for example, while the police had reason to stop the car for traffic violations, the State does not contend that there was probable cause to search the vehicle or that the search was incident to a valid arrest of any of the occupants. Yet, the search yielded tangible evidence that served as a basis for a prosecution, and provided some assurance that others, wholly innocent of the crime, were not mistakenly brought to trial. And in those cases where there is probable cause to arrest or search, but where the police lack a warrant, a consent search may still be valuable. If the search is conducted and proves fruitless, that in itself may convince the police that an arrest with its possible stigma and embarrassment is unnecessary, or that a far more extensive search pursuant to a warrant is not justified. In short, a search pursuant to consent may result in considerably less inconvenience for the subject of the search, and, properly conducted, is a constitutionally permissible and wholly legitimate aspect of effective police activity.

But the Fourth and Fourteenth Amendments require that a consent not be coerced, by explicit or implicit means, by implied threat or covert force. For, no matter how subtly the coercion was applied, the resulting "consent" would be no more than a pretext for the unjustified police intrusion against which the Fourth Amendment is directed. * * *

The problem of reconciling the recognized legitimacy of consent searches with the requirement that they be free from any aspect of official coercion cannot be resolved by any infallible touchstone. * * * Just as was true with confessions, the requirement of a "voluntary" consent reflects a fair accommodation of the constitutional requirements involved. In examining all the surrounding circumstances to determine if in fact the consent to search was coerced, account must be taken of subtly coercive police questions, as well as the possibly vulnerable subjective state of the person who consents. Those searches that are the product of police coercion can thus be filtered out without undermining the continuing validity of consent searches. In sum, there is no reason for us to depart in the area of consent searches, from the traditional definition of "voluntariness."

The approach of the Court of Appeals for the Ninth Circuit finds no support in any of our decisions that have attempted to define the meaning of "voluntariness." Its ruling, that the State must affirmatively prove that the subject of the search knew that he had a right to refuse consent, would, in practice, create serious doubt whether consent searches could continue to be conducted. There might be rare cases where it could be proved from the record that a person in fact affirmatively knew of his right to refuse * * *. But more commonly where there was no evidence of any coercion, explicit or implicit, the prosecution would nevertheless be unable to demonstrate that the subject of the search in fact had known of his right to refuse consent. * * *

One alternative that would go far toward proving that the subject of a search did know he had a right to refuse consent would be to advise him of that right before eliciting his consent. That, however, is a suggestion that has been almost universally repudiated by both federal and state courts, and, we think, rightly so. For it would be thoroughly impractical to impose on the normal consent search the detailed requirements of an effective warning. Consent searches are part of the standard investigatory techniques of law enforcement agencies. They normally occur on the highway, or in a person's home or office, and under informal and unstructured conditions. * * * These situations are a far cry from the structured atmosphere of a trial where, assisted by counsel if he chooses, a defendant is informed of his trial rights. And, while surely a closer question, these situations are still immeasurably far removed from "custodial interrogation" where, in *Miranda v. Arizona*, [p. 501], we found that the Constitution required certain now familiar warnings as a prerequisite to police interrogation. * * *

In short, neither this Court's prior cases, nor the traditional definition of "voluntariness" requires proof of knowledge of a right to refuse as the *sine qua non* of an effective consent to a search.

* * *

D

Much of what has already been said disposes of the argument that the Court's decision in the *Miranda* case requires the conclusion that knowledge of a right to refuse is an indispensable element of a valid consent. The considerations that informed the Court's holding in *Miranda* are simply inapplicable in the present case. * * *

In this case, there is no evidence of any inherently coercive tactics—either from the nature of the police questioning or the environment in which it took place. Indeed, since consent searches will normally occur on a person's own familiar territory, the specter of incommunicado police interrogation in some remote station house is simply inapposite. There is no reason to believe, under circumstances such as are present here, that the response to a policeman's question is presumptively coerced; and there is, therefore, no reason to reject the traditional test for determining the voluntariness of a person's response. * * *

It is also argued that the failure to require the Government to establish knowledge as a prerequisite to a valid consent, will relegate the Fourth Amendment to the special province of "the sophisticated, the knowledgeable and the privileged." We cannot agree. The traditional definition of voluntariness we accept today has always taken into account evidence of minimal schooling, low intelligence, and the lack of any effective warnings to a person of his rights; and the voluntariness of any statement taken under those conditions has been carefully scrutinized to determine whether it was in fact voluntarily given.

E

Our decision today is a narrow one. We hold only that when the subject of a search is not in custody and the State attempts to justify a search on the basis of his consent, the Fourth and Fourteenth Amendments require that it demonstrate that the consent was in fact voluntarily given, and not the result of duress or coercion, express or implied. Voluntariness is a question of fact to be determined from all the circumstances, and while the subject's knowledge of a right to refuse is a factor to be taken into account, the prosecution is not required to demonstrate such knowledge as a prerequisite to establishing a voluntary consent. * * *

[*The concurring opinions of JUSTICES BLACKMUN and POWELL, and the dissenting opinions of JUSTICES DOUGLAS and BRENNAN, are omitted.*]

MR. JUSTICE MARSHALL, dissenting. * * *

I * * *

A

The Court assumes that the issue in this case is: what are the standards by which courts are to determine that consent is voluntarily given? It then imports into the law of search and seizure standards developed to decide entirely different questions about coerced confessions.

The Fifth Amendment, in terms, provides that no person "shall be compelled in any criminal case to be a witness against himself." * * * The inquiry in a case where a confession is challenged as having been elicited in an unconstitutional manner is, therefore, whether the behavior of the police amounted to compulsion of the defendant. Because of the nature of the right to be free of compulsion, it would be pointless to ask whether a defendant knew of it before he made a statement; no sane person would knowingly relinquish a right to be free of compulsion. Thus, the questions of compulsion and of violation of the right itself are inextricably intertwined. The cases involving coerced confessions, therefore, pass over the question of knowledge of that right as irrelevant, and turn directly to the question of compulsion. * * *

B

In contrast, this case deals not with "coercion," but with "consent," a subtly different concept to which different standards have been applied in the past. Freedom from coercion is a substantive right, guaranteed by the Fifth and Fourteenth Amendments. Consent, however, is a mechanism by which substantive requirements, otherwise applicable, are avoided. * * * Thus, consent searches are permitted, not because * * * an exception to the requirements of probable cause and warrant is essential to proper law enforcement, but because we permit our citizens to choose whether or not they wish to exercise their constitutional rights. Our prior decisions simply do not support the view that a meaningful choice has been made solely because no coercion was brought to bear on the subject. * * *

II * * *

If consent to search means that a person has chosen to forgo his right to exclude the police from the place they seek to search, it follows that his consent cannot be considered a meaningful choice unless he knew that he could in fact exclude the police. * * * I would therefore hold, at a minimum, that the prosecution may not rely on a purported consent to search if the subject of the search did not know that he could refuse to give consent. * * *

If one accepts this view, the question then is a simple one: must the Government show that the subject knew of his rights, or must the subject show that he lacked such knowledge?

I think that any fair allocation of the burden would require that it be placed on the prosecution. * * *

The burden on the prosecutor would disappear, of course, if the police, at the time they requested consent to search, also told the subject that he had a right to refuse consent and that his decision to refuse would be respected. The Court's assertions to the contrary notwithstanding, there is nothing impractical about this method of satisfying the prosecution's burden of proof. * * *

The Court contends that if an officer paused to inform the subject of his rights, the informality of the exchange would be destroyed. I doubt that a simple statement by an officer of an individual's right to refuse consent would do much to alter the informality of the exchange, except to alert the subject to a fact that he surely is entitled to know. It is not without significance that for many years the agents of the Federal Bureau of Investigation have routinely informed subjects of their right to refuse consent, when they request consent to search. * * *

I must conclude, with some reluctance, that when the Court speaks of practicality, what it really is talking of is the continued ability of the police to capitalize on the ignorance of citizens so as to accomplish by subterfuge what they could not achieve by relying only on the knowing relinquishment of constitutional rights. Of course it would be "practical" for the police to ignore the commands of the Fourth Amendment, if by practicality we mean that more criminals will be apprehended, even though the constitutional rights of innocent people also go by the board. But such a practical advantage is achieved only at the cost of permitting the police to disregard the limitations that the Constitution places on their behavior, a cost that a constitutional democracy cannot long absorb. * * *

NOTES AND QUESTIONS

1. *A view from the trenches.* There are no precise data on how often searches are conducted on the basis of consent, but one study reported that the two most common warrant "exceptions" are consent and search incident to a lawful arrest, with one detective suggesting that as many as 98 percent of warrantless searches fall under the "consent" umbrella. Richard Van Duizend et al., The Search Warrant Process: Preconceptions, Perceptions, and Practices 21 (1984). Even if this figure is inflated, it suggests that consent issues are of profound importance in the "real world" of searches and seizures.

2. Warrant exceptions require a rationale. As we have seen, warrantless car searches are justified on the grounds of mobility and the lesser expectation of privacy we possess in vehicles. Warrantless searches incident to arrest are justified on the ground that the police must protect themselves from possible attack and prevent destruction of evidence. Why is a warrantless search based on consent allowed? Specifically, does consent waive the Fourth Amendment protections or is it simply another way to deem a search reasonable? Which theory best explains the majority opinion in *Schneckloth*? The dissent?

3. Arnold H. Loewy, *Cops, Cars, and Citizens: Fixing the Broken Balance*, 76 St. John's L. Rev. 535, 554 (2002):

> From the detainees' perspective [in *Schneckloth*], there was little that appeared voluntary. They were stopped at 2:40 in the morning, asked (ordered?) to exit the car, and witnessed the arrival of two reinforcement police officers. They were then asked to search the car without being told that "no" was an option. Can anyone not thoroughly steeped in legal fiction really believe that they thought "no" was one of their options?

Do you agree with Loewy?

4. *Why do guilty people consent?* "Every year I witness the same mass incredulity. Why, one hundred criminal procedure students jointly wonder, would someone 'voluntarily' consent to allow a police officer to search the trunk of his car, knowing that massive amounts of cocaine are easily visible there?" Marcy Strauss, *Reconstructing Consent*, 92 J. Crim. L. & Criminology 211, 211 (2001). Have you thought the same thing?

One court has gone so far as to observe that "no sane man who denies his guilt would actually be willing that policemen search his room for contraband which is certain to be discovered." Higgins v. United States, 209 F.2d 819 (D.C. Cir. 1954). Do you agree? If so, why *do* courts so often find, where criminal evidence was discovered by the police, that the consent to search was voluntary? Is it that judges "systematically overestimate the extent to which citizens in police encounters feel free to refuse [consent]"? Janice Nadler, *No Need to Shout: Bus Sweeps and the Psychology of Coercion*, 2002 Sup. Ct. Rev. 153, 156. Or, is there another explanation?

5. *More of the same.* In Ohio v. Robinette, 519 U.S. 33, 117 S.Ct. 417, 136 L.Ed.2d 347 (1996), *O*, an officer, lawfully detained *R* for speeding. After checking *R*'s license and finding no outstanding violations, *O* asked *R* to get out of the car, after which he issued *R* a verbal warning for speeding and returned the license. *O* then said, "[o]ne question before you get gone. Are you carrying any illegal contraband in your car? Any weapons of any kind, drugs, anything like that?" After *R* responded in the negative, *O* sought and obtained consent to search the car. The search turned up a small amount of marijuana and, in a film container, a pill later determined to be a controlled substance.

R argued that his consent was involuntary because he was not informed that he was free to go after return of his driver's license. As in *Schneckloth*, the Court here ruled that, although knowledge is a factor to be taken into account in voluntariness analysis, there is no categorical requirement that police officers inform "detainees that they are free to go before a consent to search may be deemed voluntary."

6. *Another view from the trenches.* The facts in *Robinette* (Note 5) repeat themselves often, with slight variations. Consider: A deputy sheriff pulled over three young men he saw drinking beer while driving in a rural area. Having open beer in the car was not a violation of state law, but the deputy surely had probable cause to think the driver might be intoxicated. The deputy ordered the driver to undergo a field sobriety test. Luckily for the driver, he had had only one beer and thus passed the test. Disgruntled, the deputy said (possibly a general question always to ask): "You boys mind if I take a look in your trunk." After a brief pause, the driver said, "No, sir." In the trunk, in plain view, was a modest amount of cocaine and some drug paraphernalia. The deputy seized these items and arrested all three men, who turned out to be college students.

Defendants retained one of the authors of this book to represent them. In the preliminary interview, their lawyer asked the obvious question: "You knew that stuff was in the trunk?" "Yes." "You're college students. College students are usually at least as smart as average people, so here it comes: why in the world did you consent?"

The sheepish response was: "I thought if I didn't consent, the deputy would hold us and get a warrant; also, I thought if we were cooperative, he might overlook the small amount."

"You thought a deputy sheriff was going to overlook Schedule 2 drugs?"

Shrug: "I thought it was our only chance. If he got a warrant, I knew we were finished."

Is this valid consent under the majority opinion in *Schneckloth*? If so, does this case persuade you that Justice Marshall got the better of the argument in the case?

7. In *Bumper v. North Carolina*, 391 U.S. 543, 88 S.Ct. 1788, 20 L.Ed.2d 797 (1968), four white law enforcement officers went to the house of Hattie Leath, a 66-year-old African-American widow. According to the Court, the house was "located in a rural area at the end of an isolated mile-long dirt road." Ms. Leath met the officers at the front door. One of the officers told her, "I have a search warrant to search your house." She replied, "go ahead," and opened the door. At trial, the Government did not rely on a warrant to justify the search, but instead claimed that Ms. Leath voluntarily consented. The Supreme Court disagreed:

> When a prosecutor seeks to rely upon consent to justify the lawfulness of a search, he has the burden of proving that the consent was, in fact, freely and voluntarily given. This burden cannot be discharged by showing no more than acquiescence to a claim of lawful authority. * * *
>
> When a law enforcement officer claims authority to search a home under a warrant, he announces in effect that the occupant has no right to resist the search. The situation is instinct with coercion—albeit colorably lawful coercion. Where there is coercion there cannot be consent.

Is *Bumper* consistent with the totality-of-circumstances test of voluntariness announced years later in *Schneckloth*?

8. *Consent, race, and class.* Apparently most or all of the occupants of the Schneckloth vehicle were Hispanic. Should the Court have considered the possible disparate effect of the rule it was announcing in *Schneckloth* on persons of different races, cultures, and economic classes? Consider:

> Such reliance on ignorance and thinly veiled coercion is deeply troubling. * * * The current system created two Fourth Amendments—one for people who are aware of their right to say no and confident enough to assert the right against a police officer, and another for those who do not know their rights or are afraid to assert them.
>
> This doubtful standard would be problematic even if it did not closely parallel race and class lines. * * * [T]he consent doctrine in application is likely to reflect race and class divisions. Because a consent search requires no objective individualized suspicion, it is more likely to be directed at poor young black men than wealthy white elderly women. In addition, those who

> are white and wealthy are more likely to know their rights and to feel secure in asserting them.

David Cole, No Equal Justice 31 (1999). Is Professor Cole correct? If so, in light of *Schneckloth's* announcement of a totality-of-circumstances test, should a court take into consideration the race and class of the suspect in determining the voluntariness of consent? In this regard, Professor Cole, *id.* at 33–34, reports:

> [O]ne of my students reports that when she attempted to teach the consent doctrine to prisoners at a federal prison in Virginia, her predominantly black and Hispanic students ridiculed the notion. They maintained that although it might be true that she, a white woman, had the right to consent, if they declined consent, the police would either beat them or go ahead and search anyway, and then testify that they had consented. It is of course difficult to verify such statements, but that perception itself will factor into a citizen's decision to assert her rights.

9. Even if a person voluntarily consents to a search, she can set limits of a temporal nature ("You may search my house for exactly two minutes and no more.") or limit the scope of the search ("You may search my kitchen and living room, but not the bedroom."). The latter issue is considered more fully later in the chapter.

A person may also withdraw consent after it is granted. The police must honor the citizen's wishes, unless their pre-withdrawal search gives them independent grounds to proceed. But, the issue of whether a defendant has truly withdrawn consent, like voluntariness, can be a difficult one to resolve. Courts generally require that the withdrawal of consent be clearly given. For example, in State v. Wantland, 828 N.W.2d 885 (Wis. App. 2013), *W* consented to a police search of his automobile. When the officer picked up a briefcase in the vehicle, *W* asked, "Got a warrant for that?" Has *W* withdrawn his consent?

ILLINOIS V. RODRIGUEZ

Supreme Court of the United States, 1990.
497 U.S. 177, 110 S.Ct. 2793, 111 L.Ed.2d 148.

In this case, we look at who can give consent to search property when more than one person may or may not live there (roommates, anyone?). The rules regarding consent over co-occupied property center around two aspects. First, anyone who has authority over the property can give, or refuse, consent to the police to search the premises. Second, if the police believe that the person granting consent to search has the authority to do so, and that belief turns out to be wrong, the search is still valid as long as the belief was *reasonable*. We will see this concept again when we look more closely at the exclusionary rule in the next chapter. Speaking of

reasonable, this case is also useful because it displays the Court's preference for using the reasonableness clause (discussed in the introduction to this chapter) to analyze consent searches.

Note also how the case ended. The Court remanded the case—sent it back to the trial court—for consideration of whether or not "the officers reasonably believed Fischer had the authority to consent". This happens a lot as appellate courts, particularly at this level, focus on matters of law and prefer to leave factual determinations to the trial court. Why do you think this might be?

JUSTICE SCALIA delivered the opinion of the Court [joined by CHIEF JUSTICE REHNQUIST, and JUSTICES WHITE, BLACKMUN, O'CONNOR, and KENNEDY]. * * *

I * * *

On July 26, 1985, police were summoned to the residence of Dorothy Jackson on South Wolcott in Chicago. They were met by Ms. Jackson's daughter, Gail Fischer, who showed signs of a severe beating. She told the officers that she had been assaulted by respondent Edward Rodriguez earlier that day in an apartment on South California Avenue. Fischer stated that Rodriguez was then asleep in the apartment, and she consented to travel there with the police in order to unlock the door with her key so that the officers could enter and arrest him. During this conversation, Fischer several times referred to the apartment on South California as "our" apartment, and said that she had clothes and furniture there. It is unclear whether she indicated that she currently lived at the apartment, or only that she used to live there.

The police officers drove to the apartment on South California, accompanied by Fischer. They did not obtain an arrest warrant for Rodriguez, nor did they seek a search warrant for the apartment. At the apartment, Fischer unlocked the door with her key and gave the officers permission to enter. They moved through the door into the living room, where they observed in plain view drug paraphernalia and containers filled with white powder that they believed (correctly, as later analysis showed) to be cocaine. * * * The officers arrested Rodriguez and seized the drugs and related paraphernalia.

Rodriguez was charged with possession of a controlled substance with intent to deliver. He moved to suppress all evidence seized at the time of his arrest, claiming that Fischer had vacated the apartment several weeks earlier and had no authority to consent to the entry. The Cook County Circuit Court granted the motion, holding that at the time she consented to the entry Fischer did not have common authority over the apartment. The Court concluded that Fischer was not a "usual resident" but rather an "infrequent visitor" at the apartment on South California, based upon its findings that Fischer's name was not on the lease, that she did not contribute to the rent, that she was not allowed to invite others to the apartment on her own, that she did not have access to the apartment when respondent was away, and that she had moved some of her possessions from the apartment. The Circuit Court also rejected the State's contention that, even if Fischer did not possess common authority over the premises, there was no Fourth Amendment violation if the police *reasonably believed* at the time of their entry that Fischer possessed the authority to consent. * * *

II * * *

As we stated in [*United States v.*] *Matlock*, [415 U.S. 164, 94 S.Ct. 988, 39 L.Ed.2d 242 (1974)], "[c]ommon authority" rests "on mutual use of the property by persons generally having joint access or control for most purposes * * *." The burden of establishing that common authority rests upon the State. On the basis of this record, it is clear that burden was not sustained. The evidence showed that although Fischer, with her two small children, had lived with Rodriguez beginning in December 1984, she had moved out on July 1, 1985, almost a month before the search at issue here, and had gone to live with her mother. * * * She had a key to the apartment, which she said at trial she had taken without Rodriguez's knowledge * * *. On these facts the State has not established that, with respect to the South California apartment, Fischer had "joint access or control for most purposes." * * *

III

A

The State contends that, even if Fischer did not in fact have authority to give consent, it suffices to validate the entry that the law enforcement officers reasonably believed she did. * * *

B * * *

* * * What he [the defendant] is assured by the Fourth Amendment itself, however, is not that no government search of his house will occur unless he consents; but that no such search will occur that is "unreasonable." There are various elements, of course, that can make a search of a person's house "reasonable"—one of which is the consent of the person or his cotenant. The essence of respondent's argument is that we should impose upon this element a requirement that we have not imposed upon other elements that regularly compel

government officers to exercise judgment regarding the facts: namely, the requirement that their judgment be not only responsible but correct.

The fundamental objective that alone validates all unconsented government searches is, of course, the seizure of persons who have committed or are about to commit crimes, or of evidence related to crimes. But "reasonableness," with respect to this necessary element, does not demand that the government be factually correct in its assessment that that is what a search will produce. Warrants need only be supported by "probable cause," which demands no more than a proper "assessment of probabilities in particular factual contexts * * *." If a magistrate, based upon seemingly reliable but factually inaccurate information, issues a warrant for the search of a house in which the sought-after felon is not present, has never been present, and was never likely to have been present, the owner of that house suffers one of the inconveniences we all expose ourselves to as the cost of living in a safe society; he does not suffer a violation of the Fourth Amendment.

Another element often, though not invariably, required in order to render an unconsented search "reasonable" is, of course, that the officer be authorized by a valid warrant. Here also we have not held that "reasonableness" precludes error with respect to those factual judgments that law enforcement officials are expected to make. [Justice Scalia then recounted the facts in *Maryland v. Garrison*, p. 212, Note 6 in which the Court upheld a search in which the police mistakenly searched the wrong residence.] * * *

It would be superfluous to multiply these examples. It is apparent that in order to satisfy the "reasonableness" requirement of the Fourth Amendment, what is generally demanded of the many factual determinations that must regularly be made by agents of the government—whether the magistrate issuing a warrant, the police officer executing a warrant, or the police officer conducting a search or seizure under one of the exceptions to the warrant requirement—is not that they always be correct, but that they always be reasonable. As we put it in *Brinegar v. United States*, 338 U.S. 160, 176, 69 S.Ct. 1302, 1311, 93 L.Ed. 1879 (1949):

> "Because many situations which confront officers in the course of executing their duties are more or less ambiguous, room must be allowed for some mistakes on their part. But the mistakes must be those of reasonable men, acting on facts leading sensibly to their conclusions of probability."

We see no reason to depart from this general rule with respect to facts bearing upon the authority to consent to a search. Whether the basis for such authority exists is the sort of recurring factual question to which law enforcement officials must be expected to apply their judgment; and all the Fourth Amendment requires is that they answer it reasonably. The Constitution is no more violated when officers enter without a warrant because they reasonably (though erroneously) believe that the person who has consented to their entry is a resident of the premises, than it is violated when they enter without a warrant because they reasonably (though erroneously) believe they are in pursuit of a violent felon who is about to escape. * * *

* * * [W]hat we hold today does not suggest that law enforcement officers may always accept a person's invitation to enter premises. Even when the invitation is accompanied by an explicit assertion that the person lives there, the surrounding circumstances could conceivably be such that a reasonable person would doubt its truth and not act upon it without further inquiry. As with other factual determinations bearing upon search and seizure, determination of consent to enter must "be judged against an objective standard: would the facts available to the officer at the moment * * * 'warrant a man of reasonable caution in the belief' " that the consenting party had authority over the premises? If not, then warrantless entry without further inquiry is unlawful unless authority actually exists. But if so, the search is valid.

In the present case, the Appellate Court found it unnecessary to determine whether the officers reasonably believed that Fischer had the authority to consent, because it ruled as a matter of law that a reasonable belief could not validate the entry. Since we find that ruling to be in error, we remand for consideration of that question. * * *

JUSTICE MARSHALL, with whom JUSTICE BRENNAN and JUSTICE STEVENS join, dissenting. * * *

* * * The Court holds that the warrantless entry into Rodriguez's home was nonetheless valid if the officers reasonably believed that Fischer had authority to consent. The majority's defense of this position rests on a misconception of the basis for third-party consent searches. That such searches do not give rise to claims of constitutional violations rests not on the premise that they are "reasonable" under the Fourth Amendment, but on the premise that a person may voluntarily limit his expectation of privacy by allowing others to exercise authority over his possessions. Thus, an individual's decision to permit another "joint access [to] or control [over the property] for most purposes," *United States v. Matlock*, limits that individual's reasonable expectation of privacy and to that extent limits his Fourth Amendment protections. If an individual has not so

limited his expectation of privacy, the police may not dispense with the safeguards established by the Fourth Amendment. * * *

I * * *

Unlike searches conducted pursuant to the recognized exceptions to the warrant requirement, third-party consent searches are not based on an exigency and therefore serve no compelling social goal. Police officers, when faced with the choice of relying on consent by a third party or securing a warrant, should secure a warrant and must therefore accept the risk of error should they instead choose to rely on consent.

II

Our prior cases discussing searches based on third-party consent have never suggested that such searches are "reasonable." In *United States v. Matlock*, this Court upheld a warrantless search conducted pursuant to the consent of a third party who was living with the defendant. The Court rejected the defendant's challenge to the search, stating that a person who permits others to have "joint access or control for most purposes * * * assume[s] the risk that [such persons] might permit the common area to be searched." As the Court's assumption-of-risk analysis makes clear, third-party consent limits a person's ability to challenge the reasonableness of the search only because that person voluntarily has relinquished some of his expectation of privacy by sharing access or control over his property with another person.

A search conducted pursuant to an officer's reasonable but mistaken belief that a third party had authority to consent is thus on an entirely different constitutional footing from one based on the consent of a third party who in fact has such authority. Even if the officers reasonably believed that Fischer had authority to consent, she did not, and Rodriguez's expectation of privacy was therefore undiminished. Rodriguez accordingly can challenge the warrantless intrusion into his home as a violation of the Fourth Amendment. * * *

III

* * * [T]he majority seeks to rely on cases suggesting that reasonable but mistaken factual judgments by police will not invalidate otherwise reasonable searches. * * *

* * * The cases the majority cites * * * provide no support for its holding. In *Brinegar v. United States*, for example, the Court confirmed the unremarkable proposition that police need only probable cause, not absolute certainty, to justify the arrest of a suspect on a highway. As *Brinegar* makes clear, the possibility of

factual error is built into the probable cause standard, and such a standard, by its very definition, will in some cases result in the arrest of a suspect who has not actually committed a crime. Because probable cause defines the reasonableness of searches and seizures outside of the home, a search is reasonable under the Fourth Amendment whenever that standard is met, notwithstanding the possibility of "mistakes" on the part of police. * * *

The majority's reliance on *Maryland v. Garrison* is also misplaced. * * * As in *Brinegar*, the Court's decision was premised on the general reasonableness of the type of police action involved. Because searches based on warrants are generally reasonable, the officers' reasonable mistake of fact did not render their search "unreasonable." * * *

IV

* * * That a person who allows another joint access to his property thereby limits his expectation of privacy does not justify trampling the rights of a person who has not similarly relinquished any of his privacy expectation.

* * * [B]y allowing a person to be subjected to a warrantless search in his home without his consent and without exigency, the majority has taken away some of the liberty that the Fourth Amendment was designed to protect.

NOTES AND QUESTIONS

1. According to Justice Scalia, what is the justification for warrantless consent searches? Do you find the rationale in accord with *Schneckloth*? Does Justice Marshall provide a plausible explanation of consent searches?

2. As developed at the trial court level and as is set out in the first paragraph of the Court's opinion, Gail Fischer told the police that she had clothing and some of her furniture at the apartment in question. Why would she have said this if it were her apartment? Don't these remarks put a reasonable officer on notice that this was not her apartment? In this regard, consider the following conversation between Michael R. Dreeben, who argued on behalf of the United States as *amicus curiae* in support of the State of Illinois, and Justices Stevens and O'Connor, during oral arguments in the *Rodriguez* case:

> QUESTION: * * * [D]o you think the police officer had any duty to ask the young lady if she lived there? * * *
>
> MR. DREEBEN: No. I don't think they did, Justice Stevens. And the reason that they didn't have a specific duty to ask that particular question is that they were summoned to the scene of what they understood was a

> battery victim. * * * They learned that she had been beaten by her boyfriend at an apartment that they—she described as "our apartment." There's testimony that she said that many of her things were there. * * *
>
> QUESTION: Well, it would have been pretty simple for them to ask a few more questions, wouldn't it?
>
> MR. DREEBEN: Yes, Justice O'Connor.
>
> QUESTION: And, you're asking for an exception to the warrant requirement which is something paramount in the Fourth Amendment requirements. It seems to me you're suggesting that we just open the door wide without any corresponding obligation on the part of the police to make reasonable inquiry.
>
> MR. DREEBEN: Justice O'Connor, I think it would be fully appropriate for this Court to hold that appropriate inquiry is necessary when the facts are ambiguous and clarification is what a reasonable police officer would do.

In your view, is this a case in which "the facts are ambiguous and clarification is what a reasonable police officer would do"? Did Ms. Fisher say something to the police that might have, perhaps should have, put them on notice that she no longer lived in the apartment?

3. Does this case have Fourth Amendment implications that extend beyond consent searches? For example, suppose that when Rodriguez was arrested, the police conducted a search incident to the arrest and discovered additional contraband in a dresser drawer thirty feet away from the handcuffed arrestee. If you represented Rodriguez and sought to have that evidence suppressed, what would you argue? If you were the prosecutor, how would you respond, based on *Rodriguez*?

4. *Scope of consent.* A consent search is invalid, even if the consent was voluntary, if the police exceed the scope of the consent granted. In Florida v. Jimeno, 500 U.S. 248, 111 S.Ct. 1801, 114 L.Ed.2d 297 (1991), Officer Trujillo, who had stopped Jimeno's car for a traffic violation, told Jimeno (based on earlier information) that he had reason to believe that Jimeno was carrying narcotics in the car. Trujillo asked permission to search the vehicle and reportedly received consent. In the search, the officer found a folded paper bag on the car's floorboard, which he opened. It contained cocaine. Jimeno moved to suppress the cocaine on the ground that his consent to search the car, even if voluntary, did not extend to the closed paper bag inside the car. The Court rejected the argument:

> The touchstone of the Fourth Amendment is reasonableness. The Fourth Amendment does not proscribe all state-initiated searches and seizures; it merely proscribes those which are unreasonable. *Illinois v.*

> *Rodriguez.* * * * The standard for measuring the scope of a suspect's consent under the Fourth Amendment is that of "objective" reasonableness—what would the typical reasonable person have understood by the exchange between the officer and the suspect? The question before us, then, is whether it is reasonable for an officer to consider a suspect's general consent to a search of his car to include consent to examine a paper bag lying on the floor of the car. We think that it is.
>
> The scope of a search is generally defined by its expressed object. In this case, the terms of the search's authorization were simple. Respondent granted Officer Trujillo permission to search his car, and did not place any explicit limitation on the scope of the search. Trujillo had informed Jimeno that he believed Jimeno was carrying narcotics, and that he would be looking for narcotics in the car. We think that it was objectively reasonable for the police to conclude that the general consent to search respondents' car included consent to search containers within that car which might bear drugs. A reasonable person may be expected to know that narcotics are generally carried in some form of a container. * * * The authorization to search in this case, therefore, extended beyond the surfaces of the car's interior to the paper bag lying on the car's floor.
>
> The facts of this case are therefore different from those in *State v. Wells*, [539 So.2d 464 (1989)], on which the Supreme Court of Florida relied in affirming the suppression order in this case. There the Supreme Court of Florida held that consent to search the trunk of a car did not include authorization to pry open a locked briefcase found inside the trunk. It is very likely unreasonable to think that a suspect, by consenting to the search of his trunk, has agreed to the breaking open of a locked briefcase within the trunk, but it is otherwise with respect to a closed paper bag.

Did the Court adequately distinguish the facts in *Wells*? What if Trujillo had told Jimeno that he wanted to search the car for a stolen large-screen television set?

5. *Problems.* In light of everything you have learned, what result in the following "consent" cases?

A. *O* obtained consent to search *D*'s luggage at a train station. Inside the luggage, he found a can labeled "tamales in gravy." *O* shook the can and it seemed to contain a dry substance, like salt. *O* proceeded to break open the can and found a bag of methamphetamine. United States v. Osage, 235 F.3d 518 (10th Cir. 2000).

B. A border agent received consent to "search" and "look in" the suspect's two mobile phones. When one phone rang, the agent answered it and pretended to be the defendant. This conversation produced evidence a prosecutor later sought to use in a smuggling prosecution. Is the evidence admissible? What if a text message, rather than a phone call, came during the mobile phone search: would the officer have a right to read the incoming message? United States v. Lopez-Cruz, 730 F.3d 803 (9th Cir. 2013).

C. At 3:30 a.m., *S,* a passenger in a vehicle stopped in a public parking lot, voluntarily consented to a search of his person for drugs. As part of that search, one of the police officers pulled open the waistbands of *S*'s sweat pants and underwear and peered inside with a flashlight. *S* objected, but by the time he did, the officer has already observed the white cap of what appeared to be a pill bottle tucked in between *S*'s inner thigh and testicles. Should the pill bottle, which was seized, be suppressed? State v. Stone, 653 S.E.2d 414 (N.C. 2007).

D. Police came to Victor's hotel room. They knocked. A woman answered. The officer asked, "Is Victor here?" According to the officer, the woman looked at him "funny—like a deer in the headlights type of look," and seemed "nervous" and "stunned." She replied, "I don't know." The officer told her truthfully that Victor asked for him to come to the hotel room. He asked consent to enter. She consented. The woman did not have authority over the premises. Is the consent valid? Commonwealth v. Lopez, 937 N.E.2d 949 (Mass. 2010).

6. *More on Consent and Co-Tenants.* We know from *Rodriguez* and *Matlock* (discussed in *Rodriguez*) that someone who appears to be a co-tenant can consent to a search; police do not have to obtain the consent of other co-tenants. But what should be the right result when one co-tenant consents and the other co-tenant, also present, refuses to consent? In Georgia v. Randolph, 547 U.S. 103, 126 S.Ct. 1515, 164 L.Ed.2d 208 (2006), the Court held, 5–4, that the refusal of one co-tenant nullifies the consent of another co-tenant. At first blush, this makes sense; the co-tenant who refuses has the same property law rights in the dwelling as the other co-tenant. But a moment's reflection discloses two complications. First, what about the property rights of the co-tenant who gives consent? Why are they less important than the property rights of the one who refuses? Second, as Chief Justice Roberts well notes in his dissent, Randolph just happened to be lucky enough to be standing near the door when his wife gave consent. Should Fourth Amendment protection really be based on luck? The property interest of an unlucky co-owner who would refuse if asked

> is not protected if a co-owner happens to be absent when the police arrive, in the backyard gardening, asleep in the next room, or listening to music through earphones so that only his co-occupant hears the knock on the door. That the rule is so random in its application confirms that it bears no real relation to the privacy protected by the Fourth Amendment. What the majority's rule protects is not so much privacy as the good luck of a co-owner who just happens to be present at the door when the police arrive.

> Usually when the development of Fourth Amendment jurisprudence leads to such arbitrary lines, we take it as a signal that the rules need to be rethought.

Rodriguez presumably would have refused had he been lucky enough to be at the door when Fisher opened it with her key. Matlock presumably would have refused if he had been in the house rather than detained in a squad car nearby. They lose; Randolph wins. Fair?

And then we have Fernandez v. California, 571 U.S. 292, 134 S.Ct. 1126, 188 L.Ed.2d 25 (2014) Police come to an apartment where Fernandez, a suspect in an assault, is living with Rojas. While police are speaking to Rojas at the door of the apartment, Fernandez appeared and told police, "You don't have any right to come in here. I know my rights." At that point, however, police had independent grounds to believe Fernandez had assaulted Rojas in the apartment. Thus, police arrest Fernandez for assault and take him to the police station. An hour later, they return to the apartment, inform Rojas that Fernandez was under arrest, and obtain consent from her to search their apartment. Does *Randolph* apply? After all, Fernandez *was* present in the apartment and *did* object to their entry an hour before the police obtained consent from Rojas.

No, the Court held. The later consent by Rojas gave police the right to search the co-occupied apartment. Justice Alito stated for the Court that "consent by one resident of jointly occupied premises is generally sufficient to justify a warrantless search." He described *Randolph* as a "narrow exception," observing that Justice Souter's opinion in *Randolph* "went to great lengths to make clear that its holding was limited to situations in which the objecting occupant is present. Again and again, the opinion of the Court stressed this controlling factor. * * * The Court's opinion could hardly have been clearer on this point * * *."

7. *What one law professor has to say about co-tenant consent.* Perhaps you agree with Professor Stuart Green who told the authors of this book: "I have always thought the Court wrong to allow one co-tenant to waive the property and privacy rights of the other co-tenant. But if that is the proper way to view the Fourth Amendment, then *Randolph* was wrongly decided because a co-tenant has the right to waive the interests of another co-tenant. But if *Randolph* is correctly decided, then *Fernandez* is wrongly decided because the co-tenant in *Fernandez* exercised his right to exclude the police. On my view, the Court is 0 for 3 in co-tenant consent cases."

8. What if the driver of a car, lawfully stopped on the highway, consents to a search of the car, but his passenger, his common law wife, objects? Does *Randolph* apply outside the home? For one court's answer, see State v. Copeland, 399 S.W.3d 159 (Tex. Crim. App. 2013).

B. FROM PROBABLE CAUSE TO REASONABLE SUSPICION: *TERRY* STOPS AND THE REASONABLENESS OF SEARCHES AND SEIZURES

1. The *Terry* Doctrine

JOSHUA DRESSLER & ALAN C. MICHAELS—UNDERSTANDING CRIMINAL PROCEDURE

(Volume 1) (6th edition 2013), 261–263.

The Fourth Amendment was once considered a monolith. "Probable cause" had a single meaning, and "searches" and "seizures" were all-or-nothing concepts. The monolith was cracked by the Supreme Court in *Camara v. Municipal Court.* In *Camara*, the justices recognized a different form of "probable cause," applicable to administrative-search cases, that does not require individualized suspicion and which is based on the general Fourth Amendment standard of "reasonableness." To determine "reasonableness," the *Camara* Court invoked a balancing test, in which the individual's and society's interests in a given type of administrative search were weighed against each other.

If *Camara* cracked the Fourth Amendment monolith, *Terry v. Ohio* broke it entirely. Although the issue in *Terry* was described by the Court as "quite narrow"—"whether it is always unreasonable for a policeman to seize a person and subject him to a limited search for weapons unless there is probable cause to arrest"—the significance of the case to Fourth Amendment jurisprudence is, quite simply, monumental. In terms of the daily activities of the police, as well as the experiences of persons "on the street," there is no Supreme Court Fourth Amendment case—not even *Katz v. United States*—of greater practical impact.

The significance of *Terry* will be seen in [the materials that follow], but a brief overview is appropriate. First, *Terry* transported *Camara*'s "reasonableness" balancing test from the realm of administrative searches to traditional criminal investigations, and used it to determine the reasonableness of certain warrantless searches and seizures, rather than merely to define "probable cause." The result has been a significant diminution in the role of the Warrant Clause in Fourth Amendment jurisprudence. That is, *Terry* provided the impetus, as well as the framework, for a move by the Supreme Court away from the proposition that "warrantless searches are *per se* unreasonable," to the competing view that the appropriate test of police conduct "is not whether it is reasonable to procure a search warrant, but whether the search was reasonable." Warrantless police conduct became much easier to justify after *Terry*.

Second, *Terry* recognized that searches and seizures can vary in their intrusiveness. The Court no longer treats all searches and all seizures alike. * * *

Third, as a corollary of the last point, because of *Terry* the police may now conduct a wide array of searches and seizures that are considered less-than-ordinarily intrusive, on the basis of a lesser standard of cause than "probable cause" * * *. * * *

At least one other aspect of *Terry* deserves note here. Professor Akhil Amar suggests that this case may provide "one of the most open Fourth Amendment discussions of race to date."[10] Whether or not this assertion is accurate,[11] there is no gainsaying that when the police forcibly stop persons on the street to question them or to conduct full or cursory searches, highly sensitive issues of racial profiling (and to a lesser extent, issues of ethnicity, class, and gender) come to the fore.

Some scholars believe that the *Terry* opinion (or, at least, the *Terry* doctrine as it has come to be interpreted over the years), and its move away from the warrant requirement, has done much to exacerbate racial tensions between the police and members of minority communities. Others believe that the Court's movement in this case to a reasonableness standard is good, in part because it will force courts to confront issues, such as race and class, "honestly and openly." Whoever is right in this regard, Chief Justice Earl Warren was surely correct when he observed in *Terry* that "[w]e would be less than candid if we did not acknowledge that this [case] thrusts to the fore, difficult and troublesome issues regarding a sensitive area of police activity."

TERRY V. OHIO

Supreme Court of the United States, 1968.
392 U.S. 1, 88 S.Ct. 1868, 20 L.Ed.2d 889.

Given the Warren Court's emphasis on the rights of defendants, this case is a little unusual in that it greatly expands the discretion granted police officers. At least, that was one of its consequences. In the cases we discussed in Chapter 5, probable cause of some type was still required in many of those exceptions to the warrant requirement: exigent

---

10 Akhil Reed Amar, *Fourth Amendment First Principles*, 107 Harv. L. Rev. 757, 808 (1994).

11 It is not a universally held view. *E.g.*, Anthony C. Thompson, *Stopping the Usual Suspects: Race and the Fourth Amendment*, 74 N.Y.U. L. Rev. 956 (1999) (contending that the Supreme Court intentionally disguised the race-based aspects of the search and seizure in *Terry*).

circumstances still required probable cause to believe the suspect was committing or had committed a crime; SILA still required probable cause to arrest; the automobile exception still required probable cause to believe that weapons or evidence of crime will be found in the car; and plain view is often derived from one of the above exceptions with the probable cause that goes along with it. In *Terry* we move to a different standard; *reasonable suspicion* instead of probable cause.

The language of *Terry* itself presents a narrow holding. "*In specific, limited situations where police have to make split-second decisions about potential threats to the safety of themselves and others, officers can engage in a brief stop of a suspect and an equally brief search or "pat-down" for weapons.*" If this brief investigation reveals no other probable cause to believe a crime is being committed, the contact ends there. These stops have come to be known as a "Terry stop," or "stop and frisk."

However, as we will see in the cases following *Terry*, the option for a *Terry* stop has been used in a far broader range of situations. It has also become the basis for much of the conduct by police departments that have resulted in charges of racial profiling. When law enforcement can stop and search suspects on less than probable cause, it becomes easier for those stops to be based on characteristics that have little to do with the defendant's conduct and far more to do with how the defendant looks or the neighborhood in which police find him. Thus, it is how *Terry* has been applied, rather than the case itself, that has generated the most controversy and criticism, some of which is explored in the Notes following *Terry*. As you read about some of the scholarly debate over *Terry*, use your own experience to decide if the creation of the reasonable suspicion standard was a good idea at the time? Is it still?

MR. CHIEF JUSTICE WARREN delivered the opinion of the Court [joined by JUSTICES BLACK, HARLAN, BRENNAN, STEWART, WHITE, FORTAS, and MARSHALL]. * * *

Petitioner Terry was convicted of carrying a concealed weapon and sentenced to the statutorily prescribed term of one to three years in the penitentiary. * * * Officer McFadden testified that while he was patrolling in plain clothes in downtown Cleveland at approximately 2:30 in the afternoon of October 31, 1963, his attention was attracted by two men, Chilton and Terry, standing on the corner of Huron Road and Euclid Avenue. He had never seen the two men before, and he was unable to say precisely what first drew his eye to them. However, he testified that he had been a policeman for 39 years and a detective for 35 and that he had been assigned to patrol this vicinity of downtown Cleveland for shoplifters and pickpockets for 30 years. He explained that he had developed routine habits of observation over the years and that he would "stand and watch people or walk and watch people at many intervals of the day." He added: "Now, in this case when I looked over they didn't look right to me at the time."

His interest aroused, Officer McFadden took up a post of observation in the entrance to a store 300 to 400 feet away from the two men. [He observed one of the men walk up the street, stop, peer into a store window, walk on, turn around, look in again, and then rejoin the second man and confer. The second man then repeated the process. This was done five or six times by each man.] At one point, while the two were standing together on the corner, a third man approached them and engaged them briefly in conversation. This man then left the two others and walked west on Euclid Avenue. Chilton and Terry resumed their measured pacing, peering, and conferring. After this had gone on for 10 to 12 minutes, the two men walked off together, heading west on Euclid Avenue, following the path taken earlier by the third man.

By this time Officer McFadden had become thoroughly suspicious. He testified that after observing their elaborately casual and oft-repeated reconnaissance of the store window on Huron Road, he suspected the two men of "casing a job, a stick-up," and that he considered it his duty as a police officer to investigate further. He added that he feared "they may have a gun." * * * Deciding that the situation was ripe for direct action, Officer McFadden approached the three men, identified himself as a police officer and asked for their names. At this point his knowledge was confined to what he had observed. * * * When the men "mumbled something" in response to his inquiries, Officer McFadden grabbed petitioner Terry, spun him around so that they were facing the other two, with Terry between McFadden and the others, and patted down the outside of his clothing. In the left breast pocket of Terry's overcoat Officer McFadden felt a pistol. He * * * removed a .38-caliber revolver from the pocket and ordered all three men to face the wall with their hands raised. Officer McFadden proceeded to pat down the outer clothing of Chilton and the third man, Katz.[1] He discovered another revolver in the outer pocket of Chilton's overcoat, but no weapons were found on Katz. The officer testified that he only patted the men down to see whether they had weapons, and that he did not put his hands beneath the outer garments of either Terry or Chilton until he felt their guns. * * * Officer McFadden seized Chilton's gun, asked the proprietor of the

---

1 Although the *Terry* opinion was not explicit, Terry and Chilton were African-Americans; Katz was white. *Id.* at 729.

store to call a police wagon, and took all three men to the station, where Chilton and Terry were formally charged with carrying concealed weapons. * * *

I * * *

* * * Unquestionably petitioner was entitled to the protection of the Fourth Amendment as he walked down the street in Cleveland. The question is whether in all the circumstances of this on-the-street encounter, his right to personal security was violated by an unreasonable search and seizure.

We would be less than candid if we did not acknowledge that this question thrusts to the fore difficult and troublesome issues regarding a sensitive area of police activity—issues which have never before been squarely presented to this Court. * * *

On the one hand, it is frequently argued that in dealing with the rapidly unfolding and often dangerous situations on city streets the police are in need of an escalating set of flexible responses, graduated in relation to the amount of information they possess. For this purpose it is urged that distinctions should be made between a "stop" and an "arrest" (or a "seizure" of a person), and between a "frisk" and a "search." Thus, it is argued, the police should be allowed to "stop" a person and detain him briefly for questioning upon suspicion that he may be connected with criminal activity. Upon suspicion that the person may be armed, the police should have the power to "frisk" him for weapons. If the "stop" and the "frisk" give rise to probable cause to believe that the suspect has committed a crime, then the police should be empowered to make a formal "arrest," and a full incident "search" of the person. This scheme is justified in part upon the notion that a "stop" and a "frisk" amount to a mere "minor inconvenience and petty indignity," which can properly be imposed upon the citizen in the interest of effective law enforcement on the basis of a police officer's suspicion.

On the other side the argument is made that the authority of the police must be strictly circumscribed by the law of arrest and search as it has developed to date in the traditional jurisprudence of the Fourth Amendment. It is contended with some force that there is not—and cannot be—a variety of police activity which does not depend solely upon the voluntary cooperation of the citizen and yet which stops short of an arrest based upon probable cause to make such an arrest. The heart of the Fourth Amendment, the argument runs, is a severe requirement of specific justification for any intrusion upon protected personal security, coupled with a highly developed system of judicial controls to enforce upon the agents of the State the commands of the Constitution. Acquiescence by the courts in the compulsion inherent in the field interrogation practices at issue here, it is urged, would constitute an abdication of judicial control over, and indeed an encouragement of, substantial interference with liberty and personal security by police officers whose judgment is necessarily colored by their primary involvement in "the often competitive enterprise of ferreting out crime." This, it is argued, can only serve to exacerbate police-community tensions in the crowded centers of our Nation's cities.

In this context we approach the issues in this case mindful of the limitations of the judicial function in controlling the myriad daily situations in which policemen and citizens confront each other on the street. * * * Ever since its inception, the rule excluding evidence seized in violation of the Fourth Amendment has been recognized as a principal mode of discouraging lawless police conduct. * * *

The exclusionary rule has its limitations, however, as a tool of judicial control. It cannot properly be invoked to exclude the products of legitimate police investigative techniques on the ground that much conduct which is closely similar involves unwarranted intrusions upon constitutional protections. Moreover, in some contexts the rule is ineffective as a deterrent. Street encounters between citizens and police officers are incredibly rich in diversity. They range from wholly friendly exchanges of pleasantries or mutually useful information to hostile confrontations of armed men involving arrests, or injuries, or loss of life. Moreover, hostile confrontations are not all of a piece. Some of them begin in a friendly enough manner, only to take a different turn upon the injection of some unexpected element into the conversation. Encounters are initiated by the police for a wide variety of purposes, some of which are wholly unrelated to a desire to prosecute for crime. Doubtless some police "field interrogation" conduct violates the Fourth Amendment. But a stern refusal by this Court to condone such activity does not necessarily render it responsive to the exclusionary rule. Regardless of how effective the rule may be where obtaining convictions is an important objective of the police, it is powerless to deter invasions of constitutionally guaranteed rights where the police either have no interest in prosecuting or are willing to forgo successful prosecution in the interest of serving some other goal.

Proper adjudication of cases in which the exclusionary rule is invoked demands a constant awareness of these limitations. The wholesale harassment by certain elements of the police community, of which minority groups, particularly Negroes, frequently complain, will not be stopped by the exclusion of any evidence from any criminal trial. Yet a rigid and unthinking application of the exclusionary rule, in futile protest against practices which it can never be used effectively to control, may exact a high toll in human injury and frustration of efforts to prevent crime. No judicial opinion can comprehend the protean variety of the street encounter, and we can only judge the facts of the case before us. Nothing we say today is to be taken as indicating approval of police conduct outside the legitimate investigative sphere. Under our decision, courts still retain their traditional responsibility to guard against police conduct which is overbearing or harassing, or which trenches upon personal security without the objective evidentiary justification which the Constitution requires. When such conduct is identified, it must be condemned by the judiciary and its fruits must be excluded from evidence in criminal trials. And, of course, our approval of legitimate and restrained investigative conduct undertaken on the basis of ample factual justification should in no way discourage the employment of other remedies than the exclusionary rule to curtail abuses for which that sanction may prove inappropriate.

Having thus roughly sketched the perimeters of the constitutional debate over the limits on police investigative conduct in general and the background against which this case presents itself, we turn our attention to the quite narrow question posed by the facts before us: whether it is always unreasonable for a policeman to seize a person and subject him to a limited search for weapons unless there is probable cause for an arrest. * * *

II

Our first task is to establish at what point in this encounter the Fourth Amendment becomes relevant. That is, we must decide whether and when Officer McFadden "seized" Terry and whether and when he conducted a "search." There is some suggestion in the use of such terms as "stop" and "frisk" that such police conduct is outside the purview of the Fourth Amendment because neither action rises to the level of a "search" or "seizure" within the meaning of the Constitution. We emphatically reject this notion. It is quite plain that the Fourth Amendment governs "seizures" of the person which do not eventuate in a trip to the station house and prosecution for crime—"arrests" in traditional terminology. It must be recognized that whenever a police officer accosts an individual and restrains his freedom to walk away, he has "seized" that person. And it is nothing less than sheer torture of the English language to suggest that a careful exploration of the outer surfaces of a person's clothing all over his or her body in an attempt to find weapons is not a "search." Moreover, it is simply fantastic to urge that such a procedure performed in public by a policeman while the citizen stands helpless, perhaps facing a wall with his hands raised, is a "petty indignity." It is a serious intrusion upon the sanctity of the person, which may inflict great indignity and arouse strong resentment, and it is not to be undertaken lightly.

The danger in the logic which proceeds upon distinctions between a "stop" and an "arrest," or "seizure" of the person, and between a "frisk" and a "search" is twofold. It seeks to isolate from constitutional scrutiny the initial stages of the contact between the policeman and the citizen. And by suggesting a rigid all-or-nothing model of justification and regulation under the Amendment, it obscures the utility of limitations upon the scope, as well as the initiation, of police action as a means of constitutional regulation. This Court has held in the past that a search which is reasonable at its inception may violate the Fourth Amendment by virtue of its intolerable intensity and scope. The scope of the search must be "strictly tied to and justified by" the circumstances which rendered its initiation permissible.

The distinctions of classical "stop-and-frisk" theory thus serve to divert attention from the central inquiry under the Fourth Amendment—the reasonableness in all the circumstances of the particular governmental invasion of a citizen's personal security. "Search" and "seizure" are not talismans. We therefore reject the notions that the Fourth Amendment does not come into play at all as a limitation upon police conduct if the officers stop short of something called a "technical arrest" or a "full-blown search."

In this case there can be no question, then, that Officer McFadden "seized" petitioner and subjected him to a "search" when he took hold of him and patted down the outer surfaces of his clothing. We must decide whether at that point it was reasonable for Officer McFadden to have interfered with petitioner's personal security as he did. And in determining whether the seizure and search were "unreasonable" our inquiry is a dual one—whether the officer's action was justified at its inception, and whether it was reasonably related in scope to the circumstances which justified the interference in the first place.

III

If this case involved police conduct subject to the Warrant Clause of the Fourth Amendment, we would have to ascertain whether "probable cause" existed to justify the search and seizure which took place. However, that is not the case. We do not retreat from our holdings that the police must, whenever practicable, obtain advance judicial approval of searches and seizures through the warrant procedure, or that in most instances failure to comply with the warrant requirement can only be excused by exigent circumstances. But we deal here with an entire rubric of police conduct—necessarily swift action predicated upon the on-the-spot observations of the officer on the beat—which historically has not been, and as a practical matter could not be, subjected to the warrant procedure.

Instead, the conduct involved in this case must be tested by the Fourth Amendment's general proscription against unreasonable searches and seizures.

Nonetheless, the notions which underlie both the warrant procedure and the requirement of probable cause remain fully relevant in this context. In order to assess the reasonableness of Officer McFadden's conduct as a general proposition, it is necessary "first to focus upon the governmental interest which allegedly justifies official intrusion upon the constitutionally protected interests of the private citizen," for there is "no ready test for determining reasonableness other than by balancing the need to search [or seize] against the invasion which the search [or seizure] entails." *Camara v. Municipal Court*, 387 U.S. 523, 534–535, 536–537, 87 S.Ct. 1727, 1735, 18 L.Ed.2d 930 (1967). And in justifying the particular intrusion the police officer must be able to point to specific and articulable facts which, taken together with rational inferences from those facts, reasonably warrant that intrusion. The scheme of the Fourth Amendment becomes meaningful only when it is assured that at some point the conduct of those charged with enforcing the laws can be subjected to the more detached, neutral scrutiny of a judge who must evaluate the reasonableness of a particular search or seizure in light of the particular circumstances. And in making that assessment it is imperative that the facts be judged against an objective standard: would the facts available to the officer at the moment of the seizure or the search "warrant a man of reasonable caution in the belief" that the action taken was appropriate? * * * Anything less would invite intrusions upon constitutionally guaranteed rights based on nothing more substantial than inarticulate hunches, a result this Court has consistently refused to sanction. * * *

Applying these principles to this case, we consider first the nature and extent of the governmental interests involved. One general interest is of course that of effective crime prevention and detection; it is this interest which underlies the recognition that a police officer may in appropriate circumstances and in an appropriate manner approach a person for purposes of investigating possibly criminal behavior even though there is no probable cause to make an arrest. It was this legitimate investigative function Officer McFadden was discharging when he decided to approach petitioner and his companions. He had observed Terry, Chilton, and Katz go through a series of acts, each of them perhaps innocent in itself, but which taken together warranted further investigation. There is nothing unusual in two men standing together on a street corner, perhaps waiting for someone. Nor is there anything suspicious about people in such circumstances strolling up and down the street, singly or in pairs. Store windows, moreover, are made to be looked in. But the story is quite different where, as here, two men hover about a street corner for an extended period of time, at the end of which it becomes apparent that they are not waiting for anyone or anything; where these men pace alternately along an identical route, pausing to stare in the same store window roughly 24 times; where each completion of this route is followed immediately by a conference between the two men on the corner; where they are joined in one of these conferences by a third man who leaves swiftly; and where the two men finally follow the third and rejoin him a couple of blocks away. It would have been poor police work indeed for an officer of 30 years' experience in the detection of thievery from stores in this same neighborhood to have failed to investigate this behavior further.

The crux of this case, however, is not the propriety of Officer McFadden's taking steps to investigate petitioner's suspicious behavior, but rather, whether there was justification for McFadden's invasion of Terry's personal security by searching him for weapons in the course of that investigation. We are now concerned with more than the governmental interest in investigating crime; in addition, there is the more immediate interest of the police officer in taking steps to assure himself that the person with whom he is dealing is not armed with a weapon that could unexpectedly and fatally be used against him. Certainly it would be unreasonable to require that police officers take unnecessary risks in the performance of their duties. American criminals have a long tradition of armed violence, and every year in this country many law enforcement officers are killed in the line of duty, and thousands more are wounded. Virtually all of these deaths and a substantial portion of the injuries are inflicted with guns and knives.

In view of these facts, we cannot blind ourselves to the need for law enforcement officers to protect themselves and other prospective victims of violence in situations where they may lack probable cause for an arrest. When an officer is justified in believing that the individual whose suspicious behavior he is investigating at close range is armed and presently dangerous to the officer or to others, it would appear to be clearly unreasonable to deny the officer the power to take necessary measures to determine whether the person is in fact carrying a weapon and to neutralize the threat of physical harm.

We must still consider, however, the nature and quality of the intrusion on individual rights which must be accepted if police officers are to be conceded the right to search for weapons in situations where probable cause to arrest for crime is lacking. Even a limited search of the outer clothing for weapons constitutes a severe, though brief, intrusion upon cherished personal security, and it must surely be an annoying, frightening, and perhaps humiliating experience. * * *

Petitioner * * * says it is unreasonable for the policeman to [frisk a suspect] * * * until such time as the situation evolves to a point where there is probable cause to make an arrest. * * *

There are two weaknesses in this line of reasoning, however. First, it fails to take account of traditional limitations upon the scope of searches, and thus recognizes no distinction in purpose, character, and extent between a search incident to an arrest and a limited search for weapons. The former, although justified in part by the acknowledged necessity to protect the arresting officer from assault with a concealed weapon, is also justified on other grounds, and can therefore involve a relatively extensive exploration of the person. A search for weapons in the absence of probable cause to arrest, however, must, like any other search, be strictly circumscribed by the exigencies which justify its initiation. Thus it must be limited to that which is necessary for the discovery of weapons which might be used to harm the officer or others nearby, and may realistically be characterized as something less than a "full" search, even though it remains a serious intrusion.

A second, and related, objection to petitioner's argument is that it assumes that the law of arrest has already worked out the balance between the particular interests involved here—the neutralization of danger to the policeman in the investigative circumstance and the sanctity of the individual. But this is not so. An arrest is a wholly different kind of intrusion upon individual freedom from a limited search for weapons, and the interests each is designed to serve are likewise quite different. An arrest is the initial stage of a criminal prosecution. It is intended to vindicate society's interest in having its laws obeyed, and it is inevitably accompanied by future interference with the individual's freedom of movement, whether or not trial or conviction ultimately follows. The protective search for weapons, on the other hand, constitutes a brief, though far from inconsiderable, intrusion upon the sanctity of the person. * * *

Our evaluation of the proper balance that has to be struck in this type of case leads us to conclude that there must be a narrowly drawn authority to permit a reasonable search for weapons for the protection of the police officer, where he has reason to believe that he is dealing with an armed and dangerous individual, regardless of whether he has probable cause to arrest the individual for a crime. The officer need not be absolutely certain that the individual is armed; the issue is whether a reasonably prudent man in the circumstances would be warranted in the belief that his safety or that of others was in danger. And in determining whether the officer acted reasonably in such circumstances, due weight must be given, not to his inchoate and unparticularized suspicion or "hunch," but to the specific reasonable inferences which he is entitled to draw from the facts in light of his experience.

IV

* * * We think on the facts and circumstances Officer McFadden detailed before the trial judge a reasonably prudent man would have been warranted in believing petitioner was armed and thus presented a threat to the officer's safety while he was investigating his suspicious behavior. The actions of Terry and Chilton were consistent with McFadden's hypothesis that these men were contemplating a daylight robbery—which, it is reasonable to assume, would be likely to involve the use of weapons—and nothing in their conduct from the time he first noticed them until the time he confronted them and identified himself as a police officer gave him sufficient reason to negate that hypothesis. Although the trio had departed the original scene, there was nothing to indicate abandonment of an intent to commit a robbery at some point. Thus, when Officer McFadden approached the three men gathered before the display window at Zucker's store he had observed enough to make it quite reasonable to fear that they were armed; and nothing in their response to his hailing them, identifying himself as a police officer, and asking their names served to dispel that reasonable belief. * * *

The manner in which the seizure and search were conducted is, of course, as vital a part of the inquiry as whether they were warranted at all. The Fourth Amendment proceeds as much by limitations upon the scope of governmental action as by imposing preconditions upon its initiation. * * *

We need not develop at length in this case, however, the limitations which the Fourth Amendment places upon a protective seizure and search for weapons. These limitations will have to be developed in the concrete factual circumstances of individual cases. * * * Suffice it to note that such a search, unlike a search without a warrant incident to a lawful arrest, is not justified by any need to prevent the disappearance or destruction of evidence of crime. The sole justification of the search in the present situation is the protection of the police officer and others nearby, and it must therefore be confined in scope to an intrusion reasonably designed to discover guns, knives, clubs, or other hidden instruments for the assault of the police officer.

The scope of the search in this case presents no serious problem in light of these standards. Officer McFadden patted down the outer clothing of petitioner and his two companions. He did not place his hands in their pockets or under the outer surface of their garments until he had felt weapons, and then he merely reached for and removed the guns. * * * Officer McFadden confined his search strictly to what was minimally necessary to learn whether the men were armed and to disarm them once he discovered the weapons. He did not conduct a general exploratory search for whatever evidence of criminal activity he might find.

V

We conclude that the revolver seized from Terry was properly admitted in evidence against him. At the time he seized petitioner and searched him for weapons, Officer McFadden had reasonable grounds to believe that petitioner was armed and dangerous, and it was necessary for the protection of himself and others to take swift measures to discover the true facts and neutralize the threat of harm if it materialized. The policeman carefully restricted his search to what was appropriate to the discovery of the particular items which he sought. Each case of this sort will, of course, have to be decided on its own facts. We merely hold today that where a police officer observes unusual conduct which leads him reasonably to conclude in light of his experience that criminal activity may be afoot and that the persons with whom he is dealing may be armed and presently dangerous, where in the course of investigating this behavior he identifies himself as a policeman and makes reasonable inquiries, and where nothing in the initial stages of the encounter serves to dispel his reasonable fear for his own or others' safety, he is entitled for the protection of himself and others in the area to conduct a carefully limited search of the outer clothing of such persons in an attempt to discover weapons which might be used to assault him. Such a search is a reasonable search under the Fourth Amendment, and any weapons seized may properly be introduced in evidence against the person from whom they were taken.

Affirmed.

[*JUSTICE BLACK concurred in the judgment and in CHIEF JUSTICE WARREN'S opinion except as to matters omitted from the excerpt above.*]

MR. JUSTICE HARLAN, concurring.

While I unreservedly agree with the Court's ultimate holding in this case, I am constrained to fill in a few gaps, as I see them, in its opinion. * * *

In the first place, if the frisk is justified in order to protect the officer during an encounter with a citizen, the officer must first have constitutional grounds to insist on an encounter, to make a *forcible* stop. Any person, including a policeman, is at liberty to avoid a person he considers dangerous. If and when a policeman has a right instead to disarm such a person for his own protection, he must first have a right not to avoid him but to be in his presence. That right must be more than the liberty (again, possessed by every citizen) to address questions to other persons, for ordinarily the person addressed has an equal right to ignore his interrogator and walk away; he certainly need not submit to a frisk for the questioner's protection. I would make it perfectly clear that the right to frisk in this case depends upon the reasonableness of a forcible stop to investigate a suspected crime.

Where such a stop is reasonable, however, the right to frisk must be immediate and automatic if the reason for the stop is, as here, an articulable suspicion of a crime of violence. Just as a full search incident to a lawful arrest requires no additional justification, a limited frisk incident to a lawful stop must often be rapid and routine. There is no reason why an officer, rightfully but forcibly confronting a person suspected of a serious crime, should have to ask one question and take the risk that the answer might be a bullet. * * *

MR. JUSTICE WHITE, concurring.

* * * I think an additional word is in order concerning the matter of interrogation during an investigative stop. There is nothing in the Constitution which prevents a policeman from addressing questions to anyone on the street. * * * Of course, the person stopped is not obliged to answer, and answers may not be compelled, and refusal to answer furnishes no basis for an arrest, although it may alert the officer to the need for continued observation. * * *

MR. JUSTICE DOUGLAS, dissenting. * * *

The opinion of the Court disclaims the existence of "probable cause." * * * Had a warrant been sought, a magistrate would * * * have been unauthorized to issue one, for he can act only if there is a showing of "probable cause." We hold today that the police have greater authority to make a "seizure" and conduct a "search" than a judge has to authorize such action. We have said precisely the opposite over and over again.

* * * [P]olice officers up to today have been permitted to effect arrests or searches without warrants only when the facts within their personal knowledge would satisfy the constitutional standard of *probable cause.* * * * The term "probable cause" rings a bell of certainty that is not sounded by phrases such as "reasonable suspicion." Moreover, the meaning of "probable cause" is deeply imbedded in our constitutional history. * * *

To give the police greater power than a magistrate is to take a long step down the totalitarian path. Perhaps such a step is desirable to cope with modern forms of lawlessness. But if it is taken, it should be the deliberate choice of the people through a constitutional amendment. * * *

NOTES AND QUESTIONS

1. The *Terry* opinion contained the following footnote (omitted from the excerpt above). Does information provided by Terry's defense counsel affect your opinion of Officer McFadden's conduct in any way? Thirty years after the case, Terry's defense counsel remembers Officer McFadden's testimony this way:

> He was asked specifically what attracted him to them. On one occasion he said, "Well, to tell the truth, I just didn't like 'em." He was asked how long he had been a police officer. "39 years." How long had he been a detective? "35 years." What did he think they were doing? "Well, "he said, "I suspected they were casing a joint for the purpose of robbing it." "Well," he was asked, "have you ever in your 39 years as a police officer, 35 as a detective, had the opportunity to observe anybody casing a place for a stickup?" He said, "No I haven't." "Then what attracted you to them?" He indicated he just didn't like them.

Louis Stokes, *Representing John W. Terry*, 72 St. John's L. Rev. 727, 729–30 (1998).

As for McFadden himself, defense counsel Stokes respected him, *id.* at 729:

> He was a real character—a tall, stately guy, and basically a good policeman. Mac, as we called him, was really a guy that we really liked. He was straight. One thing about him—as a police officer, he came straight down the line. You did not have to worry about him misrepresenting what the facts were.

2. *Follow-up tidbit.* At about the time the Court was hearing the *Terry* case, Terry was confined to an asylum for the criminally insane; and prior to the Court hearing, Chilton was shot to death while perpetrating a robbery in Columbus, Ohio. Reuben M. Payne, *The Prosecutor's Perspective on Terry: Detective McFadden Had a Right to Protect Himself*, 72 St. John's L. Rev. 733, 733 (1998). McFadden did take the third individual (Katz) into custody, but no charges were brought against him.

3. *What happened to probable cause?* Officer McFadden clearly did not have time to obtain a warrant to search Terry, Chilton, and Katz. The Supreme Court, therefore, could uncontroversially have justified the lack of a warrant on the basis of exigency, but how does the Chief Justice explain away the probable cause requirement?

4. *Thinking about the implications of* Terry. Professor Akhil Amar has written that there are "in effect two inconsistent *Terry* opinions," a "good *Terry*" and "bad *Terry*." Akhil Reed Amar, *Terry and Fourth Amendment First Principles*, 72 St. John's L. Rev. 1097, 1097 (1998). He has described the "good *Terry*" opinion this way:

> First, it embraced a broad definition of "searches" and "seizures," enabling the Fourth Amendment to apply to myriad ways in which government

> might intrude upon citizens' persons, houses, papers, and effects. Second, the good *Terry* did not insist that all such broadly defined searches and seizures be preceded by warrants. Third, and more dramatic still, the good *Terry* did not insist that all warrantless intrusions be justified by probable cause. The stunning logical lesson of the good *Terry* is thus that a warrantless search or seizure may sometimes lawfully occur in a situation where a warrant could not issue (because probable cause is lacking). Fourth, in place of the misguided notions that every search or seizure always requires a warrant, and always requires probable cause, the good *Terry* insisted that the Fourth Amendment means what it says and says what it means: All searches and seizures must be reasonable. Reasonableness—not the warrant, not probable cause—thus emerged as the central Fourth Amendment mandate and touchstone. Fifth, the good *Terry* identified some of the basic components of Fourth Amendment reasonableness so that the concept would make common sense and constitutional sense. Reasonable intrusions must be *proportionate* to legitimate governmental purposes—more intrusive government action requires more justification. Reasonableness must focus not only on privacy and secrecy but also on *bodily integrity* and *personal dignity*: Cops act unreasonably not just when they paw through my pockets without good reason, but also when they beat me up for fun or toy with me for sport. Reasonableness also implicates *race*—a complete Fourth Amendment analysis, the good *Terry* insisted, must be sensitive to the possibility of racial oppression and harassment. If we wrongly think that the basic Fourth Amendment mandates are warrants and probable cause, we will have difficulty explicitly factoring race into the equation, but the spacious concept of reasonableness allows us to look race square in the eye, constitutionally.

Id. at 1098–1099.

Do you applaud some or all of these features of *Terry*?

Professor Scott Sundby is less enamored with *Terry,* particularly with its departure from the probable cause requirement:

> It is mighty hard to argue with reasonableness. * * * After all, a flexible "reasonableness" based Fourth Amendment standard holds forth the promise of both accommodating a wide variety of governmental interests * * * while still being able to address a myriad of concerns about government overstepping * * *. * * *
>
> Let me suggest, however, that when it comes to the Fourth Amendment there can be an unreasonable side to reasonableness, that "more can be less." * * *

> My limited goal * * * is to suggest that if one looks at the Fourth Amendment's underlying values, in particular the value of mutual "government-citizen trust," probable cause should be viewed as a norm for a "reasonable" search or seizure. Consequently, any departures from probable cause should be deemed "reasonable" only as limited exceptions allowed under narrow circumstances. * * *
>
> Viewing the Fourth Amendment as founded only upon privacy as a bedrock value * * * is to ignore that the Amendment is part of a larger constitutional setting. Once placed within a broader context of our whole constitutional system, the Amendment becomes much more than merely a constitutional outpost for individual privacy. Instead, the Amendment also becomes part of the mutually reinforcing consent that flows between the citizenry and the government, a form of reciprocal trust: The citizenry gives its consent and trust to the government to be governed and the government, in turn, trusts the citizenry to exercise its liberties responsibly. * * *
>
> This idea of trust is why probable cause must be the center of the Fourth Amendment universe rather than * * * merely one satellite in orbit around a general reasonableness balancing test.

Scott E. Sundby, *An Ode to Probable Cause: A Brief Response to Professors Amar and Slobogin*, 72 St. John's L. Rev. 1133, 1133–1135, 1137–1138 (1998).

5. *Terry and race.* Professor Amar applauded *Terry* for bringing race into the Fourth Amendment picture (Note 4). Not everyone, however, believes that *Terry* handled the race issue adequately. Critics of *Terry* have argued that it effectively authorized disproportionate numbers of detentions and frisks of innocent persons of color. We will come back to this issue shortly, but consider here Tracey Maclin, *Terry v. Ohio's Fourth Amendment Legacy: Black Men and Police Discretion*, 72 St. John's L. Rev. 1271, 1275–1276, 1285–1287 (1998):

> When one examines the history and modern exercise of police "stop and frisk" practices, the old adage "the more things change, the more they stay the same," aptly describes the experience of many black men when confronted by police officers. Before the "due process revolution" of the 1960s, a retired, white Detroit police officer told the United States Civil Rights Commission the following:
>
> > I would estimate—and this I have heard in the station also—that if you stop and search 50 Negroes and you get one good arrest out of it that's a good percentage; it's a good day's work. So, in my opinion,

there are 49 Negroes whose rights have been misused, and that goes on every day.

* * * [T]hings have not changed much; black men continue to be subjected to arbitrary searches and "frisks" by police. * * *

The irony, of course, is that the police power to "frisk" suspicious persons is the product of a Supreme Court that did more to promote the legal rights of black Americans than any other court. The Warren Court, led by Chief Justice Earl Warren, played an instrumental role in ending racial * * * discrimination in the United States. * * *

Thus, it seems paradoxical to criticize the Warren Court as insensitive to the experience of blacks, particularly blacks targeted by police officials. Yet, the Court's ruling in *Terry v. Ohio*, which upheld the power of police to "frisk" persons they suspect are dangerous, merits criticism. * * *

My view that *Terry* was wrongly decided emanates from three propositions which bear emphasis. First, long before *Terry* came to the Court, the law was settled on the amount of evidence needed for a warrantless search. In a string of cases involving car searches, the Court left no doubt that the Fourth Amendment required probable cause of criminal conduct before officers could search the inside of a car. * * * If probable cause was the constitutional minimum to justify a car search, then surely an equivalent degree of evidence is required before that officer can undertake "a careful exploration of the outer surfaces of a person's clothing all over his or her body in an attempt to find weapons." * * *

Second, presenting the issue in *Terry* as a conflict between "police safety" and individual freedom, misunderstands the reality of street encounters. No matter how the Court ruled in *Terry*, police officers would continue frisking people they viewed as a threat to their safety. Once this pragmatic fact was conceded, the crucial question in *Terry* was who would bear the burden when officers searched without probable cause: The government, which would suffer the suppression of evidence, or the individual, who was the target of a search forbidden by the Constitution?

Finally, the *Terry* Court succumbed to pressure to weaken constitutional principle when it was clear that many politicians, and a large segment of the public, had signaled their disapproval of the Court's effort to extend meaningful constitutional protection to those who needed it the most: Poor and minority persons suspected of criminal behavior. A more confident Court would have surveyed the legal landscape, recognized that stop and frisk practices could not be reconciled with a robust Fourth

> Amendment, and begun the fight to ensure that blacks, the poor, and other "undesirables," would enjoy the same constitutional privileges possessed by the elite of American society.

Tracey Maclin, *Terry v. Ohio's Fourth Amendment Legacy: Black Men and Police Discretion*, 72 St. John's L. Rev. 1271, 1275–1276, 1285–1287 (1998).

6. Suppose that a police officer, based on her personal observations, reasonably suspects (but lacks probable cause to believe) that a customer in a store is about to shoplift some merchandise. Applying *Terry*, may the officer briefly detain the customer for questioning? May she pat down the suspected shoplifter?

7. *The "Terry doctrine" after a crime has been committed. Terry* and nearly all cases interpreting it have involved circumstances in which the police believed "crime was afoot." In United States v. Hensley, 469 U.S. 221, 105 S.Ct. 675, 83 L.Ed.2d 604 (1985), the Court unanimously ruled that the *Terry* doctrine also applies when an officer seeks to investigate a *completed* felony: Stops are allowed if the "police have a reasonable suspicion, grounded in specific and articulable facts, that a person they encounter was involved in or is wanted in connection with a completed felony." Left open is under what circumstances a *Terry* stop is justified to investigate a completed minor offense.

8. *Pat-downs (part 1).* When a frisk is permissible under *Terry*, what may the officer do when she feels some object during the pat-down? You will remember (p. 302, Note 2) that the Court recognized a "plain touch" doctrine in Minnesota v. Dickerson, 508 U.S. 366, 113 S.Ct. 2130, 124 L.Ed.2d 334 (1993). Consider how the officer in *Dickerson* conducted the frisk (you may assume the officer had a right to conduct the pat-down):

> The officers pulled their squad car into the alley and ordered respondent to stop and submit to a patdown search. The search revealed no weapons, but the officer conducting the search did take an interest in a small lump in respondent's nylon jacket. The officer later testified:
>
> > "[A]s I pat-searched the front of his body, I felt a lump, a small lump, in the front pocket. I examined it with my fingers and it slid and it felt to be a lump of crack cocaine in cellophane."
>
> The officer then reached into respondent's pocket and retrieved a small plastic bag containing one fifth of one gram of crack cocaine.

Although the officer in *Dickerson* had grounds to pat-down the suspect, the Court held that the crack cocaine here was improperly seized:

> [T]he dispositive question before this Court is whether the officer who conducted the search was acting within the lawful bounds marked by *Terry*

> at the time he gained probable cause to believe that the lump in respondent's jacket was contraband. * * * The Minnesota Supreme Court, after "a close examination of the record," held that the officer's own testimony "belies any notion that he 'immediately' " recognized the lump as crack cocaine. Rather, the court concluded, the officer determined that the lump was contraband only after "squeezing, sliding and otherwise manipulating the contents of the defendant's pocket"—a pocket which the officer already knew contained no weapon.
>
> Under the State Supreme Court's interpretation of the record before it, it is clear that the court was correct in holding that the police officer in this case overstepped the bounds of the "strictly circumscribed" search for weapons allowed under *Terry*. * * * Here, the officer's continued exploration of respondent's pocket after having concluded that it contained no weapon was unrelated to "[t]he sole justification of the search [under *Terry*:] * * * the protection of the police officer and others nearby." It therefore amounted to the sort of evidentiary search that *Terry* expressly refused to authorize * * *.

9. *Pat-downs (part 2)*. Do you agree with the *Terry* Court that pat-down searches are less intrusive than so-called "full searches"? Forced to choose, would *you* rather be required to empty your trouser pockets (a full search) or have your body patted-down? In a concurring opinion in *Dickerson*, *id.*, Justice Scalia expressed misgivings with this aspect of *Terry*:

> I frankly doubt * * * whether the fiercely proud men who adopted our Fourth Amendment would have allowed themselves to be subjected, on mere *suspicion* of being armed and dangerous, to such indignity [as a frisk] * * *. * * * On the other hand, even if a "frisk" prior to arrest would have been considered impermissible in 1791, perhaps it was considered permissible by 1868, when the Fourteenth Amendment (the basis for applying the Fourth Amendment to the States) was adopted. Or perhaps it is only since that time that concealed weapons capable of harming the interrogator quickly and from beyond arm's reach have become common—which might alter the judgment of what is "reasonable" under the original standard. But technological changes were no more discussed in *Terry* than was the original state of the law.
>
> If I were of the view that *Terry* was (insofar as the power to "frisk" is concerned) incorrectly decided, I might—even if I felt bound to adhere to that case—vote to exclude the evidence incidentally discovered, on the theory that half a constitutional guarantee is better than none. * * * As a

policy matter, it may be desirable to *permit* "frisks" for weapons, but not to *encourage* "frisks" for drugs by admitting evidence other than weapons.

What do you think of Scalia's half-a-constitutional-right suggestion?

10. *Pat-downs (part 3).* In a state where it is not illegal to carry a firearm, what if a police officer asks a person on the street, "Are you carrying a firearm?," and the individuals says "yes." Under *Terry*, may the officer now non-consensually pat-down the individual? State v. Serna, 331 P.3d 405 (Ariz. 2014). Look carefully at the language in the *Terry* opinion. Can you see an argument for the view that such a pat-down violates the Fourth Amendment?

11. *Pat-downs (part 4).* At 2:15 a.m., the police received a tip (not amounting to probable cause, but you may assume for current purposes constituting reasonable suspicion) that a man seated in a nearby vehicle was carrying narcotics and had a gun at his waist. The officer, *O*, approached the vehicle to investigate. He tapped on the car window and asked the occupant, *W*, to open the door. Instead, *W* rolled down the window. When he did, *O* reached inside the car and—without conducting a pat-down—removed a revolver from *W*'s waistband. (The gun was not visible to *O*, but it was in precisely the place indicated by his informant. *W*, charged with illegal possession of a handgun, moved to suppress the weapon.)

The Supreme Court in Adams v. Williams, 407 U.S. 143, 92 S.Ct. 1921, 32 L.Ed.2d 612 (1972), upheld *O*'s actions. Why would the Court have authorized this non-pat-down search under the principles of *Terry*? Beyond the pat-down issue, if you had represented *W*, can you think of another argument you could have made, based solely on language found in the majority opinion in *Terry*, to argue that *O* acted unlawfully?

12. *When the purpose of the seizure changes: traffic stops that become something more.* The Court stated in *Terry* (end of Part II) that "in determining whether the seizure and search were 'unreasonable' our inquiry is a dual one—whether the officer's action was justified at its inception, and whether it was reasonably related in scope to the circumstances which justified the interference in the first place." In *Terry*, Officer McFadden seized Terry and the other suspects in order to investigate a possible imminent robbery; the subsequent pat-down weapons search was reasonably related in scope to the purpose of the initial seizure. In contrast, in *Minnesota v. Dickerson* (Note 8), a pat-down for weapons that turned into a pat-down for drugs fell outside the scope of the *Terry* doctrine and, therefore, was unreasonable.

What if the police temporarily detain a person lawfully on a traffic violation, and then use the opportunity to conduct an investigation unrelated to the reason for the original detention? For example, in Illinois v. Caballes, 543 U.S. 405, 125 S.Ct. 834, 160 L.Ed.2d 842 (2005), the police lawfully stopped *C*, an automobile driver, to write a warning ticket for speeding. While the vehicle was by the roadside, another officer used a "well-trained narcotics-detection dog" to sniff the vehicle for drugs. The police lacked reasonable suspicion to believe that the vehicle contained drugs.

Notice that use of the dog was unrelated to the original justification for the vehicle stop. According to the defense, therefore, "the use of the dog converted the citizen-police encounter from a lawful traffic stop into a drug investigation, and because the shift in purpose was not supported by any reasonable suspicion that [*C*] possessed narcotics, it was unlawful."

The Court, 6–2, rejected this argument. Writing for the majority, Justice Stevens stated that using a dog to sniff for drugs does "not change the character of a traffic stop that is lawful at its inception and otherwise executed in a reasonable manner, unless the dog sniff itself infringed [*C*'s] constitutionally protected interest in privacy." Here, "any interest in possessing contraband cannot be deemed legitimate," and thus, governmental conduct that *only* reveals the possession of contraband "compromises no legitimate privacy interest."

Justice Ginsburg, joined by Justice Souter, disagreed:

> A drug-detection dog is an intimidating animal. Injecting such an animal into a routine traffic stop changes the character of the encounter between the police and the motorist. The stop becomes broader, more adversarial, and (in at least some cases) longer. [*C*] * * * was exposed to the embarrassment and intimidation of being investigated, on a public thoroughfare, for drugs. Even if the drug sniff is not characterized as a Fourth Amendment "search," the sniff surely broadened the scope of the traffic-violation-related seizure.

Justice Stevens *did* warn in *Caballes* that "a seizure that is justified solely by the interest in issuing a warning ticket can become unlawful if it is prolonged beyond the time reasonably required to complete that mission." Here, however, the state courts determined that the dog-sniffing procedure did not extend the duration of *C*'s seizure.

In Rodriguez v. United States, 575 U.S. ____, 135 S.Ct. 1609, 191 L.Ed.2d 492 (2015), however, Justice Stevens's warning became doctrine. Here, a police officer stopped a vehicle containing two men because it had veered onto a highway shoulder for one or two seconds, in violation of a state law prohibiting driving on highway shoulders. The officer asked the driver why he had driven onto the shoulder (the driver said he was avoiding a pothole); he then gathered the driver's license, registration and proof of insurance, and conducted a records check (no problems found); and then he obtained the passenger's license for a records check (no problems found) and questioned him as to where the two men were coming from and where they were going. At that point, the police officer issues a written traffic warning and returned all of the documents. Twenty-two minutes from the initial stop had elapsed. At this point, although the officer lacked reasonable suspicion to suspect that the automobile contained narcotics, he ordered the occupants out of the car, and eight minutes later, a dog sniffed the vehicle and indicated the presence of drugs.

The Supreme Court, 6–3 per Justice Ginsburg, held that Rodriguez's Fourth Amendment rights had been violated. She stated that a routine traffic stop is comparable to a brief *Terry v. Ohio* seizure. As part of such a stop, Ginsburg explained, ordinary inquiries incident to a traffic stop—*e.g.*, checking the driver's license, determining whether there are any outstanding warrants against the driver, and inspecting the automobile's registration and proof of insurance—are permitted. Here, however, all of that had been completed before the dog was brought to the scene. This latter process (in the language of *Caballes*) "prolonged * * * the time reasonably required to complete th[e] mission" of issuing the warning ticket.

The Government argued (and the dissent agreed) that the officer effectively was being penalized because he had "expeditiously" completed all of the traffic-related tasks. As Justice Ginsburg put it, this argument meant that "an officer can earn bonus time to pursue an unrelated criminal investigation." But, she said, "[t]he reasonableness of a seizure * * * depends on what the police in fact do. * * * The critical question * * * is not whether the dog sniff occurs before or after the officer issues a ticket, * * * but whether conducting the sniff 'prolongs'—*i.e.*, adds time to—'the stop.' "

13. *Problem.* Consider the facts in Sibron v. New York, 392 U.S. 40, 88 S.Ct. 1889, 20 L.Ed.2d 917 (1968), a companion case to *Terry*: *O*, a police officer, observed *S* talk with known drug addicts over the course of an eight-hour period. Suspecting that *S* was selling drugs, *O* confronted *S* inside a restaurant, and told him to come outside. Outside, *O* said, "You know what I am after." *S* mumbled something and reached into his pocket, at which point *O* thrust his hand into the pocket and pulled out packets of heroin.

Should the heroin be suppressed at *S*'s trial? What if the officer had not thrust his hand in *S*'s pocket, but instead had ordered him to empty his pockets. Would this be permissible under *Terry*? See United States v. Reyes, 349 F.3d 219 (5th Cir. 2003).

14. *When is a seizure a 'seizure'?* Thus far, the majority of our Fourth Amendment cases have focused on searches. But the Fourth Amendment also prohibits unreasonable seizures. Along these lines, note the following footnote from the majority opinion in *Terry*:

> We thus decide nothing today concerning the constitutional propriety of an investigative "seizure" upon less than probable cause for purposes of "detention" and/or interrogation. Obviously, not all personal intercourse

> between policeman and citizens involves "seizures" of persons. Only when the officer by means of physical force or show of authority, has in some way restrained the liberty of a citizen may we conclude that a "seizure" has occurred. We cannot tell with any certainty upon this record whether any such "seizure" took place here prior to Officer McFadden's initiation of physical contact for purposes of searching Terry for weapons, and we thus assume that up to that point no intrusions upon constitutionally protected rights had occurred.

The next several cases take up the issue of just when a "seizure" occurs and for what purpose.

2. Drawing Lines: Arrests, Seizures, and Non-Seizures

One way to look at the relationship between the Fourth Amendment, *Terry v. Ohio*, and the following seizure cases is to once again think of a simple checklist, similar to the one we used to decide if a search is constitutional or not (see Chapters 3 and 4). In this case, analyzing the constitutionality of a seizure involves three questions:

1. Was the defendant seized?
2. When was the defendant seized?
3. What type of seizure was used?
    a. *Terry*-level seizures require only reasonable suspicion.
    b. Seizures tantamount to an arrest require probable cause.

A seizure was defined in *Terry* as taking place only when "the officer by means of physical force or show of authority, has in some way restrained the liberty of a citizen."

The first case in this section deals with a seizure which the majority found to be—in most respects—the same as a traditional arrest and thus subject to the requirement of probable cause. The remaining cases found in the Notes and Questions deal with the distinction between arrests, *Terry* seizures, and encounters with the police that are not deemed to be seizures at all. As you read these cases, keep in mind the original language of *Terry v. Ohio*, and the justification the *Terry* court set forth for why we needed *Terry* stops in the first place. Assuming for the purposes of this section that you agree with the *Terry* decision, is there a point at which you feel the Court has moved too far from its original justification; that officers under the *Terry* rubric have been given too much discretion in seizing (and then presumably, searching) an individual? If so, where?

DUNAWAY V. NEW YORK

Supreme Court of the United States, 1979.
442 U.S. 200, 99 S.Ct. 2248, 60 L.Ed.2d 824.

This next case, *Dunaway*, takes placed only eleven years after *Terry*. As you will see when reading the majority opinion, the Court originally treated *Terry* as a very narrow exception. In *Dunaway*, the Court refers to *Terry* stops as a "special category of Fourth Amendment 'seizures' so substantially less intrusive than arrests that the general rule requiring probable cause to make Fourth Amendment 'seizures' reasonable could be replaced by a balancing test," but that true to the language in *Terry*, this balancing test only applied for the purpose of a pat-down for weapons. The Court goes on to reiterate its intention to maintain the "narrow scope" of *Terry*.

Applying that narrow view of *Terry* to the facts here, the Court finds that Dunaway's detention was in "important respects" the same as a traditional arrest and declines to apply the reasonable suspicion standard advocated by the State of New York. However, take a close look at Justice Rehnquist's dissent. While not disputing Justice Brennan's definition of a *Terry* stop as a narrowly drawn exception, Justice Rehnquist looks at the same set of facts and determines that nothing close to a traditional arrest took place; that no "objectively coercive or physically threatening" conduct was used by the officer. Using the checklist set out in the introduction to this section, decide for yourself if *Dunaway* was seized, and if so, which standard—probable cause or reasonable suspicion—determines if that seizure was reasonable.

The Notes and Questions after *Dunaway* is where the fun begins. The cases there expand *Terry* to a review of seizures in a wide-variety of situations. These include moving a suspect to a separate room off an airport concourse, ordering a driver out of a car, detention for an extended period of time, bus sweeps, and taking flight from police.

Remember, though, that the focus of these cases is whether or not a seizure has occurred, and if so, what standard it is analyzed under. Determining when that standard has been met comes in the next section.

MR. JUSTICE BRENNAN delivered the opinion of the Court [joined by JUSTICES STEWART, WHITE, MARSHALL, BLACKMUN, and STEVENS]. * * *

I

On March 26, 1971, the proprietor of a pizza parlor in Rochester, N.Y., was killed during an attempted robbery. On August 10, 1971, Detective Anthony Fantigrossi of the Rochester Police was told by another officer that an informant had supplied a possible lead implicating petitioner in the crime. Fantigrossi questioned the supposed source of the lead—a jail inmate awaiting trial for burglary—but learned nothing that supplied "enough information to get a warrant" for petitioner's arrest. Nevertheless, Fantigrossi ordered other detectives to "pick up" petitioner and "bring him in." Three detectives located petitioner at a neighbor's house on the morning of August 11. Petitioner was taken into custody; although he was not told he was under arrest, he would have been physically restrained if he had attempted to leave. He was driven to police headquarters in a police car and placed in an interrogation room, where he was questioned by officers after being given the warnings required by *Miranda v. Arizona* [p. 501]. Petitioner waived counsel and eventually made statements and drew sketches that incriminated him in the crime. * * *

II * * *

* * * There can be little doubt that petitioner was "seized" in the Fourth Amendment sense when he was taken involuntarily to the police station. And respondent State concedes that the police lacked probable cause to arrest petitioner before his incriminating statement during interrogation. Nevertheless respondent contends that the seizure of petitioner did not amount to an arrest and was therefore permissible under the Fourth Amendment because the police had a "reasonable suspicion" that petitioner possessed "intimate knowledge about a serious and unsolved crime." We disagree.

Before *Terry v. Ohio*, the Fourth Amendment's guarantee against unreasonable seizures of persons was analyzed in terms of arrest, probable cause for arrest, and warrants based on such probable cause. The basic principles were relatively simple and straightforward: The term "arrest" was synonymous with those seizures governed by the Fourth Amendment. While warrants were not required in all circumstances, the requirement of probable cause, as elaborated in numerous precedents, was treated as absolute. * * *

Terry for the first time recognized an exception to the requirement that Fourth Amendment seizures of persons must be based on probable cause. That case involved a brief, on-the-spot stop on the street and a frisk for weapons, a situation that did not fit comfortably within the traditional concept of an "arrest." * * * [S]ince the intrusion involved in a "stop and frisk" was so much less severe than that involved in traditional "arrests," the Court declined to stretch the concept of "arrest"—and the general rule requiring probable cause to make arrests "reasonable" under the Fourth Amendment—to cover such intrusions. Instead, the Court treated the stop-and-frisk intrusion as a *sui generis* "rubric of police conduct." * * * Thus, *Terry* departed from traditional Fourth Amendment analysis in two respects. First, it defined a special category of Fourth Amendment "seizures" so substantially less intrusive than arrests that the general rule requiring probable cause to make Fourth Amendment "seizures" reasonable could be replaced by a balancing test. Second, the application of this balancing test led the Court to approve this narrowly defined less intrusive seizure on grounds less rigorous than probable cause, but only for the purpose of a pat-down for weapons.

Because *Terry* involved an exception to the general rule requiring probable cause, this Court has been careful to maintain its narrow scope. * * *

Respondent State now urges the Court to apply a balancing test, rather than the general rule, to custodial interrogations, and to hold that "seizures" such as that in this case may be justified by mere "reasonable suspicion." *Terry* and its progeny clearly do not support such a result. * * *

In contrast to the brief and narrowly circumscribed intrusions involved in those cases, the detention of petitioner was in important respects indistinguishable from a traditional arrest. Petitioner was not questioned briefly where he was found. Instead, he was taken from a neighbor's home to a police car, transported to a police station, and placed in an interrogation room. He was never informed that he was "free to go"; indeed, he would have been physically restrained if he had refused to accompany the officers or had tried to escape their custody. The application of the Fourth Amendment's requirement of probable cause does not depend on whether an intrusion of this magnitude is termed an "arrest" under state law. The mere facts that petitioner was not told he was under arrest, was not "booked," and would not have had an arrest record if the interrogation had proved fruitless, while not insignificant for all purposes, obviously do not make petitioner's seizure even roughly analogous to the narrowly defined intrusions involved in *Terry* and its progeny. Indeed, any "exception" that could cover a seizure as intrusive as that in this case would threaten to swallow the general rule that Fourth Amendment seizures are "reasonable" only if based on probable cause.

The central importance of the probable-cause requirement to the protection of a citizen's privacy afforded by the Fourth Amendment's guarantees cannot be compromised in this fashion. * * *

In effect, respondent urges us to adopt a multifactor balancing test of "reasonable police conduct under the circumstances" to cover all seizures that do not amount to technical arrests. But the protections intended by the Framers could all too easily disappear in the consideration and balancing of the multifarious circumstances presented by different cases, especially when that balancing may be done in the first instance by police officers engaged in the "often competitive enterprise of ferreting out crime." A single, familiar standard is essential to guide police officers, who have only limited time and expertise to reflect on and balance the social and individual interests involved in the specific circumstances they confront. * * * For all but those narrowly defined intrusions, the requisite "balancing" has been performed in centuries of precedent and is embodied in the principle that seizures are "reasonable" only if supported by probable cause. * * *

* * * We accordingly hold that the Rochester police violated the Fourth and Fourteenth Amendments when, without probable cause, they seized petitioner and transported him to the police station for interrogation. * * *

MR. JUSTICE POWELL took no part in the consideration or decision of this case.

MR. JUSTICE WHITE, concurring.

The opinion of the Court might be read to indicate that *Terry v. Ohio* is an almost unique exception to a hard-and-fast standard of probable cause. As our prior cases hold, however, the key principle of the Fourth Amendment is reasonableness—the balancing of competing interests. But if courts and law enforcement officials are to have workable rules, this balancing must in large part be done on a categorical basis—not in an ad hoc, case-by-case fashion by individual police officers. * * * It is enough, for me, that the police conduct here is similar enough to an arrest that the normal level of probable cause is necessary before the interests of privacy and personal security must give way.

[*The concurring opinion of JUSTICE STEVENS is omitted.*]

MR. JUSTICE REHNQUIST, with whom CHIEF JUSTICE BURGER joins, dissenting. * * *

I

* * * In my view, this is a case where the defendant voluntarily accompanied the police to the station to answer their questions.

* * * According to the testimony of the police officers, one officer approached a house where petitioner was thought to be located and knocked on the door. When a person answered the door, the officer identified himself and asked the individual his name. After learning that the person who answered the door was petitioner, the officer asked him if he would accompany the officers to police headquarters for questioning, and petitioner responded that he would. Petitioner was not told that he was under arrest or in custody and was not warned not to resist or flee. No weapons were displayed and petitioner was not handcuffed. Each officer testified that petitioner was not touched or held during the trip downtown; his freedom of action was not in any way restrained by the police. In short, the police behavior in this case was entirely free of "physical force or show of authority." * * *

* * * I do not dispute the fact that a police request to come to the station may indeed be an "awesome experience." But I do not think that that fact alone means that in every instance where a person assents to a police request to come to headquarters, there has been a "seizure" within the meaning of the Fourth Amendment. The question turns on whether the officer's conduct is objectively coercive or physically threatening, not on the mere fact that a person might in some measure feel cowed by the fact that a request is made by a police officer.

Therefore, although I agree that the police officers in this case did not have that degree of suspicion or probable cause that would have justified them in physically compelling petitioner to accompany them to the police station for questioning, I do not believe that the record demonstrates as a fact that this is what happened. No involuntary detention for questioning was shown to have taken place. The Fourth Amendment, accordingly, does not require suppression of petitioner's statements. * * *

NOTES AND QUESTIONS

1. Does the dissent disagree with the majority's claim that the police may not compel a person to come to the police station for questioning on less than probable cause? What is the basis of the disagreement between the majority and the dissent?

2. Would the seizure have been permissible if the police had found Dunaway in his front yard and had taken him to their police vehicle and questioned him there about the crime? What if they had taken him against his will from his front yard into his home for questioning?

3. *Drawing lines: moving the suspect (part 1).* In Florida v. Royer, 460 U.S. 491, 103 S.Ct. 1319, 75 L.Ed.2d 229 (1983), two police detectives at Miami International

Airport became suspicious of Royer, whose characteristics fit a drug-courier profile and who had paid cash for a one-way ticket to New York. Royer was about to embark on the flight when the detectives approached him. Upon request, he produced his airline ticket and driver's license. The ticket was under an assumed name. The detectives informed Royer that they were narcotics investigators and that they suspected him of transporting narcotics. Without returning the ticket or license, they asked him to accompany them to a small room, which was equipped with a desk and two chairs, adjacent to the airport concourse, where he was alone with the two officers. Meanwhile, one of the detectives retrieved Royer's luggage from the airline and brought it to the room. Royer consented to a search of his luggage that turned up marijuana. During the encounter, the police concededly lacked probable cause to arrest Royer.

Justice White, joined by Justices Marshall, Powell, and Stevens, concluded that the marijuana seized from the luggage had to be suppressed:

> We have concluded * * * that at the time Royer produced the key to his suitcase, the detention to which he was then subjected was a more serious intrusion on his personal liberty than is allowable on mere suspicion of criminal activity.
>
> * * * What had begun as a consensual inquiry in a public place had escalated into an investigatory procedure in a police interrogation room * * *. The officers had Royer's ticket, they had his identification, and they had seized his luggage. Royer was never informed that he was free to board his plane if he so chose, and he reasonably believed that he was being detained. At least as of that moment, any consensual aspects of the encounter had evaporated * * *. As a practical matter, Royer was under arrest. * * *
>
> We also think that the officers' conduct was more intrusive than necessary to effectuate an investigative detention otherwise authorized by the *Terry* line of cases. First, by returning his ticket and driver's license, and informing him that he was free to go if he so desired, the officers might have obviated any claim that the encounter was anything but a consensual matter from start to finish. Second, there are undoubtedly reasons of safety and security that would justify moving a suspect from one location to another during an investigatory detention, such as from an airport concourse to a more private area. There is no indication in this case that such reasons prompted the officers to transfer the site of the encounter from the concourse to the interrogation room. * * *
>
> Third, the State has not touched on the question whether it would have been feasible to investigate the contents of Royer's bags in a more

> expeditious way. The courts are not strangers to the use of trained dogs to detect the presence of controlled substances in luggage. There is no indication here that this means was not feasible and available. If it had been used, Royer and his luggage could have been momentarily detained while this investigative procedure was carried out. Indeed, it may be that no detention at all would have been necessary. A negative result would have freed Royer in short order; a positive result would have resulted in his justifiable arrest on probable cause.

4. *Drawing lines: moving the suspect (part 2).* In Pennsylvania v. Mimms, 434 U.S. 106, 98 S.Ct. 330, 54 L.Ed.2d 331 (1977), *O* validly stopped *M* in his vehicle in order to issue him a traffic citation. *O* ordered *M* out of the car, as he routinely did with all traffic violators. When *M* complied, *O* observed a large bulge under *M*'s jacket. *O* frisked *M*, felt a gun, and seized it. The bulge would not have been observed had *O* not ordered *M* out of the car, so the issue in the case centered around that action.

The state court held that *O* did not have a right to order *M* out of the vehicle because he lacked a reasonable belief that the driver posed a threat to his safety. The Supreme Court disagreed. Balancing the competing interests, it ruled that when an officer legally stops a driver on the highway, he may order the driver out of the car without further justification. It described the interest in police safety as "legitimate and weighty." On the other side of the scale is the driver's interest, having been lawfully stopped, to be permitted to stay in his car:

> We think this additional intrusion [of getting out of the car] can only be described as *de minimis*. The driver is being asked to expose very little more of his person than is already exposed. The police have already lawfully decided that the driver shall be briefly detained: the only question is whether he shall spend that period sitting in the driver's seat of his car or standing alongside it.

What if a driver, stopped for a ticket, has a passenger in his car. Is the officer justified in ordering *her* out of the car, too? In Maryland v. Wilson, 519 U.S. 408, 117 S.Ct. 882, 137 L.Ed.2d 41 (1997), the Court, 7–2, said yes. "On the public interest side of the balance, the same weighty interest in officer safety is present regardless of whether the occupant of the stopped car is a driver or passenger."

"On the personal liberty side of the balance," the Court stated, "the case for the passengers is * * * stronger than that for the driver. There is probable cause to believe that the driver has committed a minor vehicular offense, but there is no reason to stop or detain the passengers." However, practically speaking, since innocent passengers are inevitably seized when the driver is stopped, the Court concluded that a change in circumstances—being ordered out of the car—was again too minor an additional intrusion to outweigh police safety.

Do you see the balance that way?

What if the speeding vehicle is a taxicab, and the passenger wants to leave to find another cab. May an officer order her to *remain* until he completes ticketing the driver?

5. *Drawing lines: length of the detention.* In *Terry v. Ohio*, Officer McFadden only detained Terry and Chilton briefly before he determined that he had grounds to arrest them for possession of concealed weapons. Does this mean, therefore, that a *Terry*-type seizure may not lawfully extend beyond a few minutes? Not necessarily.

In United States v. Sharpe, 470 U.S. 675, 105 S.Ct. 1568, 84 L.Ed.2d 605 (1985), federal drug agent Cooke patrolling a highway for drug trafficking observed a suspicious camper truck apparently traveling in tandem with a Pontiac. He radioed for assistance, and state highway patrolman Thrasher responded. They attempted to pull the cars over. The driver of the Pontiac pulled to the side, but the camper truck driver did not stop immediately. Thrasher successfully pursued the camper, which eventually pulled over.

Agent Cooke obtained identification from the Pontiac driver and then unsuccessfully attempted to reach Thrasher by radio. Cooke radioed for more assistance. When it arrived, he left the officers with the Pontiac and drove to the spot where Thrasher had pulled over the camper. When he smelled marijuana coming from the truck, he opened it, found bales of marijuana, and arrested the driver. The Court of Appeals held that the 20-minute detention of Savage, the driver of the camper, "failed to meet * * * [*Terry*'s] requirement of brevity." The Supreme Court, per Chief Justice Burger, saw it differently:

> Admittedly, *Terry*, *Dunaway*, [and] *Royer* [p. 356, Note 3], * * * considered together, may in some instances create difficult line-drawing problems in distinguishing an investigative stop from a *de facto* arrest. Obviously, if an investigative stop continues indefinitely, at some point it can no longer be justified as an investigative stop. But our cases impose no rigid time limitation on *Terry* stops. While it is clear that "the brevity of the invasion of the individual's Fourth Amendment interests is an important factor in determining whether the seizure is so minimally intrusive as to be justifiable on reasonable suspicion," we have emphasized the need to consider the law enforcement purposes to be served by the stop as well as the time reasonably needed to effectuate those purposes. Much as a "bright line" rule would be desirable, in evaluating whether an investigative detention is unreasonable, common sense and ordinary human experience must govern over rigid criteria. * * *
>
> In assessing whether a detention is too long in duration to be justified as an investigative stop, we consider it appropriate to examine whether the

> police diligently pursued a means of investigation that was likely to confirm or dispel their suspicions quickly, during which time it was necessary to detain the defendant. A court making this assessment should take care to consider whether the police are acting in a swiftly developing situation, and in such cases the court should not indulge in unrealistic second-guessing. * * * The question is not simply whether some other alternative was available, but whether the police acted unreasonably in failing to recognize or to pursue it.
>
> We readily conclude that, given the circumstances facing him, Agent Cooke pursued his investigation in a diligent and reasonable manner. During most of Savage's 20-minute detention, Cooke was attempting to contact Thrasher and enlisting the help of the local police who remained with Sharpe while Cooke left to pursue Officer Thrasher and the pickup. Once Cooke reached Officer Thrasher and Savage, he proceeded expeditiously * * *.
>
> * * * The delay in this case was attributable almost entirely to the evasive actions of Savage, who sought to elude the police as Sharpe moved his Pontiac to the side of the road. Except for Savage's maneuvers, only a short and certainly permissible pre-arrest detention would likely have taken place.

6. *Problem.* Customs officials at L.A. International Airport had reason to suspect Rosa Montoya De Hernandez, who was a Colombian citizen, of being a "balloon swallower," *i.e.*, one who smuggles narcotics into the country hidden in balloons in her alimentary canal. The officials gave the suspect the option of undergoing an x-ray (she refused because she claimed that she was pregnant) or of being returned to her home country. She chose the latter option, but officials could not get her on a flight home due to visa problems. Therefore, "the officers decided on an alternative course: they would simply lock De Hernandez away in an adjacent manifest room 'until her peristaltic functions produced a monitored bowel movement.' The officers explained to De Hernandez that she could not leave until she had excreted by squatting over a wastebasket pursuant to the watchful eyes of two attending matrons."

The suspect was put incommunicado in a small room that contained only hard chairs and a table, where she remained for more than 16 hours during which she did not defecate. At that point, customs officials sought and received a court order authorizing a pregnancy test, which turned out negative, and a rectal examination that confirmed the existence of a balloon containing a foreign substance. Overall, the detention lasted nearly 24 hours. Is this a *Terry* seizure or *de facto* arrest? Is it a border search? Should the defendant be able to suppress this evidence? See United States v. Montoya de Hernandez, 473 U.S. 531, 105 S.Ct. 3304, 87 L.Ed.2d 381 (1985).

7. *Drawing lines: determining the exact point of detention.* In the case of United States v. Mendenhall, 446 U.S. 544, 100 S.Ct. 1870, 64 L.Ed.2d 497 (1980), the defendant consented to a search of her person at Detroit's Metropolitan Airport. The defendant later argued that her consent was not voluntary because she did not "feel free to leave" and thus had been seized, and that her seizure was unconstitutional. It became necessary, therefore, for the Court to determine when in a series of events, a seizure, if any, took place. The facts in *Mendenhall* are as follows:

> * * * The respondent arrived at the Detroit Metropolitan Airport on a commercial airline flight from Los Angeles early in the morning on February 10, 1976. As she disembarked from the airplane, she was observed by two agents of the DEA [Drug Enforcement Administration], who were present at the airport for the purpose of detecting unlawful traffic in narcotics. After observing the respondent's conduct, which appeared to the agents to be characteristic of persons unlawfully carrying narcotics, the agents approached her as she was walking through the concourse, identified themselves as federal agents, and asked to see her identification and airline ticket. The respondent produced her driver's license, which was in the name of Sylvia Mendenhall, and, in answer to a question of one of the agents, stated that she resided at the address appearing on the license. The airline ticket was issued in the name of "Annette Ford." When asked why the ticket bore a name different from her own, the respondent stated that she "just felt like using that name." In response to a further question, the respondent indicated that she had been in California only two days. Agent Anderson then specifically identified himself as a federal narcotics agent and, according to his testimony, the respondent "became quite shaken, extremely nervous. She had a hard time speaking."
>
> After returning the airline ticket and driver's license to her, Agent Anderson asked the respondent if she would accompany him to the airport DEA office for further questions. She did so, although the record does not indicate a verbal response to the request. The office, which was located up one flight of stairs about 50 feet from where the respondent had first been approached, consisted of a reception area adjoined by three other rooms. At the office the agent asked the respondent if she would allow a search of her person and handbag and told her that she had the right to decline the search if she desired. She responded: "Go ahead." She then handed Agent Anderson her purse, which contained a receipt for an airline ticket that had been issued to "F. Bush" three days earlier for a flight from Pittsburgh

> through Chicago to Los Angeles. The agent asked whether this was the ticket that she had used for her flight to California, and the respondent stated that it was.
>
> A female police officer then arrived to conduct the search of the respondent's person. She asked the agents if the respondent had consented to be searched. The agents said that she had, and the respondent followed the policewoman into a private room. There the policewoman again asked the respondent if she consented to the search, and the respondent replied that she did. The policewoman explained that the search would require that the respondent remove her clothing. The respondent stated that she had a plane to catch and was assured by the policewoman that if she were carrying no narcotics, there would be no problem. The respondent then began to disrobe without further comment. As the respondent removed her clothing, she took from her undergarments two small packages, one of which appeared to contain heroin, and handed both to the policewoman. The agents then arrested the respondent for possessing heroin. * * *

After citing the definition of "seizure" set out in *Terry*, the Court went on to hold that "a person has been 'seized' within the meaning of the Fourth Amendment only if, in view of all the circumstances surrounding the incident, a reasonable person would have believed he was not free to leave." Applying this definition to the circumstances surrounding Mendenhall's detention, two of the Justices held that "no seizure of the respondent occurred." Three more Justices assumed for purposes of the case that a seizure had taken place, but found that the agents had sufficient reasonable suspicion of criminal activity therefore "did not violate the Fourth Amendment by stopping the respondent for routine questioning." Based on the facts set out above, do *you* believe a reasonable person in Mendenhall's position would have felt free to leave? Up to what point?

In footnote 1 of *Mendenhall*, the Court noted the following based on the testimony at trial of the DEA agents involved in the case:

> The agent testified that the respondent's behavior fit the so called "drug courier profile"—an informally compiled abstract of characteristics thought typical of persons carrying illicit drugs. In this case, the agents thought it relevant that (1) the respondent was arriving on a flight from Los Angeles, a city believed by the agents to be the place of origin for much of the heroin brought to Detroit; (2) the respondent was the last person to leave the plane, "appeared to be very nervous," and "completely scanned the whole area where [the agents] were standing"; (3) after leaving the plane the respondent proceeded past the baggage area without claiming any

luggage; and (4) the respondent changed airlines for her flight out of Detroit.

Do these facts change your view of the case in any way?

8. *The potential role of race and other characteristics in "seizure" analysis.* To what extent is it relevant to the analysis that Mendenhall was an African-American woman, and that the police were white males? Consider the following:

> * * * [M]y thesis is that police encounters involving black men contain a combination of fear, distrust, anger and coercion that make these encounters unique and always potentially explosive. * * *
>
> To be sure, when whites are stopped by the police, they too feel uneasy and often experience fear. Inherent in any police encounter, even for whites, is the fear that the officer will abuse his authority by being arrogant, or act in a manner that causes the individual to feel more nervous than necessary. * * *
>
> But I wonder whether the average white person worries that an otherwise routine police encounter may lead to a violent confrontation. When they are stopped by the police, do whites contemplate the possibility that they will be physically abused for questioning why an officer has stopped them?

Tracey Maclin, *"Black and Blue Encounters"—Some Preliminary Thoughts About Fourth Amendment Seizures: Should Race Matter?*, 26 Val. U. L. Rev. 243, 243, 254–56 (1991).

If this mutual distrust exists, and if African-Americans, especially black males, fear the police, because of experiences in their community, in a way that white males do not, should the law take this difference into account in measuring police conduct? Specifically, if the question is whether a "reasonable person" in the suspect's situation would believe that he is not free to leave, should we incorporate the suspect's race in that analysis (as Professor Maclin ultimately recommends), or should the law apply a race-blind approach? Is the latter approach unfair because it would require people "to act as if they belonged to a completely different community, one whose experiences with government officials leads to the conclusion that it is safe to assert one's rights"? Susan F. Mandiberg, *Reasonable Officers vs. Reasonable Lay Persons in the Supreme Court's Miranda and Fourth Amendment Cases*, 14 Lewis & Clark L. Rev. 1481, 1502 (2010).

If the race of the suspect *should* be considered, are there other characteristics that should be included?

9. *"Bus sweeps."* In *Terry* and *Mendenhall*, the general issue was whether (or when) a person who was in motion (walking back and forth on a Cleveland street, or moving through an airport concourse) was seized by a law enforcement officer. There

is more to be said on this subject with the next case, but before we turn to it, let's turn things around a bit: when is a person seized if he or she is already in a stationary position? One example of this scenario is the so-called "bus sweep," described this way by Justice Marshall in Florida v. Bostick, 501 U.S. 429, 111 S.Ct. 2382, 115 L.Ed.2d 389 (1991):

> At issue in this case is a "new and increasingly common tactic in the war on drugs": the suspicionless police sweep of buses in interstate or intrastate travel. Typically under this technique, a group of state or federal officers will board a bus while it is stopped at an intermediate point on its route. Often displaying badges, weapons or other indicia of authority, the officers identify themselves and announce their purpose to intercept drug traffickers. They proceed to approach individual passengers, requesting them to show identification, produce their tickets, and explain the purpose of their travels. * * * An "interview" of this type ordinarily culminates in a request for consent to search the passenger's luggage.
>
> These sweeps are conducted in "dragnet" style. The police admittedly act without an "articulable suspicion" in deciding which buses to board and which passengers to approach for interviewing. By proceeding systematically in this fashion, the police are able to engage in a tremendously high volume of searches.

So, when is one of these bus passengers seized, if at all? At what point can we say that a reasonable person would believe that her liberty has been restrained by the officer? The Court, in United States v. Drayton, 536 U.S. 194, 122 S.Ct. 2105, 153 L.Ed.2d 242 (2002), explained:

> The proper inquiry necessitates a consideration of "all the circumstances surrounding the encounter." [We have noted] * * * that the traditional rule, which states that a seizure does not occur so long as a reasonable person would feel free "to disregard the police and go about his business," is not an accurate measure of the coercive effect of a bus encounter. A passenger may not want to get off a bus if there is a risk it will depart before the opportunity to reboard. A bus rider's movements are confined in this sense, but this is the natural result of choosing to take the bus; it says nothing about whether the police conduct is coercive. The proper inquiry "is whether a reasonable person would feel free to decline the officers' requests or otherwise terminate the encounter." * * * The reasonable person test * * * "presupposes an *innocent* person."

10. *Drawing lines: to flee or not to flee.* Review the following facts from California v. Hodari D., 499 U.S. 621, 111 S.Ct. 1547, 113 L.Ed.2d 690 (1991).

> Late one evening in April 1988, Officers Brian McColgin and Jerry Pertoso were on patrol in a high-crime area of Oakland, California. They were dressed in street clothes but wearing jackets with "Police" embossed on both front and back. Their unmarked car * * * rounded the corner, [and] they saw four or five youths huddled around a small red car parked at the curb. When the youths saw the officers' car approaching they apparently panicked and took flight. The respondent here, Hodari D., and one companion ran west through an alley; the others fled south. The red car also headed south at a high rate of speed.
>
> The officers were suspicious and gave chase. [Officer Pertoso gave chase by foot. Just before he reached Hodari, the youth tossed away what appeared to be a small rock.] * * * A moment later, Pertoso tackled Hodari, handcuffed him, and radioed for assistance. Hodari was found to be carrying $130 in cash and a pager; the rock he had discarded was found to be crack cocaine.

The State of California conceded in the courts below that Pertoso did not have sufficient reasonable suspicion to stop Hodari simply because he fled. Therefore, the only issue left in the case by the time it reached the U.S. Supreme Court, was whether, "at the time he dropped the drugs, Hodari had been 'seized' within the meaning of the Fourth Amendment." Since no physical force was used on Hodari until after the threw away the 'rock', the Court's decision turned on whether the officer's pursuit met the requirement of a *show of authority* equivalent to that needed for a seizure, even when the defendant did not yield to that show of authority. Justice Scalia, writing for a 7–2 majority, held that it did not.

> The word seizure readily bears the meaning of a laying on of hands or application of physical force to restrain movement, even when it is ultimately unsuccessful. * * * It does not remotely apply, however, to the prospect of a policeman yelling "Stop in the name of the law!" at a fleeing form that continues to flee. That is no seizure. * * *
>
> We do not think it desirable, even as a policy matter, to stretch the Fourth Amendment beyond its words and beyond the meaning of arrest, as respondent urges. Street pursuits always place the public at some risk, and compliance with police orders to stop should be encouraged. Only a few of those orders, we must presume, will be without adequate basis, and since the addressee has no ready means of identifying the deficient ones it almost invariably is the responsible course to comply.

Hodari argued that he was seized based on the test laid on in *Mendenhall* (p. 361, Note 7). Not so, argues Justice Scalia in *Hodari*:

> In seeking to rely upon that test here, respondent fails to read it carefully. It says a person has been seized "only if," not that he has been seized "whenever"; it states a *necessary* but not a *sufficient*, condition for seizure—or, more precisely, for seizure effected through a "show of authority." * * *
>
> In sum, assuming that Pertoso's pursuit in the present case constituted a "show of authority" enjoining Hodari to halt, since Hodari did not comply with that injunction he was not seized until he was tackled. The cocaine abandoned while he was running was in this case not the fruit of a seizure, and his motion to exclude evidence of it was properly denied. * * *

Justices Stevens and Marshall dissented, arguing that the holding in *Hodari* relied too much on a citizen's decision regarding how to respond rather than on an officer's decision about how to act.

> In this case the officer's show of force—taking the form of a head-on chase—adequately conveyed the message that respondent was not free to leave. * * * There was an interval of time between the moment that respondent saw the officer fast approaching and the moment when he was tackled, and thus brought under control of the officer. The question is whether the Fourth Amendment was implicated at the earlier or the later moment.
>
> Because the facts of this case are somewhat unusual, it is appropriate to note that the same issue would arise if the show of force took the form of a command to "freeze", a warning shot, or the sound of sirens accompanied by a patrol car's flashing lights. In any of these situations, there may be a significant time interval between the initiation of the officer's show of force and the complete submission by the citizen. At least on the facts of this case, the Court concludes that the timing of the seizure is governed by the citizen's reaction, rather than by the officer's conduct. One consequence of this conclusion is that the point at which the interaction between citizen and police officer becomes a seizure occurs, not when a reasonable citizen believes he or she is no longer free to go, but, rather, only after the officer exercises control over the citizen.

11. Fifteen years after *Hodari*, Justice Souter, writing for a unanimous Supreme Court in Brendlin v. California, 551 U.S. 249, 127 S.Ct. 2400, 168 L.Ed.2d 132 (2007), summarized the "seizure of person" line of cases this way:

> A person is seized by the police and thus entitled to challenge the government's action under the Fourth Amendment when the officer, " 'by

means of physical force or show of authority,' " terminates or restrains his freedom of movement, "*through means intentionally applied.*" Thus, an "unintended person * * * [may be] the object of the detention," so long as the detention is "willful" and not merely the consequence of "an unknowing act." [C]f. *County of Sacramento* v. *Lewis*, 523 U.S. 833, 844, 118 S.Ct. 1708, 140 L.Ed.2d 1043 (1998) (no seizure where a police officer accidentally struck and killed a motorcycle passenger during a high-speed pursuit). A police officer may make a seizure by a show of authority and without the use of physical force, but there is no seizure without actual submission; otherwise, there is at most an attempted seizure.

When the actions of the police do not show an unambiguous intent to restrain or when an individual's submission to a show of governmental authority takes the form of passive acquiescence, there needs to be some test for telling when a seizure occurs in response to authority, and when it does not. The test was devised by Justice Stewart in *United States* v. *Mendenhall*, [p. 361, Note 7], who wrote that a seizure occurs if "in view of all of the circumstances surrounding the incident, a reasonable person would have believed that he was not free to leave." Later on, the Court adopted Justice Stewart's touchstone, but added that when a person "has no desire to leave" for reasons unrelated to the police presence, the "coercive effect of the encounter" can be measured better by asking whether "a reasonable person would feel free to decline the officers' requests or otherwise terminate the encounter"; see * * * *United States* v. *Drayton*, [p. 364, Note 9].

Based on this summary of the law, the *Brendlin* Court held that a car passenger, and not only the driver, is seized as the result of a police-ordered traffic stop.

12. *Problem.* Officers, in their police vehicle, flashed their red lights to stop a car. After two blocks, the driver pulled into the driveway of his home. Passenger *M* got out of the car. One officer called out, "Hold up." *M* replied, "What do you want?," began to back away slowly, and then fled. During pursuit, *M* threw down an object later determined to be contraband. Was *M* seized? If so, at what moment? See United States v. Morgan, 936 F.2d 1561 (10th Cir. 1991).

13. *Problem.* In an area "infamous for racial tension," a suburban police officer observed three African-American youths riding their bicycle one block south of Eight Mile Road, the dividing point between largely-black Detroit and a nearly-white suburb. "After a quick interrogation and a racist joke, the officer allegedly ordered the youths to take their bicycles 'back across Eight Mile,' and watched while they did so." Stephen E. Henderson, *"Move On" Orders as Fourth Amendment Seizures*, 2008 B.Y.U. L.

Rev. 1, 23. Assuming everything prior to this was constitutional, did the officer's "move on" order constitute a seizure?

3. Defining "Reasonable Suspicion"

ALABAMA V. WHITE

Supreme Court of the United States, 1990.
496 U.S. 325, 110 S.Ct. 2412, 110 L.Ed.2d 301.

Remember the checklist at the start of the seizure cases?

1. **Was the defendant seized?**
2. **When was the defendant seized?**
3. **What type of seizure was used?**
   a. ***Terry*-level seizures require only reasonable suspicion.**
   b. **Seizures tantamount to an arrest require probable cause.**

Once we determine that there is a seizure—and classify it as either a *Terry* stop or an arrest—we then have to apply the relevant standard; either reasonable suspicion or probable cause. We discussed the definition of probable cause in Chapter 4. Here we examine how the Court has defined *reasonable suspicion.*

Even though reasonable suspicion is viewed as a lesser burden than probable cause—and thus much easier to meet—note how similar the factors that determine probable cause are to those used to determine reasonable suspicion (see in particular *Illinois v. Gates*).

The Notes following *White* describe several cases where the Court continues to struggle with what is and is not reasonable suspicion. You will see that race and racial profiling once again enter the debate over the reasonable suspicion standard and the discretion it seems to give officers.

JUSTICE WHITE delivered the opinion of the Court [joined by CHIEF JUSTICE REHNQUIST, and JUSTICES BLACKMUN, O'CONNOR, SCALIA, and KENNEDY]. * * *

On April 22, 1987, at approximately 3 p.m., Corporal B. H. Davis of the Montgomery Police Department received a telephone call from an anonymous person, stating that Vanessa White would be leaving 235-C Lynwood Terrace Apartments at a particular time in a brown Plymouth station wagon with the right taillight lens broken, that she would be going to Dobey's Motel, and that she would be in possession of about an ounce of cocaine inside a brown attaché case.

Corporal Davis and his partner, Corporal P. A. Reynolds, proceeded to the Lynwood Terrace Apartments. The officers saw a brown Plymouth station wagon with a broken right taillight in the parking lot in front of the 235 building. The officers observed respondent leave the 235 building, carrying nothing in her hands, and enter the station wagon. They followed the vehicle as it drove the most direct route to Dobey's Motel. When the vehicle reached the Mobile Highway, on which Dobey's Motel is located, Corporal Reynolds requested a patrol unit to stop the vehicle. The vehicle was stopped at approximately 4:18 p.m., just short of Dobey's Motel. Corporal Davis asked respondent to step to the rear of her car, where he informed her that she had been stopped because she was suspected of carrying cocaine in the vehicle. He asked if they could look for cocaine, and respondent said they could look. The officers found a locked brown attaché case in the car, and, upon request, respondent provided the combination to the lock. The officers found marijuana in the attaché case and placed respondent under arrest. During processing at the station, the officers found three milligrams of cocaine in respondent's purse.

* * * The Court of Criminal Appeals of Alabama held that the officers did not have the reasonable suspicion necessary under *Terry v. Ohio* to justify the investigatory stop of respondent's car, and that the marijuana and cocaine were fruits of respondent's unconstitutional detention. * * * We now reverse. * * *

Illinois v. Gates, [p. 164], dealt with an anonymous tip in the probable-cause context. The Court there abandoned the "two-pronged test" of *Aguilar v. Texas*, 378 U.S. 108, 84 S.Ct. 1509, 12 L.Ed.2d 723 (1964), and *Spinelli v. United States*, [p. 167], in favor of a "totality of the circumstances" approach to determining whether an informant's tip establishes probable cause. *Gates* made clear, however, that those factors that had been considered critical under *Aguilar* and *Spinelli*—an informant's "veracity," "reliability," and "basis of knowledge"—remain "highly relevant in determining the value of his report." These factors are also relevant in the reasonable suspicion context, although allowance must be made in applying them for the lesser showing required to meet that standard.

The opinion in *Gates* recognized that an anonymous tip alone seldom demonstrates the informant's basis of knowledge or veracity inasmuch as ordinary citizens generally do not provide extensive recitations of the basis of their everyday observations and given that the veracity of persons supplying anonymous tips is "by hypothesis largely unknown, and unknowable." This is not to say that an anonymous caller could never provide the reasonable suspicion necessary for a *Terry* stop. But the tip in *Gates* was not an exception to the general rule, and the anonymous tip in this case is like the one in *Gates*: "[It] provides virtually nothing from which one might conclude that [the caller] is either honest or his information reliable; likewise, the [tip] gives absolutely no indication of the basis for the [caller's] predictions regarding [Vanessa White's] criminal activities." By requiring "[s]omething more," as *Gates* did, we merely apply what we said in *Adams* [*v. Williams*, 407 U.S. 143, 92 S.Ct. 1921, 32 L.Ed.2d 612 (1972)]: "Some tips, completely lacking in indicia of reliability, would either warrant no police response or require further investigation before a forcible stop of a suspect would be authorized." Simply put, a tip such as this one, standing alone, would not " 'warrant a man of reasonable caution in the belief' that [a stop] was appropriate."

As there was in *Gates*, however, in this case there is more than the tip itself. The tip was not as detailed, and the corroboration was not as complete, as in *Gates*, but the required degree of suspicion was likewise not as high. We discussed the difference in the two standards last Term in *United States v. Sokolow*, 490 U.S. 1, 109 S.Ct. 1581, 104 L.Ed.2d 1 (1989):

> "The officer [making a *Terry* stop] * * * must be able to articulate something more than an 'inchoate and unparticularized suspicion or "hunch."' The Fourth Amendment requires 'some minimal level of objective justification' for making the stop. That level of suspicion is considerably less than proof of wrongdoing by a preponderance of the evidence. We have held that probable cause means 'a fair probability that contraband or evidence of a crime will be found,' and the level of suspicion required for a *Terry* stop is obviously less demanding than for probable cause."

Reasonable suspicion is a less demanding standard than probable cause not only in the sense that reasonable suspicion can be established with information that is different in quantity or content than that required to establish probable cause, but also in the sense that reasonable suspicion can arise from information that is less reliable than that required to show probable cause. * * * Both factors—quantity and quality—are considered in the "totality of the circumstances—the whole picture," that must be taken into account when evaluating whether there is reasonable suspicion. Thus, if a tip has a relatively low degree of reliability, more information will be required to establish the requisite quantum of suspicion than would be required if the tip were more reliable. * * * Contrary to the court below, we conclude that when the officers stopped respondent, the anonymous tip had been sufficiently corroborated to furnish reasonable suspicion that respondent was engaged in criminal activity and that the investigative stop therefore did not violate the Fourth Amendment.

It is true that not every detail mentioned by the tipster was verified, such as the name of the woman leaving the building or the precise apartment from which she left; but the officers did corroborate that a woman left the 235 building and got into the particular vehicle that was described by the caller. With respect to the time of departure predicted by the informant, Corporal Davis testified that the caller gave a particular time when the woman would be leaving, but he did not state what that time was. He did testify that, after the call, he and his partner proceeded to the Lynwood Terrace Apartments to put the 235 building under surveillance. Given the fact that the officers proceeded to the indicated address immediately after the call and that respondent emerged not too long thereafter, it appears from the record before us that respondent's departure from the building was within the time frame predicted by the caller. As for the caller's prediction of respondent's destination, it is true that the officers stopped her just short of Dobey's Motel and did not know whether she would have pulled in or continued on past it. But given that the 4-mile route driven by respondent was the most direct route possible to Dobey's Motel, but nevertheless involved several turns, we think respondent's destination was significantly corroborated.

The Court's opinion in *Gates* gave credit to the proposition that because an informant is shown to be right about some things, he is probably right about other facts that he has alleged, including the claim that the object of the tip is engaged in criminal activity. Thus, it is not unreasonable to conclude in this case that the independent corroboration by the police of significant aspects of the informer's predictions imparted some degree of reliability to the other allegations made by the caller.

We think it also important that, as in *Gates*, "the anonymous [tip] contained a range of details relating not just to easily obtained facts and conditions existing at the time of the tip, but to future actions of third parties ordinarily not easily predicted." The fact that the officers found a car precisely matching the caller's description in front of the 235 building is an example of the former. Anyone could have "predicted" that fact because it was a condition presumably existing at the time of the call. What was important was the caller's ability to predict respondent's *future behavior*, because it demonstrated inside information—a special familiarity with respondent's affairs. The general public would have had no way of knowing that respondent would shortly leave the building, get in the described car, and drive the most direct route to Dobey's Motel. Because only a small number of people are generally privy to an individual's itinerary, it is reasonable for police to believe that a person with access to such information is likely to also have access to reliable information about that individual's illegal activities. When significant aspects of the caller's predictions were verified, there was reason to believe not only that the caller was honest but also that he was well informed, at least well enough to justify the stop.

Although it is a close case, we conclude that under the totality of the circumstances the anonymous tip, as corroborated, exhibited sufficient indicia of reliability to justify the investigatory stop of respondent's car. * * *

JUSTICE STEVENS, with whom JUSTICE BRENNAN and JUSTICE MARSHALL join, dissenting.

Millions of people leave their apartments at about the same time every day carrying an attaché case and heading for a destination known to their neighbors. Usually, however, the neighbors do not know what the briefcase contains. An anonymous neighbor's prediction about somebody's time of departure and probable destination is anything but a reliable basis for assuming that the commuter is in possession of an illegal substance—particularly when the person is not even carrying the attaché case described by the tipster.

The record in this case does not tell us how often respondent drove from the Lynwood Terrace Apartments to Dobey's Motel; for all we know, she may have been a room clerk or telephone operator working the evening shift. It does not tell us whether Office Davis made any effort to ascertain the informer's identity, his reason for calling, or the basis of his prediction about respondent's destination. Indeed, for all that this record tells us, the tipster may well have been another police officer who had a "hunch" that respondent might have cocaine in her attaché case.

Anybody with enough knowledge about a given person to make her the target of a prank, or to harbor a grudge against her, will certainly be able to formulate a tip about her like the one predicting Vanessa White's excursion. In addition, under the Court's holding, every citizen is subject to being seized and questioned by any officer who is prepared to testify that the warrantless stop was based on an anonymous tip predicting whatever conduct the officer just observed. Fortunately, the vast majority of those in our law enforcement community would not adopt such a practice. But the Fourth Amendment was intended to protect the citizen from the overzealous and unscrupulous officer as well as from those who are conscientious and truthful. This decision makes a mockery of that protection. * * *

NOTES AND QUESTIONS

1. Do you believe that the police had sufficient grounds to stop White?

2. The *White* Court unsurprisingly stated that reasonable suspicion "can be established with information that is different in quantity * * * than that required to establish probable cause." But, it also stated that "reasonable suspicion" is a less demanding standard "in the sense that reasonable suspicion can arise from information that is less reliable than that required to show probable cause." *Should* this be the rule?

3. The *White* Court quoted *Adams v. Williams*, the pertinent facts of which are summarized on p. 348, Note 11. Take another look at that Note. Now, here are some additional facts: The officer approached the Williams vehicle after "a person known to [the officer] * * * informed him that an individual seated in a nearby vehicle was carrying narcotics and had a gun at his waist." The officer knew the tipster because he had provided information once before, regarding homosexual activity. That information did *not* result in an arrest because the officer could not substantiate the claim. The *Williams* majority concluded, nonetheless, that reasonable suspicion in *this* case existed:

> [W]e believe that [the officer] acted justifiably in responding to his informant's tip. The informant was known to him personally and had provided him with information in the past. This is a stronger case than obtains in the case of an anonymous telephone tip. The informant here came forward personally to give information that was immediately verifiable at the scene. Indeed, under Connecticut law, the informant might have been subject to immediate arrest for making a false complaint had [the officer]'s investigation proved the tip incorrect. Thus, while the Court's decisions indicate that this informant's unverified tip may have been insufficient for a narcotics arrest or search warrant, the information carried enough indicia of reliability to justify the officer's forcible stop of Williams.

Are you persuaded that the officer had reasonable suspicion, justifying a seizure or search of Williams?

4. An important factor in *Alabama v. White*, one that put the police conduct on the proper side of the "reasonable suspicion" line, was that the anonymous informant accurately predicted future behavior of the suspect. Even with that, you will notice that the Court characterized the facts as presenting "a close case" on the issue of reasonable suspicion. In this regard, consider Florida v. J.L., 529 U.S. 266, 120 S.Ct. 1375, 146 L.Ed.2d 254 (2000).

In *J.L.*, an anonymous caller told police that "a young black male standing at a particular bus stop and wearing a plaid shirt was carrying a gun." Two officers went to the location and observed three black males, one wearing a plaid shirt, "just hanging out [there]." Nothing about their behavior apart from the tip aroused suspicion, and no gun was visible. Nonetheless, the officers seized J.L., a minor, and frisked him. The Court *unanimously* held that the anonymous tip exhibited insufficient indicia of reliability to provide reasonable suspicion for the police action. Speaking for the Court, Justice Ginsburg wrote:

> The tip in the instant case lacked the moderate indicia of reliability present in *White* and essential to the Court's decision in that case. The anonymous call concerning J.L. provided no predictive information and therefore left the police without means to test the informant's knowledge or credibility. * * * All the police had to go on in this case was the bare report of an unknown, unaccountable informant who neither explained how he knew about the gun nor supplied any basis for believing he had inside information about J.L. If *White* was a close case on the reliability of anonymous tips, this one surely falls on the other side of the line.
>
> Florida contends that the tip was reliable because its description of the suspect's visible attributes proved accurate: There really was a young black male wearing a plaid shirt at the bus stop. * * *
>
> An accurate description of a subject's readily observable location and appearance is of course reliable in this limited sense: It will help the police correctly identify the person whom the tipster means to accuse. Such a tip, however, does not show that the tipster has knowledge of concealed criminal activity. The reasonable suspicion here at issue requires that a tip be reliable in its assertion of illegality, not just in its tendency to identify a determinate person.

Reconsider *Adams v. Williams* (Note 3). Is *J.L.* distinguishable?

5. The Supreme Court had another opportunity to consider the issues raised in *Alabama v. White* and *Florida v. J.L.* (Note 4). The facts in Navarette v. California, 572 U.S. 393, 134 S.Ct. 1683, 188 L.Ed.2d 680 (2014), were fairly simple: At 3:47 p.m., a 911 call relayed an anonymous tip from the caller to the effect that a Ford pickup had run the reporting party off the road five minutes earlier at a specified point on the highway. The caller described the Ford and provided a license plate number.

At 4:00 p.m., a highway patrol officer spotted the vehicle (roughly 19 miles away from the reported incident). He did not observe anything unusual about the way the pickup was being driven. Nonetheless, at about 4:05 p.m., the officer pulled the driver over. The officer smelled marijuana. A search of the truck bed revealed 30 pounds of marijuana. Driver Navarette and his passenger were arrested.

The issue was whether the initial stop, based as it was solely on the anonymous information provided by the caller, was founded on reasonable suspicion. The Court, 5–4, in an opinion authored by Justice Clarence Thomas, concluded that the stop was lawful. He stated that "under appropriate circumstance, an anonymous tip can demonstrate sufficient indicia of reliability to provide reasonable suspicion to make [an] investigatory stop."

Here, the Court found that "[b]y reporting that she had been run off the road by a specific vehicle, * * * the caller necessarily claimed eyewitness knowledge of the alleged dangerous driving. That basis of knowledge lends significant support to the tip's reliability." Thomas contrasted these facts to *J.L.*, "where the tip provided no basis for concluding that the tipster had actually seen the gun. Even in *White*, where we upheld the stop, there was scant evidence that the tipster had actually observed cocaine in the station wagon."

What about the other prong, namely, the anonymous caller's truthfulness? Justice Thomas said that there was reason to think that the 911 caller in this case was telling the truth. The vehicle was in a location that was consistent with the call. Moreover, the "timeline of events suggests that the caller reported the incident soon after she was run off the road. That sort of contemporaneous report has long been treated as especially reliable." The Court offered still another justification for treating the call as reliable:

> A 911 call has some [technological] features that allow for identifying and tracing callers, and thus provide some safeguards against making false reports with immunity. * * * The caller's use of the 911 system is therefore one of the relevant circumstances that, taken together, justified the officer's reliance on the information reported in the 911 call.

But, even if so, what did it give the officers reasonable suspicion to believe had occurred? Actually, the Court said that the issue was not whether there was reasonable suspicion a crime had *occurred*—the Court again (see p. 346, Note 7) left open the issue of how the Court should deal with *Terry* stops for the purpose of investigating completed minor offenses—but rather whether there was reasonable suspicion that a crime was *occurring*, namely, drunk driving. But, does *that* follow?

> [T]he accumulated experience of thousands of officers suggests that * * * erratic behaviors [on the highway] are strongly correlated with drunk driving. Of course, not all traffic infractions imply intoxication. Unconfirmed reports of driving without a seatbelt or slightly over the speed limit, for example, are so tenuously connected to drunk driving that a stop on those grounds alone would be constitutionally suspect. But a reliable tip alleging the dangerous behaviors discussed above generally would justify a traffic stop on suspicion of drunk driving.

> The 911 caller * * * alleged a specific and dangerous result of the driver's conduct: running another car off the highway. That conduct bears too great a resemblance to paradigmatic manifestations of drunk driving to be dismissed as an isolated example of recklessness.

What about the fact that the officer did not observe erratic driving? Justice Thomas stated: It is hardly surprising that the appearance of a marked police car would inspire more careful driving for a time. The Court concluded:

> Like *White*, this is a "close case." * * * Under the totality of the circumstances, we find the indicia of reliability in this case sufficient to provide the officer with reasonable suspicion that the driver of the reported vehicle had run another vehicle off the road. That made it reasonable under the circumstances for the officer to execute a traffic stop.

Justice Scalia, joined by Justices Ginsburg, Kagan, and Sotomayor, dissented:

> The tipster said the truck had "[run her] off the roadway," but the police had no reason to credit that charge and many reasons to doubt it, beginning with the peculiar fact that the accusation was anonymous. "[E]liminating accountability * * * is ordinarily the very purpose of anonymity." The unnamed tipster "can lie with impunity." Anonymity is especially suspicious with respect to the call that is the subject of the present case. When does a victim complain to the police about an arguably criminal act (running the victim off the road) without giving his identity, so that he can accuse and testify when the culprit is caught?

Justice Scalia described *Alabama v. White* as "extreme," but less so than the present case:

> [In *White*], the reliability of the tip was established by the fact that it predicted the target's behavior in the finest detail—a detail that could be known only by someone familiar with the target's business * * *. Here the Court makes a big deal of the fact that the tipster was dead right about the fact that a silver Ford F-150 truck (license plate 8D94925) was traveling south on Highway 1 somewhere near mile marker 88. But everyone in the world who saw the car would have that knowledge, and anyone who wanted the car stopped would have to provide that information. Unlike the situation in *White*, that generally available knowledge in no way makes it plausible that the tipster saw the car run someone off the road.

Justice Scalia went on:

> The Court says that "[b]y reporting that she had been run off the road by a specific vehicle * * * the caller necessarily claimed eyewitness knowledge." So what? The issue is not how she claimed to know, but whether what she

> claimed to know was true. The claim to "eyewitness knowledge" of being run off the road supports *not at all* its veracity * * *.

As for the caller's veracity, the dissenters were similarly unimpressed. What about the majority's point, however, that the tipster's identity can be verified through the 911 system? Justice Scalia's response had a ring of sarcasm:

> [T]he Court says that [an] * * * "indicator of veracity" is the anonymous tipster's mere "use of the 911 emergency system." Because, you see, recent "technological and regulatory developments" suggest that the identities of unnamed 911 callers are increasingly less likely to remain unknown. Indeed, the systems are able to identify "the caller's geographic location with increasing specificity." *Amici* disagree with this, * * * and the present case surely suggests that *amici* are right—since we know neither the identity of the tipster nor even the county from which the call was made. But assuming the Court is right about the ease of identifying 911 callers, it proves absolutely nothing in the present case unless the anonymous caller was *aware* of that fact. "It is the tipster's *belief* in anonymity, not its *reality*, that will control his behavior." There is no reason to believe that your average anonymous 911 tipster is aware that 911 callers are readily identifiable.

But, Justice Scalia was not done:

> All that has been said up to now assumes that the anonymous caller made, at least in effect, an accusation of drunken driving. But in fact she did not. She said that the petitioners' truck " '[r]an [me] off the roadway.' " That neither asserts that the driver was drunk nor even raises the *likelihood* that the driver was drunk. The most it conveys is that the truck did some apparently nontypical thing that forced the tipster off the roadway, whether partly or fully, temporarily or permanently. Who really knows what (if anything) happened? The truck might have swerved to avoid an animal, a pothole, or a jaywalking pedestrian.
>
> But let us assume the worst of the many possibilities: that it was a careless, reckless, or even intentional maneuver that forced the tipster off the road. [The driver] might have been distracted by his use of a hands-free cell phone, or distracted by an intense sports argument with [the passenger]. Or, indeed, he might have intentionally forced the tipster off the road because of some personal animus, or hostility to her "Make Love, Not War" bumper sticker. I fail to see how reasonable suspicion of a *discrete instance* of irregular or hazardous driving generates a reasonable suspicion of *ongoing intoxicated driving*. What proportion of the hundreds of thousands—perhaps millions—of careless, reckless, or intentional traffic violations committed each day is attributable to drunken drivers? I say 0.1

> percent. I have no basis for that except my own guesswork. But unless the Court has some basis in reality to believe that the proportion is many orders of magnitude above that—say 1 in 10 or at least 1 in 20—it has no grounds for its unsupported assertion that the tipster's report in this case gave rise to a *reasonable suspicion* of drunken driving.
>
> It gets worse. Not only, it turns out, did the police have no good reason *at first* to believe that Lorenzo [Navarette] was driving drunk, they had very good reason *at last* to know that he was not. The Court concludes that the tip, plus confirmation of the truck's location, produced reasonable suspicion that the truck not only had been *but still was* barreling dangerously and drunkenly down Highway 1. In fact, alas, it was not, and the officers knew it. They followed the truck for five minutes, presumably to see if it was being operated recklessly. And *that* was good police work. * * * But the pesky little detail left out of the Court's reasonable-suspicion equation is that, for the five minutes that the truck was being followed (five minutes is a *long* time), [the] driving was irreproachable. * * *
>
> Resisting this line of reasoning, the Court curiously asserts that, since drunk drivers who see marked squad cars in their rearview mirrors may evade detection simply by driving "more careful[ly]," the "absence of additional suspicious conduct" is "hardly surprising" and thus largely irrelevant. Whether a drunk driver drives drunkenly, the Court seems to think, is up to him. That is not how I understand the influence of alcohol. I subscribe to the more traditional view that the dangers of intoxicated driving are the intoxicant's impairing effects on the body—effects that no mere act of the will can resist.

The dissenters closed with a warning:

> All the malevolent 911 caller need do [in light of this case] is assert a traffic violation, and the targeted car will be stopped, forcibly if necessary, by the police. If the driver turns out not to be drunk (which will almost always be the case), the caller need fear no consequences, even if 911 knows his identity. After all, he never alleged drunkenness, but merely called in a traffic violation—and on that point his word is as good as his victim's.

Whose analysis—Justice Thomas's or Justice Scalia's—do you find more persuasive in light of *White* and *J.L.*?

6. In *Illinois v. Rodriguez*, we saw that the Supreme Court observed that "in order to satisfy the 'reasonableness' requirement of the Fourth Amendment, what is generally demanded of the many *factual* determinations that must be regularly be made by [police officers] * * * is not that they always be correct, but that they always be

reasonable." (Emphasis added.) What, then, about a reasonable mistake of *law* by a police officer?

The Court spoke to this question in Heien v. North Carolina, 574 U.S. ___, 135 S.Ct. 530, 190 L.Ed.2d 475 (2014). A police officer noticed that only one of a vehicle's brake lights was working, so he pulled over the driver. While issuing a warning citation, the officer became suspicious of the conduct of Heien, the car owner, and his passenger. Consequently, the officer sought and obtained consent to search the vehicle, which turned up cocaine. Heien moved to suppress the evidence of the cocaine on the ground that his seizure—the stop of the vehicle—was unconstitutional. Indeed, it turned out that the applicable North Carolina statute only required that vehicles be equipped with a single working brake light. Therefore, the officer had no legal basis to stop the vehicle.

The Court held, 8–1, that the officer's misunderstanding of the law was reasonable (in view of an ambiguity in the code provision) and, therefore, there was reasonable suspicion justifying the stop of the vehicle. Chief Justice Roberts stated that "[w]e have recognized that searches and seizures based on mistakes of fact can be reasonable." And, he said, "reasonable men make mistakes of law, too, and such mistakes are no less compatible with the concept of reasonable suspicion [and probable cause]." Justice Sotomayor dissented.

7. *Racial profiling and reasonable suspicion.* Racial profiling (that is, the use of race or ethnicity as the primary criterion in conducting stops, searches, and other law enforcement investigative procedures) is a serious issue in light of the Supreme Court's ruling in *Whren v. United States*, but it is magnified by *Terry v. Ohio* and the lower standard of cause that an officer may use to temporarily detain a person on the street or in a car.

For example, an officer might use something as minor as an apparent crack in a vehicle windshield as justification to stop an African-American (or Hispanic, etc.) driver on the ground that it constitutes reasonable suspicion that the driver is violating a statute that prohibits driving "in such unsafe condition as to endanger any person." Muse v. State, 146 Md.App. 395, 807 A.2d 113 (2002). The officer might then use this stop in order to seek consent to conduct a drug or weapons search of the car—a search that she might not have sought to conduct if the driver had been white. Indeed, the officer might not have stopped the car with the cracked windshield in the first place but for the fact the driver was black or Hispanic.

That racial profiling is a part of this nation's experience is not speculative. In Maryland, from 1995 through 1997, a survey indicated that 70% of drivers stopped on Interstate 95 were African-American, although 17.5% of the traffic and speeders on the road were black. David Cole, No Equal Justice 36 (1999). Videotapes in one Florida county demonstrated that 5% of the drivers appeared to be dark-skinned, but

70% of the drivers stopped were African-American or Hispanic, and more than 80% of cars searched on the highway were persons of color. Traffic tickets, however, were given in less than 1% of the stops. *Id.* at 37. Or, consider the following uncontested findings of fact on stops-and-frisks in New York City, as reported in Floyd v. City of New York, 959 F.Supp.2d 540 (S.D.N.Y. 2013):

- Between January 2004 and June 2012, the NYPD conducted over 4.4 million *Terry* stops.
- The number of stops per year rose sharply from 314,000 in 2004 to a high of 686,000 in 2011.
- 52% of all stops were followed by a protective frisk for weapons. A weapon was found after 1.5% of these frisks. In other words, in 98.5% of the 2.3 million frisks, no weapon was found.
- 8% of all stops led to a search into the stopped person's clothing, ostensibly based on the officer feeling an object during the frisk that he suspected to be a weapon, or immediately perceived to be contraband other than a weapon. In 9% of these searches, the felt object was in fact a weapon. 91% of the time, it was not. In 14% of these searches, the felt object was in fact contraband. 86% of the time it was not.
- 6% of all stops resulted in an arrest, and 6% resulted in a summons. The remaining 88% of the 4.4 million stops resulted in no further law enforcement action.
- In 52% of the 4.4 million stops, the person stopped was black.
- In 31% of the stops, the person stopped was Hispanic.
- In 10% of the stops, the person stopped was white.
- In 2010, New York City's resident population was roughly 23% black, 29% Hispanic, and 33% white.
- In 23% of the stops of blacks, and 24% of the stops of Hispanics, the officer recorded using force. The number for whites was 17%.
- Weapons were seized in 1.0% of the stops of blacks, 1.1% of the stops of Hispanics, and 1.4% of the stops of whites.
- Contraband other than weapons was seized in 1.8% of the stops of blacks, 1.7% of the stops of Hispanics, and 2.3% of the stops of whites.
- For the years 2004 to 2009, the two most commonly [provided justifications] * * * for a stop were "Furtive Movements" and "Area

Has Incidence Of Reported Offense Of Type Under Investigation" ("High Crime Area"). * * * [O]fficers marked "Furtive Movements" as a basis for the stop on 42% of the forms, and "High Crime Area" on 55% of the forms. In 2009, officers indicated "Furtive Movements" as a basis for the stop nearly 60% of the time.

- Both "Furtive Movements" and "High Crime Area" are weak indicators of criminal activity. For the years 2004 to 2009, stops were 22% more likely to result in arrest if "High Crime Area" was *not* checked, and 18% more likely to result in arrest if "Furtive Movements" was not checked.

District Judge Shira Scheindlin determined that because this police tactic was employed predominantly against young African-American and Hispanic males, the stops-and-frisks violated the Constitution. The Second Circuit Court of Appeals granted New York City's motion to stay Judge Scheindlin's opinion and the case was ultimately settled out of court.

Is there a way to justify disproportionate *Terry* stops of young, male racial minorities? One commanding officer in New York was tape recorded stating that his officers should frisk "the right people at the right time, the right location," and when asked what the "right location" meant, specified a particular location, stating "I told you at roll call, and I have no problem telling you this, male blacks 14, to 20, 21." Joseph Goldstein, *Bronx Inspector, Secretly Recorded, Suggests Race Is Factor in a Police Tactic*, New York Times, March 22, 2013, at A21. If the data supported the proposition that the "particular location" was a high crime area, and if the data supported the proposition that young males of color were more prone than others to commit offenses with weapons in that area, should that justify stops of persons fitting that category? Consider this remark:

> [M]ost criminologists who have studied the matter have concluded that blacks (and men and young people) do in fact commit crime in a higher per capita rate than whites (and women and older people). Thus, all other things being equal, it is rational to be more suspicious of a young black man than an elderly white woman. But that it may be rational does not make it right.

Cole, supra, at 42. If it *is rational* to be more suspicious of young black men than elderly white women, why isn't it also *right* and *constitutional* to be more suspicious? In this regard, suppose a small town near the Mexican border experiences a large influx of Hispanics into their community in a short period of time. Would it be rational for federal agents to suspect that many of them are in the country illegally? If so, should it be constitutional for the agents to briefly detain any person in that town who appears to be of Mexican descent, solely on that basis? Consider these remarks by

Justice Sotomayor, in dissent, in Utah v. Strieff, 579 U.S. ___, 136 S.Ct. 2056, 195 L.Ed.2d 400 (2016):

> For generations, black and brown parents have given their children "the talk"—instructing them never to run down the street; always keep your hands where they can be seen; do not even think of talking back to a stranger—all out of fear of how an officer with a gun will react to them. * * *
>
> We must not pretend that the countless people who are routinely targeted by the police are "isolated." They are the canaries in the coal mine [who] * * * warn us that no one can breathe in this atmosphere. They are the ones who recognize that unlawful police stops corrode all of our civil liberties and threaten all of our lives. Until their voices matter too, our justice system will continue to be anything but.

For more on the subject, see Sherry F. Colb, *Profiling With Apologies*, 1 Ohio St. J. Crim. L. 611 (2004); Sharon L. Davies, *Profiling Terror*, 1 Ohio St. J. Crim. L. 45 (2003); Kent Greenawalt, *Probabilities, Perceptions, Consequences and "Discrimination": One Puzzle about Controversial "Stop and Frisk,"* 12 Ohio St. J. Crim. L. 181 (2014); and David A. Harris, Profiles in Injustice: Why Racial Profiling Cannot Work (2002).

8. *Converting reasonable suspicion into an arrest?* May the police leap-frog from a *Terry* seizure based on reasonable suspicion into an arrest by simply asking the seized individual for her name and, if she refuses to answer, arresting her for that failure? Perhaps so if a state enacts a law requiring a properly detained individual to identify herself to the police.

In Hiibel v. Sixth Judicial District Court of Nevada, Humboldt County, 542 U.S. 177, 124 S.Ct. 2451, 159 L.Ed.2d 292 (2004), a deputy sheriff was dispatched to investigate a report of a man assaulting a woman. When the officer arrived at the scene, he found a man standing outside a truck, with a young woman sitting inside it. The man appeared intoxicated. The deputy asked the man, later identified to be Larry Hiibel, for identification. At least eleven times Hiibel refused to provide identification. Consequently, the deputy arrested him for "willfully resist[ing], delay[ing], or obstruct[ing] a public officer in discharging or attempting to discharge any legal duty of his office." The government reasoned that Hiibel had violated this statute because another statute, a so-called "stop and identify" statute, authorized police officers to "detain any person whom the officer encounters under circumstances which reasonably indicate that the person has committed, is committing or is about to commit a crime," and to "ascertain [the individual's] identity." The latter statute provided that "[a]ny person so detained shall identify himself."

Stop-and-identify statutes cannot be enforced if the stop—the initial seizure that presages the request for identification—is unlawful for want of reasonable suspicion. But, what about here, where Hiibel conceded that the deputy had grounds to conduct a *Terry*-level seizure?

Justice Kennedy, writing for the majority, explained that properly crafted and enforced stop-and-identify laws are constitutional:

> Our decisions make clear that questions concerning a suspect's identity are a routine and accepted part of many *Terry* stops. * * *
>
> The principles of *Terry* permit a State to require a suspect to disclose his name in the course of a *Terry* stop. The reasonableness of a seizure under the Fourth Amendment is determined "by balancing its intrusion on the individual's Fourth Amendment interests against its promotion of legitimate government interests." The Nevada statute [in this case] satisfies that standard. The request for identity has an immediate relation to the purpose, rationale, and practical demands of a *Terry* stop. The threat of criminal sanction helps ensure that the request for identity does not become a legal nullity. On the other hand, the Nevada statute does not alter the nature of the stop itself: it does not change its duration, or its location. A state law requiring a suspect to disclose his name in the course of a valid *Terry* stop is consistent with Fourth Amendment prohibitions against unreasonable searches and seizures.
>
> Petitioner argues that the Nevada statute circumvents the probable cause requirement, in effect allowing an officer to arrest a person for being suspicious. According to petitioner, this creates a risk of arbitrary police conduct that the Fourth Amendment does not permit. * * * Petitioner's concerns are met by the requirement that a *Terry* stop must be justified at its inception and "reasonably related in scope to the circumstances which justified" the initial stop. Under these principles, an officer may not arrest a suspect for failure to identify himself if the request for identification is not reasonably related to the circumstances justifying the stop. * * * It is clear in this case that the request for identification was "reasonably related in scope to the circumstances which justified" the stop.

9. *Problem.* Suppose that the police know that *X* is a drug dealer. Indeed, they observed a videotape of *X* selling drugs a few weeks earlier. Now they observe *X* talking to *D*, someone about whom they have no prior information. *X* is holding a plastic sandwich container and nervously looking around; their meeting lasts only two minutes, the same length of time as the drug sale in the videotape, and takes place in the interior of *X*'s car. Do these facts justify a *Terry* stop of *D* after he leaves *X*? *Holt v. State,* 78 A.3d 415 (Md. 2013).

ILLINOIS V. WARDLOW

Supreme Court of the United States, 2000.
528 U.S. 119, 120 S.Ct. 673, 145 L.Ed.2d 570.

In *Hodari*, the State of California conceded that the officer did not have reasonable suspicion to stop the defendant, so the case rested entirely on whether or not there was a seizure before he tossed away the drugs for the officer to find—no seizure, no Fourth Amendment concerns. In response to California's concession in *Hodari*, Justice Scalia said this in a footnote:

> California conceded below that Officer Pertoso did not have the "reasonable suspicion" required to justify stopping Hodari. That it would be unreasonable to stop, for brief inquiry, young men who scatter in panic upon the mere sighting of the police is not self-evident, and arguably contradicts proverbial common sense. See Proverbs 28:1 ("The wicked flee when no man pursueth"). We do not decide that point here, but rely entirely upon the State's concession.

As a result, the Court never decided in *Hodari* whether or not flight by a suspect—particularly in a high crime area—is by itself enough reasonable suspicion to pursue and conduct a *Terry* stop on the suspect. This is precisely the issue that confronts the Court eight years later in *Illinois v. Wardlow*. Not surprisingly, Chief Justice Rehnquist, with whom Justice Scalia joins, refers to determinations of reasonable suspicion as being "based on common sense judgements and inferences of human behavior." So, the question in *Wardlow* becomes, is flight from the police in a high-crime area common sense behavior? Relying once again on the totality of the circumstances, the Court holds that, in this case, Wardlow's presence in an area known for narcotics trafficking combined with his unprovoked flight upon seeing the officers was sufficient reasonable suspicion for the stop.

Note in particular the way the Court responds to the argument that there are numerous perfectly innocent explanations for flight, as well as Justice Stevens' discussion of the perceptions of minorities and other citizens living in high crime areas. At the end, ask yourself if you agree with Chief Justice Rehnquist or Justice Stevens in how the reasonable suspicion standard should be applied to Mr. Wardlow's actions?

CHIEF JUSTICE REHNQUIST delivered the opinion of the Court [joined by JUSTICES O'CONNOR, SCALIA, KENNEDY, and THOMAS].

Respondent Wardlow fled upon seeing police officers patrolling an area known for heavy narcotics trafficking. Two of the officers caught up with him, stopped him, and conducted a protective patdown search for weapons. Discovering a .38-caliber handgun, the officers arrested Wardlow. We hold that the officers' stop did not violate the Fourth Amendment * * *.

On September 9, 1995, Officers Nolan and Harvey were working as uniformed officers in the special operations section of the Chicago Police Department. The officers were driving the last car of a four car caravan converging on an area known for heavy narcotics trafficking in order to investigate drug transactions. The officers were traveling together because they expected to find a crowd of people in the area, including lookouts and customers.

As the caravan passed 4035 West Van Buren, Officer Nolan observed respondent Wardlow standing next to the building holding an opaque bag. Respondent looked in the direction of the officers and fled. Nolan and Harvey turned their car southbound, watched him as he ran through * * * an alley, and eventually cornered him on the street. Nolan then exited his car and stopped respondent. He immediately conducted a protective pat-down search for weapons because in his experience it was common for there to be weapons in the near vicinity of narcotics transactions. During the frisk, Officer Nolan * * * felt a heavy, hard object similar to the shape of a gun. The officer then opened the bag and discovered a .38-caliber handgun with five live rounds of ammunition. The officers arrested Wardlow.

The Illinois trial court denied respondent's motion to suppress, finding the gun was recovered during a lawful stop and frisk. * * * Wardlow was convicted of unlawful use of a weapon by a felon. The Illinois Appellate Court reversed Wardlow's conviction, concluding that the gun should have been suppressed because Officer Nolan did not have reasonable suspicion sufficient to justify an investigative stop pursuant to *Terry v. Ohio.*

The Illinois Supreme Court agreed. While rejecting the Appellate Court's conclusion that Wardlow was not in a high crime area, the Illinois Supreme Court determined that sudden flight in such an area does not create a reasonable suspicion justifying a *Terry* stop. * * * [T]he court explained that although police have the right to approach individuals and ask questions, the individual has no obligation to respond. The person may decline to answer and simply go on his or her way, and the refusal to respond, alone, does not provide a legitimate basis for an investigative stop. The court then determined that flight may simply be an exercise of this right to "go on one's way," and, thus, could not constitute reasonable suspicion justifying a *Terry* stop.

The Illinois Supreme Court also rejected the argument that flight combined with the fact that it occurred in a high crime area supported a finding of reasonable suspicion * * *. Finding no independently suspicious circumstances to support an investigatory detention, the court held that the stop and subsequent arrest violated the Fourth Amendment. * * *

This case, involving a brief encounter between a citizen and a police officer on a public street, is governed by the analysis we first applied in *Terry*. * * *

* * * An individual's presence in an area of expected criminal activity, standing alone, is not enough to support a reasonable, particularized suspicion that the person is committing a crime. But officers are not required to ignore the relevant characteristics of a location in determining whether the circumstances are sufficiently suspicious to warrant further investigation. Accordingly, we have previously noted the fact that the stop occurred in a "high crime area" among the relevant contextual considerations in a *Terry* analysis.

In this case, moreover, it was not merely respondent's presence in an area of heavy narcotics trafficking that aroused the officers' suspicion but his unprovoked flight upon noticing the police. Our cases have also recognized that nervous, evasive behavior is a pertinent factor in determining reasonable suspicion. Headlong flight—wherever it occurs—is the consummate act of evasion: it is not necessarily indicative of wrongdoing, but it is certainly suggestive of such. In reviewing the propriety of an officer's conduct, courts do not have available empirical studies dealing with inferences drawn from suspicious behavior, and we cannot reasonably demand scientific certainty from judges or law enforcement officers where none exists. Thus, the determination of reasonable suspicion must be based on commonsense judgments and inferences about human behavior. We conclude Officer Nolan was justified in suspecting that Wardlow was involved in criminal activity, and, therefore, in investigating further.

Such a holding is entirely consistent with our decision in *Florida v. Royer* [p. 356, Note 3], where we held that when an officer, without reasonable suspicion or probable cause, approaches an individual, the individual has a right to ignore the police and go about his business. * * * But unprovoked flight is simply not a mere refusal to cooperate. Flight, by its very nature, is not "going about one's business"; in fact, it is just the opposite. Allowing officers confronted with such flight to stop the fugitive and investigate further is quite consistent with the individual's right to go about his business or to stay put and remain silent in the face of police questioning.

Respondent and *amici* also argue that there are innocent reasons for flight from police and that, therefore, flight is not necessarily indicative of ongoing criminal activity. This fact is undoubtedly true, but does not establish a violation of the Fourth Amendment. Even in *Terry*, the conduct justifying the stop was ambiguous and susceptible of an innocent explanation. * * * *Terry* recognized that the officers could detain the individuals to resolve the ambiguity.

In allowing such detentions, *Terry* accepts the risk that officers may stop innocent people. Indeed, the Fourth Amendment accepts that risk in connection with more drastic police action; persons arrested and detained on probable cause to believe they have committed a crime may turn out to be innocent. The *Terry* stop is a far more minimal intrusion, simply allowing the officer to briefly investigate further. * * *

The judgment of the Supreme Court of Illinois is reversed * * *. * * *

JUSTICE STEVENS, with whom JUSTICE SOUTER, JUSTICE GINSBURG, and JUSTICE BREYER join, concurring in part and dissenting in part.

The State of Illinois asks this Court to announce a "bright-line rule" authorizing the temporary detention of anyone who flees at the mere sight of a police officer. Respondent counters by asking us to adopt the opposite *per se* rule—that the fact that a person flees upon seeing the police can never, by itself, be sufficient to justify a temporary investigative stop of the kind authorized by *Terry v. Ohio*. * * *

Although I agree with the Court's rejection of the *per se* rules proffered by the parties, unlike the Court, I am persuaded that in this case the brief testimony of the officer who seized respondent does not justify the conclusion that he had reasonable suspicion to make the stop. Before discussing the specific facts of this case, I shall comment on the parties' requests for a *per se* rule.

I * * *

* * * A pedestrian may break into a run for a variety of reasons—to catch up with a friend a block or two away, to seek shelter from an impending storm, to arrive at a bus stop before the bus leaves, to get home in time for dinner, to resume jogging after a pause for rest, to avoid contact with a bore or a bully, or simply to answer the call of nature—any of which might coincide with the arrival of an officer in the vicinity. A pedestrian might also run because he or she has just sighted one or more police officers. In the latter instance, the State properly points

out "that the fleeing person may be, *inter alia*, (1) an escapee from jail, (2) wanted on a warrant, (3) in possession of contraband, (*i.e.*, drugs, weapons, stolen goods, etc.); or (4) someone who has just committed another type of crime." In short, there are unquestionably circumstances in which a person's flight is suspicious, and undeniably instances in which a person runs for entirely innocent reasons.

Given the diversity and frequency of possible motivations for flight, it would be profoundly unwise to endorse either *per se* rule. The inference we can reasonably draw about the motivation for a person's flight, rather, will depend on a number of different circumstances. Factors such as the time of day, the number of people in the area, the character of the neighborhood, whether the officer was in uniform, the way the runner was dressed, the direction and speed of the flight, and whether the person's behavior was otherwise unusual might be relevant in specific cases. This number of variables is surely sufficient to preclude either a bright-line rule that always justifies, or that never justifies, an investigative stop based on the sole fact that flight began after a police officer appeared nearby. * * *

Even assuming we know that a person runs because he sees the police, the inference to be drawn may still vary from case to case. Flight to escape police detection, we have said, may have an entirely innocent motivation * * *. [Innocent people flee, *inter alia*, out of fear of being wrongfully arrested or forced to appear as a witness to a crime.]

In addition to these concerns, a reasonable person may conclude that an officer's sudden appearance indicates nearby criminal activity. And where there is criminal activity there is also a substantial element of danger—either from the criminal or from a confrontation between the criminal and the police. These considerations can lead to an innocent and understandable desire to quit the vicinity with all speed.

Among some citizens, particularly minorities and those residing in high crime areas, there is also the possibility that the fleeing person is entirely innocent, but, with or without justification, believes that contact with the police can itself be dangerous, apart from any criminal activity associated with the officer's sudden presence. For such a person, unprovoked flight is neither "aberrant" nor "abnormal." Moreover, these concerns and fears are known to the police officers themselves, and are validated by law enforcement investigations into their own practices. Accordingly, the evidence supporting the reasonableness of these beliefs is too pervasive to be dismissed as random or rare, and too persuasive to be disparaged as inconclusive or insufficient. In any event, just as we do not require "scientific certainty" for our commonsense conclusion that unprovoked flight can sometimes indicate suspicious motives, neither do we require scientific certainty to conclude that unprovoked flight can occur for other, innocent reasons. * * *

II

Guided by that totality-of-the-circumstances test, the Court concludes that Officer Nolan had reasonable suspicion to stop respondent. In this respect, my view differs from the Court's. * * *

Officer Nolan and his partner were in the last of the four patrol cars that "were all caravaning eastbound down Van Buren." Nolan first observed respondent "in front of 4035 West Van Buren." Wardlow "looked in our direction and began fleeing." Nolan then "began driving southbound down the street observing [respondent] running through the gangway and the alley southbound," and observed that Wardlow was carrying a white, opaque bag under his arm. * * *

This terse testimony is most noticeable for what it fails to reveal. Though asked whether he was in a marked or unmarked car, Officer Nolan could not recall the answer. He was not asked whether any of the other three cars in the caravan were marked, or whether any of the other seven officers were in uniform. Though he explained that the size of the caravan was because "[n]ormally in these different areas there's an enormous amount of people, sometimes lookouts, customers," Officer Nolan did not testify as to whether *anyone* besides Wardlow was nearby 4035 West Van Buren. Nor is it clear that that address was the intended destination of the caravan. * * * Officer Nolan's testimony also does not reveal how fast the officers were driving. It does not indicate whether he saw respondent notice the other patrol cars. And it does not say whether the caravan, or any part of it, had already passed Wardlow by before he began to run.

Indeed, the Appellate Court thought the record was even "too vague to support the inference that * * * defendant's flight was related to his expectation of police focus on him." Presumably, respondent did not react to the first three cars, and we cannot even be sure that he recognized the occupants of the fourth as police officers. The adverse inference is based entirely on the officer's statement: "He looked in our direction and began fleeing."

No other factors sufficiently support a finding of reasonable suspicion. * * *

The State, along with the majority of the Court, relies as well on the assumption that this flight occurred in a high crime area. Even if that assumption is accurate, it is insufficient because even in a high crime neighborhood unprovoked flight does not invariably lead to reasonable suspicion. On the contrary, because many factors providing innocent motivations for unprovoked flight are concentrated in high crime areas, the character of the neighborhood arguably makes an inference of guilt less appropriate, rather than more so. Like unprovoked flight itself, presence in a high crime neighborhood is a fact too generic and susceptible to innocent explanation to satisfy the reasonable suspicion inquiry. * * *

NOTES AND QUESTIONS

1. In your view, should "unprovoked flight" = "reasonable suspicion"? If not, in your view should "unprovoked flight" + "high-crime area" = "reasonable suspicion"? Can you posit a set of facts in which this is *not* an accurate formula?

2. Lenese C. Herbert, *Can't You See What I'm Saying? Making Expressive Conduct a Crime in High-Crimes Areas*, 9 Geo. J. Pov. L. & Pol'y 135, 135–36, 165 (2002):

> As an eager young Assistant United States Attorney who "papered" countless complaints, conducted numerous hearings, and tried a substantial number of cases, I learned how to decode police officer jargon and law enforcement terminology. One of the most commonly used—yet seldom defined—phrases was "high-crime area." * * * Before court appearance, I would often question police officers about this characterization. In court, however, judges * * * never asked officers for data to support assertions that an area was high-crime. Even defense counsel seldom explored what this classification meant, the bases for it, or its relevance. * * *
>
> I suspected that the police were using a code language to suggest that their actions were justified because they were directed at "high-crime people": poor, undereducated, black and brown males who live in or frequent depressed * * * inner-city neighborhoods, or who look as if they do. In practice, police have the implicit authorization to create and apply an inferior set of rights to individuals in high-crime areas, presumably because those individuals are regarded as being less worthy than other citizens. * * *
>
> * * * The *Wardlow* Court * * * has virtually relinquished the protection and safeguarding of the rights of the policed to the police themselves.

Are these criticisms fair?

3. *Problem.* Officers on patrol observed a car leaving the area with one headlight out and an expired inspection sticker. The officers signaled for the car to stop. The driver complied. As the officers approached the driver's side, *B*, a passenger in the front seat, jumped out and ran away. One officer gave chase and tackled him. Reasonable suspicion for *this* seizure? United States v. Bonner, 363 F.3d 213 (3d Cir. 2004). Does your answer depend on whether this occurred: (a) near a housing project in a poor part of town; or (b) in the Beverly Hills, California business district?

4. Expanding the Scope of the *Terry* Balancing Approach

Introductory Comment

Notice that what we have covered so far regarding *Terry v. Ohio* has involved persons, rather than property—specifically, the warrantless "brief" seizures and, sometimes, "minimal" frisk-searches of persons. But, once one shifts the focus from the warrant clause to the reasonableness clause, and thus once a court balances the individual's Fourth Amendment interests against the government's interest in criminal law enforcement, there is nothing that conceptually limits this approach to stop-and-frisk (or stop-and-question) scenarios.

Indeed, as the following case and Notes demonstrate, it turns out that the *Terry* balancing approach extends to other criminal investigatory situations: to justify some warrantless, probable-cause-less, limited seizures and searches of *property*, as well as minimal *non*-frisk searches of persons, including some DNA searches.

MARYLAND V. BUIE

Supreme Court of the United States, 1990.
494 U.S. 325, 110 S.Ct. 1093, 108 L.Ed.2d 276.

The following case of *Maryland v. Buie* does two things. First, it applies a *Terry* stop analysis to a protective sweep of property—a house. Second, it expands the concept of SILA (see Chapter 5) to include a search of the house for places where an attack could be launched. Keep an eye out for how the Court distinguishes *Buie* from *Chimel.* Ask yourself which exception you think best applies to this case: *Terry* or *Chimel.* For more thoughts on this, see Justice Brennan's footnote from his dissent, set out in Note 2 after *Buie.* (For those of you who like to keep a messy room, Justice Brennan's dissent may have you rethinking that tendency.)

Also pay attention to the fine line Justice Stevens draws in his concurring opinion. He agrees with the standard for protective sweeps of a home, but he does not necessarily agree that it was met in this case. He leaves that to the trial court to determine (although he thinks the State will have a hard road to travel) and merely concurs in the decision to remand the case for retrial consistent with the standard *Buie* sets out.

In the Notes after *Buie*, the Court expands the application of *Terry* stops to property in several areas, including dog sniffs of luggage, and sweeps of automobiles, and, particularly relevant to today's justice system, the taking of DNA samples from arrestees.

JUSTICE WHITE delivered the opinion of the Court [joined by CHIEF JUSTICE REHNQUIST, and JUSTICES BLACKMUN, STEVENS, O'CONNOR, SCALIA, and KENNEDY].

A "protective sweep" is a quick and limited search of premises, incident to an arrest and conducted to protect the safety of police officers or others. It is narrowly confined to a cursory visual inspection of those places in which a person might be hiding. In this case we must decide what level of justification is required by the Fourth and Fourteenth Amendments before police officers, while effecting the arrest of a suspect in his home pursuant to an arrest warrant, may conduct a warrantless protective sweep of all or part of the premises. * * *

I

On February 3, 1986, two men committed an armed robbery of a Godfather's Pizza restaurant in Prince George's County, Maryland. One of the robbers was wearing a red running suit. That same day, Prince George's County police obtained arrest warrants for respondent Jerome Edward Buie and his suspected accomplice in the robbery, Lloyd Allen. Buie's house was placed under police surveillance.

On February 5, the police executed the arrest warrant for Buie. They first had a police department secretary telephone Buie's house to verify that he was home. The secretary spoke to a female first, then to Buie himself. Six or seven officers proceeded to Buie's house. Once inside, the officers fanned out through the first and second floors. Corporal James Rozar announced that he would "freeze" the basement so that no one could come up and surprise the officers. With his service revolver drawn, Rozar twice shouted into the basement, ordering anyone down there to come out. When a voice asked who was calling, Rozar announced three times: "this is the police, show me your hands." Eventually, a pair of hands appeared around the bottom of the stairwell and Buie emerged from the basement. He was arrested, searched, and handcuffed by Rozar. Thereafter, Detective Joseph Frolich entered the basement "in case there was someone else" down there. He noticed a red running suit lying in plain view on a stack of clothing and seized it.

The trial court denied Buie's motion to suppress the running suit * * *. * * *

II

It is not disputed that until the point of Buie's arrest the police had the right, based on the authority of the arrest warrant, to search anywhere in the house that Buie might have been found, including the basement. * * * There is also no dispute that if Detective Frolich's entry into the basement was lawful, the seizure of the red running suit, which was in plain view and which the officer had probable cause to believe was evidence of a crime, was also lawful under the Fourth Amendment. The issue in this case is what level of justification the Fourth Amendment required before Detective Frolich could legally enter the basement to see if someone else was there.

Petitioner, the State of Maryland, argues that, under a general reasonableness balancing test, police should be permitted to conduct a protective sweep whenever they make an in-home arrest for a violent crime. * * *

III

It goes without saying that the Fourth Amendment bars only unreasonable searches and seizures. Our cases show that in determining reasonableness, we have balanced the intrusion on the individual's Fourth Amendment interests against its promotion of legitimate governmental interests. Under this test, a search of the house or office is generally not reasonable without a warrant issued on probable cause. There are other contexts, however, where the public interest is such that neither a warrant nor probable cause is required.

The *Terry* [*v. Ohio*] case is most instructive for present purposes. * * * We stated [in *Terry*] that there is " 'no ready test for determining reasonableness other than by balancing the need to search * * * against the invasion which the search * * * entails.' " * * *

The ingredients to apply the balance struck in *Terry* * * * are present in this case. Possessing an arrest warrant and probable cause to believe Buie was in his home, the officers were entitled to enter and to search anywhere in the house in which Buie might be found. Once he was found, however, the search for him was over, and there was no longer that particular justification for entering any rooms that had not yet been searched.

That Buie had an expectation of privacy in those remaining areas of his house, however, does not mean such rooms were immune from entry. In *Terry* * * * we were concerned with the immediate interest of the police officer[ ] in taking steps to assure [himself] that the persons with whom [he was] dealing were not armed with, or able to gain immediate control of, a weapon that could unexpectedly and fatally be used against [him]. In the instant case, there is an analogous interest of the officers in taking steps to assure themselves that the house in which a suspect is being, or has just been, arrested is not harboring other persons who are dangerous and who could unexpectedly launch an attack. The risk of danger in the context of an arrest in the home is as great as, if not greater than, it is in an on-the-street or roadside investigatory encounter. A *Terry* * * * frisk occurs before a police-citizen confrontation has escalated to the point of arrest. A protective sweep, in contrast, occurs as an adjunct to the serious step of taking a person into custody for the purpose of prosecuting him for a crime. Moreover, unlike an encounter on the street or along a highway, an in-home arrest puts the officer at the disadvantage of being on his adversary's "turf." An ambush in a confined setting of unknown configuration is more to be feared than it is in open, more familiar surroundings.

We recognized in *Terry* that "[e]ven a limited search of the outer clothing for weapons constitutes a severe, though brief, intrusion upon cherished personal security, and it must surely be an annoying, frightening, and perhaps humiliating experience." But we permitted the intrusion, which was no more than necessary to protect the officer from harm. Nor do we here suggest, as the State does, that entering rooms not examined prior to the arrest is a *de minimis* intrusion that may be disregarded. We are quite sure, however, that the arresting officers are permitted in such circumstances to take reasonable steps to ensure their safety after, and while making, the arrest. That interest is sufficient to outweigh the intrusion such procedures may entail.

We agree with the State * * * that a warrant was not required. We also hold that as an incident to the arrest the officers could, as a precautionary matter and without probable cause or reasonable suspicion, look in closets and other spaces immediately adjoining the place of arrest from which an attack could be immediately launched. Beyond that, however, we hold that there must be articulable facts which, taken together with the rational inferences from those facts, would warrant a reasonably prudent officer in believing that the area to be swept harbors an individual posing a danger to those on the arrest scene. * * *

We should emphasize that such a protective sweep, aimed at protecting the arresting officers, if justified by the circumstances, is nevertheless not a full search of the premises, but may extend only to a cursory inspection of those spaces where a person may be found. The sweep lasts no longer than is necessary to dispel the reasonable suspicion of danger and in any event no longer than it takes to complete the arrest and depart the premises.

IV

* * * To reach our conclusion today * * *, we need not disagree with the Court's statement in *Chimel*, that "the invasion of privacy that results from a top-to-bottom search of a man's house [cannot be characterized] as 'minor,' " nor hold that "simply because some interference with an individual's privacy and freedom of movement has lawfully taken place, further intrusions should

automatically be allowed despite the absence of a warrant that the Fourth Amendment would otherwise require." The type of search we authorize today is far removed from the "top-to-bottom" search involved in *Chimel*; moreover, it is decidedly not "automati[c]," but may be conducted only when justified by a reasonable, articulable suspicion that the house is harboring a person posing a danger to those on the arrest scene. * * *

We * * * remand this case to the Court of Appeals of Maryland for further proceedings not inconsistent with this opinion. * * *

JUSTICE STEVENS, concurring.

Today the Court holds that reasonable suspicion, rather than probable cause, is necessary to support a protective sweep while an arrest is in progress. I agree with that holding and with the Court's opinion, but I believe it is important to emphasize that the standard applies only to *protective* sweeps. Officers conducting such a sweep must have a reasonable basis for believing that their search will reduce the danger of harm to themselves or of violent interference with their mission; in short, the search must be protective.

In this case, to justify Officer Frolich's entry into the basement, it is the State's burden to demonstrate that the officers had a reasonable basis for believing not only that someone in the basement might attack them or otherwise try to interfere with the arrest, but also that it would be safer to go down the stairs instead of simply guarding them from above until respondent had been removed from the house. The fact that respondent offered no resistance when he emerged from the basement is somewhat inconsistent with the hypothesis that the danger of an attack by a hidden confederate persisted after the arrest. * * *

Indeed, were the officers concerned about safety, one would expect them to do what Officer Rozar did before the arrest: guard the basement door to prevent surprise attacks. As the Court indicates, Officer Frolich might, at the time of the arrest, reasonably have "look[ed] in" the already open basement door to ensure that no accomplice had followed Buie to the stairwell. But Officer Frolich did not merely "look in" the basement; he entered it. That strategy is sensible if one wishes to search the basement. It is a surprising choice for an officer, worried about safety, who need not risk entering the stairwell at all.

The State may thus face a formidable task on remand. However, the Maryland courts are better equipped than are we to review the record. * * * I therefore agree that a remand is appropriate.

[*The concurring opinion of JUSTICE KENNEDY is omitted.*]

JUSTICE BRENNAN, with whom JUSTICE MARSHALL joins, dissenting. * * *

* * * [T]he Court's implicit judgment that a protective sweep constitutes a "minimally intrusive" search akin to that involved in *Terry* markedly undervalues the nature and scope of the privacy interests involved.

While the Fourth Amendment protects a person's privacy interests in a variety of settings, "physical entry of the home is the chief evil against which the wording of the Fourth Amendment is directed." The Court discounts the nature of the intrusion because it believes that the scope of the intrusion is limited. The Court explains that a protective sweep's scope is "narrowly confined to a cursory visual inspection of those places in which a person might be hiding," and confined in duration to a period "no longer than is necessary to dispel the reasonable suspicion of danger and in any event no longer than it takes to complete the arrest and depart the premises." But these spatial and temporal restrictions are not particularly limiting. A protective sweep would bring within police purview virtually all personal possessions within the house not hidden from view in a small enclosed space. Police officers searching for potential ambushers might enter every room including basements and attics; open up closets, lockers, chests, wardrobes, and cars; and peer under beds and behind furniture. The officers will view letters, documents, and personal effects that are on tables or desks or are visible inside open drawers; books, records, tapes, and pictures on shelves; and clothing, medicines, toiletries and other paraphernalia not carefully stored in dresser drawers or bathroom cupboards. While perhaps not a "full-blown" or "top-to-bottom" search, a protective sweep is much closer to it than to a "limited patdown for weapons" * * *. * * * The "ingredient" of a minimally intrusive search is absent, and the Court's holding today therefore unpalatably deviates from *Terry* and its progeny.

In light of the special sanctity of a private residence and the highly intrusive nature of a protective sweep, I firmly believe that police officers must have probable cause to fear that their personal safety is threatened by a hidden confederate of an arrestee before they may sweep through the entire home. * * * I respectfully dissent.

NOTES AND QUESTIONS

1. On remand, the Court of Appeals of Maryland, 4–3, upheld the sweep. Buie v. State, 320 Md. 696, 580 A.2d 167 (1990).

2. In a footnote to his dissent, Justice Brennan addressed the implications of *Buie* for the SILA exception first set out in *Chimel.*

> The Court's decision also to expand the "search incident to arrest" exception previously recognized in *Chimel v. California*, allowing police officers without *any* requisite level of suspicion to look into "closets and other spaces immediately adjoining the place of arrest from which an attack could be immediately launched," is equally disquieting. *Chimel* established that police officers may presume as a matter of law, without need for factual support in a particular case, that arrestees might take advantage of weapons or destroy evidence in the area "within [their] immediate control"; therefore, a protective search of that area is *per se* reasonable under the Fourth Amendment. I find much less plausible the Court's implicit assumption today that arrestees are likely to sprinkle hidden allies throughout the rooms in which they might be arrested. Hence there is no comparable justification for permitting arresting officers to presume as a matter of law that they are threatened by ambush from "immediately adjoining" spaces.

3. During a protective sweep, what may a police officer do if she finds a person hidden in a closet? Watching television in a family room? May she fully search the person? Automatically conduct a pat-down? May she conduct a search of the *grabbing area of that* person, even if this includes searching small areas, such as drawers, where a gun (but not another person) might be discovered?

4. *Brief seizure of property?* In United States v. Place, 462 U.S. 696, 103 S.Ct. 2637, 77 L.Ed.2d 110 (1983), the Supreme Court extended the *Terry* analysis of temporary seizures of persons to personalty. In *Place*, law enforcement officers at Miami International Airport grew suspicious of Raymond Place's behavior and, after an initial investigation, alerted Drug Enforcement Administration (DEA) authorities in New York, where Place was traveling. When Place arrived at New York's LaGuardia airport, two DEA agents were waiting for him. Place's behavior there reasonably aroused the agents' suspicion. Therefore, they approached Place, identified themselves as federal narcotics agents, requested and received his identification, and then sought consent to search Place's two pieces of luggage. When Place refused, the agents informed him that would take the bags to seek a search warrant. Instead, they took the luggage to Kennedy Airport where they subjected the two bags to a "sniff test" by a trained canine, which reacted positively to one bag. This occurred about ninety minutes after the initial seizure of the luggage. Because it was late in the afternoon on Friday, the agents held both bags until Monday morning, at which time a magistrate issued a warrant to search one bag. Upon opening it, the agents discovered a large quantity of cocaine.

Justice O'Connor, writing for six members of the Court, held that the principles of *Terry v. Ohio* * * * applied to Place's luggage:

> We examine first the governmental interest offered as a justification for a brief seizure of luggage from the suspect's custody for the purpose of pursuing a limited course of investigation. The Government contends that, where the authorities possess specific and articulable facts warranting a reasonable belief that a traveler's luggage contains narcotics, the governmental interest in seizing the luggage briefly to pursue further investigation is substantial. We agree. * * *
>
> Against this strong governmental interest, we must weigh the nature and extent of the intrusion upon the individual's Fourth Amendment rights when the police briefly detain luggage for limited investigative purposes. On this point, respondent Place urges that the rationale for a *Terry* stop of the person is wholly inapplicable to investigative detentions of personalty. Specifically, the *Terry* exception to the probable-cause requirement is premised on the notion that a *Terry*-type stop of the person is substantially less intrusive of a person's liberty interests than a formal arrest. In the property context, however, Place urges, there are no degrees of intrusion. Once the owner's property is seized, the dispossession is absolute.
>
> We disagree. The intrusion on possessory interests occasioned by a seizure of one's personal effects can vary both in its nature and extent. The seizure may be made after the owner has relinquished control of the property to a third party or, as here, from the immediate custody and control of the owner. Moreover, the police may confine their investigation to an on-the-spot inquiry—for example, immediate exposure of the luggage to a trained narcotics detection dog—or transport the property to another location. Given the fact that seizures of property can vary in intrusiveness, some brief detentions of personal effects may be so minimally intrusive of Fourth Amendment interests that strong countervailing governmental interests will justify a seizure based only on specific articulable facts that the property contains contraband or evidence of a crime.
>
> In sum, we conclude that when an officer's observations lead him reasonably to believe that a traveler is carrying luggage that contains narcotics, the principles of *Terry* and its progeny would permit the officer to detain the luggage briefly to investigate the circumstances that aroused his suspicion, provided that the investigative detention is properly limited in scope.

Although the Government won *that* legal argument, it ultimately lost the Fourth Amendment claim in *this* case:

> The precise type of detention we confront here is seizure of personal luggage from the immediate possession of the suspect for the purpose of arranging exposure to a narcotics detection dog. Particularly in the case of detention of luggage within the traveler's immediate possession, the police conduct intrudes on both the suspect's possessory interest in his luggage as well as his liberty interest in proceeding with his itinerary. The person whose luggage is detained is technically still free to continue his travels or carry out other personal activities pending release of the luggage. * * * Nevertheless, such a seizure can effectively restrain the person since he is subjected to the possible disruption of his travel plans in order to remain with his luggage or to arrange for its return. Therefore, when the police seize luggage from the suspect's custody, we think the limitations applicable to investigative detentions of the person should define the permissible scope of an investigative detention of the person's luggage on less than probable cause. Under this standard, it is clear that the police conduct here exceeded the permissible limits of a *Terry*-type investigative stop.
>
> The length of the detention of respondent's luggage alone precludes the conclusion that the seizure was reasonable in the absence of probable cause. Although we have recognized the reasonableness of seizures longer than the momentary ones involved in *Terry*, * * * the brevity of the invasion of the individual's Fourth Amendment interests is an important factor in determining whether the seizure is so minimally intrusive as to be justifiable on reasonable suspicion. Moreover, in assessing the effect of the length of the detention, we take into account whether the police diligently pursue their investigation. We note that here the New York agents knew the time of Place's scheduled arrival at LaGuardia, had ample time to arrange for their additional investigation at that location, and thereby could have minimized the intrusion on respondent's Fourth Amendment interests. Thus, although we decline to adopt any outside time limitation for a permissible *Terry* stop, we have never approved a seizure of the person for the prolonged 90-minute period involved here and cannot do so on the facts presented by this case.
>
> Although the 90-minute detention of respondent's luggage is sufficient to render the seizure unreasonable, the violation was exacerbated by the failure of the agents to accurately inform respondent of the place to which they were transporting his luggage, of the length of time he might be dispossessed, and of what arrangements would be made for return of the

> luggage if the investigation dispelled the suspicion. In short, we hold that the detention of respondent's luggage in this case went beyond the narrow authority possessed by police to detain briefly luggage reasonably suspected to contain narcotics.

Does any of the Court's analysis here seem to conflict with anything else you have read in the *Terry* materials? What was the chance that Place was armed?

5. *"Car frisks."* We have seen that the police may ordinarily search a car without a warrant if they have probable cause to do so. They may also search portions of it as an incident to a lawful arrest of a car occupant (or a recent one), even without probable cause, if the interior of the car is in the arrestee's grabbing area. But, now suppose the police conduct a lawful *Terry*-level stop of a driver. May the police, short of probable cause, search the car to protect themselves from possible weapons that might be hidden inside?

In Michigan v. Long, 463 U.S. 1032, 103 S.Ct. 3469, 77 L.Ed.2d 1201 (1983), two officers on patrol in a rural area of Michigan, shortly after midnight, observed a car driving erratically and swerve off into a shallow ditch. The officer stopped to investigate. Long, the only occupant of the car, exited his vehicle and, leaving the car door open, met the officers at the rear of his car. One officer asked Long for his driver's license, but Long—who now appeared to the officers to be "under the influence of something"—did not respond, but turned away and began walking to the open door of his car. The officers followed him, at which point they observed a large hunting knife on the floorboard of the driver's side of the car. At that point, the officers stopped Long from moving closer to the car. They subjected him to a *Terry* frisk, which revealed no weapons.

One officer then shone his flashlights into the car, "to search for other weapons." As the Court described it, "[t]he officer noticed that something was protruding from under the armrest on the front seat. He knelt in the vehicle and lifted the armrest. He saw an open pouch on the front seat, and upon flashing his light on the pouch, determined that it contained what appeared to be marihuana." A further search of the passenger compartment of the vehicle did not turn up other contraband. Long was arrested for possession of marijuana.

The Supreme Court granted certiorari in the case "to consider the important question of the authority of a police officer to protect himself by conducting a *Terry*-type search of the passenger compartment of a motor vehicle during the lawful investigatory stop of the occupant of the vehicle." The Court, per Justice O'Connor, upheld what has since been characterized as a *Terry* "frisk" of the passenger compartment of an automobile:

Contrary to Long's view, *Terry* need not be read as restricting the preventative search to the person of the detained suspect.

In two cases in which we applied *Terry* to specific factual situations, we recognized that investigative detentions involving suspects in vehicles are especially fraught with danger to police officers. In *Pennsylvania v. Mimms*, [p. 358, Note 4], we held that police may order persons out of an automobile during a stop for a traffic violation, and may frisk those persons for weapons if there is a reasonable belief that they are armed and dangerous. Our decision rested in part on the "inordinate risk confronting an officer as he approaches a person seated in an automobile." In *Adams v. Williams*, [p. 348, Note 11], we held that the police, acting on an informant's tip, may reach into the passenger compartment of an automobile to remove a gun from a driver's waistband even where the gun was not apparent to police from outside the car and the police knew of its existence only because of the tip. Again, our decision rested in part on our view of the danger presented to police officers in "traffic stop" and automobile situations.

Finally, we have also expressly recognized that suspects may injure police officers and others by virtue of their access to weapons, even though they may not themselves be armed. * * *

Our past cases indicate then that protection of police and others can justify protective searches when police have a reasonable belief that the suspect poses a danger, that roadside encounters between police and suspects are especially hazardous, and that danger may arise from the possible presence of weapons in the area surrounding a suspect. These principles compel our conclusion that the search of the passenger compartment of an automobile, limited to those areas in which a weapon may be placed or hidden, is permissible if the police officer possesses a reasonable belief based on "specific and articulable facts which, taken together with the rational inferences from those facts, reasonably warrant" the officer in believing that the suspect is dangerous and the suspect may gain immediate control of weapons. "[T]he issue is whether a reasonably prudent man in the circumstances would be warranted in the belief that his safety or that of others was in danger."

Having announced the new rule, the Court turned to the question of whether the officers here had the requisite grounds to conduct the weapons search of the passenger compartment of the car:

The circumstances of this case clearly justified Deputies Howell and Lewis in their reasonable belief that Long posed a danger if he were permitted to reenter his vehicle. The hour was late and the area rural. Long

> was driving his automobile at excessive speed, and his car swerved into a ditch. The officers had to repeat their questions to Long, who appeared to be "under the influence" of some intoxicant. Long was not frisked until the officers observed that there was a large knife in the interior of the car into which Long was about to reenter. The subsequent search of the car was restricted to those areas to which Long would generally have immediate control, and that could contain a weapon. The trial court determined that the leather pouch containing marihuana could have contained a weapon. It is clear that the intrusion was "strictly circumscribed by the exigencies which justifi[ed] its initiation."

Do you agree with the Court's new rule? Even if you do, do you think the police needed to search the vehicle in *this* case? Justice Brennan, writing also for Justice Marshall, dissented:

> [T]he scope of a search is determined not only by reference to its purpose, but also by reference to its intrusiveness. Yet the Court today holds that a search of a car (and the containers within it) that is not even occupied by the suspect is only as intrusive as, or perhaps less intrusive than, thrusting a hand into a pocket after an initial patdown has suggested the presence of concealed objects that might be used as weapons.
>
> The Court suggests no limit on the "area search" it now authorizes. * * * Presumably a weapon "may be placed or hidden" anywhere in a car. A weapon also might be hidden in a container in the car. In this case, the Court upholds the officer's search of a leather pouch because it "could have contained a weapon." In addition, the Court's requirement that an officer have a reasonable suspicion that a suspect is armed and dangerous does little to check the initiation of an area search. In this case, the officers saw a hunting knife in the car, but the Court does not base its holding that the subsequent search was permissible on the ground that possession of the knife may have been illegal under state law. An individual can lawfully possess many things that can be used as weapons. A hammer, or a baseball bat, can be used as a very effective weapon. * * * Based on these facts, one might reasonably conclude that respondent was drunk. A drunken driver is indeed dangerous while driving, but not while stopped on the roadside by the police. Even when an intoxicated person lawfully has in his car an object that could be used as a weapon, it requires imagination to conclude that he is presently dangerous. Even assuming that the facts in this case justified the officers' initial "frisk" of respondent, they hardly provide adequate justification for a search of a suspect's car and the containers within it. This represents an intrusion not just different in degree, but in kind, from the

intrusion sanctioned by *Terry*. In short, the implications of the Court's decision are frightening.

6. *DNA testing of arrestees.* In Maryland v. King, 569 U.S. 435, 133 S.Ct. 1958, 186 L.Ed.2d 1 (2013), King was arrested for first-and second-degree assault. Pursuant to a Maryland statute,[2] the police used a cheek swab to take a DNA sample from King, uploaded the information to a Maryland DNA database, and later matched his DNA sample with one taken from the victim of an unsolved rape. Later charged in the rape, King moved to suppress the DNA match on the ground that the statute authorizing the suspicionless DNA collection violated the Fourth Amendment.

In an opinion authored by Justice Kennedy, the Supreme Court held, 5–4, that "[w]hen officers make an arrest supported by probable cause to hold for a serious offense and they bring the suspect to the station to be detained in custody, taking and analyzing a cheek swab of the arrestee's DNA is, like fingerprinting and photographing, a legitimate police booking procedure that is reasonable under the Fourth Amendment." The Chief Justice and Justices Thomas, Breyer, and Alito, joined the opinion. Justice Kennedy conceded that the use of "a buccal swab on the inner tissues of a person's cheek in order to obtain DNA samples is a search. Virtually any 'intrusio[n] into the human body' will work an invasion of 'cherished personal security' that is subject to constitutional scrutiny." However, he went on, "[t]o say that the Fourth Amendment applies here is the beginning point, not the end of the analysis." The ultimate issue, he said, is whether the search is reasonable. Justice Kennedy then balanced the "privacy-related and law enforcement-related concerns to determine if the intrusion was reasonable."

Notice that while there was probable cause to arrest King, no individualized suspicion justified the cheek swab. The Court's use of a reasonableness balance to decide whether the swab is permissible reflects its commitment to the *Terry* view of the Fourth Amendment that minimizes the importance of warrants and probable cause. To the Court majority, DNA testing is reasonable in view of the "need for law enforcement officers in a safe and accurate way to process and identify the persons and possessions they must take into custody. * * * When probable cause exists to remove an individual from the normal channels of society and hold him in legal custody, DNA identification plays a critical role in serving those interests."

How does DNA provide this benefit? Justice Kennedy explained that "a name is of little value compared to the real interest in identification at stake when an

---

[2] The statute authorized the collection of DNA samples from "an individual who is charged with * * * a crime of violence or an attempt to commit a crime of violence; or * * * burglary or an attempt to commit burglary." Once taken, the sample may not be processed or placed in a database unless or until the arrestee is arraigned (which occurs approximately 48 hours after the arrest). The samples must be destroyed if the prosecution does not result in conviction of the individual or, after conviction, if the person is granted an unconditional pardon.

individual is brought into custody. Quoting a federal court, "[i]t is a well recognized aspect of criminal conduct that the perpetrator will take unusual steps to conceal not only his conduct, but also his identity. Disguises used while committing a crime may be supplemented or replaced by changed names, and even changed physical features." Justice Kennedy went on, "the only difference between DNA analysis and the accepted use of fingerprint databases is the unparalleled accuracy DNA provides."

Another benefit of DNA testing, Justice Kennedy claimed, is "ensuring that the custody of an arrestee does not create inordinate 'risks for facility staff, for the existing detainee population, and for a new detainee.' DNA identification can provide untainted information to those charged with detaining suspects [such as whether the suspect] has a record of violence or mental disorder."

The Court provided three additional law enforcement benefits of DNA testing:

> Third, looking forward to future stages of criminal prosecution, "the Government has a substantial interest in ensuring that persons accused of crimes are available for trials." A person who is arrested for one offense but knows that he has yet to answer for some past crime may be more inclined to flee the instant charges, lest continued contact with the criminal justice system expose one or more other serious offenses. For example, a defendant who had committed a prior sexual assault might be inclined to flee on a burglary charge, knowing that in every State a DNA sample would be taken from him after his conviction on the burglary charge that would tie him to the more serious charge of rape. * * *
>
> Fourth, an arrestee's past conduct is essential to an assessment of the danger he poses to the public, and this will inform a court's determination whether the individual should be released on bail. * * *
>
> Finally, in the interests of justice, the identification of an arrestee as the perpetrator of some heinous crime may have the salutary effect of freeing a person wrongfully imprisoned for the same offense.

The Court found little on the other side of the scale to call into question the DNA sampling process: the procedure involves nothing more than a "brief and * * * minimal intrusion. A gentle rub along the inside of the cheek does not break the skin, and it 'involves virtually no risk, trauma, or pain.' A * * * swab of this nature does not increase the indignity already attendant to normal incidents of arrest."

Justice Scalia, who was joined by Justices Ginsburg, Sotomayor, and Kagan, wrote a fiery dissent. He analogized the DNA testing to the British use of general warrants that the "Americans despised" at the time of the founding of the nation, and which motivated the adoption of the Fourth Amendment:

> The Fourth Amendment forbids searching a person for evidence of a crime when there is no basis for believing the person is guilty of the crime or is in possession of incriminating evidence. That prohibition is categorical and without exception; it lies at the very heart of the Fourth Amendment. Whenever this Court has allowed a suspicionless search, it has insisted upon a justifying motive apart from the investigation of crime.
>
> It is obvious that no such noninvestigative motive exists in this case. The Court's assertion that DNA is being taken, not to solve crimes, but to *identify* those in the State's custody, taxes the credulity of the credulous.

Justice Scalia explained:

> The portion of the Court's opinion that explains the identification rationale is strangely silent on the actual workings of the DNA search at issue here. To know those facts is to be instantly disabused of the notion that what happened had anything to do with identifying King.
>
> King was arrested on April 10, 2009, on charges unrelated to the case before us. That same day, April 10, the police searched him and seized the DNA evidence at issue here. What happened next? Reading the Court's opinion, particularly its insistence that the search was necessary to know "who [had] been arrested," one might guess that King's DNA was swiftly processed and his identity thereby confirmed—perhaps against some master database of known DNA profiles, as is done for fingerprints. After all, was not the suspicionless search here crucial to avoid "inordinate risks for facility staff" or to "existing detainee population"? Surely, then—*surely*—the State of Maryland got cracking on those grave risks immediately, by rushing to identify King with his DNA as soon as possible.
>
> Nothing could be further from the truth. Maryland officials did not even begin the process of testing King's DNA that day. Or, actually, the next day. Or the day after that. And that was for a simple reason: Maryland law forbids them to do so. A "DNA sample collected from an individual charged with a crime . . . *may not* be tested or placed in the statewide DNA data base system prior to the first scheduled arraignment date." And King's first appearance in court was not until three days after his arrest. (I suspect, though, that they did not wait three days to ask his name or take his fingerprints.)
>
> This places in a rather different light the Court's solemn declaration that the search here was necessary so that King could be identified at "every stage of the criminal process." I hope that the Maryland officials who read the Court's opinion do not take it seriously. Acting on the Court's

> misperception of Maryland law could lead to jail time. See Md. Pub. Saf. Code Ann. § 2–512(c)–(e) (punishing by up to five years' imprisonment anyone who obtains or tests DNA information except as provided by statute). Does the Court really believe that Maryland did not know whom it was arraigning? * * * If the purpose of this Act is to assess "whether [King] should be released on bail," why would it *possibly* forbid the DNA testing process to *begin* until King was arraigned? Why would Maryland resign itself to simply hoping that the bail decision will drag out long enough that the "identification" can succeed before the arrestee is released? The truth, known to Maryland and increasingly to the reader: this search had nothing to do with establishing King's identity.

To the dissenters, the true purpose of DNA testing of arrestees is to create a database to solve previously unsolved crimes—to help solve "cold cases." But, what is wrong with that? Justice Scalia:

> The Court disguises the vast (and scary) scope of its holding by promising a limitation it cannot deliver. The Court repeatedly says that DNA testing, and entry into a national DNA registry, will not befall thee and me, dear reader, but only those arrested for "serious offense[s]." I cannot imagine what principle could possibly justify this limitation, and the Court does not attempt to suggest any. If one believes that DNA will "identify" someone arrested for assault, he must believe that it will "identify" someone arrested for a traffic offense. This Court does not base its judgments on senseless distinctions. At the end of the day, *logic will out.* When there comes before us the taking of DNA from an arrestee for a traffic violation, the Court will predictably (and quite rightly) say, "We can find no significant difference between this case and *King.*" Make no mistake about it: As an entirely predictable consequence of today's decision, your DNA can be taken and entered into a national DNA database if you are ever arrested, rightly or wrongly, and for whatever reason. * * *
>
> Today's judgment will, to be sure, have the beneficial effect of solving more crimes; then again, so would the taking of DNA samples from anyone who flies on an airplane (surely the Transportation Security Administration needs to know the "identity" of the flying public), applies for a driver's license, or attends a public school. Perhaps the construction of such a genetic panopticon is wise. But I doubt that the proud men who wrote the charter of our liberties would have been so eager to open their mouths for royal inspection.
>
> I therefore dissent, and hope that today's incursion upon the Fourth Amendment * * * will someday be repudiated.

7. *Problem.* R's live-in girlfriend called 911 to report that R was drunk and talking about committing suicide. While she was on the telephone, two gunshots were fired. The 911 dispatcher directed her to leave the house and wait for the police. A SWAT team arrived shortly thereafter and surrounded the house. The girlfriend informed them that R was the only person inside. After a lengthy standoff, an officer used a stun gun on R, who was sitting on a windowsill with his legs hanging out an open window as he drunkenly cursed at the officers. R was formally arrested outside the house for possession of a firearm. He told the officers that nobody else was inside the house. Nonetheless, the SWAT team secured the house and then broke through a barricaded door and entered the premises. Inside they seized a shotgun and made photographs of spent shells and the holes R had shot into the ceiling. The police justified the entry as a protective sweep. Was the entry valid on that or any other ground? Commonwealth v. Robertson, 275 Va. 559, 659 S.E.2d 321 (2008).

5. Summary: A Look Back at *Terry* and Reasonable Suspicion

When we started our look at *Terry v. Ohio*, we were dealing with a very narrowly drawn exception to the requirements for probable cause and a warrant in order to protect officer and public safety—nothing more. While the reasonable suspicion standard, set out in *Terry* and defined in *Alabama v. White*, was meant to be less demanding than that of probable cause, it was more than simply a hunch on the part of the officer. There had to be reasons for his or her suspicions that the officer could articulate or describe. Thus, the standard was sometimes called "articulable suspicion".

In his dissent in *Terry,* Justice Douglas warned that "[t]o give the police greater power than a magistrate is to take a long step down the totalitarian path." Are we there yet? Perhaps not. But, we certainly have come a long way from the limited circumstance of an officer having a reasonable, and articulable, suspicion of criminal activity that could pose a danger to officers or others. In addition to persons who arouse the suspicions of law enforcement in a wide variety of situations, *Terry* stops have since been applied to cars pulled over for traffic stops, luggage that has already been through airport screening for weapons, passengers in cars pulled over for traffic stops, passengers in busses, dog sniffs of luggage, protective sweeps of homes, and DNA testing of arrestees. It is also impossible to ignore the social science evidence that *Terry* stops are disproportionately used against minority populations.

Chapter 5 began as an examination of the "exceptions" to a warrant "requirement." Once we moved away from the concept of a *probable cause* requirement in *Terry* however, the question of warrants disappeared, and we were left with the issue of the overall reasonableness of the search or seizure. Like many reasonableness inquiries in law, this requires only a balancing test between the government's interest in conducting the search and the level of intrusion involved. In view of the myriad of ways in which the facts of these cases have been interpreted in both majority and dissenting opinions, it might be argued by some that the "reasonableness" test is not as objective a test as the term "reasonableness" might suggest. What might be the dangers, if any, of that?

C. Reasonableness in a "Special Needs" (and Non-Criminal?) Context

Introduction

It is necessary to draw a distinction between searches and seizures conducted by police in furtherance of their criminal law enforcement responsibilities and searches and seizures conducted by police, and by other public officials, in furtherance of "community caretaking functions" or, more generally, non-law enforcement purposes. It is necessary to draw this line because the Supreme Court sometimes does. Unfortunately, the line-drawing is exceptionally difficult, because the distinction, if it even exists, is not easy to draw.

If you think back over this chapter, nearly every case we have considered involved a search or seizure in a criminal investigation. But, there have been some exceptions. For example, we had a Note (p. 282, Note 4) relating to automobile inventories: When an automobile is towed as the result of illegal parking, for example, the police may routinely inspect the contents of the car, not as part of a criminal investigation, but simply to make sure that belongings are properly inventoried for safekeeping and other purposes. South Dakota v. Opperman, 428 U.S. 364, 96 S.Ct. 3092, 49 L.Ed.2d 1000 (1976), held that because such inventories are not criminal investigations, the warrant clause including the probable cause requirement do not apply. The reasonableness clause, alone, must be considered, and the Court held that the police may inventory automobiles under specified circumstances in the absence of probable cause *or even reasonable suspicion*. These "special circumstances" include the existence of a written policy specifying how the inventory should be conducted.

Opperman has come to be seen as stating a special inventory "exception" to the warrant "requirement." But that may primarily be a function of history. Over time, the Supreme Court has come to recognize another general warrant "exception," sometimes described as the "special needs" exception, which could easily encompass inventories. A search or seizure comes within the "special needs" category when a perceived need, *beyond the normal need for criminal law enforcement*, makes the warrant and/or probable-cause requirements of the Fourth Amendment impracticable or, simply, irrelevant. In "special needs" circumstances, the Court evaluates the governmental activity by applying the reasonableness balancing standard.

One scholar has observed that "little or no effort has been made to explain what these 'special needs' are; the term turns out to be no more than a label that indicates when a lax standard will apply." William J. Stuntz, *Implicit Bargains, Government Power, and the Fourth Amendment*, 44 Stan. L. Rev. 553, 554 (1992). An interesting feature of the doctrine is that, in this area, often "the Court [has] one of its rare opportunities to hear face-to-face, as Fourth Amendment claimants, those law-abiding citizens for whose ultimate benefits the constitutional restraints on public power were primarily intended." Stephen J. Schulhofer, *On the Fourth Amendment Rights of the Law-Abiding Public*, 1989 Sup. Ct. Rev. 87, 88. Yet, as we will see, in these cases not only are traditional warrants inapplicable, but the Supreme Court sometimes dispenses with the requirement of suspicion of wrongdoing on the part of the "victim" of the search or seizure.

NOTES AND QUESTIONS

1. *Administrative searches.* In 1967 (long before recognition of a "special needs" doctrine), the Supreme Court considered the applicability of the Fourth Amendment in the enforcement of housing code regulations, Camara v. Municipal Court, 387 U.S. 523, 87 S.Ct. 1727, 18 L.Ed.2d 930 (1967), and safety code provisions affecting commercial buildings, See v. City of Seattle, 387 U.S. 541, 87 S.Ct. 1737, 18 L.Ed.2d 943 (1967). *Camara* and *See* were decided during the peak of the dominance of the warrant clause. In general, these cases provide that, except in the event of emergency or consent, residences and commercial buildings may not be entered to inspect for administrative code violations without an administrative search warrant. The "probable cause" for these administrative warrants can be supplied by a showing of non-arbitrary justification to inspect the particular premises, *e.g.*, that all the buildings in the area are due to being inspected. This kind of "probable cause" obviously does not require particularized suspicion of criminal wrongdoing or even of administrative code violations in a specific building.

Since the *Camara-See* doctrine was laid down, and as the Supreme Court's devotion to warrants has receded, the Court has approved *warrantless* administrative searches of "closely [governmentally] regulated industries," even in the absence of emergency or consent. As the Court explained in New York v. Burger, 482 U.S. 691, 107 S.Ct. 2636, 96 L.Ed.2d 601 (1987),

> [b]ecause the owner or operator of commercial premises in a "closely regulated" industry has a reduced expectation of privacy, the warrant and probable-cause requirements, which fulfill the traditional Fourth Amendment standard of reasonableness for a government search, have lessened application in this context. Rather, we conclude that, as in other situations of "special need," where the privacy interests of the owner are weakened and the government interests in regulating particular businesses are concomitantly heightened, a warrantless inspection of commercial premises may well be reasonable within the meaning of the Fourth Amendment.

Burger is an especially interesting case because, unlike most administrative searches that are conducted by employees of administrative agencies, the searches here were performed by police officers, who entered the defendant's automobile junkyard without a warrant or probable cause of criminal wrongdoing. Pursuant to statute, they asked to see Burger's business license and record of automobiles and parts on the premises. He admitted he had neither and thus was in plain violation of the administrative regulations for junkyards. The officers then searched the junkyard, where they discovered stolen vehicle parts that led to Burger's arrest for possession of stolen property.

The Court upheld the search. It did so despite the fact that the searches were conducted by police officers, and that the officers, serving as agents of an administrative agency, could have cited Burger for violation of administrative regulations once he admitted the lack of records to them, without ever conducting the search that turned up criminal wrongdoing. The Court did not focus on the motives of the officers in this case. All that mattered was that the administrative regulations had a non-penal purpose.

2. *Birth of the "special needs" doctrine.* The Court gave birth to the "special needs" doctrine, although its express mention arose only in a concurring opinion, in New Jersey v. T.L.O, 469 U.S. 325, 105 S.Ct. 733, 83 L.Ed.2d 720 (1985). In *T.L.O.*, two public school students were caught smoking on school grounds, in violation of school rules. When one of them denied she smoked, the vice-principal demanded her purse, opened it, and observed a package of cigarettes. As he pulled them out, he discovered cigarette paper, which is often used to make marijuana cigarettes. This led to a full search of T.L.O.'s purse, which turned up evidence implicating her in marijuana sales. The criminal evidence was handed over to the police and used in a juvenile court proceeding against her.

Although the Supreme Court had initially granted certiorari to decide whether the exclusionary rule was simply inapplicable to school searches, the Court ultimately decided the case on the much narrower ground that this particular search complied with the Fourth Amendment. The Court held that neither the warrant requirement nor probable cause applies to searches by public school officials. It quickly disposed of the warrant requirement, stating that it is "unsuited to the school environment," because it would "unduly interfere with the maintenance of the swift and informal disciplinary proceedings needed in the schools." As for probable cause, the majority observed that "[w]here a careful balancing of governmental and public interests suggests that the public interest is best served by a Fourth Amendment standard of reasonableness that stops short of probable cause, we have not hesitated to adopt such a standard." Here, the Court ruled, public school teachers and administrators may search students without a warrant if two conditions are met: (1) "there are reasonable grounds"—not necessarily "probable cause" in the criminal law context—"for suspecting that the search will turn up evidence that the student has violated or is violating either the law or the rules of the school"; and (2) once initiated, the search is "not excessively intrusive in light of the age and sex of the student and the nature of the infraction." The Supreme Court concluded that the initial search for cigarettes in this case, based on the report of her smoking, "was in no sense unreasonable for Fourth Amendment purposes."

3. *A "special needs" school search that went too far.* In Safford Unified School District #1 v. Redding, 557 U.S. 364, 129 S.Ct. 2633, 174 L.Ed.2d 354 (2009), the Court confronted the issue of "whether a 13-year-old student's Fourth Amendment right was violated when she was subjected to a search of her bra and underpants by school officials acting on reasonable suspicion that she had brought forbidden prescription and over-the-counter drugs to school." The Court stated that characterizing the search—requiring the student "to remove her clothes down to her underwear, and then 'pull out' her bra and the elastic band on her underpants"—as a "strip search is a fair way to speak of it." (The search failed to turn up any pills.)

Every member of the Court except Justice Thomas concluded that the strip search violated the Fourth Amendment. The Court, per Justice Souter, stated that it violated the "rule of reasonableness as stated in *T.L.O.*":

> Here, the content of the suspicion failed to match the degree of intrusion. [The principal who ordered the search] knew beforehand that the pills were prescription-strength ibuprofen and over-the-counter naproxen, common pain relievers equivalent to two Advil, or one Aleve. He must have been aware of the nature and limited threat of the specific drugs he was searching for * * *. * * *
>
> In sum, what was missing from the suspected facts that pointed to [the student] was any indication of danger to the students from the power of the drugs or their quantity, and any reason [specific to this student] to suppose that [she] was carrying pills in her underwear. * * *

> We * * * mean * * * to make it clear that the *T.L.O.* concern to limit a school search to reasonable scope requires the support of reasonable suspicion of danger or of resort to underwear for hiding evidence of wrongdoing before a search can reasonably make the quantum leap from outer clothes and backpacks to exposure of intimate parts. The meaning of such a search, and the degradation its subject may reasonably feel, place a search that intrusive in a category of its own demanding its own specific suspicions.

Notice, however, that Safford is a civil suit against the school district. No exclusion of evidence in a criminal case was involved.

4. *Airport searches.* Consider this scenario based roughly on the facts in United States v. Aukai, 497 F.3d 955 (9th Cir. 2007) (en banc): *A* goes to the airport and, because he has forgotten to bring his driver's license or other government-issued photographic identification, he is required to undergo a more intensive screening process in order to pass through security. First, *A* went through the ordinary screening process without difficulty. He then was informed he would have to undergo a second screening in which a Transportation and Security Administration (TSA) officer would pass a handheld "wand" close to *A*'s body. When the TSA officer used the wand, it sounded an alarm twice near one of *A*'s pockets. Although *A* continued to assert that his pockets were empty, he was ordered to empty his pockets. At this point, *A* told the TSA officer he had changed his mind and no longer wanted to board the plane and, instead, wanted to leave the airport. But, the TSA agent refused to let him leave and required that he empty his pockets. When *A* complied, the officer discovered drug paraphernalia resulting in *A*'s arrest.

Was the latter warrantless search—after *A* asked to leave—constitutional? The Ninth Circuit in *Aukai* ruled, 15–0, that the search was constitutional. The court characterized the procedure as a valid "administrative search" (see Note 1), therefore not dependent upon *A*'s consent. The Ninth Circuit also invoked the "special needs" doctrine. In doing so, however, it ruled that "the scope of such searches is not limitless. A particular airport security search is constitutionally reasonable provided that it 'is no more extensive than necessary, in the light of current technology, to detect the presence of weapons or explosives * * * [and] that it is confined in good faith to that purpose.' " The Ninth Circuit concluded that the airport screening in *A*'s case satisfied these requirements. Do you see the strongest argument on behalf of the government?

5. *Border searches.* Special rules also apply in the international border context. At the border and its functional equivalent (*e.g.*, at an airport where an international flight arrives), a person may be stopped and her belongings searched without a warrant and in the absence of individualized suspicion of wrongdoing, "pursuant to

the long-standing right of the sovereign to protect itself" from the entry of persons and things dangerous to the nation. United States v. Ramsey, 431 U.S. 606, 97 S.Ct. 1972, 52 L.Ed.2d 617 (1977). In dictum the *Ramsey* Court did state, however, that "[w]e * * * leave open the question 'whether, and under what circumstances, a border search might be deemed "unreasonable" because of the particularly offensive manner it is carried out.' "

The law of border searches is somewhat more complicated away from the border. Particularly on highways in the vicinity of the Mexican border, federal agents often stop vehicles to question occupants regarding their citizenship. The Court has distinguished here between seizures conducted by "roving border patrols" (where agents stop a car without notice on a little-traveled road) and those that occur at a fixed interior checkpoint (a permanent stop along a well-traveled highway). With *roving* border patrols, the Supreme Court has determined that the agents need reasonable suspicion of criminal activity to detain the car occupants briefly. United States v. Brignoni-Ponce, 422 U.S. 873, 95 S.Ct. 2574, 45 L.Ed.2d 607 (1975). However, in United States v. Martinez-Fuerte, 428 U.S. 543, 96 S.Ct. 3074, 49 L.Ed.2d 1116 (1976), the Court ruled that vehicle occupants may be stopped for questioning at *fixed* interior checkpoints without individualized suspicion of wrongdoing.

MICHIGAN DEPARTMENT OF STATE POLICE V. SITZ

Supreme Court of the United States, 1990.
496 U.S. 444, 110 S.Ct. 2481, 110 L.Ed.2d 412.

As discussed in the Notes above, checkpoints can either be fixed or roving. The Court has distinguished fixed checkpoints from roving patrols on two grounds. First, the subjective intrusion on the security of lawful travelers—their fear and surprise level—"is appreciably less in the case of a [fixed] checkpoint stop." Second, agents at fixed checkpoints have less discretionary enforcement authority than roving agents: the location of the checkpoint is fixed, and they may only stop those that pass through it. The case of *Michigan Department of State Police v. Sitz* looks at a fixed checkpoint. Pay close attention to the stated purpose of the checkpoint in the case that follows, *City of Indianapolis v. Edmunds.*

Also note the dissent by Justices Brennan and Marshall. As with many of their dissents, they are uncomfortable with giving law enforcement what they view as too much discretionary authority to engage in searches and seizures. The further away from a requirement for probable cause to search or seize the Court gets, the less comfortable they are. Both were passionate members of the Warren Court and both firmly believed that the role of the Court was to reign in the massive authority and power of the State as the

best way to protect the rights of the individual; no more so than with criminal defendants.

CHIEF JUSTICE REHNQUIST delivered the opinion of the Court [joined by JUSTICES WHITE, O'CONNOR, SCALIA, and KENNEDY].

This case poses the question whether a State's use of highway sobriety checkpoints violates the Fourth and Fourteenth Amendments to the United States Constitution. We hold that it does not and therefore reverse the contrary holding of the Court of Appeals of Michigan.

Petitioners, the Michigan Department of State Police and its director, established a sobriety checkpoint pilot program in early 1986. The director appointed a Sobriety Checkpoint Advisory Committee comprising representatives of the State Police force, local police forces, state prosecutors, and the University of Michigan Transportation Research Institute. Pursuant to its charge, the advisory committee created guidelines setting forth procedures governing checkpoint operations, site selection, and publicity.

Under the guidelines, checkpoints would be set up at selected sites along state roads. All vehicles passing through a checkpoint would be stopped and their drivers briefly examined for signs of intoxication. In cases where a checkpoint officer detected signs of intoxication, the motorist would be directed to a location out of the traffic flow where an officer would check the motorist's driver's license and car registration and, if warranted, conduct further sobriety tests. Should the field tests and the officer's observations suggest that the driver was intoxicated, an arrest would be made. All other drivers would be permitted to resume their journey immediately.

The first—and to date the only—sobriety checkpoint operated under the program was conducted in Saginaw County with the assistance of the Saginaw County Sheriff's Department. During the 75-minute duration of the checkpoint's operation, 126 vehicles passed through the checkpoint. The average delay for each vehicle was approximately 25 seconds. Two drivers were detained for field sobriety testing, and one of the two was arrested for driving under the influence of alcohol. A third driver who drove through without stopping was pulled over by an officer in an observation vehicle and arrested for driving under the influence.

On the day before the operation of the Saginaw County checkpoint, respondents filed a complaint in the Circuit Court of Wayne County seeking declaratory and injunctive relief from potential subjection to the checkpoints. * * *

After the trial, at which the court heard extensive testimony concerning, *inter alia*, the "effectiveness" of highway sobriety checkpoint programs, the court ruled that the Michigan program violated the Fourth Amendment * * *. On appeal, the Michigan Court of Appeals affirmed the holding * * *. * * *

To decide this case the trial court performed a balancing test derived from our opinion in *Brown v. Texas*, 443 U.S. 47, 99 S.Ct. 2637, 61 L.Ed.2d 357 (1979). As described by the Court of Appeals, the test involved "balancing the state's interest in preventing accidents caused by drunk drivers, the effectiveness of sobriety checkpoints in achieving that goal, and the level of intrusion on an individual's privacy caused by the checkpoints." The Court of Appeals agreed that "the *Brown* three-prong balancing test was the correct test to be used to determine the constitutionality of the sobriety checkpoint plan." * * *

Petitioners concede, correctly in our view, that a Fourth Amendment "seizure" occurs when a vehicle is stopped at a checkpoint. The question thus becomes whether such seizures are "reasonable" under the Fourth Amendment.

* * * We address only the initial stop of each motorist passing through a checkpoint and the associated preliminary questioning and observation by checkpoint officers. Detention of particular motorists for more extensive field sobriety testing may require satisfaction of an individualized suspicion standard.

No one can seriously dispute the magnitude of the drunken driving problem or the States' interest in eradicating it. Media reports of alcohol-related death and mutilation on the Nation's roads are legion. The anecdotal is confirmed by the statistical. "Drunk drivers cause an annual death toll of over 25,000 and in the same time span cause nearly one million personal injuries and more than five billion dollars in property damage." For decades, this Court has "repeatedly lamented the tragedy."

Conversely, the weight bearing on the other scale—the measure of the intrusion on motorists stopped briefly at sobriety checkpoints—is slight. We reached a similar conclusion as to the intrusion on motorists subjected to a brief stop at a highway checkpoint for detecting illegal aliens. See [*United States v.*] *Martinez-Fuerte*, [p. 413, Note 5]. We see virtually no difference between the levels of intrusion on law-abiding motorists from the brief stops necessary to the effectuation of these two types of checkpoints, which to the average motorist would seem identical save for the nature of the questions the checkpoint officers might ask. The trial court and the Court of Appeals, thus, accurately gauged the "objective" intrusion, measured by the duration of the seizure and the intensity of the investigation, as minimal.

With respect to what it perceived to be the "subjective" intrusion on motorists, however, the Court of Appeals found such intrusion substantial. * * *

We believe the Michigan courts misread our cases concerning the degree of "subjective intrusion" and the potential for generating fear and surprise. The "fear and surprise" to be considered are not the natural fear of one who has been drinking over the prospect of being stopped at a sobriety checkpoint but, rather, the fear and surprise engendered in law-abiding motorists by the nature of the stop. * * * The intrusion resulting from the brief stop at the sobriety checkpoint is for constitutional purposes indistinguishable from the checkpoint stops we upheld in *Martinez-Fuerte.*

The Court of Appeals went on to consider as part of the balancing analysis the "effectiveness" of the proposed checkpoint program. Based on extensive testimony in the trial record, the court concluded that the checkpoint program failed the "effectiveness" part of the test, and that this failure materially discounted petitioners' strong interest in implementing the program. We think the Court of Appeals was wrong on this point as well.

The actual language from *Brown v. Texas*, upon which the Michigan courts based their evaluation of "effectiveness," describes the balancing factor as "the degree to which the seizure advances the public interest." This passage from *Brown* was not meant to transfer from politically accountable officials to the courts the decision as to which among reasonable alternative law enforcement techniques should be employed to deal with a serious public danger. Experts in police science might disagree over which of several methods of apprehending drunken drivers is preferable as an ideal. But for purposes of Fourth Amendment analysis, the choice among such reasonable alternatives remains with the governmental officials who have a unique understanding of, and a responsibility for, limited public resources, including a finite number of police officers. * * *

In *Delaware v. Prouse*, [440 U.S. 648, 99 S.Ct. 1391, 59 L.Ed.2d 660 (1979),] we disapproved random stops made by Delaware Highway Patrol officers in an effort to apprehend unlicensed drivers and unsafe vehicles. We observed that *no* empirical evidence indicated that such stops would be an effective means of promoting roadway safety * * *. * * *

Unlike *Prouse*, this case involves neither a complete absence of empirical data nor a challenge to random highway stops. During the operation of the Saginaw County checkpoint, the detention of the 126 vehicles that entered the checkpoint resulted in the arrest of two drunken drivers. Stated as a percentage, approximately 1.6 percent of the drivers passing through the checkpoint were arrested for alcohol impairment. In addition, an expert witness testified at the trial that experience in other States demonstrated that, on the whole, sobriety checkpoints resulted in drunken driving arrests of around 1 percent of all motorists stopped. By way of comparison, the record from one of the consolidated cases in *Martinez-Fuerte* showed that in the associated checkpoint, illegal aliens were found in only 0.12 percent of the vehicles passing through the checkpoint. The ratio of illegal aliens detected to vehicles stopped (considering that on occasion two or more illegal aliens were found in a single vehicle) was approximately 0.5 percent. We concluded that this "record * * * provides a rather complete picture of the effectiveness of the San Clemente checkpoint," and we sustained its constitutionality. We see no justification for a different conclusion here.

In sum, the balance of the State's interest in preventing drunken driving, the extent to which this system can reasonably be said to advance that interest, and the degree of intrusion upon individual motorists who are briefly stopped, weighs in favor of the state program. We therefore hold that it is consistent with the Fourth Amendment. * * *

[*JUSTICE BLACKMUN'S concurrence in the judgment is omitted.*]

JUSTICE BRENNAN, with whom JUSTICE MARSHALL joins, dissenting. * * *

* * * Some level of individualized suspicion is a core component of the protection the Fourth Amendment provides against arbitrary government action. By holding that no level of suspicion is necessary before the police may stop a car for the purpose of preventing drunken driving, the Court potentially subjects the general public to arbitrary or harassing conduct by the police. * * *

* * * That stopping every car *might* make it easier to prevent drunken driving is an insufficient justification for abandoning the requirement of individualized suspicion. * * * Without proof that the police cannot develop individualized suspicion that a person is driving while impaired by alcohol, I believe the constitutional balance must be struck in favor of protecting the public against even the "minimally intrusive" seizures involved in this case. * * *

JUSTICE STEVENS, with whom JUSTICE BRENNAN and JUSTICE MARSHALL join as to Parts I and II, dissenting. * * *

I

There is a critical difference between a seizure that is preceded by fair notice and one that is effected by surprise. That is one reason why a border search, or indeed any search at a permanent and fixed checkpoint, is much less intrusive than a random stop. A motorist with advance notice of the location of a permanent checkpoint has an opportunity to avoid the search entirely, or at least to prepare for, and limit, the intrusion on her privacy.

No such opportunity is available in the case of a random stop or a temporary checkpoint, which both depend for their effectiveness on the element of surprise. A driver who discovers an unexpected checkpoint on a familiar local road will be startled and distressed. She may infer, correctly, that the checkpoint is not simply "business as usual," and may likewise infer, again correctly, that the police have made a discretionary decision to focus their law enforcement efforts upon her and others who pass the chosen point. * * *

* * * [I]t is significant that many of the stops at permanent checkpoints occur during daylight hours, whereas the sobriety checkpoints are almost invariably operated at night. A seizure followed by interrogation and even a cursory search at night is surely more offensive than a daytime stop that is almost as routine as going through a toll gate. * * *

These fears are not, as the Court would have it, solely the lot of the guilty. * * * Unwanted attention from the local police need not be less discomforting simply because one's secrets are not the stuff of criminal prosecutions. Moreover, those who have found—by reason of prejudice or misfortune—that encounters with the police may become adversarial or unpleasant without good cause will have grounds for worrying at any stop designed to elicit signs of suspicious behavior. * * *

II

The Court, unable to draw any persuasive analogy to *Martinez-Fuerte*, rests its decision today on application of a more general balancing test taken from *Brown v. Texas*. In that case the appellant, a pedestrian, had been stopped for questioning in an area of El Paso, Texas, that had "a high incidence of drug traffic" because he "looked suspicious." He was then arrested and convicted for refusing to identify himself to police officers. We set aside his conviction because the officers stopped him when they lacked any reasonable suspicion that he was engaged in criminal activity. In our opinion, we stated:

> "Consideration of the constitutionality of such seizures involves a weighing of the gravity of the public concerns served by the seizure, the degree to which the seizure advances the public interest, and the severity of the interference with individual liberty."

The gravity of the public concern with highway safety that is implicated by this case is, of course, undisputed. Yet, that same grave concern was implicated in

Delaware v. Prouse. Moreover, I do not understand the Court to have placed any lesser value on the importance of the drug problem implicated in *Brown v. Texas* * * *. A different result in this case must be justified by the other two factors in the *Brown* formulation.

As I have already explained, I believe the Court is quite wrong in blithely asserting that a sobriety checkpoint is no more intrusive than a permanent checkpoint. * * * [T]he surprise intrusion upon individual liberty is not minimal. On that issue, my difference with the Court may amount to nothing less than a difference in our respective evaluations of the importance of individual liberty, a serious, albeit inevitable, source of constitutional disagreement. On the degree to which the sobriety checkpoint seizures advance the public interest, however, the Court's position is wholly indefensible.

The Court's analysis of this issue resembles a business decision that measures profits by counting gross receipts and ignoring expenses. The evidence in this case indicates that sobriety checkpoints result in the arrest of a fraction of one percent of the drivers who are stopped, but there is absolutely no evidence that this figure represents an increase over the number of arrests that would have been made by using the same law enforcement resources in conventional patrols. Thus, although the *gross* number of arrests is more than zero, there is a complete failure of proof on the question whether the wholesale seizures have produced any *net* advance in the public interest in arresting intoxicated drivers. * * *

III

The most disturbing aspect of the Court's decision today is that it appears to give no weight to the citizen's interest in freedom from suspicionless unannounced investigatory seizures. * * * [T]he Court places a heavy thumb on the law enforcement interest by looking only at gross receipts instead of net benefits. Perhaps this tampering with the scales of justice can be explained by the Court's obvious concern about the slaughter on our highways and a resultant tolerance for policies designed to alleviate the problem by "setting an example" of a few motorists. This possibility prompts two observations.

First, my objections to random seizures or temporary checkpoints do not apply to a host of other investigatory procedures that do not depend upon surprise and are unquestionably permissible. * * * It is, for example, common practice to require every prospective airline passenger, or every visitor to a public building, to pass through a metal detector that will reveal the presence of a firearm or an explosive. Permanent, nondiscretionary checkpoints could be used to control serious dangers at other publicly operated facilities. Because concealed weapons obviously represent one such substantial threat to public safety, I would suppose that all subway passengers could be required to pass through metal detectors, so long as the detectors were permanent and every passenger was subjected to the same search. Likewise, I would suppose that a State could condition access to its toll roads upon not only paying the toll but also taking a uniformly administered breathalizer test. * * * This procedure would not be subject to the constitutional objections that control this case: The checkpoints would be permanently fixed, the stopping procedure would apply to all users of the toll road in precisely the same way, and police officers would not be free to make arbitrary choices about which neighborhoods should be targeted or about which individuals should be more thoroughly searched. * * *

This is a case that is driven by nothing more than symbolic state action—an insufficient justification for an otherwise unreasonable program of random seizures. Unfortunately, the Court is transfixed by the wrong symbol—the illusory prospect of punishing countless intoxicated motorists—when it should keep its eyes on the road plainly marked by the Constitution. * * *

NOTES AND QUESTIONS

1. Is an otherwise permissible suspicionless checkpoint valid if there is no empirical data supporting its use? What if the data suggest that the checkpoints are useless or even counter-productive?

2. In *Delaware v. Prouse*, distinguished by the Chief Justice in *Sitz*, the Court held that

> except in those situations in which there is at least articulable and reasonable suspicion that a motorist is unlicensed or that an automobile is not registered * * *, stopping an automobile and detaining the driver in order to check his driver's license and the registration of the automobile are unreasonable under the Fourth Amendment. This holding does not preclude * * * States from developing methods for spot checks that involve less intrusion or that do not involve the unconstrained exercise of discretion. Questioning of all oncoming traffic at roadblock-type stops is one possible alternative.

Why would be it less objectionable to stop and question everyone? Does this "misery loves company" approach to the Fourth Amendment make sense?

3. So checkpoints are constitutional, right? Well . . .

City of Indianapolis v. Edmond

Supreme Court of the United States, 2000.
531 U.S. 32, 121 S.Ct. 447, 148 L.Ed.2d 333.

In this case, we revisit a fixed checkpoint, but this time for the purpose of narcotics interdiction, not drunk driving. One works, the other does not. Look carefully for how the Court makes the distinction. Consider whether or not you think the distinction is workable. Put another way, where does *Edmunds* leave us? Is the legality of a checkpoint based simply on how the authorities in charge of the checkpoint word its purpose and objectives? Note 1 after *Edmunds* expands on this dilemma.

If you are headed into the criminal justice field, many of you will undoubtedly be required to undergo drug-testing as a condition of employment. These tests are viewed as a type of administrative search and their legal basis is set out in Note 3.

Finally, take a look at Note 5 in the context of our increased concerns about terrorism. Are you more likely to approve of this kind of checkpoint given the nature of the crime? Why should that matter? Do you think your opinion would be different if September 11 had not happened?

JUSTICE O'CONNOR delivered the opinion of the Court [joined by JUSTICES STEVENS, KENNEDY, SOUTER, GINSBURG, and BREYER].

In *Michigan Dept. of State Police v. Sitz* [p. 413], and *United States v. Martinez-Fuerte* [p. 413, Note 5], we held that brief, suspicionless seizures at highway checkpoints for the purposes of combating drunk driving and intercepting illegal immigrants were constitutional. We now consider the constitutionality of a highway checkpoint program whose primary purpose is the discovery and interdiction of illegal narcotics.

I

In August 1998, the city of Indianapolis began to operate vehicle checkpoints on Indianapolis roads in an effort to interdict unlawful drugs. The city conducted six such roadblocks between August and November that year, stopping 1,161 vehicles and arresting 104 motorists. Fifty-five arrests were for drug-related crimes, while 49 were for offenses unrelated to drugs. The overall "hit rate" of the program was thus approximately nine percent.

* * * At each checkpoint location, the police stop a predetermined number of vehicles. Approximately 30 officers are stationed at the checkpoint. Pursuant to written directives issued by the chief of police, at least one officer approaches the vehicle, advises the driver that he or she is being stopped briefly at a drug

checkpoint, and asks the driver to produce a license and registration. The officer also looks for signs of impairment and conducts an open-view examination of the vehicle from the outside. A narcotics-detection dog walks around the outside of each stopped vehicle.

The directives instruct the officers that they may conduct a search only by consent or based on the appropriate quantum of particularized suspicion. The officers must conduct each stop in the same manner until particularized suspicion develops, and the officers have no discretion to stop any vehicle out of sequence. * * *

The affidavit of Indianapolis Police Sergeant Marshall DePew * * * provides further insight concerning the operation of the checkpoints. According to Sergeant DePew, checkpoint locations are selected * * * based on such considerations as area crime statistics and traffic flow. The checkpoints are generally operated during daylight hours and are identified with lighted signs reading, " 'NARCOTICS CHECKPOINT ___ MILE AHEAD, NARCOTICS K-9 IN USE, BE PREPARED TO STOP.' " * * * Sergeant DePew also stated that the average stop for a vehicle not subject to further processing lasts two to three minutes or less.

Respondents were each stopped at a narcotics checkpoint in late September 1998. * * * Respondents claimed that the roadblocks violated the Fourth Amendment of the United States Constitution * * *. Respondents requested declaratory and injunctive relief for the class, as well as damages and attorney's fees for themselves. * * *

II

The Fourth Amendment requires that searches and seizures be reasonable. A search or seizure is ordinarily unreasonable in the absence of individualized suspicion of wrongdoing. While such suspicion is not an "irreducible" component of reasonableness, we have recognized only limited circumstances in which the usual rule does not apply. For example, we have upheld certain regimes of suspicionless searches where the program was designed to serve "special needs, beyond the normal need for law enforcement." We have also allowed searches for certain administrative purposes without particularized suspicion of misconduct, provided that those searches are appropriately limited. See, *e.g., New York v. Burger,* [p. 409, Note 1].

We have also upheld brief, suspicionless seizures of motorists at a fixed Border Patrol checkpoint designed to intercept illegal aliens, *Martinez-Fuerte, supra,* and at a sobriety checkpoint aimed at removing drunk drivers from the road,

Michigan Dept. of State Police v. Sitz. In addition, in *Delaware v. Prouse*, we suggested that a similar type of roadblock with the purpose of verifying drivers' licenses and vehicle registrations would be permissible. In none of these cases, however, did we indicate approval of a checkpoint program whose primary purpose was to detect evidence of ordinary criminal wrongdoing. * * *

III

* * * [W]hat principally distinguishes these checkpoints from those we have previously approved is their primary purpose.

As petitioners concede, the Indianapolis checkpoint program unquestionably has the primary purpose of interdicting illegal narcotics. In their stipulation of facts, the parties repeatedly refer to the checkpoints as "drug checkpoints" * * *. In addition, the first document attached to the parties' stipulation is entitled "DRUG CHECKPOINT CONTACT OFFICER DIRECTIVES BY ORDER OF THE CHIEF OF POLICE." These directives instruct officers to "[a]dvise the citizen that they are being stopped briefly at a drug checkpoint." * * * Further, according to Sergeant DePew, the checkpoints are identified with lighted signs [announcing a "NARCOTICS CHECKPOINT"]. * * *

We have never approved a checkpoint program whose primary purpose was to detect evidence of ordinary criminal wrongdoing. * * * [E]ach of the checkpoint programs that we have approved was designed primarily to serve purposes closely related to the problems of policing the border or the necessity of ensuring roadway safety. Because the primary purpose of the Indianapolis narcotics checkpoint program is to uncover evidence of ordinary criminal wrongdoing, the program contravenes the Fourth Amendment.

Petitioners propose several ways in which the narcotics-detection purpose of the instant checkpoint program may instead resemble the primary purposes of the checkpoints in *Sitz* and *Martinez-Fuerte*. Petitioners state that the checkpoints in those cases had the same ultimate purpose of arresting those suspected of committing crimes. Securing the border and apprehending drunk drivers are, of course, law enforcement activities, and law enforcement officers employ arrests and criminal prosecutions in pursuit of these goals. If we were to rest the case at this high level of generality, there would be little check on the ability of the authorities to construct roadblocks for almost any conceivable law enforcement purpose. Without drawing the line at roadblocks designed primarily to serve the general interest in crime control, the Fourth Amendment would do little to prevent such intrusions from becoming a routine part of American life.

Petitioners also emphasize the severe and intractable nature of the drug problem as justification for the checkpoint program. * * * But the gravity of the threat alone cannot be dispositive of questions concerning what means law enforcement officers may employ to pursue a given purpose. Rather, in determining whether individualized suspicion is required, we must consider the nature of the interests threatened and their connection to the particular law enforcement practices at issue. We are particularly reluctant to recognize exceptions to the general rule of individualized suspicion where governmental authorities primarily pursue their general crime control ends.

Nor can the narcotics-interdiction purpose of the checkpoints be rationalized in terms of a highway safety concern similar to that present in *Sitz*. The detection and punishment of almost any criminal offense serves broadly the safety of the community, and our streets would no doubt be safer but for the scourge of illegal drugs. Only with respect to a smaller class of offenses, however, is society confronted with the type of immediate, vehicle-bound threat to life and limb that the sobriety checkpoint in *Sitz* was designed to eliminate.

Petitioners also liken the anticontraband agenda of the Indianapolis checkpoints to the antismuggling purpose of the checkpoints in *Martinez-Fuerte*. Petitioners cite this Court's conclusion in *Martinez-Fuerte* that the flow of traffic was too heavy to permit "particularized study of a given car that would enable it to be identified as a possible carrier of illegal aliens," and claim that this logic has even more force here. The problem with this argument is that the same logic prevails any time a vehicle is employed to conceal contraband or other evidence of a crime. This type of connection to the roadway is very different from the close connection to roadway safety that was present in *Sitz* and *Prouse*. Further, the Indianapolis checkpoints are far removed from the border context that was crucial in *Martinez-Fuerte*. * * *

The primary purpose of the Indianapolis narcotics checkpoints is in the end to advance "the general interest in crime control." We decline to suspend the usual requirement of individualized suspicion where the police seek to employ a checkpoint primarily for the ordinary enterprise of investigating crimes. * * *

Of course, there are circumstances that may justify a law enforcement checkpoint where the primary purpose would otherwise, but for some emergency, relate to ordinary crime control. For example, * * * the Fourth Amendment would almost certainly permit an appropriately tailored roadblock set up to thwart an imminent terrorist attack or to catch a dangerous criminal who is likely to flee by way of a particular route. The exigencies created by these scenarios are far removed from the circumstances under which authorities might simply stop cars as a matter of course to see if there just happens to be a felon leaving the jurisdiction. While we do not limit the purposes that may justify a checkpoint program to any rigid set of categories, we decline to approve a program whose primary purpose is ultimately indistinguishable from the general interest in crime control.

Petitioners argue that our prior cases preclude an inquiry into the purposes of the checkpoint program. For example, they cite *Whren v. United States* [p. 268], * * * to support the proposition that "where the government articulates and pursues a legitimate interest for a suspicionless stop, courts should not look behind that interest to determine whether the government's 'primary purpose' is valid." * * *

In *Whren,* we held that an individual officer's subjective intentions are irrelevant to the Fourth Amendment validity of a traffic stop that is justified objectively by probable cause to believe that a traffic violation has occurred. * * * In so holding, we expressly distinguished cases where we had addressed the validity of searches conducted in the absence of probable cause.

Whren therefore reinforces the principle that, while "[s]ubjective intentions play no role in ordinary, probable-cause Fourth Amendment analysis," programmatic purposes may be relevant to the validity of Fourth Amendment intrusions undertaken pursuant to a general scheme without individualized suspicion. * * *

Petitioners argue that the Indianapolis checkpoint program is justified by its lawful secondary purposes of keeping impaired motorists off the road and verifying licenses and registrations. If this were the case, however, law enforcement authorities would be able to establish checkpoints for virtually any purpose so long as they also included a license or sobriety check. For this reason, we examine the available evidence to determine the primary purpose of the checkpoint program. * * * [A] program driven by an impermissible purpose may be proscribed while a program impelled by licit purposes is permitted, even though the challenged conduct may be outwardly similar. While reasonableness under the Fourth Amendment is predominantly an objective inquiry, our special needs and administrative search cases demonstrate that purpose is often relevant when suspicionless intrusions pursuant to a general scheme are at issue.

It goes without saying that our holding today does nothing to alter the constitutional status of the sobriety and border checkpoints that we approved in *Sitz* and *Martinez-Fuerte,* or of the type of traffic checkpoint that we suggested would be lawful in *Prouse.* The constitutionality of such checkpoint programs still depends on a balancing of the competing interests at stake and the effectiveness of the program. * * *

Our holding also does not affect the validity of border searches or searches at places like airports and government buildings, where the need for such measures to ensure public safety can be particularly acute. * * * Finally, we caution that the purpose inquiry in this context is to be conducted only at the programmatic level and is not an invitation to probe the minds of individual officers acting at the scene.

Because the primary purpose of the Indianapolis checkpoint program is ultimately indistinguishable from the general interest in crime control, the checkpoints violate the Fourth Amendment. * * *

CHIEF JUSTICE REHNQUIST, with whom JUSTICE THOMAS joins, and with whom JUSTICE SCALIA joins as to Part I, dissenting.

I

* * * This case follows naturally from *Martinez-Fuerte* and *Sitz*. Petitioners acknowledge that the "primary purpose" of these roadblocks is to interdict illegal drugs, but this fact should not be controlling. Even accepting the Court's conclusion that the checkpoints at issue in *Martinez-Fuerte* and *Sitz* were not primarily related to criminal law enforcement the question whether a law enforcement purpose could support a roadblock seizure is not presented in this case. The District Court found that another "purpose of the checkpoints is to check driver's licenses and vehicle registrations," and the written directives state that the police officers are to "[l]ook for signs of impairment." The use of roadblocks to look for signs of impairment was validated by *Sitz*, and the use of roadblocks to check for driver's licenses and vehicle registrations was expressly recognized in *Delaware v. Prouse*. That the roadblocks serve these legitimate state interests cannot be seriously disputed * * *. * * *

Because of the valid reasons for conducting these roadblock seizures, it is constitutionally irrelevant that petitioners also hoped to interdict drugs. * * *

With these checkpoints serving two important state interests, the remaining prongs of the *Brown v. Texas* balancing test are easily met. The seizure is objectively reasonable as it lasts, on average, two to three minutes and does not involve a search. The subjective intrusion is likewise limited as the checkpoints are clearly marked and operated by uniformed officers who are directed to stop every vehicle in the same manner. * * * Finally, the checkpoints' success rate—49 arrests for offenses unrelated to drugs—only confirms the State's legitimate interests in preventing drunken driving and ensuring the proper licensing of drivers and registration of their vehicles.

These stops effectively serve the State's legitimate interests; they are executed in a regularized and neutral manner; and they only minimally intrude upon the privacy of the motorists. They should therefore be constitutional. * * *

NOTES AND QUESTIONS

1. Here is footnote 2 of the majority opinion:

> Because petitioners concede that the primary purpose of the Indianapolis checkpoints is narcotics detection, we need not decide whether the State may establish a checkpoint program with the primary purpose of checking licenses or driver sobriety and a secondary purpose of interdicting narcotics. Specifically, we express no view on the question whether police may expand the scope of a license or sobriety checkpoint seizure in order to detect the presence of drugs in a stopped car.

The footnote resulted in the following tongue-in-cheek observation of Professor Wayne LaFave, posing as David Letterman:

> Now, I'm no Supreme Court justice, nor one of them there high-priced lawyers with the shiny suits and ring on the pinky finger, or even one of those legal pundits that jabber on TV all the time. I'm just a simple late-show host and TV celebrity, but I think I've got about an ounce of common sense, which is all it takes to see that if these drug checkpoints are bad, it shouldn't make any difference what purpose is listed first and what is listed second. And if the Court doesn't make that clear when the time comes, I guarantee that you'll hear about it on this show during our occasional "Stupid Supreme Court Tricks" segment.

Wayne R. LaFave, *The Fourth Amendment as a "Big Time" TV Fad*, 53 Hastings L.J.265, 274 (2001).

2. *How far does Edmond reach?* In Illinois v. Lidster, 540 U.S. 419, 124 S.Ct. 885, 157 L.Ed.2d 843 (2004), local police in Illinois set up a highway checkpoint designed to elicit information from motorists about a fatal hit-and-run accident that had occurred in roughly the same place a week earlier. The blockage resulted in a traffic slow-down, leading to lines of up to fifteen cars in each lane, a delay of a few minutes, and a brief ten-to-fifteen-second conversation with officers. Justice Breyer delivered the opinion of the Court:

> The checkpoint stop here differs significantly from that in *Edmond.* The stop's primary law enforcement purpose was *not* to determine whether

a vehicle's occupants were committing a crime, but to ask vehicle occupants, as members of the public, for their help in providing information about a crime in all likelihood committed by others. The police expected the information elicited to help them apprehend, not the vehicle's occupants, but other individuals.

Edmond's language, as well as its context, makes clear that the constitutionality of this latter, information-seeking kind of stop was not then before the Court. * * * We concede that *Edmond* describes the law enforcement objective there in question as a "general interest in crime control," but it specifies that the phrase "general interest in crime control" does not refer to every "law enforcement" objective. We must read this and related general language in *Edmond* as we often read general language in judicial opinions—as referring in context to circumstances similar to the circumstances then before the Court and not referring to quite different circumstances that the Court was not then considering.

Neither do we believe, *Edmond* aside, that the Fourth Amendment would have us apply an *Edmond*-type rule of automatic unconstitutionality to brief, information-seeking highway stops of the kind now before us. * * * The Fourth Amendment does not treat a motorist's car as his castle. And special law enforcement concerns will sometimes justify highway stops without individualized suspicion. Moreover, unlike *Edmond,* the context here (seeking information from the public) is one in which, by definition, the concept of individualized suspicion has little role to play. Like certain other forms of police activity, say, crowd control or public safety, an information-seeking stop is not the kind of event that involves suspicion, or lack of suspicion, of the relevant individual.

For another thing, information-seeking highway stops are less likely to provoke anxiety or to prove intrusive. The stops are likely brief. The police are not likely to ask questions designed to elicit self-incriminating information. * * *

Finally, we do not believe that an *Edmond*-type rule is needed to prevent an unreasonable proliferation of police checkpoints. Practical considerations—namely, limited police resources and community hostility to related traffic tie-ups—seem likely to inhibit any such proliferation. And, of course, the Fourth Amendment's normal insistence that the stop be reasonable in context will still provide an important legal limitation on police use of this kind of information-seeking checkpoint.

These considerations, taken together, convince us that an *Edmond*-type presumptive rule of unconstitutionality does not apply here. That does not

> mean the stop is automatically, or even presumptively, constitutional. It simply means that we must judge its reasonableness, hence, its constitutionality, on the basis of the individual circumstances.

The Court proceeded to apply *Brown* and determined that the relevant public concern was grave; the checkpoint advanced the grave public concern to a significant degree; and "[m]ost importantly, the stops interfered only minimally with liberty of the sort the Fourth Amendment seeks to protect." Justice Breyer found that, objectively, the seizures were brief and minimal, and even viewed subjectively, "the contact provided little reason for anxiety or alarm," as the police stopped all vehicles systematically and "there is no allegation here that the police acted in a discriminatory or otherwise unlawful manner while questioning motorists during stops."

3. *Drug testing.* Suspicionless drug testing (by means of urinalysis, breathalyzer, or blood) has been upheld by the Supreme Court in various circumstances: drug testing of railroad personnel involved in train accidents, Skinner v. Railway Labor Executives' Association, 489 U.S. 602, 109 S.Ct. 1402, 103 L.Ed.2d 639 (1989); random drug testing of federal customs officers who carry weapons or are involved in drug interdiction, National Treasury Employees Union v. Von Raab, 489 U.S. 656, 109 S.Ct. 1384, 103 L.Ed.2d 685 (1989); and random urine testing of school students involved in athletics, Vernonia School District 47J v. Acton, 515 U.S. 646, 115 S.Ct. 2386, 132 L.Ed.2d 564 (1995), or other extracurricular activities, Board of Education of Independent School District No. 92 of Pottawatomie County v. Earls, 536 U.S. 822, 122 S.Ct. 2559, 153 L.Ed.2d 735 (2002) (policy required all middle and high school students participating in any extracurricular activity to consent to drug testing).

In drug testing cases, the Court considers the "nature and immediacy" of the government's concerns regarding drug use. In some cases, the Court has found a "compelling," "substantial," or "important" governmental or societal need for drug testing that could not be accommodated by application of ordinary probable cause or reasonable suspicion standards. In *Skinner*, evidence was introduced that there was a link between drug and alcohol use by railroad employees and train accidents. In *Von Raab*, there was a felt need to ensure that federal officers involved in handling weapons or investigating drug offenses were themselves free of drugs. In *Vernonia*, the School District had experienced serious academic disruption due to drug use by students, especially student-athletes. In *Pottawatomie County*, the student drug problem was not as severe as in *Vernonia*, but the school district "provided sufficient evidence" of drug use in its schools "to shore up the need for its drug testing program."

Weighed against the interest in random drug testing is the privacy interest of those subjected to the testing. The *Skinner* Court concluded that the bodily intrusion involved in blood testing is minimal; and breath testing is less intrusive still. As for urine testing, however, the justices agreed that the excretory function "traditionally

[is] shielded by great privacy." But, in each of the cases, the testing regulations ensured that the individuals were not observed while they urinated. Also weighing against the privacy interests of the individuals was the fact that, with the employees, their expectation of privacy was "diminished by reason of their participation in an industry * * * regulated pervasively to ensure safety"; and in *Vernonia*, the Court stated that "[c]entral * * * to the present case is the fact that the subjects of the [drug] Policy are (1) children, who (2) have been committed to the temporary custody of the State as schoolmaster."

Not all suspicionless drug testing is allowed. The Fourth Amendment "shields society" from urinalysis drug testing that "diminishes personal privacy [solely] for a symbol's sake." In Chandler v. Miller, 520 U.S. 305, 117 S.Ct. 1295, 137 L.Ed.2d 513 (1997), the Supreme Court ruled, 8–1, that Georgia's requirement that candidates for state office pass a drug test did "not fit within the closely guarded category of constitutionally permissible suspicionless searches." The statute required candidates for state office to submit to urinalysis testing within thirty days prior to qualifying for nomination or election. A candidate who tested positive for illegal drugs could not be placed on the ballot.

The Court found no special need for the testing. First, the law was not passed in response to any suspicion of drug use by state officials. Second, because the test date was no secret, a drug-taking candidate could "abstain for a pretest period sufficient to avoid detection." Thus, the scheme was "not well designed to identify candidates who violate antidrug laws." And, finally, unlike *Skinner* and *Von Raab*, in which it was not feasible to subject employees to day-to-day scrutiny for drugs, "[c]andidates for public office * * * are subject to relentless scrutiny—by their peers, the public, and the press." Consequently, all that was left to the testing regime was "the image the State seeks to protect." "However well-meant," the Court said, "the Fourth Amendment shields society against that state action."

4. *Problem.* A Missouri police department set up a narcotics roadblock, but with a twist. One evening, they put warnings on a highway: "DRUG ENFORCEMENT CHECKPOINT ONE MILE AHEAD" and "POLICE DRUG DOGS WORKING." In fact, however, the checkpoint was set up immediately following the signs, at an exit selected because it did not provide gas or food services. The only lawful purpose for getting off at that exit was to go to a local high school or church (where no events were occurring that evening), or one of several residences.

In this case, the defendant "suddenly veered off onto the off ramp." The police at the checkpoint stopped him (as they did all others who exited at that point). The defendant appeared nervous, had glazed and bloodshot eyes, and smelled of alcohol. The defendant consented to a vehicle search, which turned up large quantities of drugs. Are the drugs admissible in a criminal prosecution? State v. Mack, 66 S.W.3d 706 (Mo.2002).

5. *Problem.* Consider the following New York City anti-terrorist checkpoint program for its subways: Officers are assigned to random-and-changing checkpoints. They are required to select every fifth or tenth person (based on passenger volume) and search the subway rider's belongings. Only belongings large enough to carry an explosive device may be opened, and the inspection is limited to "what is minimally necessary to ensure that [it] * * * does not contain an explosive device." The preferred inspection method involves physical manipulation of the contents by the subway rider or, if necessary, by the officer. The officer is not permitted to request or record a passenger's personal information (*e.g.*, name, address, demographic data). In general, the typical inspection lasts a matter of seconds. This program is conducted in the absence of any specific terrorist threat, and the City cannot provide studies demonstrating that such a program deters terrorists. Constitutional? MacWade v. Kelly, 460 F.3d 260 (2d Cir. 2006).

CHAPTER 6 SUMMARY

The theme of Chapter 5 was that while a warrant was not required in certain specific circumstances, probable cause still often was. In other words, in most cases, *both* probable cause and an established exception to the warrant requirement had to be present for the search under discussion to be reasonable. In this chapter, that is no longer the case. The exceptions discussed here—consent, *Terry* stops, and administrative/special needs searches—require neither a warrant nor the traditional requirement of probable cause.

How can a search without a warrant or probable cause be reasonable? In the case of consent, it is because there is nothing in the Fourth Amendment that prevents law enforcement officers from simply asking if they can conduct a search, and nothing that prevents us from saying yes. Along with searches incident to lawful arrests, consent searches are the most often used by law enforcement. A consent given to search is valid when given voluntarily. There is, however, no requirement that officers inform suspects of their right to say *no* to a search.

The original basis for reasonable suspicion searches—known as *Terry* stops—was that the Court recognized that there may be instances of contact between the police and the public that for safety reasons require split-second decisions on the part of an officer that necessitates an initial intrusion on someone's privacy based on something less than probable cause. Administrative and special needs searches are searches where conduct is heavily regulated and the level of intrusion deemed minor enough that the full protections of the Fourth Amendment do not apply.

The case of *Terry v. Ohio* and its reasonable suspicion standard provided one of the most significant challenges to the hitherto traditional reasonableness analysis under the Fourth Amendment. Although the original justification in *Terry*—that police may conduct a limited pat down for weapons if they have reasonable suspicion that the suspect presents a danger to police or others—seemed to promise a narrow exception to the probable cause regime, its subsequent interpretation and application has generated no end of appellate litigation and scholarly literature. One result of *Terry*, argue some Fourth Amendment scholars, is to diminish the importance of warrants altogether, making the sole inquiry one of reasonableness, which may be far more subjective than we like to admit. Others point to the wide level of discretion the standard leaves to police officers, discretion that raises issues of abuses of discretion based on race or other characteristics that have nothing to do with individualized suspicion. Finally, the *Terry* decision has affected not only searches but seizures as the Court now distinguishes between *Terry*-level seizures requiring only reasonable suspicion and seizures "tantamount" to an arrest which still require probable cause.

Searches under the rubric of administrative or special needs involve searches and seizures conducted by police, and by other public officials, in furtherance of "community caretaking functions" or, more generally, non-law enforcement purposes. Searches that fall under this rubric include such things as automobile inventory searches, housing ordinances, public health and safety inspections (think restaurants or construction sites), border searches, airport security searches, DUI checkpoints, and searches on school premises. Because such searches often do not involve criminal investigations (at least at the beginning), the warrant clause, including the probable cause requirement, does not apply. However, these searches often follow strict written guidelines detailing how and when the searches are to be conducted and how the locations of such searches are selected. For example, DUI checkpoints must use a fixed location, specify ahead of time which cars are to be stopped (every car, every third car, etc.), and cannot be for the purposes of general criminal investigation.

But there is no gainsaying that the Court has come a long way from the pre-*Terry* days when almost all non-consensual searches required probable cause and many required warrants. Whether today's more nuanced Fourth Amendment world is a better one is for each of us to decide.

CHAPTER 7

Remedies for Fourth Amendment Violations

A. STANDING

1. The Starting Point

There are two important Fourth Amendment rules considered in this chapter: the "exclusionary rule" and a doctrine that the Supreme Court used to call (and many lawyers still call) "standing."

As discussed more fully later in this chapter, the exclusionary rule—the rule that evidence obtained in violation of the Fourth Amendment is suppressed at trial—is typically justified on deterrence grounds: The police will be less likely to violate the Fourth Amendment if they know that the fruits of their unconstitutional conduct will be excluded from a criminal trial. Before evidence can be excluded, however, a court must determine whether the person seeking exclusion has the right to bring the Fourth Amendment claim. This is the "standing" requirement.

In this regard consider Alderman v. United States, 394 U.S. 165, 89 S.Ct. 961, 22 L.Ed.2d 176 (1969): Alderman and Aderisio were charged with conspiracy to transmit murderous threats in interstate commerce. They sought, as co-defendants and accused co-conspirators, to have incriminating statements they made excluded because one or both of them were the subject of unlawful governmental electronic surveillance. Justice White, writing for the Court, explained that the issue of exclusion had to be determined on an individual basis—*each* defendant would have to prove that he, *personally*, had "standing" to raise the Fourth Amendment claim. *Alderman* explained the law of standing this way:

> The established principle is that suppression of the product of a Fourth Amendment violation can be successfully urged only by those whose

rights were violated by the search itself, not by those who are aggrieved solely by the introduction of damaging evidence. Coconspirators and codefendants have been accorded no special standing. * * *

The rule is stated in Jones v. United States, 362 U.S. 257, 261, 80 S.Ct. 725, 731, 4 L.Ed.2d 697 (1960):

> "In order to qualify as a 'person aggrieved by an unlawful search and seizure' one must have been a victim of a search or seizure, one against whom the search was directed, as distinguished from one who claims prejudice only through the use of evidence gathered as a consequence of a search or seizure directed at someone else. * * *
>
> "Ordinarily, then, it is entirely proper to require of one who seeks to challenge the legality of a search as the basis for suppressing relevant evidence that he allege, and if the allegation be disputed that he establish, that he himself was the victim of an invasion of privacy." * * *

We adhere to * * * the general rule that Fourth Amendment rights are personal rights which, like some other constitutional rights, may not be vicariously asserted. * * *

The necessity for [proving standing is] * * * not eliminated by recognizing and acknowledging the deterrent aim of the [exclusionary] rule. * * * The deterrent values of preventing the incrimination of those whose rights the police have violated have been considered sufficient to justify the suppression of probative evidence even though the case against the defendant is weakened or destroyed. We adhere to that judgment. But we are not convinced that the additional benefits of extending the exclusionary rule to other defendants would justify further encroachment upon the public interest in prosecuting those accused of crime and having them acquitted or convicted on the basis of all the evidence which exposes the truth.

NOTES AND QUESTIONS

1. The Court ruled in *Alderman* that a person has standing to contest electronic surveillance, and thus is entitled to suppression of unlawfully heard conversations, if: (a) government agents unlawfully overheard that person's conversations, regardless of where they occurred; or (b) if the conversations occurred on that person's premises,

whether or not she was present or participated in the conversations. In what way is a person a "victim" in each of these circumstances?

2. *A procedural matter.* Judges hear Fourth Amendment suppression motions prior to trial. Notice the problem potentially confronting a defendant who seeks to have evidence seized by the police excluded from the trial: In order to raise the Fourth Amendment claim, she must first show that it was *her* Fourth Amendment rights that were violated. To do this, the defendant may need to testify at the suppression hearing and, for example, assert ownership of a briefcase that was searched (and in which contraband was discovered), allegedly without probable cause.

The defendant's testimony that she owned the briefcase may benefit the defendant in the suppression hearing by giving her a right to challenge the police action, but what if she loses on her Fourth Amendment claim? May the prosecutor now use at trial the defendant's inculpatory pretrial admission that it was her briefcase in which contraband was discovered? If so, defendants who need to testify to prove standing may be deterred from raising legitimate Fourth Amendment claims for fear that their testimony will be used against them at trial. To mitigate this problem, the Supreme Court held in Simmons v. United States, 390 U.S. 377, 88 S.Ct. 967, 19 L.Ed.2d 1247 (1968), that "when a defendant testifies in support of a motion to suppress evidence on Fourth Amendment grounds, his testimony may not thereafter be admitted against him at trial on the issue of guilt unless he makes no objection."

Does *Simmons* relieve a defendant of *all* risks from testifying at the suppression hearing?

3. *Can guests challenge a search of someone else's home?* In Minnesota v. Olson, 495 U.S. 91, 110 S.Ct. 1684, 109 L.Ed.2d 85 (1990), the police, without a warrant or consent, entered a residence in which they believed Olson, a robbery-murder suspect, was staying as an overnight guest. The officers searched the residence until they discovered him hiding in a closet. In an opinion written by Justice White, the Court held that Olson had standing to contest the warrantless search:

> To hold that an overnight guest has a legitimate expectation of privacy in his host's home merely recognizes the everyday expectations of privacy that we all share. Staying overnight in another's home is a longstanding social custom that serves functions recognized as valuable by society. We stay in others' homes when we travel to a strange city for business or pleasure, when we visit our parents, children, or more distant relatives out of town, when we are in between jobs or homes, or when we house-sit for a friend. We will all be hosts and we will all be guests many times in our lives. From either perspective, we think that society recognizes that a houseguest has a legitimate expectation of privacy in his host's home.

> From the overnight guest's perspective, he seeks shelter in another's home precisely because it provides him with privacy, a place where he and his possessions will not be disturbed by anyone but his host and those his host allows inside. We are at our most vulnerable when we are asleep because we cannot monitor our own safety or the security of our belongings. It is for this reason that, although we may spend all day in public places, when we cannot sleep in our own home we seek out another private place to sleep, whether it be a hotel room, or the home of a friend. Society expects at least as much privacy in these places as in a telephone booth * * *.
>
> That the guest has a host who has ultimate control of the house is not inconsistent with the guest having a legitimate expectation of privacy. The houseguest is there with the permission of his host, who is willing to share his house and his privacy with his guest. It is unlikely that the guest will be confined to a restricted area of the house; and when the host is away or asleep, the guest will have a measure of control over the premises. The host may admit or exclude from the house as he prefers, but it is unlikely that he will admit someone who wants to see or meet with the guest over the objection of the guest. On the other hand, few houseguests will invite others to visit them while they are guests without consulting their hosts; but the latter, who have the authority to exclude despite the wishes of the guest, will often be accommodating. The point is that hosts will more likely than not respect the privacy interests of their guests, who are entitled to a legitimate expectation of privacy despite the fact that they have no legal interest in the premises and do not have the legal authority to determine who may or may not enter the household. If the untrammeled power to admit and exclude were essential to Fourth Amendment protection, an adult daughter temporarily living in the home of her parents would have no legitimate expectation of privacy because her right to admit or exclude would be subject to her parents' veto.

Chief Justice Rehnquist and Justice Blackmun dissented, but did not write an opinion.

4. *Standing and the Fourth Amendment: one issue or two?* In the now famous case of Rakas v. Illinois, 439 U.S. 128, 99 S.Ct. 421, 58 L.Ed.2d 387 (1978), Justice Rehnquist dispensed with the concept of "standing," as such, in the Fourth Amendment context. Prior to *Rakas*, a defense lawyer would seek to prove that her client had standing to challenge the police action; if that obstacle was overcome, she would raise the merits of the Fourth Amendment claim. Now, *Rakas* teaches, there is just one step: to ask whether the defendant had a legitimate expectation of privacy in the area searched or

the item seized? This tells courts both whether the defendant has standing and whether the Fourth Amendment applies. But, this approach of converting a two-step process into one can result in unintended confusion, as Justice Blackmun has observed:

> In my view, *Rakas v. Illinois* recognized two analytically distinct but "invariably intertwined" issues of substantive Fourth Amendment jurisprudence. The first is "whether [a] disputed search or seizure has infringed an interest of the defendant which the Fourth Amendment was designed to protect"; the second is whether "the challenged search or seizure violated [that] Fourth Amendment righ[t]." The first of these questions is answered by determining whether the defendant has a "legitimate expectation of privacy" that has been invaded by a governmental search or seizure. The second is answered by determining whether applicable cause and warrant requirements have been properly observed.
>
> I agree with the Court that these two inquiries "merge into one," in the sense that both are to be addressed under the principles of Fourth Amendment analysis developed in *Katz v. United States* and its progeny. But I do not read today's decision, or *Rakas*, as holding that it is improper for lower courts to treat these inquiries as distinct components of a Fourth Amendment claim. Indeed, I am convinced that it would invite confusion to hold otherwise. It remains possible for a defendant to prove that his legitimate interest of privacy was invaded, and yet fail to prove that the police acted illegally in doing so. And it is equally possible for a defendant to prove that the police acted illegally, and yet fail to prove that his own privacy interest was affected.

Rawlings v. Kentucky, 448 U.S. 98, 100 S.Ct. 2556, 65 L.Ed.2d 633 (1980).

Can you see why Justice Blackmun might be correct in this regard? If not, you will hopefully see why, after you read the next case.

MINNESOTA V. CARTER

Supreme Court of the United States, 1998.
525 U.S. 83, 119 S.Ct. 469, 142 L.Ed.2d 373.

As noted at the beginning of this chapter, *Alderman* taught us that a person may not successfully assert a Fourth Amendment claim unless she has standing to contest the search, *i.e.*, that she was the victim of the Fourth Amendment violation. What *Alderman* left open was the question of how we determine when someone is a "victim" of an unlawful search. If the

approach taken in *Minnesota v. Carter*, reminds you a lot of *Katz*, you are right. We return here to questions of "legitimate expectation of privacy."

Notice in particular Justice Scalia's concurrence and in it, his criticism of *Katz*. Justice Scalia, as he does in most of his opinions, relies heavily on the precise language of the Amendment—on what the obvious meaning of the provision is—given that language, along with the meaning the Framers would have most likely attached to the Amendment when they wrote it. Justice Scalia, as we have mentioned in previous notes, was an *originalist*, one who believes that the Court can only go by the wording within the "four corners" of the Constitution. Any interpretations beyond that, including those designed to take into account how the world has changed in the past 200-plus years, is the purview of legislative bodies, not judicial ones. See if you can identify how this leads to his criticism of *Katz*. If Justice Scalia has been on the Court at the time of the *Katz* decision, how do you think he would have voted?

CHIEF JUSTICE REHNQUIST delivered the opinion of the Court [joined by JUSTICES O'CONNOR, SCALIA, KENNEDY, and THOMAS].

Respondents and the lessee of an apartment were sitting in one of its rooms, bagging cocaine. While so engaged they were observed by a police officer, who looked through a drawn window blind. The Supreme Court of Minnesota held that the officer's viewing was a search which violated respondents' Fourth Amendment rights. We hold that no such violation occurred.

James Thielen, a police officer in the Twin Cities' suburb of Eagan, Minnesota, went to an apartment building to investigate a tip from a confidential informant. The informant said that he had walked by the window of a ground-floor apartment and had seen people putting a white powder into bags. The officer looked in the same window through a gap in the closed blind and observed the bagging operation for several minutes. He then notified headquarters, which began preparing affidavits for a search warrant while he returned to the apartment building. * * *

* * * A search of the apartment pursuant to a warrant revealed cocaine residue [and plastic baggies] on the kitchen table * * *. Thielen identified Carter, Johns, and Thompson as the three people he had observed placing the powder into baggies. The police later learned that while Thompson was the lessee of the apartment, Carter and Johns lived in Chicago and had come to the apartment for the sole purpose of packaging the cocaine. Carter and Johns had never been to the apartment before and were only in the apartment for approximately 2½ hours.

In return for the use of the apartment, Carter and Johns had given Thompson one-eighth of an ounce of the cocaine.

Carter and Johns * * * moved to suppress all evidence obtained from the apartment * * *. * * * The Minnesota trial court held that since, unlike the defendant in *Minnesota v. Olson* [p. 435, Note 3], Carter and Johns were not overnight social guests but temporary out-of-state visitors, they were not entitled to claim the protection of the Fourth Amendment against the government intrusion into the apartment. The trial court also concluded that Thielen's observation was not a search within the meaning of the Fourth Amendment. After a trial, Carter and Johns were each convicted of * * * [two controlled substance] offenses. * * *

A divided Minnesota Supreme Court reversed, holding that respondents had "standing" to claim the protection of the Fourth Amendment because they had " 'a legitimate expectation of privacy in the invaded place.' " * * * Based upon its conclusion that the respondents had "standing" to raise their Fourth Amendment claims, the court went on to hold that Thielen's observation constituted a search of the apartment under the Fourth Amendment, and that the search was unreasonable. * * *

The Minnesota courts analyzed whether respondents had a legitimate expectation of privacy under the rubric of "standing" doctrine, an analysis which this Court expressly rejected 20 years ago in *Rakas*. * * * Central to our analysis [in *Rakas*] was the idea that in determining whether a defendant is able to show the violation of his (and not someone else's) Fourth Amendment rights, the "definition of those rights is more properly placed within the purview of substantive Fourth Amendment law than within that of standing." Thus, we held that in order to claim the protection of the Fourth Amendment, a defendant must demonstrate that he personally has an expectation of privacy in the place searched, and that his expectation is reasonable * * *. * * *

The text of the Amendment suggests that its protections extend only to people in "their" houses. But we have held that in some circumstances a person may have a legitimate expectation of privacy in the house of someone else. In *Minnesota v. Olson*, for example, we decided that an overnight guest in a house had the sort of expectation of privacy that the Fourth Amendment protects. * * *

Respondents here were obviously not overnight guests, but were essentially present for a business transaction and were only in the home a matter of hours. There is no suggestion that they had a previous relationship with Thompson, or that there was any other purpose to their visit. Nor was there anything similar to the overnight guest relationship in *Olson* to suggest a degree of acceptance into the household. While the apartment was a dwelling place for Thompson, it was for these respondents simply a place to do business.

Property used for commercial purposes is treated differently for Fourth Amendment purposes than residential property. "An expectation of privacy in commercial premises, however, is different from, and indeed less than, a similar expectation in an individual's home." And while it was a "home" in which respondents were present, it was not their home. Similarly, the Court has held that in some circumstances a worker can claim Fourth Amendment protection over his own workplace. See, *e.g.*, *O'Connor v. Ortega*, 480 U.S. 709, 107 S.Ct. 1492, 94 L.Ed.2d 714 (1987). But there is no indication that respondents in this case had nearly as significant a connection to Thompson's apartment as the worker in *O'Connor* had to his own private office.

If we regard the overnight guest in *Minnesota v. Olson* as typifying those who may claim the protection of the Fourth Amendment in the home of another, and one merely "legitimately on the premises" as typifying those who may not do so, the present case is obviously somewhere in between. But the purely commercial nature of the transaction engaged in here, the relatively short period of time on the premises, and the lack of any previous connection between respondents and the householder, all lead us to conclude that respondents' situation is closer to that of one simply permitted on the premises. We therefore hold that any search which may have occurred did not violate their Fourth Amendment rights.

Because we conclude that respondents had no legitimate expectation of privacy in the apartment, we need not decide whether the police officer's observation constituted a "search." The judgment of the Supreme Court of Minnesota is accordingly reversed * * *. * * *

JUSTICE SCALIA, with whom JUSTICE THOMAS joins, concurring.

I join the opinion of the Court because I believe it accurately applies our recent case law, including *Minnesota v. Olson*. I write separately to express my view that that case law * * * gives short shrift to the text of the Fourth Amendment, and to the well and long understood meaning of that text. Specifically, it leaps to apply the fuzzy standard of "legitimate expectation of privacy"—a consideration that is often relevant to whether a search or seizure covered by the Fourth Amendment is "unreasonable"—to the threshold question whether a search or seizure covered by the Fourth Amendment *has occurred.* If that latter question is addressed first and analyzed under the text of the Constitution as traditionally understood, the present case is not remotely difficult.

The Fourth Amendment protects "[t]he right of the people to be secure *in their* persons, houses, papers, and effects, against unreasonable searches and seizures * * *." It must be acknowledged that the phrase "their * * * houses" in this provision is, in isolation, ambiguous. It could mean "their respective houses," so that the protection extends to each person only in his *own* house. But it could also mean "their respective and each other's houses," so that each person would be protected even when visiting the house of someone else. As today's opinion for the Court suggests, however, it is not linguistically possible to give the provision the latter, expansive interpretation with respect to "houses" without giving it the same interpretation with respect to the nouns that are parallel to "houses"—"persons, * * * papers, and effects"—which would give me a constitutional right not to have your person unreasonably searched. This is so absurd that it has to my knowledge never been contemplated. The obvious meaning of the provision is that *each* person has the right to be secure against unreasonable searches and seizures in *his own* person, house, papers, and effects. * * *

That "their * * * houses" was understood to mean "their respective houses" would have been clear to anyone who knew the English and early American law of arrest and trespass that underlay the Fourth Amendment. The people's protection against unreasonable search and seizure in their "houses" was drawn from the English common-law maxim, "A man's home is *his* castle." As far back as *Semayne's Case* of 1604, the leading English case for that proposition * * *, the King's Bench proclaimed that "the house of any one is not a castle or privilege but for himself, and shall not extend to protect any person who flies to his house." * * *

Of course this is not to say that the Fourth Amendment protects only the Lord of the Manor who holds his estate in fee simple. People call a house "their" home when legal title is in the bank, when they rent it, and even when they merely occupy it rent-free—*so long as they actually live there.* * * *

Thus, in deciding the question presented today we write upon a slate that is far from clean. The text of the Fourth Amendment, the common-law background against which it was adopted, and the understandings consistently displayed after its adoption make the answer clear. * * * We went to the absolute limit of what text and tradition permit in *Minnesota v. Olson*, when we protected a mere overnight guest against an unreasonable search of his hosts' apartment. But whereas it is plausible to regard a person's overnight lodging as at least his "temporary" residence, it is entirely impossible to give that characterization to an apartment that he uses to package cocaine. Respondents here were not searched in "their

* * * hous[e]" under any interpretation of the phrase that bears the remotest relationship to the well understood meaning of the Fourth Amendment.

The dissent believes that "[o]ur obligation to produce coherent results" requires that we ignore this clear text and four-century-old tradition, and apply instead the notoriously unhelpful test adopted in a "benchmar[k]" decision that is 31 years old[,] citing *Katz v. United States*. In my view, the only thing the past three decades have established about the *Katz* test (which has come to mean the test enunciated by Justice Harlan's separate concurrence in *Katz*) is that, unsurprisingly, those "actual (subjective) expectation[s] of privacy" "that society is prepared to recognize as 'reasonable,' " bear an uncanny resemblance to those expectations of privacy that this Court considers reasonable. When that self-indulgent test is employed (as the dissent would employ it here) to determine whether a "search or seizure" within the meaning of the Constitution has *occurred* (as opposed to whether that "search or seizure" is an "unreasonable" one), it has no plausible foundation in the text of the Fourth Amendment. That provision did not guarantee some generalized "right of privacy" and leave it to this Court to determine which particular manifestations of the value of privacy "society is prepared to recognize as 'reasonable.' " Rather, it enumerated ("persons, houses, papers, and effects") the objects of privacy protection to which the *Constitution* would extend, leaving further expansion to the good judgment, not of this Court, but of the people through their representatives in the legislature.

The dissent may be correct that a person invited into someone else's house to engage in a common business (even common monkey-business, so to speak) *ought* to be protected against government searches of the room in which that business is conducted; and that persons invited in to deliver milk or pizza (whom the dissent dismisses as "classroom hypotheticals," as opposed, presumably, to flesh-and-blood hypotheticals) ought *not* to be protected against government searches of the rooms that they occupy. I am not sure of the answer to those policy questions. But I am sure that the answer is not remotely contained in the Constitution, which means that it is left—as *many*, indeed *most*, important questions are left—to the judgment of state and federal legislators. We go beyond our proper role as judges in a democratic society when we restrict the people's power to govern themselves over the full range of policy choices that the Constitution has left available to them.

[JUSTICE KENNEDY's concurring opinion is omitted.]

[JUSTICE BREYER concurred in the judgment. He agreed with JUSTICE GINSBURG that Carter had a Fourth Amendment interest in the apartment but he would have held that there was no search—i.e., that the police officer viewing the interior of the apartment through a "gap

in the closed blind" did not invade Carter's legitimate expectation of privacy. BREYER*'s opinion justifies the concern raised earlier that it is potentially confusing to collapse standing into the substantive Fourth Amendment issue.* BREYER *is the only justice who separated the question of whether Carter can litigate the Fourth Amendment issue, what the Court once called standing (yes), from the question whether the Fourth Amendment itself was violated by the police action (no).*]

JUSTICE GINSBURG, with whom JUSTICE STEVENS and JUSTICE SOUTER join, dissenting.

The Court's decision undermines not only the security of short-term guests, but also the security of the home resident herself. In my view, when a homeowner or lessor personally invites a guest into her home to share in a common endeavor, whether it be for conversation, to engage in leisure activities, or for business purposes licit or illicit, that guest should share his host's shelter against unreasonable searches and seizures.

* * * First, the disposition I would reach in this case responds to the unique importance of the home—the most essential bastion of privacy recognized by the law. Second, even within the home itself, the position to which I would adhere would not permit "a casual visitor who has never seen, or been permitted to visit, the basement of another's house to object to a search of the basement if the visitor happened to be in the kitchen of the house at the time of the search." *Rakas*. Further, I would here decide only the case of the homeowner who chooses to share the privacy of her home and her company with a guest, and would not reach classroom hypotheticals like the milkman or pizza deliverer.

My concern centers on an individual's choice to share her home and her associations there with persons she selects. Our decisions indicate that people have a reasonable expectation of privacy in their homes in part because they have the prerogative to exclude others. The power to exclude implies the power to include. Our Fourth Amendment decisions should reflect these complementary prerogatives. * * *

Through the host's invitation, the guest gains a reasonable expectation of privacy in the home. *Minnesota v. Olson* so held with respect to an overnight guest. The logic of that decision extends to shorter term guests as well. * * * One need not remain overnight to anticipate privacy in another's home * * *. In sum, when a homeowner chooses to share the privacy of her home and her company with a short-term guest, the twofold requirement "emerg[ing] from prior decisions" has been satisfied: Both host and guest "have exhibited an actual (subjective) expectation of privacy"; that "expectation [is] one [our] society is prepared to recognize as 'reasonable.' " *Katz v. United States.*

As the Solicitor General acknowledged, the illegality of the host-guest conduct, the fact that they were partners in crime, would not alter the analysis. * * * Indeed, it must be this way. If the illegality of the activity made constitutional an otherwise unconstitutional search, such Fourth Amendment protection, reserved for the innocent only, would have little force in regulating police behavior toward either the innocent or the guilty.

Our leading decision in *Katz* is key to my view of this case. * * * We were mindful that "the Fourth Amendment protects people, not places," and held that this electronic monitoring of a business call "violated the privacy upon which [the caller] justifiably relied while using the telephone booth." Our obligation to produce coherent results in this often visited area of the law requires us to inform our current expositions by benchmarks already established. * * * The Court's decision in this case veers sharply from the path marked in *Katz*. I do not agree that we have a more reasonable expectation of privacy when we place a business call to a person's home from a public telephone booth on the side of the street, than when we actually enter that person's premises to engage in a common endeavor.

* * *

NOTES AND QUESTIONS

1. *Problem. S*, who was wanted by federal authorities in connection with a drug conspiracy and murder, drove all night from Michigan to Georgia. He arrived in the morning and promptly entered an apartment he had sublet from *L*, the leaseholder, for $2000. He went to sleep. Six hours later, the police entered, arrested *S*, and searched the premises, resulting in the seizure of evidence. United States v. Stuckey, 325 F.Supp.2d 793 (E.D. Mich. 2004). Standing?

2. In *Rakas v. Illinois* (p. 436, Note 4), the Court repeatedly observed that the petitioners in that case had not claimed ownership of the property seized. The implication seemed to be that if a person owns seized property, she has standing to contest the search resulting in its seizure. That implication, however, has proved false. In Rawlings v. Kentucky, 448 U.S. 98, 100 S.Ct. 2556, 65 L.Ed.2d 633 (1980), the Court ruled that the test enunciated in *Rakas*—whether the petitioner had a reasonable expectation of privacy in the area searched—is the exclusive test for determining whether a defendant may successfully challenge a search.

In *Rawlings*, the police, armed with a warrant to arrest *X*, entered a residence occupied by five persons. While unsuccessfully searching for *X*, the police smelled burnt marijuana and observed some marijuana seeds on the mantel in one bedroom. While two officers left to obtain a search warrant, other officers detained the occupants of the house, allowing them to leave only if they consented to a body search. Two of the occupants consented to a search and left.

Less than an hour later, the two officers returned with a search warrant. One of them walked over to Cox, a female sitting on the couch, and ordered her to empty the contents of her purse, which she did. Among the contents was a jar containing 1,800 tablets of LSD. At that point, Cox turned to Rawlings, a male who had been sitting next to her, and told him "to take what was his." He claimed ownership of the controlled substances. The trial court determined that Rawlings had known Cox for a few days and had recently slept on her couch at least twice, and—although there was a factual dispute on the matter—Rawlings had dumped the drugs in Cox's purse, with her knowledge, on the afternoon of the search.

The Court agreed with the lower court that Rawlings had not made a sufficient showing that his legitimate expectation of privacy was violated by the search of Cox's purse:

> We believe that the record in this case supports that conclusion. Petitioner, of course, bears the burden of proving not only that the search of Cox's purse was illegal, but also that he had a legitimate expectation of privacy in that purse. At the time petitioner dumped thousands of dollars' worth of illegal drugs into Cox's purse, he had known her for only a few days. According to Cox's uncontested testimony, petitioner had never sought or received access to her purse prior to that sudden bailment. Nor did petitioner have any right to exclude other persons from access to Cox's purse. In fact, Cox testified that Bob Stallons, a longtime acquaintance and frequent companion of Cox's, had free access to her purse and on the very morning of the arrest had rummaged through its contents in search of a hairbrush. Moreover, even assuming that petitioner's version of the bailment is correct and that Cox did consent to the transfer of possession, the precipitous nature of the transaction hardly supports a reasonable inference that petitioner took normal precautions to maintain his privacy. * * *
>
> Petitioner contends nevertheless that, because he claimed ownership of the drugs in Cox's purse, he should be entitled to challenge the search regardless of his expectation of privacy. We disagree. While petitioner's ownership of the drugs is undoubtedly one fact to be considered in this case, *Rakas* emphatically rejected the notion that "arcane" concepts of

property law ought to control the ability to claim the protections of the Fourth Amendment.

Are you persuaded by the Court's reasoning?

3. *Variations on Rawlings.* Assume the following variations on the facts in *Rawlings*. Would Rawlings have standing to challenge the police conduct in these circumstances?

A. When Cox emptied her purse as ordered, a police officer observed the drug vial, picked it up, but was unable to determine what was in it. He removed the lid and inspected the contents. Based on his observations, he concluded that the vial contained controlled substances and, therefore, seized it.

B. When Cox emptied her purse, the officer discovered a sealed envelope belonging to Rawlings. Based on a hunch that the envelope contained illegal drugs, the officer seized the envelope and, four days later, subjected it to a dog sniff, which confirmed his hunch. The officer then opened the envelope and seized the drugs inside.

B. EXCLUSIONARY RULE

The thrust of *Mapp v. Ohio* (Chapter 2, is straight-forward: when the police violate a defendant's Fourth Amendment rights—whether the violation is intentional, reckless, negligent, or even innocent—the evidence obtained in violation of the amendment may not be used at *that* defendant's (don't forget the standing requirement!) criminal trial in the case-in-chief. We will see later, however, that this bright-line approach no longer applies. For now, however, let's look at the exclusionary rule in its robust form and consider the scope of the exclusionary rule when it does apply.

1. The Rule Is Recognized

MAPP V. OHIO

Supreme Court of the United States, 1961.
367 U.S. 643, 81 S.Ct. 1684, 6 L.Ed.2d 1081.

[See p. 58 for the text of the case.]

NOTES AND QUESTIONS

1. Go back carefully over the language in *Mapp* regarding the purpose of the exclusionary rule. According to *Mapp*, is the exclusionary rule constitutionally

required? Look carefully at the language in Justice Clark's majority opinion and Justice Harlan's dissent for clues.

2. *United States v. Calandra and the constitutionality of the exclusionary rule.* The Supreme Court held in United States v. Calandra, 414 U.S. 338, 94 S.Ct. 613, 38 L.Ed.2d 561 (1974), that the Fourth Amendment exclusionary rule does not apply in grand jury proceedings. The Court's reasoning is significant well beyond grand juries:

> [T]he [exclusionary] rule is a judicially created remedy designed to safeguard Fourth Amendment rights generally through its deterrent effect, rather than a personal constitutional right of the party aggrieved.
>
> Despite its broad deterrent purpose, the exclusionary rule has never been interpreted to proscribe the use of illegally seized evidence in all proceedings or against all persons. As with any remedial device, the application of the rule has been restricted to those areas where its remedial objectives are thought most efficaciously served. * * *
>
> Any incremental deterrent effect which might be achieved by extending the rule to grand jury proceedings is uncertain at best. Whatever deterrence of police misconduct may result from the exclusion of illegally seized evidence from criminal trials, it is unrealistic to assume that application of the rule to grand jury proceedings would significantly further that goal. Such an extension would deter only police investigation consciously directed toward the discovery of evidence solely for use in a grand jury investigation. The incentive to disregard the requirement of the Fourth Amendment solely to obtain an indictment from a grand jury is substantially negated by the inadmissibility of the illegally seized evidence in a subsequent criminal prosecution of the search victim. * * * We therefore decline to embrace a view that would achieve a speculative and undoubtedly minimal advance in the deterrence of police misconduct at the expense of substantially impeding the role of the grand jury.

What is the significance of the Court's statement that "the rule is a judicially created remedy * * *, rather than a personal constitutional right of the party aggrieved"? What are the implications of this assertion?

3. *The "judicial integrity" rationale of the exclusionary rule.* As seen in the last Note, the Court in *United States v. Calandra* weighed the purported costs of the exclusionary rule against the incremental deterrent benefits of invoking the rule in grand jury proceedings. As the dissenters pointed out there, however, the majority did *not* consider a second rationale for the exclusionary doctrine mentioned in *Mapp*:

> For the first time, the Court today discounts to the point of extinction the vital function of the rule to insure that the judiciary avoid even the slightest

> appearance of sanctioning illegal government conduct. This rejection of "the imperative of judicial integrity," openly invites "[t]he conviction that all government is staffed by * * * hypocrites[, a conviction] easy to instill and difficult to erase." When judges appear to become "accomplices in the willful disobedience of a Constitution they are sworn to uphold," we imperil the very foundation of our people's trust in their Government on which our democracy rests.

Why might "extinction" of the judicial integrity rationale undermine the position of advocates of the exclusionary rule? Think about how a defendant might show incremental deterrence from the application of the exclusionary rule beyond the criminal trial itself.

4. As the Court has observed, even "[i]n the complex and turbulent history of the [exclusionary] rule, the Court never has applied it to exclude evidence from a civil proceeding, federal or state." United States v. Janis, 428 U.S. 433, 96 S.Ct. 3021, 49 L.Ed.2d 1046 (1976). According to *Janis*, the deterrence benefit of extending the exclusionary rule to non-criminal proceedings (*e.g.*, civil suits, deportation or disbarment proceedings, etc.) would be comparatively slight, whereas the social costs of exclusion would be severe.

Moreover, as we have already seen in the context of grand juries (Note 2), the exclusionary rule does not apply in all criminal proceedings. For example, courts have also allowed the introduction of unconstitutionally seized evidence at pre-trial preliminary hearings, after the guilt phase of a trial during sentencing, and at probation and parole revocation hearings.

And, for a long time, there has been one circumstance in which the exclusionary rule does not apply during the guilt phase of criminal trials: a prosecutor may impeach a defendant's testimony by introducing evidence previously excluded on Fourth Amendment grounds. For example, in Walder v. United States, 347 U.S. 62, 74 S.Ct. 354, 98 L.Ed. 503 (1954), the Supreme Court held that a defendant may not take advantage of a court's exclusion of narcotics found in his possession by testifying in direct examination that he has never possessed narcotics. In such circumstances, as Justice Frankfurter wrote for the Court:

> It is one thing to say that the Government cannot make an affirmative use of evidence unlawfully obtained. It is quite another to say that the defendant can turn the illegal method by which evidence in the Government's possession was obtained to his own advantage, and provide himself with a shield against contradiction of his untruths. Such an extension of the [exclusionary] doctrine would be a perversion of the Fourth Amendment.

5. In Silverthorne Lumber Company v. United States, 251 U.S. 385, 40 S.Ct. 182, 64 L.Ed. 319 (1920), the great Justice Holmes wrote: "The essence of a provision forbidding the acquisition of evidence in a certain way is that not merely evidence so acquired shall not be used before the Court *but that it shall not be used at all*"? What is he getting at by the words we have italicized? Walder v. United States, 347 U.S. 62, 74 S.Ct. 354, 98 L.Ed. 503 (1954) explained its meaning this way:

> The Government cannot violate the Fourth Amendment * * * and use the fruits of such unlawful conduct to secure a conviction. *Nor can the Government make indirect use of such evidence for its case, or support a conviction on evidence obtained through leads from the unlawfully obtained evidence.* All these methods are outlawed, and convictions obtained by means of them are invalidated, because they encourage the kind of society that is obnoxious to free men. (Emphasis added.)

In other words, if the police seize item A in violation of the Fourth Amendment, they also are barred from introducing item B at Citizen's criminal trial if B was obtained as a result of the unconstitutional seizure of item A. In this example, B is what lawyers call "a fruit of a poisonous tree." But, read on.

6. *"Independent source" doctrine.* The fruit-of-the-poisonous-tree doctrine is not as simple and straightforward as just stated. Notice what Justice Holmes wrote immediately after the words quoted in Note 5: "Of course, this does not mean that the facts thus obtained become sacred and inaccessible. If knowledge of them is gained from an independent source they may be proved like any others * * *."

In other words, perhaps there *is* a poisonous tree (a Fourth Amendment violation), but we must consider the possibility that a particular "fruit" comes from a different, *un*poisoned tree. This is an expression of the so-called "independent source" doctrine. It and the related "inevitable discovery" (or "hypothetical independent source") rule are considered in subsection b. below.

7. *"Attenuation" or "dissipation of taint" doctrine.* Even if particular evidence *is* a fruit of the poisonous tree, it may still be admissible, notwithstanding the sweeping italicized language in *Silverthorne* (Note 5). As Justice Frankfurter explained in Nardone v. United States, 308 U.S. 338, 60 S.Ct. 266, 84 L.Ed. 307 (1939), "[s]ophisticated argument may prove a causal connection between information obtained through illicit [police conduct] and the Government's proof. As a matter of good sense, however, such connection may have become so attenuated as to dissipate the taint." At some point, in other words, the law stops looking backwards in time and essentially says, "enough is enough, we are prepared to eat this fruit," i.e., to allow use of the secondary evidence at trial even if it is causally linked to a previous Fourth Amendment violation. This attenuation factor in considered below.

8. *Yet another checklist.* Given one of your author's fondness for checklists, here is another one.

In analyzing any fruit-of-the-poisonous-tree case, study the facts carefully to:

1. identify the "tree" (the constitutional violation);
2. identify the fruit (the evidence the government seeks to introduce);
3. determine whether the fruit comes from the tree (is there a causal link?); and,
4. if the fruit *did* come from a poisonous tree, identify any facts that may justify the conclusion that the fruit no longer is poisoned (the "attenuation" or "dissipation" doctrine).

2. "Independent Source" and "Inevitable Discovery" Doctrines

MURRAY V. UNITED STATES

Supreme Court of the United States, 1988.
487 U.S. 533, 108 S.Ct. 2529, 101 L.Ed.2d 472.

When reading *Murray v. United States*, take a close look at Justice Marshall's dissent. It is another good example of the Justice's famous distrust of the power of the state and the exercise of what was considered normal police practice at the time.

The case in Note 5 is one we will see again in Chapter 8 as *Brewer v. Williams*. This is a very famous case, not the least because of the tragic facts involved. When you read *Brewer*, you will see some very stirring language about the difficult need to follow the rules even in the most emotional of cases; a good reminder that all these opinions we read have very human consequences.

JUSTICE SCALIA delivered the opinion of the Court [joined by CHIEF JUSTICE REHNQUIST, and JUSTICES WHITE and BLACKMUN].

I

* * * [T]he facts are as follows: Based on information received from informants, federal law enforcement agents had been surveilling petitioner Murray and several of his co-conspirators. At about 1:45 p.m. on April 6, 1983, they observed Murray drive a truck and Carter drive a green camper, into a warehouse in South Boston. When the petitioners drove the vehicles out about 20 minutes later, the surveilling agents saw within the warehouse two individuals and a tractor-trailer rig bearing a long, dark container. Murray and [petitioner] Carter later

turned over the truck and camper to other drivers, who were in turn followed and ultimately arrested, and the vehicles lawfully seized. Both vehicles were found to contain marijuana.

After receiving this information, several of the agents converged on the South Boston warehouse and forced entry. They found the warehouse unoccupied, but observed in plain view numerous burlap-wrapped bales that were later found to contain marijuana. They left without disturbing the bales, kept the warehouse under surveillance, and did not reenter it until they had a search warrant. In applying for the warrant, the agents did not mention the prior entry, and did not rely on any observations made during that entry. When the warrant was issued—at 10:40 p.m., approximately eight hours after the initial entry—the agents immediately reentered the warehouse and seized 270 bales of marijuana and notebooks listing customers for whom the bales were destined.

Before trial, petitioners moved to suppress the evidence found in the warehouse. The District Court denied the motion, rejecting petitioners' arguments that the warrant was invalid because the agents did not inform the Magistrate about their prior warrantless entry, and that the warrant was tainted by that entry. The First Circuit affirmed, assuming for purposes of its decision that the first entry into the warehouse was unlawful. * * *

II * * *

Almost simultaneously with our development of the exclusionary rule, in the first quarter of this century, we also announced what has come to be known as the "independent source" doctrine. * * * The dispute here is over the scope of this doctrine. Petitioners contend that it applies only to evidence obtained for the first time during an independent lawful search. The Government argues that it applies also to evidence initially discovered during, or as a consequence of, an unlawful search, but later obtained independently from activities untainted by the initial illegality. We think the Government's view has better support in both precedent and policy. * * *

Petitioners' asserted policy basis for excluding evidence which is initially discovered during an illegal search, but is subsequently acquired through an independent and lawful source, is that a contrary rule will remove all deterrence to, and indeed positively encourage, unlawful police searches. As petitioners see the incentives, law enforcement officers will routinely enter without a warrant to make sure that what they expect to be on the premises is in fact there. If it is not, they will have spared themselves the time and trouble of getting a warrant; if it is, they can get the warrant and use the evidence despite the unlawful entry. We see the incentives differently. An officer with probable cause sufficient to obtain a search warrant would be foolish to enter the premises first in an unlawful manner. By doing so, he would risk suppression of all evidence on the premises, both seen and unseen, since his action would add to the normal burden of convincing a magistrate that there is probable cause the much more onerous burden of convincing a trial court that no information gained from the illegal entry affected either the law enforcement officers' decision to seek a warrant or the magistrate's decision to grant it. Nor would the officer *without* sufficient probable cause to obtain a search warrant have any added incentive to conduct an unlawful entry, since whatever he finds cannot be used to establish probable cause before a magistrate. * * *

III

To apply what we have said to the present cases: Knowledge that the marijuana was in the warehouse was assuredly acquired at the time of the unlawful entry. But it was also acquired at the time of entry pursuant to the warrant, and if that later acquisition was not the result of the earlier entry there is no reason why the independent source doctrine should not apply. Invoking the exclusionary rule would put the police (and society) not in the *same* position they would have occupied if no violation occurred, but in a *worse* one.

We think this is also true with respect to the tangible evidence, the bales of marijuana. * * * So long as a later, lawful seizure is genuinely independent of an earlier, tainted one (which may well be difficult to establish where the seized goods are kept in the police's possession) there is no reason why the independent source doctrine should not apply.

The ultimate question, therefore, is whether the search pursuant to warrant was in fact a genuinely independent source of the information and tangible evidence at issue here. This would not have been the case if the agents' decision to seek the warrant was prompted by what they had seen during the initial entry or if information obtained during that entry was presented to the Magistrate and affected his decision to issue the warrant. [The District Court, however, did not explicitly determine whether the agents would have sought the warrant even if they had not illegally entered the warehouse.] * * *

Accordingly, we vacate the judgment and remand these cases to the Court of Appeals with instructions that it remand to the District Court for determination whether the warrant-authorized search of the warehouse was an independent source of the challenged evidence in the sense we have described. * * *

[JUSTICE BRENNAN and JUSTICE KENNEDY took no part in the consideration or decision of these cases.]

JUSTICE MARSHALL, with whom JUSTICE STEVENS and JUSTICE O'CONNOR join, dissenting. * * *

* * * In holding that the independent source exception may apply to the facts of these cases, I believe the Court loses sight of the practical moorings of the independent source exception and creates an affirmative incentive for unconstitutional searches. * * *

Under the circumstances of these cases, the admission of the evidence "reseized" during the second search severely undermines the deterrence function of the exclusionary rule. Indeed, admission in these cases affirmatively encourages illegal searches. The incentives for such illegal conduct are clear. Obtaining a warrant is inconvenient and time consuming. Even when officers have probable cause to support a warrant application, therefore, they have an incentive first to determine whether it is worthwhile to obtain a warrant. Probable cause is much less than certainty, and many "confirmatory" searches will result in the discovery that no evidence is present, thus saving the police the time and trouble of getting a warrant. If contraband is discovered, however, the officers may later seek a warrant to shield the evidence from the taint of the illegal search. The police thus know in advance that they have little to lose and much to gain by forgoing the bother of obtaining a warrant and undertaking an illegal search.

The Court, however, "see[s] the incentives differently." Under the Court's view, today's decision does not provide an incentive for unlawful searches, because the officer undertaking the search would know that "his action would add to the normal burden of convincing a magistrate that there is probable cause the much more onerous burden of convincing a trial court that no information gained from the illegal entry affected either the law enforcement officers' decision to seek a warrant or the magistrate's decision to grant it." The Court, however, provides no hint of why this risk would actually seem significant to the officers. Under the circumstances of these cases, the officers committing the illegal search have both knowledge and control of the factors central to the trial court's determination. First, it is a simple matter, as was done in these cases, to exclude from the warrant application any information gained from the initial entry so that the magistrate's determination of probable cause is not influenced by the prior illegal search. Second, today's decision makes the application of the independent source exception turn entirely on an evaluation of the officers' intent. It normally will be difficult for the trial court to verify, or the defendant to rebut, an assertion by officers that they always intended to obtain a warrant, regardless of the results of the illegal search. The testimony of the officers conducting the illegal search is the only direct evidence of intent, and the defendant will be relegated simply to arguing that the officers should not be believed. Under these circumstances, the litigation risk described by the Court seems hardly a risk at all; it does not significantly dampen the incentive to conduct the initial illegal search. * * *

* * * In the instant cases, there are no "demonstrated historical facts" capable of supporting a finding that the subsequent warrant search was wholly unaffected by the prior illegal search. The same team of investigators was involved in both searches. The warrant was obtained immediately after the illegal search, and no effort was made to obtain a warrant prior to the discovery of the marijuana during the illegal search. The only evidence available that the warrant search was wholly independent is the testimony of the agents who conducted the illegal search. Under these circumstances, the threat that the subsequent search was tainted by the illegal search is too great to allow for the application of the independent source exception. The Court's contrary holding lends itself to easy abuse, and offers an incentive to bypass the constitutional requirement that probable cause be assessed by a neutral and detached magistrate before the police invade an individual's privacy. * * *

In sum, under circumstances as are presented in these cases, when the very law enforcement officers who participate in an illegal search immediately thereafter obtain a warrant to search the same premises, I believe the evidence discovered during the initial illegal entry must be suppressed. Any other result emasculates the Warrant Clause and provides an intolerable incentive for warrantless searches. * * *

[*The dissenting opinion of JUSTICE STEVENS is omitted.*]

NOTES AND QUESTIONS

1. Notice that only three justices joined Scalia's opinion announcing the Court's judgment. But because Justices Brennan and Kennedy did not participate in the case, four justices is a majority and Scalia's is thus a majority opinion.

2. In *Murray*, the failure of the police to inform the magistrate of their unlawful confirmatory search strengthened their Fourth Amendment claim by avoiding possible taint in the warrant process. But, should an officer have a duty of candor that is violated by such non-disclosure when he seeks a warrant?

3. In *Murray*, suppose that a police officer had testified at the suppression hearing, "We were sure we had probable cause, so we planned on getting a warrant, but we were kinda worried that the defendants were going to come back and destroy

the evidence. So, we went in, just in case, and then, when we saw we were wrong about the emergency, we went for the warrant. But, sure, if we had found nothing in the warehouse, we would not have applied for a warrant. Why would we have?" According to Justice Scalia, based on this testimony, would the independent source doctrine apply? Should it?

4. Consider Craig M. Bradley, *Murray v. United States: The Bell Tolls for the Search Warrant Requirement*, 64 Ind. L.J. 907, 915–18 (1989):

> While *Murray* will encourage the police to find evidence without a warrant, the most serious problem caused by the decision affects the innocent rather than the guilty. The purpose of the warrant requirement is not to slow the police down in their pursuit of the guilty, but to require that the decision of a "neutral and detached magistrate" is interposed between the police's impulse to search and their action on that impulse.
>
> * * * When * * * [non-exigent] warrantless searches are allowed to occur without any exclusionary sanction attaching, as in *Murray*, it greatly increases the chance that the police will search the innocent.
>
> Consider the position of the rational police officer. Assume that it is true, as the Court avers, that if he has ample probable cause and ample time, he will go ahead and get a warrant in order to avoid the additional explanations that a warrantless search will entail. But suppose, as is frequently the case, that his probable cause is shaky or nonexistent. *Murray* positively encourages him to proceed with an illegal search. If he finds nothing, he simply shrugs his shoulders and walks away. If he finds evidence, he leaves his partner to watch over it, repairs to the magistrate, and reports that "an anonymous reliable informant who has given information on three occasions in the past that has led to convictions called to tell me that he had just seen bales of marijuana stored at a warehouse at 123 Elm Street." The warrant issues and the marijuana is seized. Before trial (assuming that the defense has found out about the illegal search), the officer admits it, chalks it up to a fear that the evidence would be lost if the warehouse were not immediately secured, apologizes for being wrong in this assessment, and introduces the warrant affidavit to demonstrate an independent source. The Court, in allowing such behavior, has missed the point of the warrant requirement and the exclusionary rule—that it "reduce[s] the Fourth Amendment to a nullity" to allow warrantless searches to go unpunished. * * *
>
> Of course, it has always been the case that the police could make up the existence of "Old Reliable," the informant, and use his fictitious "tip" as the basis for a search warrant. The problem with this tactic is that, if the

police are wrong and no evidence is found, they are forced to return to the magistrate empty-handed. This is embarrassing to the police department and would only have to happen a few times before the magistrates and defense attorneys would realize that the police were liars. After *Murray*, there is no such fear, because the fictitious "Old Reliable" will *always be right*! His "tip" will always lead to evidence because the police will have found it in advance.

5. *Inevitable discovery doctrine.* In Nix v. Williams, 467 U.S. 431, 104 S.Ct. 2501, 81 L.Ed.2d 377 (1984), Williams was arraigned for the abduction of Pamela Powers, a 10-year-old girl who disappeared from a YMCA building in Des Moines, Iowa, where she had accompanied her parents to observe a sporting event. While in custody, the police subjected Williams to a so-called "Christian Burial Speech" that motivated him to lead authorities to the victim's body, so that she could receive a "Christian burial." At the time, a search for her body was underway and one search team was within two-and-a-half miles of the victim, but the search effort was called off when Williams agreed to cooperate. Williams was convicted of first-degree murder, in part based on his incriminating statements to the police while leading them to the body.

Williams appealed his conviction. As examined in *Brewer v. Williams* (Chapter 8), the Supreme Court overturned the conviction because the police violated Williams's Sixth Amendment right to counsel when they engaged in the Christian Burial Speech. Consequently, at Williams's second trial, the State was not permitted to introduce the defendant's statements to the police, nor did they seek to show that Williams led the police to the body, but they presented evidence of the condition of the victim's body when it was found, as well as articles and photographs of her clothing, and the results of post mortem medical and chemical tests on the body, all of which were concededly a fruit of the poisonous Sixth Amendment tree.

Because the State could not show that they found the body independently, the independent-source doctrine was unavailable. Instead, the prosecution reasoned that, if the search had *not* been suspended and Williams had *not* led the police to the victim, her body would inevitably have been discovered in essentially the same condition within a short time. Therefore, the State argued, the contested evidence should be admissible.

The Supreme Court unanimously agreed that the fruit-of-the-poisonous-tree doctrine (here, the Sixth Amendment version, but similarly pursuant to the Fourth Amendment) is subject to an "inevitable discovery" rule. As the Court put the rule: "If the prosecution can establish * * * that the information ultimately or inevitably would have been discovered by lawful means—here the volunteers' search—then the deterrence rationale has so little basis that the evidence should be received." If it were otherwise, the Court concluded, the Government would be put in a worse position than if no illegality had transpired.

3. "Attenuation" (or "Dissipation of Taint") Doctrine

WONG SUN V. UNITED STATES

Supreme Court of the United States, 1963.
371 U.S. 471, 83 S.Ct. 407, 9 L.Ed.2d 441.

In Note 7 on p. 449 we introduced the "attenuation" or "dissipation of taint" doctrine. *Wong Sun v. United States* explores that doctrine in more detail.

According to Webster's Dictionary, to attenuate means "to lessen the amount, force, magnitude, or value" of something; "to weaken". To dissipate means "to cause to spread thin or scatter and gradually vanish." In the context of the Fourth Amendment, the doctrine applies when the connection between misconduct by the police and the securing of incriminating evidence has become so distant or weak that it no longer makes sense to use the earlier misconduct as a reason to exclude perfectly good evidence.

The facts in *Wong Sun v. United States* are somewhat confusing, but keeping straight what party did what is vital to understanding the Court's opinion (don't you just love when that happens?). Therefore, it may useful to map out the facts early in your reading of the case using the checklist from p. 450, Note 8:

1. **identify the "tree" (the constitutional violation);**
2. **identify the fruit (the evidence the government seeks to introduce);**
3. **determine whether the fruit comes from the tree (is there a causal link?); and,**
4. **if the fruit *did* come from a poisonous tree, identify any facts that may justify the conclusion that the fruit no longer is poisoned (the "attenuation" or "dissipation" doctrine).**

Note 2 after *Wong Sun* sets out the factors courts use to determine when the taint of police misconduct has dissipated under the totality of the circumstances approach we have seen in other contexts. Note 3 explores the implications when police misconduct leads, not to physical evidence, but to a live witness who can choose for herself whether to testify.

MR. JUSTICE BRENNAN delivered the opinion of the Court [joined by CHIEF JUSTICE WARREN, and JUSTICES BLACK, DOUGLAS, and GOLDBERG].

* * *

About 2 a.m. on the morning of June 4, 1959, federal narcotics agents in San Francisco, after having had one Hom Way under surveillance for six weeks, arrested him and found heroin in his possession. Hom Way, who had not before been an informant, stated after his arrest that he had bought an ounce of heroin the night before from one known to him only as "Blackie Toy," proprietor of a laundry on Leavenworth Street.

About 6 a.m. that morning six or seven federal agents went to a laundry at 1733 Leavenworth Street. The sign above the door of this establishment said "Oye's Laundry." It was operated by the petitioner James Wah Toy. There is, however, nothing in the record which identifies James Wah Toy and "Blackie Toy" as the same person. The other federal officers remained nearby out of sight while Agent Alton Wong, who was of Chinese ancestry, rang the bell. When petitioner Toy appeared and opened the door, Agent Wong told him that he was calling for laundry and dry cleaning. Toy replied that he didn't open until 8 o'clock and told the agent to come back at that time. Toy started to close the door. Agent Wong thereupon took his badge from his pocket and said, "I am a federal narcotics agent." Toy immediately "slammed the door and started running" down the hallway through the laundry to his living quarters at the back where his wife and child were sleeping in a bedroom. Agent Wong and the other federal officers broke open the door and followed Toy down the hallway to the living quarters and into the bedroom. Toy reached into a nightstand drawer. Agent Wong thereupon drew his pistol, pulled Toy's hand out of the drawer, placed him under arrest and handcuffed him. There was nothing in the drawer and a search of the premises uncovered no narcotics.

One of the agents said to Toy "* * * [Hom Way] says he got narcotics from you." Toy responded, "No, I haven't been selling any narcotics at all. However, I do know somebody who has." When asked who that was, Toy said, "I only know him as Johnny. I don't know his last name." However, Toy described a house on Eleventh Avenue where he said Johnny lived; he also described a bedroom in the house where he said "Johnny kept about a piece" [an ounce—Eds.] of heroin, and where he and Johnny had smoked some of the drug the night before. The agents left immediately for Eleventh Avenue and located the house. They entered and found one Johnny Yee in the bedroom. After a discussion with the agents, Yee took from a bureau drawer several tubes containing in all just less than one ounce of heroin, and surrendered them. Within the hour Yee and Toy were taken to the

Office of the Bureau of Narcotics. Yee there stated that the heroin had been brought to him some four days earlier by petitioner Toy and another Chinese known to him only as "Sea Dog."

Toy was questioned as to the identity of "Sea Dog" and said that "Sea Dog" was Wong Sun. Some agents, including Agent Alton Wong, took Toy to Wong Sun's neighborhood where Toy pointed out a multifamily dwelling where he said Wong Sun lived. Agent Wong rang a downstairs door bell and a buzzer sounded, opening the door. The officer identified himself as a narcotics agent to a woman on the landing and asked "for Mr. Wong." The woman was the wife of petitioner Wong Sun. She said that Wong Sun was "in the back room sleeping." Alton Wong and some six other officers climbed the stairs and entered the apartment. One of the officers went into the back room and brought petitioner Wong Sun from the bedroom in handcuffs. A thorough search of the apartment followed, but no narcotics were discovered.

Petitioner Toy and Johnny Yee were arraigned before a United States Commissioner on June 4 on a complaint charging a violation of 21 U.S.C. § 174. Later that day, each was released on his own recognizance. Petitioner Wong Sun was arraigned on a similar complaint filed the next day and was also released on his own recognizance. Within a few days, both petitioners and Yee were interrogated at the office of the Narcotics Bureau by Agent William Wong, also of Chinese ancestry. The agent advised each of the three of his right to withhold information which might be used against him, and stated to each that he was entitled to the advice of counsel, though it does not appear that any attorney was present during the questioning of any of the three. The officer also explained to each that no promises or offers of immunity or leniency were being or could be made.

The agent interrogated each of the three separately. After each had been interrogated the agent prepared a statement in English from rough notes. The agent read petitioner Toy's statement to him in English and interpreted certain portions of it for him in Chinese. Toy also read the statement in English aloud to the agent, said there were corrections to be made, and made the corrections in his own hand. Toy would not sign the statement, however; in the agent's words "he wanted to know first if the other persons involved in the case had signed theirs." Wong Sun had considerable difficulty understanding the statement in English and the agent restated its substance in Chinese. Wong Sun refused to sign the statement although he admitted the accuracy of its contents.

Hom Way did not testify at petitioners' trial. The Government offered Johnny Yee as its principal witness but excused him after he invoked the privilege against self-incrimination and flatly repudiated the statement he had given to Agent William Wong. That statement was not offered in evidence nor was any testimony elicited from him identifying either petitioner as the source of the heroin in his possession, or otherwise tending to support the charges against the petitioners.

The statute expressly provides that proof of the accused's possession of the drug will support a conviction under the statute unless the accused satisfactorily explains the possession. The Government's evidence tending to prove the petitioners' possession (the petitioners offered no exculpatory testimony) consisted of four items which the trial court admitted over timely objections that they were inadmissible as "fruits" of unlawful arrests or of attendant searches: (1) the statements made orally by petitioner Toy in his bedroom at the time of his arrest; (2) the heroin surrendered to the agents by Johnny Yee; (3) petitioner Toy's pretrial unsigned statement; and (4) petitioner Wong Sun's similar statement. The dispute below and here has centered around the correctness of the rulings of the trial judge allowing these items in evidence. * * *

We believe that significant differences between the cases of the two petitioners require separate discussion of each. We shall first consider the case of petitioner Toy.

I.

The Court of Appeals found there was neither reasonable grounds nor probable cause for Toy's arrest. * * *

* * * It remains to be seen what consequences flow from this conclusion.

II.

It is conceded that Toy's declarations in his bedroom are to be excluded if they are held to be "fruits" of the agents' unlawful action. * * *

The exclusionary rule has traditionally barred from trial physical, tangible materials obtained either during or as a direct result of an unlawful invasion. It follows from our holding in *Silverman v. United States*, 365 U.S. 505, 81 S.Ct. 679, 5 L.Ed.2d 734, that the Fourth Amendment may protect against the overhearing of verbal statements as well as against the more traditional seizure of "papers and effects." Similarly, testimony as to matters observed during an unlawful invasion has been excluded in order to enforce the basic constitutional policies. Thus, verbal evidence which derives so immediately from an unlawful entry and an unauthorized arrest as the officers' action in the present case is no less the "fruit" of official illegality than the more common tangible fruits of the unwarranted intrusion. Nor do the policies underlying the exclusionary rule invite any logical distinction between physical and verbal evidence. Either in terms of deterring lawless conduct by federal officers, or of closing the doors of the federal courts to any use of evidence unconstitutionally obtained, the danger in relaxing the exclusionary rules in the case of verbal evidence would seem too great to warrant introducing such a distinction.

The Government argues that Toy's statements to the officers in his bedroom, although closely consequent upon the invasion which we hold unlawful, were nevertheless admissible because they resulted from "an intervening independent act of a free will." This contention, however, takes insufficient account of the circumstances. Six or seven officers had broken the door and followed on Toy's heels into the bedroom where his wife and child were sleeping. He had been almost immediately handcuffed and arrested. Under such circumstances it is unreasonable to infer that Toy's response was sufficiently an act of free will to purge the primary taint of the unlawful invasion. * * *

III.

We now consider whether the exclusion of Toy's declarations requires also the exclusion of the narcotics taken from Yee, to which those declarations led the police. The prosecutor candidly told the trial court that "we wouldn't have found those drugs except that Mr. Toy helped us to." Hence this is not the case envisioned by this Court where the exclusionary rule has no application because the Government learned of the evidence "from an independent source"; nor is this a case in which the connection between the lawless conduct of the police and the discovery of the challenged evidence has "become so attenuated as to dissipate the taint." We need not hold that all evidence is "fruit of the poisonous tree" simply because it would not have come to light but for the illegal actions of the police. Rather, the more apt question in such a case is "whether, granting establishment of the primary illegality, the evidence to which instant objection is made has been come at by exploitation of that illegality or instead by means sufficiently distinguishable to be purged of the primary taint." Maguire, Evidence of Guilt, 221 (1959). We think it clear that the narcotics were "come at by the exploitation of that illegality" and hence that they may not be used against Toy.

IV.

[The Court determined that Toy's unsigned statement was inadmissible on non-constitutional grounds. Therefore, it did not reach the issue of "whether, in light of the fact that Toy was free on his own recognizance when he made the statement, that statement was a fruit of the illegal arrest."]

V.

We turn now to the case of the other petitioner, Wong Sun. We have no occasion to disagree with the finding of the Court of Appeals that his arrest, also, was without probable cause or reasonable grounds. At all events no evidentiary consequences turn upon that question. For Wong Sun's unsigned confession was not the fruit of that arrest, and was therefore properly admitted at trial. On the evidence that Wong Sun had been released on his own recognizance after a lawful arraignment, and had returned voluntarily several days later to make the statement, we hold that the connection between the arrest and the statement had "become so attenuated as to dissipate the taint." The fact that the statement was unsigned, whatever bearing this may have upon its weight and credibility, does not render it inadmissible; Wong Sun understood and adopted its substance, though he could not comprehend the English words. The petitioner has never suggested any impropriety in the interrogation itself which would require the exclusion of this statement.

We must then consider the admissibility of the narcotics surrendered by Yee. Our holding, *supra*, that this ounce of heroin was inadmissible against Toy does not compel a like result with respect to Wong Sun. The exclusion of the narcotics as to Toy was required solely by their tainted relationship to information unlawfully obtained from Toy, and not by any official impropriety connected with their surrender by Yee. The seizure of this heroin invaded no right of privacy of person or premises which would entitle Wong Sun to object to its use at his trial. * * *

[The concurring opinion of JUSTICE DOUGLAS, and the dissenting opinion of JUSTICE CLARK, joined by JUSTICES HARLAN, STEWART, and WHITE, are omitted.]

NOTES AND QUESTIONS

1. What was the poisonous tree, *i.e.*, the initial illegality, in *Wong Sun*? What were the alleged fruits? Why did the Supreme Court treat Wong Sun differently than Toy?

2. *Removing the taint: factors.* Typically, dissipation-of-taint claims are decided on their own facts, based on the totality of the circumstances. The Supreme Court in Brown v. Illinois, 422 U.S. 590, 95 S.Ct. 2254, 45 L.Ed.2d 416 (1975), and lower courts apply various factors in determining whether the connection between the Fourth Amendment violation and the fruit has become so attenuated as to dissipate the taint: (1) the length of time that has elapsed between the initial illegality and the seizure of the fruit in question; (2) the flagrancy of the initial misconduct (dissipation of bad-

faith violations takes longer than with good-faith violations); (3) the existence or absence of intervening causes of the seizure of the fruit; and, closely related to the third factor, (4) the presence or absence of an act of free will by the defendant resulting in the seizure of the fruit.

For example, in *Brown*, he was arrested at his apartment without probable cause, in violation of the Fourth Amendment (the "tree"). While in custody, he made incriminating statements (the "fruit" from the poisonous tree) after being read the *Miranda* warnings and voluntarily waiving his constitutional rights pursuant to *Miranda*. Did the *Miranda* warning dissipate the taint? The Court rejected a proposed bright-line rule that *Miranda* warnings automatically untaint subsequent confessions. Whether a post-*Miranda*-warning statement, which is a fruit of a Fourth Amendment violation, is untainted is resolved like all other cases: on a case-by-case basis, based on the totality of the circumstances.

In *Brown*, the Court held that the State of Illinois had failed to sustain its burden of showing the requisite dissipation of taint, notwithstanding the *Miranda* warnings and waiver. The statement (the fruit) came less than two hours after the illegal arrest, and "there was no intervening event of significance whatsoever." Also, the Court noted that the illegality here (the unlawful arrest) "had a quality of purposefulness," in that the officers knew they were acting in violation of the Fourth Amendment. In essence, the purposefulness of the violation created substantial poison, and thus required more to be dissipated.

3. In *Wong Sun*, the Court considered the admissibility of both tangible evidence (heroin) and verbal statements. The Court stated that "the policies underlying the exclusionary rule [do not] invite any logical distinction between physical and verbal evidence" in regard to the dissipation of taint.

But, it turns out, there *is* a distinction between verbal evidence and the existence of a witness who later provides verbal evidence. In United States v. Ceccolini, 435 U.S. 268, 98 S.Ct. 1054, 55 L.Ed.2d 268 (1978), the police unlawfully seized information that led them to a witness to a crime perpetrated by Ceccolini. Some months later, the witness agreed to testify against Ceccolini. According to the Court of Appeals, the witness's testimony should not have been permitted because "the road to [the] testimony from the [officer's] concededly unconstitutional search [was] both straight and uninterrupted."

The Supreme Court reversed. According to *Ceccolini*, "the exclusionary rule should be invoked with much greater reluctance where the claim is based on a causal relationship between a constitutional violation and the discovery of a live witness than when a similar claim is advanced to support suppression of an inanimate object." The Court reasoned as follows:

> The greater the willingness of the witness to freely testify, the greater the likelihood that he or she will be discovered by legal means and, concomitantly, the smaller the incentive to conduct an illegal search to discover the witness. Witnesses are not like guns or documents which remain hidden from view until one turns over a sofa or opens a filing cabinet. Witnesses can, and often do, come forward and offer evidence entirely of their own volition. And evaluated properly, the degree of free will necessary to dissipate the taint will very likely be found more often in the case of live-witness testimony than other kinds of evidence. * * *
>
> Another factor which * * * seems to us to differentiate the testimony of all live witnesses—even putative defendants—from the exclusion of the typical documentary evidence, is that such exclusion would perpetually disable a witness from testifying about relevant and material facts, regardless of how unrelated such testimony might be to the purpose of the originally illegal search or the evidence discovered thereby. Rules which disqualify knowledgeable witnesses from testifying at trial are, in the words of Professor McCormick, "serious obstructions to the ascertainment of truth" * * *. * * * In short, since the cost of excluding live-witness testimony often will be greater, a closer, more direct link between the illegality and that kind of testimony is required.

Are you persuaded?

4. Assume the following general scenario. The police temporarily detain *D* without the requisite reasonable suspicion. Because of the unconstitutional seizure, the officer learns *D*'s name, which in turn leads to discovery of an outstanding warrant for *D*'s arrest. The officer arrests *D* pursuant to the warrant and conducts a warrantless search of *D*, which turns up contraband. Applying the attenuation factors set out in Note 2, is the contraband admissible against *D*? Federal and state courts reached conflicting answers to this question.

Now the Supreme Court has resolved the conflict, at least based on the facts presented to it in Utah v. Strieff, 579 U.S. ___, 136 S.Ct. 2056, 195 L.Ed.2d 400 (2016). In *Strieff*, based on an anonymous tip that drug activities were occurring at a specified residence, South Salt Lake City narcotics officers placed the residence under surveillance for a week. They observed "visitors who left a few minutes after arriving at the house." One of the visitors was Edward Strieff.

After Strieff left the home, and approached a nearby store, Officer Douglas Fackrell accosted him, identified himself, and asked Strieff what he was doing at the residence. The officer also requested identification, which he received, and then relayed that information to a police dispatcher who reported that Strieff had an outstanding arrest warrant for a traffic violation. The officer therefore arrested Strieff on the warrant, conducted a search incident to the arrest, and discovered a baggie of methamphetamine and drug paraphernalia on Stieff, resulting in his arrest on drug charges. At the suppression hearing, the officer acknowledged that the stop was designed for investigatory purposes—to "find out what was going on [in] the house"—and he admitted that he had no other basis for stopping Strieff. He also testified that it was "normal" practice by South Salt Lake City police to check for outstanding arrest warrants during all *Terry* stops.

It was conceded by the State that the initial stop of Strieff was unconstitutional, for lack of reasonable suspicion. The issue, therefore, was whether the drugs subsequently found on him were inadmissible as a fruit of the initial illegality. The Court, per Justice Thomas, by a vote of 5–3, held that "the officer's discovery of the [valid] arrest warrant attenuated the connection between the unlawful stop and the evidence seized incident to arrest."

Justice Thomas applied "three factors articulated in *Brown v. Illinois*" [Note 2 above]. First, the Court looked at the temporal proximity between the unconstitutional seizure of Strieff and the discovery of the drugs on his person. In view of the fact that the discovery occurred closely after Strieff's unlawful seizure, "such a short time interval counsels in favor of suppression."

The Court then turned to a second factor, "the presence of intervening circumstances." Here, Justice Thomas noted that the warrant was valid, "predated Officer Fackrell's investigation, and * * * was entirely unconnected with the stop." In view of the fact that, once discovered, the warrant obligated the officer to arrest Strieff, this factor "strongly favor[ed] the State." (Justice Thomas did not explain how this factor, which indeed predated the illegal seizure, could constitute an "intervening" circumstance).

Finally, the Court looked at "the purpose and flagrancy of the official misconduct." Justice Thomas found this "strongly" favored the State: "Officer Fackrell was at most negligent"; he "should have asked Strieff whether he would speak with him, instead of demanding that [he] do so." But the officer's "errors in judgment hardly rise to a purposeful or flagrant violation of Strieff's Fourth Amendment rights," meriting the exclusionary rule sanction.

Justice Kagan, joined by Justice Ginsburg dissented. She disagreed with the majority, which "chalks up Fackrell's Fourth Amendment violation to a couple of innocent 'mistakes.' But far from a Barney-Fife-type mishap, Fackrell's seizure of Strieff was a calculated decision, taken with so little justification that the State has never tried to defend its legality."

Justice Sotomayor, also joined by Justice Ginsburg, wrote a separate, stinging dissent. She wrote:

> Do not be soothed by the opinion's technical language: This case allows the police to stop you on the street, demand your identification, and check it for outstanding traffic warrants—even if you are doing nothing wrong. If the officer discovers a warrant for a fine you forgot to pay, courts will now excuse his illegal stop and will admit into evidence anything he happens to find by searching you after arresting you for a warrant.

Sotomayor observed that Utah listed over 180,000 misdemeanor warrants in its database. Therefore, she wrote, "[t]he warrant check * * * was not an 'intervening circumstance' separating the stop from the search for drugs. It was part and parcel of the officer's illegal 'expedition for evidence in the hope that something might turn up.' " She warned that, in light of this decision, "[t]he mere existence of a warrant * * * forgives an officer who, with no knowledge of the warrant at all, unlawfully stops that person on a whim or hunch."

Justice Sotomayor, then writing only for herself and "drawing on [her] professional experiences," indicated that "unlawful 'stops' have severe consequences much greater than the inconvenience suggested by the name":

> [T]his case tells everyone, white and black, guilty and innocent, that an officer can verify your legal status at any time. It says that your body is subject to invasion while courts excuse the violation of your rights. It implies that you are not a citizen of a democracy but the subject of a carceral state, just waiting to be catalogued.

Moreover, consider the following set of incentives created by *Strieff*: officers can stop anyone for any reason, run a warrant check, arrest and search those for whom there is an outstanding warrant, and let the rest go without searching them. In the latter case, there is a Fourth Amendment violation but no evidence to suppress and not much in the way of civil damages to deter the police. Presumably, this possibility was discussed by the justices because the majority found no indication that the stop was part of "systematic or recurrent police misconduct." But Justice Sotomayor pointed out that the majority offered no guidance as to how a defendant could prove such widespread misconduct.

Any idea why the State conceded a lack of reasonable suspicion for the stop? Can you make an argument that the officer *did have* reasonable suspicion?

C. THE EXCLUSIONARY RULE IS NARROWED (AND ON LIFE SUPPORT?)

UNITED STATES V. LEON

Supreme Court of the United States, 1984.
468 U.S. 897, 104 S.Ct. 3405, 82 L.Ed.2d 677.

The Court in *United States v. Leon* established for the first time the "good-faith" exception to the exclusionary rule; an exception that starts here and, as many legal scholars argue, ends up eviscerating the exclusionary rule altogether (more on this later).

An important starting point in understanding *Leon* is to remember that the warrant was facially valid. In other words, there was nothing to give the officers any indication that there would be a problem with the warrant later on. As far as the officers knew, they followed the rules and never intended to do otherwise.

It is also useful to keep in mind that other countries—including ones with criminal justice systems just as fair as ours—think we are crazy for systematically excluding vital evidence in cases, evidence that sometimes rises to the level of "the knife with victim's DNA and defendant's fingerprints on it" (a bit of an exaggeration perhaps, but you get the idea).

From there, note the debate between the majority and the dissent. This is the essence of the longer-term impact of *Leon.* Despite language in *Mapp* to the contrary, Justice White, writing for the *Leon* Court, characterizes the exclusionary rule as a "judicially-engineered remedy" that does nothing more than balance the original purpose of the exclusionary rule—deterrence of police misconduct—against the significant social costs of excluding evidence of a crime. Only when the deterrent effect outweighs those significant costs should exclusion be considered. See if you can identify the precise social costs the majority is concerned about.

Justices Brennan and Marshall vehemently disagree. To them, the exclusionary rule, as stated clearly in *Weeks* and in *Mapp*, is part and parcel of the constitutional concerns embedded in the Fourth Amendment. Without a rule excluding any evidence gathered in violation of its strictures, the Amendment becomes meaningless. In addition, to retain its meaning, the rule must apply to the entire system, not just to mistakes by the police. As Justice Brennan states in writing the dissent: "A more direct answer may

be supplied by recognizing that the Amendment, like other provisions of the Bill of Rights, restrains the power of the government as a whole; it does not specify only a particular agency and exempt all others. The judiciary is responsible, no less than the executive, for ensuring that constitutional rights are respected."

JUSTICE WHITE delivered the opinion of the Court [joined by CHIEF JUSTICE BURGER, and JUSTICES BLACKMUN, POWELL, REHNQUIST, and O'CONNOR].

This case presents the question whether the Fourth Amendment exclusionary rule should be modified so as not to bar the use in the prosecution's case in chief of evidence obtained by officers acting in reasonable reliance on a search warrant issued by a detached and neutral magistrate but ultimately found to be unsupported by probable cause. * * *

I

In August 1981, a confidential informant of unproven reliability informed an officer of the Burbank Police Department that two persons known to him as "Armando" and "Patsy" were selling large quantities of cocaine and methaqualone from their residence at 620 Price Drive in Burbank, Cal. [Based on this and other claims of the informant, the Burbank police initiated an investigation that focused on the Price Drive residence and, later, on two other residences.]

* * * Based on * * * observations summarized in the affidavit, Officer Cyril Rombach of the Burbank Police Department, an experienced and well-trained narcotics investigator, prepared an application for a warrant to search [three residences] and automobiles registered to each of the respondents for an extensive list of items believed to be related to respondents' drug-trafficking activities. Officer Rombach's extensive application was reviewed by several Deputy District Attorneys.

A facially valid search warrant was issued in September 1981 by a State Superior Court Judge. * * *

The respondents * * * filed motions to suppress the evidence seized pursuant to the warrant. The District Court held an evidentiary hearing and, while recognizing that the case was a close one, granted the motions to suppress * * *. It concluded that the affidavit was insufficient to establish probable cause * * *. In response to a request from the Government, the court made clear that Officer Rombach had acted in good faith, but it rejected the Government's suggestion that the Fourth Amendment exclusionary rule should not apply where evidence is seized in reasonable, good-faith reliance on a search warrant. * * *

The Government's petition for certiorari * * * presented only the question "[w]hether the Fourth Amendment exclusionary rule should be modified so as not to bar the admission of evidence seized in reasonable, good-faith reliance on a search warrant that is subsequently held to be defective." We granted certiorari to consider the propriety of such a modification. * * *

II * * *

A

The Fourth Amendment contains no provision expressly precluding the use of evidence obtained in violation of its commands, and an examination of its origin and purposes makes clear that the use of fruits of a past unlawful search or seizure "work[s] no new Fourth Amendment wrong." The wrong condemned by the Amendment is "fully accomplished" by the unlawful search or seizure itself, and the exclusionary rule is neither intended nor able to "cure the invasion of the defendant's rights which he has already suffered." The rule thus operates as "a judicially created remedy designed to safeguard Fourth Amendment rights generally through its deterrent effect, rather than a personal constitutional right of the party aggrieved."

Whether the exclusionary sanction is appropriately imposed in a particular case, our decisions make clear, is "an issue separate from the question whether the Fourth Amendment rights of the party seeking to invoke the rule were violated by police conduct." Only the former question is currently before us, and it must be resolved by weighing the costs and benefits of preventing the use in the prosecution's case in chief of inherently trustworthy tangible evidence obtained in reliance on a search warrant issued by a detached and neutral magistrate that ultimately is found to be defective.

The substantial social costs exacted by the exclusionary rule for the vindication of Fourth Amendment rights have long been a source of concern. "Our cases have consistently recognized that unbending application of the exclusionary sanction to enforce ideals of governmental rectitude would impede unacceptably the truth-finding functions of judge and jury." An objectionable collateral consequence of this interference with the criminal justice system's truth-finding function is that some guilty defendants may go free or receive reduced sentences as a result of favorable plea bargains. Particularly when law enforcement officers have acted in objective good faith or their transgressions have been minor, the magnitude of the benefit conferred on such guilty defendants offends basic concepts of the criminal justice system. Indiscriminate application of the exclusionary rule, therefore, may well "generat[e] disrespect for the law and administration of justice." Accordingly, "[a]s with any remedial device, the application of the rule has been restricted to those areas where its remedial objectives are thought most efficaciously served."

B

Close attention to those remedial objectives has characterized our recent decisions concerning the scope of the Fourth Amendment exclusionary rule. The Court has, to be sure, not seriously questioned, "in the absence of a more efficacious sanction, the continued application of the rule to suppress evidence from the [prosecution's] case where a Fourth Amendment violation has been substantial and deliberate * * *." Nevertheless, the balancing approach that has evolved in various contexts—including criminal trials—"forcefully suggest[s] that the exclusionary rule be more generally modified to permit the introduction of evidence obtained in the reasonable good-faith belief that a search or seizure was in accord with the Fourth Amendment." * * *

As yet, we have not recognized any form of good-faith exception to the Fourth Amendment exclusionary rule. But the balancing approach that has evolved during the years of experience with the rule provides strong support for the modification currently urged upon us. As we discuss below, our evaluation of the costs and benefits of suppressing reliable physical evidence seized by officers reasonably relying on a warrant issued by a detached and neutral magistrate leads to the conclusion that such evidence should be admissible in the prosecution's case in chief.

III

A

Because a search warrant "provides the detached scrutiny of a neutral magistrate, which is a more reliable safeguard against improper searches than the hurried judgment of a law enforcement officer 'engaged in the often competitive enterprise of ferreting out crime,'" we have expressed a strong preference for warrants and declared that "in a doubtful or marginal case a search under a warrant may be sustainable where without one it would fall." Reasonable minds frequently may differ on the question whether a particular affidavit establishes probable cause, and we have thus concluded that the preference for warrants is most appropriately effectuated by according "great deference" to a magistrate's determination.

Deference to the magistrate, however, is not boundless. It is clear, first, that the deference accorded to a magistrate's finding of probable cause does not preclude inquiry into the knowing or reckless falsity of the affidavit on which that determination was based. *Franks v. Delaware*, [p. 179, Note 7]. Second, the courts must also insist that the magistrate purport to "perform his 'neutral and detached' function and not serve merely as a rubber stamp for the police." A magistrate failing to "manifest that neutrality and detachment demanded of a judicial officer when presented with a warrant application" and who acts instead as "an adjunct law enforcement officer" cannot provide valid authorization for an otherwise unconstitutional search. *Lo-Ji Sales, Inc. v. New York*, [p.199].

Third, reviewing courts will not defer to a warrant based on an affidavit that does not "provide the magistrate with a substantial basis for determining the existence of probable cause." "Sufficient information must be presented to the magistrate to allow that official to determine probable cause; his action cannot be a mere ratification of the bare conclusions of others." Even if the warrant application was supported by more than a "bare bones" affidavit, a reviewing court may properly conclude that, notwithstanding the deference that magistrates deserve, the warrant was invalid because the magistrate's probable-cause determination reflected an improper analysis of the totality of the circumstances, or because the form of the warrant was improper in some respect.

Only in the first of these three situations, however, has the Court set forth a rationale for suppressing evidence obtained pursuant to a search warrant; in the other areas, it has simply excluded such evidence without considering whether Fourth Amendment interests will be advanced. To the extent that proponents of exclusion rely on its behavioral effects on judges and magistrates in these areas, their reliance is misplaced. First, the exclusionary rule is designed to deter police misconduct rather than to punish the errors of judges and magistrates. Second, there exists no evidence suggesting that judges and magistrates are inclined to ignore or subvert the Fourth Amendment or that lawlessness among these actors requires application of the extreme sanction of exclusion.

Third, and most important, we discern no basis, and are offered none, for believing that exclusion of evidence seized pursuant to a warrant will have a significant deterrent effect on the issuing judge or magistrate. Many of the factors that indicate that the exclusionary rule cannot provide an effective "special" or "general" deterrent for individual offending law enforcement officers apply as well to judges or magistrates. And, to the extent that the rule is thought to operate as a "systemic" deterrent on a wider audience, it clearly can have no such effect on individuals empowered to issue search warrants. Judges and magistrates are not adjuncts to the law enforcement team; as neutral judicial officers, they have no stake in the outcome of particular criminal prosecutions. The threat of exclusion thus cannot be expected significantly to deter them. Imposition of the exclusionary sanction is not necessary meaningfully to inform judicial officers of their errors, and we cannot conclude that admitting evidence obtained pursuant to a warrant while at the same time declaring that the warrant was somehow defective will in any way reduce judicial officers' professional incentives to comply with the Fourth Amendment, encourage them to repeat their mistakes, or lead to the granting of all colorable warrant requests.

B

If exclusion of evidence obtained pursuant to a subsequently invalidated warrant is to have any deterrent effect, therefore, it must alter the behavior of individual law enforcement officers or the policies of their departments. One could argue that applying the exclusionary rule in cases where the police failed to demonstrate probable cause in the warrant application deters future inadequate presentations or "magistrate shopping" and thus promotes the ends of the Fourth Amendment. Suppressing evidence obtained pursuant to a technically defective warrant supported by probable cause also might encourage officers to scrutinize more closely the form of the warrant and to point out suspected judicial errors. We find such arguments speculative and conclude that suppression of evidence obtained pursuant to a warrant should be ordered only on a case-by-case basis and only in those unusual cases in which exclusion will further the purposes of the exclusionary rule.

We have frequently questioned whether the exclusionary rule can have any deterrent effect when the offending officers acted in the objectively reasonable belief that their conduct did not violate the Fourth Amendment. "No empirical researcher, proponent or opponent of the rule, has yet been able to establish with any assurance whether the rule has a deterrent effect * * *." But even assuming that the rule effectively deters some police misconduct and provides incentives for the law enforcement profession as a whole to conduct itself in accord with the Fourth Amendment, it cannot be expected, and should not be applied, to deter objectively reasonable law enforcement activity. * * *

This is particularly true, we believe, when an officer acting with objective good faith has obtained a search warrant from a judge or magistrate and acted within its scope. In most such cases, there is no police illegality and thus nothing to deter. It is the magistrate's responsibility to determine whether the officer's allegations establish probable cause and, if so, to issue a warrant comporting in form with the requirements of the Fourth Amendment. In the ordinary case, an officer cannot be expected to question the magistrate's probable-cause determination or his judgment that the form of the warrant is technically sufficient. "[O]nce the warrant issues, there is literally nothing more the policeman can do in seeking to comply with the law." Penalizing the officer for the magistrate's error, rather than his own, cannot logically contribute to the deterrence of Fourth Amendment violations.

C

We conclude that the marginal or nonexistent benefits produced by suppressing evidence obtained in objectively reasonable reliance on a subsequently invalidated search warrant cannot justify the substantial costs of exclusion. We do not suggest, however, that exclusion is always inappropriate in cases where an officer has obtained a warrant and abided by its terms. * * * [T]he officer's reliance on the magistrate's probable-cause determination and on the technical sufficiency of the warrant he issues must be objectively reasonable, and it is clear that in some circumstances the office will have no reasonable grounds for believing that the warrant was properly issued.

Suppression therefore remains an appropriate remedy if the magistrate or judge in issuing a warrant was misled by information in an affidavit that the affiant knew was false or would have known was false except for his reckless disregard of the truth. *Franks v. Delaware.* The exception we recognize today will also not apply in cases where the issuing magistrate wholly abandoned his judicial role in the manner condemned in *Lo-Ji Sales, Inc. v. New York*; in such circumstances, no reasonably well trained officer should rely on the warrant. Nor would an officer manifest objective good faith in relying on a warrant based on an affidavit "so lacking in indicia of probable cause as to render official belief in its existence entirely unreasonable." Finally, depending on the circumstances of the particular case, a warrant may be so facially deficient—*i.e.*, in failing to particularize the place to be searched or the things to be seized—that the executing officers cannot reasonably presume it to be valid.

In so limiting the suppression remedy, we leave untouched the probable cause standard and the various requirements for a valid warrant. The good-faith exception for searches conducted pursuant to warrants is not intended to signal our unwillingness strictly to enforce the requirements of the Fourth Amendment, and we do not believe that it will have this effect. * * *

IV

When the principles we have enunciated today are applied to the facts of this case, it is apparent that the judgment of the Court of Appeals cannot stand. * * *

In the absence of an allegation that the magistrate abandoned his detached and neutral role, suppression is appropriate only if the officers were dishonest or reckless in preparing their affidavit or could not have harbored an objectively reasonable belief in the existence of probable cause. * * * Officer Rombach's application for a warrant clearly was supported by much more than a "bare bones" affidavit. The affidavit related the results of an extensive investigation and, as the opinions of the divided panel of the Court of Appeals make clear, provided evidence sufficient to create disagreement among thoughtful and competent judges as to the existence of probable cause. Under these circumstances, the officers' reliance on the magistrate's determination of probable cause was objectively reasonable, and application of the extreme sanction of exclusion is inappropriate.

JUSTICE BLACKMUN, concurring. * * *

As the Court's opinion in this case makes clear, the Court has narrowed the scope of the exclusionary rule because of an empirical judgment that the rule has little appreciable effect in cases where officers act in objectively reasonable reliance on search warrants. * * *

What must be stressed, however, is that any empirical judgment about the effect of the exclusionary rule in a particular class of cases necessarily is a provisional one. By their very nature, the assumptions on which we proceed today cannot be cast in stone. To the contrary, they now will be tested in the real world of state and federal law enforcement, and this Court will attend to the results. If it should emerge from experience that, contrary to our expectations, the good-faith exception to the exclusionary rule results in a material change in police compliance with the Fourth Amendment, we shall have to reconsider what we have undertaken here. The logic of a decision that rests on untested predictions about police conduct demands no less. * * *

JUSTICE BRENNAN, with whom JUSTICE MARSHALL joins, dissenting. * * *

I * * *

A

At bottom, the Court's decision turns on the proposition that the exclusionary rule is merely a " 'judicially created remedy designed to safeguard Fourth Amendment rights generally through its deterrent effect, rather than a personal constitutional right.' " The germ of that idea is found in *Wolf v. Colorado*, [p. 54], and although I had thought that such a narrow conception of the rule had been forever put to rest by our decision in *Mapp v. Ohio*, it has been revived by the present Court and reaches full flower with today's decision. The essence of this view * * * is that the sole "purpose of the Fourth Amendment is to prevent unreasonable governmental intrusions into the privacy of one's person, house, papers, or effects. The wrong condemned is the unjustified governmental invasion of these areas of an individual's life. That wrong * * * is *fully accomplished* by the original search without probable cause." This reading of the Amendment implies that its proscriptions are directed solely at those government agents who may actually invade an individual's constitutionally protected privacy. The courts are not subject to any direct constitutional duty to exclude illegally obtained evidence, because the question of the admissibility of such evidence is not addressed by the Amendment. This view of the scope of the Amendment relegates the judiciary to the periphery. Because the only constitutionally cognizable injury has already been "fully accomplished" by the police by the time a case comes before the courts, the Constitution is not itself violated if the judge decides to admit the tainted evidence. Indeed, the most the judge *can* do is wring his hands and hope that perhaps by excluding such evidence he can deter future transgressions by the police.

Such a reading appears plausible, because, as critics of the exclusionary rule never tire of repeating, the Fourth Amendment makes no express provision for the exclusion of evidence secured in violation of its commands. A short answer to this claim, of course, is that many of the Constitution's most vital imperatives are stated in general terms and the task of giving meaning to these precepts is therefore left to subsequent judicial decisionmaking in the context of concrete cases. * * *

A more direct answer may be supplied by recognizing that the Amendment, like other provisions of the Bill of Rights, restrains the power of the government as a whole; it does not specify only a particular agency and exempt all others. The judiciary is responsible, no less than the executive, for ensuring that constitutional rights are respected.

When that fact is kept in mind, the role of the courts and their possible involvement in the concerns of the Fourth Amendment comes into sharper focus. Because seizures are executed principally to secure evidence, and because such evidence generally has utility in our legal system only in the context of a trial supervised by a judge, it is apparent that the admission of illegally obtained evidence implicates the same constitutional concerns as the initial seizure of that evidence. Indeed, by admitting unlawfully seized evidence, the judiciary becomes a part of what is in fact a single governmental action prohibited by the terms of the Amendment. Once that connection between the evidence-gathering role of the police and the evidence-admitting function of the courts is acknowledged, the plausibility of the Court's interpretation becomes more suspect. * * * It is difficult to give any meaning at all to the limitations imposed by the Amendment if they are read to proscribe only certain conduct by the police but to allow other agents of the same government to take advantage of evidence secured by the police in violation of its requirements. The Amendment therefore must be read to condemn not only the initial unconstitutional invasion of privacy—which is done, after all, for the purpose of securing evidence—but also the subsequent use of any evidence so obtained. * * *

B * * *

* * * [T]he Court * * * has gradually pressed the deterrence rationale for the rule back to center stage. The various arguments advanced by the Court in this campaign have only strengthened my conviction that the deterrence theory is both misguided and unworkable. First, the Court has frequently bewailed the "cost" of excluding reliable evidence. In large part, this criticism rests upon a refusal to acknowledge the function of the Fourth Amendment itself. If nothing else, the Amendment plainly operates to disable the government from gathering information and securing evidence in certain ways. In practical terms, of course, this restriction of official power means that some incriminating evidence inevitably will go undetected if the government obeys these constitutional restraints. It is the loss of that evidence that is the "price" our society pays for enjoying the freedom and privacy safeguarded by the Fourth Amendment. Thus, some criminals will go free *not*, in Justice (then Judge) Cardozo's misleading epigram, "because the constable has blundered," but rather because official compliance with Fourth Amendment requirements makes it more difficult to catch criminals. Understood in this way, the Amendment directly contemplates that some reliable and incriminating evidence will be lost to the government; therefore, it is not the exclusionary rule, but the Amendment itself that has imposed this cost.

In addition, the Court's decisions over the past decade have made plain that the entire enterprise of attempting to assess the benefits and costs of the exclusionary rule in various contexts is a virtually impossible task for the judiciary to perform honestly or accurately. Although the Court's language in those cases suggests that some specific empirical basis may support its analyses, the reality is that the Court's opinions represent inherently unstable compounds of intuition, hunches, and occasional pieces of partial and often inconclusive data. * * *

By remaining within its redoubt of empiricism and by basing the rule solely on the deterrence rationale, the Court has robbed the rule of legitimacy. * * * The extent of this Court's fidelity to Fourth Amendment requirements, however, should not turn on such statistical uncertainties. * * *

III

Even if I were to accept the Court's general approach to the exclusionary rule, I could not agree with today's result. * * *

At the outset, the Court suggests that society has been asked to pay a high price—in terms either of setting guilty persons free or of impeding the proper functioning of trials—as a result of excluding relevant physical evidence in cases where the police, in conducting searches and seizing evidence, have made only an "objectively reasonable" mistake concerning the constitutionality of their actions. But what evidence is there to support such a claim?

Significantly, the Court points to none, and, indeed, as the Court acknowledges, recent studies have demonstrated that the "costs" of the exclusionary rule—calculated in terms of dropped prosecutions and lost convictions—are quite low. Contrary to the claims of the rule's critics that exclusion leads to "the release of countless guilty criminals," these studies have demonstrated that federal and state prosecutors very rarely drop cases because of potential search and seizure problems. For example, a 1979 study prepared at the request of Congress by the General Accounting Office reported that only 0.4% of all cases actually declined for prosecution by federal prosecutors were declined primarily because of illegal search problems. If the GAO data are restated as a percentage of *all* arrests, the study shows that only 0.2% of all felony arrests are declined for prosecution because of potential exclusionary rule problems. Of course, these data describe only the costs attributable to the exclusion of evidence in all cases; the costs due to the exclusion of evidence in the narrower category of cases where police have made objectively reasonable mistakes must necessarily be even smaller. The Court, however, ignores this distinction and mistakenly weighs the aggregated costs of exclusion in *all* cases, irrespective of the circumstances that led to exclusion, against the potential benefits associated with only those cases in which evidence is excluded because police reasonably but mistakenly believe that their conduct does not violate the Fourth Amendment. When such faulty scales are used, it is little wonder that the balance tips in favor of restricting the application of the rule.

What then supports the Court's insistence that this evidence be admitted? Apparently, the Court's only answer is that even though the costs of exclusion are not very substantial, the potential deterrent effect in these circumstances is so marginal that exclusion cannot be justified. The key to the Court's conclusion in this respect is its belief that the prospective deterrent effect of the exclusionary rule operates only in those situations in which police officers, when deciding whether to go forward with some particular search, have reason to know that their planned conduct will violate the requirements of the Fourth Amendment. * * *

The flaw in the Court's argument, however, is that its logic captures only one comparatively minor element of the generally acknowledged deterrent purposes of the exclusionary rule. To be sure, the rule operates to some extent to deter future misconduct by individual officers who have had evidence suppressed in their own cases. But what the Court overlooks is that the deterrence rationale for the rule is not designed to be, nor should it be thought of as, a form of "punishment" of individual police officers for their failures to obey the restraints imposed by the Fourth Amendment. Instead, the chief deterrent function of the rule is its tendency to promote institutional compliance with Fourth Amendment requirements on the part of law enforcement agencies generally. Thus, as the Court has previously recognized, "over the long term, [the] demonstration [provided by the exclusionary rule] that our society attaches serious consequences to violation of constitutional rights is thought to encourage those who formulate law enforcement policies, and the officers who implement them, to incorporate Fourth Amendment ideals into their value system." It is only through such an institution wide mechanism that information concerning Fourth Amendment standards can be effectively communicated to rank-and-file officers.

If the overall educational effect of the exclusionary rule is considered, application of the rule to even those situations in which individual police officers have acted on the basis of a reasonable but mistaken belief that their conduct was authorized can still be expected to have a considerable long-term deterrent effect. If evidence is consistently excluded in these circumstances, police departments will surely be prompted to instruct their officers to devote greater care and attention to providing sufficient information to establish probable cause when applying for a warrant, and to review with some attention the form of the warrant that they have been issued, rather than automatically assuming that whatever document the magistrate has signed will necessarily comport with Fourth Amendment requirements.

After today's decisions, however, that institutional incentive will be lost. * * *

[*The dissenting opinion of* JUSTICE STEVENS *is omitted.*]

NOTES AND QUESTIONS

1. According to Justice White, what is the purpose of the exclusionary rule? Does Justice Brennan, in dissent, suggest another justification for the rule?

2. Based on what you have learned this semester, and taking into consideration the various opinions in *Leon*, do you believe the Fourth Amendment exclusionary rule should be abolished? If so, how should the law deal with Fourth Amendment violations?

3. However you answered the questions in Note 2, who has the better side of the argument on the narrow issue in *Leon*: Should "evidence obtained by officers acting in reasonable reliance on a search warrant issued by a detached and neutral magistrate * * * ultimately found to be unsupported by probable cause," be admissible in the prosecutor's case-in-chief?

4. The Supreme Court applied the *Leon* exception in a second case decided the same day. In Massachusetts v. Sheppard, 468 U.S. 981, 104 S.Ct. 3424, 82 L.Ed.2d 737 (1984), the Court permitted introduction of evidence obtained from a search conducted pursuant to a warrant that violated the Fourth Amendment particularity requirement. The Court explained how the problem arose:

> Because it was Sunday, the local court was closed, and the police had a difficult time finding a warrant application form. Detective O'Malley finally found a warrant form previously in use in the Dorchester District. The form was entitled "Search Warrant—Controlled Substance G. L. c. 276 §§ 1 through 3A." Realizing that some changes had to be made before the form could be used to authorize the search requested in the affidavit, Detective O'Malley deleted the subtitle "controlled substance" with a typewriter. He also substituted "Roxbury" for the printed "Dorchester" and typed Sheppard's name and address into blank spaces provided for that information. However, the reference to "controlled substance" was not deleted in the portion of the form that constituted the warrant application and that, when signed, would constitute the warrant itself.
>
> Detective O'Malley then took the affidavit and the warrant form to the residence of a judge who had consented to consider the warrant application. The judge examined the affidavit and stated that he would authorize the search as requested. Detective O'Malley offered the warrant form and stated that he knew the form as presented dealt with controlled substances. He showed the judge where he had crossed out the subtitles. After unsuccessfully searching for a more suitable form, the judge informed O'Malley that he would make the necessary changes so as to provide a proper search warrant. The judge then took the form, made some changes on it, and dated and signed the warrant. However, he did not change the substantive portion of the warrant, which continued to authorize a search for controlled substances; nor did he alter the form so as to incorporate the affidavit. The judge returned the affidavit and the warrant to O'Malley,

> informing him that the warrant was sufficient authority in form and content to carry out the search as requested. O'Malley took the two documents and, accompanied by other officers, proceeded to Sheppard's residence.

Although the warrant that was executed violated the Fourth Amendment, the Supreme Court concluded that the officers executing the warrant, which included Detective O'Malley, acted in objective good-faith.

> The officers in this case took every step that could reasonably be expected of them. Detective O'Malley prepared an affidavit which was reviewed and approved by the District Attorney. He presented that affidavit to a neutral judge. The judge concluded that the affidavit established probable cause * * *. He was told by the judge that the necessary changes would be made. He then observed the judge make some changes and received the warrant and the affidavit. At this point, a reasonable police officer would have concluded, as O'Malley did, that the warrant authorized a search for the materials outlined in the affidavit.
>
> Sheppard contends that since O'Malley knew the warrant form was defective, he should have examined it to make sure that the necessary changes had been made. However, that argument is based on the premise that O'Malley had a duty to disregard the judge's assurances that the requested search would be authorized and the necessary changes would be made. Whatever an officer may be required to do when he executes a warrant without knowing beforehand what items are to be seized, we refuse to rule that an officer is required to disbelieve a judge who has just advised him, by word and by action, that the warrant he possesses authorizes him to conduct the search he has requested.

Justices Brennan and Marshall also dissented in *Sheppard.*

5. Is the *Leon* standard exclusively objective, or are there circumstances in which a court may inquire into the thought processes of the officers seeking or executing a warrant? For example, suppose that an officer takes her warrant affidavit to the prosecutor for a legal judgment of its sufficiency. The prosecutor unequivocally states that it fails to show probable cause. Although the officer now believes that the affidavit is inadequate, she applies for a warrant anyway, "just in case" she finds a sympathetic magistrate. Based on the same affidavit, a magistrate improperly issues a warrant. In determining whether the *Leon* exception to the exclusionary rule applies, is the officer's visit to the prosecutor relevant? If so, may defense counsel inquire into the officer's reasons for seeking a warrant despite the advice? May the lawyer elicit testimony, for example, that the officer had doubted that she had probable cause, but went ahead because she believed that the magistrate was "police-friendly"? See 1

Wayne R. LaFave, Search and Seizure 71–73 (4th ed. 2004). Along these lines, note the following two footnotes from Justice White's opinion in *Leon*:

> We emphasize that the standard of reasonableness we adopt is an objective one. Many objections to a good-faith exception assume that the exception will turn on the subjective good faith of individual officers. "Grounding the modification in objective reasonableness, however, retains the value of the exclusionary rule as an incentive for the law enforcement profession as a whole to conduct themselves in accord with the Fourth Amendment." The objective standard we adopt, moreover, requires officers to have a reasonable knowledge of what the law prohibits. As Professor Jerold Israel has observed:
>
>> "The key to the [exclusionary] rule's effectiveness as a deterrent lies, I believe, in the impetus it has provided to police training programs that make officers aware of the limits imposed by the fourth amendment and emphasize the need to operate within those limits. [An objective good-faith exception] is not likely to result in the elimination of such programs, which are now viewed as an important aspect of police professionalism. Neither is it likely to alter the tenor of those programs; the possibility that illegally obtained evidence may be admitted in borderline cases is unlikely to encourage police instructors to pay less attention to fourth amendment limitations. Finally, [it] should not encourage officers to pay less attention to what they are taught, as the requirement that the officer act in 'good faith' is inconsistent with closing one's mind to the possibility of illegality."

And:

> * * * [W]e * * * eschew inquiries into the subjective beliefs of law enforcement officers who seize evidence pursuant to a subsequently invalidated warrant. Although we have suggested that, "[o]n occasion, the motive with which the officer conducts an illegal search may have some relevance in determining the propriety of applying the exclusionary rule," we believe that "sending state and federal courts on an expedition into the minds of police officers would produce a grave and fruitless misallocation of judicial resources." Accordingly, our good-faith inquiry is confined to the objectively ascertainable question whether a reasonably well trained officer would have known that the search was illegal despite the magistrate's authorization. In making this determination, all of the circumstances—including whether the warrant application had previously been rejected by a different magistrate—may be considered.

6. Does the *Leon* exception apply if a magistrate signs a warrant without looking at the supporting affidavit? What if she skims the affidavit and signs the warrant five seconds later?

7. Professor Tonja Jacobi asserts that the exclusionary rule actually *over*-deters, and thus leads to avoidance and under-enforcement. She reports that police avoid the exclusionary rule by perjury, among other means; and "judges resist and distort the rule for the same reason." This leads to under-enforcement of the Fourth Amendment, precisely the opposite, of course, of what the *Mapp* Court intended. Tonja Jacobi, *The Law and Economics of the Exclusionary Rule*, 87 Notre Dame L. Rev. 585, 675 (2012).

1. Does the Good-Faith Exception Doom the Exclusionary Rule?

Between 2006 and 2011, three cases—Hudson v. Michigan, 547 U.S. 586, 126 S.Ct. 2159, 165 L.Ed.2d 56 (2006); Herring v. United States, 555 U.S. 135, 129 S.Ct. 695, 172 L.Ed.2d 496 (2009); and Davis v. United States, 564 U.S. 229, 131 S.Ct. 2149, 180 L.Ed.2d 285 (2011)—took up the issue of when and how the good-faith exception applies. In doing so, these cases also raised questions about the purpose of the exclusionary rule and its role in preserving the constitutional protections inherent in the Fourth Amendment. In the end, the dissenters in these cases, along with a number of legal scholars, accuse the majority of the Court of eviscerating the exclusionary rule to the point where it applies only to a small category of cases, thus, rendering the Fourth Amendment itself almost meaningless.

As we start our journey through these three cases, it is interesting to note how the Justices lined up on these issues. There is most definitely a pattern. In all three cases the majority consisted of Justices Scalia, Roberts, Kennedy, Thomas, and Alito (Justice Kagan joined in on *Davis*). On the dissenting side in *Hudson* and *Herring* were Justices Breyer, Stevens, Souter and Ginsberg. By the time we get to *Davis*, Justices Breyer and Ginsberg are as passionate as ever in their dissents, but Justices Stevens and Souter are no longer on the Court.

The Justices on the majority side of this divide were considered part of the conservative wing of the Court; those dissenting considered to be its liberal backbone. To the extent that "conservative" and "liberal" are still useful terms, this affects the patterns of the arguments on both sides. Conservative justices, of which Justice Scalia was probably one of the most famous, tend to view the Constitution through the *originalist* lens; a requirement not clearly stated in the Constitution, or obviously intended at the time the provision was written, is the purview of the legislature not the courts. Judicial bodies can only uphold the Constitution as it was written. Liberal justices, on the other hand, tend to be *realists*. They view the Constitution as a living, breathing document designed to be interpreted in the context of the changing needs of society. To realists, it is absolutely the purview of the judicial system to make these needed adjustments when the legislative bodies fail to do so. Conservative Justices also tend to be more law enforcement oriented; feeling more comfortable—at least via judicial rulings—of erring on the side of leaving officers the discretion needed to do their jobs. If that discretion needs to be reined in, that is the role of the legislature or the particular police department. On this second point, though, Justice Scalia is an outlier. As we saw in cases like *Jones, Hicks,* and *Kyllo*, Scalia took the libertarian position that police should not have easy access to our homes or our personal property.

Liberal justices—of which Justice Marshall and Justice Brennan are probably the best examples—view the role of the courts as protecting individuals against overly aggressive law enforcement practices and see the Court as the last option for defendants in standing up to the overwhelming power and advantage of the State in criminal proceedings. As we work through *Hudson*, *Herring*, and *Davis*, see if you can identify how these views affected the debate over the good-faith exception, and even the exclusionary rule itself.

2. *Hudson* and the Knock-and-Announce Rule

To begin our look at *Hudson*, let's start with a look back at the language in *Mapp* in 1961 on the importance of the exclusionary rule, and its constitutional underpinnings. Remember, even though the exclusionary rule had applied to federal criminal proceedings since *Weeks* was handed down in 1914, this was the first time it had been applied to the states via the Fourteenth Amendment. In applying the exclusionary rule to the states, the Court stated the following:

- This Court has ever since [the ruling in *Weeks*] required of federal officers a strict adherence to that command which this Court has held to be a clear, specific, and constitutionally required—even if judicially implied—deterrent safeguard without insistence upon which the Fourth Amendment would have been reduced to "a form of words."
- There are in the cases of this Court some passing references to the *Weeks* rule as being one of evidence. But the plain and unequivocal language of *Weeks*—and its later paraphrase in *Wolf*—to the effect

that the *Weeks* rule is of constitutional origin, remains entirely undisturbed.

- Since the Fourth Amendment's right of privacy has been declared [in *Wolf*] enforceable against the States through the Due Process Clause of the Fourteenth, it is enforceable against them by the same sanction of exclusion as is used against the Federal Government. Were it otherwise, then just as without the *Weeks* rule the assurance against unreasonable federal searches and seizures would be a "form of words," valueless and undeserving of mention * * *. * * * Therefore, in extending the substantive protections of due process to all constitutionally unreasonable searches—state or federal—it was logically and constitutionally necessary that the exclusion doctrine be also insisted upon * * *.

- But, * * * "there is another consideration [beyond the deterrence of police misconduct]—the imperative of judicial integrity." The criminal goes free, if he must, but it is the law that sets him free. Nothing can destroy a government more quickly that its failure to observe its own laws, or worse, its disregard of the charter of its own existence.

- Our decision, founded on reason and truth, gives to the individual no more than that which the Constitution guarantees him * * *.

Compare this language in 1961 with the language in *Hudson* in 2006.

> Suppression of evidence, however, has always been our last resort, not our first impulse. The exclusionary rule generates "substantial social costs" which sometimes include setting the guilty free and the dangerous at large. We have therefore been "cautio[us] against expanding" it, and "have repeatedly emphasized that the rule's 'costly toll' upon truth-seeking and law enforcement objectives presents a high obstacle for those urging [its] application." We have rejected "[i]ndiscriminate application" of the rule, and have held it to be applicable only "where its remedial objectives are thought most efficaciously served"—that is, "where its deterrence benefits outweigh its 'substantial social costs.' "
>
> We did not always speak so guardedly. Expansive dicta in *Mapp*, for example, suggested wide scope for the exclusionary rule. * * * But we have long since rejected that approach. * * * [starting with *Leon*].

The language in *Mapp* compared to the language in *Hudson* almost makes it sound like we are talking about two different exclusionary rules. So how did we get here from there? Let's start by looking at the facts of *Hudson.*

> Police obtained a warrant authorizing a search for drugs and firearms at the home of petitioner Booker Hudson. They discovered both. Large quantities of drugs were found, including cocaine rocks in Hudson's pocket. A loaded gun was lodged between the cushion and armrest of the chair in which he was sitting. Hudson was charged under Michigan law with unlawful drug and firearm possession.
>
> This case is before us only because of the method of entry into the house. When the police arrived to execute the warrant, they announced their presence, but waited only a short time—perhaps "three to five seconds"—before turning the knob of the unlocked front door and entering Hudson's home. Hudson moved to suppress all the inculpatory evidence, arguing that the premature entry violated his Fourth Amendment rights.

Note that unlike in *Leon,* there was no problem with the warrant itself. The only thing that made the entry into Booker Hudson's home illegal was the failure by the police to follow the "knock and announce" requirement. The Court began its analysis by looking at the purpose of the "knock and announce rule and identified three interests the rule was designed to protect: 1) the protection of life and limb; 2) the protection of property; and 3) protection against those elements of privacy and dignity that can be destroyed by a sudden entrance. Unlike the warrant requirement, however, the interests protected by the "knock and announce" rule "do not include the shielding of potential evidence from the government's eyes." The Court went on to hold that: "Since the interests that *were* violated in this case have nothing to do with the seizure of the evidence, the exclusionary rule in inapplicable."

In coming to this conclusion, Justice Scalia noted that not much was deterred by the violation of the "knock and announce" rule since the warrant in this case was valid and could simply have been re-executed (something of an independent source or inevitable discovery argument). In addition, not every action that might have *some* deterrent effect on police misconduct needs to rise to the level of a Fourth Amendment requirement.

Also key to the broad reading *Hudson* is given in later cases is the way Justice Scalia defines "attenuation," melding it with the issue of the level of deterrence versus the social costs involved. "Attenuation can occur, of course, when the causal connection is remote. Attenuation also occurs when, even give a direct causal connection, the interest protected by the constitutional guarantee that has been violated would not be served by suppression of the evidence obtained." In other words, even when the taint of the poisonous tree has not dissipated—there is a direct connection between the misconduct and the seizure of the evidence—attenuation can still be found if the costs of the suppression outweigh the interests—even constitutional ones—being protected. This balancing test thus becomes the main focus of the exclusion cases that follow *Hudson*.

Justice Scalia also spent significant time in his opinion noting the alternative remedies available to defendants since *Mapp*. These included lawsuits for damages against police departments under 42 U.S.C. § 1983, the professionalism of policing, and internal review boards. The availability of these remedies made the argument for the application of the exclusionary rule to these facts much weaker than it would have been in 1961. Although the ruling in *Hudson* applied to the narrow fact pattern surrounding violations of the "knock and announce" rule, Justice Scalia's list of remedies made reference to many that would apply to police violations of the Fourth Amendment in general, suggesting that he was making an argument for overruling the exclusionary rule itself.

Justice Breyer, in dissent, took issue with this view, arguing that the "knock and announce" rule was not separate from the warrant requirement, but was part and parcel of the assurance of a reasonable search and seizure. Violation of that rule makes the search unreasonable, and evidence from unreasonable searches and seizures is to be suppressed. Justice Breyer goes on to note that the Court could not specifically identify any social costs of applying the exclusionary rule to the "knock and announce" rule that did not apply to all Fourth Amendment violations.

> [The majority cannot] justify its failure to respect the need for deterrence, as set forth consistently in the Court's prior case law, through its claim of "substantial social costs"—at least if it means that those "social costs" are somehow special here. The only costs it mentions are those that typically accompany *any* use of the Fourth Amendment's exclusionary principle: (1) that where the constable blunders, a guilty defendant may be set free (consider *Mapp* itself); (2) that defendants may assert claims where Fourth Amendment rights are uncertain * * *, and (3) that sometimes it is difficult to decide the merits of those uncertain claims. * * * The majority's "substantial social costs" argument is an argument against the Fourth Amendment's exclusionary

principle itself. And it is an argument that this Court, until now, has consistently rejected.

3. *Herring* and Negligent Conduct by the Police

Was *Hudson* indeed an argument for the end of the exclusionary rule itself? Certainly the dissenters thought so, and they once again accused the majority of doing so three years later.

In *Leon*, the mistake made regarding the warrant was made by the magistrate—the police acted entirely in good-faith in believing they could rely on the warrant in conducting the search. In *Herring*, the mistake was made by the police department itself; the very conduct the exclusionary rule was designed to prevent. Yet the same majority as in *Hudson* held that the good-faith exception applied here as well. In *Herring*, an investigator with the Coffee County Sheriff's Department learned that Bennie Dean Herring, a known felon, was at the department's impound lot trying to retrieve an item from his impounded truck. According to the Court:

> * * *Anderson asked the county's warrant clerk, Sandy Pope, to check for any outstanding warrants for Herring's arrest. When she found none, Anderson asked Pope to check with Sharon Morgan, her counterpart in neighboring Dale County. After checking Dale County's computer database, Morgan replied that there was an active arrest warrant for Herring's failure to appear on a felony charge. Pope relayed the information to Anderson and asked Morgan to fax over a copy of the warrant as confirmation. Anderson and a deputy followed Herring as he left the impound lot, pulled him over, and arrested him. A search incident to the arrest revealed methamphetamine in Herring's pocket, and a pistol (which as a felon he could not possess) in his vehicle.
>
> There had, however, been a mistake about the warrant. The Dale County sheriff's computer records are supposed to correspond to actual arrest warrants, which the office also maintains. But when Morgan went to the files to retrieve the actual warrant to fax to Pope, Morgan was unable to find it. She called a court clerk and learned that the warrant had been recalled five months earlier. Normally when a warrant is recalled the court clerk's office or a judge's chambers calls Morgan, who enters the information in the sheriff's computer database and disposes of the physical copy. For whatever reason, the information about the recall of the warrant for Herring did not appear in the database. Morgan immediately called Pope to alert her to the mixup, and Pope contacted

Anderson over a secure radio. This all unfolded in 10 to 15 minutes, but Herring had already been arrested and found with the gun and drugs, just a few hundred yards from the sheriff's office.

The lower courts found that the conduct in question, even though engaged in by law enforcement officials, involved "a negligent failure to act, not a deliberate or tactical choice to act." As a result, the Court upheld the Eleventh Circuit's ruling that "the benefit of suppressing the evidence 'would be marginal or nonexistent," and the evidence was therefore admissible under the good-faith rule of *United States v. Leon*."

This time, Chief Justice Roberts wrote the majority opinion, in which Justices Scalia, Kennedy, Thomas, and Alito joined. Once again referring to the exclusionary rule as a judicially-engineered rule "designed to safeguard Fourth Amendment rights generally through its deterrent effect", Chief Justice Roberts reiterated what he saw as the three key aspects of the exclusionary rule. First, that exclusion "has always been our last resort, not our first impulse." Second, that the exclusionary rule is not an individual right and applies only where it 'result[s] in appreciable deterrence.' Finally, that "the benefits of deterrence must outweigh the costs."

After acknowledging the flagrant misconduct demonstrated in *Weeks* and *Mapp*, the Court compared those original cases to the conduct in *Herring*:

> To trigger the exclusionary rule, police conduct must be sufficiently deliberate that exclusion can meaningfully deter it, and sufficiently culpable that such deterrence is worth the price paid by the judicial system. As laid out in our cases, the exclusionary rule serves to deter deliberate, reckless, or grossly negligent conduct, or in some circumstances recurring or systemic negligence. The error in this case does not rise to that level.

In short, applying the exclusionary rule to mere negligent police behavior does not create sufficient deterrence to justify the social cost of excluding probative evidence.

In dissent, Justice Ginsburg returned to her theme in *Hudson* of the broader role for the exclusionary rule envisioned by *Mapp,* rather than relying on a simple cost-benefit analysis. In the view of the dissenters, the exclusionary rule continues to be inseparable from the strictures of the Fourth Amendment. Strict adherence to the rule is the only way to prevent the Amendment from being rendered meaningless. In addition, Ginsburg took issue with the majority's characterization of the deterrent effect on negligent behavior as minimal, and saw a much higher social cost in allowing even negligent database errors:

> Is the potential deterrence here worth the costs it imposes? In light of the paramount importance of accurate recordkeeping in law enforcement, I would answer yes * * *.
>
> Electronic databases form the nervous system of contemporary criminal justice operations. In recent years, their breadth and influence have dramatically expanded. Police today can access databases that include not only the updated National Crime Information Center (NCIC), but also terrorist watchlists, the Federal Government's employee eligibility system, and various commercial databases. Moreover, States are actively expanding information sharing between jurisdictions. As a result, law enforcement has an increasing supply of information within its easy electronic reach.
>
> The risk of error stemming from these databases is not slim. Herring's *amici* warn that law enforcement databases are insufficiently monitored and often out of date. Government reports describe, for example, flaws in NCIC databases, terrorist watchlist databases, and databases associated with the Federal Government's employment eligibility verification system
>
> Inaccuracies in expansive, interconnected collections of electronic information raise grave concerns for individual liberty. * * *

4. *Davis* and a Mistake of Law

Both *Hudson* and *Herring* involved police misconduct—whether deliberate or negligent. What happens, though, if in the midst of a case, the law changes and the police in their conduct followed the old law—which now makes the search unreasonable. Does the good-faith exception apply then. The Court in *Davis* said yes.

In *Davis*, the defendant was a passenger in an automobile subjected to a "routine traffic stop" that resulted in his arrest for giving a false name to the police. The driver of the car was arrested for driving while intoxicated. The driver and passenger were handcuffed and placed in separate patrol cars, after which the arresting officers conducted a warrantless search of the passenger compartment of the automobile, pursuant to the Fourth Amendment law set out in *Belton v. New York*. A firearm was discovered in the pocket of Davis's coat in the automobile, resulting in his federal indictment and conviction on one count of possession of a firearm by a convicted felon. While Davis's appeal was pending in the Eleventh Circuit, the Supreme Court decided *Arizona v. Gant*, which adopted a new rule relating to searches of automobiles incident to lawful arrests. The Eleventh Circuit held that, under the new law announced in *Gant*, the police search violated the Fourth Amendment. However, based on *Herring v. United States*, the appellate court concluded that "penalizing" the officers for following the law that existed at the time of his conduct would not deter Fourth Amendment violations. It therefore refused to apply the exclusionary rule to the unconstitutional search and affirmed Davis's conviction.

The language of the majority opinion, written by Justice Alito, suggested that the cost-benefit analysis that so bothered the dissenters in *Hudson* and *Herring* had, by 2011, won over the constitutional language of *Mapp*.

> The Fourth Amendment protects the "right of the people to be secure in their persons, houses, papers, and effects, against unreasonable searches and seizures." The Amendment says nothing about suppressing evidence obtained in violation of this command. That rule—the exclusionary rule—is a "prudential" doctrine, created by this Court to "compel respect for the constitutional guaranty." Exclusion is "not a personal constitutional right," nor is it designed to "redress the injury" occasioned by an unconstitutional search. The rule's sole purpose, we have repeatedly held, is to deter future Fourth Amendment violations. Our cases have thus limited the rule's operation to situations in which this purpose is "thought most efficaciously served." Where suppression fails to yield "appreciable deterrence," exclusion is "clearly * * * unwarranted."
>
> Real deterrent value is a "necessary condition for exclusion," but it is not "a sufficient" one. The analysis must also account for the "substantial social costs" generated by the rule. Exclusion exacts a heavy toll on both the judicial system and society at large. It almost always requires courts to ignore reliable, trustworthy evidence bearing on guilt or innocence. And its bottom-line effect, in many cases, is to suppress the truth and set the criminal loose in the community without punishment. Our cases hold that society must swallow this bitter pill when necessary, but only as a "last resort." For exclusion to be appropriate, the deterrence benefits of suppression must outweigh its heavy costs.
>
> Admittedly, there was a time when our exclusionary-rule cases were not nearly so discriminating in their approach to the doctrine.

> "Expansive dicta" in several decisions suggested that the rule was a self-executing mandate implicit in the Fourth Amendment itself. * * * In time, however, we came to acknowledge the exclusionary rule for what it undoubtedly is—a "judicially created remedy" of this Court's own making. * * * In a line of cases beginning with *United States* v. *Leon,* we also recalibrated our cost-benefit analysis in exclusion cases to focus the inquiry on the "flagrancy of the police misconduct" at issue.

Using similar language as that of *Hudson* in discussing police culpability, the Court applied the good-faith exception to the officers conduct in *Davis*:

> The search incident to Davis's arrest in this case followed [the Eleventh Circuit's] * * * precedent to the letter. Although the search turned out to be unconstitutional under *Gant*, all agree that the officers' conduct was in strict compliance with then-binding * * * law and was not culpable in any way. * * * The officers who conducted the search did not violate Davis's Fourth Amendment rights deliberately, recklessly, or with gross negligence. Nor does this case involve any "recurring or systemic negligence" on the part of law enforcement. The police acted in strict compliance with binding precedent, and their behavior was not wrongful. Unless the exclusionary rule is to become a strict-liability regime, it can have no application in this case. * * *
>
> About all that exclusion would deter in this case is conscientious police work. * * *

Justices Breyer and Ginsburg dissent here again. Although it is hard to find anything to blame in the officer's conduct in following what was then the law, Justice Breyer criticizes the majority for leaving Davis "with a right [under *Gant*] but not a remedy." For Justices Breyer and Ginsburg, the importance of the exclusionary rule to the protections of the Fourth Amendment demands a strict liability approach to its enforcement. To leave a right with no remedy is to spell doom for the exclusionary rule:

> Thus, if the Court means what it now says, if it would place determinative weight upon the culpability of an individual officer's conduct, and if it would apply the exclusionary rule only where a Fourth Amendment violation was "deliberate, reckless, or grossly negligent," then the "good faith" exception will swallow the exclusionary rule. Indeed, our broad dicta in *Herring*—dicta the Court repeats and expands upon today—may already be leading lower courts in this direction. Today's decision will doubtless accelerate this trend.

But, notice, the number of dissenters to these good-faith cases has shrunk from four (*Hudson*, *Herring*) to two. What do you think the implications are for future good-faith cases?

5. The Future of the Exclusionary Rule

Consider where we have been and where we are now. For a long period of this nation's history, including the colonial era, only a civil remedy, a tort suit, was available to an individual who asserted that his "person, house, paper, or effects" were the subject of an unreasonable search of seizure. In the twentieth century, however, with the Supreme Court's rulings in *Weeks v. United States* and *Mapp v. Ohio*, the Fourth Amendment exclusionary rule was recognized as a right defendants enjoyed in the federal (*Weeks*) and, later, state (*Mapp*) courts.

Notice, as well, that the *Weeks-Mapp* rule was strict in its nature. It was essentially a strict liability rule: if a law enforcement agent violated the Fourth Amendment rights of a person, *even inadvertently*, the evidence obtained as a result of that violation (and subsequent, causally linked, tainted fruits thereof) was inadmissible in the prosecutor's case-in-chief.

What is the scope of the rule now? Do you believe the narrower or broader version of the rule is preferable, and why? For that matter, do you think that the exclusionary rule still exists, or, like Justices Ginsberg and Breyer, do you believe it was doomed by the decisions in *Leon, Hudson, Herring,* and *Davis*?

NOTES AND QUESTIONS

1. Consider again *Kyllo v. United States*, where the police, on the street, beamed a "thermal imager" at a house in order to determine if it was emitting unusual levels of heat consistent with indoor marijuana growing. The information secured in that procedure was used to obtain a search warrant. The Court held, 5–4, that this constituted a search and, under the circumstances of the case, an improper intrusion on Kyllo's rights. If the case had arisen for the first time today rather than in 2001, would the evidence unconstitutionally seized in *Kyllo* be admissible? What issue do you need to resolve to answer this question?

What if the police conduct a warrantless search of your home because they believe they have probable cause to search it for weapons and that an exigency justifies the warrantless entry. The police don't find what they are looking for, but they do discover a small quantity of illegal drugs. Later, at a suppression hearing, a magistrate determines that the police lacked probable cause to search your home and that the facts available to the officers did not justify their belief that an exigency existed. After the trilogy of cases just discussed, would the drugs be inadmissible at your trial?

2. *Problem. H* challenged the introduction of evidence at his trial, obtained as a result of an arrest, pursuant to three misdemeanor arrest warrants. Here are the facts regarding the arrest warrants, as described by the Ohio Supreme Court, in State v. Hoffman, 25 N.E.3d 993 (Ohio 2014):

> The deputy clerk who signed and issued the three arrest warrants had been employed by the Toledo Municipal Court for 17 years. She testified that when an officer came in for a warrant, she would verify that the complaint included the offender's correct name and address, the violation codes, the charge, the offense classification, the date of the offense, a description of the offense, and the signature of the officer. But she also stated that she never asked an officer any questions. With regard to the warrants issued against Hoffman, the deputy clerk specifically testified that she did not make a probable-cause determination. When asked if she knew what probable cause is, she said, "no, I don't." She denied that it was part of her job responsibility to make a finding of probable cause. She simply gave the officer the oath, issued the warrants, and placed them into the computer system.

It appears that, in 2000, an Ohio lower court had upheld an arrest warrant under similar factual circumstances in a one-paragraph analysis. The Ohio Supreme Court in that case declined to accept jurisdiction of the petitioner's appeal.

Based on everything you have learned to this moment, should the evidence seized in *Hoffman* be excluded from his trial?

3. *Where do we go now?* If the *Mapp* exclusionary rule in its robust form is no more, it is worth thinking about alternatives to the rule as it presently exists. Justice Scalia, in dictum, mused on the possibility of resolving Fourth Amendment violations through civil litigation, but there are obstacles to this approach. Can you think of any other remedy that would deter police misconduct at least as well as the exclusionary rule?

On a comparative note, Section 8 of the Canadian Charter of Rights and Freedoms provides that "[e]veryone has a right to be secure against unreasonable search or seizure." Unlike our Constitution, however, the Canadian charter expressly recognizes a general exclusionary rule. Section 24 of the Charter provides that

> [w]here * * * a court concludes that evidence was obtained in a manner that infringed or denied any rights or freedoms guaranteed by this Charter, the evidence shall be excluded if it is established that, having regard to all of

the circumstances, the admission of it in the proceedings would bring the administration of justice into disrepute.

What does "bring[ing] the administration of justice into disrepute" mean? Essentially it is linked to the concept of judicial integrity: "to exclude any evidence whose admission might be seen as judicially condoning a 'serious' violation of Canada's Charter." Apparently, the "seriousness" of the violation depends on whether it was deliberate or inadvertent. Craig M. Bradley, *Reconceiving the Fourth Amendment and the Exclusionary Rule*, 73 Law & Contemp. Probs. 211, 217 (2010).

In England and Wales, judges have discretion to exclude evidence if admitting it would make the proceedings unfair. The House of Lords, however, has not developed a body of search-and-seizure case law, nor guidelines for exclusion. *Id.* at 220–21.

In New Zealand, as a result of a 2002 court decision, "[e]vidence is now excluded * * * only if the exclusion is held to be a proportional remedial response to the breach of the Bill of Rights at issue in the case. In order to make that determination, judges have to settle on what best serves the due administration of justice." Scott Optican, *Lessons From Down Under: A Dialogue on Police Search and Seizure in New Zealand and the United States*, 3 Ohio St. J. Crim. L. 257, 269 (2005). New Zealand courts balance various factors, including the nature of the violation, the seriousness of the crime allegedly committed by the defendant, and the importance of the evidence to the prosecutor's case. *Id.* at 269–70.

4. One of casebook-author Thomas's students (not at Rutgers) told him that a magistrate he worked for routinely pre-signed arrest warrants. Thomas said he did not believe the student, who later produced a stack of blank arrest warrants—blank that is, except for the signature of the magistrate!!

CHAPTER 7 SUMMARY

As shown in Chapter 2, the exclusionary rule—the rule that evidence obtained in violation of the Fourth Amendment is suppressed at trial at both the state and federal level—is typically justified on deterrence grounds: The police will be less likely to violate the Fourth Amendment if they know that the fruits of their unconstitutional conduct will be excluded from a criminal trial. Before evidence can be excluded, however, a court must determine whether the person seeking exclusion has the right to bring the Fourth Amendment claim. This is known as the "standing" requirement.

The standing requirement holds that in order for a person to raise a Fourth Amendment claim, it had to be the claimant's expectation of privacy that was violated. Thus if the police search your friend's house without a warrant and find incriminating evidence against you that you have left at your friend's house, your friend may have the right to challenge the warrantless search of the house, but you do not. It's her house, not yours.

In addition to issues of standing, there are several exceptions to the exclusionary rule. The *independent source* doctrine holds that if the illegally obtained evidence can later be obtained from a valid source independent of the Fourth Amendment violation, it can come in. Similarly, the *inevitable discovery* doctrine holds that if the evidence would have been discovered anyway, even without the violation, the evidence may be used at trial. Finally, since deterrence of improper conduct is not a factor when the police could not reasonably know that a Fourth Amendment violation has occurred, evidence is not suppressed when it is illegally obtained in so-called "good faith."

Later cases have further weakened the exclusionary rule, arguing that the exclusion of evidence should only be used as a last resort and that only when any deterrent effect outweighs the significant social costs of excluding otherwise credible evidence of a crime. Not every action that might have some deterrent effect on police misconduct will require application of the exclusionary rule. As a result, evidence resulting from negligence on the part of the police is allowed in under the good-faith exception. Evidence is only excluded if police conduct demonstrates culpability.

CHAPTER 8

Police Interrogation: Constitutional Limits

A. THE *MIRANDA* DOCTRINE

Most of this chapter focuses on the right to keep compelled or involuntary confessions from being offered in criminal cases. There are, essentially, two protections against compelled confessions. For centuries, the Anglo-American law forbade the use against criminal defendants of involuntary confessions. The classic American case on this is Brown v. Mississippi, 297 US 278, 56 S.Ct. 461, 80 L.Ed. 682 (1936), where a gang of white vigilantes, assisted by law enforcement officers, used torture to obtain confessions from two black men who were probably innocent. The officer who guided the torture even admitted in court the details of the torture. You saw this case in Chapter 1.

The basis for *Brown*, and almost all the confessions cases before we get to Miranda v. Arizona, 384 US 436, 86 S.Ct. 1602, 16 L.Ed. 2d 694 (1966), was found in the right to due process. There is a due process clause that applies to federal actors in the Fifth Amendment and an identical due process clause that applies to state actors in the Fourteenth Amendment. In effect, the United States Supreme Court found that due process of law forbids the use of an involuntary confession in court.

Voluntariness of human action, however, is not an easy empirical or philosophical "fact" to determine. If someone stronger than you takes your hand and forces you to hit someone, we can say that is an involuntary action. But if you decide between alternatives, in one sense that choice is always voluntary. Even the robber's demand—"your money or your life"—involves an element of choice. You could refuse to turn over your money and see whether he is serious about killing you. Few people would make that choice, which leads courts to say that turning over the money in such circumstances is involuntary. Similarly, as in *Brown*, a confession obtained by torture would universally be thought to be involuntary.

But as we move away from the obvious cases, the question becomes much more complicated.

In Chambers v. Florida, 309 U.S. 227, 60 S.Ct. 472, 84 L.Ed. 716 (1940), an elderly white man was robbed and murdered, and the community was "enraged." The sheriff rounded up twenty-five to forty black men. Defendants claimed that they "were continually threatened and physically mistreated." The State, perhaps learning a lesson from *Brown*, denied the mistreatment. In the Court's view, however, it did not matter whether the authorities threatened the suspects. It was enough that they were arrested by "dragnet methods" and then subjected to "protracted questioning * * * without friends, advisers or counselors, and under circumstances calculated to break the strongest nerves and the stoutest resistance." The "undisputed facts," the Court unanimously held, "showed that compulsion was applied." Notice that the critical inquiry was not whether compulsion *moved* the suspect to confess, as it surely did in *Brown*, but whether "compulsion was applied." The Court seemed to be searching for a test of "voluntariness" that was easier to apply.

In Ashcraft v. Tennessee, 322 US 143, 64 S.Ct. 921, 88 L.Ed. 1192 (1944), the Supreme Court held that a confession taken after thirty-six hours of non-stop interrogation was involuntary. The Court concluded that the interrogation by relays was "so inherently coercive that its very existence is irreconcilable with the possession of mental freedom by a lone suspect against whom its full coercive force is brought to bear." That seems intuitively correct. But Justice Jackson asked the critical question in his dissent:

> If the constitutional admissibility of a confession is no longer to be measured by the mental state of the individual confessor but by a general doctrine dependent on the clock, it should be capable of statement in definite terms. If thirty-six hours is more than is permissible, what about 24? or 12? or 6? or 1? All are "inherently coercive."

In sum, what exactly is an involuntary confession?

As Lawrence Herman has cogently put the problems with voluntariness:

> A careful reading of the Court's more than forty involuntary confession cases discloses not one but five different objectives. * * * (1) to deter the police from engaging in conduct that may produce an unreliable confession; (2) to deter the police from engaging in conduct so offensive to the minimum standards of a civilized society that it shocks the conscience of the Court; (3) to deter the police from engaging in less-than-shocking misconduct; (4) to deter the police from using the

> techniques of an inquisitorial system and to encourage them to use the techniques of an accusatorial system; and (5) to deter the police from overbearing the suspect's will.
>
> Your initial reaction may be that these objectives at last give us the definitional tool we need. Precisely the opposite is true, however. Each of the objectives is problematic in one or more ways, and the very number of them obfuscates rather than clarifies.

Given the vagaries of the voluntariness inquiry and the different goals the Court had identified, we should not be surprised at the need for an alternative. Herman writes:

> Small wonder, then, that in a period of thirty years or so, the Supreme Court granted review in over thirty-five cases in which confessions had been held voluntary. Small wonder, too, that the Court reversed the conviction in most of these cases. And small wonder that the Court became disaffected from its own work product. All students of the Court recognize that it cannot police the application of doctrine by lower courts. All it can hope to do is make doctrine intelligible and give illustrative examples. The Court tried to do that in the confession cases, and it failed. Given the inherent vagueness of the crucial concepts and the many rationales underlying the rule, failure was foreordained. So also was the search for an alternative.

Lawrence Herman, *The Supreme Court, the Attorney General, and the Good Old Days of Police Interrogation*, 48 Ohio St. L.J. 733, 749–50, 754–55 (1987).

One attempt to provide an alternative limit on interrogation more precise than the voluntariness test was Escobedo v. Illinois, 378 U.S. 478, 84 S.Ct. 1758, 12 L.Ed.2d 977 (1964). Two years before *Miranda*, the Court held that the Sixth Amendment was violated when the police denied Escobedo's request to speak to his lawyer who was present in the police station; Escobedo was being interrogated before charges were filed but after the investigation had focused on him. The Sixth Amendment provides: "In all criminal prosecutions, the accused shall enjoy the right * * * to have the Assistance of Counsel for his defence." The dissents soundly criticized the majority for applying the Sixth Amendment right to counsel in a pre-indictment case. Do you see the interpretive difficulty? Moreover, the narrow holding in *Escobedo* would not benefit many suspects because very few would have a lawyer or know to request his presence.

Justice White's dissent in *Escobedo* presaged what the Court would do in *Miranda*:

> The Court may be concerned with a narrower matter: the unknowing defendant who responds to police questioning because he mistakenly believes that he must, and that his admissions will not be used against him. But this worry hardly calls for the broadside the Court has now fired. The failure to inform an accused that he need not answer and that his answers may be used against him is very relevant indeed to whether the disclosures are compelled. Cases in this Court, to say the least, have never placed a premium on ignorance of constitutional rights. If an accused is told he must answer and does not know better, it would be very doubtful that the resulting admissions could be used against him.

Justice White lost the *Escobedo* battle over the meaning of the Sixth Amendment but won the war. The Court would, in *Miranda*, change the textual basis for its interrogation rules from the Sixth Amendment right to counsel to the Fifth Amendment right against compelled self-incrimination. White dissented in *Miranda* as well.

We looked at *Ashcraft* a moment ago on the issue of what constitutes an involuntary confession. Thirty-six hours of nonstop questioning does the trick. But there is also an important image that the *Ashcraft* Court uses that will support its analysis in *Miranda*. The Court drew an explicit analogy between a suspect who is being interrogated by the police and a criminal defendant on the witness stand in court. Justice Black stressed that no court would permit "prosecutors serving in relays to keep a defendant witness under continuous cross examination" for long periods. "Nor can we, consistently with Constitutional due process of law, hold voluntary a confession where prosecutors do the same thing away from the restraining influences of a public trial in an open court room." Notice, when we get to *Miranda*, that Justice Black, who wrote the majority opinion in *Ashcraft*, joins the majority opinion in *Miranda*.

Ashcraft explicitly based its analogy to the courtroom questioning on the due process clause. The Fifth Amendment right against being compelled to be a witness against oneself had always been thought to apply only to criminal trials and other formal proceedings, such as congressional hearings. In 1965, a year after *Escobedo* attempted to ground interrogation limits in the Sixth Amendment, and a year before *Miranda*, Professor Yale Kamisar argued that the Fifth Amendment right should be extended to the interrogation room. In probably the most influential article yet written on the American law of interrogation, Kamisar argued that a privilege limited to the courtroom setting was not particularly valuable to defendants:

> The courtroom is a splendid place where defense attorneys bellow and strut and prosecuting attorneys are hemmed in at many turns. But what happens before an accused reaches the safety and enjoys the comfort of this veritable mansion? Ah, there's the rub. Typically he must first pass through a much less pretentious edifice, a police station with bare back rooms and locked doors.

Yale Kamisar, *Equal Justice in the Gatehouses and Mansions of American Criminal Procedure: From Powell to Gideon, from Escobedo to * * **, in Criminal Justice in Our Time, 19 (A.E. Dick Howard, ed. 1965).Noting that wealthy privileged suspects routinely faced police interrogators with counsel at their side, Kamisar argued that "respect for the individual and securing equal treatment in law enforcement" require the State to make counsel available to suspects who face police interrogation and to warn them that they need not answer. He concluded: "To the extent the Constitution permits the wealthy and educated to 'defeat justice,' if you will, why shouldn't all defendants be given a like opportunity?" Id. at 79–80.

MIRANDA V. ARIZONA

Supreme Court of the United States, 1966.
384 U.S. 436, 86 S.Ct. 1602, 16 L.Ed.2d 694.

By 1966 it must have been clear to the Court that a more precise rule was needed to govern police interrogation. It was also clear that *Escobedo* was not a rule that would benefit the typical suspect. No, what the Court needed was an all-encompassing rule that applied to all police interrogations. Enter *Miranda.*

MR. CHIEF JUSTICE WARREN delivered the opinion of the Court [joined by JUSTICES BLACK, DOUGLAS, BRENNAN and FORTAS].

The cases before us raise questions which go to the roots of our concepts of American criminal jurisprudence: the restraints society must observe consistent with the Federal Constitution in prosecuting individuals for crime. More specifically, we deal with the admissibility of statements obtained from an individual who is subjected to custodial police interrogation and the necessity for procedures which assure that the individual is accorded his privilege under the Fifth Amendment to the Constitution not to be compelled to incriminate himself.
* * *

We start here * * * with the premise that our holding is not an innovation in our jurisprudence, but is an application of principles long recognized and applied in other settings. We have undertaken a thorough re-examination of the Escobedo decision and the principles it announced, and we reaffirm it. That case was but an explication of basic rights that are enshrined in our Constitution—that "No person * * * shall be compelled in any criminal case to be a witness against himself," and that "the accused shall * * * have the Assistance of Counsel"—rights which were put in jeopardy in that case through official overbearing. These precious rights were fixed in our Constitution only after centuries of persecution and struggle. And in the words of Chief Justice Marshall, they were secured "for ages to come, and * * * designed to approach immortality as nearly as human institutions can approach it." * * *

Our holding will be spelled out with some specificity in the pages which follow but briefly stated it is this: the prosecution may not use statements, whether exculpatory or inculpatory, stemming from custodial interrogation of the defendant unless it demonstrates the use of procedural safeguards effective to secure the privilege against self-incrimination. By custodial interrogation, we mean questioning initiated by law enforcement officers after a person has been taken into custody or otherwise deprived of his freedom of action in any significant way. * * *

I

The constitutional issue we decide in each of these cases is the admissibility of statements obtained from a defendant questioned while in custody or otherwise deprived of his freedom of action in any significant way. In each, the defendant was questioned by police officers, detectives, or a prosecuting attorney in a room in which he was cut off from the outside world. In none of these cases was the defendant given a full and effective warning of his rights at the outset of the interrogation process. In all the cases, the questioning elicited oral admissions, and in three of them, signed statements as well which were admitted at their trials. They all thus share salient features—incommunicado interrogation of individuals in a police-dominated atmosphere, resulting in self-incriminating statements without full warnings of constitutional rights.

An understanding of the nature and setting of this in-custody interrogation is essential to our decisions today. The difficulty in depicting what transpires at such interrogations stems from the fact that in this country they have largely taken place incommunicado. * * *

Again we stress that the modern practice of in-custody interrogation is psychologically rather than physically oriented. As we have stated before, "* * * [T]his Court has recognized that coercion can be mental as well as physical, and that the blood of the accused is not the only hallmark of an unconstitutional inquisition." Interrogation still takes place in privacy. Privacy results in secrecy and this in turn results in a gap in our knowledge as to what in fact goes on in the interrogation rooms. A valuable source of information about present police practices, however, may be found in various police manuals and texts which document procedures employed with success in the past, and which recommend various other effective tactics. These texts are used by law enforcement agencies themselves as guides. It should be noted that these texts professedly present the most enlightened and effective means presently used to obtain statements through custodial interrogation. By considering these texts and other data, it is possible to describe procedures observed and noted around the country.

[The methods described in Inbau & Reid, Criminal Interrogation and Confessions (1962), are a revision and enlargement of material presented in three prior editions of a predecessor text, Lie Detection and Criminal Interrogation (3d ed. 1953). * * * Similarly, the techniques described in O'Hara, Fundamentals of Criminal Investigation (1956), were gleaned from long service as observer, lecturer in police science, and work as a federal criminal investigator. All these texts have had rather extensive use among law enforcement agencies and among students of police science, with total sales and circulation of over 44,000. Eds.]

The officers are told by the manuals that the "principal psychological factor contributing to a successful interrogation is privacy—being alone with the person under interrogation." The efficacy of this tactic has been explained as follows:

> "If at all practicable, the interrogation should take place in the investigator's office or at least in a room of his own choice. The subject should be deprived of every psychological advantage. In his own home he may be confident, indignant, or recalcitrant. He is more keenly aware of his rights and more reluctant to tell of his indiscretions or criminal behavior within the walls of his home. Moreover his family and other friends are nearby, their presence lending moral support. In his own office, the investigator possesses all the advantages. The atmosphere suggests the invincibility of the forces of the law."

To highlight the isolation and unfamiliar surroundings, the manuals instruct the police to display an air of confidence in the suspect's guilt and from outward appearance to maintain only an interest in confirming certain details. The guilt of the subject is to be posited as a fact. The interrogator should direct his comments toward the reasons why the subject committed the act, rather than court failure by asking the subject whether he did it. Like other men, perhaps the subject has had a bad family life, had an unhappy childhood, had too much to drink, had an unrequited desire for women. The officers are instructed to minimize the moral seriousness of the offense, to cast blame on the victim or on society. These tactics are designed to put the subject in a psychological state where his story is but an elaboration of what the police purport to know already—that he is guilty. Explanations to the contrary are dismissed and discouraged.

The texts thus stress that the major qualities an interrogator should possess are patience and perseverance. One writer describes the efficacy of these characteristics in this manner:

> "In the preceding paragraphs emphasis has been placed on kindness and stratagems. The investigator will, however, encounter many situations where the sheer weight of his personality will be the deciding factor. Where emotional appeals and tricks are employed to no avail, he must rely on an oppressive atmosphere of dogged persistence. He must interrogate steadily and without relent, leaving the subject no prospect of surcease. He must dominate his subject and overwhelm him with his inexorable will to obtain the truth. He should interrogate for a spell of several hours pausing only for the subject's necessities in acknowledgment of the need to avoid a charge of duress that can be technically substantiated. In a serious case, the interrogation may continue for days, with the required intervals for food and sleep, but with no respite from the atmosphere of domination. It is possible in this way to induce the suspect to talk without resorting to duress or coercion. The method should be used only when the guilt of the suspect appears highly probable."

The manuals suggest that the suspect be offered legal excuses for his actions in order to obtain an initial admission of guilt. Where there is a suspected revenge-killing, for example, the interrogator may say:

> "Joe, you probably didn't go out looking for this fellow with the purpose of shooting him. My guess is, however, that you expected something from him and that's why you carried a gun—for your own protection. You knew him for what he was, no good. Then when you met him he probably started using foul, abusive language and he gave some indication that he was about to pull a gun on you, and that's when you had to act to save your own life. That's about it, isn't it, Joe?"

Having then obtained the admission of shooting, the interrogator is advised to refer to circumstantial evidence which negates the self-defense explanation. This should enable him to secure the entire story. One text notes that "Even if he fails to do so, the inconsistency between the subject's original denial of the shooting and his present admission of at least doing the shooting will serve to deprive him of a self-defense 'out' at the time of trial." * * *

The interrogators sometimes are instructed to induce a confession out of trickery. The technique here is quite effective in crimes which require identification or which run in series. In the identification situation, the interrogator may take a break in his questioning to place the subject among a group of men in a line-up. "The witness or complainant (previously coached, if necessary) studies the line-up and confidently points out the subject as the guilty party." Then the questioning resumes "as though there were now no doubt about the guilt of the subject." A variation on this technique is called the "reverse line-up":

> "The accused is placed in a line-up, but this time he is identified by several fictitious witnesses or victims who associated him with different offenses. It is expected that the subject will become desperate and confess to the offense under investigation in order to escape from the false accusations." * * *

[The Court described other strategies, including the "Mutt and Jeff" act in which one officer plays the good cop and one the brutal bad cop who can be kept under control only if the suspect cooperates with the good cop. Another strategy discourages silence: "Suppose you were in my shoes and I were in yours and you called me in to ask me about this and I told you 'I don't want to answer any of your questions.' You'd think I had something to hide, and you'd probably be right in thinking that." Finally, one strategy discourages requests to talk to a lawyer or to a relative: "Joe I'm only looking for the truth, and if you're telling the truth, that's it. You can handle this by yourself." The Court noted, "Few will persist in their initial refusal to talk, it is said, if this monologue is employed correctly." Eds.]

From these representative samples of interrogation techniques, the setting prescribed by the manuals and observed in practice becomes clear. In essence, it is this: To be alone with the subject is essential to prevent distraction and to deprive him of any outside support. The aura of confidence in his guilt undermines his will to resist. He merely confirms the preconceived story the police seek to have him describe. Patience and persistence, at times relentless questioning, are employed. To obtain a confession, the interrogator must "patiently maneuver himself or his quarry into a position from which the desired objective may be attained." When normal procedures fail to produce the needed result, the police may resort to deceptive stratagems such as giving false legal advice. It is important to keep the subject off balance, for example, by trading on his insecurity about himself or his surroundings. The police then persuade, trick, or cajole him out of exercising his constitutional rights. * * *

In the cases before us today, given this background, we concern ourselves primarily with this interrogation atmosphere and the evils it can bring. In No. 759, *Miranda v. Arizona*, the police arrested the defendant and took him to a special interrogation room where they secured a confession. In No. 760, *Vignera v. New York*, the defendant made oral admissions to the police after interrogation in the afternoon, and then signed an inculpatory statement upon being questioned by an assistant district attorney later the same evening. In No. 761, *Westover v. United States*, the defendant was handed over to the Federal Bureau of Investigation by local authorities after they had detained and interrogated him for a lengthy period, both at night and the following morning. After some two hours of questioning, the federal officers had obtained signed statements from the defendant. Lastly, in No. 584, *California v. Stewart*, the local police held the defendant five days in the station and interrogated him on nine separate occasions before they secured his inculpatory statement.

In these cases, we might not find the defendants' statements to have been involuntary in traditional terms. Our concern for adequate safeguards to protect precious Fifth Amendment rights is, of course, not lessened in the slightest. In each of the cases, the defendant was thrust into an unfamiliar atmosphere and run through menacing police interrogation procedures. The potentiality for compulsion is forcefully apparent, for example, in *Miranda*, where the indigent Mexican defendant was a seriously disturbed individual with pronounced sexual fantasies, and in Stewart, in which the defendant was an indigent Los Angeles Negro who had dropped out of school in the sixth grade. To be sure, the records do not evince overt physical coercion or patent psychological ploys. The fact remains that in none of these cases did the officers undertake to afford appropriate safeguards at the outset of the interrogation to insure that the statements were truly the product of free choice.

It is obvious that such an interrogation environment is created for no purpose other than to subjugate the individual to the will of his examiner. This atmosphere carries its own badge of intimidation. To be sure, this is not physical intimidation, but it is equally destructive of human dignity. The current practice of incommunicado interrogation is at odds with one of our Nation's most cherished principles—that the individual may not be compelled to incriminate himself. Unless adequate protective devices are employed to dispel the compulsion inherent in custodial surroundings, no statement obtained from the defendant can truly be the product of his free choice.

From the foregoing, we can readily perceive an intimate connection between the privilege against self-incrimination and police custodial questioning. It is fitting to turn to history and precedent underlying the Self-Incrimination Clause to determine its applicability in this situation.

II.

We sometimes forget how long it has taken to establish the privilege against self-incrimination, the sources from which it came and the fervor with which it was defended. Its roots go back into ancient times. * * *

Thus we may view the historical development of the privilege as one which groped for the proper scope of governmental power over the citizen. As a "noble principle often transcends its origins," the privilege has come rightfully to be recognized in part as an individual's substantive right, a "right to a private enclave where he may lead a private life. That right is the hallmark of our democracy." We have recently noted that the privilege against self-incrimination—the essential mainstay of our adversary system—is founded on a complex of values. All these policies point to one overriding thought: the constitutional foundation underlying the privilege is the respect a government—state or federal—must accord to the dignity and integrity of its citizens. To maintain a "fair state-individual balance," to require the government "to shoulder the entire load," to respect the inviolability of the human personality, our accusatory system of criminal justice demands that the government seeking to punish an individual produce the evidence against him by its own independent labors, rather than by the cruel, simple expedient of compelling it from his own mouth. In sum, the privilege is fulfilled only when the person is guaranteed the right "to remain silent unless he chooses to speak in the unfettered exercise of his own will."

The question in these cases is whether the privilege is fully applicable during a period of custodial interrogation. In this Court, the privilege has consistently been accorded a liberal construction. We are satisfied that all the principles embodied in the privilege apply to informal compulsion exerted by law-enforcement officers during in-custody questioning. An individual swept from familiar surroundings into police custody, surrounded by antagonistic forces, and subjected to the techniques of persuasion described above cannot be otherwise than under compulsion to speak. As a practical matter, the compulsion to speak in the isolated setting of the police station may well be greater than in courts or other official investigations, where there are often impartial observers to guard against intimidation or trickery. * * *

III

Today, then, there can be no doubt that the Fifth Amendment privilege is available outside of criminal court proceedings and serves to protect persons in all settings in which their freedom of action is curtailed in any significant way from being compelled to incriminate themselves. We have concluded that without proper safeguards the process of in-custody interrogation of persons suspected or accused of crime contains inherently compelling pressures which work to undermine the individual's will to resist and to compel him to speak where he would not otherwise do so freely. In order to combat these pressures and to permit a full opportunity to exercise the privilege against self-incrimination, the accused must be adequately and effectively apprised of his rights and the exercise of those rights must be fully honored.

It is impossible for us to foresee the potential alternatives for protecting the privilege which might be devised by Congress or the States in the exercise of their creative rule-making capacities. Therefore we cannot say that the Constitution necessarily requires adherence to any particular solution for the inherent compulsions of the interrogation process as it is presently conducted. Our decision in no way creates a constitutional straitjacket which will handicap sound efforts at reform, nor is it intended to have this effect. We encourage Congress and the States to continue their laudable search for increasingly effective ways of protecting the rights of the individual while promoting efficient enforcement of our criminal laws. However, unless we are shown other procedures which are at least as effective in apprising accused persons of their right of silence and in assuring a continuous opportunity to exercise it, the following safeguards must be observed.

At the outset, if a person in custody is to be subjected to interrogation, he must first be informed in clear and unequivocal terms that he has the right to remain silent. For those unaware of the privilege, the warning is needed simply to make them aware of it—the threshold requirement for an intelligent decision as to its exercise. More important, such a warning is an absolute prerequisite in overcoming the inherent pressures of the interrogation atmosphere. It is not just the subnormal or woefully ignorant who succumb to an interrogator's imprecations, whether implied or expressly stated, that the interrogation will continue until a confession is obtained or that silence in the face of accusation is itself damning and will bode ill when presented to a jury. Further, the warning will show the individual that his interrogators are prepared to recognize his privilege should he choose to exercise it.

The Fifth Amendment privilege is so fundamental to our system of constitutional rule and the expedient of giving an adequate warning as to the availability of the privilege so simple, we will not pause to inquire in individual cases whether the defendant was aware of his rights without a warning being given. Assessments of the knowledge the defendant possessed, based on information as to his age, education, intelligence, or prior contact with authorities, can never be more than a speculation. More important, whatever the background of the person interrogated, a warning at the time of the interrogation is indispensable to overcome its pressures and to insure that the individual knows he is free to exercise the privilege at that point in time.

The warning of the right to remain silent must be accompanied by the explanation that anything said can and will be used against the individual in court. This warning is needed in order to make him aware not only of the privilege, but also of the consequences of forgoing it. It is only through an awareness of these consequences that there can be any assurance of real understanding and intelligent exercise of the privilege. Moreover, this warning may serve to make the individual more acutely aware that he is faced with a phase of the adversary system—that he is not in the presence of persons acting solely in his interest.

The circumstances surrounding in-custody interrogation can operate very quickly to overbear the will of one merely made aware of his privilege by his interrogators. Therefore, the right to have counsel present at the interrogation is indispensable to the protection of the Fifth Amendment privilege under the system we delineate today. Our aim is to assure that the individual's right to choose between silence and speech remains unfettered throughout the interrogation process. A once-stated warning, delivered by those who will conduct the interrogation, cannot itself suffice to that end among those who most require knowledge of their rights. A mere warning given by the interrogators is not alone sufficient to accomplish that end. Prosecutors themselves claim that the admonishment of the right to remain silent without more "will benefit only the recidivist and the professional." Even preliminary advice given to the accused by his own attorney can be swiftly overcome by the secret interrogation process. Thus, the need for counsel to protect the Fifth Amendment privilege comprehends not merely a right to consult with counsel prior to questioning, but also to have counsel present during any questioning if the defendant so desires.

The presence of counsel at the interrogation may serve several significant subsidiary functions as well. If the accused decides to talk to his interrogators, the assistance of counsel can mitigate the dangers of untrustworthiness. With a lawyer present the likelihood that the police will practice coercion is reduced, and if coercion is nevertheless exercised the lawyer can testify to it in court. The presence of a lawyer can also help to guarantee that the accused gives a fully accurate statement to the police and that the statement is rightly reported by the prosecution at trial.

An individual need not make a pre-interrogation request for a lawyer. While such request affirmatively secures his right to have one, his failure to ask for a lawyer does not constitute a waiver. No effective waiver of the right to counsel during interrogation can be recognized unless specifically made after the warnings we here delineate have been given. The accused who does not know his rights and therefore does not make a request may be the person who most needs counsel. * * *

Accordingly we hold that an individual held for interrogation must be clearly informed that he has the right to consult with a lawyer and to have the lawyer with him during interrogation under the system for protecting the privilege we delineate today. As with the warnings of the right to remain silent and that anything stated can be used in evidence against him, this warning is an absolute prerequisite to interrogation. No amount of circumstantial evidence that the person may have been aware of this right will suffice to stand in its stead. Only through such a warning is there ascertainable assurance that the accused was aware of this right.

If an individual indicates that he wishes the assistance of counsel before any interrogation occurs, the authorities cannot rationally ignore or deny his request on the basis that the individual does not have or cannot afford a retained attorney. The financial ability of the individual has no relationship to the scope of the rights involved here. The privilege against self-incrimination secured by the Constitution applies to all individuals. The need for counsel in order to protect the privilege exists for the indigent as well as the affluent. In fact, were we to limit these constitutional rights to those who can retain an attorney, our decisions today would be of little significance. The cases before us as well as the vast majority of confession cases with which we have dealt in the past involve those unable to retain counsel. While authorities are not required to relieve the accused of his poverty, they have the obligation not to take advantage of indigence in the administration of justice. * * *

In order fully to apprise a person interrogated of the extent of his rights under this system then, it is necessary to warn him not only that he has the right to consult with an attorney, but also that if he is indigent a lawyer will be appointed to represent him. Without this additional warning, the admonition of the right to consult with counsel would often be understood as meaning only that he can consult with a lawyer if he has one or has funds to obtain one. The warning of a right to counsel would be hollow if not couched in terms that would convey to the indigent—the person most often subjected to interrogation—the knowledge that he too has a right to have counsel present. As with the warnings of the right to remain silent and of the general right to counsel, only by effective and express explanation to the indigent of this right can there be assurance that he was truly in a position to exercise it.

Once warnings have been given, the subsequent procedure is clear. If the individual indicates in any manner, at any time prior to or during questioning, that he wishes to remain silent, the interrogation must cease. At this point he has shown that he intends to exercise his Fifth Amendment privilege; any statement taken after the person invokes his privilege cannot be other than the product of compulsion, subtle or otherwise. Without the right to cut off questioning, the setting of in-custody interrogation operates on the individual to overcome free choice in producing a statement after the privilege has been once invoked. If the individual states that he wants an attorney, the interrogation must cease until an attorney is present. At that time, the individual must have an opportunity to confer with the attorney and to have him present during any subsequent questioning. If the individual cannot obtain an attorney and he indicates that he wants one before speaking to police, they must respect his decision to remain silent. * * *

If the interrogation continues without the presence of an attorney and a statement is taken, a heavy burden rests on the government to demonstrate that the defendant knowingly and intelligently waived his privilege against self-incrimination and his right to retained or appointed counsel. This Court has always set high standards of proof for the waiver of constitutional rights, and we re-assert these standards as applied to in-custody interrogation. Since the State is responsible for establishing the isolated circumstances under which the interrogation takes place and has the only means of making available corroborated evidence of warnings given during incommunicado interrogation, the burden is rightly on its shoulders.

An express statement that the individual is willing to make a statement and does not want an attorney followed closely by a statement could constitute a waiver. But a valid waiver will not be presumed simply from the silence of the accused after warnings are given or simply from the fact that a confession was in fact eventually obtained. A statement we made in Carnley v. Cochran, 369 U.S. 506, 516, 82 S.Ct. 884, 8 L.Ed.2d 70 (1962), is applicable here:

> "Presuming waiver from a silent record is impermissible. The record must show, or there must be an allegation and evidence which show, that an accused was offered counsel but intelligently and understandingly rejected the offer. Anything less is not waiver."

Moreover, where in-custody interrogation is involved, there is no room for the contention that the privilege is waived if the individual answers some questions or gives some information on his own prior to invoking his right to remain silent when interrogated.

Whatever the testimony of the authorities as to waiver of rights by an accused, the fact of lengthy interrogation or incommunicado incarceration before a statement is made is strong evidence that the accused did not validly waive his rights. In these circumstances the fact that the individual eventually made a statement is consistent with the conclusion that the compelling influence of the interrogation finally forced him to do so. It is inconsistent with any notion of a voluntary relinquishment of the privilege. Moreover, any evidence that the accused was threatened, tricked, or cajoled into a waiver will, of course, show that the defendant did not voluntarily waive his privilege. The requirement of warnings and waiver of rights is a fundamental with respect to the Fifth Amendment privilege and not simply a preliminary ritual to existing methods of interrogation.

The warnings required and the waiver necessary in accordance with our opinion today are, in the absence of a fully effective equivalent, prerequisites to the admissibility of any statement made by a defendant. No distinction can be drawn between statements which are direct confessions and statements which amount to "admissions" of part or all of an offense. The privilege against self-incrimination protects the individual from being compelled to incriminate himself in any manner; it does not distinguish degrees of incrimination. Similarly, for precisely the same reason, no distinction may be drawn between inculpatory statements and statements alleged to be merely "exculpatory." If a statement made were in fact truly exculpatory it would, of course, never be used by the prosecution. In fact, statements merely intended to be exculpatory by the defendant are often used to impeach his testimony at trial or to demonstrate untruths in the statement given under interrogation and thus to prove guilt by implication. These statements are incriminating in any meaningful sense of the word and may not be used without the full warnings and effective waiver required for any other statement. In Escobedo itself, the defendant fully intended his accusation of another as the slayer to be exculpatory as to himself.

The principles announced today deal with the protection which must be given to the privilege against self-incrimination when the individual is first subjected to police interrogation while in custody at the station or otherwise deprived of his freedom of action in any significant way. It is at this point that our adversary system of criminal proceedings commences, distinguishing itself at the outset from the inquisitorial system recognized in some countries. Under the system of warnings we delineate today or under any other system which may be devised and found effective, the safeguards to be erected about the privilege must come into play at this point.

Our decision is not intended to hamper the traditional function of police officers in investigating crime. When an individual is in custody on probable cause, the police may, of course, seek out evidence in the field to be used at trial against him. Such investigation may include inquiry of persons not under restraint. General on-the-scene questioning as to facts surrounding a crime or other general questioning of citizens in the fact-finding process is not affected by our holding. It is an act of responsible citizenship for individuals to give whatever information they may have to aid in law enforcement. In such situations the compelling atmosphere inherent in the process of in-custody interrogation is not necessarily present. * * *

To summarize, we hold that when an individual is taken into custody or otherwise deprived of his freedom by the authorities in any significant way and is subjected to questioning, the privilege against self-incrimination is jeopardized. Procedural safeguards must be employed to protect the privilege, and unless other fully effective means are adopted to notify the person of his right to silence and to assure that the exercise of the right will be scrupulously honored, the following measures are required. He must be warned prior to any questioning that he has the right to remain silent, that anything he says can be used against him in a court of law, that he has the right to the presence of an attorney, and that if he cannot afford an attorney one will be appointed for him prior to any questioning if he so desires. Opportunity to exercise these rights must be afforded to him throughout the interrogation. After such warnings have been given, and such opportunity afforded him, the individual may knowingly and intelligently waive these rights and agree to answer questions or make a statement. But unless and until such warnings and waiver are demonstrated by the prosecution at trial, no evidence obtained as a result of interrogation can be used against him. * * *

V

Because of the nature of the problem and because of its recurrent significance in numerous cases, we have to this point discussed the relationship of the Fifth Amendment privilege to police interrogation without specific concentration on the facts of the cases before us. We turn now to these facts to consider the application to these cases of the constitutional principles discussed above. In each instance, we have concluded that statements were obtained from the defendant under circumstances that did not meet constitutional standards for protection of the privilege.

No. 759. *Miranda v. Arizona.*

On March 13, 1963, petitioner, Ernesto Miranda, was arrested at his home and taken in custody to a Phoenix police station. He was there identified by the complaining witness. The police then took him to "Interrogation Room No. 2" of the detective bureau. There he was questioned by two police officers. The officers admitted at trial that Miranda was not advised that he had a right to have an attorney present. Two hours later, the officers emerged from the interrogation room with a written confession signed by Miranda. At the top of the statement was a typed paragraph stating that the confession was made voluntarily, without threats or promises of immunity and "with full knowledge of my legal rights, understanding any statement I make may be used against me."

At his trial before a jury, the written confession was admitted into evidence over the objection of defense counsel, and the officers testified to the prior oral confession made by Miranda during the interrogation. Miranda was found guilty of kidnapping and rape. He was sentenced to 20 to 30 years' imprisonment on each count, the sentences to run concurrently. On appeal, the Supreme Court of Arizona held that Miranda's constitutional rights were not violated in obtaining the confession and affirmed the conviction. In reaching its decision, the court emphasized heavily the fact that Miranda did not specifically request counsel.

We reverse. From the testimony of the officers and by the admission of respondent, it is clear that Miranda was not in any way apprised of his right to consult with an attorney and to have one present during the interrogation, nor was his right not to be compelled to incriminate himself effectively protected in any other manner. Without these warnings the statements were inadmissible. The mere fact that he signed a statement which contained a typed-in clause stating that he had "full knowledge" of his "legal rights" does not approach the knowing and intelligent waiver required to relinquish constitutional rights. * * *

[*The Court reversed the other three convictions as well. The opinion of* J*USTICE* C*LARK, dissenting in three of the cases, including Miranda, and concurring in the result in one of the cases, is omitted.*]

MR. JUSTICE HARLAN, with whom MR. JUSTICE STEWART and MR. JUSTICE WHITE join, dissenting. * * *

I * * *

While the fine points of [the majority's] scheme are far less clear than the Court admits, the tenor is quite apparent. The new rules are not designed to guard against police brutality or other unmistakably banned forms of coercion. Those who use third-degree tactics and deny them in court are equally able and destined to lie as skillfully about warnings and waivers. Rather, the thrust of the new rules is to negate all pressures, to reinforce the nervous or ignorant suspect, and ultimately to discourage any confession at all. The aim in short is toward "voluntariness" in a utopian sense, or to view it from a different angle, voluntariness with a vengeance.

To incorporate this notion into the Constitution requires a strained reading of history and precedent and a disregard of the very pragmatic concerns that alone may on occasion justify such strains. * * *

III * * *

What the Court largely ignores is that its rules impair, if they will not eventually serve wholly to frustrate, an instrument of law enforcement that has long and quite reasonably been thought worth the price paid for it. There can be little doubt that the Court's new code would markedly decrease the number of confessions. * * *

While passing over the costs and risks of its experiment, the Court portrays the evils of normal police questioning in terms which I think are exaggerated. Albeit stringently confined by the due process standards interrogation is no doubt often inconvenient and unpleasant for the suspect. However, it is no less so for a man to be arrested and jailed, to have his house searched, or to stand trial in court, yet all this may properly happen to the most innocent given probable cause, a warrant, or an indictment. Society has always paid a stiff price for law and order, and peaceful interrogation is not one of the dark moments of the law. * * *

MR. JUSTICE WHITE, with whom MR. JUSTICE HARLAN and MR. JUSTICE STEWART join, dissenting. * * *

III * * *

Although in the Court's view in-custody interrogation is inherently coercive, the Court says that the spontaneous product of the coercion of arrest and detention is still to be deemed voluntary. An accused, arrested on probable cause, may blurt out a confession which will be admissible despite the fact that he is alone and in custody, without any showing that he had any notion of his right to remain silent or of the consequences of his admission. Yet, under the Court's rule, if the police ask him a single question such as "Do you have anything to say?" or "Did you kill your wife?" his response, if there is one, has somehow been compelled, even if the accused has been clearly warned of his right to remain silent. Common sense informs us to the contrary. While one may say that the response was "involuntary" in the sense the question provoked or was the occasion for the response and thus the defendant was induced to speak out when he might have remained silent if not arrested and not questioned, it is patently unsound to say the response is compelled. * * *

On the other hand, even if one assumed that there was an adequate factual basis for the conclusion that all confessions obtained during in-custody interrogation are the product of compulsion, the rule propounded by the Court would still be irrational, for, apparently, it is only if the accused is also warned of his right to counsel and waives both that right and the right against self-incrimination that the inherent compulsiveness of interrogation disappears. But if the defendant may not answer without a warning a question such as "Where were you last night?" without having his answer be a compelled one, how can the Court ever accept his negative answer to the question of whether he wants to consult his retained counsel or counsel whom the court will appoint? And why if counsel is present and the accused nevertheless confesses, or counsel tells the accused to tell the truth, and that is what the accused does, is the situation any less coercive insofar as the accused is concerned? The Court apparently realizes its dilemma of foreclosing questioning without the necessary warnings but at the same time permitting the accused, sitting in the same chair in front of the same policemen, to waive his right to consult an attorney. It expects, however, that the accused will not often waive that right; and if it is claimed that he has, the State faces a severe, if not impossible, burden of proof. * * *

In sum, for all the Court's expounding on the menacing atmosphere of police interrogation procedures, it has failed to supply any foundation for the conclusions it draws or the measures it adopts.

IV * * *

The most basic function of any government is to provide for the security of the individual and of his property. These ends of society are served by the criminal laws which for the most part are aimed at the prevention of crime. Without the reasonably effective performance of the task of preventing private violence and retaliation, it is idle to talk about human dignity and civilized values. * * *

In some unknown number of cases the Court's rule will return a killer, a rapist or other criminal to the streets and to the environment which produced him, to repeat his crime whenever it pleases him. As a consequence, there will not be a gain, but a loss, in human dignity. The real concern is not the unfortunate consequences of this new decision on the criminal law as an abstract, disembodied series of authoritative proscriptions, but the impact on those who rely on the public authority for protection and who without it can only engage in violent self-help with guns, knives and the help of their neighbors similarly inclined. There is, of course, a saving factor: the next victims are uncertain, unnamed and unrepresented in this case. * * *

NOTES AND QUESTIONS

1. Is *Miranda* legitimate? The point to a Constitution, of course, is to enshrine certain principles so fundamental that they should stand even when a majority of the country thinks otherwise. This role is often called "counter-majoritarian" because it stands in the way of the ordinary democratic process. Some parts of the Constitution are clear enough not to need much interpretation—the First Amendment provides that "Congress shall make no law respecting an establishment of religion, or prohibiting the free exercise thereof; or abridging the freedom of speech, or of the press." There are some issues at the margin of these rights but their core meanings are clear and obvious: Congress cannot create a State religion or forbid newspapers or political speech.

But when the Court indulges an interpretation of the text that is not obvious, its counter-majoritarian function is more controversial, and its legitimacy potentially weakened. No better example of that exists than the Court's abortion decision, Roe v. Wade, 410 US 113, 93 S.Ct. 705, 35 L.Ed. 2d 147 (1973), where the Court inferred a right to privacy (not mentioned in the Bill of Rights) from the "liberty" protected by the due process clause. But all the due process clause says is that a state cannot "deprive any person of life, liberty, or property, without due process of law." The content of this nebulous "liberty" is not immediately obvious. Reading that "liberty" to include the right to terminate a pregnancy has proved to be controversial. While *Miranda* is hardly as controversial as *Roe*, it was for a time a lightning rod for critics of the Court, as we will shortly see.

The Fifth Amendment provides that no person "shall be compelled in any criminal case to be a witness against himself." Do you think the Court is right that this protection applies to the police interrogation room? What is the contrary argument? One doctrinal fact is clear: The Court first faced the issue of whether the suspect had to be warned of his right to remain silent in 1896 and squarely held that warnings were not required. See Wilson v. United States, 162 U.S. 613, 16 S.Ct. 895, 40 L.Ed. 1090 (1896). Thus, for seventy years, the law was precisely the opposite of what the *Miranda* Court said it was. It bears noting that the *Miranda* majority opinion does not bother to overrule *Wilson*; indeed, the opinion does not even mention *Wilson.*

When the Court is tempted to find new rights in old, vague language, perhaps it should pause to consider how our society has become more partisan, the tenor of our discussions more shrill, the debates over Supreme Court nominees more contentious, and the decisions of the Court more indecipherable to the majority of our citizenry. Judging from the large percentage of our society that chooses not to take advantage of its right to vote, it appears that we have become increasingly disengaged from and cynical towards the democratic process as a means of effective societal change. Application of the Constitution as a counter-majoritarian check has not come without a price.

2. Does the *Miranda* Court see the interrogation problem as police compulsion or, rather, as the police cajoling suspects in a way that creates or exploits the natural tendency of persons to appear co-operative? That tendency would naturally lead suspects to talk even when it is not in their best interests. Perhaps the *Miranda* warnings were intended to create a set of preferences that exist in opposition to the preferences that police wish suspects to have. See Louis Michael Seidman, Rubashov's Question: Self-Incrimination and the Problem of Coerced Preferences, 2 Yale J. L. & Human. 149 (1990).

Police are, of course, quintessential authority figures. Moreover, as Professor Kent Greenawalt provocatively argued in *Silence as a Moral and Constitutional Right*, 23 Wm. & Mary L. Rev. 15 (1981), the ordinary morality we apply in our day-to-day lives usually requires a response when someone accuses us of malfeasance or misfeasance. If your co-worker, for instance, asks why you failed to cover for her as you promised, the future working relationship will be strained if you respond, "I don't have to answer that question." If you do answer, moreover, it is odd to think of that answer as compelled by the questioner. It seems more likely that you evaluated the consequences of answering and not answering, and chose by an exercise of your will to answer. Why consider this choice to be "compulsion"? Examine the text of the Fifth Amendment. What is the textual basis for a "right to remain silent"?

3. *The fox-hunt analogy.* The *Miranda* dissents raise, in one form or another, the normative question: What is wrong with taking advantage of guilty suspects to obtain a confession? One answer is Professor William Stuntz's. He argued that the *Miranda* Court misread the self-incrimination clause as protecting privacy rather than freedom from coercion. *Miranda*'s limits on police questioning, on this view, began with the premise that "the information belonged to the defendant, it was private, and the government had no right to get it unless the defendant chose—really chose—to give

it up." William J. Stuntz, *The Substantive Origins of Criminal Procedure*, 105 Yale L.J. 393, 441 (1995).

Professor Gerald Caplan put it as follows:

> Perhaps the impulse to allow even the unquestionably guilty some prospect of escaping detection or conviction is universal. Wigmore referred to this impulse as the "instinct of giving the game fair play." Pound characterized it as "the sporting theory" of justice, and Bentham derisively labeled it "the fox hunter's reason." Under this view, fairness is given that special definition that sportsmen reserve for their games. Bentham elaborated on his analogy to the fox hunt: "The fox is to have a fair chance for his life: he must have * * * leave to run a certain length of way, for the express purpose of giving him a chance for escape." Fairness, so defined, dictates that neither side should have an undue advantage; the police and the criminal should be on roughly equal footing and the rules of the game should be drawn to avoid favoring one side or the other. As Justice Fortas put it in a well-known article (written before he joined the Court), the accused and the accuser are "equals, meeting in battle." The state was sovereign, but so was the individual. The individual possessed the "sovereign right * * * to meet the state on terms as equal as their respective strength would permit * * * strength against strength, resource against resource, argument against argument." * * *
>
> [T]he *Miranda* approach reflects a bias against self-accusation on principle. This bias has roots in the desire to treat suspects equally. Suspects who do not know their rights, or do not assert them, as a consequence of some handicap—poverty, lack of education, emotional instability—should not, it is felt, fare worse than more accomplished suspects who know and have the capacity to assert their rights. This "equal protection" appeal finds its way repeatedly into judicial opinions and legal commentary. In *Miranda* itself, Chief Justice Warren referred approvingly to [a] California Supreme Court's decision * * *, which stressed that "the defendant who does not realize his rights under the law and who therefore does not request counsel is the very defendant who most needs counsel." A few years earlier, Professor Beisel similarly argued that only the "frightened, the insecure, the weak, and untrained, the bewildered, the stupid, the naive, the credulous" confess. * * * To the extent that these observations are true—and they seem true enough—they suggest two distinct remedies. One would be to make it more difficult to convict those who are most vulnerable; the other would be to develop ways to bring those hardier, more knowledgeable persons—the hired killer, the calculating embezzler, the experienced

> burglar—to justice. The critics * * * have preferred the former. They do not see the lack of stamina and professionalism of the suspect as conferring a benefit on society by facilitating the identification of wrongdoers.
>
> But guilt is personal. That another, equally guilty, person got away with murder because of some fortuitous factor—he was more experienced in dealing with the police, he had a poorly developed sense of guilt, he had a smart lawyer, he knew his rights—or even because of discrimination, does not make the more vulnerable murderer less guilty. To hold otherwise is to confuse justice with equality. "Both are desirable. However, neither can replace the other." Since sophisticated suspects ordinarily will choose not to confess (with or without knowledge of their rights), "[t]o strive for equality * * * is to strive to eliminate confessions." Thus, the *Miranda* Court elected to let one person get away with murder because of the advantage possessed by another.

Gerald M. Caplan, *Questioning Miranda*, 38 Vand. L. Rev. 1417, 1441–42, 1456–58 (1985).

4. *Miranda: more pros and cons.* The Supreme Court has spoken of the privilege in stirring language. For example, "the roots of the privilege * * * tap the basic stream of religious and political principle because the privilege reflects the limits of the individual's attornment to the state and—in a philosophical sense—insists upon the equality of the individual and the state." In re Gault, 387 U.S. 1, 87 S.Ct. 1428, 18 L.Ed.2d 527 (1967). Before he joined the Court, Abe Fortas wrote: "A man may be punished, even put to death by the state, but * * * he should not be made to prostrate himself before its majesty. Mea culpa belongs to a man and his God. It is a plea that cannot be exacted from free men by human authority." Abe Fortas, *The Fifth Amendment: Nemo Tenetur Prodere Seipsum*, 25 Clev. B. Ass'n J. 91, 100 (1954).

The Court noted in 1964 that "the privilege, while sometimes 'a shelter to the guilty,' is often 'a protection to the innocent.' " Does the privilege only "sometimes" shelter the guilty but "often" protect the innocent? It does not seem likely. To be sure, an innocent defendant might make a poor witness or have a felony record that can be introduced to impeach his credibility if he testifies. Professor Stephen Schulhofer notes that the defendant "may look sleazy. He may be inarticulate, nervous, or easily intimidated. His vague memory on some of the details may leave him vulnerable to a clever cross-examination." Stephen J. Schulhofer, *Some Kind Words for the Privilege Against Self-Incrimination*, 26 Val. U. L. Rev. 311, 330 (1991). But Judge Henry Friendly concluded that the privilege "so much more often shelters the guilty" that its "occasional effect in protecting the innocent would be an altogether insufficient reason" to find the privilege beneficial. Henry J. Friendly, *The Fifth Amendment Tomorrow: The Case for Constitutional Change*, 37 U. Cin. L. Rev. 671, 687 (1968).

Professor Donald Dripps has remarked, with characteristic economy, that "[t]he privilege is at best an anachronism and at worst a constitutional blunder." Donald Dripps, *Akhil Amar On Criminal Procedure and Constitutional Law: "Here I Go Down That Wrong Road Again,"* 74 N. C. L. Rev. 1559, 1635 (1996). As you proceed through this chapter, you should consider whether you agree more with Professor Dripps's characterization of the Fifth Amendment privilege or, instead, the sentiments in the first paragraph of this Note.

5. *Where are they now?* The Court's sweeping judgment in *Miranda* was hardly the end of Ernest Miranda's contact with the criminal justice system. The state re-prosecuted—without the confession given to the police, of course—and the second trial ended again in a conviction. The principal evidence was a confession Miranda made to his girlfriend when she visited him in jail a few days after he had confessed to the police. Liva Baker, *Miranda*: Crime, Law and Politics 291 (1983). Miranda's second conviction was affirmed on appeal, and the United States Supreme Court denied certiorari. Thus, Ernest Miranda served a prison term for the very rape that led to the most controversial criminal procedure ruling in the history of the Supreme Court.

But that is still not the end of the story. After Miranda was paroled, he returned to Phoenix, and worked for a time as an appliance store deliveryman. On January 31, 1976, he played poker with two Mexican immigrants in La Ampola, a "dusty bar in the Deuce section of Phoenix." A fistfight escalated into a knife attack on Miranda. He was stabbed twice and was dead on arrival at Good Samaritan Hospital. Miranda was 34 years old. The police apprehended one of the immigrants, later charged as an accomplice in the killing of Miranda. The officers read the suspect his *Miranda* rights. Baker, at 408.

6. What is the narrow holding in *Miranda*? If you said, police must give warnings whenever they question a suspect who is in custody, you would be right as a general matter. But there is an exception. Can you imagine a set of circumstances in which the police are questioning a suspect who is in custody and yet police do not have to give warnings? The next case answers that riddle. It also makes plain that application of *Miranda* is not always as neat and easy as Chief Justice Warren's opinion implies and, perhaps the *Miranda* majority desired.

ILLINOIS V. PERKINS

Supreme Court of the United States, 1990.
496 US 292, 110 S.Ct. 2394, 110 L.Ed. 2d 243.

Lloyd Perkins was in jail when an undercover officer asked him whether he had ever murdered anyone. He confessed in detail to an unsolved murder. He was in jail; he was questioned by a police officer. Is

this custodial interrogation as defined by *Miranda*? Read on and see what it means to think like a lawyer!

JUSTICE KENNEDY delivered the opinion of the Court [joined by CHIEF JUSTICE REHNQUIST and JUSTICES WHITE, BLACKMUN, STEVENS, O'CONNOR, and SCALIA].

An undercover government agent was placed in the cell of respondent Perkins, who was incarcerated on charges unrelated to the subject of the agent's investigation. Respondent made statements that implicated him in the crime that the agent sought to solve. Respondent claims that the statements should be inadmissible because he had not been given *Miranda* warnings by the agent. We hold that the statements are admissible. *Miranda* warnings are not required when the suspect is unaware that he is speaking to a law enforcement officer and gives a voluntary statement.

I

In November 1984, Richard Stephenson was murdered in a suburb of East St. Louis, Illinois. The murder remained unsolved until March 1986, when one Donald Charlton told police that he had learned about a homicide from a fellow inmate at the Graham Correctional Facility, where Charlton had been serving a sentence for burglary. The fellow inmate was Lloyd Perkins, who is the respondent here. Charlton told police that, while at Graham, he had befriended respondent, who told him in detail about a murder that respondent had committed in East St. Louis. On hearing Charlton's account, the police recognized details of the Stephenson murder that were not well known, and so they treated Charlton's story as a credible one.

By the time the police heard Charlton's account, respondent had been released from Graham, but police traced him to a jail in Montgomery County, Illinois, where he was being held pending trial on a charge of aggravated battery, unrelated to the Stephenson murder. The police wanted to investigate further respondent's connection to the Stephenson murder, but feared that the use of an eavesdropping device would prove impracticable and unsafe. They decided instead to place an undercover agent in the cellblock with respondent and Charlton. The plan was for Charlton and undercover agent John Parisi to pose as escapees from a work release program who had been arrested in the course of a burglary. Parisi and Charlton were instructed to engage respondent in casual conversation and report anything he said about the Stephenson murder.

Parisi, using the alias "Vito Bianco," and Charlton, both clothed in jail garb, were placed in the cellblock with respondent at the Montgomery County jail. The cellblock consisted of 12 separate cells that opened onto a common room. Respondent greeted Charlton who, after a brief conversation with respondent, introduced Parisi by his alias. Parisi told respondent that he "wasn't going to do any more time" and suggested that the three of them escape. Respondent replied that the Montgomery County jail was "rinky-dink" and that they could "break out." The trio met in respondent's cell later that evening, after the other inmates were asleep, to refine their plan. Respondent said that his girlfriend could smuggle in a pistol. Charlton said: "Hey, I'm not a murderer, I'm a burglar. That's your guys' profession." After telling Charlton that he would be responsible for any murder that occurred, Parisi asked respondent if he had ever "done" anybody. Respondent said that he had and proceeded to describe at length the events of the Stephenson murder. Parisi and respondent then engaged in some casual conversation before respondent went to sleep. Parisi did not give respondent *Miranda* warnings before the conversations. Respondent was charged with the Stephenson murder. Before trial, he moved to suppress the statements made to Parisi in the jail. The trial court granted the motion to suppress, and the State appealed. The Appellate Court of Illinois affirmed, holding that *Miranda* prohibits all undercover contacts with incarcerated suspects that are reasonably likely to elicit an incriminating response.

We granted certiorari to decide whether an undercover law enforcement officer must give *Miranda* warnings to an incarcerated suspect before asking him questions that may elicit an incriminating response. We now reverse.

II

In *Miranda*, the Court held that the Fifth Amendment privilege against self-incrimination prohibits admitting statements given by a suspect during "custodial interrogation" without a prior warning. Custodial interrogation means "questioning initiated by law enforcement officers after a person has been taken into custody * * *." The warning mandated by *Miranda* was meant to preserve the privilege during "incommunicado interrogation of individuals in a police-dominated atmosphere." That atmosphere is said to generate "inherently compelling pressures which work to undermine the individual's will to resist and to compel him to speak where he would not otherwise do so freely." "Fidelity to the doctrine announced in *Miranda* requires that it be enforced strictly, but only in those types of situations in which the concerns that powered the decision are implicated."

Conversations between suspects and undercover agents do not implicate the concerns underlying *Miranda*. The essential ingredients of a "police-dominated atmosphere" and compulsion are not present when an incarcerated person speaks freely to someone whom he believes to be a fellow inmate. Coercion is determined from the perspective of the suspect. When a suspect considers himself in the company of cellmates and not officers, the coercive atmosphere is lacking. There is no empirical basis for the assumption that a suspect speaking to those whom he assumes are not officers will feel compelled to speak by the fear of reprisal for remaining silent or in the hope of more lenient treatment should he confess.

It is the premise of *Miranda* that the danger of coercion results from the interaction of custody and official interrogation. We reject the argument that *Miranda* warnings are required whenever a suspect is in custody in a technical sense and converses with someone who happens to be a government agent. Questioning by captors, who appear to control the suspect's fate, may create mutually reinforcing pressures that the Court has assumed will weaken the suspect's will, but where a suspect does not know that he is conversing with a government agent, these pressures do not exist. The state court here mistakenly assumed that because the suspect was in custody, no undercover questioning could take place. When the suspect has no reason to think that the listeners have official power over him, it should not be assumed that his words are motivated by the reaction he expects from his listeners. "[W]hen the agent carries neither badge nor gun and wears not 'police blue,' but the same prison gray" as the suspect, there is no "interplay between police interrogation and police custody."

Miranda forbids coercion, not mere strategic deception by taking advantage of a suspect's misplaced trust in one he supposes to be a fellow prisoner. As we recognized in *Miranda*: "Confessions remain a proper element in law enforcement. Any statement given freely and voluntarily without any compelling influences is, of course, admissible in evidence.". Ploys to mislead a suspect or lull him into a false sense of security that do not rise to the level of compulsion or coercion to speak are not within *Miranda*'s concerns.

Miranda was not meant to protect suspects from boasting about their criminal activities in front of persons whom they believe to be their cellmates. This case is illustrative. Respondent had no reason to feel that undercover agent Parisi had any legal authority to force him to answer questions or that Parisi could affect respondent's future treatment. Respondent viewed the cellmate-agent as an equal and showed no hint of being intimidated by the atmosphere of the jail. In recounting the details of the Stephenson murder, respondent was motivated solely by the desire to impress his fellow inmates. He spoke at his own peril.

The tactic employed here to elicit a voluntary confession from a suspect does not violate the Self-Incrimination Clause. * * *

This Court's Sixth Amendment decisions * * * also do not avail respondent. We held in those cases that the government may not use an undercover agent to circumvent the Sixth Amendment right to counsel once a suspect has been charged with the crime. After charges have been filed, the Sixth Amendment prevents the government from interfering with the accused's right to counsel. In the instant case no charges had been filed on the subject of the interrogation, and our Sixth Amendment precedents are not applicable.

Respondent can seek no help from his argument that a bright-line rule for the application of *Miranda* is desirable. Law enforcement officers will have little difficulty putting into practice our holding that undercover agents need not give *Miranda* warnings to incarcerated suspects. The use of undercover agents is a recognized law enforcement technique, often employed in the prison context to detect violence against correctional officials or inmates, as well as for the purposes served here. The interests protected by *Miranda* are not implicated in these cases, and the warnings are not required to safeguard the constitutional rights of inmates who make voluntary statements to undercover agents.

We hold that an undercover law enforcement officer posing as a fellow inmate need not give *Miranda* warnings to an incarcerated suspect before asking questions that may elicit an incriminating response. The statements at issue in this case were voluntary, and there is no federal obstacle to their admissibility at trial. We now reverse and remand for proceedings not inconsistent with our opinion.

JUSTICE BRENNAN, concurring in the judgment [omitted].

JUSTICE MARSHALL, dissenting.

This Court clearly and simply stated its holding in *Miranda*: "[T]he prosecution may not use statements, whether exculpatory or inculpatory, stemming from custodial interrogation of the defendant unless it demonstrates the use of procedural safeguards effective to secure the privilege against self-incrimination." The conditions that require the police to apprise a defendant of his constitutional rights—custodial interrogation conducted by an agent of the police—were present in this case. Because Lloyd Perkins received no *Miranda* warnings before he was subjected to custodial interrogation, his confession was not admissible.

The Court reaches the contrary conclusion by fashioning an exception to the *Miranda* rule that applies whenever "an undercover law enforcement officer posing as a fellow inmate * * * ask[s] questions that may elicit an incriminating response" from an incarcerated suspect. This exception is inconsistent with the rationale supporting *Miranda* and allows police officers intentionally to take advantage of suspects unaware of their constitutional rights. I therefore dissent. * * *

While Perkins was confined, an undercover police officer, with the help of a police informant, questioned him about a serious crime. Although the Court does not dispute that Perkins was interrogated, it downplays the nature of the 35-minute questioning by disingenuously referring to it as a "conversatio[n]." The officer's narration of the "conversation" at Perkins' suppression hearing however, reveals that it clearly was an interrogation. * * *

The compulsion proscribed by *Miranda* includes deception by the police. * * *

The Court's adoption of an exception to the *Miranda* doctrine is incompatible with the principle, consistently applied by this Court, that the doctrine should remain simple and clear. * * *

Even if *Miranda*, as interpreted by the Court, would not permit such obviously compelled confessions, the ramifications of today's opinion are still disturbing. The exception carved out of the *Miranda* doctrine today may well result in a proliferation of departmental policies to encourage police officers to conduct interrogations of confined suspects through undercover agents, thereby circumventing the need to administer *Miranda* warnings. Indeed, if *Miranda* now requires a police officer to issue warnings only in those situations in which the suspect might feel compelled "to speak by the fear of reprisal for remaining silent or in the hope of more lenient treatment should he confess," presumably it allows custodial interrogation by an undercover officer posing as a member of the clergy or a suspect's defense attorney. Although such abhorrent tricks would play on a suspect's need to confide in a trusted adviser, neither would cause the suspect to "think that the listeners have official power over him." The Court's adoption of the "undercover agent" exception to the *Miranda* rule thus is necessarily also the adoption of a substantial loophole in our jurisprudence protecting suspects' Fifth Amendment rights.

NOTES AND QUESTIONS

1. Can you explain the difference between the interrogation that occurred in *Perkins* and the interrogations that the Court considered in *Miranda*? How does Justice Marshall respond to this argument? Which opinion would you have joined?

2. Do you see a policy argument in favor of the majority's approach?

Thinking About *Miranda*: A Lawyer's Checklist

You have read *Miranda*, seen the *Perkins* exception, and learned what happened to Miranda the man. Now we begin the road of learning what happened to *Miranda*—the doctrine—after the case was decided. Before we begin the story, it is worth setting out the basic issues that a lawyer or student needs to consider when a *Miranda* issue potentially arises in a specific case.

First, there is the triggering mechanism for *Miranda* warnings—custodial interrogation. We will see later that the Supreme Court treats this concept as if it were two independent elements, "custody" and "interrogation." And, both elements can be difficult to discern in cases at the margin.

Second, assuming a finding of "custody" and a finding of "interrogation," *Miranda* warnings are ordinarily required. But, as *Miranda* teaches, a suspect may waive her "*Miranda* rights." What constitutes a valid waiver can also be a complicated matter. By far, waiver is the most litigated *Miranda* issue in criminal proceedings.

Third, if *Miranda* warnings are not given when they should be, or if they are given but a valid waiver is not secured, the suspect's statements received by the police are generally inadmissible. But, there is another question that may come to your mind: What about any "fruits" of the *Miranda* violation? Are they subject to exclusion as well, in the same way as "fruits of the poisonous tree" are handled in the Fourth Amendment? Wait until you see what the Supreme Court has said about that!

Fourth, are there other exceptions to the *Miranda* rule? That is, are there circumstances other than the *Perkins* jail plant situation in which the police do not have to give *Miranda* warnings in advance of custodial interrogation, or are there circumstances in which the remedy for violation of the *Miranda* rule does not include total exclusion of the original *Miranda*-less statement?

We will now examine those sub-issues in more detail.

B. *Miranda* Custody

BERKEMER V. MCCARTY

Supreme Court of the United States, 1984.
468 U.S. 420, 104 S.Ct. 3138, 82 L.Ed.2d 317.

Rick McCarty was forced to pull his car off the road and was then questioned by the police officer while he was standing alongside his car on

the side of the road. Was he in custody for purposes of *Miranda*? No. Now you *really* need to think like a lawyer.

JUSTICE MARSHALL delivered the opinion of the Court [joined by CHIEF JUSTICE BURGER, and JUSTICES BRENNAN, WHITE, BLACKMUN, POWELL, REHNQUIST, and O'CONNOR].

This case presents two related questions: First, does our decision in *Miranda v. Arizona* govern the admissibility of statements made during custodial interrogation by a suspect accused of a misdemeanor traffic offense? Second, does the roadside questioning of a motorist detained pursuant to a traffic stop constitute custodial interrogation for the purposes of the doctrine enunciated in *Miranda*?

I

A

The parties have stipulated to the essential facts. On the evening of March 31, 1980, Trooper Williams of the Ohio State Highway Patrol observed respondent's car weaving in and out of a lane on Interstate Highway 270. After following the car for two miles, Williams forced respondent to stop and asked him to get out of the vehicle. When respondent complied, Williams noticed that he was having difficulty standing. At that point, "Williams concluded that [respondent] would be charged with a traffic offense and, therefore, his freedom to leave the scene was terminated." However, respondent was not told that he would be taken into custody. Williams then asked respondent to perform a field sobriety test, commonly known as a "balancing test." Respondent could not do so without falling.

While still at the scene of the traffic stop, Williams asked respondent whether he had been using intoxicants. Respondent replied that "he had consumed two beers and had smoked several joints of marijuana a short time before." Respondent's speech was slurred, and Williams had difficulty understanding him. Williams thereupon formally placed respondent under arrest and transported him in the patrol car to the Franklin County Jail.

At the jail, respondent was given an intoxilyzer test to determine the concentration of alcohol in his blood. The test did not detect any alcohol whatsoever in respondent's system. Williams then resumed questioning respondent in order to obtain information for inclusion in the State Highway Patrol Alcohol Influence Report. Respondent answered affirmatively a question whether he had been drinking. When then asked if he was under the influence of alcohol, he said, "I guess, barely." Williams next asked respondent to indicate on the form whether the marihuana he had smoked had been treated with any chemicals. In the section of the report headed "Remarks," respondent wrote, "No ang[el] dust or PCP in the pot. Rick McCarty."

At no point in this sequence of events did Williams or anyone else tell respondent that he had a right to remain silent, to consult with an attorney, and to have an attorney appointed for him if he could not afford one.

B

Respondent was charged with operating a motor vehicle while under the influence of alcohol and/or drugs * * *.

Respondent moved to exclude the various incriminating statements he had made to Trooper Williams on the ground that introduction into evidence of those statements would violate the Fifth Amendment insofar as he had not been informed of his constitutional rights prior to his interrogation. * * *

II * * *

In the years since the decision in *Miranda,* we have frequently reaffirmed the central principle established by that case: if the police take a suspect into custody and then ask him questions without informing him of the rights enumerated [in *Miranda*], his responses cannot be introduced into evidence to establish his guilt.

Petitioner asks us to carve an exception out of the foregoing principle. When the police arrest a person for allegedly committing a misdemeanor traffic offense and then ask him questions without telling him his constitutional rights, petitioner argues, his responses should be admissible against him. We cannot agree.

One of the principal advantages of the doctrine that suspects must be given warnings before being interrogated while in custody is the clarity of that rule. * * *

The exception to *Miranda* proposed by petitioner would substantially undermine this crucial advantage of the doctrine. The police often are unaware when they arrest a person whether he may have committed a misdemeanor or a felony. Consider, for example, the reasonably common situation in which the driver of a car involved in an accident is taken into custody. Under Ohio law, both driving while under the influence of intoxicants and negligent vehicular homicide are misdemeanors, while reckless vehicular homicide is a felony. When arresting a person for causing a collision, the police may not know which of these offenses he may have committed. Indeed, the nature of his offense may depend upon circumstances unknowable to the police, such as whether the suspect has previously committed a similar offense or has a criminal record of some other kind. It may even turn upon events yet to happen, such as whether a victim of the accident dies. It would be unreasonable to expect the police to make guesses as to the nature of the criminal conduct at issue before deciding how they may interrogate the suspect.

Equally importantly, the doctrinal complexities that would confront the courts if we accepted petitioner's proposal would be Byzantine. Difficult questions quickly spring to mind: For instance, investigations into seemingly minor offenses sometimes escalate gradually into investigations into more serious matters; at what point in the evolution of an affair of this sort would the police be obliged to give *Miranda* warnings to a suspect in custody? What evidence would be necessary to establish that an arrest for a misdemeanor offense was merely a pretext to enable the police to interrogate the suspect (in hopes of obtaining information about a felony) without providing him the safeguards prescribed by *Miranda*? The litigation necessary to resolve such matters would be time-consuming and disruptive of law enforcement. And the end result would be an elaborate set of rules, interlaced with exceptions and subtle distinctions, discriminating between different kinds of custodial interrogations. Neither the police nor criminal defendants would benefit from such a development.

Absent a compelling justification we surely would be unwilling so seriously to impair the simplicity and clarity of the holding of *Miranda*. Neither of the two arguments proffered by petitioner constitutes such a justification. Petitioner first contends that *Miranda* warnings are unnecessary when a suspect is questioned about a misdemeanor traffic offense, because the police have no reason to subject such a suspect to the sort of interrogation that most troubled the Court in *Miranda*. We cannot agree that the dangers of police abuse are so slight in this context. For example, the offense of driving while intoxicated is increasingly regarded in many jurisdictions as a very serious matter. Especially when the intoxicant at issue is a narcotic drug rather than alcohol, the police sometimes have difficulty obtaining evidence of this crime. Under such circumstances, the incentive for the police to try to induce the defendant to incriminate himself may well be substantial. Similar incentives are likely to be present when a person is arrested for a minor offense but the police suspect that a more serious crime may have been committed. * * *

Petitioner's second argument is that law enforcement would be more expeditious and effective in the absence of a requirement that persons arrested for traffic offenses be informed of their rights. Again, we are unpersuaded. The occasions on which the police arrest and then interrogate someone suspected only of a misdemeanor traffic offense are rare. The police are already well accustomed to giving *Miranda* warnings to persons taken into custody. Adherence to the principle that all suspects must be given such warnings will not significantly hamper the efforts of the police to investigate crimes.

We hold therefore that a person subjected to custodial interrogation is entitled to the benefit of the procedural safeguards enunciated in *Miranda*, regardless of the nature or severity of the offense of which he is suspected or for which he was arrested.

The implication of this holding is that * * * the statements made by respondent at the County Jail were inadmissible. There can be no question that respondent was "in custody" at least as of the moment he was formally placed under arrest and instructed to get into the police car. Because he was not informed of his constitutional rights at that juncture, respondent's subsequent admissions should not have been used against him.

III

To assess the admissibility of the self-incriminating statements made by respondent prior to his formal arrest, we are obliged to address a second issue concerning the scope of our decision in *Miranda*: whether the roadside questioning of a motorist detained pursuant to a routine traffic stop should be considered "custodial interrogation." Respondent urges that it should, on the ground that *Miranda* by its terms applies whenever "a person has been taken into custody or otherwise deprived of his freedom of action in any significant way." Petitioner contends that a holding that every detained motorist must be advised of his rights before being questioned would constitute an unwarranted extension of the *Miranda* doctrine.

It must be acknowledged at the outset that a traffic stop significantly curtails the "freedom of action" of the driver and the passengers, if any, of the detained vehicle. Under the law of most States, it is a crime either to ignore a policeman's signal to stop one's car or, once having stopped, to drive away without permission. Certainly few motorists would feel free either to disobey a directive to pull over or to leave the scene of a traffic stop without being told they might do so. Partly for these reasons, we have long acknowledged that "stopping an automobile and detaining its occupants constitute a 'seizure' within the meaning of [the Fourth] Amendmen[t], even though the purpose of the stop is limited and the resulting detention quite brief."

However, we decline to accord talismanic power to the phrase in the *Miranda* opinion emphasized by respondent. Fidelity to the doctrine announced in *Miranda* requires that it be enforced strictly, but only in those types of situations in which the concerns that powered the decision are implicated. Thus, we must decide whether a traffic stop exerts upon a detained person pressures that sufficiently impair his free exercise of his privilege against self-incrimination to require that he be warned of his constitutional rights.

Two features of an ordinary traffic stop mitigate the danger that a person questioned will be induced "to speak where he would not otherwise do so freely." First, detention of a motorist pursuant to a traffic stop is presumptively temporary and brief. The vast majority of roadside detentions last only a few minutes. A motorist's expectations, when he sees a policeman's light flashing behind him, are that he will be obliged to spend a short period of time answering questions and waiting while the officer checks his license and registration, that he may then be given a citation, but that in the end he most likely will be allowed to continue on his way. In this respect, questioning incident to an ordinary traffic stop is quite different from stationhouse interrogation, which frequently is prolonged, and in which the detainee often is aware that questioning will continue until he provides his interrogators the answers they seek.

Second, circumstances associated with the typical traffic stop are not such that the motorist feels completely at the mercy of the police. To be sure, the aura of authority surrounding an armed, uniformed officer and the knowledge that the officer has some discretion in deciding whether to issue a citation, in combination, exert some pressure on the detainee to respond to questions. But other aspects of the situation substantially offset these forces. Perhaps most importantly, the typical traffic stop is public, at least to some degree. Passersby, on foot or in other cars, witness the interaction of officer and motorist. This exposure to public view both reduces the ability of an unscrupulous policeman to use illegitimate means to elicit self-incriminating statements and diminishes the motorist's fear that, if he does not cooperate, he will be subjected to abuse. The fact that the detained motorist typically is confronted by only one or at most two policemen further mutes his sense of vulnerability. In short, the atmosphere surrounding an ordinary traffic stop is substantially less "police dominated" than that surrounding the kinds of interrogation at issue in *Miranda* itself, and in the subsequent cases in which we have applied *Miranda*.

In both of these respects, the usual traffic stop is more analogous to a so-called "*Terry* stop," than to a formal arrest. Under the Fourth Amendment, we have held, a policeman who lacks probable cause but whose "observations lead him reasonably to suspect" that a particular person has committed, is committing, or is about to commit a crime, may detain that person briefly in order to "investigate the circumstances that provoke suspicion." "[T]he stop and inquiry must be 'reasonably related in scope to the justification for their initiation.' "

Typically, this means that the officer may ask the detainee a moderate number of questions to determine his identity and to try to obtain information confirming or dispelling the officer's suspicions. But the detainee is not obliged to respond. And, unless the detainee's answers provide the officer with probable cause to arrest him, he must then be released. The comparatively nonthreatening character of detentions of this sort explains the absence of any suggestion in our opinions that *Terry* stops are subject to the dictates of *Miranda*. The similarly noncoercive aspect of ordinary traffic stops prompts us to hold that persons temporarily detained pursuant to such stops are not "in custody" for the purposes of *Miranda*.

Respondent contends that to "exempt" traffic stops from the coverage of *Miranda* will open the way to widespread abuse. Policemen will simply delay formally arresting detained motorists, and will subject them to sustained and intimidating interrogation at the scene of their initial detention. The net result, respondent contends, will be a serious threat to the rights that the *Miranda* doctrine is designed to protect.

We are confident that the state of affairs projected by respondent will not come to pass. It is settled that the safeguards prescribed by *Miranda* become applicable as soon as a suspect's freedom of action is curtailed to a "degree associated with formal arrest." If a motorist who has been detained pursuant to a traffic stop thereafter is subjected to treatment that renders him "in custody" for practical purposes, he will be entitled to the full panoply of protections prescribed by *Miranda*.

Admittedly, our adherence to the doctrine just recounted will mean that the police and lower courts will continue occasionally to have difficulty deciding exactly when a suspect has been taken into custody. Either a rule that *Miranda* applies to all traffic stops or a rule that a suspect need not be advised of his rights until he is formally placed under arrest would provide a clearer, more easily administered line. However, each of these two alternatives has drawbacks that make it unacceptable. The first would substantially impede the enforcement of the Nation's traffic laws—by compelling the police either to take the time to warn all detained motorists of their constitutional rights or to forgo use of self-incriminating statements made by those motorists—while doing little to protect citizens' Fifth Amendment rights. The second would enable the police to circumvent the constraints on custodial interrogations established by *Miranda*.

Turning to the case before us, we find nothing in the record that indicates that respondent should have been given *Miranda* warnings at any point prior to the time Trooper Williams placed him under arrest. For the reasons indicated above, we reject the contention that the initial stop of respondent's car, by itself, rendered him "in custody." And respondent has failed to demonstrate that, at any time between the initial stop and the arrest, he was subjected to restraints comparable to those associated with a formal arrest. Only a short period of time elapsed between the stop and the arrest. At no point during that interval was respondent informed that his detention would not be temporary. Although Trooper Williams apparently decided as soon as respondent stepped out of his car that respondent would be taken into custody and charged with a traffic offense, Williams never communicated his intention to respondent. A policeman's unarticulated plan has no bearing on the question whether a suspect was "in custody" at a particular time; the only relevant inquiry is how a reasonable man in the suspect's position would have understood his situation. Nor do other aspects of the interaction of Williams and respondent support the contention that respondent was exposed to "custodial interrogation" at the scene of the stop. From aught that appears in the stipulation of facts, a single police officer asked respondent a modest number of questions and requested him to perform a simple balancing test at a location visible to passing motorists. Treatment of this sort cannot fairly be characterized as the functional equivalent of formal arrest.

We conclude, in short, that respondent was not taken into custody for the purposes of *Miranda* until Williams arrested him. Consequently, the statements respondent made prior to that point were admissible against him. * * *

[*The opinion of JUSTICE STEVENS, concurring in part and concurring in the judgment is omitted.*]

NOTES AND QUESTIONS

1. Notice that the ultimate holding is a compromise. The State argued for a blanket *Miranda* exception for traffic stops on the ground that they are generically different from other kinds of police interference with liberty, and that *Miranda* would interfere with the efficient prosecution of traffic offenders. The Court rather casually rejected that argument. Yet in the part of the opinion holding that traffic stops do not always constitute custody, the Court embraced the argument that traffic stops are different from the custody that *Miranda* had in mind. How can the Court have it both ways? One answer is that the Court likes *Miranda* bright lines but at the same time realizes that bright lines do not always provide the best set of outcomes; thus, sometimes, as in defining custody in *Berkemer*, the Court introduces complexity to provide better results. Limiting custody to a formal arrest obviously invites police to delay formal arrest as long as possible.

2. It might also be helpful to remember that while *Miranda* was handed down by the Warren Court, *Berkermer* was a Burger Court decision. By the time we get to

the Burger Court, we see a tendency in the Court decisions to be more law enforcement oriented; to pull back somewhat on the Warren decisions as overly hamstringing the ability of law enforcement to effectively do their jobs. In this context, it is somewhat surprising that the core of the opinion was unanimous and that it was written by Justice Marshall, one of the Warren Court liberal justices.

A. Consider the *Berkemer* fact pattern with the following change: Before the officer administers the sobriety test, Rick says, "My house is right over there. My mother is expecting me home. Can I go tell her what's happening?" The officer says, "No." Custody? What if Rick tries to leave and the officer physically stops him? Would it matter if Rick were sixteen and driving on a learner's permit? What if the officer handcuffs him? See Stone v. City of Huntsville, 656 So.2d 404 (Ala.Crim.App.1994).

B. A fight breaks out between rival fraternities late at night and several college students are running from the melee when police officers intercept them. With guns drawn, police order them to lie face down on the ground "and do not move." Are the students in *Miranda* custody the moment the police give the order or only if they comply and lie on the ground?

C. Six law enforcement officers (three uniformed officers and three parole officers) knocked on *N*'s door. He opened the door dressed only in his underwear. One of the officers asked him to step into the hallway, which he did. The officer then handcuffed *N*, telling him that he was not under arrest but was being restrained for his owns safety and that of the officers. Police led him into his apartment, where they discovered three other adults present. They asked *N* whether there was a gun in the apartment (a bullet had been shot through the wall of *N*'s apartment into the apartment next door). *Miranda* warnings were never given. Custody? See United States v. Newton, 369 F.3d 659 (2d. Cir. 2004).

3. Is the custody test wholly objective? Put yourself in Rick McCarty's place after the officer orders him to perform a "simple balancing test," and he falls down. Would you expect the officer to let you climb to your feet, get into your car, and drive away? Suppose that, while prone on the ground, Rick McCarty had said, "I guess I'm in a whole lot of trouble," and the officer did not respond. Custody? What if the officer had answered, "Yes"?

But if the test is wholly objective, perhaps courts cannot take into account that Rick flunked the balancing test; instead, the question might be whether a motorist pulled over and asked to take a balancing test would feel that he was subject to restraints comparable to an arrest. The Court's sharply divided opinion in J.D.B. v. North Carolina, 564 U.S. 261, 131 S.Ct. 2394, 180 L.Ed.2d 310 (2011), suggests that the test is almost wholly objective. The issue in J.D.B. was whether to take into account that the suspect was thirteen years old when determining whether he was in custody. The Court, 5–4, held that "so long as the child's age was known to the officer at the time of police questioning, or would have been objectively apparent to a reasonable officer, its inclusion in the custody analysis is consistent with the objective nature of that test." Reasoning that a child's age is "a fact that 'generates commonsense conclusions about behavior and perception,' " the Court concluded:

> In some circumstances, a child's age "would have affected how a reasonable person" in the suspect's position "would perceive his or her freedom to leave." That is, a reasonable child subjected to police questioning will sometimes feel pressured to submit when a reasonable adult would feel free to go. We think it clear that courts can account for that reality without doing any damage to the objective nature of the custody analysis.

Only five votes could be mustered to take account of the fact that the suspect was thirteen, and the holding is narrowly stated. This suggests that other arguments to consider a particular characteristic of a suspect will likely fall on deaf ears.

4. *In prison but not in custody?* We saw in *Illinois v. Perkins* that a jail inmate who does not know he is talking to the police is not entitled to warnings. The Court would later decide that being in the general prison population is not even "custody" for purposes of *Miranda.* In prison, police interrogated Shatzer about a crime other than the one for which he was serving time. When he requested counsel, police terminated the interrogation and Shatzer returned to the general population. Was this a break in *Miranda* custody? Can a prisoner be said not to be in custody when he is incarcerated? Yes, the Court held in Maryland v. Shatzer, 559 U.S 98, 130 S.Ct. 1213, 175 L.Ed.2d 1045 (2010).

The Court acknowledged that being in prison met the *Berkemer* test whether "there is a 'formal arrest or restraint on freedom of movement' of the degree associated with a formal arrest." But the Court said "that the freedom-of-movement test identifies only a necessary and not a sufficient condition for *Miranda* custody." It is not a sufficient condition because "*Miranda* is to be enforced 'only in those types of situations in which the concerns that powered the decision are implicated.' "

> Interrogated suspects who have previously been convicted of crime live in prison. When they are released back into the general prison population, they return to their accustomed surroundings and daily routine—they regain the degree of control they had over their lives prior to the interrogation. Sentenced prisoners, in contrast to the *Miranda* paradigm, are not isolated with their accusers. They live among other inmates, guards, and workers, and often can receive visitors and communicate with people on the outside by mail or telephone.

In the Court's view, "The 'inherently compelling pressures' of [Shatzer's] custodial interrogation ended when he returned to his normal life."

5. In an early *Miranda* custody case, a police officer telephoned a parolee named Mathiason to ask where it would be convenient to meet. Mathiason said he had no preference, and the officer asked him to come to the station. When he arrived, the officer told him he was not under arrest and took him into an office where he told him he was a suspect in a burglary and told him (falsely) that his fingerprints had been found at the scene of the burglary. He confessed and then was allowed to leave the police station. Finding the atmosphere a coercive one, the state court held that the suspect had been in custody. By a 7–2 vote, the Court held that in the absence of any "restraint on freedom of movement," there could be no custody. See Oregon v. Mathiason, 429 U.S. 492, 97 S.Ct. 711, 50 L.Ed.2d 714 (1977). Would a parolee such as Mathiason have felt coerced by his circumstances? If so, can it be said that he was "coerced" to answer questions and yet was not in "custody"? Did the bright-line rule of *Miranda* take precedence over the policy of reducing coercion? In any event, lacking custody, it did not matter whether he felt compelled to answer police questions.

Apply *Mathiason* to the following facts. *D* threatens his wife when she moves out, and a week later her daughter and grandchildren are murdered in her new apartment. The police approach *D* at work and tell him that he is not a suspect but they need to ask him some questions in light of his prior threats. He agrees to accompany them to the police station. They inform him that department policy requires them to handcuff him and put him in the back of the car for the ride to the station. Police remove the handcuffs as soon as they reach the station and take him to an interview room. There he is interrogated, makes incriminating statements, and is released, just as Mathiason was. Custody? Dye v. State, 717 N.E.2d 5 (Ind.1999). What if they release him, wait fifteen minutes, and then arrest him. Does that change the analysis?

6. *Problems.*

A. R is a non-commissioned officer in the Air Force. Suspecting *R* of having downloaded child pornography on his computer, civilian authorities ask his commanding officer to order him to meet with them. As a result of this order, *R* meets the police in his home, where he is assured that he is "not about to be arrested" and "that the police were concerned not with the mere presence of child pornography on the computer but its production." Questioned by the police, *R* eventually admitted downloading the material. No *Miranda* warnings were given. Was he in custody? See United States v. Rogers, 659 F.3d 74 (1st Cir. 2011).

B. D has "hired" an undercover officer to kill his wife. Six police cars surround D's house where he is having a pool party to provide himself an alibi. Trees prevent anyone at the party from observing the cars. A single officer (with arrest warrant in back pocket) goes to the pool area and tells D that someone just shot his wife.

Feigning shock and dismay, D answers questions the officer asks (without giving *Miranda* warnings). This exchange takes place in front of fourteen of D's closest friends. After the questioning, officer pulls out an arrest warrant and arrests D. Are the answers to the questions admissible under Berkemer?

C. A prostitute is found murdered and police interview her former high-school boyfriend, D, on three separate occasions. He was told each time that he was not under arrest; each time he voluntarily appeared at the police station. The third interview lasted eleven hours, with bathroom breaks and three other brief breaks where D was left alone. His car keys were taken from him to perform a consensual search of his car and never returned. Roughly ten hours into the interview, D asked if he could leave and return the next day to continue and the police said, "No, you're here now. Why don't we go ahead and get this all wrapped up." An hour later, he confessed. Only after the confession was reduced to writing did the police give him *Miranda* warnings. The trial court held the confession admissible because, like Mathiason, D was told he was not under arrest and showed up voluntarily for the interview. Do you agree? Do you believe this outcome is consistent with the rationale of *Miranda*? See Commonwealth v. DiStefano, 782 A.2d 574 (Pa.Super.2001).

C. *Miranda* Interrogation

RHODE ISLAND V. INNIS

Supreme Court of the United States, 1980.
446 U.S. 291, 100 S.Ct. 1682, 64 L.Ed.2d 297.

Here, police have a murder suspect in the squad car. Police have a conversation that causes the suspect to lead the officers to the murder weapon. Is this interrogation for purposes of *Miranda*? Now you are starting to catch on to that "thinking like a lawyer" business.

MR. JUSTICE STEWART delivered the opinion of the Court joined by JUSTICES WHITE, BLACKMUN, POWELL, and REHNQUIST]. * * *

I

On the night of January 12, 1975, John Mulvaney, a Providence, R.I., taxicab driver, disappeared after being dispatched to pick up a customer. His body was discovered four days later buried in a shallow grave in Coventry, R.I. He had died from a shotgun blast aimed at the back of his head.

On January 17, 1975, shortly after midnight, the Providence police received a telephone call from Gerald Aubin, also a taxicab driver, who reported that he had just been robbed by a man wielding a sawed-off shotgun. Aubin further reported that he had dropped off his assailant near Rhode Island College in a section of Providence known as Mount Pleasant. [Aubin later identified a photo of respondent. Eds.] * * *

At approximately 4:30 a. m. on the same date, Patrolman Lovell, while cruising the streets of Mount Pleasant in a patrol car, spotted the respondent standing in the street facing him. When Patrolman Lovell stopped his car, the respondent walked towards it. Patrolman Lovell then arrested the respondent, who was unarmed, and advised him of his so-called *Miranda* rights. While the two men waited in the patrol car for other police officers to arrive, Patrolman Lovell did not converse with the respondent other than to respond to the latter's request for a cigarette.

Within minutes, Sergeant Sears arrived at the scene of the arrest, and he also gave the respondent the *Miranda* warnings. Immediately thereafter, Captain Leyden and other police officers arrived. Captain Leyden advised the respondent of his *Miranda* rights. The respondent stated that he understood those rights and wanted to speak with a lawyer. Captain Leyden then directed that the respondent be placed in a "caged wagon," a four-door police car with a wire screen mesh between the front and rear seats, and be driven to the central police station. Three officers, Patrolmen Gleckman, Williams, and McKenna, were assigned to accompany the respondent to the central station. They placed the respondent in the vehicle and shut the doors. Captain Leyden then instructed the officers not to question the respondent or intimidate or coerce him in any way. The three officers then entered the vehicle, and it departed.

While en route to the central station, Patrolman Gleckman initiated a conversation with Patrolman McKenna concerning the missing shotgun. As Patrolman Gleckman later testified:

> "A. At this point, I was talking back and forth with Patrolman McKenna stating that I frequent this area while on patrol and [that because a school for handicapped children is located nearby,] there's a lot of handicapped children running around in this area, and God forbid one of them might find a weapon with shells and they might hurt themselves."

Patrolman McKenna apparently shared his fellow officer's concern:

> "A. I more or less concurred with him [Gleckman] that it was a safety factor and that we should, you know, continue to search for the weapon and try to find it."

While Patrolman Williams said nothing, he overheard the conversation between the two officers:

> "A. He [Gleckman] said it would be too bad if the little—I believe he said a girl—would pick up the gun, maybe kill herself."

The respondent then interrupted the conversation, stating that the officers should turn the car around so he could show them where the gun was located. At this point, Patrolman McKenna radioed back to Captain Leyden that they were returning to the scene of the arrest and that the respondent would inform them of the location of the gun. At the time the respondent indicated that the officers should turn back, they had traveled no more than a mile, a trip encompassing only a few minutes.

The police vehicle then returned to the scene of the arrest where a search for the shotgun was in progress. There, Captain Leyden again advised the respondent of his *Miranda* rights. The respondent replied that he understood those rights but that he "wanted to get the gun out of the way because of the kids in the area in the school." The respondent then led the police to a nearby field, where he pointed out the shotgun under some rocks by the side of the road.

On March 20, 1975, a grand jury returned an indictment charging the respondent with the kidnaping, robbery, and murder of John Mulvaney. Before trial, the respondent moved to suppress the shotgun and the statements he had made to the police regarding it. After an evidentiary hearing at which the respondent elected not to testify, the trial judge found that the respondent had been "repeatedly and completely advised of his *Miranda* rights." He further found that it was "entirely understandable that [the officers in the police vehicle] would voice their concern [for the safety of the handicapped children] to each other." The judge then concluded that the respondent's decision to inform the police of the location of the shotgun was "a waiver, clearly, and on the basis of the evidence that I have heard, and [sic] intelligent waiver, of his [*Miranda*] right to remain silent." Thus, without passing on whether the police officers had in fact "interrogated" the respondent, the trial court sustained the admissibility of the shotgun and testimony related to its discovery. That evidence was later introduced at the respondent's trial, and the jury returned a verdict of guilty on all counts. * * *

II * * *

In the present case, the parties are in agreement that the respondent was fully informed of his *Miranda* rights and that he invoked his *Miranda* right to counsel when he told Captain Leyden that he wished to consult with a lawyer. It is also uncontested that the respondent was "in custody" while being transported to the police station.

The issue, therefore, is whether the respondent was "interrogated" by the police officers in violation of the respondent's undisputed right under *Miranda* to remain silent until he had consulted with a lawyer. In resolving this issue, we first define the term "interrogation" under *Miranda* before turning to a consideration of the facts of this case.

A

The starting point for defining "interrogation" in this context is, of course, the Court's *Miranda* opinion. There the Court observed that "[b]y custodial interrogation, we mean questioning initiated by law enforcement officers after a person has been taken into custody or otherwise deprived of his freedom of action in any significant way." This passage and other references throughout the opinion to "questioning" might suggest that the *Miranda* rules were to apply only to those police interrogation practices that involve express questioning of a defendant while in custody.

We do not, however, construe the *Miranda* opinion so narrowly. The concern of the Court in *Miranda* was that the "interrogation environment" created by the interplay of interrogation and custody would "subjugate the individual to the will of his examiner" and thereby undermine the privilege against compulsory self-incrimination. The police practices that evoked this concern included several that did not involve express questioning. For example, one of the practices discussed in *Miranda* was the use of line-ups in which a coached witness would pick the defendant as the perpetrator. This was designed to establish that the defendant was in fact guilty as a predicate for further interrogation. A variation on this theme discussed in *Miranda* was the so-called "reverse line-up" in which a defendant would be identified by coached witnesses as the perpetrator of a fictitious crime, with the object of inducing him to confess to the actual crime of which he was suspected in order to escape the false prosecution. The Court in *Miranda* also included in its survey of interrogation practices the use of psychological ploys, such as to "posi[t]" "the guilt of the subject," to "minimize the moral seriousness of the offense," and "to cast blame on the victim or on society." It is clear that these techniques of persuasion, no less than express questioning, were thought, in a custodial setting, to amount to interrogation.

This is not to say, however, that all statements obtained by the police after a person has been taken into custody are to be considered the product of interrogation. * * * [T]he special procedural safeguards outlined in *Miranda* are required not where a suspect is simply taken into custody, but rather where a suspect in custody is subjected to interrogation. "Interrogation," as conceptualized in the *Miranda* opinion, must reflect a measure of compulsion above and beyond that inherent in custody itself.

We conclude that the *Miranda* safeguards come into play whenever a person in custody is subjected to either express questioning or its functional equivalent. That is to say, the term "interrogation" under *Miranda* refers not only to express questioning, but also to any words or actions on the part of the police (other than those normally attendant to arrest and custody) that the police should know are reasonably likely to elicit an incriminating response from the suspect. The latter portion of this definition focuses primarily upon the perceptions of the suspect, rather than the intent of the police. This focus reflects the fact that the *Miranda* safeguards were designed to vest a suspect in custody with an added measure of protection against coercive police practices, without regard to objective proof of the underlying intent of the police. A practice that the police should know is reasonably likely to evoke an incriminating response from a suspect thus amounts to interrogation. But, since the police surely cannot be held accountable for the unforeseeable results of their words or actions, the definition of interrogation can extend only to words or actions on the part of police officers that they should have known were reasonably likely to elicit an incriminating response.

B

Turning to the facts of the present case, we conclude that the respondent was not "interrogated" within the meaning of *Miranda.* It is undisputed that the first prong of the definition of "interrogation" was not satisfied, for the conversation between Patrolmen Gleckman and McKenna included no express questioning of the respondent. Rather, that conversation was, at least in form, nothing more than a dialogue between the two officers to which no response from the respondent was invited.

Moreover, it cannot be fairly concluded that the respondent was subjected to the "functional equivalent" of questioning. It cannot be said, in short, that Patrolmen Gleckman and McKenna should have known that their conversation was reasonably likely to elicit an incriminating response from the respondent. There is nothing in the record to suggest that the officers were aware that the respondent was peculiarly susceptible to an appeal to his conscience concerning the safety of handicapped children. Nor is there anything in the record to suggest that the police knew that the respondent was unusually disoriented or upset at the time of his arrest. The case thus boils down to whether, in the context of a brief conversation, the officers should have known that the respondent would suddenly be moved to make a self-incriminating response. Given the fact that the entire conversation appears to have consisted of no more than a few off hand remarks, we cannot say that the officers should have known that it was reasonably likely that Innis would so respond. This is not a case where the police carried on a lengthy harangue in the presence of the suspect. Nor does the record support the respondent's contention that, under the circumstances, the officers' comments were particularly "evocative." It is our view, therefore, that the respondent was not subjected by the police to words or actions that the police should have known were reasonably likely to elicit an incriminating response from him.

The Rhode Island Supreme Court erred, in short, in equating "subtle compulsion" with interrogation. That the officers' comments struck a responsive chord is readily apparent. Thus, it may be said, as the Rhode Island Supreme Court did say, that the respondent was subjected to "subtle compulsion." But that is not the end of the inquiry. It must also be established that a suspect's incriminating response was the product of words or actions on the part of the police that they should have known were reasonably likely to elicit an incriminating response. This was not established in the present case. * * *

[*The opinion of* JUSTICE WHITE*, concurring, is omitted.*]

MR. CHIEF JUSTICE BURGER, concurring in the judgment. * * *

The meaning of *Miranda* has become reasonably clear and law enforcement practices have adjusted to its strictures; I would neither overrule *Miranda*, disparage it, nor extend it at this late date. * * *

MR. JUSTICE MARSHALL, with whom MR. JUSTICE BRENNAN joins, dissenting.

I am substantially in agreement with the Court's definition of "interrogation" within the meaning of *Miranda*. In my view, the *Miranda* safeguards apply whenever police conduct is intended or likely to produce a response from a suspect in custody. As I read the Court's opinion, its definition of "interrogation" for *Miranda* purposes is equivalent, for practical purposes, to my formulation, since it contemplates that "where a police practice is designed to elicit an incriminating response from the accused, it is unlikely that the practice will not also be one which the police should have known was reasonably likely to have that effect." Thus, the Court requires an objective inquiry into the likely effect of police conduct on a typical individual, taking into account any special susceptibility of the suspect to certain kinds of pressure of which the police know or have reason to know.

I am utterly at a loss, however, to understand how this objective standard as applied to the facts before us can rationally lead to the conclusion that there was no interrogation. * * *

One can scarcely imagine a stronger appeal to the conscience of a suspect—any suspect—than the assertion that if the weapon is not found an innocent person will be hurt or killed. And not just any innocent person, but an innocent child—a little girl—a helpless, handicapped little girl on her way to school. The notion that such an appeal could not be expected to have any effect unless the suspect were known to have some special interest in handicapped children verges on the ludicrous. As a matter of fact, the appeal to a suspect to confess for the sake of others, to "display some evidence of decency and honor," is a classic interrogation technique. * * *

I firmly believe that this case is simply an aberration, and that in future cases the Court will apply the standard adopted today in accordance with its plain meaning.

MR. JUSTICE STEVENS, dissenting. * * *

I * * *

In * * * order to give full protection to a suspect's right to be free from any interrogation at all, the definition of "interrogation" must include any police statement or conduct that has the same purpose or effect as a direct question. Statements that appear to call for a response from the suspect, as well as those that are designed to do so, should be considered interrogation. By prohibiting only those relatively few statements or actions that a police officer should know are likely to elicit an incriminating response, the Court today accords a suspect considerably less protection. Indeed, since I suppose most suspects are unlikely to incriminate themselves even when questioned directly, this new definition will almost certainly exclude every statement that is not punctuated with a question mark from the concept of "interrogation."

The difference between the approach required by a faithful adherence to *Miranda* and the stinted test applied by the Court today can be illustrated by comparing three different ways in which Officer Gleckman could have communicated his fears about the possible dangers posed by the shotgun to handicapped children. He could have:

(1) directly asked Innis:

> Will you please tell me where the shotgun is so we can protect handicapped school children from danger?

(2) announced to the other officers in the wagon:

> If the man sitting in the back seat with me should decide to tell us where the gun is, we can protect handicapped children from danger.

or (3) stated to the other officers:

It would be too bad if a little handicapped girl would pick up the gun that this man left in the area and maybe kill herself.

In my opinion, all three of these statements should be considered interrogation because all three appear to be designed to elicit a response from anyone who in fact knew where the gun was located. Under the Court's test, on the other hand, the form of the statements would be critical. The third statement would not be interrogation because in the Court's view there was no reason for Officer Gleckman to believe that Innis was susceptible to this type of an implied appeal; therefore, the statement would not be reasonably likely to elicit an incriminating response. Assuming that this is true, then it seems to me that the first two statements, which would be just as unlikely to elicit such a response, should also not be considered interrogation. But, because the first statement is clearly an express question, it would be considered interrogation under the Court's test. The second statement, although just as clearly a deliberate appeal to Innis to reveal the location of the gun, would presumably not be interrogation because (a) it was not in form a direct question and (b) it does not fit within the "reasonably likely to elicit an incriminating response" category that applies to indirect interrogation.

As this example illustrates, the Court's test creates an incentive for police to ignore a suspect's invocation of his rights in order to make continued attempts to extract information from him. If a suspect does not appear to be susceptible to a particular type of psychological pressure, the police are apparently free to exert that pressure on him despite his request for counsel, so long as they are careful not to punctuate their statements with question marks. And if, contrary to all reasonable expectations, the suspect makes an incriminating statement, that statement can be used against him at trial. The Court thus turns *Miranda*'s unequivocal rule against any interrogation at all into a trap in which unwary suspects may be caught by police deception. * * *

NOTES AND QUESTIONS

1. Do you think Chief Justice Burger concurs in the judgment out of respect for *stare decisis* or for some other reason?

2. Do you agree with the majority or either of the two dissents? In predicting the outcome of the case in the United States Supreme Court, Professor Welsh White predicted that Innis would win:

> Since the conversation indicates a strong desire to know the location of the shotgun, any person with knowledge of the weapon's location would be likely to believe that the officers wanted him to disclose its location. Thus, a reasonable person in Innis's position would believe that the officers were seeking to solicit precisely the type of response that was given.

See White, Rhode Island v. Innis: The Significance of a Suspect's Assertion of His Right to Counsel, 17 Am.Crim.L.Rev. 53, 68 (1979).

3. Is the test for interrogation objective or subjective? Some of both? Why should the officer's intent make any difference? Indeed, why should the test focus on the officer at all? Here's what the Court said in a footnote:

> This is not to say that the intent of the police is irrelevant, for it may well have a bearing on whether the police should have known that their words or actions were reasonably likely to evoke an incriminating response. In particular, where a police practice is designed to elicit an incriminating response from the accused, it is unlikely that the practice will not also be one which the police should have known was reasonably likely to have that effect.

4. *The question-mark rule.* J found one of two men in the drunk tank lying in a pool of blood. The other inmate was asleep on his bunk. As J was unlocking the door, she yelled to the sleeping inmate: "What happened?" The inmate awoke and said, "I killed the son of a bitch last night; he would not shut up." State v. Bennett, 30 Utah 2d 343, 517 P.2d 1029 (1973). This case implies a common-sense rule that one should not irritate cell-mates, but does it fit the Innis doctrinal rule about express questioning? What argument can you make to have the answer introduced even if a court were to hold that the jailer interrogated the prisoner?

5. *The functional equivalent of questioning.* The second half of the *Innis* test is designed to cover situations in which the police create a situation that produces the same kind of pressure on the suspect that a direct question would. As the Court said in a footnote: "To limit the ambit of *Miranda* to express questioning would 'place a premium on the ingenuity of police to devise methods of indirect interrogation, rather than to implement the plain mandate of *Miranda*.' "

Given that the pressure in Innis itself was held insufficient to constitute the functional equivalent of questioning, consider the following cases:

A. F was arrested for murdering a woman during a robbery in which furs were stolen. F declined to answer questions. Later, the detective placed some of the stolen furs (recovered from the apartment of a co-defendant) in front of F's cell, about a foot away from F. F immediately grabbed the wire mesh and asked to speak to the district attorney. Told that the D.A. could not do anything for him, he said, "I can't afford to do a lot of time. What can I tell you?" Was this statement obtained through interrogation? See People v. Ferro, 63 N.Y.2d 316, 472 N.E.2d 13, 482 N.Y.S.2d 237 (1984).

B. Police took J into custody for the murder of his baby. They gave him *Miranda* warnings, and he said he understood his rights and would talk to them "but I want my lawyer present when I talk." The police said no lawyer was then available, but one would be appointed for him when he was transferred to the jail. J said, "Well, I want to tell you about it." One detective said to J, "God takes care of little babies. The baby is already in heaven." J asked the detective: "Are you a religious man?" The detective responded, "Not as religious as I should be." J then began telling police how he hit the baby and threw it into the back yard. Interrogation? See State v. Jones, 386 So.2d 1363 (La.1980).

C. H was a suspect in a burglary and sexual assault of V. H permitted two police officers to take his picture and agreed to accompany them to V's home. En route, H told the officers that he knew nothing about the crime. Upon arrival, one officer remained with H in the squad car and the other officer entered V's home, where V identified H from a photograph array. The officer returned to the squad car and said to H, "You're a liar." H responded, "You're right. I did it." Was H subject to interrogation? Was he in custody? See People v. Huffman, 61 N.Y.2d 795, 473 N.Y.S.2d 945, 462 N.E.2d 122 (1984).

D. Police arrested Y for robbery and took him to the station, where he waived his *Miranda* rights. Agent S interrogated Y, who continually denied his involvement. When Y's accomplice confessed in another room, S told Y, who then invoked his right to counsel. S terminated the interview and got up to leave the room. As he reached the door, however, he turned around and said, "I want you to remember me, and I want you to remember my face, and I want you to remember that I gave you a chance." Did this constitute interrogation? See United States v. Young, 46 M.J. 768 (Army Crim.App.1997).

6. S walks into the sheriff's office and states, "I done it; I done it; arrest me; arrest me." A deputy asks, "What did you do?" He replies, "I killed my wife." "What did you kill her with?" asks the deputy. "With an axe, that's all I had." Are any of these statements admissible under *Miranda*? People v. Savage, 102 Ill.App.2d 477, 242 N.E.2d 446 (1968). What if the deputy's second response is "calm down; you're no murderer"? Interrogation? Custody?

D. *Miranda* Special Situations

A fair reading of the *Miranda* opinion suggests that the Court thought it was creating a self-executing seamless rule that would be easily applied by lower courts.

There would no longer be agonizing over whether a confession was voluntary or even whether the pressure the police used constituted coercion or compulsion. But the course of law is never true, and particularly when the law proved intensely controversial, as was the case with *Miranda.* We will shortly see that in 1968 Congress passed a statute designed to "overrule" *Miranda.* Even more telling, Republican candidate Richard Nixon made the Warren Court in general, and *Miranda* in particular, the subject of attacks on the campaign trail. In one of his speeches just days before the 1968 election, Nixon said, "Some of our courts have gone too far in their decisions weakening the peace forces as against the criminal forces in the United States of America, and we are going to change that." Just as telling, Democratic candidate Hubert Humphrey made no effect to defend *Miranda.*

Nixon won the election and quickly appointed two justices who were either on record as hostile to *Miranda* or likely to be hostile (Warren Burger and Harry Blackmun). Two more appointments of conservative justices followed in Nixon's first term (Lewis Powell and William Rehnquist). Most of those who followed the Supreme Court, including the two senior authors of this book, thought *Miranda* would soon be overruled. But as Yogi Berra said, "Predictions are difficult, particularly about the future." Instead, a Court unfriendly to *Miranda* began to create "special situations"—categories of cases from which the Court has withdrawn the protective cover of *Miranda.*

1. "Jail Plant" Exception

You have already seen one exception to the *Miranda* rule that a suspect who is interrogated while in custody must be given warnings of the right to remain silent and to a lawyer. The case that followed *Miranda* in this chapter, *Illinois v. Perkins*, reasoned that if the suspect in jail does not know that he is being interrogated by the police, he is not subject to the same coercive atmosphere that concerned the Court in *Miranda.* Indeed, at one point, the *Perkins* Court noted, "*Miranda* was not meant to protect suspects from boasting about their criminal activities in front of persons whom they believe to be their cellmates." Thus, although this would not be the result under the Court's Sixth Amendment right to counsel doctrine, see part G, the police are free under *Miranda* to recruit "jail plants" to work for the police and place the "plants" in a cell to question suspects. And we know from our study of the Fourth Amendment, that the "plant" can wear a wire and have the police hear and record what the suspect says to the "plant."

Is this entirely fair? Who knows, but one doctrinal fact is clear from the post-*Miranda* cases: *Miranda* did not create any kind of global right to be treated fairly by the police. Consider what happened to *Innis*, for example.

2. Impeachment Exception

The earliest *Miranda* exception was the use of statements taken in violation of *Miranda* to impeach the testimony of a defendant. Evidence law permits the opposing lawyer to introduce out-of-court statements that are inconsistent with what the witness says in court. The judge will instruct the jury that it may consider the out-of-court statements as bearing on the credibility of the witness but not as evidence (because it was made out of court). One does not have to be too cynical, however, to assume that jurors who hear damaging out-of-court statements will consider them as part of the case and not just on credibility.

In Harris v. New York, 401 US 222, 91 S.Ct. 643, 28 L.Ed. 2d 1 (1971), police did not provide Harris with *Miranda* warnings before questioning him, and the State thus did not attempt to use his statements made to police to prove his guilt of the crime of selling heroin to an undercover officer. But when Harris testified in his own defense in a way that contradicted some of what he had told police, the judge permitted the prosecutor to ask him about the contradictory *Miranda*-less statements he had made to the police. As required by state evidence law, the judge "instructed the jury that the statements attributed to [Harris] by the prosecution could be considered only in passing on petitioner's credibility and not as evidence of guilt."

Because the statements in the *Miranda* cases were used to prove guilt, the narrow holding of *Miranda* did not reach the issue in *Harris*. There was language in *Miranda* that could be read to say that statements taken in violation of *Miranda* could not be used for any purpose, but that language is what lawyers and judges call "dicta." Dicta is language that explains why a court reaches the result it reaches but is not part of the result. *Miranda*'s narrow holding is that the prosecution cannot use, at trial to prove guilt, statements made without a waiver of the right to remain silent and the right to counsel. The Court had no occasion to decide whether other uses of these statements are permitted; that language is thus dicta. The *Harris* Court conceded that "[s]ome comments in the *Miranda* opinion can indeed be read as indicating a bar to use of an uncounseled statement for any purpose," but the Court dismissed those comments because "discussion of that issue was not at all necessary to the Court's holding and cannot be regarded as controlling." The Court, now with new members appointed by Nixon, disregarded the dicta from *Miranda* that it did not like.

Determining what is "dicta" that is unnecessary to the holding is difficult for judges, lawyers, and students. As a general matter, when courts speak of narrow holding, they mean the facts that are necessary to the outcome of the case. We saw earlier the case of *Brown v. Mississippi*, where the State participated in torture to obtain confessions. At one point, the Court condemns confessions "obtained by violence." That probably represents the narrow holding. At another point, the Court condemns methods that violate fundamental principles of liberty and justice. That statement is probably broader than confessions obtained by violence and can be viewed as dicta. It helps explain *why* confessions obtained by violence are inadmissible but it has no independent meaning and would provide no limits on courts deciding cases involving confessions that were not obtained by violence.

Similarly, the *Miranda* language that statements taken in violation of the warnings and waiver rule cannot be used for any purpose is broader than necessary to hold that the statements in *Miranda* must be suppressed. Thus, *Harris* rejected that broad statement from *Miranda* and held that statements taken in violation of *Miranda* can be used to impeach the credibility of the defendant if he testifies inconsistently with what he told police. Unlike the public safety exception you are about to see, the impeachment exception probably affects many cases. Defendants who testify are likely to want to shade their testimony in a way that is more favorable to them than what they told police. But if they do that, at least some of the suppressed statements will be heard by the jury.

Is this a bad outcome? Assuming what the suspect told the police is closer to the truth than what he testifies to months or years later, why should the jury not hear the more truthful statements? Chief Justice Burger, writing for the *Harris* majority, invoked a powerful metaphor to justify the holding: "The shield provided by *Miranda* cannot be perverted into a license to use perjury by way of a defense, free from the risk of confrontation with prior inconsistent utterances."

3. Public Safety Exception

NEW YORK V. QUARLES

Supreme Court of the United States, 1984.
467 U.S. 649, 104 S.Ct. 2626, 81 L.Ed.2d 550.

Should *Miranda* apply when a police officer responds to a rapidly unfolding crime scene and takes action designed to protect the public? The Court splits 5–4 on this question.

JUSTICE REHNQUIST delivered the opinion of the Court [joined by CHIEF JUSTICE BURGER, and JUSTICES WHITE, BLACKMUN and POWELL]. * * *

On September 11, 1980, at approximately 12:30 a.m., Officer Frank Kraft and Officer Sal Scarring were on road patrol in Queens, N.Y., when a young woman approached their car. She told them that she had just been raped by a black male, approximately six feet tall, who was wearing a black jacket with the name "Big Ben" printed in yellow letters on the back. She told the officers that the man had just entered an A & P supermarket located nearby and that the man was carrying a gun.

The officers drove the woman to the supermarket, and Officer Kraft entered the store while Officer Scarring radioed for assistance. Officer Kraft quickly spotted respondent, who matched the description given by the woman, approaching a checkout counter. Apparently upon seeing the officer, respondent turned and ran toward the rear of the store, and Officer Kraft pursued him with a drawn gun. When respondent turned the corner at the end of an aisle, Officer Kraft lost sight of him for several seconds, and upon regaining sight of respondent, ordered him to stop and put his hands over his head.

Although more than three other officers had arrived on the scene by that time, Officer Kraft was the first to reach respondent. He frisked him and discovered that he was wearing a shoulder holster which was then empty. After handcuffing him, Officer Kraft asked him where the gun was. Respondent nodded in the direction of some empty cartons and responded, "the gun is over there." Officer Kraft thereafter retrieved a loaded .38-caliber revolver from one of the cartons, formally placed respondent under arrest, and read him his *Miranda* rights from a printed card. Respondent indicated that he would be willing to answer questions without an attorney present. Officer Kraft then asked respondent if he owned the gun and where he had purchased it. Respondent answered that he did own it and that he had purchased it in Miami, Fla.

In the subsequent prosecution of respondent for criminal possession of a weapon, the judge excluded the statement, "the gun is over there," and the gun because the officer had not given respondent the warnings required by our decision in *Miranda v. Arizona* before asking him where the gun was located. The judge excluded the other statements about respondent's ownership of the gun and the place of purchase, as evidence tainted by the prior *Miranda* violation. * * *

[The New York Court of Appeals] * * * rejected the State's argument that the exigencies of the situation justified Officer Kraft's failure to read respondent his *Miranda* rights until after he had located the gun. * * * For the reasons which follow, we believe that this case presents a situation where concern for public safety must be paramount to adherence to the literal language of the prophylactic rules enunciated in *Miranda.*

The Fifth Amendment guarantees that "[n]o person * * * shall be compelled in any criminal case to be a witness against himself." In *Miranda* this Court for the first time extended the Fifth Amendment privilege against compulsory self-incrimination to individuals subjected to custodial interrogation by the police. The Fifth Amendment itself does not prohibit all incriminating admissions; "[a]bsent some officially coerced self-accusation, the Fifth Amendment privilege is not violated by even the most damning admissions." The *Miranda* Court, however, presumed that interrogation in certain custodial circumstances is inherently coercive and held that statements made under those circumstances are inadmissible unless the suspect is specifically informed of his *Miranda* rights and freely decides to forgo those rights. The prophylactic *Miranda* warnings therefore are "not themselves rights protected by the Constitution but [are] instead measures to insure that the right against compulsory self-incrimination [is] protected." Requiring *Miranda* warnings before custodial interrogation provides "practical reinforcement" for the Fifth Amendment right.

In this case we have before us no claim that respondent's statements were actually compelled by police conduct which overcame his will to resist. Thus the only issue before us is whether Officer Kraft was justified in failing to make available to respondent the procedural safeguards associated with the privilege against compulsory self-incrimination since *Miranda.*

The New York Court of Appeals was undoubtedly correct in deciding that the facts of this case come within the ambit of the *Miranda* decision as we have subsequently interpreted it. We agree that respondent was in police custody * * *. Here Quarles was surrounded by at least four police officers and was handcuffed when the questioning at issue took place. As the New York Court of Appeals observed, there was nothing to suggest that any of the officers were any longer concerned for their own physical safety. The New York Court of Appeals' majority declined to express an opinion as to whether there might be an exception to the *Miranda* rule if the police had been acting to protect the public, because the lower courts in New York had made no factual determination that the police had acted with that motive.

We hold that on these facts there is a "public safety" exception to the requirement that *Miranda* warnings be given before a suspect's answers may be admitted into evidence, and that the availability of that exception does not depend upon the motivation of the individual officers involved. In a kaleidoscopic situation such as the one confronting these officers, where spontaneity rather than adherence to a police manual is necessarily the order of the day, the application of the exception which we recognize today should not be made to depend on post hoc findings at a suppression hearing concerning the subjective motivation of the arresting officer. Undoubtedly most police officers, if placed in Officer Kraft's position, would act out of a host of different, instinctive, and largely unverifiable motives—their own safety, the safety of others, and perhaps as well the desire to obtain incriminating evidence from the suspect.

Whatever the motivation of individual officers in such a situation, we do not believe that the doctrinal underpinnings of *Miranda* require that it be applied in all its rigor to a situation in which police officers ask questions reasonably prompted by a concern for the public safety. The *Miranda* decision was based in large part on this Court's view that the warnings which it required police to give to suspects in custody would reduce the likelihood that the suspects would fall victim to constitutionally impermissible practices of police interrogation in the presumptively coercive environment of the station house. The dissenters warned that the requirement of *Miranda* warnings would have the effect of decreasing the number of suspects who respond to police questioning. The *Miranda* majority, however, apparently felt that whatever the cost to society in terms of fewer convictions of guilty suspects, that cost would simply have to be borne in the interest of enlarged protection for the Fifth Amendment privilege.

The police in this case, in the very act of apprehending a suspect, were confronted with the immediate necessity of ascertaining the whereabouts of a gun which they had every reason to believe the suspect had just removed from his empty holster and discarded in the supermarket. So long as the gun was concealed somewhere in the supermarket, with its actual whereabouts unknown, it obviously posed more than one danger to the public safety: an accomplice might make use of it, a customer or employee might later come upon it.

In such a situation, if the police are required to recite the familiar *Miranda* warnings before asking the whereabouts of the gun, suspects in Quarles' position might well be deterred from responding. Procedural safeguards which deter a suspect from responding were deemed acceptable in *Miranda* in order to protect the Fifth Amendment privilege; when the primary social cost of those added protections is the possibility of fewer convictions, the *Miranda* majority was willing to bear that cost. Here, had *Miranda* warnings deterred Quarles from responding to Officer Kraft's question about the whereabouts of the gun, the cost would have been something more than merely the failure to obtain evidence useful in convicting Quarles. Officer Kraft needed an answer to his question not simply to make his case against Quarles but to insure that further danger to the public did not result from the concealment of the gun in a public area.

We conclude that the need for answers to questions in a situation posing a threat to the public safety outweighs the need for the prophylactic rule protecting the Fifth Amendment's privilege against self-incrimination. We decline to place officers such as Officer Kraft in the untenable position of having to consider, often in a matter of seconds, whether it best serves society for them to ask the necessary questions without the *Miranda* warnings and render whatever probative evidence they uncover inadmissible, or for them to give the warnings in order to preserve the admissibility of evidence they might uncover but possibly damage or destroy their ability to obtain that evidence and neutralize the volatile situation confronting them.

In recognizing a narrow exception to the *Miranda* rule in this case, we acknowledge that to some degree we lessen the desirable clarity of that rule. * * * But as we have pointed out, we believe that the exception which we recognize today lessens the necessity of that on-the-scene balancing process. The exception will not be difficult for police officers to apply because in each case it will be circumscribed by the exigency which justifies it. We think police officers can and will distinguish almost instinctively between questions necessary to secure their own safety or the safety of the public and questions designed solely to elicit testimonial evidence from a suspect.

The facts of this case clearly demonstrate that distinction and an officer's ability to recognize it. Officer Kraft asked only the question necessary to locate the missing gun before advising respondent of his rights. It was only after securing the loaded revolver and giving the warnings that he continued with investigatory questions about the ownership and place of purchase of the gun. The exception which we recognize today, far from complicating the thought processes and the on-the-scene judgments of police officers, will simply free them to follow their legitimate instincts when confronting situations presenting a danger to the public safety.

We hold that the Court of Appeals in this case erred in excluding the statement, "the gun is over there," and the gun because of the officer's failure to read respondent his *Miranda* rights before attempting to locate the weapon. Accordingly we hold that it also erred in excluding the subsequent statements as illegal fruits of a *Miranda* violation. We therefore reverse and remand for further proceedings not inconsistent with this opinion. * * *

JUSTICE O'CONNOR, concurring in the judgment in part and dissenting in part.

* * * Were the Court writing from a clean slate, I could agree with its holding. But *Miranda* is now the law and, in my view, the Court has not provided sufficient justification for departing from it or for blurring its now clear strictures. Accordingly, I would require suppression of the initial statement taken from respondent in this case. [In an omitted part of her opinion, Justice O'Connor agreed that the gun was admissible and thus concurred in that part of the Court's judgment. Her view, which later formed the holding in Oregon v. Elstad, next sub-section, was that a *Miranda* violation has no "fruit" beyond the statement itself.] * * *

I * * *

In my view, a "public safety" exception unnecessarily blurs the edges of the clear line heretofore established and makes *Miranda*'s requirements more difficult to understand. In some cases, police will benefit because a reviewing court will find that an exigency excused their failure to administer the required warnings. But in other cases, police will suffer because, though they thought an exigency excused their noncompliance, a reviewing court will view the "objective" circumstances differently and require exclusion of admissions thereby obtained. The end result will be a finespun new doctrine on public safety exigencies incident to custodial interrogation, complete with the hair-splitting distinctions that currently plague our Fourth Amendment jurisprudence. * * *

* * * In my view, since there is nothing about an exigency that makes custodial interrogation any less compelling, a principled application of *Miranda* requires that respondent's statement be suppressed. * * *

JUSTICE MARSHALL, with whom JUSTICE BRENNAN and JUSTICE STEVENS join, dissenting. * * *

III

* * * The majority has lost sight of the fact that *Miranda v. Arizona* and our earlier custodial-interrogation cases all implemented a constitutional privilege against self-incrimination. The rules established in these cases were designed to protect criminal defendants against prosecutions based on coerced self-incriminating statements. The majority today turns its back on these constitutional considerations, and invites the government to prosecute through the use of what necessarily are coerced statements.

A

The majority's error stems from a serious misunderstanding of *Miranda v. Arizona* and of the Fifth Amendment upon which that decision was based. The majority implies that *Miranda* consisted of no more than a judicial balancing act in which the benefits of "enlarged protection for the Fifth Amendment privilege" were weighed against "the cost to society in terms of fewer convictions of guilty suspects." Supposedly because the scales tipped in favor of the privilege against self-incrimination, the *Miranda* Court erected a prophylactic barrier around statements made during custodial interrogations. The majority now proposes to return to the scales of social utility to calculate whether *Miranda*'s prophylactic rule remains cost-effective when threats to the public's safety are added to the balance. * * *

Whether society would be better off if the police warned suspects of their rights before beginning an interrogation or whether the advantages of giving such warnings would outweigh their costs did not inform the *Miranda* decision. On the contrary, the *Miranda* Court was concerned with the proscriptions of the Fifth Amendment, and, in particular, whether the Self-Incrimination Clause permits the government to prosecute individuals based on statements made in the course of custodial interrogations. * * *

In fashioning its "public-safety" exception to *Miranda*, the majority makes no attempt to deal with the constitutional presumption established by that case. The majority does not argue that police questioning about issues of public safety is any less coercive than custodial interrogations into other matters. The majority's only contention is that police officers could more easily protect the public if *Miranda* did not apply to custodial interrogations concerning the public's safety. But *Miranda* was not a decision about public safety; it was a decision about coerced confessions. Without establishing that interrogations concerning the public's safety are less likely to be coercive than other interrogations, the majority cannot endorse the "public-safety" exception and remain faithful to the logic of *Miranda v. Arizona.*

B

The majority's avoidance of the issue of coercion may not have been inadvertent. It would strain credulity to contend that Officer Kraft's questioning of respondent Quarles was not coercive. In the middle of the night and in the back of an empty supermarket, Quarles was surrounded by four armed police officers. His hands were handcuffed behind his back. The first words out of the mouth of the arresting officer were: "Where is the gun?" In the majority's phrase, the situation was "kaleidoscopic." Police and suspect were acting on instinct. Officer Kraft's abrupt and pointed question pressured Quarles in precisely the way that the *Miranda* Court feared the custodial interrogations would coerce self-incriminating testimony.

That the application of the "public-safety" exception in this case entailed coercion is no happenstance. The majority's ratio decidendi is that interrogating suspects about matters of public safety will be coercive. In its cost-benefit analysis, the Court's strongest argument in favor of a "public-safety" exception to *Miranda* is that the police would be better able to protect the public's safety if they were not always required to give suspects their *Miranda* warnings. The crux of this argument is that, by deliberately withholding *Miranda* warnings, the police can get information out of suspects who would refuse to respond to police questioning were they advised of their constitutional rights. The "public-safety" exception is efficacious precisely because it permits police officers to coerce criminal defendants into making involuntary statements.

* * * Though the majority's opinion is cloaked in the beguiling language of utilitarianism, the Court has sanctioned sub silentio criminal prosecutions based on compelled self-incriminating statements. I find this result in direct conflict with the Fifth Amendment's dictate that "[n]o person * * * shall be compelled in any criminal case to be a witness against himself."

The irony of the majority's decision is that the public's safety can be perfectly well protected without abridging the Fifth Amendment. If a bomb is about to explode or the public is otherwise imminently imperiled, the police are free to interrogate suspects without advising them of their constitutional rights. Such unconsented questioning may take place not only when police officers act on instinct but also when higher faculties lead them to believe that advising a suspect of his constitutional rights might decrease the likelihood that the suspect would reveal life-saving information. If trickery is necessary to protect the public, then the police may trick a suspect into confessing. While the Fourteenth Amendment sets limits on such behavior, nothing in the Fifth Amendment or our decision in *Miranda v. Arizona* proscribes this sort of emergency questioning. All the Fifth Amendment forbids is the introduction of coerced statements at trial. * * *

NOTES AND QUESTIONS

1. Justice Marshall, in an omitted part of his dissent, took issue with the majority's conclusion that there was a legitimate threat to public safety on these facts. What do you think? How would you phrase that threat? Would the case come out

differently if a suspect was handcuffed in a motel room when the officer asked the location of the gun? See State v. Stephenson, 350 N.J.Super. 517, 796 A.2d 274 (App. Div. 2002).

2. For those who are curious about what happened to the rape charge, Quarles could of course have been prosecuted separately for rape and for the gun charge.

3. The majority further explained the basis of its holding in two footnotes. In footnote 5, the Court wrote:

> The dissent curiously takes us to task for "endors[ing] the introduction of coerced self-incriminating statements in criminal prosecutions," and for "sanction[ing] sub silentio criminal prosecutions based on compelled self-incriminating statements." Of course our decision today does nothing of the kind. As the *Miranda* Court itself recognized, the failure to provide *Miranda* warnings in and of itself does not render a confession involuntary, and respondent is certainly free on remand to argue that his statement was coerced under traditional due process standards. Today we merely reject the only argument that respondent has raised to support the exclusion of his statement, that the statement must be presumed compelled because of Officer Kraft's failure to read him his *Miranda* warnings.

In footnote 7, the Court once again emphasized that there was no constitutional imperative that limited the officer's questioning of Quarles:

> The dissent argues that a public safety exception to *Miranda* is unnecessary because in every case an officer can simply ask the necessary questions to protect himself or the public, and then the prosecution can decline to introduce any incriminating responses at a subsequent trial. But absent actual coercion by the officer, there is no constitutional imperative requiring the exclusion of the evidence that results from police inquiry of this kind; and we do not believe that the doctrinal underpinnings of *Miranda* require us to exclude the evidence, thus penalizing officers for asking the very questions which are the most crucial to their efforts to protect themselves and the public.

4. Broadly construed, a "public safety" exception might swallow up much of the *Miranda* rule. One might think that in every arrest for a drug or violent crime, the police officer would ask whether the suspect was armed and lots of suspects would say something against their interest. But when author Thomas in 2002 drew a sample of 216 state and federal cases that discuss *Miranda,* he found that only four cases presented the public safety issue. See George C. Thomas III, Stories About *Miranda,* 102 Mich. L. Rev. 1959 (2004). Three courts applied it to admit the statements and one found that the case did not fit *Quarles.*

5. *Quarles and terror suspects.* F.B.I. agents did not provide *Miranda* warnings to Faisal Shahzad before questioning him "extensively" about the attempted Times Square car bombing in 2010. Mark Hosenball, Obama Officials on Shahzad Case: We Did It Right, Newsweek, May 6, 2010. Agents did not warn Shahzad until he had "provided what the F.B.I. called 'valuable intelligence and evidence.' " Peter Baker, A Renewed Debate Over Suspect Rights, The New York Times, May 4, 2010. Once the agents had "determined there was no imminent threat to be headed off," they read Mr. Shahzad his rights, "but he waived them and continued talking."

The Court said in *Quarles*: "We conclude that the need for answers to questions in a situation posing a threat to the public safety outweighs the need for the prophylactic rule protecting the Fifth Amendment's privilege against self-incrimination." Would the need to determine whether there were other bombs about to go off in a crowded city outweigh the need to protect the privilege of a suspect believed to be connected to at least one bomb?

Does *Quarles* justify what the agents did in the Times Square case? Can you point to language or reasoning in the case that would support the defense assertion that the agents went too far under *Quarles*?

Attorney General Eric Holder explicitly relied on *Quarles* to justify withholding *Miranda* warnings in Shahzad's case, though he said that it was time that *Quarles* was "updated. That's one of the things that I think we're going to be reaching out to Congress to do, to come up with a proposal that is both constitutional, but that is also relevant to our time and the threat that we now face." Anne E. Kornblut, Obama Administration Looks into Modifying *Miranda* Law in the Age of Terrorism, The Washington Post, May 10, 2010.

6. *911 calls and Quarles.* Police responded to a 911 call reporting that Ms. B had attempted suicide. The officers who answered the call were aware that Ms. B had obtained a restraining order against her estranged husband, who opened the door and admitted the police. He attempted to hand his cell phone to the officer, stating, "Can you speak to my attorney?" The officer ignored the phone and tried to assist Ms. B who was bleeding and motionless on the couch. After calling for assistance, an officer asked Mr. B when he had last heard from his wife. He said he had seen or talked to her around four o'clock. He then asked again "can you please talk to my attorney?" Two other officers arrived and Mr. B asked them to please talk to his attorney. Police ignored the request because they were attending to Ms. B. At one point, an officer took the phone and threw it across the room.

Does *Miranda* bar admission in Mr. B's murder trial of his answer to the question of when had he last heard from his wife? See State v. Boretsky, 186 N.J. 271, 894 A.2d 659 (2006).

7 *Problems.* Assume that no *Miranda* warnings were given in the following Problems, and concern yourself only with whether the statements would be admissible under the "public safety" exception.

A. L walks into the police station and cries out, "I killed her, I killed her, I killed her." The police officer knew that L's wife was missing. "Are you L?" "Yes." "Where is Mrs. L?" "At the boathouse." "Where exactly at the boathouse?" "In the last bay, in the van." Police take L to the boathouse. They inspect the van and find a large fiberglass box but no other sign of the victim. Police ask L, "Is she in the box?" "Yes." See State v. Lockhart, 830 A.2d 433 (Me. 2003).

B. A bank robber, F, is shot by the bank security guard but manages to flee a Dallas bank. As he runs from the bank, a salesman from a nearby car dealership chases him. When F collapses in a field near the bank, the car salesman draws his gun and covers the wounded F. Two police officers arrive and draw their guns on the car salesman until they are persuaded that F is the suspect. The officers then aim their guns at F and tell him to put his hands over his head. He responds that he is wounded and cannot raise his arms. After frisking F, the police officers ascertain that he is wounded, yet keep their guns pointed at him. The officers ask the following questions: "Who shot you?", "Who was with you?", and "Where is the gun?" Are the answers admissible? See Fleming v. Collins, 954 F.2d 1109 (5th Cir. 1992) (en banc).

C. After police arrest L on outstanding warrants, the officer notices that he is chewing and swallowing plastic bags. When she asks what is in the bags, the "savvy" suspect replies, "Methamphetamine." The State seeks to introduce the statement on the ground that the officer was concerned about the suspect's health and needed to know what he was ingesting. Which way do you rule as judge? See United States v. Lutz, 207 F.Supp.2d 1247 (D. Kan. 2002).

D. C was arrested for conspiracy to distribute a large quantity of cocaine. Before searching C prior to placing him in detention at the station, the officer asked whether he had any drugs or needles on his person. He responded, "I don't use drugs. I sell them." Admissible? Would it matter if the officer testified that he asked the same question of every person arrested for a drug offense? See United States v. Carrillo, 16 F.3d 1046 (9th Cir. 1994).

8. *Quarles* recognized a "public safety" exception to *Miranda.* It did so by distinguishing between compulsion—a pure violation of the Fifth Amendment—and a violation of the mere "prophylactic *Miranda* warnings." In *Oregon v. Elstad*, next subsection, we see this distinction made more explicit, and the Supreme Court again finds that the implications of a *Miranda* violation are not the same as a violation of the Fifth Amendment in its pristine form.

4. Booking Question Exception

In Pennsylvania v. Muniz, 496 U.S. 582, 110 S.Ct. 2638, 110 L.Ed.2d 528 (1990), eight members of the Court agreed that police do not have to provide *Miranda* warnings before asking a suspect routine booking questions, such as name, address, height, weight, eye color, date of birth, and current age. Four members of the Court were of the view that there exists a routine booking question exception to *Miranda*, making it unnecessary to decide whether those questions could ever constitute interrogation under *Miranda* and *Rhode Island v. Innis*.

A different set of four justices adopted a more foundational approach. Recall that the Fifth Amendment forbids being compelled to be a witness against oneself. What does it mean to be a witness against oneself? In Schmerber v. California, 384 US 757, 86 S.Ct. 1826, 16 L.Ed. 2d 908 (1966), the Court reasoned that one is a witness only if one gives testimonial evidence; blood is not "testimonial" and thus compelling a suspect to provide blood is not making him be a witness against himself. The rough and ready test for "testimonial" is whether it requires a mental calculation. Thus, neither compelling a suspect to wear a particular item of clothing in a lineup nor compelling him to give a handwriting sample is testimonial because neither requires a mental calculation. For four justices, questions about age, height, weight, etc. do not require sufficient mental calculation to qualify as testimonial. For those justices there was no need to create a booking question exception. Differing theories aside, the point to *Muniz* is that there is no need to provide *Miranda* warnings before police ask routine booking questions.

5. Warnings Cure Earlier Failure to Warn

OREGON V. ELSTAD

Supreme Court of the United States, 1985.
470 U.S. 298, 105 S.Ct. 1285, 84 L.Ed.2d 222.

This case is a special situation because it involves "half a loaf" for defendants. The statements taken without warnings are inadmissible. But a robust *Miranda* world could also condemn later statements even if warnings and "waiver" precede the later statements. A court might, as the state court did here, hold that the failure to warn before the initial questioning poisons the later statements as well as the statements made without warnings. But the United States Supreme Court did not agree.

JUSTICE O'CONNOR delivered the opinion of the Court [joined by CHIEF JUSTICE BURGER, and JUSTICES WHITE, BLACKMUN, POWELL, and REHNQUIST].

This case requires us to decide whether an initial failure of law enforcement officers to administer the warnings required by *Miranda v. Arizona*, without more, "taints" subsequent admissions made after a suspect has been fully advised of and has waived his *Miranda* rights. Respondent, Michael James Elstad, was convicted of burglary by an Oregon trial court. The Oregon Court of Appeals reversed, holding that respondent's signed confession, although voluntary, was rendered inadmissible by a prior remark made in response to questioning without benefit of *Miranda* warnings. * * *

I

In December 1981, the home of Mr. and Mrs. Gilbert Gross, in the town of Salem, Polk County, Ore., was burglarized. Missing were art objects and furnishings valued at $150,000. A witness to the burglary contacted the Polk County Sheriff's office, implicating respondent Michael Elstad, an 18-year-old neighbor and friend of the Grosses' teenage son. Thereupon, Officers Burke and McAllister went to the home of respondent Elstad, with a warrant for his arrest. Elstad's mother answered the door. She led the officers to her son's room where he lay on his bed, clad in shorts and listening to his stereo. The officers asked him to get dressed and to accompany them into the living room. Officer McAllister asked respondent's mother to step into the kitchen, where he explained that they had a warrant for her son's arrest for the burglary of a neighbor's residence. Officer Burke remained with Elstad in the living room. He later testified:

> "I sat down with Mr. Elstad and I asked him if he was aware of why Detective McAllister and myself were there to talk with him. He stated no, he had no idea why we were there. I then asked him if he knew a person by the name of Gross, and he said yes, he did, and also added that he heard that there was a robbery at the Gross house. And at that point I told Mr. Elstad that I felt he was involved in that, and he looked at me and stated, 'Yes, I was there.' "

The officers then escorted Elstad to the back of the patrol car. As they were about to leave for the Polk County Sheriff's office, Elstad's father arrived home and came to the rear of the patrol car. The officers advised him that his son was a suspect in the burglary. Officer Burke testified that Mr. Elstad became quite agitated, opened the rear door of the car and admonished his son: "I told you that you were going to get into trouble. You wouldn't listen to me. You never learn."

Elstad was transported to the Sheriff's headquarters and approximately one hour later, Officers Burke and McAllister joined him in McAllister's office. McAllister then advised respondent for the first time of his *Miranda* rights, reading from a standard card. Respondent indicated he understood his rights, and, having these rights in mind, wished to speak with the officers. Elstad gave a full statement, explaining that he had known that the Gross family was out of town and had been paid to lead several acquaintances to the Gross residence and show them how to gain entry through a defective sliding glass door. The statement was typed, reviewed by respondent, read back to him for correction, initialed and signed by Elstad and both officers. As an afterthought, Elstad added and initialed the sentence, "After leaving the house Robby & I went back to [the] van & Robby handed me a small bag of grass." Respondent concedes that the officers made no threats or promises either at his residence or at the Sheriff's office. * * *

* * * The State conceded that Elstad had been in custody when he made his statement, "I was there," and accordingly agreed that this statement was inadmissible as having been given without the prescribed *Miranda* warnings. But the State maintained that any conceivable "taint" had been dissipated prior to the respondent's written confession by McAllister's careful administration of the requisite warnings. * * *

II

The arguments advanced in favor of suppression of respondent's written confession rely heavily on metaphor. One metaphor, familiar from the Fourth Amendment context, would require that respondent's confession, regardless of its integrity, voluntariness, and probative value, be suppressed as the "tainted fruit of the poisonous tree" of the *Miranda* violation. A second metaphor questions whether a confession can be truly voluntary once the "cat is out of the bag." Taken out of context, each of these metaphors can be misleading. They should not be used to obscure fundamental differences between the role of the Fourth Amendment exclusionary rule and the function of *Miranda* in guarding against the prosecutorial use of compelled statements as prohibited by the Fifth Amendment. The Oregon court assumed and respondent here contends that a failure to administer *Miranda* warnings necessarily breeds the same consequences as police infringement of a constitutional right, so that evidence uncovered following an unwarned statement must be suppressed as "fruit of the poisonous tree." We believe this view misconstrues the nature of the protections afforded by *Miranda* warnings and therefore misreads the consequences of police failure to supply them.

A * * *

Respondent's contention that his confession was tainted by the earlier failure of the police to provide *Miranda* warnings and must be excluded as "fruit of the poisonous tree" assumes the existence of a constitutional violation. This figure of speech is drawn from Wong Sun v. United States, 371 US 471, 83 S.Ct. 407, 9 L.Ed. 2d 441 (1963), in which the Court held that evidence and witnesses discovered as a result of a search in violation of the Fourth Amendment must be excluded from evidence. The *Wong Sun* doctrine applies as well when the fruit of the Fourth Amendment violation is a confession. It is settled law that "a confession obtained through custodial interrogation after an illegal arrest should be excluded unless intervening events break the causal connection between the illegal arrest and the confession so that the confession is 'sufficiently an act of free will to purge the primary taint.' "

But as we explained in *Quarles* [last sub-section] * * * a procedural *Miranda* violation differs in significant respects from violations of the Fourth Amendment, which have traditionally mandated a broad application of the "fruits" doctrine. The purpose of the Fourth Amendment exclusionary rule is to deter unreasonable searches, no matter how probative their fruits. * * * Where a Fourth Amendment violation "taints" the confession, a finding of voluntariness for the purposes of the Fifth Amendment is merely a threshold requirement in determining whether the confession may be admitted in evidence. Beyond this, the prosecution must show a sufficient break in events to undermine the inference that the confession was caused by the Fourth Amendment violation.

The *Miranda* exclusionary rule, however, serves the Fifth Amendment and sweeps more broadly than the Fifth Amendment itself. It may be triggered even in the absence of a Fifth Amendment violation. The Fifth Amendment prohibits use by the prosecution in its case in chief only of compelled testimony. Failure to administer *Miranda* warnings creates a presumption of compulsion. Consequently, unwarned statements that are otherwise voluntary within the meaning of the Fifth Amendment must nevertheless be excluded from evidence under *Miranda.* Thus, in the individual case, *Miranda*'s preventive medicine provides a remedy even to the defendant who has suffered no identifiable constitutional harm.

But the *Miranda* presumption, though irrebuttable for purposes of the prosecution's case in chief, does not require that the statements and their fruits be discarded as inherently tainted. Despite the fact that patently voluntary statements taken in violation of *Miranda* must be excluded from the prosecution's case, the presumption of coercion does not bar their use for impeachment purposes on cross-examination. * * * Where an unwarned statement is preserved for use in situations that fall outside the sweep of the *Miranda* presumption, "the primary criterion of admissibility [remains] the 'old' due process voluntariness test."

In Michigan v. Tucker, 417 US 433, 94 S.Ct. 2357, 41 L.Ed. 2d 182 (1974), the Court was asked to extend the *Wong Sun* fruits doctrine to suppress the testimony of a witness for the prosecution whose identity was discovered as the result of a statement taken from the accused without benefit of full *Miranda* warnings. As in respondent's case, the breach of the *Miranda* procedures in Tucker involved no actual compulsion. The Court concluded that the unwarned questioning "did not abridge respondent's constitutional privilege * * * but departed only from the prophylactic standards later laid down by this Court in *Miranda* to safeguard that privilege." Since there was no actual infringement of the suspect's constitutional rights, the case was not controlled by the doctrine expressed in Wong Sun that fruits of a constitutional violation must be suppressed. In deciding "how sweeping the judicially imposed consequences" of a failure to administer *Miranda* warnings should be, the *Tucker* Court noted that neither the general goal of deterring improper police conduct nor the Fifth Amendment goal of assuring trustworthy evidence would be served by suppression of the witness' testimony. The unwarned confession must, of course, be suppressed, but the Court ruled that introduction of the third-party witness' testimony did not violate Tucker's Fifth Amendment rights.

We believe that this reasoning applies with equal force when the alleged "fruit" of a noncoercive *Miranda* violation is neither a witness nor an article of evidence but the accused's own voluntary testimony. As in *Tucker*, the absence of any coercion or improper tactics undercuts the twin rationales—trustworthiness and deterrence—for a broader rule. Once warned, the suspect is free to exercise his own volition in deciding whether or not to make a statement to the authorities. The Court has often noted: " '[A] living witness is not to be mechanically equated with the proffer of inanimate evidentiary objects illegally seized. * * * [T]he living witness is an individual human personality whose attributes of will, perception, memory and volition interact to determine what testimony he will give.' " * * *

* * * If errors are made by law enforcement officers in administering the prophylactic *Miranda* procedures, they should not breed the same irremediable consequences as police infringement of the Fifth Amendment itself. It is an unwarranted extension of *Miranda* to hold that a simple failure to administer the warnings, unaccompanied by any actual coercion or other circumstances calculated to undermine the suspect's ability to exercise his free will, so taints the investigatory process that a subsequent voluntary and informed waiver is ineffective for some indeterminate period. Though *Miranda* requires that the

unwarned admission must be suppressed, the admissibility of any subsequent statement should turn in these circumstances solely on whether it is knowingly and voluntarily made.

B

The Oregon court, however, believed that the unwarned remark compromised the voluntariness of respondent's later confession. It was the court's view that the prior answer and not the unwarned questioning impaired respondent's ability to give a valid waiver and that only lapse of time and change of place could dissipate what it termed the "coercive impact" of the inadmissible statement. When a prior statement is actually coerced, the time that passes between confessions, the change in place of interrogations, and the change in identity of the interrogators all bear on whether that coercion has carried over into the second confession. The failure of police to administer *Miranda* warnings does not mean that the statements received have actually been coerced, but only that courts will presume the privilege against compulsory self-incrimination has not been intelligently exercised. * * * In these circumstances, a careful and thorough administration of *Miranda* warnings serves to cure the condition that rendered the unwarned statement inadmissible. The warning conveys the relevant information and thereafter the suspect's choice whether to exercise his privilege to remain silent should ordinarily be viewed as an "act of free will." * * *

* * * We must conclude that, absent deliberately coercive or improper tactics in obtaining the initial statement, the mere fact that a suspect has made an unwarned admission does not warrant a presumption of compulsion. A subsequent administration of *Miranda* warnings to a suspect who has given a voluntary but unwarned statement ordinarily should suffice to remove the conditions that precluded admission of the earlier statement. In such circumstances, the finder of fact may reasonably conclude that the suspect made a rational and intelligent choice whether to waive or invoke his rights.

III

Though belated, the reading of respondent's rights was undeniably complete. McAllister testified that he read the *Miranda* warnings aloud from a printed card and recorded Elstad's responses. There is no question that respondent knowingly and voluntarily waived his right to remain silent before he described his participation in the burglary. It is also beyond dispute that respondent's earlier remark was voluntary, within the meaning of the Fifth Amendment. Neither the environment nor the manner of either "interrogation" was coercive. The initial conversation took place at midday, in the living room area of respondent's own home, with his mother in the kitchen area, a few steps away. Although in retrospect the officers testified that respondent was then in custody [and thus warnings were required, eds.], at the time he made his statement he had not been informed that he was under arrest. The arresting officers' testimony indicates that the brief stop in the living room before proceeding to the station house was not to interrogate the suspect but to notify his mother of the reason for his arrest.

The State has conceded the issue of custody and thus we must assume that Burke breached *Miranda* procedures in failing to administer *Miranda* warnings before initiating the discussion in the living room. This breach may have been the result of confusion as to whether the brief exchange qualified as "custodial interrogation" or it may simply have reflected Burke's reluctance to initiate an alarming police procedure before McAllister had spoken with respondent's mother. Whatever the reason for Burke's oversight, the incident had none of the earmarks of coercion. Nor did the officers exploit the unwarned admission to pressure respondent into waiving his right to remain silent.

Respondent, however, has argued that he was unable to give a fully informed waiver of his rights because he was unaware that his prior statement could not be used against him. Respondent suggests that Officer McAllister, to cure this deficiency, should have added an additional warning to those given him at the Sheriff's office. Such a requirement is neither practicable nor constitutionally necessary. In many cases, a breach of *Miranda* procedures may not be identified as such until long after full *Miranda* warnings are administered and a valid confession obtained. The standard *Miranda* warnings explicitly inform the suspect of his right to consult a lawyer before speaking. Police officers are ill-equipped to pinch-hit for counsel, construing the murky and difficult questions of when "custody" begins or whether a given unwarned statement will ultimately be held admissible. * * *

JUSTICE BRENNAN, with whom JUSTICE MARSHALL joins, dissenting. * * *

Even while purporting to reaffirm [*Miranda*'s] constitutional guarantees, the Court has engaged of late in a studied campaign to strip the *Miranda* decision piecemeal and to undermine the rights *Miranda* sought to secure. Today's decision not only extends this effort a further step, but delivers a potentially crippling blow to *Miranda* and the ability of courts to safeguard the rights of persons accused of crime. For at least with respect to successive confessions, the Court today appears to strip remedies for *Miranda* violations of the "fruit of the poisonous tree" doctrine prohibiting the use of evidence presumptively derived from official illegality. * * *

Today's decision, in short, threatens disastrous consequences far beyond the outcome in this case. * * *

I * * *

The Court today * * * [adopts] a rule that "the psychological impact of voluntary disclosure of a guilty secret" neither "qualifies as state compulsion" nor "compromises the voluntariness" of subsequent confessions. So long as a suspect receives the usual *Miranda* warnings before further interrogation, the Court reasons, the fact that he "is free to exercise his own volition in deciding whether or not to make" further confessions "ordinarily" is a sufficient "cure" and serves to break any causal connection between the illegal confession and subsequent statements.

The Court's marble-palace psychoanalysis is tidy, but it flies in the face of our own precedents, demonstrates a startling unawareness of the realities of police interrogation, and is completely out of tune with the experience of state and federal courts over the last 20 years. Perhaps the Court has grasped some psychological truth that has eluded persons far more experienced in these matters; if so, the Court owes an explanation of how so many could have been so wrong for so many years. * * *

[*The opinion of* JUSTICE STEVENS*, dissenting, is omitted.*]

NOTES AND QUESTIONS

1. *Custody.* Referring back to the custody materials, do you think the State might have won the custody issue? If so, why do you suppose the State conceded the custody question?

2. Does the Court hold that no second statement would ever be suppressed if it followed an unwarned incriminating statement or only that in this case the statement was admissible? Or is there a third way to read *Elstad*?

3. *An exception to the Elstad exception!* In 2004, the Court discovered a very narrow exception to the rule that warnings and waiver cure any prior *Miranda* violation. In Missouri v. Seibert, 542 U.S. 600, 124 S.Ct. 2601, 159 L.Ed.2d 643 (2004), the police used a two-stage interrogation technique designed to induce the suspect to waive her *Miranda* rights at the second stage, Without providing warnings, the police interrogated Seibert for 30–40 minutes and finally got her to admit her role in killing a mentally ill teenager. After a short break, the police provided warnings, reminded Seibert that she had already admitted the crime, and then obtained a "waiver."

Though there was no majority opinion, five members of the Court agreed that the waiver did not cleanse the deliberate violation of *Miranda* when the "warning was withheld to obscure both the practical and legal significance" of the warning that was given later." Kennedy, J., concurring in the judgment. Justice Breyer concurred, expressing his view that courts "should exclude the 'fruits' of the initial unwarned questioning unless the failure to warn was in good faith." The "good faith" approach is probably the best way to understand the *Seibert* exception to the *Elstad* exception to *Miranda.*

4. *Problem.* Police question a 17-year-old suspect held in custody without providing *Miranda* warnings. He admits his involvement in a burglary. One officer turns to the other and, in ear-shot of the suspect, asks him to let the suspect "know about his rights" because he has "already told us about going into the house [and] I don't think that's going to change [his] desire to cooperate with us." Police give *Miranda* warnings. He asks whether he is under arrest and the police tell him he is not. He later confesses to a murder as well as the burglary. Argue for suppression of this confession. Ramirez v. State, 739 So.2d 568 (Fla. 1999).

5. Do you think the *Elstad* Court is saying that *Miranda* is not required by the Constitution?

E. *Miranda* and Politics

We mentioned earlier that Richard Nixon in 1968 campaigned against *Miranda* and other of the Warren Court decisions. The time was ripe for this campaign strategy as the crime rate in general, and the violent crime rate in particular, had skyrocketed in the mid-1960s. The number of violent crimes reported by the FBI almost doubled between 1963 and 1968, from 317,000 to 595,000. Total property crimes were up about 50% in the same period, from roughly 2 million to roughly 3 million.

George Wallace, a third party candidate for president, played the "law and order" card even more blatantly than Nixon. During a rally in Cicero, Illinois, he made remarks that were a standard part of his campaign speech. The Supreme Court, Wallace said, was a "sorry, lousy, no-account outfit." Murderers and rapists are "just laughing while the police are crying for help." If a criminal "knocks you over the head," he will be "out of jail before you're out of the hospital and the policeman who arrested him will be on trial. But some psychologist says, 'well he's not to blame, society's to blame. His father didn't take him to see the Pittsburgh Pirates when he was a little boy.' " Then, a promise from Wallace: "If we were President now, you wouldn't get stabbed or raped in the shadow of the White House, even if we had to call out 30,000 troops and equip them with two-foot-long bayonets and station them every few feet apart." Liva Baker, *Miranda*: Crime, Law and Politics 243–44 (1983).

Nixon attacked *Miranda* specifically: At a rally in Ohio just days before the election, Nixon said:

> I found that a cab driver who had been cruelly murdered and robbed, and the man who murdered and robbed him had confessed the crime, was set free because of a Supreme Court decision. An old woman, who had been brutally robbed and then murdered—the man who confessed the crime was set free because of a Supreme Court decision. * * * And an old man who had been robbed and clubbed to death—and the man who confessed the crime was set free in Las Vegas.

In another campaign speech, Nixon promised "legislation to restore the balance" between the "peace forces" and "criminal forces." Baker, supra, at 245–46. Congress beat him to the punch, passing in the summer of 1968 the Omnibus Crime Control and Safe Streets Act. What follows gives some sense of the rhetoric on the floor of the Congress.

> [Senator McClellan:] [C]rime and the threat of crime, rioting, and violence, stalk America. Our streets are unsafe. Our Citizens are fearful, terrorized, and outraged. * * *
>
> The war on crime must be fought on many fronts. * * * Court decisions that dispense "unequal" justice to society and which protect and liberate guilty and confirmed criminals to pursue and repeat their nefarious crimes should be reversed and overruled. * * * The confusion and disarray injected into law enforcement by [*Miranda* and other cases] are deplorable and demoralizing. * * *
>
> * * * Look at that chart [of the crime rate]. Look at it and weep for your country. * * *
>
> * * * [I]f this effort to deal with these erroneous Court decisions is defeated, every gangster and overlord of the underworld; every syndicate chief, racketeer, captain, lieutenant, sergeant, private, punk, and hoodlum in organized crime; every murderer, rapist, robber, burglar, arsonist, thief, and conman will have cause to rejoice and celebrate.
>
> * * * [A]nd every innocent, law-abiding, and God-fearing citizen in this land will have cause to weep and despair.

114 Cong. Rec. 11,200–01, 14,146, 14,155.

Part of the resulting bill was 18 U.S.C. § 3501, the 1968 Omnibus Crime Control and Safe Streets Act, a statute intended to "overrule" *Miranda.*

Two of its provisions follow.

§ 3501. Admissibility of confessions

(a) In any criminal prosecution brought by the United States or by the District of Columbia, a confession, as defined in subsection (e) hereof, shall be admissible in evidence if it is voluntarily given. Before such confession is received in evidence, the trial judge shall, out of the presence of the jury, determine any issue as to voluntariness. If the trial judge determines that the confession was voluntarily made it shall be admitted in evidence and the trial judge shall permit the jury to hear relevant evidence on the issue of voluntariness and shall instruct the jury to give such weight to the confession as the jury feels it deserves under all the circumstances.

(b) The trial judge in determining the issue of voluntariness shall take into consideration all the circumstances surrounding the giving of the confession, including (1) the time elapsing between arrest and arraignment of the defendant making the confession, if it was made after arrest and before arraignment, (2) whether such defendant knew the nature of the offense with which he was charged or of which he was suspected at the time of making the confession, (3) whether or not such defendant was advised or knew that he was not required to make any statement and that any such statement could be used against him, (4) whether or not such defendant had been advised prior to questioning of his right to the assistance of counsel, and (5) whether or not such defendant was without the assistance of counsel when questioned and when giving such confession.

These provisions were not tested in the United States Supreme Court until 2000.

DICKERSON V. UNITED STATES

Supreme Court of the United States, 2000.
530 U.S. 428, 120 S.Ct. 2326, 147 L.Ed.2d 405.

In several cases that you have read, the Court suggested that a *Miranda* violation is not a violation of the "real" Fifth Amendment right against compelled self-incrimination. That "loose language" produces the next case, where the Court tries to have its cake and eat it, too. A *Miranda* violation is, well, sort of a constitutional violation.

Chief Justice Rehnquist delivered the opinion of the Court [joined by Justices Stevens, O'Connor, Kennedy, Souter, Ginsberg, and Breyer].

In *Miranda v. Arizona*, we held that certain warnings must be given before a suspect's statement made during custodial interrogation could be admitted in evidence. In the wake of that decision, Congress enacted 18 U.S.C. § 3501, which in essence laid down a rule that the admissibility of such statements should turn only on whether or not they were voluntarily made. We hold that *Miranda*, being a constitutional decision of this Court, may not be in effect overruled by an Act of Congress, and we decline to overrule *Miranda* ourselves. We therefore hold that *Miranda* and its progeny in this Court govern the admissibility of statements made during custodial interrogation in both state and federal courts.

Petitioner Dickerson was indicted for bank robbery, conspiracy to commit bank robbery, and using a firearm in the course of committing a crime of violence * * *. Before trial, Dickerson moved to suppress a statement he had made at a Federal Bureau of Investigation field office, on the grounds that he had not received "*Miranda* warnings" before being interrogated. [The Fourth Circuit held] that petitioner had not received *Miranda* warnings before making his statement. But it went on to hold that § 3501, which in effect makes the admissibility of statements such as Dickerson's turn solely on whether they were made voluntarily, was satisfied in this case. It then concluded that our decision in *Miranda* was not a constitutional holding, and that therefore Congress could by statute have the final say on the question of admissibility. * * *

In *Miranda*, we noted that the advent of modern custodial police interrogation brought with it an increased concern about confessions obtained by coercion. Because custodial police interrogation, by its very nature, isolates and pressures the individual, we stated that "even without employing brutality, the 'third degree' or [other] specific stratagems, * * * custodial interrogation exacts a heavy toll on individual liberty and trades on the weakness of individuals." We concluded that the coercion inherent in custodial interrogation blurs the line between voluntary and involuntary statements, and thus heightens the risk that an individual will not be "accorded his privilege under the Fifth Amendment * * * not to be compelled to incriminate himself." Accordingly, we laid down "concrete constitutional guidelines for law enforcement agencies and courts to follow." Those guidelines established that the admissibility in evidence of any statement given during custodial interrogation of a suspect would depend on whether the police provided the suspect with four warnings. * * *

Given § 3501's express designation of voluntariness as the touchstone of admissibility, its omission of any warning requirement, and the instruction for trial courts to consider a nonexclusive list of factors relevant to the circumstances of a confession, we agree with the Court of Appeals that Congress intended by its enactment to overrule *Miranda*. Because of the obvious conflict between our decision in *Miranda* and § 3501, we must address whether Congress has constitutional authority to thus supersede *Miranda*. If Congress has such authority, § 3501's totality-of-the-circumstances approach must prevail over *Miranda*'s requirement of warnings; if not, that section must yield to *Miranda*'s more specific requirements.

The law in this area is clear. This Court has supervisory authority over the federal courts, and we may use that authority to prescribe rules of evidence and procedure that are binding in those tribunals. However, the power to judicially create and enforce nonconstitutional "rules of procedure and evidence for the federal courts exists only in the absence of a relevant Act of Congress." Congress retains the ultimate authority to modify or set aside any judicially created rules of evidence and procedure that are not required by the Constitution.

But Congress may not legislatively supersede our decisions interpreting and applying the Constitution. This case therefore turns on whether the *Miranda* Court announced a constitutional rule or merely exercised its supervisory authority to regulate evidence in the absence of congressional direction. * * * Relying on the fact that we have created several exceptions to *Miranda*'s warnings requirement and that we have repeatedly referred to the *Miranda* warnings as "prophylactic," the Court of Appeals concluded that the protections announced in *Miranda* are not constitutionally required.

We disagree with the Court of Appeals' conclusion, although we concede that there is language in some of our opinions that supports the view taken by that court. But first and foremost of the factors on the other side—that *Miranda* is a constitutional decision—is that both *Miranda* and two of its companion cases applied the rule to proceedings in state courts—to wit, Arizona, California, and New York. Since that time, we have consistently applied *Miranda*'s rule to prosecutions arising in state courts. It is beyond dispute that we do not hold a supervisory power over the courts of the several States. * * *

The *Miranda* opinion itself begins by stating that the Court granted certiorari "to explore some facets of the problems * * * of applying the privilege against self-incrimination to in-custody interrogation, and to give concrete constitutional guidelines for law enforcement agencies and courts to follow." (emphasis added). * * *

Additional support for our conclusion that *Miranda* is constitutionally based is found in the *Miranda* Court's invitation for legislative action to protect the constitutional right against coerced self-incrimination. After discussing the "compelling pressures" inherent in custodial police interrogation, the *Miranda* Court concluded that, "in order to combat these pressures and to permit a full opportunity to exercise the privilege against self-incrimination, the accused must be adequately and effectively appraised of his rights and the exercise of those rights must be fully honored." However, the Court emphasized that it could not foresee "the potential alternatives for protecting the privilege which might be devised by Congress or the States," and it accordingly opined that the Constitution would not preclude legislative solutions that differed from the prescribed *Miranda* warnings but which were "at least as effective in apprising accused persons of their right of silence and in assuring a continuous opportunity to exercise it."

The Court of Appeals also relied on the fact that we have, after our *Miranda* decision, made exceptions from its rule in cases such as *New York v. Quarles* and *Harris v. New York* [see section E]. But we have also broadened the application of the *Miranda* doctrine * * *. These decisions illustrate the principle—not that *Miranda* is not a constitutional rule—but that no constitutional rule is immutable. No court laying down a general rule can possibly foresee the various circumstances in which counsel will seek to apply it, and the sort of modifications represented by these cases are as much a normal part of constitutional law as the original decision.

The Court of Appeals also noted that in *Oregon v. Elstad*, we stated that " 'the *Miranda* exclusionary rule * * * serves the Fifth Amendment and sweeps more broadly than the Fifth Amendment itself.' " Our decision in that case—refusing to apply the traditional "fruits" doctrine developed in Fourth Amendment cases—does not prove that *Miranda* is a nonconstitutional decision, but simply recognizes the fact that unreasonable searches under the Fourth Amendment are different from unwarned interrogation under the Fifth Amendment. * * *

The dissent argues that it is judicial overreaching for this Court to hold § 3501 unconstitutional unless we hold that the *Miranda* warnings are required by the Constitution, in the sense that nothing else will suffice to satisfy constitutional requirements. But we need not go farther than *Miranda* to decide this case. In *Miranda*, the Court noted that reliance on the traditional totality-of-the-circumstances test raised a risk of overlooking an involuntary custodial confession, a risk that the Court found unacceptably great when the confession is offered in the case in chief to prove guilt. The Court therefore concluded that something more than the totality test was necessary. As discussed above, § 3501 reinstates the totality test as sufficient. Section 3501 therefore cannot be sustained if *Miranda* is to remain the law.

Whether or not we would agree with *Miranda*'s reasoning and its resulting rule, were we addressing the issue in the first instance, the principles of stare decisis weigh heavily against overruling it now. While " 'stare decisis is not an inexorable command,' " particularly when we are interpreting the Constitution, "even in constitutional cases, the doctrine carries such persuasive force that we have always required a departure from precedent to be supported by some 'special justification.' "

We do not think there is such justification for overruling *Miranda*. *Miranda* has become embedded in routine police practice to the point where the warnings have become part of our national culture. While we have overruled our precedents when subsequent cases have undermined their doctrinal underpinnings, we do not believe that this has happened to the *Miranda* decision. If anything, our subsequent cases have reduced the impact of the *Miranda* rule on legitimate law enforcement while reaffirming the decision's core ruling that unwarned statements may not be used as evidence in the prosecution's case in chief.

The disadvantage of the *Miranda* rule is that statements which may be by no means involuntary, made by a defendant who is aware of his "rights," may nonetheless be excluded and a guilty defendant go free as a result. But experience suggests that the totality-of-the-circumstances test which § 3501 seeks to revive is more difficult than *Miranda* for law enforcement officers to conform to, and for courts to apply in a consistent manner. The requirement that *Miranda* warnings be given does not, of course, dispense with the voluntariness inquiry. But as we said in *Berkemer v. McCarty*, "cases in which a defendant can make a colorable argument that a self-incriminating statement was 'compelled' despite the fact that the law enforcement authorities adhered to the dictates of *Miranda* are rare."

In sum, we conclude that *Miranda* announced a constitutional rule that Congress may not supersede legislatively. Following the rule of stare decisis, we decline to overrule *Miranda* ourselves. * * *

JUSTICE SCALIA, with whom JUSTICE THOMAS joins, dissenting [omitted].

F. Waiver and Invocation of the *Miranda* Rights

The *Miranda* Court was careful to emphasize that suspects could waive the rights that the Court found implicit in the privilege against self-incrimination. Once a court determines that the suspect made statements in response to custodial police interrogation, the next issue is whether police gave the *Miranda* warnings and whether the suspect waived those rights.

These issues are obviously linked and can prove confusing. After police provide warnings, there are three possible suspect responses. The suspect can waive and talk to the police; the suspect can invoke her right to remain silent and/or her right to counsel; or the suspect can do nothing. Doing nothing simply kicks the can down the road. At any point, the "do nothing" suspect can waive or invoke. Of course, the can may be kicked all the way down the road: The "do nothing" suspect might do nothing until police tire of the game and stop asking questions.

To further complicate matters, the invocation of the right to silence, it turns out, has different doctrinal and on-the-ground consequences than the invocation of the right to counsel. It is always helpful to ask yourself which suspect response is being analyzed: waiver or invocation of silence or invocation of counsel.

NOTES AND QUESTIONS

1. *What did Miranda say about waiver?* Here is part of what the *Miranda* Court had to say about waiver:

> An express statement that the individual is willing to make a statement and does not want an attorney followed closely by a statement could constitute a waiver. But a valid waiver will not be presumed simply from the silence of the accused after warnings are given or simply from the fact that a confession was in fact eventually obtained.

2. *Waiver evolves.* By 1979, the Court was backtracking on what is required to show waiver. The Court made clear in North Carolina v. Butler, 441 U.S. 369, 99 S.Ct. 1755, 60 L.Ed.2d 286 (1979), that waiver of *Miranda* does not require an "express statement that the individual is willing to make a statement *and* does not want an attorney." It is sufficient if the suspect says he is willing to talk to police, and it does not matter that he also said "but I am not signing any form." Though the Court sent the case back to the state courts for a final resolution, it seems clear from the opinion that this course of conduct was sufficient to prove waiver.

Part of showing waiver, of course, is showing that the suspect understands the warnings. If the warnings are given in English, and the suspect does not understand English, the resulting "waiver" is almost certainly invalid.

3. *Waiver continues to evolve.* By 2010, it was no longer necessary for the suspect even to say he was willing to talk to police. If the suspect understands the *Miranda* warnings, and answers questions, he has waived *Miranda*, the Court recently held. See

Berghuis v. Thompkins, 560 U.S. 370, 130 S.Ct. 2250, 176 L.Ed.2d 1098 (2010). The police gave the warnings and had the suspect demonstrate that he understood English. The police then questioned the suspect for almost three hours. He did not respond to any question about his involvement in a murder. Then at roughly the three hour mark, the police discovered the suspect's vulnerability.

The detective asked Thompkins, "Do you believe in God?" Thompkins looked at the detective and said "Yes," as his eyes filled with tears. The next question was "Do you pray to God?" Thompkins said "Yes." Then the final move: "Do you pray to God to forgive you for shooting that boy down?" Thompkins answered "Yes." The Court held, 5–4, that this was an adequate waiver even though Thompkins never explicitly waived his rights. The Court also made clear that any invocation of the right to remain silent must be unambiguous. See *Davis v. United States*, p. 583, Note 2.

4. *And what other information must suspects have before they can waive?* The answer: Not much. For instance, suspects are not entitled to know what crime the police are questioning them about. In Colorado v. Spring, 479 U.S. 564, 107 S.Ct. 851, 93 L.Ed.2d 954 (1987), S was arrested for interstate possession of stolen firearms. He waived his *Miranda* rights, and the police questioned him not about the stolen firearms but about a murder with which S had not been charged. The Court held that a waiver of *Miranda* is to interrogation in general and not to interrogation about a particular crime.

Suspects are also not entitled to know that a lawyer is seeking to talk to him. In Moran v. Burbine, 475 U.S. 412, 106 S.Ct. 1135, 89 L.Ed.2d 410 (1986), the suspect waived his *Miranda* rights multiple times while his lawyer was attempting to communicate with him. The Court held that these were valid *Miranda* waivers even though he did not know his lawyer was trying to reach him. The Court noted, "Events occurring outside of the presence of the suspect and entirely unknown to him surely can have no bearing on the capacity to comprehend and knowingly relinquish a constitutional right. * * * No doubt the additional information would have been useful to respondent; perhaps even it might have affected his decision to confess. But we have never read the Constitution to require that the police supply a suspect with a flow of information to help him calibrate his self-interest in deciding whether to speak or stand by his rights."

5. *And how many suspects waive Miranda?* Studies show that roughly eighty percent of suspects waive their *Miranda* rights. See Paul G. Cassell & Bret S. Hayman, Police Interrogation in the 1990s: An Empirical Study of the Effects of *Miranda*, 43 UCLA L. Rev. 839 (1996); Richard A. Leo, Inside the Interrogation Room, 86 J. Crim. L. & Criminology 266, 282–83 (1996). George C. Thomas III, Stories About *Miranda*, 102 Mich. L. Rev. 1959 (2004).

Does this mean *Miranda* is ineffective or only that most suspects want to tell their side of the story? For an argument that the latter character trait explains more of the waiver rate than most scholars believe, see George C. Thomas III, *Miranda*'s Illusion: Telling Stories in the Police Interrogation Room, 81 Texas L. Rev. 1091 (2003) (essay on Welsh S. White, *Miranda*'s Waning Protections (2001)).

6. *Invocation.* As we said earlier, one road open to suspects is to invoke either the right to counsel or the right to remain silent. We begin with invocation of the right to counsel.

EDWARDS V. ARIZONA

Supreme Court of the United States, 1981.
451 U.S. 477, 101 S.Ct. 1880, 68 L.Ed.2d 378.

The next case raises yet one more question left unanswered by the *Miranda* opinion: what must police do, or not do, after a suspect has invoked the right to counsel? It turns out the answer is not what you might expect: police do NOT have to actually provide a lawyer.

JUSTICE WHITE delivered the opinion of the Court [joined by JUSTICES BRENNAN, STEWART, MARSHALL, BLACKMUN, and STEVENS]. * * *

I

On January 19, 1976, a sworn complaint was filed against Edwards in Arizona state court charging him with robbery, burglary, and first-degree murder. An arrest warrant was issued pursuant to the complaint, and Edwards was arrested at his home later that same day. At the police station, he was informed of his rights as required by *Miranda v. Arizona.* Petitioner stated that he understood his rights, and was willing to submit to questioning. After being told that another suspect already in custody had implicated him in the crime, Edwards denied involvement and gave a taped statement presenting an alibi defense. He then sought to "make a deal." The interrogating officer told him that he wanted a statement, but that he did not have the authority to negotiate a deal. The officer provided Edwards with the telephone number of a county attorney. Petitioner made the call, but hung up after a few moments. Edwards then said: "I want an attorney before making a deal." At that point, questioning ceased and Edwards was taken to county jail.

At 9:15 the next morning, two detectives, colleagues of the officer who had interrogated Edwards the previous night, came to the jail and asked to see Edwards. When the detention officer informed Edwards that the detectives wished to speak with him, he replied that he did not want to talk to anyone. The guard told him that "he had" to talk and then took him to meet with the detectives. The officers identified themselves, stated they wanted to talk to him, and informed him of his *Miranda* rights. Edwards was willing to talk, but he first wanted to hear the taped statement of the alleged accomplice who had implicated him. After listening to the tape for several minutes, petitioner said that he would make a statement so long as it was not tape-recorded. The detectives informed him that the recording was irrelevant since they could testify in court concerning whatever he said. Edwards replied: "I'll tell you anything you want to know, but I don't want it on tape." He thereupon implicated himself in the crime.

Prior to trial, Edwards moved to suppress his confession on the ground that his *Miranda* rights had been violated when the officers returned to question him after he had invoked his right to counsel. * * * The [trial] court stated without explanation that it found Edwards' statement to be voluntary. Edwards was tried twice and convicted. Evidence concerning his confession was admitted at both trials.

On appeal, the Arizona Supreme Court held that Edwards had invoked both his right to remain silent and his right to counsel during the interrogation conducted on the night of January 19. The court then went on to determine, however, that Edwards had waived both rights during the January 20 meeting when he voluntarily gave his statement to the detectives after again being informed that he need not answer questions and that he need not answer without the advice of counsel. * * *

II

In *Miranda v. Arizona*, the Court determined that the Fifth and Fourteenth Amendments' prohibition against compelled self-incrimination required that custodial interrogation be preceded by advice to the putative defendant that he has the right to remain silent and also the right to the presence of an attorney. The Court also indicated the procedures to be followed subsequent to the warnings. If the accused indicates that he wishes to remain silent, "the interrogation must cease." If he requests counsel, "the interrogation must cease until an attorney is present."

Miranda thus declared that an accused has a Fifth and Fourteenth Amendment right to have counsel present during custodial interrogation. Here, the critical facts as found by the Arizona Supreme Court are that Edwards asserted his right to counsel and his right to remain silent on January 19, but that the police, without furnishing him counsel, returned the next morning to confront him and as a result of the meeting secured incriminating oral admissions. Contrary to the holdings of the state courts, Edwards insists that having exercised his right on the

19th to have counsel present during interrogation, he did not validly waive that right on the 20th. For the following reasons, we agree.

First, the Arizona Supreme Court applied an erroneous standard for determining waiver where the accused has specifically invoked his right to counsel. It is reasonably clear under our cases that waivers of counsel must not only be voluntary, but must also constitute a knowing and intelligent relinquishment or abandonment of a known right or privilege, a matter which depends in each case "upon the particular facts and circumstances surrounding that case, including the background, experience, and conduct of the accused." * * *

* * * Here, however sound the conclusion of the state courts as to the voluntariness of Edwards' admission may be, neither the trial court nor the Arizona Supreme Court undertook to focus on whether Edwards understood his right to counsel and intelligently and knowingly relinquished it. It is thus apparent that the decision below misunderstood the requirement for finding a valid waiver of the right to counsel, once invoked.

Second, although we have held that after initially being advised of his *Miranda* rights, the accused may himself validly waive his rights and respond to interrogation, the Court has strongly indicated that additional safeguards are necessary when the accused asks for counsel; and we now hold that when an accused has invoked his right to have counsel present during custodial interrogation, a valid waiver of that right cannot be established by showing only that he responded to further police-initiated custodial interrogation even if he has been advised of his rights. We further hold that an accused, such as Edwards, having expressed his desire to deal with the police only through counsel, is not subject to further interrogation by the authorities until counsel has been made available to him, unless the accused himself initiates further communication, exchanges, or conversations with the police.

Miranda itself indicated that the assertion of the right to counsel was a significant event and that once exercised by the accused, "the interrogation must cease until an attorney is present." Our later cases have not abandoned that view. * * * We reconfirm these [cases] and, to lend them substance, emphasize that it is inconsistent with *Miranda* and its progeny for the authorities, at their instance, to reinterrogate an accused in custody if he has clearly asserted his right to counsel.

In concluding that the fruits of the interrogation initiated by the police on January 20 could not be used against Edwards, we do not hold or imply that Edwards was powerless to countermand his election or that the authorities could in no event use any incriminating statements made by Edwards prior to his having access to counsel. Had Edwards initiated the meeting on January 20, nothing in the Fifth and Fourteenth Amendments would prohibit the police from merely listening to his voluntary, volunteered statements and using them against him at the trial. The Fifth Amendment right identified in *Miranda* is the right to have counsel present at any custodial interrogation. Absent such interrogation, there would have been no infringement of the right that Edwards invoked and there would be no occasion to determine whether there had been a valid waiver. Rhode Island v. Innis makes this sufficiently clear.

But this is not what the facts of this case show. Here, the officers conducting the interrogation on the evening of January 19 ceased interrogation when Edwards requested counsel as he had been advised he had the right to do. The Arizona Supreme Court was of the opinion that this was a sufficient invocation of his *Miranda* rights, and we are in accord. It is also clear that without making counsel available to Edwards, the police returned to him the next day. This was not at his suggestion or request. Indeed, Edwards informed the detention officer that he did not want to talk to anyone. At the meeting, the detectives told Edwards that they wanted to talk to him and again advised him of his *Miranda* rights. Edwards stated that he would talk, but what prompted this action does not appear. He listened at his own request to part of the taped statement made by one of his alleged accomplices and then made an incriminating statement, which was used against him at his trial. We think it is clear that Edwards was subjected to custodial interrogation on January 20 within the meaning of Rhode Island v. Innis, and that this occurred at the instance of the authorities. His statement made without having had access to counsel, did not amount to a valid waiver and hence was inadmissible.

Accordingly, the holding of the Arizona Supreme Court that Edwards had waived his right to counsel was infirm, and the judgment of that court is reversed. * * *

[*The opinion of* CHIEF JUSTICE BURGER, *concurring in the judgment, is omitted.*]

JUSTICE POWELL, with whom JUSTICE REHNQUIST joins, concurring in the result.

Although I agree that the judgment of the Arizona Supreme Court must be reversed, I do not join the Court's opinion because I am not sure what it means. * * *

* * * [T]he Court—after reiterating the familiar principles of waiver—goes on to say:

> "We further hold that an accused, such as Edwards, having expressed his desire to deal with the police only through counsel, is not subject to further interrogation by the authorities until counsel has been made available to him, unless the accused [has] himself initiate[d] further communication, exchanges, or conversations with the police."

In view of the emphasis placed on "initiation," I find the Court's opinion unclear. If read to create a new per se rule, requiring a threshold inquiry as to precisely who opened any conversation between an accused and state officials, I cannot agree. I would not superimpose a new element of proof on the established doctrine of waiver of counsel. * * *

In sum, once warnings have been given and the right to counsel has been invoked, the relevant inquiry—whether the suspect now desires to talk to police without counsel—is a question of fact to be determined in light of all of the circumstances. Who "initiated" a conversation may be relevant to the question of waiver, but it is not the sine qua non to the inquiry. The ultimate question is whether there was a free and knowing waiver of counsel before interrogation commenced.

If the Court's opinion does nothing more than restate these principles, I am in agreement with it. I hesitate to join the opinion only because of what appears to be an undue and undefined, emphasis on a single element: "initiation." * * *.

NOTES AND QUESTIONS

1. *Problems of initiation/waiver.* In a footnote, the *Edwards* Court made plain that the question of waiver after invocation of the right to counsel is often a two-step process:

> If, as frequently would occur in the course of a meeting initiated by the accused, the conversation is not wholly one-sided, it is likely that the officers will say or do something that clearly would be "interrogation." In that event, the question would be whether a valid waiver of the right to counsel and the right to silence had occurred, that is, whether the purported waiver was knowing and intelligent and found to be so under the totality of the circumstances, including the necessary fact that the accused, not the police, reopened the dialogue with the authorities.

A plurality of the Court sought to explain "initiation" two years after *Edwards* in Oregon v. Bradshaw, 462 U.S. 1039, 103 S.Ct. 2830, 77 L.Ed.2d 405 (1983). Initiation occurs only when an inquiry from the suspect can "be fairly said to represent a desire on the part of an accused to open up a more generalized discussion relating directly or indirectly to the investigation." Asking for a drink of water or to use a telephone would not constitute initiation because they are "routine incidents of the custodial relationship."

A. Police arrested B for a misdemeanor after B admitted minor involvement in an offense. At that point, B requested counsel, and the police terminated the conversation. Later, when B was being transferred from the police station to the jail, B asked, "Well, what is going to happen to me now?" The officer responded, "You do not have to talk to me. You have requested an attorney, and I don't want you talking to me unless you so desire because anything you say—because—since you have requested an attorney, you know, it has to be at your own free will." B said he understood. During the following conversation, the officer suggested that B might "help himself" by taking a polygraph examination. B agreed, took the test, was told that the test revealed he was not telling the truth, and he then confessed. What are the issues under *Edwards*, and how would you resolve them?

B. A uniformed police officer arrested C and provided warnings, to which he responded by clearly requesting counsel. Later, at the station and after the complaining witness identified C, a detective said that he needed to ask C some questions for the booking process. The detective said that he was not going to ask C about the crime because he knew C had invoked his right to counsel. C became upset and said he wasn't about to talk to a patrol officer about the crime but that he wanted to talk to a detective. The detective read C his rights again, and C waived and made a statement. Admissible? See Cross v. State, 144 S.W.3d 521 (Tex. Crim. App. 2004).

2. *Invocation must be unambiguous.* Davis v. United States, 512 U.S. 452, 114 S.Ct. 2350, 129 L.Ed.2d 362 (1994), presented the question of what constitutes an invocation. Davis initially waived his rights to remain silent and to a lawyer, both orally and in writing.

> About an hour and a half into the interview, petitioner said, "Maybe I should talk to a lawyer." According to the uncontradicted testimony of one of the interviewing agents, the interview then proceeded as follows:
>
> > "[We m]ade it very clear that we're not here to violate his rights, that if he wants a lawyer, then we will stop any kind of questioning with him, that we weren't going to pursue the matter unless we have it clarified is he asking for a lawyer or is he just making a comment about a lawyer, and he said, [']No, I'm not asking for a lawyer,' and then he continued on, and said, 'No, I don't want a lawyer.' "
>
> After a short break, the agents reminded petitioner of his rights to remain silent and to counsel. The interview then continued for another

> hour, until petitioner said, "I think I want a lawyer before I say anything else." At that point, questioning ceased.

The Court characterized Davis's argument that his statements be suppressed as an "invitation to extend *Edwards* and require law enforcement officers to cease questioning immediately upon the making of an ambiguous or equivocal reference to an attorney." It declined to accept the argument, holding instead that

> the suspect must unambiguously request counsel. As we have observed, "a statement either is such an assertion of the right to counsel or it is not." Although a suspect need not "speak with the discrimination of an Oxford don," he must articulate his desire to have counsel present sufficiently clearly that a reasonable police officer in the circumstances would understand the statement to be a request for an attorney. If the statement fails to meet the requisite level of clarity, *Edwards* does not require that the officers stop questioning the suspect.

Four members of the *Davis* Court concurred in the judgment in an opinion by Justice Souter, agreeing that on the facts of the case no violation of *Edwards* occurred, but challenging the majority's assertion that *Edwards* did not require clarifying questions when officers are faced with an ambiguous request for counsel.

> Indeed, it is easy, amidst the discussion of layers of protection, to lose sight of a real risk in the majority's approach, going close to the core of what the Court has held that the Fifth Amendment requires. * * * When a suspect understands his (expressed) wishes to have been ignored (and by hypothesis, he has said something that an objective listener could "reasonably," although not necessarily, take to be a request), in contravention of the "rights" just read to him by his interrogator, he may well see further objection as futile and confession (true or not) as the only way to end his interrogation. * * *
>
> The other justifications offered for the "requisite level of clarity" rule, are that, whatever its costs, it will further society's strong interest in "effective law enforcement," and maintain the "ease of application" that has long been a concern of our *Miranda* jurisprudence. With respect to the first point, the margin of difference between the clarification approach advocated here and the one the Court adopts is defined by the class of cases in which a suspect, if asked, would make it plain that he meant to request counsel (at which point questioning would cease). While these lost confessions do exact a real price from society, it is one that *Miranda* itself determined should be borne.

3. *The "woman" question.* Professor Janet Ainsworth has argued that requiring an unambiguous invocation is unfair to certain subgroups within the population.

> * * * [S]ociolinguistic research on typical male and female speech patterns indicates that men tend to use direct and assertive language, whereas women more often adopt indirect and deferential speech patterns. Because majority legal doctrine governing a person's rights during police interrogation favors linguistic behavior more typical of men than of women, asking the "woman question" reveals a hidden bias in this ostensibly gender-neutral doctrine.
>
> The sociolinguistic evidence that women disproportionately adopt indirect speech patterns predicts that legal rules requiring the use of direct and unqualified language will adversely affect female defendants more often than male defendants. * * *
>
> The detrimental consequences of interrogation law, however, are not limited to female defendants. Asking the "woman question" provokes related inquiry into whether legal doctrine may similarly fail to incorporate the experiences and perspectives of other marginalized groups. * * * [T]he available evidence demonstrates that there are a number of ethnic speech communities whose members habitually adopt a speech register including indirect and qualified modes of expression very much like those observed in typical female language use.
>
> Even within communities whose speech is not characterized by indirect modes of expression, individual speakers who are socially or situationally powerless frequently adopt an indirect speech register. In fact, several prominent researchers have concluded that the use of this characteristically "female" speech style correlates better with powerlessness than with gender. The psychosocial dynamics of the police interrogation setting inherently involve an imbalance of power between the suspect, who is situationally powerless, and the interrogator, whose role entails the exercise of power. Such asymmetries of power in the interrogation session increase the likelihood that a particular suspect will adopt an indirect, and thus seemingly equivocal, mode of expression. This study, which begins by focusing on the disadvantages to women defendants of current invocation doctrine, ultimately has far-reaching implications for various other classes of speakers that do not share the linguistic norm of assertive and direct expression.

Janet E. Ainsworth, *The Pragmatics of Powerlessness in Police Interrogation*, 103 Yale L.J. 259, 262–264 (1993).

4. *How broad is the Edwards rule?* In their separate *Edwards* opinions, Chief Justice Burger and Justice Powell expressed concern that the majority opinion could be read to require a rigid prophylactic rule as a way of protecting the prophylactic rule of *Miranda.* They were quite the prophets. In Minnick v. Mississippi, 498 U.S. 146, 111 S.Ct. 486, 112 L.Ed.2d 489 (1990), Minnick answered a few questions posed by FBI agents and then said, "Come back Monday when I have a lawyer." The agents ceased interrogation, and Minnick consulted with his lawyer on at least two occasions before Monday when Mississippi police re-advised him of his rights and secured incriminating statements. The Court held that Minnick's statements were inadmissible even though he had consulted with counsel. As Justice Scalia put it in dissent, Minnick's

> confession must be suppressed, not because it was "compelled," nor even because it was obtained from an individual who could realistically be assumed to be unaware of his rights, but simply because this Court sees fit to prescribe as a "systemic assuranc[e]," that a person in custody who has once asked for counsel cannot thereafter be approached by the police unless counsel is present. Of course the Constitution's proscription of compelled testimony does not remotely authorize this incursion upon state practices; and even our recent precedents are not a valid excuse. * * *
>
> Today's extension of the *Edwards* prohibition is the latest stage of prophylaxis built upon prophylaxis, producing a veritable fairyland castle of imagined constitutional restriction upon law enforcement. This newest tower, according to the Court, is needed to avoid "inconsisten[cy] with [the] purpose" of *Edwards'* prophylactic rule, which was needed to protect *Miranda*'s prophylactic right to have counsel present, which was needed to protect the right against compelled self-incrimination found (at last!) in the Constitution.
>
> It seems obvious to me that, even in *Edwards* itself but surely in today's decision, we have gone far beyond any genuine concern about suspects who do not know their right to remain silent, or who have been coerced to abandon it. Both holdings are explicable, in my view, only as an effort to protect suspects against what is regarded as their own folly. The sharp-witted criminal would know better than to confess; why should the dull-witted suffer for his lack of mental endowment? Providing him an attorney at every stage where he might be induced or persuaded (though not coerced) to incriminate himself will even the odds. Apart from the fact that this protective enterprise is beyond our authority under the Fifth Amendment or any other provision of the Constitution, it is unwise. The procedural protections of the Constitution protect the guilty as well as the

> innocent, but it is not their objective to set the guilty free. That some clever criminals may employ those protections to their advantage is poor reason to allow criminals who have not done so to escape justice.

Do you agree with Justice Scalia? What is the purpose of counsel in the *Miranda* context, as contrasted with the Sixth Amendment?

5. *How long does Edwards invocation last?* In 2010, in an opinion by Justice Scalia, the Court held that suspects who invoke their right to counsel and then are released from custody can, at some point, be asked again if they wish to waive their rights. In Maryland v. Shatzer, 559 U.S. 98, 130 S.Ct. 1213, 175 L.Ed.2d 1045 (2010), two and a half years elapsed between the *Edwards* invocation and the second waiver request, and the Court unanimously agreed that his waiver was valid. What split the Court was the dicta intended to provide "certainty" about "when renewed interrogation is lawful." The majority chose two weeks as the "cleansing period" because that "provides plenty of time for the suspect to get reacclimated to his [non-custodial] normal life, to consult with friends and counsel, and to shake off any residual coercive effects of his prior custody." Rejecting fourteen days as "arbitrary," Justice Thomas wrote: "This ipse dixit does not explain why extending the Edwards presumption for 14 days following a break in custody—as opposed to 0, 10, or 100 days—provides the 'closest possible fit' with the Self-Incrimination Clause." Justice Stevens concurred in the judgment, arguing that a two-week period between attempted interrogations was not long enough if the police did not provide a lawyer as requested. The suspect who is approached fourteen days later, Stevens wrote, "is likely to feel that the police lied to him or are ignoring his rights."

6. *How does an invocation of the right to remain silent compare to Edwards?* A single standard could measure the effect of all invocations of *Miranda*. The *Edwards* rule could apply to invocations of the right to remain silent as well as the right to counsel; the police would not then be permitted to attempt to question the suspect who invoked either right unless the suspect initiated the exchange. But the Court has not seen fit to apply the same broad rule to requests to remain silent.

In Michigan v. Mosley, 423 U.S. 96, 96 S.Ct. 321, 46 L.Ed.2d 313 (1975), decided five years before *Edwards*, Mosley was questioned by a detective of the armed robbery section of the detective bureau. The interrogation ended as soon as Mosley "said he did not want to answer any questions about the robberies." A few hours later, a detective from the homicide section questioned Mosley about a fatal shooting during a holdup attempt (not the same robbery that was the subject of the earlier interrogation).

> Before questioning Mosley about this homicide, Detective Hill carefully advised him of his "*Miranda* rights." Mosley read the notification form both silently and aloud, and Detective Hill then read and explained

> the warnings to him and had him sign the form. Mosley at first denied any involvement in the Williams murder, but after the officer told him that Anthony Smith had confessed to participating in the slaying and had named him as the "shooter," Mosley made a statement implicating himself in the homicide. The interrogation by Detective Hill lasted approximately 15 minutes, and at no time during its course did Mosley ask to consult with a lawyer or indicate that he did not want to discuss the homicide. In short, there is no claim that the procedures followed during Detective Hill's interrogation of Mosley, standing alone, did not fully comply with the strictures of the *Miranda* opinion.

The Court considered the various meanings that the *Miranda* Court could have intended when it stated that "interrogation must cease" when the person in custody indicates that "he wishes to remain silent."

> A reasonable and faithful interpretation of the *Miranda* opinion must rest on the intention of the Court in that case to adopt "fully effective means * * * to notify the person of his right of silence and to assure that the exercise of the right will be scrupulously honored * * *." The critical safeguard identified in the passage at issue is a person's "right to cut off questioning." Through the exercise of his option to terminate questioning he can control the time at which questioning occurs, the subjects discussed, and the duration of the interrogation. The requirement that law enforcement authorities must respect a person's exercise of that option counteracts the coercive pressures of the custodial setting. We therefore conclude that the admissibility of statements obtained after the person in custody has decided to remain silent depends under *Miranda* on whether his "right to cut off questioning" was "scrupulously honored."

The Court held that, under the facts of the case, the previous request not to talk to a different detective, from a different police section, about a different crime, did not extend to a second interrogation that was also preceded by warnings. Thus, the suspect who requests her right to silence is protected differently from the one who demands her right to counsel.

Why might it seem odd to some that, if the Court was going to develop different rules regarding the invocation of the right to remain silent and the right to counsel, that the Court makes it easier for the State to prove waiver of the former than the latter? Hint: notice that the right to silence is created by the explicit text of the Fifth Amendment that creates the right not to be compelled to be a witness against oneself. But the *Miranda* right to counsel is created out of whole cloth as a way to protect the right to silence. Why, then, would invoking the right to counsel gives suspects more protection than invoking the right to silence?

7. *Problems of invocation and waiver of the right to counsel or silence.* Here are some Problems with which to wrestle. Do not forget in working on them that *Davis* and *Berghuis* created a rule that invocation of the right to counsel and to silence must be unambiguous.

A. Officers arrest a suspect and place him in a squad car. An officer reads him his *Miranda* rights and asks if he understands them. He says that he does. The officer then reads a waiver form and asks him if he is willing to waive his rights. He responds: "Get the f--- out of my face. I don't have nothing to say. I refuse to sign [the waiver form]." Is this invocation? See United States v. Banks, 78 F.3d 1190, 1196–98 (7th Cir. 1996).

B. Police ask B to come to the station to discuss a "police matter." When he arrives, police tell him he is not under arrest and is free to leave at any time. "Great," he says. "But I want a lawyer anyway, and I want a lawyer now." Police ignore the request and ask B questions. He quickly answers in an incriminating way. Police allow him to leave but, of course, arrest him later. Are his answers admissible? See Burket v. Angelone, 208 F.3d 172, 198 (4th Cir. 2000).

C. Police want to question H about a forgery charge. Police provide *Miranda* warnings, and H executes a standard waiver form. Over the course of approximately three hours, H freely answers questions about the forgeries. Sometime during the interrogation, the detectives begin questioning H about a murder that had not until then been mentioned. At this point, he says: "I think I need a lawyer because if I tell everything I know, how do I know I'm not going to wind up with a complicity charge?" Invocation? See State v. Henness, 79 Ohio St.3d 53, 679 N.E.2d 686 (1997).

D. J is fifteen years old and a suspect in a murder. His mother is with him at the police station. When police give him warnings and ask whether he wishes to answer questions, J answers "no." His mother turns to him and says, "No, we need to get this straightened out. We'll talk with him anyway." J looks at his mother for a time and then nods his head. The detective asks if he wishes to answer without a lawyer being present and this time he answers "yes." Is this a valid waiver? See State v. Johnson, 136 N.C.App. 683, 525 S.E.2d 830 (2000).

E. Federal agents give D his *Miranda* warnings and he first signs a waiver but then requests counsel. At this point, the agents ask booking questions—age, birth date and place, address, height, weight, Social Security number. They also request a hair sample, telling him that if he refuses, they will get a court order. He agrees to permit the agents to take a hair sample at the local hospital. He then begins to talk about the crime and signs a second waiver. He talks more after which he requests a lawyer and falls silent. The agents sit in silence for a time. D begins to talk again and then confesses. Is any of what D said admissible? See United States v. Dougall, 919 F.2d 932 (5th Cir. 1990). Hint: Don't forget that some evidence is not testimonial.

F. Police arrest H for a fire in the apartment of his girlfriend, Deb. She is dead but police do not initially reveal this fact. They give him warnings and he signs a waiver form. He admits seeing her the evening of the fire. The officers tell him that others in the apartment complex heard H and Deb in a heated argument that afternoon. H repeatedly tells police he does not know what they are talking to him about. After the officers finally tell H that Deb is dead, the following exchange occurs:

H: What are you saying here?

Detective: What are we saying? We're saying that you took Deb's life.

H: You're saying I killed Deb?

Detective: Absolutely. There's no doubt about that. OK? We know that. * * * We just need to know why you did that, OK? We know you did that. That's not even a question here, Kevin. Understand that? We know that. We talked to a bunch of people here and—and we—we put the evidence together at the scene and it clearly points to you. OK? So, we need to know why. What was your—?

H: You think I killed her?

Detective: Did you—did you kill her because you were upset with her? Did you kill her because—

H: You think I killed—

Detective: Kevin, it's not that we think that, we know that. We need to know why you did that. That's all, OK? Tha—it's no question as to did you do that. That's not a question here, Kevin, OK? So—

H: Can I have a drink of water and then lock me up—I think we really should have an attorney.

Detective: We'll get you a drink of water.

H: I don't want to talk anymore please. (Pause). This is—this is really wrong. This woman has scars all over her from this [other man.] He's callin' her 50 times a week.

Detective: 'Kay. If you want to talk to an attorney, you understand that we have to stop talking to you. OK? And—and then your side of this story will never be known. That's your choice. That's a choice you're making.

H: So, that means what?

Detective: That means we're gonna put this thing together and we're gonna convict you of murder.

H: Of murder?

Detective: Absolutely. Yup.

H: Convict me of murdering her?

The interrogation continued and H made numerous statements regarding his involvement in Deb's death.

Did H invoke the right to counsel? To silence? Did the police violate any aspect of *Miranda* or did the original waiver solve any *Miranda* problems? See State v. Hannon, 636 N.W.2d 796 (Minn. 2001).

8. *Voluntariness problems persist.* As noted earlier, roughly 80% of suspects waive *Miranda*. In those cases, courts are still sometimes presented with the problem of whether the confession that followed post-waiver interrogation was voluntary under the old due process voluntariness test used, for example, in *Brown v. Mississippi.* In one case, detective Boyce questioned suspect Miller about the brutal murder of a seventeen-year-old girl after Miller waived his *Miranda* rights. Audio tapes of the interview showed that Detective Boyce made no threats while questioning Miller. Instead, Boyce assumed a friendly, understanding manner and spoke in a soft tone of voice. Boyce's major theme throughout the interrogation was that whoever had committed such a heinous crime had mental problems and was desperately in need of psychological treatment. The New Jersey court described the facts as follows:

> Deborah's body was found face down in a stream. Her throat had been slashed, severing her windpipe and jugular vein. The girl was nude except for a part of her bathing suit around her waist. Stab and cutting wounds had been inflicted in her pelvic area and vagina. Her right breast had been cut.

State v. Miller, 76 N.J. 392, 388 A.2d 218, 220 (1978).

Here is a portion of the post-waiver interrogation of Miller by Detective Boyce.

> Boyce: You can see it, Frank, you can feel it, you can feel it but you are not responsible. This is what I'm trying to tell you, but you've got to come forward and tell me. Don't, don't, don't let it eat you up, don't, don't fight it. You've got to rectify it, Frank. We've got to get together on this thing, or I, I mean really, you need help, you need proper help, and you know it, my God, you know, in God's name, you, you, you know it. You are not a criminal, you are not a criminal. * * * Frank, listen to me, honest to God, I'm, I'm telling you, Frank (inaudible). I know, it's going to bother you, Frank, it's going to bother you. It's there, it's not going to go away, it's there. It's right in front of you, Frank. Am I right or wrong?
>
> Miller: Yeah. * * *

> Boyce: First thing we have to do is let it all come out. Don't fight it because it's worse, Frank, it's worse. It's hurting me because I feel it. I feel it wanting to come out, but it's hurting me, Frank. * * * Let it come out, Frank. I'm here, I'm here with you now. I'm on your side, I'm on your side, Frank. I'm your brother, you and I are brothers, Frank. We are brothers, and I want to help my brother. * * * We have, we have a relationship, don't we? Have I been sincere with you, Frank? * * * No, listen to me, Frank, please listen to me. The issue now is what happened. The issue now is truth. Truth is the issue now. You've got to believe this, and the truth prevails in the end, Frank. You have to believe that and I'm sincere when I'm saying it to you. You've got to be truthful with yourself. * * * That's the most important thing, not, not what has happened, Frank. The fact that you were truthful, you came forward and you said, look I have a problem. I didn't mean to do what I did. I have a problem, this is what's important, Frank. This is very important, I got, I, I got to get closer to you, Frank, I got to make you believe this and I'm, and I'm sincere when I tell you this. You got to tell me exactly what happened, Frank. That's very important. I know how you feel inside, Frank, it's eating you up, am I right? It's eating you up, Frank. You've got to come forward. You've got to do it for yourself, for your family, for your father, this is what's important, the truth, Frank.

The interview lasted less than an hour. After Miller confessed, he collapsed in a state of shock. He slid off his chair and onto the floor with a blank stare on his face. The police officers sent for a first-aid squad that took him to the hospital. Is the confession voluntary? Does *Miranda* help in any way with this kind of issue? See Miller v. Fenton, 796 F.2d 598 (3d Cir. 1986).

9. *Does Miranda "work?"* If 80% of suspects waive *Miranda*, and wind up being protected by the old common law voluntariness test, is it even worth keeping? One scholar put the point this way:

> One of two things is true: Either there is a significant amount of abusive police questioning, or there isn't. If there is, *Miranda* is a failure; it does not protect the suspects who need protecting. If there isn't, *Miranda* is pointless—it gives a few Silent Types [those who invoke prior to interrogation] a very valuable entitlement, but to no good end. Either way, *Miranda* accomplishes nothing save distributive perversity. After thirty-five years, we can be reasonably confident of this much: Suspects cannot regulate police interrogation. The law of police interrogation is broken, and needs fixing.

William J. Stuntz, *Miranda's Mistake*, 99 Mich. L. Rev. 975 (2001).

Another scholar agrees with Stuntz, noting that

> if *Miranda*'s system of warnings and waivers is not effective in protecting the Fifth Amendment privilege for many suspects, this wholesale displacement of the voluntariness doctrine is a sleight-of-hand; it is bottomed on a falsehood. I am not against warnings and waivers per se, just the assumed effect of them. For me, the main problem with *Miranda* is the judiciary's unjustified confidence in *Miranda*'s safeguards. There is an almost religious belief that the warnings and waivers actually work, and an apparent deafness to claims that they do not. I am not the first to observe that *Miranda* can be an obstacle to the more important assessment of voluntariness; Professor Alfredo Garcia has made the point with particular force. I once was a proponent of *Miranda*, but I now believe that its critics are right.

Charles D. Weisselberg, *Mourning Miranda*, 96 Cal. L. Rev. 1519, 1595–96 (2008).

The provocative Garcia article to which Weisselberg refers is Alfredo Garcia, *Is Miranda Dead, Was It Overruled, or Is It Irrelevant?*, 10 St. Thomas L. Rev. 461 (1988).

Professor Weisselberg also offers the following eulogy to *Miranda*:

> *Miranda* launched a forty-year experiment in reforming police practices. I think the Court was right to try; sometimes there can be no progress without experimentation. Now, four decades later, we know that a set of bright-line rules is not a panacea for the issues endemic in police interrogation. I mourn the passing of *Miranda*. I deeply regret that the justices' ambitions and expectations were not met. However, I think that the best way to mourn the loss is to learn from the experiment called *Miranda*, acknowledge its failures, and move forward.

G. A Sixth Amendment Limit on Police Questioning

1. Eliciting Statements in the Absence of Counsel

MASSIAH V. UNITED STATES

Supreme Court of the United States, 1964.
377 U.S. 201, 84 S.Ct. 1199, 12 L.Ed.2d 246.

In 1964, about the only constitutional limit on police pressure during police interrogation was the old common law prohibition of the use of involuntary confessions, which had been moved by courts to the due process clauses of the Bill of Rights. But as we have seen, unless police used quite obvious coercion, it was not easy to decide whether a confession was voluntary or involuntary. In 1964, the Court decided to develop an

additional tool for policing the police—the Sixth Amendment right to counsel. You saw early in this chapter the Court's decision in *Escobedo v. Illinois*, also decided in 1964, suppressing statements taken from a suspect who had asked to speak to his lawyer. The next case applies the right to counsel to surreptitious elicitation of incriminating statements.

MR. JUSTICE STEWART delivered the opinion of the Court [joined by CHIEF JUSTICE WARREN, and JUSTICES BLACK, DOUGLAS, CLARK, and GOLDBERG].

The petitioner was indicted for violating the federal narcotics laws. He retained a lawyer, pleaded not guilty, and was released on bail. * * *

A few days later, and quite without the petitioner's knowledge, [co-defendant] Colson decided to cooperate with the government agents in their continuing investigation of the narcotics activities in which the petitioner, Colson, and others had allegedly been engaged. Colson permitted an agent named Murphy to install a Schmidt radio transmitter under the front seat of Colson's automobile, by means of which Murphy, equipped with an appropriate receiving device, could overhear from some distance away conversations carried on in Colson's car.

On the evening of November 19, 1959, Colson and the petitioner held a lengthy conversation while sitting in Colson's automobile, parked on a New York street. By prearrangement with Colson, and totally unbeknown to the petitioner, the agent Murphy sat in a car parked out of sight down the street and listened over the radio to the entire conversation. The petitioner made several incriminating statements during the course of this conversation. At the petitioner's trial these incriminating statements were brought before the jury through Murphy's testimony, despite the insistent objection of defense counsel. The jury convicted the petitioner of several related narcotics offenses, and the convictions were affirmed by the Court of Appeals.

The petitioner argues that it was an error of constitutional dimensions to permit the agent Murphy at the trial to testify to the petitioner's incriminating statements which Murphy had overheard under the circumstances disclosed by this record. This argument is based upon two distinct and independent grounds. [The Court did not reach the Fourth Amendment argument.] Secondly, it is said that the petitioner's Fifth and Sixth Amendment rights were violated by the use in evidence against him of incriminating statements which government agents had deliberately elicited from him after he had been indicted and in the absence of his retained counsel. * * *

In Spano v. New York, 360 US 315, 79 S.Ct. 1202, 3 L.Ed. 2d 1265 (1959), this Court reversed a state criminal conviction because a confession had been wrongly admitted into evidence against the defendant at his trial. In that case the defendant had already been indicted for first-degree murder at the time he confessed. The Court held that the defendant's conviction could not stand under the Fourteenth Amendment. While the Court's opinion relied upon the totality of the circumstances under which the confession had been obtained, four concurring Justices pointed out that the Constitution required reversal of the conviction upon the sole and specific ground that the confession had been deliberately elicited by the police after the defendant had been indicted, and therefore at a time when he was clearly entitled to a lawyer's help. It was pointed out that under our system of justice the most elemental concepts of due process of law contemplate that an indictment be followed by a trial, "in an orderly courtroom, presided over by a judge, open to the public, and protected by all the procedural safeguards of the law." It was said that a Constitution which guarantees a defendant the aid of counsel at such a trial could surely vouchsafe no less to an indicted defendant under interrogation by the police in a completely extrajudicial proceeding. Anything less, it was said, might deny a defendant "effective representation by counsel at the only stage when legal aid and advice would help him." * * *

This view no more than reflects a constitutional principle established as long ago as *Powell v. Alabama* [Chapter 1] where the Court noted that "* * * during perhaps the most critical period of the proceedings * * * that is to say, from the time of their arraignment until the beginning of their trial, when consultation, thorough-going investigation and preparation [are] vitally important, the defendants * * * [are] as much entitled to such aid [of counsel] during that period as at the trial itself." * * *

Here we deal not with a state court conviction, but with a federal case, where the specific guarantee of the Sixth Amendment directly applies. We hold that the petitioner was denied the basic protections of that guarantee when there was used against him at his trial evidence of his own incriminating words, which federal agents had deliberately elicited from him after he had been indicted and in the absence of his counsel. It is true that in the *Spano* case the defendant was interrogated in a police station, while here the damaging testimony was elicited from the defendant without his knowledge while he was free on bail. But, as Judge Hays pointed out in his dissent in the Court of Appeals, "if such a rule is to have any efficacy it must apply to indirect and surreptitious interrogations as well as those conducted in the jailhouse. In this case, Massiah was more seriously imposed upon * * * because he did not even know that he was under interrogation by a government agent."

* * * We do not question that in this case, as in many cases, it was entirely proper to continue an investigation of the suspected criminal activities of the defendant and his alleged confederates, even though the defendant had already been indicted. All that we hold is that the defendant's own incriminating statements, obtained by federal agents under the circumstances here disclosed, could not constitutionally be used by the prosecution as evidence against him at his trial. * * *

MR. JUSTICE WHITE, with whom MR. JUSTICE CLARK and MR. JUSTICE HARLAN join, dissenting. * * *

It is * * * a rather portentous occasion when a constitutional rule is established barring the use of evidence which is relevant, reliable and highly probative of the issue which the trial court has before it—whether the accused committed the act with which he is charged. Without the evidence, the quest for truth may be seriously impeded and in many cases the trial court, although aware of proof showing defendant's guilt, must nevertheless release him because the crucial evidence is deemed inadmissible. This result is entirely justified in some circumstances because exclusion serves other policies of overriding importance, as where evidence seized in an illegal search is excluded, not because of the quality of the proof, but to secure meaningful enforcement of the Fourth Amendment. But this only emphasizes that the soundest of reasons is necessary to warrant the exclusion of evidence otherwise admissible and the creation of another area of privileged testimony. With all due deference, I am not at all convinced that the additional barriers to the pursuit of truth which the Court today erects rest on anything like the solid foundations which decisions of this gravity should require. * * *

Whatever the content or scope of the rule may prove to be, I am unable to see how this case presents an unconstitutional interference with Massiah's right to counsel. Massiah was not prevented from consulting with counsel as often as he wished. No meetings with counsel were disturbed or spied upon. Preparation for trial was in no way obstructed. It is only a sterile syllogism—an unsound one, besides—to say that because Massiah had a right to counsel's aid before and during the trial, his out-of-court conversations and admissions must be excluded if obtained without counsel's consent or presence. The right to counsel has never meant as much before, and its extension in this case requires some further explanation, so far unarticulated by the Court. * * *

Applying the new exclusionary rule is peculiarly inappropriate in this case. At the time of the conversation in question, petitioner was not in custody but free on bail. He was not questioned in what anyone could call an atmosphere of official coercion. What he said was said to his partner in crime who had also been indicted. There was no suggestion or any possibility of coercion. What petitioner did not know was that Colson had decided to report the conversation to the police. Had there been no prior arrangements between Colson and the police, had Colson simply gone to the police after the conversation had occurred, his testimony relating Massiah's statements would be readily admissible at the trial, as would a recording which he might have made of the conversation. In such event, it would simply be said that Massiah risked talking to a friend who decided to disclose what he knew of Massiah's criminal activities. But if, as occurred here, Colson had been cooperating with the police prior to his meeting with Massiah, both his evidence and the recorded conversation are somehow transformed into inadmissible evidence despite the fact that the hazard to Massiah remains precisely the same—the defection of a confederate in crime. * * *

* * * It is one thing to establish safeguards against procedures fraught with the potentiality of coercion and to outlaw "easy but self-defeating ways in which brutality is substituted for brains as an instrument of crime detection." But here there was no substitution of brutality for brains, no inherent danger of police coercion justifying the prophylactic effect of another exclusionary rule. Massiah was not being interrogated in a police station, was not surrounded by numerous officers or questioned in relays, and was not forbidden access to others. Law enforcement may have the elements of a contest about it, but it is not a game. Massiah and those like him receive ample protection from the long line of precedents in this Court holding that confessions may not be introduced unless they are voluntary. In making these determinations the courts must consider the absence of counsel as one of several factors by which voluntariness is to be judged. This is a wiser rule than the automatic rule announced by the Court, which requires courts and juries to disregard voluntary admissions which they might well find to be the best possible evidence in discharging their responsibility for ascertaining truth.

NOTES AND QUESTIONS

1. Notice that *Massiah* predates *Miranda* by two years. Justice White's dissent characterized the *Massiah* rationale as a "thinly disguised constitutional policy of minimizing or entirely prohibiting the use in evidence of voluntary out-of-court admissions and confessions made by the accused." As we have seen, the Court would

soon apply this policy with a vengeance in *Miranda* by giving all suspects the right to remain silent and the right to counsel. Predictably, Justice White dissented in *Miranda* as well.

2. In the mid-eighteenth century, the role of defense counsel was minimal. In one sample of New Jersey cases from 1749–57, roughly half of the defendants represented themselves, presenting evidence as best they could. But even when lawyers appeared for defendants, their role appeared to be summing up at the end of the trial by making any points of law that might be helpful. This is consistent with English law of the time that prohibited lawyers in felony cases from presenting the defendant's case, though lawyers could argue "points of law." In one colonial New Jersey case, the judge appointed counsel but apparently not until after the defendant had already presented her case; the lawyer's job presumably was to sum up the case and argue points of law (she lost and was sentenced to hang). See George C. Thomas III, *Colonial Criminal Law and Procedure: The Royal Colony of New Jersey 1749–57*, 1 N.Y.U. J. L. & Liberty 671, 687–88 (2005).

Assuming that this was the model the Framers had in mind when they guaranteed the "assistance of counsel" for defendants, was it illegitimate for the *Massiah* Court to radically expand the meaning of assistance of counsel? Inappropriate? The wrong road taken?

3. Think back to what constituted a valid waiver of *Miranda*. Using that test, do you think Massiah could have waived his right to counsel? Turning the question around, what purpose would Massiah's lawyer have served if he had been in the car with Massiah and Colson? If you don't like what the Government did in this case, what precisely is it that you think was improper?

Deliberate Elicitation: The Doctrine Evolves

In *Massiah*, the Government was actively seeking to elicit statements from the accused in the absence of counsel. But the Court has decided two cases in which this was not so clear. In United States v. Henry, 447 U.S. 264, 100 S.Ct. 2183, 65 L.Ed.2d 115 (1980), Henry was indicted for bank robbery and held in jail. The government agents working on the robbery contacted Nichols, an inmate at the same jail as Henry, who "had been engaged to provide confidential information to the Federal Bureau of Investigation as a paid informant. * * * Nichols informed the agent that he was housed in the same cellblock with several federal prisoners awaiting trial, including Henry." Nichols testified at trial that Henry told him about the robbery.

As Henry had been indicted, he was in the same position as Massiah with regard to his right to counsel. But had Nichols deliberately elicited the admissions from Henry? Here is what the government agent said in his affidavit concerning the instructions given Nichols:

> "I recall telling Nichols at this time to be alert to any statements made by these individuals [the federal prisoners] regarding the charges against them. I specifically recall telling Nichols that he was not to question Henry or these individuals about the charges against them, however, if they engaged him in conversation or talked in front of him, he was requested to pay attention to their statements. I recall telling Nichols not to initiate any conversations with Henry regarding the bank robbery charges against Henry, but that if Henry initiated the conversations with Nichols, I requested Nichols to pay attention to the information furnished by Henry."

Was this "deliberate elicitation"? In an opinion by Chief Justice Burger, the Court held that it was. The Court reasoned that "[e]ven if the agent's statement that he did not intend that Nichols would take affirmative steps to secure incriminating information is accepted, he must have known that such propinquity likely would lead to that result." Moreover, the Court noted that "[i]n *Massiah*, no inquiry was made as to whether Massiah or his codefendant first raised the subject of the crime under investigation."

True enough, but the *Massiah* Court concluded that the agents had "deliberately elicited" statements from Massiah. Could the same be said in *Henry*? What does "deliberate" usually mean? It seems that the Court in *Henry* was rejecting a narrow meaning of "deliberate elicitation." *Henry* seems to stand for the proposition that "deliberate elicitation" means "deliberately put an agent in a situation where it is likely that he will hear incriminating statements." Perhaps there is no Sixth Amendment distinction between intending to elicit statements and intending to put an agent in a position where he was likely to obtain statements.

The reason to treat those two situations alike, as *Massiah* noted, is that a defendant like Massiah is "more seriously imposed upon because he did not know that his codefendant was a Government agent." This, of course, is because "[a]n accused speaking to a known Government agent is typically aware that his statements may be used against him," but not when "the accused is in the company of a fellow inmate who is acting by prearrangement as a Government agent."

But Kuhlmann v. Wilson, 477 U.S. 436, 106 S.Ct. 2616, 91 L.Ed.2d 364 (1986), makes clear that the informant must do more than merely listen. The Court accepted as true for purposes of federal habeas review of a state conviction that the informant placed in the cell functioned only as an "ear" to listen to his cell mate. The Court then stressed that

> the primary concern of the *Massiah* line of decisions is secret interrogation by investigatory techniques that are the equivalent of direct police interrogation. Since "the Sixth Amendment is not violated whenever—by luck or happenstance—the State obtains incriminating statements from the accused after the right to counsel has attached," a defendant does not make out a violation of that right simply by showing that an informant, either through prior arrangement or voluntarily, reported his incriminating statements to the police. Rather, the defendant must demonstrate that the police and their informant took some action, beyond merely listening, that was designed deliberately to elicit incriminating remarks.

As *Kuhlmann* is the more recent case, it represents the Court's current view on how best to understand "deliberate elicititation."

NOTES AND QUESTIONS

1. The cases so far have involved covert police interrogation. But what about overt police interrogation? *Massiah* was decided two years before *Miranda.* It might seem (it seemed to one of the authors of this book) that *Miranda* rendered *Massiah* superfluous in the context of overt police interrogation. *Miranda*, after all, created its own right to counsel that protected suspects from having to face police interrogation without the aid of counsel. Why wouldn't a violation of *Massiah* in the context of police interrogation always be a violation of *Miranda*? The next case raises, but does not dispose of, this question.

2. *Massiah* Waiver, 1977

BREWER V. WILLIAMS

Supreme Court of the United States, 1977.
430 U.S. 387, 97 S.Ct. 1232, 51 L.Ed.2d 424.

You saw the difficulty the Court has had determining what "counts" as a valid waiver of *Miranda.* The issue is just as difficult in the *Massiah* context. One question to ask yourself as you read these materials is whether *Massiah* waiver is any different from *Miranda* waiver when the defendant knows he is being questioned by police.

MR. JUSTICE STEWART delivered the opinion of the Court [joined by JUSTICES BRENNAN, MARSHALL, POWELL, and STEVENS]. * * *

I

On the afternoon of December 24, 1968, a 10-year-old girl named Pamela Powers went with her family to the YMCA in Des Moines, Iowa, to watch a wrestling tournament in which her brother was participating. When she failed to return from a trip to the washroom, a search for her began. The search was unsuccessful.

Robert Williams, who had recently escaped from a mental hospital, was a resident of the YMCA. Soon after the girl's disappearance Williams was seen in the YMCA lobby carrying some clothing and a large bundle wrapped in a blanket. He obtained help from a 14-year-old boy in opening the street door of the YMCA and the door to his automobile parked outside. When Williams placed the bundle in the front seat of his car the boy "saw two legs in it and they were skinny and white." Before anyone could see what was in the bundle Williams drove away. His abandoned car was found the following day in Davenport, Iowa, roughly 160 miles east of Des Moines. A warrant was then issued in Des Moines for his arrest on a charge of abduction.

On the morning of December 26, a Des Moines lawyer named Henry McKnight went to the Des Moines police station and informed the officers present that he had just received a long-distance call from Williams, and that he had advised Williams to turn himself in to the Davenport police. Williams did surrender that morning to the police in Davenport, and they booked him on the charge specified in the arrest warrant and gave him the warnings required by *Miranda v. Arizona*. The Davenport police then telephoned their counterparts in Des Moines to inform them that Williams had surrendered. McKnight, the lawyer, was still at the Des Moines police headquarters, and Williams conversed with McKnight on the telephone. In the presence of the Des Moines chief of police and a police detective named Leaming, McKnight advised Williams that Des Moines police officers would be driving to Davenport to pick him up, that the officers would not interrogate him or mistreat him, and that Williams was not to talk to the officers about Pamela Powers until after consulting with McKnight upon his return to Des Moines. As a result of these conversations, it was agreed between McKnight and the Des Moines police officials that Detective Leaming and a fellow officer would drive to Davenport to pick up Williams, that they would bring him directly back to Des Moines, and that they would not question him during the trip.

In the meantime Williams was arraigned before a judge in Davenport on the outstanding arrest warrant. The judge advised him of his *Miranda* rights and committed him to jail. Before leaving the courtroom, Williams conferred with a lawyer named Kelly, who advised him not to make any statements until consulting with McKnight back in Des Moines.

Detective Leaming and his fellow officer arrived in Davenport about noon to pick up Williams and return him to Des Moines. Soon after their arrival they met with Williams and Kelly, who, they understood, was acting as Williams' lawyer. Detective Leaming repeated the *Miranda* warnings, and told Williams:

> "[W]e both know that you're being represented here by Mr. Kelly and you're being represented by Mr. McKnight in Des Moines, and * * * I want you to remember this because we'll be visiting between here and Des Moines."

Williams then conferred again with Kelly alone, and after this conference Kelly reiterated to Detective Leaming that Williams was not to be questioned about the disappearance of Pamela Powers until after he had consulted with McKnight back in Des Moines. When Leaming expressed some reservations, Kelly firmly stated that the agreement with McKnight was to be carried out—that there was to be no interrogation of Williams during the automobile journey to Des Moines. Kelly was denied permission to ride in the police car back to Des Moines with Williams and the two officers.

The two detectives, with Williams in their charge, then set out on the 160-mile drive. At no time during the trip did Williams express a willingness to be interrogated in the absence of an attorney. Instead, he stated several times that "[w]hen I get to Des Moines and see Mr. McKnight, I am going to tell you the whole story." Detective Leaming knew that Williams was a former mental patient, and knew also that he was deeply religious.

The detective and his prisoner soon embarked on a wide-ranging conversation covering a variety of topics, including the subject of religion. Then, not long after leaving Davenport and reaching the interstate highway, Detective Leaming delivered what has been referred to in the briefs and oral arguments as the "Christian burial speech." Addressing Williams as "Reverend," the detective said:

> "I want to give you something to think about while we're traveling down the road. * * * Number one, I want you to observe the weather conditions, it's raining, it's sleeting, it's freezing, driving is very treacherous, visibility is poor, it's going to be dark early this evening.

> They are predicting several inches of snow for tonight, and I feel that you yourself are the only person that knows where this little girl's body is, that you yourself have only been there once, and if you get a snow on top of it you yourself may be unable to find it. And, since we will be going right past the area on the way into Des Moines, I feel that we could stop and locate the body, that the parents of this little girl should be entitled to a Christian burial for the little girl who was snatched away from them on Christmas [E]ve and murdered. And I feel we should stop and locate it on the way in rather than waiting until morning and trying to come back out after a snow storm and possibly not being able to find it at all."

Williams asked Detective Leaming why he thought their route to Des Moines would be taking them past the girl's body, and Leaming responded that he knew the body was in the area of Mitchellville—a town they would be passing on the way to Des Moines. [Leaming had no such knowledge; he was bluffing.] Leaming then stated: "I do not want you to answer me. I don't want to discuss it any further. Just think about it as we're riding down the road."

As the car approached Grinnell, a town approximately 100 miles west of Davenport, Williams asked whether the police had found the victim's shoes. When Detective Leaming replied that he was unsure, Williams directed the officers to a service station where he said he had left the shoes; a search for them proved unsuccessful. As they continued towards Des Moines, Williams asked whether the police had found the blanket, and directed the officers to a rest area where he said he had disposed of the blanket. Nothing was found. The car continued towards Des Moines, and as it approached Mitchellville, Williams said that he would show the officers where the body was. He then directed the police to the body of Pamela Powers.

Williams was indicted for first-degree murder. Before trial, his counsel moved to suppress all evidence relating to or resulting from any statements Williams had made during the automobile ride from Davenport to Des Moines. After an evidentiary hearing the trial judge denied the motion. He found that "an agreement was made between defense counsel and the police officials to the effect that the Defendant was not to be questioned on the return trip to Des Moines," and that the evidence in question had been elicited from Williams during "a critical stage in the proceedings requiring the presence of counsel on his request." The judge ruled, however, that Williams had "waived his right to have an attorney present during the giving of such information."

The evidence in question was introduced over counsel's continuing objection at the subsequent trial. The jury found Williams guilty of murder [and the Iowa Supreme Court affirmed]. * * *

[The federal district court granted a petition for a writ of habeas corpus, concluding] as a matter of law that the evidence in question had been wrongly admitted at Williams' trial. This conclusion was based on three alternative and independent grounds: (1) that Williams had been denied his constitutional right to the assistance of counsel; (2) that he had been denied the constitutional protections defined by this Court's decisions in *Escobedo v. Illinois* and *Miranda v. Arizona*; and (3) that in any event, his self-incriminatory statements on the automobile trip from Davenport to Des Moines had been involuntarily made. Further, the District Court ruled that there had been no waiver by Williams of the constitutional protections in question. * * *

II * * *

B

As stated above, the District Court based its judgment in this case on three independent grounds. The Court of Appeals appears to have affirmed the judgment on two of those grounds. We have concluded that only one of them need be considered here.

Specifically, there is no need to review in this case the doctrine of *Miranda v. Arizona*, a doctrine designed to secure the constitutional privilege against compulsory self-incrimination. It is equally unnecessary to evaluate the ruling of the District Court that Williams' self-incriminating statements were, indeed, involuntarily made. For it is clear that the judgment before us must in any event be affirmed upon the ground that Williams was deprived of a different constitutional right—the right to the assistance of counsel. * * *

There has occasionally been a difference of opinion within the Court as to the peripheral scope of this constitutional right. * * * Whatever else it may mean, the right to counsel granted by the Sixth and Fourteenth Amendments means at least that a person is entitled to the help of a lawyer at or after the time that judicial proceedings have been initiated against him "whether by way of formal charge, preliminary hearing, indictment, information, or arraignment."

There can be no doubt in the present case that judicial proceedings had been initiated against Williams before the start of the automobile ride from Davenport to Des Moines. A warrant had been issued for his arrest, he had been arraigned on that warrant before a judge in a Davenport courtroom, and he had been committed by the court to confinement in jail. The State does not contend otherwise.

There can be no serious doubt, either, that Detective Leaming deliberately and designedly set out to elicit information from Williams just as surely as—and perhaps more effectively than—if he had formally interrogated him. Detective Leaming was fully aware before departing for Des Moines that Williams was being represented in Davenport by Kelly and in Des Moines by McKnight. Yet he purposely sought during Williams' isolation from his lawyers to obtain as much incriminating information as possible. Indeed, Detective Leaming conceded as much when he testified at Williams' trial:

> "Q. In fact, Captain, whether he was a mental patient or not, you were trying to get all the information you could before he got to his lawyer, weren't you?
>
> "A. I was sure hoping to find out where that little girl was, yes, sir.
>
> * * *
>
> "Q. Well, I'll put it this way: You was [sic] hoping to get all the information you could before Williams got back to McKnight, weren't you?
>
> "A. Yes, sir."

The state courts clearly proceeded upon the hypothesis that Detective Leaming's "Christian burial speech" had been tantamount to interrogation. * * *

The circumstances of this case are thus constitutionally indistinguishable from those presented in *Massiah v. United States.* * * *

That the incriminating statements were elicited surreptitiously in the *Massiah* case, and otherwise here, is constitutionally irrelevant. Rather, the clear rule of *Massiah* is that once adversary proceedings have commenced against an individual, he has a right to legal representation when the government interrogates him.[8] It thus requires no wooden or technical application of the *Massiah* doctrine to conclude that Williams was entitled to the assistance of counsel guaranteed to him by the Sixth and Fourteenth Amendments.

III

The Iowa courts recognized that Williams had been denied the constitutional right to the assistance of counsel. They held, however, that he had waived that

8 The only other significant factual difference between the present case and Massiah is that here the police had agreed that they would not interrogate Williams in the absence of his counsel. This circumstance plainly provides petitioner with no argument for distinguishing away the protection afforded by Massiah. * * *

right during the course of the automobile trip from Davenport to Des Moines. * * *

In its lengthy opinion affirming this determination, the Iowa Supreme Court applied "the totality-of-circumstances test for a showing of waiver of constitutionally-protected rights in the absence of an express waiver," and concluded that "evidence of the time element involved on the trip, the general circumstances of it, and the absence of any request or expressed desire for the aid of counsel before or at the time of giving information, were sufficient to sustain a conclusion that defendant did waive his constitutional rights as alleged."

In the federal habeas corpus proceeding the District Court, believing that the issue of waiver was not one of fact but of federal law, held that the Iowa courts had "applied the wrong constitutional standards" in ruling that Williams had waived the protections that were his under the Constitution. * * *

The District Court and the Court of Appeals were * * * correct in their understanding of the proper standard to be applied in determining the question of waiver as a matter of federal constitutional law—that it was incumbent upon the State to prove "an intentional relinquishment or abandonment of a known right or privilege." Johnson v. Zerbst, [304 U.S. 458, 464, 58 S.Ct. 1019, 1023, 82 L.Ed. 1461 (1938)]. That standard has been reiterated in many cases. We have said that the right to counsel does not depend upon a request by the defendant, and that courts indulge in every reasonable presumption against waiver. This strict standard applies equally to an alleged waiver of the right to counsel whether at trial or at a critical stage of pretrial proceedings.

We conclude, finally, that the Court of Appeals was correct in holding that, judged by these standards, the record in this case falls far short of sustaining petitioner's burden. It is true that Williams had been informed of and appeared to understand his right to counsel. But waiver requires not merely comprehension but relinquishment, and Williams' consistent reliance upon the advice of counsel in dealing with the authorities refutes any suggestion that he waived that right. He consulted McKnight by long-distance telephone before turning himself in. He spoke with McKnight by telephone again shortly after being booked. After he was arraigned, Williams sought out and obtained legal advice from Kelly. Williams again consulted with Kelly after Detective Leaming and his fellow officer arrived in Davenport. Throughout, Williams was advised not to make any statements before seeing McKnight in Des Moines, and was assured that the police had agreed not to question him. His statements while in the car that he would tell the whole story after seeing McKnight in Des Moines were the clearest expressions by Williams himself that he desired the presence of an attorney before any interrogation took place. But even before making these statements, Williams had effectively asserted his right to counsel by having secured attorneys at both ends of the automobile trip, both of whom, acting as his agents, had made clear to the police that no interrogation was to occur during the journey. Williams knew of that agreement and, particularly in view of his consistent reliance on counsel, there is no basis for concluding that he disavowed it.

Despite Williams' express and implicit assertions of his right to counsel, Detective Leaming proceeded to elicit incriminating statements from Williams. Leaming did not preface this effort by telling Williams that he had a right to the presence of a lawyer, and made no effort at all to ascertain whether Williams wished to relinquish that right. The circumstances of record in this case thus provide no reasonable basis for finding that Williams waived his right to the assistance of counsel.

The Court of Appeals did not hold, nor do we, that under the circumstances of this case Williams could not, without notice to counsel, have waived his rights under the Sixth and Fourteenth Amendments. It only held, as do we, that he did not.

IV

The crime of which Williams was convicted was senseless and brutal, calling for swift and energetic action by the police to apprehend the perpetrator and gather evidence with which he could be convicted. No mission of law enforcement officials is more important. Yet "[d]isinterested zeal for the public good does not assure either wisdom or right in the methods it pursues." Although we do not lightly affirm the issuance of a writ of habeas corpus in this case, so clear a violation of the Sixth and Fourteenth Amendments as here occurred cannot be condoned. The pressures on state executive and judicial officers charged with the administration of the criminal law are great, especially when the crime is murder and the victim a small child. But it is precisely the predictability of those pressures that makes imperative a resolute loyalty to the guarantees that the Constitution extends to us all. * * *

MR. JUSTICE MARSHALL, concurring.

I concur wholeheartedly in my Brother Stewart's opinion for the Court, but add these words in light of the dissenting opinions filed today. The dissenters have, I believe, lost sight of the fundamental constitutional backbone of our criminal law. They seem to think that Detective Leaming's actions were perfectly proper, indeed laudable, examples of "good police work." In my view, good police work is something far different from catching the criminal at any price. It is equally important that the police, as guardians of the law, fulfill their responsibility to obey its commands scrupulously. For "in the end life and liberty can be as much endangered from illegal methods used to convict those thought to be criminals as from the actual criminals themselves."

In this case, there can be no doubt that Detective Leaming consciously and knowingly set out to violate Williams' Sixth Amendment right to counsel and his Fifth Amendment privilege against self-incrimination, as Leaming himself understood those rights. * * *

Leaming knowingly isolated Williams from the protection of his lawyers and during that period he intentionally "persuaded" him to give incriminating evidence. It is this intentional police misconduct—not good police practice—that the Court rightly condemns. The heinous nature of the crime is no excuse, as the dissenters would have it, for condoning knowing and intentional police transgression of the constitutional rights of a defendant. If Williams is to go free—and given the ingenuity of Iowa prosecutors on retrial or in a civil commitment proceeding, I doubt very much that there is any chance a dangerous criminal will be loosed on the streets, the bloodcurdling cries of the dissents notwithstanding—it will hardly be because he deserves it. It will be because Detective Leaming, knowing full well that he risked reversal of Williams' conviction, intentionally denied Williams the right of every American under the Sixth Amendment to have the protective shield of a lawyer between himself and the awesome power of the State. * * *

MR. JUSTICE POWELL, concurring. * * *

I * * *

* * * It is clear from the record, as both of the federal courts below found, that there was no evidence of a knowing and voluntary waiver of the right to have counsel present beyond the fact that Williams ultimately confessed. It is settled law that an inferred waiver of a constitutional right is disfavored. I find no basis in the record of this case—or in the dissenting opinions—for disagreeing with the conclusion of the District Court that "the State has produced no affirmative evidence whatsoever to support its claim of waiver."

The dissenting opinion of the Chief Justice states that the Court's holding today "conclusively presumes a suspect is legally incompetent to change his mind and tell the truth until an attorney is present." I find no justification for this view. On the contrary, the opinion of the Court is explicitly clear that the right to assistance of counsel may be waived, after it has attached, without notice to or consultation with counsel. We would have such a case here if petitioner had proved that the police refrained from coercion and interrogation, as they had agreed, and that Williams freely on his own initiative had confessed the crime. * * *

MR. JUSTICE STEVENS, concurring. * * *

Nothing that we write, no matter how well reasoned or forcefully expressed, can bring back the victim of this tragedy or undo the consequences of the official neglect which led to the respondent's escape from a state mental institution. The emotional aspects of the case make it difficult to decide dispassionately, but do not qualify our obligation to apply the law with an eye to the future as well as with concern for the result in the particular case before us. * * *

MR. CHIEF JUSTICE BURGER, dissenting.

The result in this case ought to be intolerable in any society which purports to call itself an organized society. It continues the Court—by the narrowest margin—on the much-criticized course of punishing the public for the mistakes and misdeeds of law enforcement officers, instead of punishing the officer directly, if in fact he is guilty of wrongdoing. It mechanically and blindly keeps reliable evidence from juries whether the claimed constitutional violation involves gross police misconduct or honest human error.

Williams is guilty of the savage murder of a small child; no member of the Court contends he is not. While in custody, and after no fewer than five warnings of his rights to silence and to counsel, he led police to the concealed body of his victim. The Court concedes Williams was not threatened or coerced and that he spoke and acted voluntarily and with full awareness of his constitutional rights. In the face of all this, the Court now holds that because Williams was prompted by the detective's statement—not interrogation but a statement—the jury must not be told how the police found the body.

Today's holding fulfills Judge (later Mr. Justice) Cardozo's grim prophecy that someday some court might carry the exclusionary rule to the absurd extent that its operative effect would exclude evidence relating to the body of a murder victim because of the means by which it was found. In so ruling the Court regresses to playing a grisly game of "hide and seek," once more exalting the sporting theory of criminal justice which has been experiencing a decline in our jurisprudence. With Justices White, Blackmun, and Rehnquist, I categorically reject the remarkable notion that the police in this case were guilty of unconstitutional misconduct, or any conduct justifying the bizarre result reached by the Court. * * *

Under well-settled precedents which the Court freely acknowledges, it is very clear that Williams had made a valid waiver of his Fifth Amendment right to silence and his Sixth Amendment right to counsel when he led police to the child's body. Indeed, even under the Court's analysis I do not understand how a contrary conclusion is possible. * * *

The evidence is uncontradicted that Williams had abundant knowledge of his right to have counsel present and of his right to silence. Since the Court does not question his mental competence, it boggles the mind to suggest that Williams could not understand that leading police to the child's body would have other than the most serious consequences. All of the elements necessary to make out a valid waiver are shown by the record and acknowledged by the Court; we thus are left to guess how the Court reached its holding.

One plausible but unarticulated basis for the result reached is that once a suspect has asserted his right not to talk without the presence of an attorney, it becomes legally impossible for him to waive that right until he has seen an attorney. But constitutional rights are personal, and an otherwise valid waiver should not be brushed aside by judges simply because an attorney was not present. The Court's holding operates to "imprison a man in his privileges"; it conclusively presumes a suspect is legally incompetent to change his mind and tell the truth until an attorney is present. It denigrates an individual to a nonperson whose free will has become hostage to a lawyer so that until the lawyer consents, the suspect is deprived of any legal right or power to decide for himself that he wishes to make a disclosure. * * *

MR. JUSTICE WHITE, with whom MR. JUSTICE BLACKMUN and MR. JUSTICE REHNQUIST join, dissenting.

The respondent in this case killed a 10-year-old child. * * *

I

[During his recitation of the facts, Justice White noted that Williams began directing the police in search of incriminating evidence "[s]ome considerable time" after Leaming's "Christian burial speech." In footnote 3, White observed: "The trip was 160 miles long and was made in bad weather. Leaming's statement was made shortly after leaving Davenport. Respondent's statements about the victim's clothes were made shortly before arriving in Mitchellville, a near suburb of Des Moines." Eds.]

II

The strictest test of waiver which might be applied to this case is that set forth in *Johnson v. Zerbst*, and quoted by the majority. In order to show that a right has been waived under this test, the State must prove "an intentional relinquishment or abandonment of a known right or privilege." The majority creates no new rule preventing an accused who has retained a lawyer from waiving his right to the lawyer's presence during questioning. The majority simply finds that no waiver was proved in this case. I disagree. That respondent knew of his right not to say anything to the officers without advice and presence of counsel is established on this record to a moral certainty. He was advised of the right by three officials of the State—telling at least one that he understood the right—and by two lawyers. Finally, he further demonstrated his knowledge of the right by informing the police that he would tell them the story in the presence of McKnight when they arrived in Des Moines. The issue in this case, then, is whether respondent relinquished that right intentionally.

Respondent relinquished his right not to talk to the police about his crime when the car approached the place where he had hidden the victim's clothes. Men usually intend to do what they do, and there is nothing in the record to support the proposition that respondent's decision to talk was anything but an exercise of his own free will. Apparently, without any prodding from the officers, respondent—who had earlier said that he would tell the whole story when he arrived in Des Moines—spontaneously changed his mind about the timing of his disclosures when the car approached the places where he had hidden the evidence. However, even if his statements were influenced by Detective Leaming's above-quoted statement, respondent's decision to talk in the absence of counsel can hardly be viewed as the product of an overborne will. The statement by Leaming was not coercive; it was accompanied by a request that respondent not respond to it; and it was delivered hours before respondent decided to make any statement. Respondent's waiver was thus knowing and intentional.

The majority's contrary conclusion seems to rest on the fact that respondent "asserted" his right to counsel by retaining and consulting with one lawyer and by consulting with another. How this supports the conclusion that respondent's later relinquishment of his right not to talk in the absence of counsel was unintentional is a mystery. The fact that respondent consulted with counsel on the question whether he should talk to the police in counsel's absence makes his later decision to talk in counsel's absence better informed and, if anything, more intelligent.

The majority recognizes that even after this "assertion" of his right to counsel, it would have found that respondent waived his right not to talk in counsel's absence if his waiver had been express—i.e., if the officers had asked him in the car whether he would be willing to answer questions in counsel's absence and if he had answered "yes." But waiver is not a formalistic concept. Waiver is shown whenever the facts establish that an accused knew of a right and intended to relinquish it. Such waiver, even if not express, was plainly shown here. The only other conceivable basis for the majority's holding is the implicit suggestion that the right involved in *Massiah v. United States*, as distinguished from the right involved in *Miranda v. Arizona*, is a right not to be asked any questions in counsel's absence rather than a right not to answer any questions in counsel's absence, and that the right not to be asked questions must be waived before the questions are asked. Such wafer-thin distinctions cannot determine whether a guilty murderer should go free. The only conceivable purpose for the presence of counsel during questioning is to protect an accused from making incriminating answers. Questions, unanswered, have no significance at all. Absent coercion—no matter how the right involved is defined—an accused is amply protected by a rule requiring waiver before or simultaneously with the giving by him of an answer or the making by him of a statement.

III

The consequence of the majority's decision is, as the majority recognizes, extremely serious. A mentally disturbed killer whose guilt is not in question may be released. Why? Apparently the answer is that the majority believes that the law enforcement officers acted in a way which involves some risk of injury to society and that such conduct should be deterred. However, the officers' conduct did not, and was not likely to, jeopardize the fairness of respondent's trial or in any way risk the conviction of an innocent man—the risk against which the Sixth Amendment guarantee of assistance of counsel is designed to protect. The police did nothing "wrong," let alone anything "unconstitutional." To anyone not lost in the intricacies of the prophylactic rules of *Miranda v. Arizona*, the result in this case seems utterly senseless; and for the reasons stated in Part II, even applying those rules as well as the rule of *Massiah v. United States*, the statements made by respondent were properly admitted. In light of these considerations, the majority's protest that the result in this case is justified by a "clear violation" of the Sixth and Fourteenth Amendments has a distressing hollow ring. I respectfully dissent.

[*The dissenting opinion of JUSTICE BLACKMUN, joined by JUSTICES WHITE and REHNQUIST, is omitted.*]

NOTES AND QUESTIONS

1. While a law student, one of the authors of this book, worked on *Brewer* when it was on appeal to the Eighth Circuit; his view was that the issue was better analyzed under *Miranda* than under *Massiah*. Others thought so, too. *Brewer* was widely viewed as the case the Court would use to overrule *Miranda*. Justice Blackmun noted in his *Brewer* dissent that twenty-two states "and others, as amicus curiae, strongly urge that" *Miranda* "be re-examined and overruled." Perhaps sensing *Miranda*'s vulnerability, the University of Iowa law professor in charge of the case—Robert Bartels—insisted that the Sixth Amendment argument was the defendant's best hope. As usual, the teacher was wiser than the student. But the key question is why the Court was more comfortable deciding the case under *Massiah*. What do you think?

2. The bitter dispute in *Brewer* is framed in terms of waiver, not whether Leaming deliberately elicited Williams's statements. Are these different inquiries or just two sides of the same coin? Here's what Justice White had to say about the issue in a footnote to his dissent: "If an intentional relinquishment of the right to counsel under *Miranda* is established by proof that the accused was informed of his right and then voluntarily answered questions in counsel's absence, then similar proof establishes an intentional relinquishment of the *Massiah* right to counsel."

3. What did Officer Leaming do wrong? Is the problem the "Christian burial speech" or the "waiver" after the speech? If you think it is the latter, did the Court conclude that this was an involuntary waiver? An unintelligent one? Or is there another basis? The classic treatment of this question is Yale Kamisar, *Brewer v. Williams*, *Massiah* and *Miranda*: What is "Interrogation"? When Does It Matter?, 67 Geo. L.J. 1 (1978).

4. Chief Justice Burger stated in his dissent that, following the majority's reasoning, "[I]t becomes legally impossible for [Williams] to waive that right until he has seen an attorney." Is this what the majority says? Would that be a sensible outcome? Could Officer Leaming have done something differently that would have permitted Williams to waive before seeing McKnight?

Assume Officer Leaming gave the Christian burial speech, three hours passed, and Williams asked to telephone his boyhood minister. After a lengthy telephone call in private, Williams tells the police: "I am a religious man. Having thought of nothing these last three hours except the nature of sin and forgiveness, I decided to call my minister, who said that my religious duty is to direct you to where I hid the body." A violation of *Massiah*, as amplified by *Brewer*? What if, instead, Williams tells police he is going to call his lawyer and returns after the call to say he is ready to talk? Does it matter what the lawyer advised him?

5. *Massiah "fruit."* What evidence is rendered inadmissible by the Sixth Amendment violation in *Brewer*? The Court held that the statements Williams made leading the police to the body were inadmissible, of course, but what about the body itself? This is one way to ask whether a *Massiah* violation has poisoned fruit, as in the case of a Fourth Amendment violation. You will recall that *Miranda* is in most cases "fruitless." Is a *Massiah* violation more like a Fourth Amendment violation or more like a *Miranda* violation?

The Court in *Brewer* suggested in a footnote that the body might be admissible if it would have been discovered in any event. In Nix v. Williams, 467 US 431, 104 S.Ct. 2501, 81 L.Ed. 2d 377 (1984), the Court later made a holding of this dicta. Notice, however, that this "inevitable discovery" exception is precisely that—an exception to a general rule that the fruit of a violation of *Massiah* must be suppressed. Do you see why *Massiah*, but not *Miranda*, generally requires suppression of evidence found by means of the violation?

6. *Brewer v. Williams: the rest of the story.* The State of Iowa retried Williams. For details on the retrial, including the defense theory of how Williams was factually innocent, see Phillip E. Johnson, *The Return of the "Christian Burial Speech"* Case, 32 Emory L.J. 349 (1983). In brief, the theory was that the victim was killed by a janitor at the YMCA who then hid the body in Williams's room. Upon discovering the body, and fearing the inevitable inference, Williams panicked, fled, and hid the body where it was ultimately found. According to the Eighth Circuit, the defense theory of innocence "is not so far-fetched as it sounds." Williams v. Nix, 700 F.2d 1164, 1168 (8th Cir. 1983). Some evidence in Williams's favor: A witness heard the sounds of a struggle coming from the janitor's room shortly after the victim's disappearance, and the janitor made what one witness called "furtive preparations to depart" shortly after the crime occurred. Moreover, according to defense lawyers, the janitor had a history of child molestation. He could not be located for the first trial; by the time of the second trial, he had been killed in an auto accident.

Williams was again convicted, mostly on the testimony of the person who saw skinny white legs sticking out of the bundle that Williams put in his car. Iowa does not have the death penalty. Williams is still serving a life sentence at the Fort Madison, Iowa prison.

7. *Brewer v. Williams irony.* As you can see from the dissents and concurring opinions in *Brewer*, it created a firestorm of controversy, particularly in the state of Iowa. The notion that the Court would vacate the murder conviction of the man everyone believed kidnaped, raped, and murdered a child on Christmas Eve seemed to some an attack on our way of life. Chief Justice Burger's dissent pretty much says this. Then imagine the irony: In the last thirty years the Court has decided two *Massiah*

cases that, taken together, would have allowed the Court to affirm the murder conviction in *Brewer.*

In McNeil v. Wisconsin, 501 U.S. 171, 111 S.Ct. 2204, 115 L.Ed.2d 158 (1991), the Court held that the *Massiah* right to counsel exists only for interrogations about the offense for which the suspect is being prosecuted. In *McNeil*, the suspect appeared before a judge on an armed robbery charge. Two days later, police from a different town approached to ask him questions about an unrelated murder, attempted murder, and armed burglary. As there had been no adversary proceedings commenced for those offenses, *Massiah* did not bar the questioning.

Without getting too technical, suffice it to say that the child abduction charge on which Williams made a court appearance would not be the same *Massiah* offense as murder. See Texas v. Cobb, 532 U.S. 162, 121 S.Ct. 1335, 149 L.Ed.2d 321 (2001). Thus, as Justice Breyer noted in his *Cobb* dissent: "Because first-degree murder and child abduction" are not the same offense under the Court's *Cobb* test, "and because at the time of the impermissible interrogation Williams had been charged only with abduction of a child, Williams' murder conviction should have remained undisturbed."

3. *Massiah* Waiver, 1988–2017

Williams did not explicitly waive *Miranda*, and the case was analyzed as a Sixth Amendment waiver case. One issue left undecided after *Brewer v. Williams* was whether an explicit waiver of *Miranda* would also waive a suspect's Sixth Amendment right to counsel under *Massiah.* The Court answered that question, 5–4, in Patterson v. Illinois, 487 U.S. 285, 108 S.Ct. 2389, 101 L.Ed.2d 261 (1988), A valid waiver of *Miranda* is also a waiver of *Massiah.* The Court wrote that

> the *Miranda* warnings given petitioner made him aware of his right to have counsel present during the questioning. By telling petitioner that he had a right to consult with an attorney, to have a lawyer present while he was questioned, and even to have a lawyer appointed for him if he could not afford to retain one on his own, Officer Gresham and ASA Smith conveyed to petitioner the sum and substance of the rights that the Sixth Amendment provided him. "Indeed, it seems self-evident that one who is told he" has such rights to counsel "is in a curious posture to later complain" that his waiver of these rights was unknowing. There is little more petitioner could have possibly been told in an effort to satisfy this portion of the waiver inquiry.
>
> Second, the *Miranda* warnings also served to make petitioner aware of the consequences of a decision by him to waive his Sixth Amendment

> rights during postindictment questioning. Petitioner knew that any statement that he made could be used against him in subsequent criminal proceedings. This is the ultimate adverse consequence petitioner could have suffered by virtue of his choice to make uncounseled admissions to the authorities. This warning also sufficed—contrary to petitioner's claim here—to let petitioner know what a lawyer could "do for him" during the postindictment questioning: namely, advise petitioner to refrain from making any such statements. By knowing what could be done with any statements he might make, and therefore, what benefit could be obtained by having the aid of counsel while making such statements, petitioner was essentially informed of the possible consequences of going without counsel during questioning. If petitioner nonetheless lacked "a full and complete appreciation of all of the consequences flowing" from his waiver, it does not defeat the State's showing that the information it provided to him satisfied the constitutional minimum.

Patterson's goose was cooked, at least for five members of the Court, when his lawyer could not explain to the Court during oral argument what additional information his client needed to be able to waive his Sixth Amendment right to counsel. Here is a portion of the oral argument:

> QUESTION [from the bench]: [Patterson] * * * was told that he had a right to counsel.
>
> "MR. HONCHELL [Patterson's counsel]: He was told—the word 'counsel' was used. He was told he had a right to counsel. But not through information by which it would become meaningful to him, because the method that was used was not designed to alert the accused to the Sixth Amendment rights to counsel * * *.
>
> "QUESTION: * * * You mean they should have said you have a Sixth Amendment right to counsel instead of just, you have a right to counsel?
>
> "He knew he had a right to have counsel present before [he] made the confession. Now, what in addition did he have to know to make the waiver an intelligent one?
>
> "MR. HONCHELL: He had to meaningfully know he had a Sixth Amendment right to counsel present because—
>
> "QUESTION: What is the difference between meaningfully knowing and knowing?

> "MR. HONCHELL: Because the warning here used did not convey or express what counsel was intended to do for him after indictment. * * * That there is a right to counsel who would act on his behalf and represent him.
>
> "QUESTION: Well, okay. So it should have said, in addition to saying counsel, counsel who would act on your behalf and represent you? That would have been the magic solution?
>
> "MR. HONCHELL: That is a possible method, yes."

The dissent focused on the fact that one of the interviews in which Patterson waived his *Miranda* rights was conducted by a prosecutor. According to the dissent,

> without a careful discussion of the pitfalls of proceeding without counsel, the Sixth Amendment right cannot properly be waived. An adversary party, moreover, cannot adequately provide such advice. As a result, once the right to counsel attaches and the adversary relationship between the state and the accused solidifies, a prosecutor cannot conduct a private interview with an accused party without "dilut[ing] the protection afforded by the right to counsel."

Montejo v. Louisiana, 556 U.S. 778, 129 S.Ct. 2079, 173 L.Ed.2d 955 (2009), extends the *Patterson* logic to include defendants who have been appointed counsel. The Court held in *Montejo* that despite the appointment of counsel at a preliminary hearing, a waiver of *Miranda* still works to waive *Massiah*. Montejo argued that the appointment of counsel put his case in a different posture from Patterson and that police should be prevented from "badgering" him to give up his Sixth Amendment right to counsel. The Court rejected the argument:

> Under *Miranda*'s prophylactic protection of the right against compelled self-incrimination, any suspect subject to custodial interrogation has the right to have a lawyer present if he so requests, and to be advised of that right. Under *Edwards*' prophylactic protection of the *Miranda* right, once such a defendant "has invoked his right to have counsel present," interrogation must stop. And under *Minnick*'s [Minnick v. Mississippi, 498 U.S. 146, 111 S.Ct. 486, 112 L.Ed. 2d 489 (1990)] prophylactic protection of the *Edwards* right, no subsequent interrogation may take place until counsel is present, "whether or not the accused has consulted with his attorney."
>
> These three layers of prophylaxis are sufficient. Under the *Miranda-Edwards-Minnick* line of cases (which is not in doubt), a defendant who

> does not want to speak to the police without counsel present need only say as much when he is first approached and given the *Miranda* warnings. At that point, not only must the immediate contact end, but "badgering" by later requests is prohibited. If that regime suffices to protect the integrity of "a suspect's voluntary choice not to speak outside his lawyer's presence" before his arraignment, it is hard to see why it would not also suffice to protect that same choice after arraignment, when Sixth Amendment rights have attached. And if so, then [additional protection] is simply superfluous. * * *

Williams did not need *Massiah* to win his case; the Court could have ruled in his favor under *Miranda*. Indeed, as we pointed out in Note 7 after *Brewer v. Williams*, he would lose his *Massiah* argument if made today. Given the post-*Brewer* cases like *Patterson* and *Montejo*, it appears that the Court has effectively limited *Massiah* to the fact of surreptitious elicitation of statements after adversarial proceedings have begun. Perhaps that is a good development. Sherry Colb has pointed out that, when applied to police interrogation, *Massiah* is an empty formalism. *Massiah* treats similarly situated defendants differently depending on whether charges have been filed. But, Colb argues, indictment is a meaningless threshold when the issue is whether defendants need legal advice about how to respond to police who are seeking statements from them. Why doesn't a defendant need advice of counsel the day before indictment just as much as he needs advice the day after indictment? Thus, in cases where the suspect knows he faces police interrogation, Colb believes that *Miranda* is all suspects need. See Sherry F. Colb, Why the Supreme Court Should Overrule the *Massiah* Doctrine and Permit *Miranda* Alone to Govern Interrogations, at http://writ.news.findlaw.com/colb/20010509.html.

As one of us argued in 1975 when working on the appeal in *Brewer v. Williams*, all Williams needed in that patrol car the snowy night after Christmas in 1968 (and today all he would have) is *Miranda*.

CHAPTER 8 SUMMARY

For centuries in Anglo-American law, courts have stressed the need to treat criminal suspects fairly when interrogating them. For most of this time, English and American courts insisted that a suspect's statements could be used against him only if the statements were voluntary. While this principle is easy enough to apply in cases of extreme coercion—recall the torture in *Brown v. Mississippi* from Chapter 1—voluntariness is not so easy to determine in the absence of obvious coercion. *Ashcraft v. Tennessee* held involuntary a confession taken after 36 hours of uninterrupted interrogation. Fair enough. But what about 30 hours? Or 24?

Perhaps all police interrogation of suspects in custody is, to some degree, coercive. Enter *Miranda v. Arizona*, which held that custodial police interrogation is always potentially a violation of the Fifth Amendment right not be compelled in a criminal case to be a witness against oneself. The remedy, the Court held, was to require police to give the famous *Miranda* warnings of the right to silence and to counsel. *Miranda* is the most famous of the Court's criminal procedure cases and was, for a time, controversial. The controversy has subsided, however, at least in part because subsequent cases have reduced its effect on police interrogation.

A parallel development in the law of interrogation involved the right to counsel. This right is located in the Sixth Amendment right to counsel and is, conceptually at least, independent of the *Miranda* right to counsel located in the Fifth Amendment privilege against compelled self-incrimination. The Sixth Amendment right to counsel is triggered when criminal charges are filed and forbids police from eliciting incriminating statements in the absence of counsel or the waiver of counsel. The Fifth and Sixth Amendment rights are largely co-extensive in routine criminal interrogations, but situations arise in which one, but not the other, applies to protect suspects.

CHAPTER 9

The Role of Defense Counsel

In all criminal prosecutions, the accused shall enjoy the right * * * to have the Assistance of Counsel for his defence. U.S. Const. amend. VI.

* * *

"How can you defend those people?" is a question frequently put to criminal defense attorneys, often in a tone suggesting that it is not so much a question as a demand for an apology, as though a defense attorney needs to justify his work, in a way that a prosecutor doesn't. Because the question presumes that "those people" accused of crime are guilty, and that people who are guilty of crimes ought not to be defended, it reflects a profound misunderstanding of our criminal justice system and the defense attorney's role in it.

James S. Kunen, How Can You Defend Those People?: The Making of a Criminal Lawyer xi (1983).

* * *

In the Laws of Henry I, collected around 1115, "counsel" was meant quite literally:

In [most] cases an accused person may seek counsel and obtain it from his friends and relatives (no law should forbid this), in particular the advice of those whom he brings with him or invites to attend his [case]; and in taking counsel he shall faithfully state the truth of the matter so that circumstances may appear to the best advantage with respect to the [case] or its peaceful settlement. * * *

For it is often the case that a person sees less in his own cause than in someone else's and it is generally possible to amend in another person's mouth what may not be amended in his own.

Leges Henrici Primi, laws 46.4 & 46.6

Notice that even in the twelfth century, scribes recognized that to take maximum advantage of counsel, the accused should "faithfully state the truth of the matter." Beyond that, it is clear that the principal role of counsel was to provide advice about how to proceed in a case. That is still true today.

It is difficult to exaggerate the importance of the lawyer to the criminal process. The norms that we identified in Chapter 1 as underlying the process—accuracy, efficiency, fairness, and limiting the power of government—simply cannot be achieved if the lawyer for the defense or the prosecution is inept, incompetent, indifferent, or corrupt. Consider a hypothetical based on a real case. *D* is charged with a rape-murder. He denies guilt, claiming he wasn't there that night. While preparing for trial, the lawyer learns that the rapist was sterile *but the lawyer never asks D whether he was sterile and does not even tell D this fact about the case.* Thus, the client never had a chance to offer his thoughts on whether he should take a sperm test. Without evidence that he was not sterile, *D* is convicted and given a long sentence. On appeal, a different lawyer discovered the sterility issue, has *D* tested, and (guess what?) *D* is not sterile. Whether the original lawyer was guilty of ineffective assistance of counsel is an issue for Part D. For present purposes, it is easy to see that had the lawyer performed at a higher level, *D* would have been acquitted in the first place, an outcome that serves the norms of accuracy, fairness, and efficiency.

The ethics of representing criminal defendants thus include zealous and competent representation. The ethics of lawyering also include duties owed to the court. Prosecutors, of course, also have ethical duties to provide competent representation and, above that, to seek justice rather than merely to be an advocate.

The problem of representing *indigent* defendants is particularly complicated because of funding problems. While we lack data on the provision of counsel to indigent defendants in all state courts, the Bureau of Justice Statistics determined that, in 1996, 82% of indigent felony defendants in the 75 most populous counties were represented by counsel paid for by the State; 66% of federal felony defendants in the same year were represented by publicly-financed counsel. Bureau of Justice Statistics, "Two of Three Felony Defendants Represented by Publicly-Financed Counsel," http://www.bjs.gov/content/pub/press/iddcpr.cfm. Caseloads for public defenders vary widely but in some states are astronomical: 340 in Colorado (229 of which were felonies), 367 in Wisconsin (122 felonies), and 374 in Delaware (83 felonies). We will return to this problem in Part B, where we examine one state public defender system on the verge of collapse.

A. THE ETHICS OF DEFENDING "THOSE" PEOPLE

1. A Case Study: Defending the Defenseless Client

What follows is based on the New York City police treatment of suspect named Abner Louima in 1997. The worst of the abuse, allegedly committed by Officer Justin Volpe, was shoving a broom handle into Louima's rectum so violently that it caused serious internal injuries. Volpe was charged, along with three other officers, with violating the civil rights of Louima. Volpe faced life in prison for his part in the brutal treatment. For the facts of the case, as well as the commentary on the duties of defense counsel representing Volpe, we draw heavily from Abbe Smith, *Defending Defending: The Case for Unmitigated Zeal on Behalf of People Who Do Terrible Things*, 28 Hofstra L. Rev. 925 (2000).

First, let us assume you are a lawyer specializing in criminal defense work and Officer Volpe asks you to represent him. Does it matter to you whether Volpe is guilty? Should it? If he admits that he is guilty, you might decide you do not want to represent him. If so, do you have any obligation to provide him a defense?

Suppose Volpe denies any role in the abuse, but you do not believe him. You think you have before you "a sadistic, racist cop who, in some sort of monstrous rage, had brutalized an innocent, hard-working immigrant who had the misfortune to cross Volpe's path." Smith, *supra*, at 927. Now assume that you decide to represent Volpe. You have a sign on your desk that says "Presumption of Innocence Commences With Payment of Retainer." *Id.* Volpe pays. You are his lawyer. You have suspended your judgment about Volpe's moral culpability and your job is to minimize the legal consequences of what he did. Now should your belief about his guilt or innocence make any difference in how you approach your job?

Do you think the prosecutor will offer a favorable plea bargain in Volpe's case? Suppose a hard but fair plea offer is made and you suspect, the well-known "blue wall of silence" notwithstanding, that some of the police officers involved in the incident will testify against Volpe. You decide that it is in the best interests of your client to plead guilty. Should you simply provide advice and leave it up to Volpe or should you advocate for a guilty plea? If the latter, how intensely should you advocate?

> Although much has been written about lawyer-client counseling and the proper allocation of power in decision-making, nothing can prepare a criminal lawyer for the intensity of counseling clients about

> the decision to plead guilty or go to trial, especially where the stakes are high. The timing of this conversation is crucial and can sorely test even a good lawyer-client relationship. Sometimes the moment of reckoning is early on, and sometimes not until the eve of trial.
>
> Most experienced criminal defense lawyers have had grueling sessions during which they urge recalcitrant clients to plead guilty. These intense and often unpleasant encounters can ultimately be enlightening and even redemptive for the client. Sometimes there is enormous relief in accepting the reality of a situation, putting an end to the uncertainty, and admitting guilt. Of course, sometimes the client simply sees the writing on the wall and wishes to cut his or her losses.

Smith, *supra*, at 946–47.

If no plausible plea bargain is forthcoming, or Volpe simply refuses to accept, you must prepare a defense. Whether other police officers will incriminate Volpe is not certain, but you have one very real problem. Mr. Louima suffered a torn colon, lacerated bladder, and ruptured intestine, all of which is documented in the medical evidence. How to explain these injuries without admitting that *someone* put a broom stick violently into his rectum? And if someone did that, and if the other officers point the finger at Volpe, his case is hopeless.

One way to explain the terrible injuries—the way Volpe's lawyer chose in real life—is to suggest that "Louima's injuries were not the result of police brutality, but of consensual anal sex with another man." Smith, *supra*, at 930. Would you choose this path? Is there any ethical reason not to? Turning the question around, if this is the *only* half-way plausible alternative explanation, are you ethically obligated to present the explanation?

Perhaps. Alan Dershowitz has argued, "What a defense attorney 'may' do, he must do, if it is necessary to defend his client. A zealous defense attorney has a professional obligation to take every legal and ethically permissible step that will serve the client's best interest—even if the attorney finds the step personally distasteful." Smith, *supra*, at 958, quoting Alan M. Dershowitz, Reasonable Doubts: The O.J. Simpson Case and the Criminal Justice System 145 (1996).

But we have yet to answer the question of *whether* this is permissible defense conduct. Many commentators were harshly condemning of the "rough sex" defense, denouncing it as a "vile insinuation," a "vile fantasy," and as "a second rape." Smith, *supra*, at 930–31. Does it matter if you believe that Volpe is guilty and thus that your story cannot be true? What if you are not certain of Volpe's guilt, but you have no evidence to support the allegation of homosexual conduct?

Even if you believe Volpe is innocent, can you allege "rough sex" without *any* evidence? Does it matter that Abner Louima is married and has two children?

To Lord Brougham in the early nineteenth century, the answer was that you can present the explanation without regard to your belief in your client's innocence or the truth of the story. Here is how Brougham put it:

> [A]n advocate, in the discharge of his duty, knows but one person in all the world, and that person is his client. To save that client by all means and expedients, and at all hazards and costs to other persons, and, amongst them to himself, is his first and only duty; and in performing this duty he must not regard the alarm, the torments, the destruction which he may bring upon others. Separating the duty of a patriot from that of an advocate, he must go on reckless of consequences, though it should be his unhappy fate to involve his country in confusion.

Smith, *supra*, at 928 n.23, citing 2 Trial of Queen Caroline 8 (London, Shackell & Arrowsmith 1820–21).

Justice White contrasted the role of defense counsel with that of the prosecutor in United States v. Wade, 388 U.S. 218, 87 S.Ct. 1926, 18 L.Ed.2d 1149 (1967) (White, J., dissenting in part):

> [D]efense counsel has no comparable obligation to ascertain or present the truth. Our system assigns him a different mission. * * * Defense counsel need present nothing, even if he knows what the truth is. He need not furnish any witnesses to the police, or reveal any confidences of his client, or furnish any other information to help the prosecution's case. If he can confuse a witness, even a truthful one, or make him appear at a disadvantage, unsure or indecisive, that will be his normal course. Our interest in not convicting the innocent permits counsel to put the State to its proof, to put the State's case in the worst possible light, regardless of what he thinks or knows to be the truth. Undoubtedly there are some limits which defense counsel must observe but more often than not, defense counsel will cross-examine a prosecution witness, and impeach him if he can, even if he thinks the witness is telling the truth, just as he will attempt to destroy a witness who he thinks is lying. In this respect, as part of our modified adversary system and as part of the duty imposed on the most honorable defense counsel, we countenance or require conduct which in many instances has little, if any, relation to the search for truth.

Now return to the Volpe case. What if part of your calculation is not just to create doubt among the jury by offering an alternative explanation of the facts in evidence but, rather, to invoke jury antipathy toward homosexuals, to invite homophobia to cloud the minds of the jurors? Does this take the case out of Lord Brougham's prescription for defending defenseless clients?

Some argue yes, that it crosses an ethical line when a criminal defense lawyer exploits racism, sexism, homophobia, or ethnic bias. But why would it be ethically improper to exploit homophobia if it is ethically desirable (or at least ethically neutral) for a defense lawyer to suggest through cross-examination that the eyewitness is lying when the lawyer knows she is telling the truth? To answer that challenge, some have argued that criminal defense lawyers sometimes have a duty to the community that is at least as important as the duty to the client. Exploiting various nefarious attitudes that exist in society would presumably be more injurious than suggesting that eyewitnesses are lying. But Professor Abbe Smith is unpersuaded by this "progressive" scholarship.

> Anthony Alfieri, the most prominent progressive scholar on this subject, wants to have it both ways: He would like criminal defense lawyers to be more "community-centered," and to embrace a "color-conscious, pluralist approach to advocacy that honors the integrity of diverse individual and collective * * * identities *without sacrificing effective representation*." This is both untenable and disingenuous. In truth, he wants to transform criminal defense lawyers from defenders of individuals accused of crime to defenders of the community and of certain values he holds dear.
>
> It is difficult, if not impossible, to zealously represent the criminally accused and simultaneously tend to the feelings of others. This is so in any political climate, but even more so in a time when criminal punishment is regarded as the answer to almost all of our social problems. We cannot seem to build prisons fast enough, and we are on the road to the virtual banishment of young African American men from society. It is simply wrong to place an additional burden on criminal defense lawyers to make the world a better place as they labor to represent individuals facing loss of liberty or life. * * *
>
> There is nothing unethical about using racial, gender, ethnic, or sexual stereotypes in criminal defense. It is simply an aspect of zealous advocacy. Prejudice exists in the community and in the courthouse, and criminal defense lawyers would be foolhardy not to recognize this as a fact of life. Of course, most bias and prejudice works against the

> accused, disproportionate numbers of whom are poor and nonwhite. Defense lawyers must incorporate this knowledge, as well as knowledge about the stereotypes that might apply, to the prosecution and defense witnesses in all their trial decisions.
>
> A trial is theater. Defense lawyers cannot afford to be color-blind, gender-blind, or even slightly near-sighted when it comes to race, gender, sexual orientation, and ethnicity, because jurors will be paying close attention and they have come to the trial with their own feelings about these issues. Many stereotypes arise in a criminal trial, whether or not they are actively exploited by either party. Sometimes the exploitation of stereotypes is unavoidable.

Smith, *supra*, at 951–52, 954–55, citing Anthony V. Alfieri, *Defending Racial Violence*, 95 Colum. L. Rev. 1301, 1320–21 (1995); Anthony V. Alfieri, *Race Trials*, 76 Tex. L. Rev. 1293, 1305–23 (1998).

For Professor Smith, defending the defenseless with vigorous arguments, even those designed to appeal to prejudices, poses no ethical problems.

> Justin Volpe did a terrible thing, and he will pay the price for his brutal crime for a long time. Given his client's insistence on going to trial, Volpe's lawyer had no choice but to try to mount a vigorous defense, however ill fated. This was the right thing for Volpe's lawyer to do—for his client and for the rest of us.

Smith, *supra*, at 961.

NOTES AND QUESTIONS

1. Would you represent Volpe and, if so, under what conditions concerning your belief as to his guilt?

A. If you say you would not represent Volpe under any circumstances as a retained lawyer, assume that you are a public defender, the case has been assigned to you, and all your efforts to get it assigned elsewhere have failed. Given the Sixth Amendment, Volpe has the right to have *somebody* represent him. Do you think you could provide zealous representation? For an example of an appointed lawyer who might have faced an even more hopeless case, see Messer v. Kemp, 760 F.2d 1080 (11th Cir. 1985), where two appointed lawyers had asked to be "relieved," citing "community pressure," but the third lawyer had to try the death penalty case all the way to the gruesome end.

B. If a hard, but fair, guilty plea were offered, how strongly would you urge Volpe to take it?

C. If the case goes to trial, would you (should you) raise the "rough sex" defense if you have no evidence that it is true? Would your degree of certainty of Volpe's guilt or innocence make any difference to your thinking on this issue?

In this regard, consider American Bar Association, Criminal Justice Standards for the Defense Function (4th ed. 2015), Standard 4–7.7(d): "Defense counsel should not ask a question which implies the existence of a factual predicate for which a good faith belief is lacking." Does this mean that, in the absence of proof, you cannot ask Louima whether anal sex caused his injuries?

2. Do you agree with Professor Alfieri (quoted in the Smith excerpt) that a criminal defense lawyer can adopt a "community-centered" approach and provide zealous defense at the same time?

3. Midway through his federal trial for violating Louima's civil rights, Volpe changed his plea to guilty. He was sentenced to 30 years in federal prison. In 2012, he married Caroline Rose DeMaso in a ceremony in a federal correctional facility in Florida, officiated by a priest. "While it's unclear if the bride wore white, prison policy barred Volpe from wearing a suit. Inmate No. 49477–053 likely sported a prison-issued wedding ensemble of khaki pants and matching shirt with sneakers." Federal prisoners are not permitted conjugal visits. The earliest date for his release is August 3, 2025. Rocco Parascandola, Kerry Burke, Barry Paddock, Larry McShane, "Justin Volpe, cop who sodomized Abner Louima with broomstick inside Brooklyn police station, marries Staten Island woman in Florida prison," New York Daily News, December 5, 2012, http://www.nydailynews.com/new-york/sodomized-abner-louima-marries-staten-island-woman-article-1.1213532.

4. Of course, Justin Volpe is not the only high-profile defendant who would prove difficult to represent. How would you like to be assigned to represent the surviving Boston Marathon bomber, Dzhokhar Tsarnaev? His lawyers argued "that he was pulled into the plot by his radicalized Muslim older brother." Massachusetts has no state death penalty, reflecting the anti-death penalty of many residents. Despite this aversion, the federal jury imposed the death penalty; when it was announced in court, some of the jurors wept. Tom Winter, Andy Thibault and Jon Schuppe, "Tsarnaev Sentenced to Death in Boston Bombing Trial," NBC News, May 15, 2015.

Or consider representing Jerry Sandusky who was tried for 48 counts of child sexual abuse that occurred while he was an assistant football coach at Penn State University. At trial, eight witnesses testified to the details of the sexual acts that Sandusky performed on them. The jury deliberated for two days before convicting on 45 of the 48 charges. Sandusky did not testify. The judge sentenced him to 30–60 years and declared him a "dangerous" child molester who should never be allowed to be free again. As his lawyer, your job would be to cross-examine these men, seeking to discredit their testimony; you could ask why they waited so long to report the alleged abuse and whether they were motivated to lie by the financial gain and publicity. Sandusky made similar allegations in public statements about the case. "Jerry Sandusky," https://en.wikipedia.org/wiki/Jerry_Sandusky (and sources cited by Wikipedia). In sum, you would be putting the victims on trial.

Your client would deny guilt to the end. Sandusky's case ended after the verdict, "as it began: in denial and delusion. 'In my heart, I know I did not do these alleged disgusting acts,' Mr. Sandusky said in a call from the jailhouse * * *. 'My wife has been my only sex partner, and that was after marriage.' " Editorial, "The Sandusky Rape Trial," *New York Times*, October 9, 2012.

2. Ethics and Duties of Defense Counsel

GERALD B. LEFCOURT—RESPONSIBILITIES OF A CRIMINAL DEFENSE ATTORNEY

30 Loyola of Los Angeles Law Review 59 (1996), 59–63.

In twenty-five years of practice, I have seen all sides of the criminal defense bar. I have represented indigent defendants accused of killing police officers, college protesters accused of violating student codes, politicians accused of corruption, and wealthy professionals accused of sophisticated financial crimes. The fact is, in some ways, it is always the same. I truly believe that my responsibility as a lawyer to a client is the same no matter who the defendant and no matter what the crime, and I endeavor to discharge that responsibility as zealously as possible for all.

Society expects a lot from us, all the while bashing us in every possible way. Under the Sixth Amendment we are expected to provide the criminal defendant with a rigorous defense undivided by conflicts. At the same time, in many cases we must fight with judges and prosecutors just to get paid out of frozen funds. We have to worry about whether we will be subpoenaed or have our law offices searched. We have to worry about whether the government is secretly courting our clients to turn against us. And we are told by our friends and by the media that we should not be representing guilty defendants.

These are all situations that drive wedges between our clients and our solemn responsibilities. How do we handle this? What are our fundamental obligations?

I. Responsibilities to the Client

First and foremost, defense attorneys must zealously and uncompromisingly represent the client. They must do so with all their ability and creativity, within the bounds of law. Defense attorneys must accept this duty as sacrosanct and be prepared to do whatever it takes to improve the client's position. That means they may have to offend. They may have to do the uncomfortable thing. They may have to have prosecutors and judges think of them as "the other," not one of them.

Of course, paramount is making use of one's own good judgment. While defense attorneys must take into consideration what the client wants, it is the lawyer's judgment that is being offered to the client, and the lawyer must not be afraid to use it. Defense counsel must be both an advisor and an advocate with courage and devotion. Indeed, some have described the role as a "learned friend," often the only one to whom a criminal defendant may turn in total confidence. The defendant needs counsel to evaluate the risks and advantages of alternative courses of action. But the defendant also needs a broad and comprehensive approach to the predicament.

Devoted service to the client does raise the issue of whether the attorney must do whatever the client wants. I believe that we must allow the client to make informed decisions about all matters, including strategy. An informed and participating client is a critical component of discharging our responsibilities. That is not the same thing as doing something illegal, and a lawyer should leave a case if a serious conflict arises. If defense counsel is truly repulsed by the client, the lawyer should not represent the individual. Lawyers are not busses, and they are not obligated to stop at every stop. * * *

Representing an innocent client is an easy situation for the public to support. In practice it is the hardest because of the overwhelming fear of loss. A factually guilty client, where guilt is apparent, raises society's challenge to the defense attorney: "How can you go into court knowing your client is guilty and try to get him or her off?" If this is a problem for you, you should not be a defense attorney. The committed defense attorney must be prepared to ensure that before the government takes away the client's liberty, the process of doing so is fair and true. Defense attorneys are not advocates for crime. They are as interested as anyone in a safe environment in which to live and raise their families. But they are, or should be, overwhelmingly interested in making sure that the government deprives no one of liberty without doing so consistent with the law. Otherwise, the government is just another thug interfering with a citizen's freedom.

NOTES AND QUESTIONS

1. In the Volpe case study, you considered how it might feel to represent someone who is guilty of a horrific crime. Yet, as Lefcourt suggests, it might be worse to represent an innocent defendant; and this does happen. The father one of the authors of this text—a criminal defense attorney for over 40 years – always maintained this was the hardest part of his job. How would you feel if your innocent client were sentenced to a long prison sentence? To die?

2. Does the Lefcourt excerpt make you more or less likely to make criminal defense work part of your career? More or less likely to go to work for a public defender's office?

3. For those who are thinking about becoming prosecutors, what is your reaction to the picture drawn by Lefcourt?

4. If you had to name one personality aspect that Lefcourt might say was crucial to providing consistent, competent representation of "those people," what would it be?

5. *American Bar Association standards.* The overarching function of defense counsel is "to serve as their clients' counselor and advocate with courage and devotion; to ensure that constitutional and other legal rights of their clients are protected; and to render effective, high-quality legal representation with integrity." American Bar Association, Criminal Justice Standards for the Defense Function (4th ed. 2015). Beyond interviewing the client, there is of course a duty to investigate the case, put this way in Standard 4–4.1:

> Defense counsel's investigation of the merits of the criminal charges should include efforts to secure relevant information in the possession of the prosecution, law enforcement authorities, and others, as well as independent investigation. Counsel's investigation should also include evaluation of the prosecution's evidence (including possible re-testing or re-evaluation of physical, forensic, and expert evidence) and consideration of inconsistencies, potential avenues of impeachment of prosecution witnesses, and other possible suspects and alternative theories that the evidence may raise

For over seven hundred years, counsel in England provided advice but the accused actually pled the case. Though lawyers today do much of the pleading of the case, in some ways the client is still the principal and the lawyer merely the agent or the specialized assistant. For example, Standard 4–5.2. sets out eight categories of decisions belonging to the client:

(i) whether to proceed without counsel;

(ii) what pleas to enter;

(iii) whether to accept a plea offer;

(iv) whether to cooperate with or provide substantial assistance to the government;

(v) whether to waive jury trial;

(vi) whether to testify in his or her own behalf;

(vii) whether to speak at sentencing; and

(viii) whether to appeal.

Other decisions in trial strategy and tactics "should be made by defense counsel, after consultation with the client where feasible and appropriate. Such decisions include how to pursue plea negotiations, how to craft and respond to motions and, at hearing or trial, what witnesses to call, whether and how to conduct cross-examination, what jurors to accept or strike, what motions and objections should be made, and what and how evidence should be introduced." Standard 4–5.2(d).

6. Suppose your client insists on calling his girlfriend as an alibi witness. Having interviewed her, you think the prosecutor will destroy her on cross examination because you believe she is lying about the alibi. Must you call her? Apply Note 5.

7. *And what is a lawyer to do if she thinks her client is going to testify falsely?* Below are the facts in Nix v. Whiteside, 475 U.S. 157, 106 S.Ct. 988, 89 L.Ed.2d 123 (1986).

> Whiteside was convicted of second-degree murder by a jury verdict which was affirmed by the Iowa courts. The killing took place on February 8, 1977, in Cedar Rapids, Iowa. Whiteside and two others went to one Calvin Love's apartment late that night, seeking marihuana. Love was in bed when Whiteside and his companions arrived; an argument between Whiteside and Love over the marihuana ensued. At one point, Love directed his girlfriend to get his "piece," and at another point got up, then returned to his bed. According to Whiteside's testimony, Love then started to reach under his pillow and moved toward Whiteside. Whiteside stabbed Love in the chest, inflicting a fatal wound.
>
> * * * Gary L. Robinson was then appointed and immediately began an investigation. Whiteside gave him a statement that he had stabbed Love as the latter "was pulling a pistol from underneath the pillow on the bed." Upon questioning by Robinson, however, Whiteside indicated that he had not actually seen a gun, but that he was convinced that Love had a gun. No

pistol was found on the premises; shortly after the police search following the stabbing, which had revealed no weapon, the victim's family had removed all of the victim's possessions from the apartment. Robinson interviewed Whiteside's companions who were present during the stabbing, and none had seen a gun during the incident. Robinson advised Whiteside that the existence of a gun was not necessary to establish the claim of self-defense, and that only a reasonable belief that the victim had a gun nearby was necessary even though no gun was actually present.

Until shortly before trial, Whiteside consistently stated to Robinson that he had not actually seen a gun, but that he was convinced that Love had a gun in his hand. About a week before trial, during preparation for direct examination, Whiteside for the first time told Robinson and his associate Donna Paulsen that he had seen something "metallic" in Love's hand. When asked about this, Whiteside responded:

> "[I]n Howard Cook's case there was a gun. If I don't say I saw a gun, I'm dead."

Robinson told Whiteside that such testimony would be perjury and repeated that it was not necessary to prove that a gun was available but only that Whiteside reasonably believed that he was in danger. On Whiteside's insisting that he would testify that he saw "something metallic," Robinson told him, according to Robinson's testimony:

> "[W]e could not allow him to [testify falsely] because that would be perjury, and as officers of the court we would be suborning perjury if we allowed him to do it; * * * I advised him that if he did do that it would be my duty to advise the Court of what he was doing and that I felt he was committing perjury; also, that I probably would be allowed to attempt to impeach that particular testimony."

Robinson also indicated he would seek to withdraw from the representation if Whiteside insisted on committing perjury.

Whiteside testified in his own defense at trial and stated that he "knew" that Love had a gun and that he believed Love was reaching for a gun and he had acted swiftly in self-defense. On cross-examination, he admitted that he had not actually seen a gun in Love's hand. Robinson presented evidence that Love had been seen with a sawed-off shotgun on other occasions, that the police search of the apartment may have been careless, and that the victim's family had removed everything from the apartment shortly after the crime. Robinson presented this evidence to show a basis for Whiteside's asserted fear that Love had a gun.

> The jury returned a verdict of second-degree murder, and Whiteside moved for a new trial, claiming that he had been deprived of a fair trial by Robinson's admonitions not to state that he saw a gun or "something metallic."

Now that you have seen the facts in the case, be sure to notice that the narrow legal issue is not the ethics of defense counsel Robinson in threatening to withdraw. The question for the Court was whether Robinson's threat violated his duty to provide effective assistance of counsel under the Sixth Amendment. We will turn to that issue more broadly later in this chapter.

To answer whether counsel was effective, the Supreme Court considered the ethical question that is the focus of these Notes. The Court examined the "range of professional responses to threatened client perjury acceptable under the Sixth Amendment" right to counsel. From this examination, the Court concluded that "the legal profession has accepted that an attorney's ethical duty to advance the interests of his client is limited by an equally solemn duty to comply with the law and standards of professional conduct; it specifically ensures that the client may not use false evidence."

Writing for the majority, Chief Justice Burger noted that under the norms of professional conduct, a lawyer could ethically reveal a client's perjury to the court or could withdraw from representation if the client threatens perjury. Applying the norms to Robinson's conduct, the Chief Justice noted that the threat to withdraw from representation if Whiteside went through with his false testimony, at most, "deprived Whiteside of his contemplated perjury. Nothing counsel did in any way undermined Whiteside's claim that he believed the victim was reaching for a gun." The Court went on to hold that:

> Considering Robinson's representation of respondent in light of these accepted norms of professional conduct, we discern no failure to adhere to reasonable professional standards that would in any sense make out a deprivation of the Sixth Amendment right to counsel. Whether Robinson's conduct is seen as a successful attempt to dissuade his client from committing the crime of perjury, or whether seen as a "threat" to withdraw from representation and disclose the illegal scheme, Robinson's representation of Whiteside falls well within accepted standards of professional conduct and the range of reasonable professional conduct acceptable under *Strickland*" (see *Strickland v. Washington*, p. 679).

8. Of course, the critical question, largely avoided by the Court, is how did Robinson know that the proposed testimony would be perjury? Suppose Whiteside had said "I recently underwent hypnosis and it refreshed my recollection of what I saw that night." You're his lawyer; you talk to the hypnotist, and she confirms the

client's story and is willing to testify to the general reliability of hypnotically refreshed recollection. What do you do in this case?

9. Or suppose your client said, "I saw something metallic in Love's hand that night, which is why I told you I thought he had a gun. I never told you I didn't see something metallic. I told you I wasn't sure what I saw was a gun. If you thought I said otherwise, you were mistaken." Consider Justice Stevens' concurring opinion in *Whiteside*:

> As we view this case, it appears perfectly clear that respondent intended to commit perjury, that his lawyer knew it, and that the lawyer had a duty . . . to take extreme measures to prevent the perjury from occurring.
> * * *
>
> Nevertheless, beneath the surface of this case there are areas of uncertainty that cannot be resolved today. A lawyer's certainty that a change in his client's recollection is a harbinger of intended perjury—as well as judicial review of such apparent certainty—should be tempered by the realization that, after reflection, the most honest witness may recall (or sincerely believes he recalls) details that he previously overlooked. * * * Thus, one can be convinced—as I am—that this lawyer's actions were a proper way to provide his client with effective representation without confronting the much more difficult questions of what a lawyer must, should, or may do after his client has given testimony that the lawyer does not believe. The answer to such questions may well be colored by the particular circumstances attending the actual event and its aftermath. * * *

Note the difference between not believing one's client and *knowing* the client is committing perjury? Can you tell from Justice Stevens' concurrence how he might have handled this situation if he had been Whiteside's trial lawyer?

10. In examining the norms of professional conduct, the Court in *Whiteside* relied heavily on the Model Rules of Professional Conduct. The current version of Model Rule 3.3 appears to forbid what Whiteside's lawyer did—refuse to allow his client to testify when he believes, but does not know, the testimony to be false. Comment 9 makes plain that the lawyer cannot refuse to offer a defendant's testimony in a criminal case unless he knows it is false:

> Because of the special protections historically provided criminal defendants, . . . this Rule does not permit a lawyer to refuse to offer the testimony of such a client where the lawyer reasonably believes but does not know that the testimony will be false. Unless the lawyer knows the testimony will be false, the lawyer must honor the client's decision to testify.

Did the lawyer in *Nix* have the level of certainty required by Comment 9? What would you have wanted to do in his situation? Notice that the ABA rule and comment are merely models. States are free to adopt their own approach to the perjury problem. Many states, however, have adopted the new Model Rule 3.3.

And, finally, notice that the holding in *Nix v. Whiteside* is not about the ethics of what the defense lawyer did but, rather, whether his actions violated his client's right to effective assistance of counsel. Thus, the holding in *Nix* is unaffected by any changes in the ethical rules. A lawyer who did what Whiteside's lawyer did, whatever the ethical consequences, would still presumably be providing effective assistance of counsel.

11. *Going beyond Comment 9.* The ethical dilemma in *Nix* arises from the easy assumption that the lawyer has co-equal duties to her client and to the court. One does not have to accept this premise. Professor Monroe Freedman argues forcefully that the lawyer's first duty is to the client, which requires the lawyer to facilitate and argue the client's perjured testimony if the client cannot be persuaded not to commit perjury. See Monroe Freedman, *Professional Responsibility of the Criminal Defense Lawyer: The Three Hardest Questions*, 64 Mich. L. Rev. 1469 (1966). Does this appeal to you as a solution to the perjury dilemma?

12. What if *the lawyer learns at trial that the client intends to commit perjury?* Consider the following footnote written by Chief Justice Burger in his *Whiteside* opinion.

> In the evolution of the contemporary standards promulgated by the American Bar Association, an early draft reflects a compromise suggesting that when the disclosure of intended perjury is made during the course of trial, when the withdrawal of counsel would raise difficult questions of a mistrial holding, counsel had the option to let the defendant take the stand but decline to affirmatively assist the presentation of perjury by traditional direct examination. Instead, counsel would stand mute while the defendant undertook to present the false version in narrative form in his own words unaided by any direct examination. This conduct was thought to be a signal at least to the presiding judge that the attorney considered the testimony to be false and was seeking to disassociate himself from that course. Additionally, counsel would not be permitted to discuss the known false testimony in closing arguments. Most courts treating the subject rejected this approach and insisted on a more rigorous standard [refusing to allow the client to testify]. The Eighth Circuit in this case and the Ninth Circuit have expressed approval of the "free narrative" standards.

Which approach do you prefer? Remember, this situation only comes up once a trial is in progress, at which point double jeopardy has attached.

13. *Dealing with pain.* Writing about defense counsel, Susan Bandes concludes that "[t]here may be no other profession whose practitioners are required to deal with so much pain with so little support and guidance." Susan Bandes, *Repression and Denial in Criminal Lawyering*, 9 Buffalo Crim. L. Rev. 339, 342 (2006). As a result, defense lawyers adopt mechanisms to minimize the pain, "including avoidance, denial, suppression, repression," and splitting one's personal and professional life. *Id.* at 366. While some of these mechanisms are healthy in moderation, "the danger is that they will be used to excess, leading to burnout and other forms of distress—both personal and professional." *Id.* at 380.

B. THE RIGHT TO HAVE APPOINTED COUNSEL

The first case in which the Court required a state to provide counsel for indigent defendants was *Powell v. Alabama*, Chapter 1, holding that "in a capital case, where the defendant is unable to employ counsel, and is incapable adequately of making his own defense because of ignorance, feeble-mindedness, illiteracy, or the like, it is the duty of the court, whether requested or not, to assign counsel for him as a necessary requisite of due process of law * * *." The inevitable question after *Powell* was whether its counsel rule would be limited to the narrow set of circumstances set out in the holding or expanded to include most or all indigent defendants.

In Betts v. Brady, 316 U.S. 455, 62 S.Ct. 1252, 86 L.Ed. 1595 (1942), the Court held that there was a due process right to appointed counsel at state expense only when the failure to appoint counsel would be "offensive to the common and fundamental ideas of fairness." This required a case by case determination, with much discretion held by trial judges. At least viewed in light of present-day attitudes about fairness, *Betts* was highly unstable. Could courts continue to say that it is fair to convict indigent defendants of felonies without providing counsel? If not, then why not have a rule requiring appointment? Enter Clarence Gideon, a drifter convicted of breaking and entering a poolroom in Florida. He would provide the Court with a vehicle to change the law.

GIDEON V. WAINWRIGHT

Supreme Court of the United States, 1963.
372 U.S. 335, 83 S.Ct. 792, 9 L.Ed.2d 799.

Along with *Miranda v. Arizona, Gideon v. Wainwright* is probably one of the most famous criminal justice cases to come out of the Warren Court (and co-author Mizrahi's favorite). The fact that this case becomes one of the great legacies of the Warren Court is all the more amazing because the

petition asking the U.S. Supreme Court to hear the case was handwritten by an ill-educated drifter who believed his rights had been violated by the State of Florida and would not back down.

***Gideon* is also another part of the incorporation story we began in Chapter 2. Keep in mind as you read the case that the right to have counsel appointed on felony matters in federal court had long been accepted. It is the question of whether or not that right is applied to the states via the Fourteenth Amendment that puts us on the long road from *Powell v. Alabama*—through *Betts v. Brady* (overruled in *Gideon*)—to *Gideon v. Wainwright.* Thus the decision in *Gideon* hinged on whether or not the "appointment of counsel for indigent defendants in a criminal trial" is a "fundamental right, essential to a fair trial?"**

As you read *Gideon*, note how the Court describes the role of defense counsel and its relationship to a fair trial. If the words sound eerily like the ones you read in *Powell*, they are. What amazes many students, and legal scholars, is that it took our judicial system over thirty years to figure out "that obvious truth."

Also, take a look at Justice Harlan's concurring opinion. Justice Harlan, who believed in the notions of developing due process, argues that *Betts* was not wrongly decided when it was decided but should be decided differently now. The notion of evolving standards of due process gave Justice Black, who wrote *Gideon*, apoplexy. Justice Black was an originalist, although not as stringently as Justice Scalia. Thus, Black clung to the idea (unwisely in the view of the authors of this book) that a ruling in the defendant's favor in *Betts* was dictated by *Powell*.

MR. JUSTICE BLACK delivered the opinion of the Court [joined by CHIEF JUSTICE WARREN, and JUSTICES DOUGLAS, HARLAN, BRENNEN, STEWART, WHITE, and GOLDBERG].

Petitioner was charged in a Florida state court with having broken and entered a poolroom with intent to commit a misdemeanor. This offense is a felony under Florida law. Appearing in court without funds and without a lawyer, petitioner asked the court to appoint counsel for him, whereupon the following colloquy took place:

> "The COURT: Mr. Gideon, I am sorry, but I cannot appoint Counsel to represent you in this case. Under the laws of the State of Florida, the only time the Court can appoint Counsel to represent a Defendant is when that person is charged with a capital offense. I am

> sorry, but I will have to deny your request to appoint Counsel to defend you in this case.
>
> "The DEFENDANT: The United States Supreme Court says I am entitled to be represented by Counsel."

Put to trial before a jury, Gideon conducted his defense about as well as could be expected from a layman. He made an opening statement to the jury, cross-examined the State's witnesses, presented witnesses in his own defense, declined to testify himself, and made a short argument "emphasizing his innocence to the charge contained in the Information filed in this case." The jury returned a verdict of guilty, and petitioner was sentenced to serve five years in the state prison. * * * Since 1942, when *Betts v. Brady* was decided by a divided Court, the problem of a defendant's federal constitutional right to counsel in a state court has been a continuing source of controversy and litigation in both state and federal courts. To give this problem another review here, we granted certiorari. Since Gideon was proceeding *in forma pauperis*, we appointed counsel to represent him and requested both sides to discuss in their briefs and oral arguments the following: "Should this Court's holding in *Betts v. Brady* be reconsidered?"

I

The facts upon which Betts claimed that he had been unconstitutionally denied the right to have counsel appointed to assist him are strikingly like the facts upon which Gideon here bases his federal constitutional claim. Betts was indicted for robbery in a Maryland state court. On arraignment, he told the trial judge of his lack of funds to hire a lawyer and asked the court to appoint one for him. Betts was advised that it was not the practice in that county to appoint counsel for indigent defendants except in murder and rape cases. He then pleaded not guilty, had witnesses summoned, cross-examined the State's witnesses, examined his own, and chose not to testify himself. He was found guilty by the judge, sitting without a jury, and sentenced to eight years in prison. Like Gideon, Betts sought release by habeas corpus, alleging that he had been denied the right to assistance of counsel in violation of the Fourteenth Amendment. Betts was denied any relief, and on review this Court affirmed. It was held that a refusal to appoint counsel for an indigent defendant charged with a felony did not necessarily violate the Due Process Clause of the Fourteenth Amendment, which for reasons given the Court deemed to be the only applicable federal constitutional provision. The Court said:

> "Asserted denial [of due process] is to be tested by an appraisal of the totality of facts in a given case. That which may, in one setting, constitute a denial of fundamental fairness, shocking to the universal sense of

> justice, may, in other circumstances, and in the light of other considerations, fall short of such denial."

Treating due process as "a concept less rigid and more fluid than those envisaged in other specific and particular provisions of the Bill of Rights," the Court held that refusal to appoint counsel under the particular facts and circumstances in the *Betts* case was not so "offensive to the common and fundamental ideas of fairness" as to amount to a denial of due process. Since the facts and circumstances of the two cases are so nearly indistinguishable, we think the *Betts v. Brady* holding if left standing would require us to reject Gideon's claim that the Constitution guarantees him the assistance of counsel. Upon full reconsideration we conclude that *Betts v. Brady* should be overruled.

II

The Sixth Amendment provides, "In all criminal prosecutions, the accused shall enjoy the right * * * to have the Assistance of Counsel for his defence." We have construed this to mean that in federal courts counsel must be provided for defendants unable to employ counsel unless the right is competently and intelligently waived. Betts argued that this right is extended to indigent defendants in state courts by the Fourteenth Amendment. * * * In order to decide whether the Sixth Amendment's guarantee of counsel is of this fundamental nature, the Court in *Betts* set out and considered "[r]elevant data on the subject * * * afforded by constitutional and statutory provisions subsisting in the colonies and the states prior to the inclusion of the Bill of Rights in the national Constitution, and in the constitutional, legislative, and judicial history of the states to the present date." On the basis of this historical data the Court concluded that "appointment of counsel is not a fundamental right, essential to a fair trial." It was for this reason the *Betts* Court refused to accept the contention that the Sixth Amendment's guarantee of counsel for indigent federal defendants was extended to or, in the words of that Court, "made obligatory upon the states by the Fourteenth Amendment." Plainly, had the Court concluded that appointment of counsel for an indigent criminal defendant was "a fundamental right, essential to a fair trial," it would have held that the Fourteenth Amendment requires appointment of counsel in a state court, just as the Sixth Amendment requires in a federal court. * * *

We accept *Betts v. Brady*'s assumption, based as it was on our prior cases, that a provision of the Bill of Rights which is "fundamental and essential to a fair trial" is made obligatory upon the States by the Fourteenth Amendment. We think the Court in *Betts* was wrong, however, in concluding that the Sixth Amendment's guarantee of counsel is not one of these fundamental rights. Ten years before *Betts* *v. Brady*, this Court, after full consideration of all the historical data examined in *Betts*, had unequivocally declared that "the right to the aid of counsel is of this fundamental character." *Powell v. Alabama*. While the Court at the close of its *Powell* opinion did by its language, as this Court frequently does, limit its holding to the particular facts and circumstances of that case, its conclusions about the fundamental nature of the right to counsel are unmistakable. * * *

* * * The fact is that in deciding as it did—that "appointment of counsel is not a fundamental right, essential to a fair trial"—the Court in *Betts v. Brady* made an abrupt break with its own well-considered precedents. In returning to these old precedents, sounder we believe than the new, we but restore constitutional principles established to achieve a fair system of justice. Not only these precedents but also reason and reflection require us to recognize that in our adversary system of criminal justice, any person haled into court, who is too poor to hire a lawyer, cannot be assured a fair trial unless counsel is provided for him. This seems to us to be an obvious truth. Governments, both state and federal, quite properly spend vast sums of money to establish machinery to try defendants accused of crime. Lawyers to prosecute are everywhere deemed essential to protect the public's interest in an orderly society. Similarly, there are few defendants charged with crime, few indeed, who fail to hire the best lawyers they can get to prepare and present their defenses. That government hires lawyers to prosecute and defendants who have the money hire lawyers to defend are the strongest indications of the wide-spread belief that lawyers in criminal courts are necessities, not luxuries. The right of one charged with crime to counsel may not be deemed fundamental and essential to fair trials in some countries, but it is in ours. From the very beginning, our state and national constitutions and laws have laid great emphasis on procedural and substantive safeguards designed to assure fair trials before impartial tribunals in which every defendant stands equal before the law. This noble ideal cannot be realized if the poor man charged with crime has to face his accusers without a lawyer to assist him. * * *

The Court in *Betts v. Brady* departed from the sound wisdom upon which the Court's holding in *Powell v. Alabama* rested. Florida, supported by two other States, has asked that *Betts v. Brady* be left intact. Twenty-two States, as friends of the Court, argue that *Betts* was "an anachronism when handed down" and that it should now be overruled. We agree.

[*The separate opinion of* JUSTICE DOUGLAS, *and the opinion of* JUSTICE CLARK, *concurring in the result, are omitted.*]

MR. JUSTICE HARLAN, concurring.

I agree that *Betts v. Brady* should be overruled, but consider it entitled to a more respectful burial than has been accorded, at least on the part of those of us who were not on the Court when that case was decided.

I cannot subscribe to the view that *Betts v. Brady* represented "an abrupt break with its own well-considered precedents." In 1932, in *Powell v. Alabama*, a capital case, this Court declared that under the particular facts there presented—"the ignorance and illiteracy of the defendants, their youth, the circumstances of public hostility * * * and above all that they stood in deadly peril of their lives"—the state court had a duty to assign counsel for the trial as a necessary requisite of due process of law. It is evident that these limiting facts were not added to the opinion as an after-thought; they were repeatedly emphasized, and were clearly regarded as important to the result.

Thus when this Court, a decade later, decided *Betts v. Brady*, it did no more than to admit of the possible existence of special circumstances in noncapital as well as capital trials, while at the same time insisting that such circumstances be shown in order to establish a denial of due process. The right to appointed counsel had been recognized as being considerably broader in federal prosecutions, see *Johnson v. Zerbst*, 304 U.S. 458, 58 S.Ct. 1019, 82 L.Ed. 1461, but to have imposed these requirements on the States would indeed have been "an abrupt break" with the almost immediate past. The declaration that the right to appointed counsel in state prosecutions, as established in *Powell v. Alabama*, was not limited to capital cases was in truth not a departure from, but an extension of, existing precedent. * * *

The special circumstances rule has been formally abandoned in capital cases, and the time has now come when it should be similarly abandoned in noncapital cases, at least as to offenses which, as the one involved here, carry the possibility of a substantial prison sentence. (Whether the rule should extend to all criminal cases need not now be decided.) This indeed does no more than to make explicit something that has long since been foreshadowed in our decisions. * * *

NOTES AND QUESTIONS

1. In considering whether *Betts* was a "break" with precedent, Black reads *Powell* broadly while Harlan reads it narrowly. Just based on what these two opinions tell us about *Powell*, which do you think is the better reading of *Powell*?

2. Look again at the language of the Sixth Amendment. Does the "right to the Assistance of Counsel" carry with it the correlative duty on the part of state governments to appoint and compensate counsel for indigent defendants?

Not according to *Betts*, which noted the English rule that denied representation by counsel in felony cases (oddly enough, counsel could represent misdemeanor, but not felony, defendants in England at that time). *Betts* read the eighteenth century state constitutional provisions as abrogating the English rule and thus *permitting* the assistance of counsel but not *compelling* appointment of counsel at state expense. The two ideas are conceptually very different. To have the right to do something (own property, for example) is not always the same as having the means to that right guaranteed. But some rights create a correlative duty on the part of government. The right to vote, for example, creates a duty on government to make available the means to vote (voting booths, ballots, etc.), and a duty to ensure that every vote is weighted roughly the same.

Betts accepted that the Sixth Amendment right to counsel creates a correlative duty on the *federal* government to provide counsel to all indigent federal defendants. But it did not find that duty in the due process clause of the Fourteenth Amendment and thus did not find any similar duty on States. *Betts* can thus be explained by the historic importance of federalism in the United States, but it does seem anachronistic in light of the crucial role that lawyers play in trials.

3. *Gideon's Trumpet.* When Clarence Earl Gideon's case was called for trial, the judge asked if he was ready. He responded: "I am not ready, your Honor." After more questioning from the judge, Gideon asked for counsel and the colloquy followed that you saw in *Gideon.* Anthony Lewis, Gideon's Trumpet 9–10 (1964). From prison, he filed a handwritten habeas petition in the Florida Supreme Court and, when he lost there, a handwritten petition for certiorari in the United States Supreme Court. *Id.* at 34–35. Perhaps signaling that the Supreme Court was ready to change its mind about the rule of *Betts*, the Court appointed Abe Fortas to represent Gideon. Fortas, who, of course, went on to become a justice, was in 1962, "a high-powered example of that high-powered species, the Washington lawyer." *Id.* at 48.

After preparing a brief on Gideon's behalf, Fortas sent a copy to Gideon at the state prison. He responded by thanking Fortas for the copy and added: "Everone [sic] and myself thinks it is a very wonderful and brilliant document. I do not know how you have enticed the general public to take such a [sic] interest in this cause. But I must say it makes me feel very good." *Id.* at 138.

During oral argument Fortas sought rather ingeniously to make the federalism argument work for, rather than against, Gideon. He responded to Justice Harlan's argumentative question about federalism by stating that it was "a fundamental principle for which I personally have the highest regard and concern." Then he added the *tour de force*: "Betts against Brady does not incorporate a proper regard for federalism. It requires a case-by-case supervision by this Court of state criminal proceedings, and that cannot be wholesome. * * * Intervention should be in the least abrasive, the least corrosive way possible." *Id.* at 171–72. For Fortas, the "least abrasive" intervention was a bright-line rule that state judges could apply without having federal judges looking over their shoulder. And, as you saw in the case, Fortas won Harlan's vote.

Justice Black dissented in *Betts*. He said to a friend shortly after *Gideon* was announced, "When *Betts v. Brady* was decided, I never thought I'd live to see it overruled." Lewis, *supra* at 192.

And what of Clarence Earl Gideon? Facing a second prosecution after remand, he rejected the trial lawyer the ACLU provided; after interviewing Gideon, this lawyer characterized him as "an irascible but spunky" man. *Id.* at 224. The trial judge then appointed a lawyer whom Gideon grudgingly accepted, the case proceeded to trial, and the jury acquitted. "After nearly two years in the state penitentiary Gideon was a free man. There were tears in his eyes, and he trembled even more than usual * * *." A newspaper reporter asked, "Do you feel like you accomplished something?" Gideon replied: "Well I did." *Id.* at 238.

In 1980, Anthony Lewis's book was turned into a movie of the same name. The great actor Henry Fonda played Clarence Gideon in what was to be one of his last performances. He died in 1982. Dramatic license aside, the movie does a fascinating job portraying Gideon's two trials; the one without counsel and the one with. In the first trial, where Gideon was forced to try and represent himself, you can tell that he is making a reasonable effort, and you can almost grasp the points he is trying to make with his witnesses, but he never quite gets there. In the second trial, his appointed counsel eviscerates the prosecution witnesses to the point where you are left wondering how Gideon ever got charged with this mess in the first place.

Here is something for all of you trivia buffs out there. In the movie, *Gideon's Trumpet,* Gideon's elderly landlady is played by actress Faye Wray. It was her last movie performance. What was her most famous?

4. The *Gideon* Court was unanimous that *Betts* should be overruled, and that the right to counsel should extend at least to indigent state defendants like Gideon, who face felony charges. Can you determine from Justice Black's opinion whether *Gideon* applies more broadly than to felonies?

5. Suppose the judge told *Gideon* prior to trial, "If you are convicted, I won't send you to prison, so I'm not going to give you a lawyer." Would that violate the Constitution as interpreted by *Gideon*?

6. *Is the state prosecuting and defending?* As should be obvious, and we will see in the next Comment, the only way to provide counsel to indigent defendants is some form of public financing. The net effect is that the State is paying the lawyers on both sides. While this fact could hardly be characterized as a formal conflict of interest, it might lead to a more subtle problem. As long as the only client is the State, doesn't this create an incentive for everyone involved to process the cases as smoothly as possible? To plea bargain rather than engage in pre-trial discovery, investigation, and motion practice?

What would you say, as public defender, if your client said to you, "Who's paying your salary, dude? The same dudes as for the [bleeping] DA, right?"

In this context, Justice Blackmun once observed:

> The right to privately chosen and compensated counsel * * * serves broader institutional interests. The "virtual socialization of criminal defense work in this country that would be the result of a widespread abandonment of the right to retain chosen counsel too readily would standardize the provision of criminal-defense services and diminish defense counsel's independence. There is a place in our system of criminal justice for the maverick and the risk taker and for approaches that might not fit into the structured environment of a public defender's office, or that might displease a judge whose preference for nonconfrontational styles of advocacy might influence the judge's appointment decisions.

Caplin & Drysdale, Chartered v. United States, 491 U.S. 617, 109 S.Ct. 2646, 105 L.Ed.2d 528 (1989) (Blackmun, J., dissenting).

Perhaps the public financed "system is designed to institutionalize cost-efficient lawyering arrangements that depend on routinized case processing and discourage individual lawyers assigned to the poor from providing them with adversarial advocacy." Perhaps the "principal effects" of public financed criminal defense "have been to strengthen the private bar's monopoly over fee-paying cases and to enable the state to discipline the poor through the implementation of the criminal sanction." Perhaps the system is "in reality a triumph of the alliance between the organized bar and the state." That, at least, is the view of two scholars. *See* Michael McConville & Chester L. Mirsky, *Understanding Defense of the Poor in State Courts*, 10 Studies in Law, Politics, and Society 217 (1990).

1. And How Is That Working Out for You? A Gathering Storm

Comment on *Gideon's* Legacy

None of the Justices in *Gideon* mentioned the problem of funding the new right to counsel in state courts. In 1963, relatively few federal crimes existed. The problem of paying for lawyers to represent indigent federal defendants was minuscule by comparison to indigent criminal defendants in state court. Three basic forms of public financing have evolved: public-defender programs, contract-attorney representation; and assigned-lawyer programs.

> A public-defender system is an organization of lawyers designated by a jurisdiction to provide representation to indigents in criminal cases. The attorneys who work in a public defender office are full-time salaried government employees working together under a single head defender who has responsibility for indigent representation in a particular jurisdiction—just as prosecutors are typically salaried government employees working under a single district attorney for a jurisdiction. Virtually all states have at least a minority of counties with such defender programs.
>
> Many counties have an assigned-counsel program. Under this approach, often inexperienced or underemployed private practitioners are placed on a list to provide representation to poor defendants on a case-by-case basis. They are paid by the hour (usually well below ordinary rates for attorneys in the community) or receive a flat fee per case. * * *
>
> A contract-attorney program is one in which a jurisdiction enters into an agreement with private attorneys, law firms, or bar associations to represent indigents in the community. Attorneys in such a system often maintain a substantial private practice apart from their contract work. They are paid either on a fixed-price basis (they agree to accept an undetermined number of cases for a determined flat fee) or on a fixed-fee-per-case basis. Frequently, the fees are so low that quality representation, particularly in capital cases, is difficult to obtain.
>
> Today, most large counties employ some combination of these programs.

1 Joshua Dressler & Alan C. Michaels, Understanding Criminal Procedure § 28.03 [B][5] (6th ed. 2013). And sometimes the combination is not the result of a choice

made by the legislature! In March, 2016, the Louisiana public defender system faced an existential crisis.

> The constitutional obligation to provide criminal defense for the poor has been endangered by funding problems across the country, but nowhere else is a system in statewide free fall like Louisiana's, where public defenders represent more than eight out of 10 criminal defendants. Offices throughout the state have been forced to lay off lawyers, leaving those who remain with caseloads well into the hundreds. In seven of the state's 42 judicial districts, poor defendants are already being put on wait lists; here in the 15th, the list is over 2,300 names long and growing.
>
> A system that less than a decade ago was set on a course of long-needed improvement is succumbing to years of draining resources, just as the state is facing a fiscal crisis that could make things much worse. Judges throughout the state have ordered private lawyers to represent people for free, prompting objections from members of the private bar. Some lawyers being conscripted are tax and real estate lawyers without any background in courtrooms or criminal law: "No prior experience is necessary," wrote a district judge in Lafayette in a recent plea for volunteers.
>
> Here in the state with the country's highest incarceration rate, hundreds of those without counsel are sitting in prison, including more than 60 people in New Orleans whose cases have either been put on a wait list or refused altogether by the local public defender's office.
>
> With felony caseloads already far above the professional standard, the public defender concluded that turning down cases was the only ethical option. In January, the American Civil Liberties Union sued over this in federal court.
>
> With the state in deep fiscal distress, and with higher education and health care funding already slashed, further cuts to the public defenders are possible, and perhaps likely.
>
> "Obviously, it's an obligation that they have to be adequately funded," said E. Pete Adams, the executive director of the Louisiana District Attorneys Association. "But it's also an obligation to fund a lot of other things in this state that are right now in jeopardy."

Campbell Robertson, "In Louisiana, the Poor Lack Legal Defense," *New York Times*, March 16, 2016. In the words of Jay Dixon, the chief executive of the

Louisiana Public Defender Board, "We have essentially been managing a financial collapse."

In Vermilion Parish, Louisiana, a public defender office of ten lawyers was, in March, 2016, reduced to a single lawyer, Natasha George. Ms. George handed out applications for defense counsel, telling them they would be put on a "wait list," a list "that is over 2,300 names long and growing." For those denied bail, the waiting would be done in jail.

This is not the first time Louisiana has been accused of systematically failing to provide effective assistance of counsel to indigent defendants. In 1993, Orleans Parish, which includes the city of New Orleans did not even have a public defender's office. Instead, indigent defendants relied on the Orleans Indigent Defender Program (OIDP) which operated under a public defender model and was funded mostly and inconsistently through traffic fines. In the case of State v. Peart, 621 So.2d 780 (1993), the Louisiana Supreme Court found that "the services being provided to indigent defendants in Section E of Orleans Criminal District Court do not in all cases meet constitutionally mandated standards for effective assistance of counsel" and that "the provision of indigent defense services in Section E is in many respects so lacking that defendants who must depend on it are not likely to receive the reasonably effective assistance of counsel the constitution guarantees." The case resulted when OIDP attorney Rick Teissier sued himself for ineffective assistance of counsel after he was denied the funds with which to hire an investigator needed to prepare a case for a defendant charged with armed robbery, aggravated rape, aggravated burglary, attempted armed robbery, and first-degree murder.

The trial court, after a series of hearings on Teissier's motion found the following facts regarding the indigent defense system in New Orleans in the early 1990s.

> At the time of his appointment, Teissier was handling 70 active felony cases. His clients are routinely incarcerated 30 to 70 days before he meets with them. In the period between January 1 and August 1, 1991, Teissier represented 418 defendants. Of these, he entered 130 guilty pleas at arraignment. He had at least one serious case set for trial for every trial date during that period. OIDP has enough funds to hire three investigators. They are responsible for rendering assistance in more than 7,000 cases per year in the ten sections of Criminal District Court, plus cases in Juvenile Court, Traffic Court, and Magistrates' Court. In a routine case, Teissier receives no investigative support at all. There are no funds for expert witnesses. OIDP's library is inadequate.

The trial judge ordered a number of short and long-term remedies including reduced case-loads, funding for an improved library and an investigator for Teissier, and appointment of members of the bar to represent indigent defendants. In addition, the trial judge ordered that the state legislature "provide funds to OIDP to pay additional attorneys, secretaries, paralegals, law clerks, investigators, and expert witnesses." (Done correctly, criminal defense is not cheap). Although agreeing with the trial court regarding the constitutional failures of the OIDP, the Louisiana Supreme Court reversed the remedies ordered at the trial court level:

> If legislative action is not forthcoming and indigent defense reform does not take place, this Court, in the exercise of its constitutional and inherent power and supervisory jurisdiction, may find it necessary to employ the more intrusive and specific measures it has thus far avoided to ensure indigent defendants receive reasonably effective assistance of counsel. * * * We decline at this time to undertake these more intrusive and specific measures because this Court should not tread lightly tread in the affairs of other branches of government and because the legislature ought to assess such measures in the first instance.

In 2007, at least partly in response to *Peart* and later cases finding the statewide public defender system to be inadequate, the Louisiana legislature passed the Louisiana Public Defender Act of 2007, "designed to provide effective legal representation to criminal defendants who are unable to afford an attorney, consistent with the right to counsel in our criminal courts, mindful of the need for law and order and an appreciation of victims' rights." It would appear, given what we now see happening in Louisiana, that the public defender funding act was not successful.

The problem of underfunded public defense is not, of course, limited to Louisiana. As Professor John Pfaff notes:

> [S]ince 1995, real spending on indigent defense has fallen, by 2 percent, even as the number of felony cases has risen by approximately 40 percent.
>
> Not surprisingly, public defense finds itself starved of resources while facing impossible caseloads that mock the idea of justice for the poor.
>
> In Fresno, Calif., for instance, public defenders have caseloads that are four times the recommended maximum of around 150. In Minnesota, one public defender followed by a reporter estimated that

> he had about 12 minutes to devote to each client that day. There is no way these lawyers can manage the cases being thrown at them. * * *
>
> To make things worse, 43 states now require indigent defendants to pay at least a portion of their lawyers' fees, even though these defendants are by definition indisputably poor. [And in at least one state, failure] to pay is a crime. Someone who qualifies as indigent may be acquitted, only to be convicted of being too poor to pay for the legal services the Constitution requires the state to provide.

John Pfaff, "A Mockery of Justice for the Poor," *New York Times*, April 29, 2016.

2. When Does the State Foot the Bill?: Applying *Gideon*

From the time of *Gideon v. Wainwright*, all indigent defendants charged with a felony in state courts must have an attorney appointed for them at the State's expense. But while broader than the very narrow holding in *Powell* (which applied only to particularly vulnerable defendants in capital cases), the holding in *Gideon* raised as many questions as it answered. In Scott v. Illinois, 440 U.S. 367, 99 S.Ct. 1158, 59 L.Ed.2d 383 (1979), Justice Rehnquist described some of the difficulties in applying rights developed for the federal government to the states:

> The process of incorporation creates special difficulties, for the state and federal contexts are often different and application of the same principle may have ramifications distinct in degree and kind. The range of human conduct regulated by state criminal laws is much broader than that of the federal criminal laws, particularly on the "petty" offense part of the spectrum. As a matter of constitutional adjudication, we are, therefore, less willing to extrapolate an already extended line when, although the general nature of the principle sought to be applied is clear, its precise limits and their ramifications become less so.

Applying Gideon at Trial

At the end of *Gideon*, Justice Black specified that "whether the rule should extend to all criminal cases need not now be decided." It did not take long for this question to return to the Court as states struggled to figure out when they had to provide counsel and when they did not. *Gideon*, while rightly decided, imposed a heavy financial cost on the states that they were not—and in many cases are still not—prepared to handle. Not surprisingly, states sought to limit the types of cases where the appointment of counsel for indigent defendants was required; to limit the impact of *Gideon*.

A logical distinction to draw might have been between felonies and misdemeanors and many states argued for just this distinction. But in *Argersinger v. Hamlin*, 407 U.S. 25, 92 S.Ct. 2006, 32 L.Ed.2d 530 (1972), the Court declined to go in this direction. Instead, the distinction drawn was between imprisonment or not; a sentence of incarceration, even for one day, could not be imposed if the defendant did not have, or waive, counsel.

Argersinger was charged in state court in Florida with carrying a concealed weapon. Under Florida law, that offense was punishable by up to six months in prison, a $1000 fine, or both. Unrepresented, Argersinger was convicted and sentenced to 90 days in jail after a bench trial. Appealing, Argersinger argued that "being deprived of his right to counsel, he was unable as an indigent layman properly to raise and present to the trial court good and sufficient defenses to the charge for which he stands convicted." The Florida Supreme Court affirmed the conviction, holding that "the right to court-appointed counsel extends only to trials 'for non-petty offenses punishable by more than six months imprisonment'."

The U.S. Supreme Court, in an opinion written by Justice Douglas, disagreed. After noting that the assistance of counsel was often part and parcel of misdemeanor cases in England and in the original thirteen colonies, Justice Douglas argued that there was nothing in the language or history of the Sixth Amendment right to counsel "to indicate that it was intended to embody a retraction of the right in petty offenses wherein the common law previously did require that counsel be provided." Moving to more modern times, Justice Douglas quoted some of the eloquent language from *Gideon* setting out the importance of counsel:

> [I]n our adversary system of criminal justice, any person haled into court, who is too poor to hire a lawyer, cannot be assured a fair trial unless counsel is provided for him. This seems to us to be an obvious truth. Governments, both state and federal, quite properly spend vast sums of money to establish machinery to try defendants accused of crime. Lawyers to prosecute are everywhere deemed essential to protect the public's interest in an orderly society. * * * That government hires lawyers to prosecute and defendants *who have the money* [emphasis added] hire lawyers to defend are the strongest indications of the widespread belief that lawyers in criminal courts are necessities, not luxuries.

Even though both *Powell* and *Gideon* involved felonies, Justice Douglas went on to note that the rationale for both cases applied to any trial where the accused might be deprived of liberty, even for a short time.

> The requirement of counsel may well be necessary for a fair trial even in a petty-offense prosecution. We are by no means convinced that legal and constitutional questions involved in a case that actually leads to imprisonment even for a brief period are any less complex than when a person can be sent off for six months or more.

In a fascinating discussion of the problems found in misdemeanor courts in 1972, ones that sound depressingly familiar today, the Court in *Argersinger* went on to set out the obstacles and challenges defendants face when charged with 'petty offenses' including the pressure to plead guilty, the volume of cases leading to a preference for speedy dispositions, and inadequate attention paid to individual defendants during busy court calendars. The Court even cited an ACLU study that concluded that defendants represented by counsel in misdemeanor cases were "five times as likely to emerge from police court with all charges dismissed as . . . defendants who face similar charges without counsel." The Court concluded that:

> * * * the problems associated with misdemeanor and petty offenses often require the presence of counsel to insure the accused a fair trial. * * * [Furthermore] the prospect of imprisonment for however short a time will seldom be viewed by the accused as a trivial or 'petty' matter and may well result in quite serious repercussions affecting his career and his reputation. We hold, therefore, that absent a knowing and intelligent waiver, no person may be imprisoned for any offense, whether classified as petty, misdemeanor, or felony, unless he was represented by counsel at his trial."

The defendant in *Argersinger* was in actuality deprived of his liberty. But what happens when imprisonment is an option—an *authorized* penalty—but not imposed. In *Scott v. Illinois*, the defendant was fined $50 following a conviction for shoplifting merchandise worth less than $150. The maximum penalty for that offense was a $500 fine or one year in jail, or both. Scott argued that his conviction violated his Sixth and Fourteenth Amendment rights because *Argersinger* required the appointment of counsel any time imprisonment was a possible sentence. The Illinois Supreme Court upheld Scott's conviction and the U.S. Supreme Court agreed:

> Although the intentions of the *Argersinger* Court are not unmistakably clear from its opinion, we conclude today that *Argersinger* did indeed delimit the constitutional right to appointed counsel in state criminal proceedings. Even were the matter *res nova*, we believe that the central premise of *Argersinger*—that actual imprisonment is a penalty different in kind from fines or the mere threat of imprisonment—is

> eminently sound and warrants adoption of actual imprisonment as the line defining the constitutional right to appointment of counsel. *Argersinger* has proved reasonably workable, whereas any extension would create confusion and impose unpredictable, but necessarily substantial, costs on 50 quite diverse States. We therefore hold that the Sixth and Fourteenth Amendments to the United States Constitution require only that no indigent criminal defendant be sentenced to a term of imprisonment unless the State has afforded him the right to assistance of appointed counsel in his defense. * * *

Thus, after *Argersinger* and *Scott*, the dividing line for appointment of indigent defense counsel is one of actual imprisonment. If counsel is not appointed, the judge cannot use the imprisonment option even if it is available.

In his dissent, Justice Brennan, joined by Justices Marshall and Stevens, argue for a more bright-line rule: that if imprisonment is an *authorized* penalty, appointment of counsel is required under the Sixth and Fourteenth Amendments:

> *Argersinger* thus [after *Scott*] established a "two dimensional" test for the right to counsel: the right attaches to any "nonpetty" offense punishable by more than six months in jail and in addition to any offense where actual incarceration is likely regardless of the maximum authorized penalty.
>
> The offense of "theft" with which Scott was charged is certainly not a "petty" one. It is punishable by a sentence of up to one year in jail. Unlike many traffic or other "regulatory" offenses, it carries the moral stigma associated with common-law crimes traditionally recognized as indicative of moral depravity. The State indicated at oral argument that the services of a professional prosecutor were considered essential to the prosecution of this offense. Likewise, nonindigent defendants charged with this offense would be well advised to hire the "best lawyers they can get." Scott's right to the assistance of appointed counsel is thus plainly mandated by the logic of the Court's prior cases, including *Argersinger* itself.

In addition to the concerns noted in the dissent to *Scott*, the *Argersinger* and *Scott* rulings have also been criticized for requiring trial judges to come equipped with crystal balls on their bench. Absent *Argersinger*, a judge in a misdemeanor or traffic court would not be called upon to make a prediction about the sanction to be imposed if the defendant is found guilty. *Argersinger* requires precisely that prediction. (See Sherry F. Colb, *Freedom From Incarceration: Why Is This Right Different*

From All Other Rights?, 69 N.Y.U. L. Rev. 781 (1994), arguing that freedom from incarceration is a separate due process right and using *Argersinger* to demonstrate the Court's commitment to that right).

Many states also require restitution from those convicted of crimes. One way to create incentives for defendants to pay these sums is to impose a jail sentence and suspend it on the condition that the defendant pay restitution plus any fines and court costs that might also be imposed. If the defendant does not pay, within whatever time period the court sets, the jail sentence can be "activated" by a showing of non-payment. Do indigent defendants facing that sentencing structure have a right to counsel under *Argersinger*? Yes, the Court held by a 5–4 margin in Alabama v. Shelton, 535 U.S. 654, 122 S.Ct. 1764, 152 L.Ed.2d 888 (2002). Focusing on the fact that the Alabama probation revocation hearing would not permit the defendant to inquire into the basis of his conviction, the Court adopted what amounts to a prophylactic rule. Because defendants might later face incarceration without having had counsel at the trial where guilt was determined, the Court held that courts cannot impose suspended sentences on indigent defendants without providing counsel at trial or finding waiver.

Applying Gideon on Appeal

So far we have been looking at cases at the trial court level where the law is settled that the assistance of counsel is essential for a fair trial (at least where imprisonment is concerned) and that the right to counsel cannot be predicated on a defendants ability to pay. But what happens when a convicted defendant wants to appeal? How long, and through how many proceedings, is the State required to foot the bill for appointed counsel?

Every defendant convicted at trial gets one appeal of right in a criminal case; "one bite at the apple" as the saying goes. But does a side of appointed counsel go with that apple? In Douglas v. California, 372 U.S. 353, 83 S.Ct. 814, 9 L.Ed.2d 811 (1963), the Court said yes. In *Douglas*:

> Petitioners, Bennie Will Meyes and William Douglas, were jointly tried and convicted in a California court on an information charging them with 13 felonies. A single public defender was appointed to represent them. At the commencement of the trial, the defender moved for a continuance, stating that the case was very complicated, that he was not as prepared as he felt he should be because he was handling a different defense every day, and that there was a conflict of interest between the petitioners requiring the appointment of separate counsel for each of them. This motion was denied. Thereafter, petitioners

> dismissed the defender, claiming he was unprepared, and again renewed motions for separate counsel and for a continuance. These motions also were denied, and petitioners were ultimately convicted by a jury of all 13 felonies, which included robbery, assault with a deadly weapon, and assault with intent to commit murder. Both were given prison terms. Both appealed as of right to the California District Court of Appeal. That court affirmed their convictions. Both Meyes and Douglas then petitioned for further discretionary review in the California Supreme Court, but their petitions were denied without a hearing.
>
> Although several questions are presented in the petition for certiorari, we address ourselves to only one of them. The record shows that petitioners requested, and were denied, the assistance of counsel on appeal, even though it plainly appeared they were indigents. In denying petitioners' requests, the California District Court of Appeal stated that it had "gone through" the record and had come to the conclusion that "no good whatever could be served by appointment of counsel." The District Court of Appeal was acting in accordance with a California rule of criminal procedure which provides that state appellate courts, upon the request of an indigent for counsel, may make "an independent investigation of the record and determine whether it would be of advantage to the defendant or helpful to the appellate court to have counsel appointed. * * * After such investigation, appellate courts should appoint counsel if in their opinion it would be helpful to the defendant or the court, and should deny the appointment of counsel only if in their judgment such appointment would be of no value to either the defendant or the court."

The Court found that California's procedures discriminated against certain convicted defendants because of their poverty, noting that "there can be no equal justice where the kind of appeal a man enjoys depends on the amount of money he has." In the same way that *Powell* and *Gideon* described the importance of counsel at the trial level, Justice Douglas described the important role counsel plays on appeal.

> In spite of California's forward treatment of indigents, under its present practice the type of an appeal a person is afforded in the District Court of Appeal hinges upon whether or not he can pay for the assistance of counsel. If he can the appellate court passes on the merits of his case only after having the full benefit of written briefs and oral argument by counsel. If he cannot the appellate court is forced to

> prejudge the merits before it can even determine whether counsel should be provided. At this stage in the proceedings only the barren record speaks for the indigent, and, unless the printed pages show that an injustice has been committed, he is forced to go without a champion on appeal. Any real chance he may have had of showing that his appeal has hidden merit is deprived him when the court decides on an *ex parte* examination of the record that the assistance of counsel is not required.

In his dissent, Justice Harlan viewed the need for counsel on appeal differently, and saw a distinction at the appellate level from the principles enunciated in *Gideon.*

> We have today held that in a case such as the one before us, there is an absolute right to the services of counsel at trial. *Gideon v. Wainwright.* But the appellate procedures involved here stand on an entirely different constitutional footing. *First,* appellate review is in itself not required by the Fourteenth Amendment, and thus the question presented is the narrow one whether the State's rules with respect to the appointment of counsel are so arbitrary or unreasonable, *in the context of the particular appellate procedure that it has established,* as to require their invalidation. *Second,* the kinds of questions that may arise on appeal are circumscribed by the record of the proceedings that led to the conviction; they do not encompass the large variety of tactical and strategic problems that must be resolved at the trial. *Third,* as California applies its rule, the indigent appellant receives the benefit of expert and conscientious legal appraisal of the merits of his case on the basis of the trial record, and whether or not he is assigned counsel, is guaranteed full consideration of his appeal. It would be painting with too broad a brush to conclude that under these circumstances an appeal is just like a trial. * * *

Whose approach do you agree with: Justice Douglas or Justice Harlan? Does it matter that the *Douglas* case dealt with a defendant's first appeal, granted as a matter of right from every criminal conviction?

In Ross v. Moffitt, 417 U.S. 600, 94 S.Ct. 2437, 41 L.Ed.2d 341 (1974), the Court said yes, it does matter. An appeal of right (mandatory review) is normally held at a state's intermediate level of appellate review. If either party is unhappy with the decision, they can appeal to the state's Supreme Court (In New York, the state's highest court is called the Court of Appeals while the trial court is called the Supreme Court—just in case the law is not confusing enough at times). In almost all cases in all states (death penalty appeals aside), appeals at the State Supreme Court level are at the court's discretion (discretionary review); it is the court's choice whether to hear the appeal or not. In *Ross*, the key to Justice Rehnquist's opinion is the process that takes place in requesting discretionary review:

> The facts show that respondent, in connection with his Mecklenburg County conviction, received the benefit of counsel in examining the record of his trial and in preparing an appellate brief on his behalf for the state Court of Appeals. Thus, prior to his seeking discretionary review in the State Supreme Court, his claims had "once been presented by a lawyer and passed upon by an appellate court." We do not believe that it can be said, therefore, that a defendant in respondent's circumstances is denied meaningful access to the North Carolina Supreme Court simply because the State does not appoint counsel to aid him in seeking review in that court. At that stage he will have, at the very least, a transcript or other record of trial proceedings, a brief on his behalf in the Court of Appeals setting forth his claims of error, and in many cases an opinion by the Court of Appeals disposing of his case. These materials, supplemented by whatever submission respondent may make *pro se*, would appear to provide the Supreme Court of North Carolina with an adequate basis for its decision to grant or deny review.
>
> We are fortified in this conclusion by our understanding of the function served by discretionary review in the North Carolina Supreme Court. The critical issue in that court, as we perceive it, is not whether there has been "a correct adjudication of guilt" in every individual case, see *Griffin v. Illinois*, but rather whether "the subject matter of the appeal has significant public interest," whether "the cause involves legal principles of major significance to the jurisprudence of the State," or whether the decision below is in probable conflict with a decision of the Supreme Court. The Supreme Court may deny certiorari even though it believes that the decision of the Court of Appeals was incorrect, since a decision which appears incorrect may nevertheless fail to satisfy any of the criteria discussed above. Once a defendant's claims of error are organized and presented in a lawyerlike fashion to the Court of Appeals, the justices of the Supreme Court of North Carolina who make the decision to grant or deny discretionary review should be able to ascertain whether his case satisfies the standards established by the legislature for such review.

Do you agree with Justice Rehnquist? If you think a state Supreme Court has considerable discretion over the cases it hears, consider appeals to the U.S. Supreme Court. Out of between 7,000–8,000 requests (petitions for certiorari) each year, only about 80 are set for oral argument. That does not mean that every case that was refused was correctly decided in the courts below—far from it. But as Justice Rehnquist noted in *Ross*, not every incorrect decision gets reviewed by the state's highest court, let alone the highest court in the land. More often than not, "one bite at the apple" means just that.

NOTES AND QUESTIONS

1. *Free transcripts.* Griffin v. Illinois, 351 U.S. 12, 76 S.Ct. 585, 100 L.Ed. 891 (1956), held that a state must provide a transcript free of charge to indigent defendants when it is necessary for them to obtain "adequate appellate review of their alleged trial errors." Can you distinguish *Griffin* from *Douglas*? Justice Harlan dissented in both, but could you have joined the majority in *Griffin* and the dissent in *Douglas*?

2. *Another (losing) war story.* You may be cynical about the value of having had a lawyer prepare the first appeal if the defendant has to face the second level of appeal without a lawyer. We invite the cynics to read Tansil v. Tansil, 673 S.W.2d 131 (Tenn.1984), a case in which a civil appellant discharged the lawyer who had represented him at trial and in the intermediate appellate court. The appellant represented himself for the rest of the process. He filed a handwritten petition for discretionary review in the state supreme court, which was granted, and then a badly-typed and poorly-organized brief roughly based on his lawyer's brief in the court of appeals. He also argued the case before the Tennessee Supreme Court, at one point rising from his seat among the spectators to yell that appellee's lawyer was a liar. The Chief Justice threatened appellant with expulsion, and no more outbursts occurred. The *pro se* appellant won 5–0. (One of the authors of the present casebook represented appellee; how do you explain to your client that you lost to a *pro se* appellant?).

3. The easiest way to read *Ross* is as a distinction between an appeal of right and a discretionary appeal. But a later case suggests more of a distinction between a defendant's first appeal and any subsequent appeals. In Halbert v. Michigan, 545 U.S. 605, 125 S.Ct. 2582, 162 L.Ed.2d 552 (2005), Michigan did not allow automatic appeal from a conviction resulting from a guilty plea or a plea of nolo contendere. Instead, the state court of appeals could *permit* an appeal in those cases, depending on the merits of the application. The state in *Halbert* argued that the discretionary nature of the appeal meant that the case was governed by *Ross*, while the defendant argued that the lack of a lawyer to brief and file the first appeal moved the case within the ambit of *Douglas*. The Court agreed with the defendant, noting the emphasis in *Ross* on the

fact that, under the state system there, a lawyer had already prepared one appeal and thus

> will have reviewed the trial court record, researched the legal issues, and prepared a brief reflecting that review and research. The defendant seeking second-tier review may also be armed with an opinion of the intermediate appellate court addressing the issues counsel raised. A first-tier review applicant, forced to act *pro se*, will face a record unreviewed by appellate counsel, and will be equipped with no attorney's brief prepared for, or reasoned opinion by, a court of review.

In Michigan, the court of appeals ruling on the application from a plea-convicted defendant "provides the first, and likely the only, direct review the defendant's conviction and sentence will receive." The Court then noted: "Navigating the appellate process without a lawyer's assistance is a perilous endeavor for a layperson, and well beyond the competence of individuals, like Halbert, who have little education, learning disabilities, and mental impairments." Michigan's system was thus unconstitutional under the authority of *Douglas* because it did not require lawyers for all defendants who wish to appeal their convictions to the first appellate court.

Justice Thomas's dissent, joined by Justice Scalia and, in large part by Chief Justice Rehnquist, argued that the risk to the innocent is less significant in *Halbert* than in *Douglas* because defendants who accept a conviction are less likely to be innocent. Moreover, "When a defendant pleads in open court, there is less need for counsel to develop the record and refine claims to present to an appellate court." Thus, because lawyers are less necessary, and the risk to the innocent, lower, the dissent did not find a violation of due process.

Which view of the right to counsel in the Michigan appellate system do you prefer?

C. The Right to Decide Whether to Have Counsel

Does the right "to have the Assistance of Counsel for his defense" imply the right *not* to have a lawyer—that is the right to represent oneself?

FARETTA V. CALIFORNIA

Supreme Court of the United States, 1975.
422 U.S. 806, 95 S.Ct. 2525, 45 L.Ed.2d 562.

Up until now we have looked at the establishment of the right to counsel and when it applies. What if you do not want counsel? That is the choice made by the defendant in *Faretta v. California.* In law, a defendant representing himself is referred to as proceeding *pro se*—otherwise known

as a prosecutor's worst nightmare. Note that waivers of the right to counsel, as with other waivers we have seen, must be voluntary and intelligent.

The Notes and Case Study after *Faretta* discuss the right to represent oneself in appeals and also raise the issue of how to approach a defendant is suffering from mental illness that renders him incompetent to represent himself.

MR. JUSTICE STEWART delivered the opinion of the Court [joined by JUSTICES DOUGLAS, BRENNAN, WHITE, MARSHALL, and POWELL].

The Sixth and Fourteenth Amendments of our Constitution guarantee that a person brought to trial in any state or federal court must be afforded the right to the assistance of counsel before he can be validly convicted and punished by imprisonment. This clear constitutional rule has emerged from a series of cases decided here over the last 50 years. The question before us now is whether a defendant in a state criminal trial has a constitutional right to proceed *without* counsel when he voluntarily and intelligently elects to do so. Stated another way, the question is whether a State may constitutionally hale a person into its criminal courts and there force a lawyer upon him, even when he insists that he wants to conduct his own defense. It is not an easy question, but we have concluded that a State may not constitutionally do so.

I

Anthony Faretta was charged with grand theft in an information filed in the Superior Court of Los Angeles County, Cal. At the arraignment, the Superior Court Judge assigned to preside at the trial appointed the public defender to represent Faretta. Well before the date of trial, however, Faretta requested that he be permitted to represent himself. Questioning by the judge revealed that Faretta had once represented himself in a criminal prosecution, that he had a high school education, and that he did not want to be represented by the public defender because he believed that that office was "very loaded down with * * * a heavy case load." The judge responded that he believed Faretta was "making a mistake" and emphasized that in further proceedings Faretta would receive no special favors. Nevertheless, after establishing that Faretta wanted to represent himself and did not want a lawyer, the judge, in a "preliminary ruling," accepted Faretta's waiver of the assistance of counsel. The judge indicated, however, that he might reverse this ruling if it later appeared that Faretta was unable adequately to represent himself.

Several weeks thereafter, but still prior to trial, the judge *sua sponte* held a hearing to inquire into Faretta's ability to conduct his own defense, and questioned him specifically about both the hearsay rule and the state law governing the challenge of potential jurors. After consideration of consideration of Faretta's answers, and observation of his demeanor, the judge ruled that Faretta had not made an intelligent and knowing waiver of his right to the assistance of counsel, and also ruled that Faretta had no constitutional right to conduct his own defense. The judge, accordingly, reversed his earlier ruling permitting self-representation and again appointed the public defender to represent Faretta. Faretta's subsequent request for leave to act as co-counsel was rejected, as were his efforts to make certain motions on his own behalf. Throughout the subsequent trial, the judge required that Faretta's defense be conducted only through the appointed lawyer from the public defender's office. At the conclusion of the trial, the jury found Faretta guilty as charged, and the judge sentenced him to prison. * * *

II

In the federal courts, the right of self-representation has been protected by statute since the beginnings of our Nation. Section 35 of the Judiciary Act of 1789, 1 Stat. 73, 92, enacted by the First Congress and signed by President Washington one day before the Sixth Amendment was proposed, provided that "in all the courts of the United States, the parties may plead and manage their own causes personally or by the assistance of * * * counsel * * *." The right is currently codified in 28 U.S.C. § 1654.

With few exceptions, each of the several States also accords a defendant the right to represent himself in any criminal case. The constitutions of 36 States explicitly confer that right. Moreover, many state courts have expressed the view that the right is also supported by the Constitution of the United States. * * *

III

This consensus is soundly premised. The right of self-representation finds support in the structure of the Sixth Amendment, as well as in the English and colonial jurisprudence from which the Amendment emerged.

A

The Sixth Amendment includes a compact statement of the rights necessary to a full defense:

> "In all criminal prosecutions, the accused shall enjoy the right * * * to be informed of the nature and cause of the accusation; to be confronted with the witnesses against him; to have compulsory process for obtaining witnesses in his favor, and to have the Assistance of Counsel for his defence."

Because these rights are basic to our adversary system of criminal justice, they are part of the "due process of law" that is guaranteed by the Fourteenth Amendment to defendants in the criminal courts of the States. The rights to notice, confrontation, and compulsory process, when taken together, guarantee that a criminal charge may be answered in a manner now considered fundamental to the fair administration of American justice—through the calling and interrogation of favorable witnesses, the cross-examination of adverse witnesses, and the orderly introduction of evidence. In short, the Amendment constitutionalizes the right in an adversary criminal trial to make a defense as we know it.

The Sixth Amendment does not provide merely that a defense shall be made for the accused; it grants to the accused personally the right to make his defense. It is the accused, not counsel, who must be "informed of the nature and cause of the accusation," who must be "confronted with the witnesses against him," and who must be accorded "compulsory process for obtaining witnesses in his favor." Although not stated in the Amendment in so many words, the right to self-representation—to make one's own defense personally—is thus necessarily implied by the structure of the Amendment. The right to defend is given directly to the accused; for it is he who suffers the consequences if the defense fails.

The counsel provision supplements this design. It speaks of the "assistance" of counsel, and an assistant, however expert, is still an assistant. The language and spirit of the Sixth Amendment contemplate that counsel, like the other defense tools guaranteed by the Amendment, shall be an aid to a willing defendant—not an organ of the State interposed between an unwilling defendant and his right to defend himself personally. To thrust counsel upon the accused, against his considered wish, thus violates the logic of the Amendment. In such a case, counsel is not an assistant, but a master; and the right to make a defense is stripped of the personal character upon which the Amendment insists. It is true that when a defendant chooses to have a lawyer manage and present his case, law and tradition may allocate to the counsel the power to make binding decisions of trial strategy in many areas. This allocation can only be justified, however, by the defendant's consent, at the outset, to accept counsel as his representative. An unwanted counsel "represents" the defendant only through a tenuous and unacceptable legal fiction. Unless the accused has acquiesced in such representation, the defense presented is not the defense guaranteed him by the Constitution, for, in a very real sense, it is not *his* defense.

B

The Sixth Amendment, when naturally read, thus implies a right of self-representation. This reading is reinforced by the Amendment's roots in English legal history. * * *

By the common law of [the 17th century], it was not representation by counsel but self-representation that was the practice in prosecutions for serious crime. At one time, every litigant was required to "appear before the court in his own person and conduct his own cause in his own words." While a right to counsel developed early in civil cases and in cases of misdemeanor, a prohibition against the assistance of counsel continued for centuries in prosecutions for felony or treason. Thus, in the 16th and 17th centuries the accused felon or traitor stood alone, with neither counsel nor the benefit of other rights—to notice, confrontation, and compulsory process—that we now associate with a genuinely fair adversary proceeding. The trial was merely a "long argument between the prisoner and the counsel for the Crown." As harsh as this now seems, at least "the prisoner was allowed to make what statements he liked. * * * Obviously this public oral trial presented many more opportunities to a prisoner than the secret enquiry based on written depositions, which, on the continent, had taken the place of a trial * * *." * * *

C

In the American Colonies the insistence upon a right of self-representation was, if anything, more fervent than in England.

The colonists brought with them an appreciation of the virtues of self-reliance and a traditional distrust of lawyers. When the Colonies were first settled, "the lawyer was synonymous with the cringing Attorneys-General and Solicitors-General of the Crown and the arbitrary Justices of the King's Court, all bent on the conviction of those who opposed the King's prerogatives, and twisting the law to secure convictions." This prejudice gained strength in the Colonies where "distrust of lawyers became an institution." Several Colonies prohibited pleading for hire in the 17th century. The prejudice persisted into the 18th century as "the lower classes came to identify lawyers with the upper class." The years of Revolution and Confederation saw an upsurge of antilawyer sentiment, a "sudden revival, after the War of the Revolution, of the old dislike and distrust of lawyers as a class." In the heat of these sentiments the Constitution was forged.

This is not to say that the Colonies were slow to recognize the value of counsel in criminal cases. Colonial judges soon departed from ancient English practice and allowed accused felons the aid of counsel for their defense. At the same time, however, the basic right of self-representation was never questioned. We have found no instance where a colonial court required a defendant in a criminal case to accept as his representative an unwanted lawyer. Indeed, even where counsel was permitted, the general practice continued to be self-representation.

The right of self-representation was guaranteed in many colonial charters and declarations of rights. These early documents establish that the "right to counsel" meant to the colonists a right to choose between pleading through a lawyer and representing oneself. After the Declaration of Independence, the right of self-representation, along with other rights basic to the making of a defense, entered the new state constitutions in wholesale fashion. The right to counsel was clearly thought to supplement the primary right of the accused to defend himself, utilizing his personal rights to notice, confrontation, and compulsory process. And when the Colonies or newly independent States provided by statute rather than by constitution for court appointment of counsel in criminal cases, they also meticulously preserved the right of the accused to defend himself personally. * * *

In sum, there is no evidence that the colonists and the Framers ever doubted the right of self-representation, or imagined that this right might be considered inferior to the right of assistance of counsel. To the contrary, the colonists and the Framers, as well as their English ancestors, always conceived of the right to counsel as an "assistance" for the accused, to be used at his option, in defending himself. The Framers selected in the Sixth Amendment a form of words that necessarily implies the right of self-representation. That conclusion is supported by centuries of consistent history.

IV

There can be no blinking the fact that the right of an accused to conduct his own defense seems to cut against the grain of this Court's decisions holding that the Constitution requires that no accused can be convicted and imprisoned unless he has been accorded the right to the assistance of counsel. For it is surely true that the basic thesis of those decisions is that the help of a lawyer is essential to assure the defendant a fair trial. And a strong argument can surely be made that the whole thrust of those decisions most inevitably lead to the conclusion that a State may constitutionally impose a lawyer upon even an unwilling defendant.

But it is one thing to hold that every defendant, rich or poor, has the right to the assistance of counsel, and quite another to say that a State may compel a defendant to accept a lawyer he does not want. The value of state-appointed counsel was not unappreciated by the Founders, yet the notion of compulsory counsel was utterly foreign to them. And whatever else may be said of those who wrote the Bill of Rights, surely there can be no doubt that they understood the inestimable worth of free choice.

It is undeniable that in most criminal prosecutions defendants could better defend with counsel's guidance than by their own unskilled efforts. But where the defendant will not voluntarily accept representation by counsel, the potential advantage of a lawyer's training and experience can be realized, if at all, only imperfectly. To force a lawyer on a defendant can only lead him to believe that the law contrives against him. Moreover, it is not inconceivable that in some rare instances, the defendant might in fact present his case more effectively by conducting his own defense. Personal liberties are not rooted in the law of averages. The right to defend is personal. The defendant, and not his lawyer or the State, will bear the personal consequences of a conviction. It is the defendant, therefore, who must be free personally to decide whether in his particular case counsel is to his advantage. And although he may conduct his own defense ultimately to his own detriment, his choice must be honored out of "that respect for the individual which is the lifeblood of the law."

V

When an accused manages his own defense, he relinquishes, as a purely factual matter, many of the traditional benefits associated with the right to counsel. For this reason, in order to represent himself, the accused must "knowingly and intelligently" forgo those relinquished benefits. Although a defendant need not himself have the skill and experience of a lawyer in order competently and intelligently to choose self-representation, he should be made aware of the dangers and disadvantages of self-representation, so that the record will establish that "he knows what he is doing and his choice is made with eyes open."

Here, weeks before trial, Faretta clearly and unequivocally declared to the trial judge that he wanted to represent himself and did not want counsel. The record affirmatively shows that Faretta was literate, competent, and understanding, and that he was voluntarily exercising his informed free will. The trial judge had warned Faretta that he thought it was a mistake not to accept the assistance of counsel, and that Faretta would be required to follow all the "ground rules" of trial procedure. We need make no assessment of how well or poorly Faretta had mastered the intricacies of the hearsay rule and the California code provisions that govern challenges of potential jurors on *voir dire*. For his technical legal knowledge, as such, was not relevant to an assessment of his knowing exercise of the right to defend himself.

In forcing Faretta, under these circumstances, to accept against his will a state-appointed public defender, the California courts deprived him of his constitutional right to conduct his own defense. * * *

MR. CHIEF JUSTICE BURGER, with whom MR. JUSTICE BLACKMUN and MR. JUSTICE REHNQUIST join, dissenting. * * *

I

The most striking feature of the Court's opinion is that it devotes so little discussion to the matter which it concedes is the core of the decision, that is, discerning an independent basis in the Constitution for the supposed right to represent oneself in a criminal trial. Its ultimate assertion that such a right is tucked between the lines of the Sixth Amendment is contradicted by the Amendment's language and its consistent judicial interpretation.

As the Court seems to recognize, the conclusion that the rights guaranteed by the Sixth Amendment are "personal" to an accused reflects nothing more than the obvious fact that it is he who is on trial and therefore has need of a defense. But neither that nearly trivial proposition nor the language of the Amendment, which speaks in uniformly mandatory terms, leads to the further conclusion that the right to counsel is merely supplementary and may be dispensed with at the whim of the accused. Rather, this Court's decisions have consistently included the right to counsel as an integral part of the bundle making up the larger "right to a defense as we know it." * * *

In short, both the "spirit and the logic" of the Sixth Amendment are that every person accused of crime shall receive the fullest possible defense; in the vast majority of cases this command can be honored only by means of the expressly guaranteed right to counsel, and the trial judge is in the best position to determine whether the accused is capable of conducting his defense. True freedom of choice and society's interest in seeing that justice is achieved can be vindicated only if the trial court retains discretion to reject any attempted waiver of counsel and insist that the accused be tried according to the Constitution. This discretion is as critical an element of basic fairness as a trial judge's discretion to decline to accept a plea of guilty. * * *

III

* * * I hesitate to participate in the Court's attempt to use history to take it where legal analysis cannot. Piecing together shreds of English legal history and early state constitutional and statutory provisions, without a full elaboration of the context in which they occurred or any evidence that they were relied upon by the drafters of our Federal Constitution, creates more questions than it answers and

hardly provides the firm foundation upon which the creation of new constitutional rights should rest. We are well reminded that this Court once employed an exhaustive analysis of English and colonial practices regarding the right to counsel to justify the conclusion that it was fundamental to a fair trial and, less than 10 years later, used essentially the same material to conclude that it was not.

As if to illustrate this point, the single historical fact cited by the Court which would appear truly relevant to ascertaining the meaning of the Sixth Amendment proves too much. As the Court points out, § 35 of the Judiciary Act of 1789 provided a statutory right to self-representation in federal criminal trials. The text of the Sixth Amendment, which expressly provides only for a right to counsel, was proposed the day after the Judiciary Act was signed. It can hardly be suggested that the Members of the Congress of 1789, then few in number, were unfamiliar with the Amendment's carefully structured language, which had been under discussion since the 1787 Constitutional Convention. And it would be most remarkable to suggest, had the right to conduct one's own defense been considered so critical as to require constitutional protection, that it would have been left to implication. Rather, under traditional canons of construction, *inclusion* of the right in the Judiciary Act and its *omission* from the constitutional amendment drafted at the same time by many of the same men, supports the conclusion that the omission was intentional.

There is no way to reconcile the idea that the Sixth Amendment impliedly guaranteed the right of an accused to conduct his own defense with the contemporaneous action of the Congress in passing a statute explicitly giving that right. If the Sixth Amendment created a right to self-representation it was unnecessary for Congress to enact any statute on the subject at all. In this case, therefore, history ought to lead judges to conclude that the Constitution leaves to the judgment of legislatures, and the flexible process of statutory amendment, the question whether criminal defendants should be permitted to conduct their trials *pro se*. And the fact that we have not hinted at a contrary view for 185 years is surely entitled to some weight in the scales. * * *

[JUSTICE BLACKMUN's dissent, joined by CHIEF JUSTICE BURGER and JUSTICE REHNQUIST is omitted.]

NOTES AND QUESTIONS

1. Recall from p. 631, Note 5 that a defense lawyer makes countless strategic and tactical decisions about how to present a defense, how to challenge the

prosecution's case, and how best to argue to the judge and jury. When a criminal defendant exercises his *Faretta* right to represent himself, he must make all those decisions. Which *Faretta* position, majority or dissent, do you prefer as a matter of policy? Does it seem at all odd to you that the eloquent defenders of *Gideon* in this case are the "conservative" justices?

Prior to trial, the following colloquy (set out in footnote 3 of the majority opinion) between the judge and Mr. Faretta took place:

> "THE COURT: In the Faretta matter, I brought you back down here to do some reconsideration as to whether or not you should continue to represent yourself.
>
> How have you been getting along on your research?
>
> THE DEFENDANT: Not bad, your Honor.
>
> Last night I put in the mail a 995 motion and it should be with the Clerk within the next day or two.
>
> THE COURT: Have you been preparing yourself for the intricacies of the trial of the matter?
>
> THE DEFENDANT: Well, your Honor, I was hoping that the case could possibly be disposed of on the 995.
>
> Mrs. Ayers informed me yesterday that it was the Court's policy to hear the pretrial motions at the time of trial. If possible, your Honor, I would like a date set as soon as the Court deems adequate after they receive the motion, sometime before trial.
>
> THE COURT: Let's see how you have been doing on your research.
>
> How many exceptions are there to the hearsay rule?
>
> THE DEFENDANT: Well, the hearsay rule would, I guess, be called the best evidence rule, your Honor. And there are several exceptions in case law, but in actual statutory law, I don't feel there is none.
>
> THE COURT: What are the challenges to the jury for cause?
>
> THE DEFENDANT: Well, there is twelve peremptory challenges.
>
> THE COURT: And how many for cause?
>
> THE DEFENDANT: Well, as many as the Court deems valid.
>
> THE COURT: And what are they? What are the grounds for challenging a juror for cause?
>
> THE DEFENDANT: Well, numerous grounds to challenge a witness—I mean, a juror, your Honor, one being the juror is perhaps

suffered, was a victim of the same type of offense, might be prejudiced toward the defendant. Any substantial ground that might make the juror prejudice[d] toward the defendant.

THE COURT: Anything else?

THE DEFENDANT: Well, a relative perhaps of the victim.

THE COURT: Have you taken a look at that code section to see what it is?

THE DEFENDANT: Challenge a juror?

THE COURT: Yes.

THE DEFENDANT: Yes, your Honor. I have done—

THE COURT: What is the code section?

THE DEFENDANT: On voir diring a jury, your Honor?

THE COURT: Yes.

THE DEFENDANT: I am not aware of the section right offhand.

THE COURT: What code is it in?

THE DEFENDANT: Well, the research I have done on challenging would be in Witkins Jurisprudence.

THE COURT: Have you looked at any of the codes to see where these various things are taken up?

THE DEFENDANT: No, your Honor, I haven't.

THE COURT: Have you looked in any of the California Codes with reference to trial procedure?

THE DEFENDANT: Yes, your Honor.

THE COURT: What codes?

THE DEFENDANT: I have done extensive research in the Penal Code, your Honor, and the Civil Code.

THE COURT: If you have done extensive research into it, then tell me about it.

THE DEFENDANT: On empaneling a jury, your Honor?

THE COURT: Yes.

THE DEFENDANT: Well, the District Attorney and the defendant, defense counsel, has both the right to 12 peremptory challenges of a jury. These 12 challenges are undisputable. Any reason that the defense or

> prosecution should feel that a juror would be inadequate to try the case or to rule on a case, they may then discharge that juror.
>
> But if there is a valid challenge due to grounds of prejudice or some other grounds, that these aren't considered in the 12 peremptory challenges. There are numerous and the defendant, the defense and the prosecution both have the right to make any inquiry to the jury as to their feelings toward the case."

Does this conversation change your view about the case at all? About a right to represent oneself?

How many peremptory challenges do criminal defendants get in non-capital cases under your state law? If you don't know, and the authors of your book do not know about their state, perhaps Faretta was in better shape to defend himself than it might first appear. Why do you think the Court included footnote 3?

2. Who gets the better of the argument from history? Perhaps more importantly, *why* does history seem to count so much on this issue?

3. *Defense counsel is not what it once was.* In footnote 16 of his opinion in *Faretta*, Justice Stewart had this to say:

> Such a result [forcing a defendant to accept counsel] would sever the concept of counsel from its historic roots. The first lawyers were personal friends of the litigant, brought into court by him so that he might "take 'counsel' with them" before pleading. 1 F. Pollock & F. Maitland, The History of English Law 211 (2d ed. 1909). Similarly, the first "attorneys" were personal agents, often lacking any professional training, who were appointed by those litigants who had secured royal permission to carry on their affairs through a representative, rather than personally. *Id.*, at 212–213.

4. The Court says that "even where counsel was permitted, the general practice continued to be self-representation" during the colonial era. Author Thomas reviewed the records of forty-eight trials in the New Jersey criminal courts from 1749 to 1757. In those records, defendants were represented by counsel in twenty-six cases. See George C. Thomas III, *Colonial Criminal Law and Procedure: The Royal Colony of New Jersey, 1749–57*, 1 N.Y.U. J. L. & Liberty 671, 689 (2005). These data suggest that the colonial cases were roughly evenly split between counseled and un-counseled criminal defendants. The acquittal rate was much higher (77%) in cases where the defendant was represented by counsel than in *pro se* cases (18%). Id. at 691. Before we feel too smug about those data, it is possible that a good deal of the difference is explained by self-selection. Defendants whose guilt was obvious, or who had worked out some kind of sentence deal with the king's counsel, would be less likely to spend money or try to persuade a friend to represent them.

5. Should the *Faretta* arguments, sounding in autonomy, history, and the text of the Sixth Amendment, apply equally to defendants who want to represent themselves on appeal? In Martinez v. Court of Appeal of California, 528 U.S. 152, 120 S.Ct. 684, 145 L.Ed.2d 597 (2000), the Court concluded that these concerns were less weighty. There was no right to appeal at common law, and no statutory right to appeal in federal court or state court until, at the earliest, the late nineteenth century. As to the textual argument, the Court reiterated that the Sixth Amendment applies only to rights "that are available in preparation for trial and at the trial itself. The Sixth Amendment does not include any right to appeal."

There remain the *Faretta* autonomy interests but, given that there is no Sixth Amendment right at stake, the Court found that the autonomy question had to be analyzed under the due process clause. One autonomy interest is the value of not forcing a lawyer on an appellant, who might "be skeptical of whether a lawyer, who is employed by the same government that is prosecuting him, will serve his cause with undivided loyalty." The other autonomy interest is that it is the appellant, just like the defendant in *Faretta*, who personally will bear the consequences of the proceeding. But there are costs associated with the exercise of autonomy in this context. As the Court noted, no one argues that *pro se* representation "is wise, desirable or efficient." Rather, it is usually a "bad defense, particularly when compared to a defense provided by an experienced criminal defense attorney."

Martinez concluded that the autonomy interests weigh less in the appellate context. "The status of the accused defendant, who retains a presumption of innocence throughout the trial process, changes dramatically when a jury returns a guilty verdict." Any autonomy interests "that survive a felony conviction are less compelling than those motivating the decision in *Faretta*. Yet the overriding state interest in the fair and efficient administration of justice remains as strong as at the trial level. Thus, the States are clearly within their discretion to conclude that the government's interests outweigh an invasion of the appellant's interest in self-representation."

Do you agree that the existence of a conviction impairs the autonomy interest implicit in deciding whether to represent oneself in an appellate procedure?

6. *Standby counsel.* In footnote 46 of *Faretta*, the Court anticipated the desire of trial courts to appoint standby counsel:

> The right of self-representation is not a license to abuse the dignity of the courtroom. Neither is it a license not to comply with relevant rules of procedural and substantive law. Thus, whatever else may or may not be open to him on appeal, a defendant who elects to represent himself cannot thereafter complain that the quality of his own defense amounted to a denial of "effective assistance of counsel."

In McKaskle v. Wiggins, 465 U.S. 168, 104 S.Ct. 944, 79 L.Ed.2d 122 (1984), the issue was whether unwanted intervention by standby counsel was an unconstitutional erosion of the *pro se* defendant's right of self-representation.

The Court approached this difficult inquiry by keeping its focus on the autonomy dimension of the *Faretta* doctrine:

> First, the *pro se* defendant is entitled to preserve actual control over the case he chooses to present to the jury. This is the core of the *Faretta* right. If standby counsel's participation over the defendant's objection effectively allows counsel to make or substantially interfere with any significant tactical decision, or to control the questioning of witnesses, or to speak instead of the defendant on any matter of importance, the *Faretta* right is eroded.
>
> Second, participation by standby counsel without the defendant's consent should not be allowed to destroy the jury's perception that the defendant is representing himself. The defendant's appearance in the status of one conducting his own defense is important in a criminal trial, since the right to appear *pro se* exists to affirm the accused's individual dignity and autonomy.

Is this statement inconsistent with at least the surface meaning of *Faretta* footnote 46? Can you reconcile the two?

Professor Anne Bowen Poulin offers insight into why the relationship between the *pro se* defendant and standby counsel might be fractious. Anne Bowen Poulin, *The Role of Standby Counsel in Criminal Cases: In the Twilight Zone of the Criminal Justice System*, 75 N.Y.U. L. Rev. 676 (2000). Many requests to proceed *pro se* result from a trial judge's refusal to appoint substitute counsel when the defendant has concluded that a fair trial is not possible with current counsel. If the judge grants the *pro se* request somewhat late in the process, which is when the motion is usually made, efficiency suggests not appointing a different lawyer to act as standby counsel. But to appoint the lawyer that the defendant has already rejected is only asking for trouble.

7. *Professor Poulin on the role of standby counsel.* Professor Poulin's comprehensive examination of the proper role for standby counsel, Note 7, concludes that the role varies substantially by the stage of the proceedings at issue. The threat to the jury's "perception that the defendant is representing himself" is a problem only at the trial stage. But even at trial, Professor Poulin argues that standby counsel should do more than merely sit passively and wait for a plea for help. Instead, standby counsel "should actively guide the defendant through the procedures of the trial" and should "identify hurdles, inform the defendant, and help the defendant surmount them." *Id.* at 718.

Do you think this a sound idea? Is it consistent with *Faretta* and *McKaskle*, discussed earlier in this Note?

According to Poulin, at the pre-trial, evidence-gathering stage, the standby lawyer should be as active as possible. "Only if the defendant rejects standby counsel's offer of assistance has the professional obligation of standby counsel been satisfied." *Id.* at 716. Under this conception of the role of standby counsel, the lawyer would be the client's specialized assistant, much as serjeants assisted clients in English courts in the sixteenth and seventeenth centuries.

8. *Competency to waive counsel.* In Godinez v. Moran, 509 U.S. 389, 113 S.Ct. 2680, 125 L.Ed.2d 321 (1993), the defendant had committed three cold blooded murders, including that of his ex-wife. He was evaluated by two psychiatrists, "both of whom concluded that he was competent to stand trial." The doctors prescribed medications because he was depressed and suicidal. While being treated for his depression, he sought to discharge his public defender and represent himself, with the plan of pleading guilty and not resisting the State's attempt to impose the death penalty.

The issue in *Godinez* was whether defendants who are competent to stand trial are also competent to waive counsel and plead guilty. The standard for competence to stand trial is whether the defendant has both a "sufficient present ability to consult with his lawyer with a reasonable degree of rational understanding" and "a rational as well as factual understanding of the proceedings against him." *Godinez* reasoned that while defendants who plead guilty have to make many decisions and waive several rights, the defendant who stands trial has additional decisions to make about how to present a defense. Thus, the Court held that if the competence standard "is adequate for defendants who plead not guilty, it is necessarily adequate for those who plead guilty." The Court also held that a defendant who is competent to stand trial is competent to waive counsel en route to a guilty plea.

The Court then explained why the waiver of right to counsel does not require a greater capacity:

> Nor do we think that a defendant who waives his right to the assistance of counsel must be more competent than a defendant who does not, since there is no reason to believe that the decision to waive counsel requires an appreciably higher level of mental functioning than the decision to waive other constitutional rights. [Moran] suggests that a higher competency standard is necessary because a defendant who represents himself " 'must have greater powers of comprehension, judgment, and reason than would be necessary to stand trial with the aid of an attorney.' " But this argument has a flawed premise; the competence that is required of a defendant seeking to waive his right to counsel is the competence to *waive the right*, not the competence to represent himself. In *Faretta v. California*, we held that a defendant choosing self-representation must do so

> "competently and intelligently," but we made it clear that the defendant's "technical legal knowledge" is "not relevant" to the determination whether he is competent to waive his right to counsel, and we emphasized that although the defendant "may conduct his own defense ultimately to his own detriment, his choice must be honored."

The Court stressed that the validity of the guilty plea or the waiver of the right to counsel requires more than competence or capacity. It requires a finding that the plea or the waiver "is knowing and voluntary. In this sense there is a 'heightened' standard for pleading guilty and for waiving the right to counsel, but it is not a heightened standard of *competence*."

Justice Blackmun, joined by Justice Stevens, dissented on the ground that the trial judge was on notice of Moran's "self-destructive behavior" and "his deep depression" and should therefore "have conducted another competency evaluation to determine Moran's capacity to waive the right to counsel and represent himself, instead of relying upon the psychiatrists' reports that he was able to stand trial with the assistance of counsel."

On March 30, 1996, Moran was executed. *Nevada Executes Man Who Killed 3 People*, New York Times, March 31, 1996, Sect. 1, at 27.

9. *How far can pro-se defendants go?* See the following from footnote 46 in Faretta:

> We are told that many criminal defendants representing themselves may use the courtroom for deliberate disruption of their trials. But the right of self-representation has been recognized from our beginnings by federal law and by most of the States, and no such result has thereby occurred. Moreover, the trial judge may terminate self-representation by a defendant who deliberately engages in serious and obstructionist misconduct. Of course, a State may—even over objection by the accused—appoint a "standby counsel" to aid the accused if and when the accused requests help, and to be available to represent the accused in the event that termination of the defendant's self-representation is necessary.
>
> Faretta is far from the worst *pro se* defendant one can have. How would you like to have been the prosecutor in the next case?

Faretta Hell: Do Judges Look Like Grapefruits?

Colin Ferguson was charged with killing six railroad commuters and wounding nineteen others in a 1993 shooting rampage on the Long Island Railroad. Ferguson chose this location, rather than the New York City subways, because he did not want to embarrass African-American Mayor David Dinkins. *Gunman's Shooting Spree on Commuter Train Racially Motivated: Police Say*, Agence

France-Presse (France), December 8, 1993, at 1. He entered the train with more than 100 rounds of ammunition already loaded in magazine clips. James Barron, *Suspect's Notes Suggest Motive*, The Patriot Ledger (Quincy, Mass.), December 9, 1993, at 17. He fired thirty to fifty rounds in the train, hitting the twenty-five victims. Pat Milton, *Race-Obsessed Loner Blamed in Train Tragedy*, Associated Press, December 8, 1993. All of his victims were either Caucasian or Asian, and these individuals were deliberately targeted as evidenced by four pages of handwritten notes. The notes listed racism by these groups as his primary motivation. Two examples: "That Chinese fascist will never put me to shame again without cause"; and "The sloppy running of the No. 2 train. It is racism by Caucasians and Uncle Tom Negroes." *Id.*

While in jail awaiting trial, Ferguson accused guards of throwing a fire extinguisher and a milk crate at him. *Train Suspect Claims Abuse From Jailers*, The New Orleans Times-Picayune, December 18, 1993, at A10. He also claimed that the light in his cell was kept on twenty-four hours a day to prevent him from sleeping, and that guards were plotting to poison his food. *Id.* Nassau County Sheriff officials investigated these allegations and found no evidence of mistreatment. *Id.* Despite Ferguson's mental state while in jail, two court-appointed experts found him to be competent to stand trial. *Court Psychiatrist Says Ferguson is Competent to Stand Trial*, Associated Press, January 4, 1994.

His lawyers claimed he was paranoid and delusional. He accused the lawyers of plotting against him, fired them, and requested his right to represent himself. The trial judge found him fit to stand trial and, therefore, under *Godinez*, capable of representing himself. John T. McQuiston, *Accused Killer Asks Search for "Real Killer,"* N.Y. Times, December 15, 1994, at 12. While representing himself, Ferguson asked the court to allow him to hire a private investigator so he could find the real killer. *Id.*

During the ten-day trial, he attempted to subpoena President Clinton and former New York Governor Mario Cuomo because they met with some of the survivors of the shooting. Pat Milton, *Man Convicted of Murdering Six in Train Massacre*, Associated Press, February 17, 1995. He claimed that the only reason the indictment against him had ninety-three counts was that the shootings occurred in 1993. He also claimed that he was a victim of a government conspiracy. *Id.*

His claim that he was not the killer prompted ridicule throughout the trial. On cross-examination of a detective, Ferguson asked if the suspect was ever searched. The detective replied, "Did I ever search you, no." *Id.* Ferguson cross-examined the victims he was accused of wounding. One victim, Maryanne Phillips, responded to his cross-examination by stating, "I saw you shoot me." *Id.* When he made a reference to "the gunman," the witnesses would correct him by responding with the pronoun "you." Janet Cawley, *In Bizarre Trial, Accused Gunman Defends Self; "You Shot Us," Train Survivors Testify*, Chicago Tribune, February 16, 1995, at 4. Ferguson changed his mind at least once but finally decided not to testify. In a twenty-minute monologue to the judge, with the jury out of the room, Ferguson alleged that he was the victim of a conspiracy that was somehow connected to the slaying in prison of mass murderer Jeffrey Dahmer. Pat Milton, *Ferguson Decides Not to Testify in Train-Massacre Trial*, Associated Press, February 16, 1995. He claimed the Dahmer murder was "a prelude against me. There's a conspiracy to murder me if I'm convicted." *Id.*

After ten hours of deliberation, the jury found Ferguson guilty of six counts of murder, nineteen counts of attempted murder, and three other counts. The sentencing hearing for Ferguson took three days because so many victims and family members wanted to speak. "In those three days, I don't think I was ever so moved in 30 years of being a judge," the trial judge said. The judge sentenced Ferguson to 315 years. Ferguson, now 55, is serving his sentence at the Upstate Correctional Facility in Malone, N.Y He is eligible for parole in 2309 (and that is not a typo). "20 years later: Long Island Rail Road shooting remembered as day killer Colin Ferguson went off the rails," Associated Press, *New York Daily News*, December 6, 2013.

On appeal, his lawyer, Richard Barbuto, asked the New York courts to require a higher standard of competency for self-representation than the federal standard in *Godinez*. The Ferguson case, argued Barbuto, "resulted in a perversion of the criminal justice system process." The standard for self-representation "has to be more than being able to tell the difference between a judge and a grapefruit." Robin Topping, *LIRR Gunman Didn't Have a Clue in Court*, Newsday, June 25, 1996, at A29.

These antics might appear a "perversion" of the process to Ferguson's appellate lawyer, or to you, or to the editors of this casebook. But the New York Appellate Division devoted exactly one sentence to the argument that Ferguson was not competent to represent himself: "The [trial] court properly permitted the defendant to appear *pro se,* since a defendant who is competent to stand trial is necessarily competent to waive his right to counsel and proceed *pro se*." People v. Ferguson, 670 N.Y.S.2d 327, 248 A.D.2d 725 (1998). The highest New York court denied leave to appeal.

NOTES AND QUESTIONS

1. *A third way.* The Court in *Godinez* (Note 8, p. 673) held that a defendant who is competent to stand trial is competent to waive counsel and plead guilty. But as the Court realized in Indiana v. Edwards, 554 U.S. 164, 128 S.Ct. 2379, 171 L.Ed.2d 345 (2008), the competence to waive counsel and plead guilty is not necessarily the same as the competence to waive counsel and represent oneself at trial. Edwards had been found to be schizophrenic but, after a stay in the state mental hospital, competent to stand trial. The trial judge, however, drew a distinction between competence to stand trial and competence to be his own lawyer: "With these findings, he's competent to stand trial but I'm not going to find he's competent to defend himself."

Edwards proceeded to trial represented by appointed counsel, was convicted of attempted murder, and claimed on appeal that his Sixth Amendment self-representation rights were violated. The Indiana Supreme Court agreed, concluding that *Faretta* and *Godinez* stood for the proposition that a defendant has a right to represent himself at trial if he is competent to stand trial. The Court disagreed, 7–2, finding nothing in the Sixth Amendment or the Court's precedents that would deny the state the right to force counsel on a defendant who is not mentally competent to represent himself:

> [T]he Constitution permits judges to take realistic account of the particular defendant's mental capacities by asking whether a defendant who seeks to conduct his own defense at trial is mentally competent to do so. That is to say, the Constitution permits States to insist upon representation by counsel for those competent enough to stand trial * * * but who still suffer from severe mental illness to the point where they are not competent to conduct trial proceedings by themselves.

Notably, the Court in *Edwards* did not elaborate on its standard of "not competent to conduct trial proceedings." Presumably, a defendant like Colin Ferguson would not meet whatever standard is finally adopted.

After *Edwards*, three levels of defendant competence seem to exist. A defendant might be *incompetent to stand trial* and thus must be released or made the subject of civil commitment proceedings. See Jackson v. Indiana, 406 U.S. 715, 92 S.Ct. 1845, 32 L.Ed.2d 435 (1972). If competent to stand trial, a defendant might be *competent to waive counsel and plead guilty but not competent to represent himself at trial.* Finally, a defendant might be *competent to waive counsel and represent himself at trial*, in which case *Faretta* gives him the absolute right to do so.

2. *What Edwards fails to answer. Edwards* held that a state is *permitted* to require counsel when defendants fall below the standard of "not competent to conduct trial

proceedings." Is the converse of this holding also implied—is a state *required* to appoint counsel for all defendants who wish to represent themselves but are not mentally competent to do so?

Though *Edwards* does not decide this issue, the Court offered a comment on the perception of fairness, noting that "proceedings must not only be fair, they must 'appear fair to all who observe them.' " The majority referred to an *amicus* brief in which a psychiatrist observed his patient represent himself at trial and asked "how in the world can our legal system allow an insane man to defend himself?" Taken to its logical conclusion, this comment suggests that there may be a constitutional requirement for appointed counsel when defendants who are "not competent to conduct trial proceedings" seek to represent themselves at trial. The possibility that this issue might be raised on appeal will probably encourage trial judges to err on the side of appointing counsel in close cases.

3. *The Unabomber client.* Suppose you were appointed to represent "Unabomber" Ted Kaczynski, charged with several bombings and killings. The Government has asked for the death penalty, and the prosecutors have overwhelming evidence of guilt—*e.g.*, a fully-armed bomb found in his tiny cabin, bomb-making parts and chemicals, carbon copies of the Unabomber's manifesto and taunting letters to victims and the news media, thousands of pages of diaries and journals that Kaczynski kept over a twenty-year period. The journals are filled with observations of a man who wanted only to kill his enemies by building a perfect bomb. All of this evidence, and more, will almost certainly be presented to the jury.

You believe your client is mentally ill. If his mental illness is insufficient to qualify for an insanity defense, at the very least it will be his best argument to the jury to impose life without parole rather than the death penalty. You have repeatedly given your client the benefit of your advice on this point, but he refuses to cooperate in the mental illness defense, and orders you not to raise it at trial or at the penalty phase. He tells you that if you raise the issue in court, even indirectly, he will fire you on the spot and represent himself.

What do you do? Let us assume that you are convinced that, without a mental illness defense, your client will be given the death penalty. Can you ignore his orders? What if you also believe that his decision not to plead mental illness is itself caused by his mental illness? Can you proceed with the defense without his permission?

For an argument that "the criminal process failed Kaczynski, his counsel, and the public," see Martin Sabelli & Stacey Leyton, *Train Wrecks and Freeway Crashes: An Argument For Fairness and Against Self Representation in the Criminal Justice System*, 91 J. Crim. L. & Criminology 161, 164 (2000). The authors conclude that to help avoid this kind of failure in the future, "the ethical rules must be modified to clearly allocate the authority to present evidence of mental illness to defense counsel, regardless of the defendant's wishes." *Id.* at 217. What do you think of that solution?

D. The Right to Effective Assistance of Counsel

The right to counsel cases considered so far, from *Powell* to *Faretta*, can be described as the "structural" right to counsel. The Court in these cases decided *when* defendants have a right to counsel at state expense (or the right to proceed without counsel), but not *what* constitutes the "Assistance of Counsel." But there must also be a substantive component to the right to counsel. If the defense lawyer were in a coma during the trial, it could not be said that the accused had received the "Assistance of Counsel." From there, it is merely a matter of degree to questions about lawyers who are drunk, incompetent, depressed, asleep part of the time, or representing a co-defendant with conflicting interests. These questions of substance are not easy, and many commentators think the Supreme Court has failed to grapple meaningfully with them.

STRICKLAND V. WASHINGTON

Supreme Court of the United States, 1984.
466 U.S. 668, 104 S.Ct. 2052, 80 L.Ed.2d 674.

Is the right to counsel simply the right to have counsel present? Is it the right to have the best counsel present? Adequate counsel? A warm body? *Strickland v. Washington* stands for the proposition that the right is to have "effective assistance of counsel". But what is "effective assistance". *Strickland* also attempts to answer that question. However, as you will see from the case and the Notes that follow, given that every case that goes to trial is exceedingly different, that question is excruciatingly difficult to answer. As you read the cases and Notes, ask yourself, should it be that hard to define?

Pay close attention in *Strickland* to what the defense attorney did and did not do (and why), as well as the list of claims the defendant made to show that his counsel was "ineffective". As you do, consider the two main components of an "effective assistance counsel" analysis. First, there must be errors made that go beyond what a reasonable defense attorney would do in that situation. Second, those errors had to be bad enough to have made a difference in the verdict. In other words, absent the errors, the case would have had a different outcome.

As you will see in *Strickland*, the reasonableness of an attorney's conduct is determined by the prevailing norms in the profession. Does this

mean that "effective assistance of counsel" is what lawyers say it means? Read the rest of the case to find out.

JUSTICE O'CONNOR delivered the opinion of the Court [joined by CHIEF JUSTICE BURGER and JUSTICES WHITE, BLACKMUN, POWELL, REHNQUIST, and STEVENS; and joined in part by JUSTICE BRENNAN].

This case requires us to consider the proper standards for judging a criminal defendant's contention that the Constitution requires a conviction or death sentence to be set aside because counsel's assistance at the trial or sentencing was ineffective.

I

A

During a 10-day period in September 1976, respondent planned and committed three groups of crimes, which included three brutal stabbing murders, torture, kidnaping, severe assaults, attempted murders, attempted extortion, and theft. After his two accomplices were arrested, respondent surrendered to police and voluntarily gave a lengthy statement confessing to the third of the criminal episodes. The State of Florida indicted respondent for kidnaping and murder and appointed an experienced criminal lawyer to represent him.

Counsel actively pursued pretrial motions and discovery. He cut his efforts short, however, and he experienced a sense of hopelessness about the case, when he learned that, against his specific advice, respondent had also confessed to the first two murders. By the date set for trial, respondent was subject to indictment for three counts of first-degree murder and multiple counts of robbery, kidnaping for ransom, breaking and entering and assault, attempted murder, and conspiracy to commit robbery. Respondent waived his right to a jury trial, again acting against counsel's advice, and pleaded guilty to all charges, including the three capital murder charges.

In the plea colloquy, respondent told the trial judge that, although he had committed a string of burglaries, he had no significant prior criminal record and that at the time of his criminal spree he was under extreme stress caused by his inability to support his family. He also stated, however, that he accepted responsibility for the crimes. The trial judge told respondent that he had "a great deal of respect for people who are willing to step forward and admit their responsibility" but that he was making no statement at all about his likely sentencing decision.

Counsel advised respondent to invoke his right under Florida law to an advisory jury at his capital sentencing hearing. Respondent rejected the advice and waived the right. He chose instead to be sentenced by the trial judge without a jury recommendation.

In preparing for the sentencing hearing, counsel spoke with respondent about his background. He also spoke on the telephone with respondent's wife and mother, though he did not follow up on the one unsuccessful effort to meet with them. He did not otherwise seek out character witnesses for respondent. Nor did he request a psychiatric examination, since his conversations with his client gave no indication that respondent had psychological problems.

Counsel decided not to present and hence not to look further for evidence concerning respondent's character and emotional state. That decision reflected trial counsel's sense of hopelessness about overcoming the evidentiary effect of respondent's confessions to the gruesome crimes. It also reflected the judgment that it was advisable to rely on the plea colloquy for evidence about respondent's background and about his claim of emotional stress: the plea colloquy communicated sufficient information about these subjects, and by forgoing the opportunity to present new evidence on these subjects, counsel prevented the State from cross-examining respondent on his claim and from putting on psychiatric evidence of its own.

Counsel also excluded from the sentencing hearing other evidence he thought was potentially damaging. He successfully moved to exclude respondent's "rap sheet." Because he judged that a presentence report might prove more detrimental than helpful, as it would have included respondent's criminal history and thereby would have undermined the claim of no significant history of criminal activity, he did not request that one be prepared.

At the sentencing hearing, counsel's strategy was based primarily on the trial judge's remarks at the plea colloquy as well as on his reputation as a sentencing judge who thought it important for a convicted defendant to own up to his crime. Counsel argued that respondent's remorse and acceptance of responsibility justified sparing him from the death penalty. Counsel also argued that respondent had no history of criminal activity and that respondent committed the crimes under extreme mental or emotional disturbance, thus coming within the statutory list of mitigating circumstances. He further argued that respondent should be spared death because he had surrendered, confessed, and offered to testify against a codefendant and because respondent was fundamentally a good person who had briefly gone badly wrong in extremely stressful circumstances. The State put on evidence and witnesses largely for the purpose of describing the details of the crimes. Counsel did not cross-examine the medical experts who testified about the manner of death of respondent's victims.

The trial judge found several aggravating circumstances with respect to each of the three murders. He found that all three murders were especially heinous, atrocious, and cruel, all involving repeated stabbings. All three murders were committed in the course of at least one other dangerous and violent felony, and since all involved robbery, the murders were for pecuniary gain. All three murders were committed to avoid arrest for the accompanying crimes and to hinder law enforcement. In the course of one of the murders, respondent knowingly subjected numerous persons to a grave risk of death by deliberately stabbing and shooting the murder victim's sisters-in-law, who sustained severe—in one case, ultimately fatal—injuries.

With respect to mitigating circumstances, the trial judge made the same findings for all three capital murders. First, although there was no admitted evidence of prior convictions, respondent had stated that he had engaged in a course of stealing. In any case, even if respondent had no significant history of criminal activity, the aggravating circumstances "would still clearly far outweigh" that mitigating factor. Second, the judge found that, during all three crimes, respondent was not suffering from extreme mental or emotional disturbance and could appreciate the criminality of his acts. Third, none of the victims was a participant in, or consented to, respondent's conduct. Fourth, respondent's participation in the crimes was neither minor nor the result of duress or domination by an accomplice. Finally, respondent's age (26) could not be considered a factor in mitigation, especially when viewed in light of respondent's planning of the crimes and disposition of the proceeds of the various accompanying thefts.

In short, the trial judge found numerous aggravating circumstances and no (or a single comparatively insignificant) mitigating circumstance. With respect to each of the three convictions for capital murder, the trial judge concluded: "A careful consideration of all matters presented to the court impels the conclusion that there are insufficient mitigating circumstances * * * to outweigh the aggravating circumstances." He therefore sentenced respondent to death on each of the three counts of murder and to prison terms for the other crimes. The Florida Supreme Court upheld the convictions and sentences on direct appeal.

B

Respondent subsequently sought collateral relief in state court on numerous grounds, among them that counsel had rendered ineffective assistance at the sentencing proceeding. Respondent challenged counsel's assistance in six respects. He asserted that counsel was ineffective because he failed to move for a continuance to prepare for sentencing, to request a psychiatric report, to investigate and present character witnesses, to seek a presentence investigation report, to present meaningful arguments to the sentencing judge, and to investigate the medical examiner's reports or cross-examine the medical experts. In support of the claim, respondent submitted 14 affidavits from friends, neighbors, and relatives stating that they would have testified if asked to do so. He also submitted one psychiatric report and one psychological report stating that respondent, though not under the influence of extreme mental or emotional disturbance, was "chronically frustrated and depressed because of his economic dilemma" at the time of his crimes.

* * *

D

* * * [This case] presents a type of Sixth Amendment claim that this Court has not previously considered in any generality. The Court has considered Sixth Amendment claims based on actual or constructive denial of the assistance of counsel altogether, as well as claims based on state interference with the ability of counsel to render effective assistance to the accused. With the exception of *Cuyler v. Sullivan*, 446 U.S. 335, 100 S.Ct. 1708, 64 L.Ed.2d 333 (1980), however, which involved a claim that counsel's assistance was rendered ineffective by a conflict of interest, the Court has never directly and fully addressed a claim of "actual ineffectiveness" of counsel's assistance in a case going to trial. * * *

II * * *

Because of the vital importance of counsel's assistance, this Court has held that, with certain exceptions, a person accused of a federal or state crime has the right to have counsel appointed if retained counsel cannot be obtained. That a person who happens to be a lawyer is present at trial alongside the accused, however, is not enough to satisfy the constitutional command. The Sixth Amendment recognizes the right to the assistance of counsel because it envisions counsel's playing a role that is critical to the ability of the adversarial system to produce just results. An accused is entitled to be assisted by an attorney, whether retained or appointed, who plays the role necessary to ensure that the trial is fair.

For that reason, the Court has recognized that "the right to counsel is the right to the effective assistance of counsel." * * *

The Court has not elaborated on the meaning of the constitutional requirement of effective assistance in the latter class of cases—that is, those presenting claims of "actual ineffectiveness." In giving meaning to the requirement, however, we must take its purpose—to ensure a fair trial—as the guide. The benchmark for judging any claim of ineffectiveness must be whether counsel's conduct so undermined the proper functioning of the adversarial process that the trial cannot be relied on as having produced a just result.

The same principle applies to a capital sentencing proceeding such as that provided by Florida law. * * *

III

A convicted defendant's claim that counsel's assistance was so defective as to require reversal of a conviction or death sentence has two components. First, the defendant must show that counsel's performance was deficient. This requires showing that counsel made errors so serious that counsel was not functioning as the "counsel" guaranteed the defendant by the Sixth Amendment. Second, the defendant must show that the deficient performance prejudiced the defense. This requires showing that counsel's errors were so serious as to deprive the defendant of a fair trial, a trial whose result is reliable. Unless a defendant makes both showings, it cannot be said that the conviction or death sentence resulted from a breakdown in the adversary process that renders the result unreliable.

A

As all the Federal Courts of Appeals have now held, the proper standard for attorney performance is that of reasonably effective assistance. * * * When a convicted defendant complains of the ineffectiveness of counsel's assistance, the defendant must show that counsel's representation fell below an objective standard of reasonableness.

More specific guidelines are not appropriate. The Sixth Amendment refers simply to "counsel," not specifying particular requirements of effective assistance. It relies instead on the legal profession's maintenance of standards sufficient to justify the law's presumption that counsel will fulfill the role in the adversary process that the Amendment envisions. The proper measure of attorney performance remains simply reasonableness under prevailing professional norms.

Representation of a criminal defendant entails certain basic duties. Counsel's function is to assist the defendant, and hence counsel owes the client a duty of loyalty, a duty to avoid conflicts of interest. From counsel's function as assistant to the defendant derive the overarching duty to advocate the defendant's cause and the more particular duties to consult with the defendant on important decisions and to keep the defendant informed of important developments in the course of the prosecution. Counsel also has a duty to bring to bear such skill and knowledge as will render the trial a reliable adversarial testing process.

These basic duties neither exhaustively define the obligations of counsel nor form a checklist for judicial evaluation of attorney performance. In any case presenting an ineffectiveness claim, the performance inquiry must be whether counsel's assistance was reasonable considering all the circumstances. Prevailing norms of practice as reflected in American Bar Association standards and the like are guides to determining what is reasonable, but they are only guides. No particular set of detailed rules for counsel's conduct can satisfactorily take account of the variety of circumstances faced by defense counsel or the range of legitimate decisions regarding how best to represent a criminal defendant. Any such set of rules would interfere with the constitutionally protected independence of counsel and restrict the wide latitude counsel must have in making tactical decisions. Indeed, the existence of detailed guidelines for representation could distract counsel from the overriding mission of vigorous advocacy of the defendant's cause. Moreover, the purpose of the effective assistance guarantee of the Sixth Amendment is not to improve the quality of legal representation, although that is a goal of considerable importance to the legal system. The purpose is simply to ensure that criminal defendants receive a fair trial.

Judicial scrutiny of counsel's performance must be highly deferential. It is all too tempting for a defendant to second-guess counsel's assistance after conviction or adverse sentence, and it is all too easy for a court, examining counsel's defense after it has proved unsuccessful, to conclude that a particular act or omission of counsel was unreasonable. A fair assessment of attorney performance requires that every effort be made to eliminate the distorting effects of hindsight, to reconstruct the circumstances of counsel's challenged conduct, and to evaluate the conduct from counsel's perspective at the time. Because of the difficulties inherent in making the evaluation, a court must indulge a strong presumption that counsel's conduct falls within the wide range of reasonable professional assistance; that is, the defendant must overcome the presumption that, under the circumstances, the challenged action "might be considered sound trial strategy." There are countless ways to provide effective assistance in any given case. Even the best criminal defense attorneys would not defend a particular client in the same way.

The availability of intrusive post-trial inquiry into attorney performance or of detailed guidelines for its evaluation would encourage the proliferation of ineffectiveness challenges. Criminal trials resolved unfavorably to the defendant would increasingly come to be followed by a second trial, this one of counsel's unsuccessful defense. Counsel's performance and even willingness to serve could be adversely affected. Intensive scrutiny of counsel and rigid requirements for acceptable assistance could dampen the ardor and impair the independence of defense counsel, discourage the acceptance of assigned cases, and undermine the trust between attorney and client.

Thus, a court deciding an actual ineffectiveness claim must judge the reasonableness of counsel's challenged conduct on the facts of the particular case, viewed as of the time of counsel's conduct. A convicted defendant making a claim of ineffective assistance must identify the acts or omissions of counsel that are alleged not to have been the result of reasonable professional judgment. The court must then determine whether, in light of all the circumstances, the identified acts or omissions were outside the wide range of professionally competent assistance. In making that determination, the court should keep in mind that counsel's function, as elaborated in prevailing professional norms, is to make the adversarial testing process work in the particular case. At the same time, the court should recognize that counsel is strongly presumed to have rendered adequate assistance and made all significant decisions in the exercise of reasonable professional judgment.

* * *

The reasonableness of counsel's actions may be determined or substantially influenced by the defendant's own statements or actions. Counsel's actions are usually based, quite properly, on informed strategic choices made by the defendant and on information supplied by the defendant. In particular, what investigation decisions are reasonable depends critically on such information. For example, when the facts that support a certain potential line of defense are generally known to counsel because of what the defendant has said, the need for further investigation may be considerably diminished or eliminated altogether. And when a defendant has given counsel reason to believe that pursuing certain investigations would be fruitless or even harmful, counsel's failure to pursue those investigations may not later be challenged as unreasonable. In short, inquiry into counsel's conversations with the defendant may be critical to a proper assessment of counsel's investigation decisions, just as it may be critical to a proper assessment of counsel's other litigation decisions.

B

An error by counsel, even if professionally unreasonable, does not warrant setting aside the judgment of a criminal proceeding if the error had no effect on the judgment. The purpose of the Sixth Amendment guarantee of counsel is to ensure that a defendant has the assistance necessary to justify reliance on the outcome of the proceeding. Accordingly, any deficiencies in counsel's performance must be prejudicial to the defense in order to constitute ineffective assistance under the Constitution. * * *

Accordingly, the appropriate test for prejudice finds its roots in the test for materiality of exculpatory information not disclosed to the defense by the prosecution, and in the test for materiality of testimony made unavailable to the defense by Government deportation of a witness, *United States v. Valenzuela-Bernal*, [458 U.S. 858, 102 S.Ct. 3440, 73 L.Ed.2d 1193 (1982)]. The defendant must show that there is a reasonable probability that, but for counsel's unprofessional errors, the result of the proceeding would have been different. A reasonable probability is a probability sufficient to undermine confidence in the outcome.

In making the determination whether the specified errors resulted in the required prejudice, a court should presume, absent challenge to the judgment on grounds of evidentiary insufficiency, that the judge or jury acted according to law. An assessment of the likelihood of a result more favorable to the defendant must exclude the possibility of arbitrariness, whimsy, caprice, "nullification," and the like. A defendant has no entitlement to the luck of a lawless decisionmaker, even if a lawless decision cannot be reviewed. The assessment of prejudice should proceed on the assumption that the decisionmaker is reasonably, conscientiously, and impartially applying the standards that govern the decision. * * *

The governing legal standard plays a critical role in defining the question to be asked in assessing the prejudice from counsel's errors. When a defendant challenges a conviction, the question is whether there is a reasonable probability that, absent the errors, the factfinder would have had a reasonable doubt respecting guilt. When a defendant challenges a death sentence such as the one at issue in this case, the question is whether there is a reasonable probability that, absent the errors, the sentencer—including an appellate court, to the extent it independently reweighs the evidence—would have concluded that the balance of aggravating and mitigating circumstances did not warrant death.

In making this determination, a court hearing an ineffectiveness claim must consider the totality of the evidence before the judge or jury. Some of the factual findings will have been unaffected by the errors, and factual findings that were affected will have been affected in different ways. Some errors will have had a pervasive effect on the inferences to be drawn from the evidence, altering the entire evidentiary picture, and some will have had an isolated, trivial effect. Moreover, a verdict or conclusion only weakly supported by the record is more likely to have been affected by errors than one with overwhelming record support.

Taking the unaffected findings as a given, and taking due account of the effect of the errors on the remaining findings, a court making the prejudice inquiry must ask if the defendant has met the burden of showing that the decision reached would reasonably likely have been different absent the errors.

IV

A number of practical considerations are important for the application of the standards we have outlined. Most important, in adjudicating a claim of actual ineffectiveness of counsel, a court should keep in mind that the principles we have stated do not establish mechanical rules. Although those principles should guide the process of decision, the ultimate focus of inquiry must be on the fundamental fairness of the proceeding whose result is being challenged. In every case the court should be concerned with whether, despite the strong presumption of reliability, the result of the particular proceeding is unreliable because of a breakdown in the adversarial process that our system counts on to produce just results. * * *

Although we have discussed the performance component of an ineffectiveness claim prior to the prejudice component, there is no reason for a court deciding an ineffective assistance claim to approach the inquiry in the same order or even to address both components of the inquiry if the defendant makes an insufficient showing on one. In particular, a court need not determine whether counsel's performance was deficient before examining the prejudice suffered by the defendant as a result of the alleged deficiencies. The object of an ineffectiveness claim is not to grade counsel's performance. If it is easier to dispose of an ineffectiveness claim on the ground of lack of sufficient prejudice, which we expect will often be so, that course should be followed. Courts should strive to ensure that ineffectiveness claims not become so burdensome to defense counsel that the entire criminal justice system suffers as a result. * * *

V

Having articulated general standards for judging ineffectiveness claims, we think it useful to apply those standards to the facts of this case in order to illustrate the meaning of the general principles. The record makes it possible to do so. There are no conflicts between the state and federal courts over findings of fact, and the principles we have articulated are sufficiently close to the principles applied both in the Florida courts and in the District Court that it is clear that the factfinding was not affected by erroneous legal principles.

Application of the governing principles is not difficult in this case. The facts as described above make clear that the conduct of respondent's counsel at and before respondent's sentencing proceeding cannot be found unreasonable. They also make clear that, even assuming the challenged conduct of counsel was unreasonable, respondent suffered insufficient prejudice to warrant setting aside his death sentence.

With respect to the performance component, the record shows that respondent's counsel made a strategic choice to argue for the extreme emotional distress mitigating circumstance and to rely as fully as possible on respondent's acceptance of responsibility for his crimes. Although counsel understandably felt hopeless about respondent's prospects, nothing in the record indicates, as one possible reading of the District Court's opinion suggests, that counsel's sense of hopelessness distorted his professional judgment. Counsel's strategy choice was well within the range of professionally reasonable judgments, and the decision not to seek more character or psychological evidence than was already in hand was likewise reasonable.

The trial judge's views on the importance of owning up to one's crimes were well known to counsel. The aggravating circumstances were utterly overwhelming. Trial counsel could reasonably surmise from his conversations with respondent that character and psychological evidence would be of little help. Respondent had already been able to mention at the plea colloquy the substance of what there was to know about his financial and emotional troubles. Restricting testimony on respondent's character to what had come in at the plea colloquy ensured that contrary character and psychological evidence and respondent's criminal history, which counsel had successfully moved to exclude, would not come in. On these facts, there can be little question, even without application of the presumption of adequate performance, that trial counsel's defense, though unsuccessful, was the result of reasonable professional judgment.

With respect to the prejudice component, the lack of merit of respondent's claim is even more stark. The evidence that respondent says his trial counsel should have offered at the sentencing hearing would barely have altered the sentencing profile presented to the sentencing judge. As the state courts and District Court found, at most this evidence shows that numerous people who knew respondent thought he was generally a good person and that a psychiatrist and a psychologist believed he was under considerable emotional stress that did not rise to the level of extreme disturbance. Given the overwhelming aggravating factors, there is no reasonable probability that the omitted evidence would have changed the conclusion that the aggravating circumstances outweighed the mitigating circumstances and, hence, the sentence imposed. Indeed, admission of the evidence respondent now offers might even have been harmful to his case: his "rap sheet" would probably have been admitted into evidence, and the psychological reports would have directly contradicted respondent's claim that the mitigating circumstance of extreme emotional disturbance applied to his case. * * *

Failure to make the required showing of either deficient performance or sufficient prejudice defeats the ineffectiveness claim. Here there is a double failure. More generally, respondent has made no showing that the justice of his sentence was rendered unreliable by a breakdown in the adversary process caused by deficiencies in counsel's assistance. Respondent's sentencing proceeding was not fundamentally unfair. * * *

JUSTICE BRENNAN, concurring in part and dissenting in part.

I join the Court's opinion but dissent from its judgment. Adhering to my view that the death penalty is in all circumstances cruel and unusual punishment forbidden by the Eighth and Fourteenth Amendments, I would vacate respondent's death sentence and remand the case for further proceedings. * * *

I join the Court's opinion because I believe that the standards it sets out today will both provide helpful guidance to courts considering claims of actual ineffectiveness of counsel and also permit those courts to continue their efforts to achieve progressive development of this area of the law. * * *

JUSTICE MARSHALL, dissenting. * * *

I * * *

A

My objection to the performance standard adopted by the Court is that it is so malleable that, in practice, it will either have no grip at all or will yield excessive variation in the manner in which the Sixth Amendment is interpreted and applied by different courts. To tell lawyers and the lower courts that counsel for a criminal defendant must behave "reasonably" and must act like "a reasonably competent attorney," is to tell them almost nothing. In essence, the majority has instructed judges called upon to assess claims of ineffective assistance of counsel to advert to their own intuitions regarding what constitutes "professional" representation, and has discouraged them from trying to develop more detailed standards governing the performance of defense counsel. In my view, the Court has thereby not only abdicated its own responsibility to interpret the Constitution, but also impaired the ability of the lower courts to exercise theirs. * * *

The majority defends its refusal to adopt more specific standards primarily on the ground that "[n]o particular set of detailed rules for counsel's conduct can satisfactorily take account of the variety of circumstances faced by defense counsel or the range of legitimate decisions regarding how best to represent a criminal defendant." I agree that counsel must be afforded "wide latitude" when making "tactical decisions" regarding trial strategy, but many aspects of the job of a criminal defense attorney are more amenable to judicial oversight. For example, much of the work involved in preparing for a trial, applying for bail, conferring with one's client, making timely objections to significant, arguably erroneous rulings of the trial judge, and filing a notice of appeal if there are colorable grounds therefor could profitably be made the subject of uniform standards. * * *

B

I object to the prejudice standard adopted by the Court for two independent reasons. First, it is often very difficult to tell whether a defendant convicted after a trial in which he was ineffectively represented would have fared better if his lawyer had been competent. Seemingly impregnable cases can sometimes be dismantled by good defense counsel. On the basis of a cold record, it may be impossible for a reviewing court confidently to ascertain how the government's evidence and arguments would have stood up against rebuttal and cross-examination by a shrewd, well-prepared lawyer. The difficulties of estimating prejudice after the fact are exacerbated by the possibility that evidence of injury to the defendant may be missing from the record precisely because of the incompetence of defense counsel. In view of all these impediments to a fair evaluation of the probability that the outcome of a trial was affected by ineffectiveness of counsel, it seems to me senseless to impose on a defendant whose lawyer has been shown to have been incompetent the burden of demonstrating prejudice.

Second and more fundamentally, the assumption on which the Court's holding rests is that the only purpose of the constitutional guarantee of effective assistance of counsel is to reduce the chance that innocent persons will be convicted. In my view, the guarantee also functions to ensure that convictions are obtained only through fundamentally fair procedures. The majority contends that the Sixth Amendment is not violated when a manifestly guilty defendant is convicted after a trial in which he was represented by a manifestly ineffective attorney. I cannot agree. Every defendant is entitled to a trial in which his interests are vigorously and conscientiously advocated by an able lawyer. A proceeding in which the defendant does not receive meaningful assistance in meeting the forces of the State does not, in my opinion, constitute due process. * * *

II

Even if I were inclined to join the majority's two central holdings, I could not abide the manner in which the majority elaborates upon its rulings. * * *

A

In defining the standard of attorney performance required by the Constitution, the majority appropriately notes that many problems confronting criminal defense attorneys admit of "a range of legitimate" responses. And the majority properly cautions courts, when reviewing a lawyer's selection amongst a set of options, to avoid the hubris of hindsight. The majority goes on, however, to suggest that reviewing courts should "indulge a strong presumption that counsel's conduct" was constitutionally acceptable, and should "appl[y] a heavy measure of deference to counsel's judgments."

I am not sure what these phrases mean, and I doubt that they will be self-explanatory to lower courts. If they denote nothing more than that a defendant claiming he was denied effective assistance of counsel has the burden of proof, I would agree. But the adjectives "strong" and "heavy" might be read as imposing upon defendants an unusually weighty burden of persuasion. If that is the majority's intent, I must respectfully dissent. The range of acceptable behavior defined by "prevailing professional norms" seems to me sufficiently broad to allow defense counsel the flexibility they need in responding to novel problems of trial strategy. To afford attorneys more latitude, by "strongly presuming" that their behavior will fall within the zone of reasonableness, is covertly to legitimate convictions and sentences obtained on the basis of incompetent conduct by defense counsel. * * *

IV

The views expressed in the preceding section oblige me to dissent from the majority's disposition of the case before us. It is undisputed that respondent's trial counsel made virtually no investigation of the possibility of obtaining testimony from respondent's relatives, friends, or former employers pertaining to respondent's character or background. Had counsel done so, he would have found several persons willing and able to testify that, in their experience, respondent was a responsible, non-violent man, devoted to his family, and active in the affairs of his church. Respondent contends that his lawyer could have and should have used that testimony to "humanize" respondent, to counteract the impression conveyed by the trial that he was little more than a cold-blooded killer. Had this evidence been admitted, respondent argues, his chances of obtaining a life sentence would have been significantly better.

Measured against the standards outlined above, respondent's contentions are substantial. Experienced members of the death-penalty bar have long recognized the crucial importance of adducing evidence at a sentencing proceeding that establishes the defendant's social and familial connections. See Goodpaster, The Trial for Life: Effective Assistance of Counsel in Death Penalty Cases, 58 N.Y.U. L.Rev. 299, 300–303, 334–335 (1983). The State makes a colorable—though in my view not compelling—argument that defense counsel in this case might have made a reasonable "strategic" decision not to present such evidence at the sentencing hearing on the assumption that an unadorned acknowledgment of respondent's responsibility for his crimes would be more likely to appeal to the trial judge, who was reputed to respect persons who accepted responsibility for their actions. But however justifiable such a choice might have been after counsel had fairly assessed the potential strength of the mitigating evidence available to him, counsel's failure to make any significant effort to find out what evidence might be garnered from respondent's relatives and acquaintances surely cannot be described as "reasonable." Counsel's failure to investigate is particularly suspicious in light of his candid admission that respondent's confessions and conduct in the course of the trial gave him a feeling of "hopelessness" regarding the possibility of saving respondent's life.

That the aggravating circumstances implicated by respondent's criminal conduct were substantial does not vitiate respondent's constitutional claim; judges and juries in cases involving behavior at least as egregious have shown mercy, particularly when afforded an opportunity to see other facets of the defendant's personality and life. Nor is respondent's contention defeated by the possibility that the material his counsel turned up might not have been sufficient to establish a statutory mitigating circumstance under Florida law; Florida sentencing judges and the Florida Supreme Court sometimes refuse to impose death sentences in cases "in which, even though *statutory* mitigating circumstances do not outweigh statutory aggravating circumstances, the addition of nonstatutory mitigating circumstances tips the scales in favor of life imprisonment."

If counsel had investigated the availability of mitigating evidence, he might well have decided to present some such material at the hearing. If he had done so, there is a significant chance that respondent would have been given a life sentence. In my view, those possibilities, conjoined with the unreasonableness of counsel's failure to investigate, are more than sufficient to establish a violation of the Sixth Amendment and to entitle respondent to a new sentencing proceeding. * * *

NOTES AND QUESTIONS

1. It is important, when representing clients who committed gruesome crimes, to attempt to see the defendant as a person. There are few individuals who are truly evil, who commit crimes for no reason or for reasons that are unfathomable to those of us who do not commit crimes. According to David von Drehle, David Washington, the defendant in *Strickland v. Washington*, "could often be heard weeping in his cell" on death row. Most of the men on death row "have nothing but empty space where their conscience should be," but observers thought that Washington's "remorse was real and gut-wrenching." David von Drehle, Among the Lowest of the Dead 134 (1995).

And how did someone who felt real remorse do the awful deeds that he did? Out of work, depressed, and worried about supporting his family, he was in a laundromat when a man identified himself as a minister and made a proposition—if Washington came to the minister's home, there might be money in it for him. What he did not know until later was that the proposition was sexual in nature; it included "that Washington strip and straddle his face." Washington would later explain: "I stabbed him about five times. The only thing going through my mind, I said, 'Here I am out here trying to get some money to feed my family, and here go a minister supposed to be a minister in the church, running around doing stuff like this.' " *Id.*

2. With this knowledge of David Washington, and attempting to put out of your mind that the evidence against him was overwhelming, how would you grade counsel's performance in handling the case? Consider yourself a professor who teaches a course in representing criminal defendants, forget about the crime committed, focus on the details of what counsel did and did not do, and give the lawyer in this case a grade from the following list: C (competent); D (less than competent but within the range of reasonable); D- (barely above the line of incompetence); F (incompetent). (If you think a grade of A or B is justified, see us after class!)

Put another way, imagine you were the lawyer in *Strickland* and you are later describing your performance to your spouse, your parents, or your children. Would you be proud of your accomplishment? Satisfied? Embarrassed?

(We do not minimize the harm that David Washington caused or his blameworthiness for that harm. According to von Drehle, one of Washington's crimes was to kidnap a student from the University of Miami, rob him, and stab him to death "as the young man recited the Lord's prayer." *Id.* at 134.)

3. The Court in *Strickland* said that "[p]revailing norms of practice as reflected in the American Bar Association standards and the like are guidelines to determining what is reasonable [representation] * * *." The 2015 standards about the duty to

investigate the case have been substantially revised since the version in effect when Strickland's lawyer felt "hopeless" about the defense. Standard 4–4.1(b) now states: "The duty to investigate is not terminated by factors such as the apparent force of the prosecution's evidence, a client's alleged admissions to others of facts suggesting guilt, a client's expressed desire to plead guilty or that there should be no investigation, or statements to defense counsel supporting guilt."

It's almost as if the writer had the *Strickland* facts in front of her when she crafted the 2015 standard about the duty to investigate. Using the 2015 standard, would you find the lawyer's representation reasonable?

4. *Criticisms of lawyers.* After an exhaustive study of the American indigent defense system, the Reporters for the National Committee on the Right to Counsel concluded in 2006 that a national crisis existed.

> By every measure in every report analyzing the U.S. criminal justice system, the defense function for poor people is drastically underfinanced. This lack of money is reflected in a wide range of problems, including poor people's limited access to attorneys and the resulting ineffective assistance of counsel, * * * excessive public defender caseloads and insufficient salaries and compensation for defense lawyers.

Mary Sue Backus & Paul Marcus, *The Right to Counsel in Criminal Cases, A National Crisis*, 57 Hastings L. J. 1031, 1045–46 (2006).

Backus and Marcus offered many examples of the crisis in indigent representation. For example:

> Poor people account for more than 80% of individuals prosecuted. These criminal defendants plead guilty approximately 90% of the time. In those cases, more than half the lawyers entered pleas for their clients without spending any significant time on the cases, without interviewing witnesses or filing motions. Sometimes they barely spoke with their clients.
>
> An attorney was found to have entered pleas of guilty for more than 300 defendants without ever taking a matter to trial. In one case from Mississippi, a woman accused of a minor shoplifting offense spent a year in jail, before any trial, without even speaking to her appointed counsel. In some places, one lawyer may handle more than twenty criminal cases in a single day, with a flat rate of $50 per case. In others, some defense lawyers providing counsel to indigent defendants under a state contract system can be responsible for more than 1000 cases per year. In one major metropolitan area, San Jose, California, numerous defense attorneys failed to take simple steps to investigate and prepare their cases for trial. Some attorneys went to trial without ever meeting their clients outside the

> courtroom. Some neglected to interview obvious alibi witnesses. Some accepted without question reports from prosecutors' medical and forensic experts that were ripe for challenge.

Id. at 1034–35.

The National Committee on the Right to Counsel included prosecutors, judges, defense lawyers, and academics. The honorary co-chairs were Walter Mondale, Democratic candidate for president in 1984, and William Sessions, former director of the FBI. In 2009, the committee issued a report entitled *Justice Denied: America's Continuing Neglect of our Constitutional Right to Counsel.* The report details systemic and endemic failures of indigent defense in this country. It found "overwhelming" evidence that, in most of the country, "quality defense work is simply impossible because of inadequate funding, excessive caseloads, a lack of genuine independence, and insufficient availability of other essential resources."

The report provides twenty-two recommendations for improvement and can be found at https://constitutionproject.org/documents/?tcp_search=Justice+Denied&tcp_datestart=&tcp_dateend=&sortbutton=Search+Library#tcplib.

5. *Criticisms of Strickland.* The Court's opinion in *Strickland* has not met with favor among the commentators. "Scholars have concluded that the *Strickland* approach is a cynical dead end, designed to affirm all but the most deeply flawed convictions." George C. Thomas III, *History's Lesson for the Right to Counsel*, 2004 U. Ill. L. Rev. 543, 547. One problem, identified by Professor Donald Dripps, is that the appellate review is of a record made by the lawyer charged with incompetence: "It is all but ludicrous to ask a reviewing court to assess a record made by counsel to determine how counsel erred. As one might expect, this inquiry has done little to improve the quality of defense representation." Donald A. Dripps, *Ineffective Assistance of Counsel: The Case for an Ex Ante Parity Standard*, 88 J. Crim. L. & Criminology 242, 243 (1997). As the title of this article implies, Professor Dripps would replace the *Strickland* after-the-fact inquiry with an ex ante standard that requires the judge to determine, prior to the trial, "whether the defendant's lawyer can effectively represent him. Because the effectiveness of counsel is relative to the opposition, the test should be whether the defendant is represented by a lawyer roughly as good and roughly as well-prepared as counsel for the prosecution." *Id.* at 244.

6. Consider Justice Marshall's dissent in *Strickland.* Justice Marshall views the role of the Sixth Amendment right to counsel differently than the majority. Given his history and previous opinions, this should not surprise anyone. Also consider how Justice Marshall views the conduct of the defense attorney. Do you think that further action or investigation by counsel would have made a difference? Does Justice Marshall believe that should be the standard?

7. *Why did Justice Brennan concur in Strickland?* Professor Vivian Berger, in the excerpt that follows, calls Brennan's concurrence "puzzling." We agree.

VIVIAN O. BERGER—THE SUPREME COURT AND DEFENSE COUNSEL: OLD ROADS, NEW PATHS—A DEAD END?

86 Columbia Law Review 9 (1986), 112–116.

The "moral bases of attribution in the counsel/client relationship" * * * are most tenuous in criminal proceedings. The bulk of clients do not choose their own lawyers and the stakes are liberty and, at times, even life. Yet in our complex, adversarial system, practical responsibility for the accused's cause will inevitably fall upon his professional representative unless he forgoes a lawyer entirely. * * *

Given this fact, the Court's long-awaited treatment of the subject was disappointing. The *Strickland* majority's weighty presumption of lawyer competence (despite an otherwise acceptable test of "reasonable" performance) appeared to abolish the problem by fiat. If the language of presumption and deference can be relegated to some extent to the realm of rhetoric, the burden that the Court imposed on defendants to demonstrate actual prejudice cannot. Altogether, the justices signaled an intent to shield at least appellate courts from more than minimal involvement with claims of inadequate representation, leaving it to defendants themselves and conscientious trial court judges to deal with the problem as best they can.

But if the Court paid mere lip service to the importance of effective assistance by defense counsel while offering little by way of concrete vindication of the right, one must ask, nonetheless, how much difference it would have made had a better opinion been written in *Strickland.* Few people would disagree that upsetting convictions is an inefficient way to guarantee effective assistance—not to mention the systemic costs that vacating judgments invariably inflicts. One can only speculate whether reversals of judgments or grants of the writ [of habeas corpus] educate the target population of lawyers. Very likely, these decisions have greater impact on the judiciary, teaching courts what types of conduct by attorneys will not pass constitutional muster.

I believe that the justices might have at least increased the probability of such beneficial fallout by declining to make the element of prejudice the centerpiece of their analysis. However, reformers attempting to enhance the quality of counsel's representation have fielded much more ambitious programs than simply varying the legal standards used to evaluate lawyer performance after the fact. Suggestions range from exhortations to trial judges to monitor attorneys in pending cases—

by inquiring into counsel preparation and client satisfaction—to calls for broad systemic improvements. The latter include continuing legal education, professional certification or specialization requirements for practice in certain courts or subjects, more clinically oriented law school training, higher pay and greater auxiliary resources for assigned counsel, and structural changes in the delivery of defense services.

* * * Not surprisingly, none [of these proposals] promises to yield a ready panacea for the problem of ineffective assistance, and a number pose difficulties of their own; yet some merit further exploration. For present purposes, I wish to make only one point concerning such ideas: individually and as a group, they largely resist constitutionalization. In *Strickland*—which involved a state conviction—the Court was, of course, necessarily expounding the Constitution.

* * * [I]t is hard to find power in the federal courts to order expansive structural remedies addressed to the qualifications of counsel or the organization or funding of defender associations. The most generous conception of the Court's authority to mold constitutional "common law" could hardly sustain many needed forms of systemic relief, although it might conceivably permit some form of mandated trial court procedures designed to smoke out lawyer incompetence before irremediable damage occurs. * * * I believe that there is little in a practical vein the Court could have done, or can do in the future, to promote competent performance by counsel. If I am correct, perhaps Justice Brennan's puzzling concurrence with the *Strickland* majority stems from understandable reluctance to face that extremely discomfiting fact. * * *

In short, the Court's visions of the right to counsel and the role of counsel are incoherent, or downright cynical. In this area, most of the justices have failed to speak thoughtfully and candidly about the issues, an obligation that the Court as teacher owes us always. With regard to inadequate representation, even an honest acknowledgment of the Court's limitations might have encouraged further thought about solutions transcending the factual and legal bounds of particular cases as well as the jurisdictional constraints of a Court construing the Constitution. Thus, the road mapped in *Powell*, *Gideon*, and *Douglas* has petered out in a dead end, at least for now. Signposts for new directions for counsel will have to come from a different source.

NOTES AND QUESTIONS

1. *The end of the David Washington story.*

> He was ashamed and remorseful to the very end; he had that small credit. As his twelve-year-old daughter sobbed through their final visit, he cupped her trembling chin in his hand and said: "I want you to look at me, and I want you to see where I am * * * and I want you to do better."

David von Drehle, Among the Lowest of the Dead 254 (1995).

2. *Startling ignorance.* In Kimmelman v. Morrison, 477 U.S. 365, 106 S.Ct. 2574, 91 L.Ed.2d 305 (1986), the charge was rape, the defense was that it never happened, and an important piece of evidence was a bedsheet taken without a warrant from defendant's apartment. Here is how Justice Powell, concurring in the judgment, characterized the performance issue:

> [Defendant]'s ineffective-assistance claim is uncomplicated. [Defendant] argues that his trial counsel incompetently failed to conduct any pretrial discovery. Had counsel conducted discovery, he would have known that the police had seized a bedsheet from [defendant]'s apartment without a warrant. The bedsheet contained hair samples matching hair of both [defendant] and the rape victim. The sheet also contained semen stains matching those found in the victim's underpants. The State introduced the bedsheet and accompanying expert analysis at trial, and the trial judge denied [defendant]'s belated motion to suppress on the ground that it was untimely. [Defendant] contends that the sheet would have been excluded on Fourth Amendment grounds had the suppression motion been timely filed. Thus, [defendant] argues, counsel's failure to conduct discovery led to the admission of evidence that was both damning and excludible.

Counsel's "explanation" for his failure to conduct discovery was two-fold. First, he "asserted that it was the State's obligation to inform him of its case against his client, even though he made no request for discovery." Second, counsel said "he had not expected to go to trial because he had been told that the victim did not wish to proceed." The Supreme Court unanimously held that these explanations were not sufficient to bring the case under the *Strickland* rule that trial strategy is generally not to be second-guessed. As the Court put it: "The justifications [defendant]'s attorney offered for his omission betray a startling ignorance of the law—or a weak attempt to shift blame for inadequate preparation." The Court remanded for a hearing on prejudice.

3. *Another failure to know the relevant law.* The critical aspect of *Kimmelman*, Note 2, seems to be defense counsel's "ignorance" of law that was easily known. Continuing in that vein is Padilla v. Kentucky, 559 U.S. 356, 130 S.Ct. 1473, 176 L.Ed.2d 284

(2010), where counsel did not advise his client that a state narcotics conviction would make him subject to automatic deportation under federal law. Padilla had been "a lawful permanent resident of the United States for more than 40 years" and had "served this Nation with honor as a member of the U.S. Armed Forces during the Vietnam War." His lawyer not only failed to advise him of the automatic deportation but also affirmatively misled him by telling him that he " 'did not have to worry about immigration status since he had been in the country so long.' " Thus unaware of his situation, Padilla pled guilty to drug transportation charges.

The Court held that counsel's failure to warn Padilla of the consequences of his guilty plea (automatic deportation) "fell below" *Strickland*'s "objective standard of reasonableness." and thus constituted constitutionally deficient performance. "[W]hen the deportation consequence is truly clear, as it was in this case, the duty to give correct advice is equally clear." Justice Scalia, joined by Justice Thomas, dissented.

Justice Alito, concurring in the judgment, would have accepted the Solicitor General's request to limit the holding to "affirmative misadvice," but the majority refused to do so. "It is quintessentially the duty of counsel to provide her client with available advice about an issue like deportation and the failure to do so 'clearly satisfies the first prong of the *Strickland* analysis.' "

Notice that the deportation law in *Padilla* was "not within the sentencing authority of the state trial court." As the Court conceded, many courts had taken the position that failure to advise a client about "collateral consequences" of a conviction could never be constitutionally deficient performance. That is no longer true, though the full scope of *Padilla* is unknown. Will it be limited to collateral consequences spelled out in a statute that is, in the Court's words, "succinct, clear, and explicit"? Will it also be limited to the consequence of deportation, which the Court noted it had "long recognized" as a "particularly severe" penalty?

Finally, the Court did not reach *Strickland*'s second prong—whether the constitutionally deficient performance resulted in constitutionally recognized prejudice, which is likely to prove a particularly daunting challenge for most defendants. In Hill v. Lockhart, 474 U.S. 52, 58, 106 S.Ct. 366, 88 L.Ed.2d 203 (1985), the Court suggested that proving prejudice when ineffective assistance led to a guilty plea entails more than merely proving that the client would have insisted on pleading not guilty. At one point, *Hill* phrased the prejudice inquiry as whether the outcome of the *trial* "would have been different" had the defendant pled not guilty. In *Padilla*, the Court phrased the issue as "whether 'there is a reasonable probability that, but for counsel's unprofessional errors, the result of the *proceeding* would have been different.' " (Emphasis added.) And in a footnote, the Court ominously noted "that it is often quite difficult for petitioners who have acknowledged their guilt to satisfy *Strickland*'s prejudice prong."

Padilla pled guilty to three drug-related charges and agreed to serve five years in prison and be on probation for five years after his release from prison. See Commonwealth v. Padilla, 253 S.W.3d 482 (Ky. 2008). Presumably, he made that decision because the State had a strong case. So, even if he persuades a reviewing court that he would have gone to trial, the State can seek to show that a conviction was likely and thus would have resulted in the same deportation order. How likely a conviction would have to be to avoid a finding of prejudice is yet one more unknown left in the wake of *Padilla.*

4. *Yet one more failure to know the relevant law.* In Hinton v. Alabama, 571 U.S. 263, 134 S.Ct. 1081, 188 L.Ed.2d 1 (2014) (per curiam), the defendant was tried in 1985 for two murders. The critical—and essentially the only—evidence against defendant was the testimony of the state forensics experts that the bullets that killed the victims came from defendant's gun. Thus, the testimony of a defense expert was central to the defense. Both the trial judge and the defense lawyer believed that the State only allowed $1,000 to pay an expert witness. The judge invited the defense lawyer to request more if needed and he would check to see whether more money could be awarded. The lawyer, however, did not request additional funding. Had he done so, the judge would presumably have discovered that Alabama had removed the limit on reimbursing defense experts in capital cases more than a year before Hinton's trial.

The lawyer made an "extensive search for a well-regarded expert," but could find only one expert, Andrew Payne, willing to testify for $1,000. Hinton's lawyer "testified that Payne did not have the expertise he thought he needed and that he did not consider Payne's testimony to be effective." Indeed, that might be an understatement. Here is how the Court characterized Payne's effectiveness:

> On cross-examination, the prosecutor badly discredited Payne. Payne admitted that he'd testified as an expert on firearms and toolmark identification just twice in the preceding eight years and that one of the two cases involved a shotgun rather than a handgun. Payne also conceded that he had had difficulty operating the microscope at the state forensic laboratory and had asked for help from one of the state experts. The prosecutor ended the cross-examination with this colloquy:
>
> "Q. Mr. Payne, do you have some problem with your vision?
>
> "A. Why, yes.
>
> "Q. How many eyes do you have?
>
> "A. One."

The jury convicted, and Hinton was sentenced to die. Both on direct appeal and in post-conviction review, the Alabama courts held that Payne was qualified as an expert witness under the Alabama standard, which required only that the witness have "knowledge of firearms and toolmarks examination beyond that of an average layperson."

The Supreme Court unanimously reversed the state courts, holding that the defense lawyer's "failure to request additional funding in order to replace an expert he knew to be inadequate because he mistakenly believed that he had received all he could get under Alabama law constituted deficient performance." The Court stressed that the deficient performance was not hiring the wrong expert: "We do not today launch federal courts into examination of the relative qualifications of experts hired and experts that might have been hired." Instead, the "inadequate assistance of counsel here was the inexcusable mistake of law—the unreasonable failure to understand the resources that state law made available to him—that caused counsel to employ an expert that he *himself* deemed inadequate." (Emphasis in original).

Holding that "no court has yet evaluated the prejudice question by applying the proper inquiry to the facts of this case," the Court remanded on that issue. But the Court seemed to be sending a broad hint that it considered prejudicial the failure to hire a competent expert. Notice the emphasis on the possibility that Hinton might be innocent:

> That the State presented testimony from two experienced expert witnesses that tended to inculpate Hinton does not, taken alone, demonstrate that Hinton is guilty. Prosecution experts, of course, can sometimes make mistakes. * * * This threat is minimized when the defense retains a competent expert to counter the testimony of the prosecution's expert witnesses; it is maximized when the defense instead fails to understand the resources available to it by law.

5. *Hinton, the man, and the rest of the story.* On remand, the Alabama trial court held "that counsel, in fact, would have hired a different and more qualified expert had counsel known that the statutory-funding limit had been lifted and that there was a reasonable probability that the testimony of a different and more qualified expert would have instilled in the jury a reasonable doubt as to Hinton's guilt." Hinton v. State, 172 So.3d 355 (Ct. Crim. App. Ala. 2014). The trial judge thus granted Hinton's petition to vacate his two convictions.

Faced with the prospect of retrying Hinton, state prosecutors conceded that his guilt "depends upon an absolute, conclusive determination that the bullets recovered from their bodies were in fact fired through the barrel of the firearm taken from the defendant's home." After new tests, the State's own experts "found that they could not conclusively determine that any of the six bullets were or were not fired through the same firearm or that they were fired through the firearm recovered from the defendant's home." Prosecutors moved to dismiss the case against Hinton. Alan

Blinder, "Alabama Man Freed After Decades on Death Row," *New York Times*, April 3, 2015.

Hinton "spoke of unjustly losing three decades of his life, under fear of execution, for something he didn't do. 'All they had to do was to test the gun, but when you think you're high and mighty and you're above the law, you don't have to answer to nobody,' " Hinton told reporters.

"But I've got news for you—everybody that played a part in sending me to death row, you will answer to God." Jason Hanna and Ed Payne, "Alabama Inmate Freed After Nearly 30 Years on Death Row," *CNN*, April 3, 2015.

"And, haltingly, he began to talk about mercy. 'I've got to forgive,' he said. 'I lived in hell for 30 years, so I don't want to die and go to hell. So I've got to forgive. I don't have a choice.' " Blinder, *New York Times*.

6. *And more about Alabama indigent defense.* In Maples v. Thomas, 565 U.S. 266, 132 S.Ct. 912, 181 L.Ed.2d 807 (2012), the defendant procedurally defaulted his state post-conviction proceedings by missing a filing deadline. Normally, defaulting state remedies precludes federal habeas corpus relief. The Court held, however, that there was "cause" for his failure to meet the deadline.

The Court began its opinion in *Maples* by describing the Alabama procedure for appointing counsel in capital cases:

> Alabama sets low eligibility requirements for lawyers appointed to represent indigent capital defendants at trial. Appointed counsel need only be a member of the Alabama bar and have "five years' prior experience in the active practice of criminal law." Experience with capital cases is not required. Nor does the State provide, or require appointed counsel to gain, any capital-case-specific professional education or training.
>
> Appointed counsel in death penalty cases are also undercompensated. Until 1999, the State paid appointed capital defense attorneys just "$40.00 per hour for time expended in court and $20.00 per hour for time reasonably expended out of court in the preparation of [the defendant's] case." Although death penalty litigation is plainly time intensive, the State capped at $1,000 fees recoverable by capital defense attorneys for out-of-court work. Even today, court-appointed attorneys receive only $70 per hour.
>
> Nearly alone among the States, Alabama does not guarantee representation to indigent capital defendants in postconviction proceedings. The State has elected, instead, "to rely on the efforts of typically well-funded [out-of-state] volunteers." Thus, as of 2006, 86% of the attorneys representing Alabama's death row inmates in state collateral

review proceedings "either worked for the Equal Justice Initiative (headed by NYU Law professor Bryan Stevenson), out-of-state public interest groups like the Innocence Project, or an out-of-state mega-firm." On occasion, some prisoners sentenced to death receive no postconviction representation at all. See ABA Report 112 ("[A]s of April 2006, approximately fifteen of Alabama's death row inmates in the final rounds of state appeals had no lawyer to represent them.").

For a biting critique of the representation of counsel in death cases, see Vivian O. Berger, *The Chiropractor as Brain Surgeon: Defense Lawyering in Capital Cases*, 18 N.Y.U. Rev. L. & Social Change 245 (1990); Stephen B. Bright, *Death By Lottery—Procedural Bar of Constitutional Claims in Capital Cases Due to Inadequate Representation of Indigent Defendants*, 92 W. Va. L. Rev. 679 (1990).

BRUCE A. GREEN—LETHAL FICTION: THE MEANING OF "COUNSEL" IN THE SIXTH AMENDMENT

78 Iowa Law Review 433 (1993), 433, 437.

Charles Bell, Donald Paradis, and Shirley Tyler were tried in different states for murder. Each was convicted and sentenced to death. Charles Bell was represented at trial by a recent law school graduate who had never before tried a criminal case to completion. Donald Paradis's lawyer had passed the bar exam six months earlier, had never previously represented a criminal accused, and had not elected courses in criminal law, criminal procedure, or trial advocacy while in law school. Shirley Tyler's trial lawyer was also a member of the bar for only a few months. He had defended one previous assault case and one previous robbery case, each lasting half a day. Each condemned prisoner later asserted that he or she had been denied the Sixth Amendment right of a criminal accused "to have the assistance of counsel for his defence" on the ground that the defense attorney had rendered ineffective legal assistance. In asserting this claim, each undertook the difficult burden of demonstrating the likelihood that he or she had received a sentence of death only because of the attorney's unreasonably poor performance.

Not surprisingly, none of the three death-row defendants claimed to have been deprived of "counsel" altogether, since courts unwaveringly adhere to the view that "counsel" under the Sixth Amendment includes any duly licensed attorney. This Article argues, however, that a narrower construction of the constitutional term is warranted: "counsel" should include only those attorneys who are qualified to render legal assistance to a person accused of a crime. By that standard, these three defendants, and many others who similarly have been tried, convicted, and sentenced to death with an unqualified attorney by their side, have been deprived of their right to "counsel." * * *

[This Article] describes what redefining "counsel" would mean for the criminal justice system. To be regarded as "counsel" for constitutional purposes, a member of the bar should possess the skill and knowledge understood within the profession as prerequisites to defending criminal cases adequately. The right to "counsel," meaning a qualified advocate, would not supplant the presently recognized right to effective assistance of counsel, but would supplement it. Criminal defendants would be entitled, at the threshold, to a qualified attorney. In individual cases in which a seemingly capable lawyer provided substandard representation, a convicted defendant could claim that he was denied the right to effective assistance of counsel.

Because most lawyers do not possess the requisite skill and knowledge to be qualified to defend a criminal case, some mechanism to train and certify those lawyers must be established. Courts are undoubtedly capable of establishing such a mechanism. The judiciary is, after all, responsible for the existing licensing process, and some courts already have established processes either for certifying criminal lawyers as specialists or for determining which lawyers are qualified to serve by assignment in criminal cases. Moreover, legislatures are equally capable of devising a process for upgrading the quality of criminal defense lawyers. Congress, for one, recently considered legislation designed in part to improve the quality of defense lawyers in death penalty cases.

NOTES AND QUESTIONS

1. *Sleeping beauty.* According to a court clerk assigned to the trial judge, Calvin Burdine's lawyer slept "a lot" and "for long periods of time" during the prosecution's questioning of witnesses in a death penalty trial. Yet a Fifth Circuit panel held that this fact, by itself, did not automatically require a finding that the counsel was ineffective. Burdine v. Johnson, 231 F.3d 950 (5th Cir. 2000). To be sure, an en banc decision overturned the panel, by a vote of nine to five—see Burdine v. Johnson, 262 F.3d 336 (5th Cir. 2001)—but it might give one pause that five members of the Fifth Circuit did not believe that a sleeping lawyer is necessarily an ineffective one.

2. *Awake but little more.* Prior to jury selection in a capital murder trial, defense counsel files a motion for continuance, stating that he is "totally unprepared to begin with this case." The judge denied the motion. Defense counsel questions the jury but at the close of *voir dire* refuses to exercise any of his client's peremptory challenges (available to exclude potential jurors if a challenge for cause fails). He renews his motion for a continuance and when the judge again denies it, states: "[I]f we are going ahead with this trial, * * * I will be physically present because I am sure the Court would require that, but I do not in any way intend to participate in the trial of this

matter." He again asserts that he is unprepared and physically exhausted. He attends the trial but does not participate in any way. The jury convicted and, after a sentencing hearing, the judge sentenced *H* to die. State v. Harvey, 692 S.W.2d 290 (Mo.1985).

This is either the most fundamental failure imaginable or a clever strategy. Do you see how it could be a strategy? Is there a way for the judge to defeat the strategy short of having to grant the continuance?

3. *Does this sound like effective assistance to you?* Cronic was "indicted on mail fraud charges involving the transfer of over $9,400,000 in checks." About a month before the scheduled trial date, respondent's retained counsel withdrew. (Dressler and Thomas speculate that the fee was not paid).

> The court appointed a young lawyer with a real estate practice to represent respondent, but allowed him only 25 days for pretrial preparation, even though it had taken the Government over four and one-half years to investigate the case and it had reviewed thousands of documents during that investigation. The two codefendants agreed to testify for the Government; respondent was convicted on 11 of the 13 counts in the indictment and received a 25-year sentence.

The Court unanimously held that these facts, standing alone, did not justify a finding of ineffective assistance of counsel (Justice Marshall concurred in the judgment). See United States v. Cronic, 466 U.S. 648, 104 S.Ct. 2039, 80 L.Ed. 2d 657 (1984). On the assumption that the Court did not temporarily lose its mind, explain the narrow holding.

4. *The simple closing argument.* Death penalty cases require a separate sentencing phase, as you saw in *Strickland*. What if the defense lawyer failed to present *any* mitigating evidence in the sentencing phase and a court later found "sufficient grounds" to argue several mitigating factors, including "youth, intoxication, and family background"? The only defense at sentencing consisted of the following closing argument:

> Defense Counsel: Ladies and Gentlemen, I appreciate the time you took deliberating and the thought you put into this. I'm going to be extremely brief. I have a reputation for not being brief.
>
> Jesse, stand up. Jesse?
>
> The Defendant: Sir?
>
> Defense Counsel: Stand up.
>
> You are an extremely intelligent jury. You've got that man's life in your hands. You can take it or not. That's all I have to say.

Is this effective assistance under *Strickland*? See Romero v. Lynaugh, 884 F.2d 871 (5th Cir. 1989).

5. *Thank God it's over.* In another capital case, the crime was a brutal rape and murder of an eight-year-old girl; she suffered six stab wounds to the body and five knife slashes traversing her abdomen, along with numerous lacerations and abrasions on her face, neck, and upper chest. At the close of the *guilt* phase, defense counsel argued as follows:

> I would be [dishonest] with each and every one of you if I tried to tell you the evidence said something other than what [the prosecutor] indicates occurred on that day so I'm not going to. * * * I don't think in a situation like this there's anything that I can say except to say thank God this is over. * * * I pray to God that none of you or myself, or the other people in this court room, will ever see anything like this again. I'm not going to be dishonest to y'all and say something to change what is, the evidence is, what the evidence is, the law the judge gives you as to how to consider this evidence. That's all I have. Thank you.

Assuming the evidence of guilt was overwhelming, does this closing argument at the guilt phase meet the *Strickland* standard? See Messer v. Kemp, 760 F.2d 1080 (11th Cir. 1985).

6. *Forgiveness from heaven.* Same case as Note 5. The jury convicts. At the sentencing phase, the lawyer presents a single witness, the defendant's mother, and elicits from her that she and the defendant both expected the death penalty. She also testified that the defendant "has got saved, he's confessed his sins to Christ, and he told me, he said 'mama, the Lord has forgiven me * * *.' "

In the closing argument in the sentencing phase, the lawyer said to the jury, "[Your decision] is an awesome responsibility and I dare say I would rather be over here than in y'all's seats, because as a parent under these circumstances"—here he paused before continuing—"but that's for y'all to decide." Is this effective representation under *Strickland*?

7. *Is the Court quietly requiring more competent lawyering in death cases?* Two of the Court's recent death cases suggest that *Strickland*'s refusal to engage in "Monday-morning quarter-backing" seems to be receding a bit. To be sure, *Strickland* claims in death cases are even more fact-sensitive and complex than in ordinary run-of-the mill cases, and it is difficult to generalize.

The defendant in Wiggins v. Smith, 539 U.S. 510, 123 S.Ct. 2527, 156 L.Ed.2d 471 (2003), convinced the Court that his lawyer was ineffective because he did not investigate the severe physical and sexual abuse at the hands of his mother and under the care of a series of foster parents. Notably, the Court was willing to rely on the standards for capital defense work articulated by the American Bar Association, which require "efforts to discover *all reasonably available* mitigating evidence and evidence to rebut any aggravating evidence that may be introduced by the prosecutor." ABA Guidelines for the Appointment and Performance of Counsel in Death Penalty Cases 11.4.1(C), p. 93 (1989) (emphasis added). Might Washington have proven lack of competence of his counsel if the *Strickland* Court had applied that standard? To be sure, the ABA Guidelines appeared five years after *Strickland* was decided, but evolving guidelines can be viewed as part of a partial retreat from *Strickland.*

In Rompilla v. Beard, 545 U.S. 374, 125 S.Ct. 2456, 162 L.Ed.2d 360 (2005), the defendant's trial lawyers worked harder than did Wiggins's lawyers to find mitigating evidence. They interviewed five family members in a "detailed manner" and reviewed the reports of three mental health experts who examined Rompilla. But the lawyers did not review a court file, readily available in the courthouse, containing material about one of Rompilla's prior convictions. The prosecutor had told defense counsel that he was going to use the rape victim's testimony in the prior case to prove Rompilla's violent character, which was relevant to an aggravating circumstance under the state death penalty law. Defense lawyers read the victim's testimony in the court file but did not examine the rest of the file. If defense lawyers had examined the file completely, they would have found mitigating evidence. The Court held that this constituted deficient defense. Is this really more deficient than the utter failure of the lawyer in *Strickland* to investigate his client's possible emotional disturbance? Perhaps. Justice O'Connor, the author of *Strickland*, joined the *Rompilla* majority.

8. *Foggy mirrors.* Perhaps the pithiest criticism of the *Strickland* test is that some defense lawyers call it the "foggy mirror" test. "If you place a mirror in front of defense counsel during trial and it fogs, counsel is in fact effective." Randall Coyne, Capital Punishment and the Judicial Process, Teacher's Manual 148 (1995).

9. *Can an indigent defendant sue his foggy mirror for malpractice?* The answer, in Minnesota at least, is no. See Dziubak v. Mott, 503 N.W.2d 771 (Minn. 1993). But, wait, you say: privately-retained lawyers can be sued by criminal clients for malpractice so why not publicly-financed lawyers? The state court offered two reasons. First, unlike private counsel, public defenders have no choice about which clients to accept: the defender "is obligated to represent whomever is assigned to her or him, regardless of her or his current caseload or the degree of difficulty the case presents." Second, public defenders are grossly underfunded. "It would be an unfair burden to subject the public defender to possible malpractice for acts or omissions due to impossible caseloads and an under-funded office: something completely out of the defender's control."

10. *Chances of winning an ineffective assistance claim.* The Center for Capital Litigators in Columbia, South Carolina has collected citations and summaries of all published

successful ineffective assistance of counsel claims since *Strickland*. As of December, 2001, the list contained roughly 1,200 state and federal cases. Running *Strickland* in Westlaw for the same time period produced about 37,000 entries. Thus, as the lower courts have understood and applied *Strickland*, lawyers provided constitutionally competent assistance in roughly 97% of the cases where their performance was challenged. Perhaps Justice O'Connor would say that this demonstrates the basic soundness of lawyering in criminal cases. Perhaps it does.

CHAPTER 9 SUMMARY

The role of defense counsel is vital to the fairness of our criminal justice system. While prosecutors play an obviously important role in holding people accountable when they violate society's laws, it is the defense counsel that keeps the system honest; that ensures the system's credibility so that society accepts its results

For this to work, however, defense counsel must be well-educated, well-trained, competent, dedicated, and even passionate in the defense of his or her client. The norms that we identified in Chapter 1 as underlying the process—accuracy, efficiency, fairness, and limiting the power of government—simply cannot be achieved if the lawyer for the defense (or the prosecution, for that matter) is inept, incompetent, indifferent, or corrupt.

Defense attorneys must be more than competent, however. They must also zealously represent their client regardless of what they think of the client or the crime committed. This means that attorneys must—within the bounds of law and ethics—do everything they can to defend their client. This includes making arguments that the attorney may find distasteful or that society would normally condemn.

Competent, passionate, and well-funded defense counsel is the ideal of our criminal justice system, but one that is far from met. This chapter identified several areas where we as a society need to do considerably better; most importantly in the need for proper funding, resources, and workloads for indigent defense. Some of the effects of our failure as a society to do so are discussed in the next chapter.

CHAPTER 10

Wrongful Convictions

Having spent the previous chapters examining the requirements for a properly conducted criminal investigation and adjudication process, we turn now to cases where the system has gone wrong—concentrating on cases where, either through police misconduct during the investigation, or through systemic problems inherent in our current criminal justice system, an innocent person gets convicted. In Chapter 1, we examined what an ideal or successful criminal justice system might look like. No one can credibly claim that we have met that ideal. Our criminal justice system is indeed a work in progress and likely always will be. In this chapter, we look in more detail at some of the areas where more progress is needed.

A. GUILTY UNTIL PROVEN INNOCENT?

1. Introduction

We do not know how frequently a factually innocent defendant is convicted of a crime. But we do know some root causes. Underlying most of these causes is an arrogance about our methods of investigating and prosecuting crime. For example, police interrogators think they are quite good at identifying who is lying or telling the truth. Many studies, however, show that the ability of police to be a "human lie detector" is little better than flipping a coin. See, e.g., Dan Simon, In Doubt 120–132 (2102). Moreover, though difficult to believe, a non-trivial number of normally functioning suspects falsely confess when interrogated by police.

Once police have identified a likely suspect, tunnel vision sets in. Police and prosecutors tend to see every piece of evidence as confirming their belief in guilt. To make matters worse, one investigative technique that might seem very helpful turns out to be unreliable—that of eyewitness identification. We do not know how often eyewitness identifications are wrong, but we do know that of the 350 or so

DNA exonerations, over 70% included an identification of a suspect who turned out to be factually innocent. Lab studies suggest that the error rate in eyewitness identifications is quite high. It turns out that humans are not very good at remembering faces and we now know that memory decays even over relatively brief periods of time. Thus, convictions of assault, robbery, and rape that depend crucially on eyewitness identification are inherently suspect.

Compounding the problem, almost all forensic science is, at best, an educated guess. DNA is in a class by itself; properly conducted and applied to the facts of a case, DNA testing is scientifically accurate. But fingerprints are, in cases at the margin, not as scientific as examiners claim. And the reliability problems with fingerprints pale by comparison to "expert" testimony about hair matches, crowbar markings, tire tracks, bite marks, blood spatter and other "forensic science." In 2015, the FBI admitted that between 2,000 and 3,000 cases contained deeply flawed FBI hair match evidence. In the first 268 cases reviewed, twenty-six of twenty-eight examiners in the FBI microscopic hair comparison unit "overstated forensic matches in ways that favored prosecutors in more than 95 percent" of the cases. Spencer S. Hsu, "FBI admits flaws in hair analysis over decades," The Washington Post, April 18, 2015. Thirty-two of those defendants were sentenced to death and fourteen "have been executed or died in prison."

The Norfolk Four

The following account of the Norfolk Four, based on Tom Wells & Richard A. Leo, *The Wrong Guys: Murder, False Confessions and Norfolk Four* (2008), is an example of extreme tunnel vision and arrogance on the part of police and prosecutors. Police suspected Danial Williams in the brutal rape and murder of Michelle Moore-Bosko. He confessed after eleven hours of coercive police interrogation, convincing the Norfolk police that the case was solved. Then the lab report came back: Williams's DNA did not match what was found in the victim. So, to explain that anomaly, the police fastened on a second suspect and interrogated him relentlessly until he confessed to committing the crime with Williams. But the police were no closer to the real criminal because suspect #2's DNA did not match. One would hope that the DNA evidence to this point would move police to revisit their theory that these two suspects had raped and murdered the victim. But police kept bringing in more men in the hopes of finding a DNA match; eventually a dozen men were suspects in what had become a gang rape even though police initially thought it had been committed by one man. And still no one's DNA matched that found on the victim.

After one suspect pleaded guilty and cases were proceeding against three others, the real killer/rapist was found. In a twist that belongs in a novel, Omar

Ballard, admitted his crime in a letter to a woman who had not written him while he was in jail. Ballard threatened to kill her like he had killed Michelle, unless she wrote him. She went to the police.

Ballard's DNA matched. He confessed that he had acted alone. But the detectives made clear that he would get a plea deal and no death penalty only if he told the "truth," and the "truth" they wanted was that he had met the four defendants in the parking lot and the five of them committed the gruesome crime. He initially stuck to his story that he acted alone but eventually told the "truth." He failed two lie detector tests with this fabricated story. Yet the State continued to pursue, achieve, and defend on appeal convictions against four innocent men.

The Norfolk Four saga shows how tenaciously police can hold to their original theory of the case. They had to find a way to make Danial Williams part of the crime because he had confessed. All of the original evidence pointed to a single rapist, but the State persuaded itself, somehow, that it was a gang rape even though only one man's DNA was found at the crime scene. Other than tunnel vision and deluded thinking, the only other possibility is that the State was trying to cover up the fact that it was putting the freedom of four innocent men in jeopardy. But that possibility is just too awful to put forward seriously. Wells and Leo are willing to accept tunnel vision and deluded thinking as an explanation for the almost inexplicable actions of police and prosecutors; Wells and Leo suggest it is likely that the detectives still believed their gang rape story and thought Ballard simply lying about committing the crime alone.

Ray Krone's Case

> At 8:10 in the morning on December 29, 1991, a female bartender was found, dead, in the men's room of the C.B.S. Lounge in Phoenix. She was nude. The killer left behind no physical evidence save bite marks on her breast and neck. The victim had told a friend that Ray Krone was going to help close the bar that night. Police asked Krone to make a bite impression, and an expert witness prepared a videotape that purported to show a match by moving Krone's bite impression onto the marks on the victim. According to the Arizona Supreme Court, the videotape "presented evidence in ways that would have been impossible using static exhibits." State v. Krone, 897 P.2d 621, 622 (Ariz. 1995). Although defense counsel had been given the opportunity to examine the dental expert, counsel was not informed of the existence of the videotape until the eve of trial.

The only other evidence against Krone was that he was "evasive with the police about his relationship" with the victim. Id. Of course, without the bite mark identification, being "evasive" about a relationship is practically worthless as evidence. The case turned on the bite mark evidence, and the court-appointed defense expert had no experience in video production. Accordingly, counsel moved for a continuance to obtain an expert who could evaluate the videotape. Alternatively, counsel moved to suppress the videotape or to allow testimony about an earlier case in which the same expert's testimony was successfully challenged as not sufficiently scientific. The trial court overruled all the defense motions. The prosecution expert used the videotape in his testimony, and no defense expert challenged his presentation. The jury convicted Krone of murder and kidnaping. The trial judge sentenced Krone to death.

On appeal, the Arizona Supreme Court held that the trial judge had acted improperly in refusing to allow a continuance. The jury had not yet been selected when the motion was made, the court noted, and the State would have suffered little prejudice. If substantial prejudice would have been caused, the right course of action, according to the state supreme court, was to preclude use of the videotape. What the trial judge could not do was what he did—allow use of the tape without giving defense counsel ample opportunity to prepare a defense.

So far, so good. The case was remanded for a new trial, the defense secured an expert, and the jury convicted again. This time, though, the judge sentenced Krone to life in prison, "citing doubts about whether or not Krone was the true killer." See Innocence Project web site (case of Ray Krone). This borders on the unbelievable. A trial judge who had "doubts about whether or not Krone was the true killer" sentenced him to life in prison. Krone served over ten years in prison before DNA testing conducted on the saliva and blood found on the victim excluded him as the killer. The DNA matched a man who lived close to the bar but who had never been considered a suspect in the killing.

Ray Krone's case is an example of how the current system fails innocent defendants. Police seized on the first plausible suspect and looked no further. The prosecution built a case on a Styrofoam bite impression and mumbo-jumbo scientific evidence. That the case was so weak perhaps explains why the prosecutor did not want the defense to be able to challenge the videotaped "expert" testimony. If true, that

> violates the first rule of prosecution—to do justice rather than try to win all cases. "Doing justice" in Ray Krone's case meant allowing the defense to challenge the prosecution's expert testimony.
>
> The first trial judge failed to give Krone a chance to demonstrate his innocence, and the second one sentenced him to life in prison even though he had doubts about his guilt. These are fundamental failures. To be sure, some parts of the system worked. Krone received what appears to have been effective representation by his counsel, and the Arizona Supreme Court recognized the errors of the first trial judge. Nonetheless, despite these successes, Ray Krone would have spent the rest of his life in prison for a crime he did not commit were it not for DNA testing and the Innocence Project at Cardozo Law School, founded by Barry Scheck and Peter Neufeld.
>
> What has gone wrong? In a work published in 1713, Matthew Hale acclaimed the English common law jury trial as the "best Trial in the World." Matthew Hale, The History and Analysis of the Common Law 252 (1713). For example, Hale said that having witnesses testify in person—subject to being questioned by the parties, the judge, and the jury—was the "best Method of searching and sifting out the Truth." Today * * * any rational system of justice should care more about protecting innocent defendants than any other value. But DNA testing has made plain that our modern adversary system just isn't very good at protecting innocent defendants.

George C. Thomas III—The Supreme Court on Trial—How the American System of Justice Sacrifices Innocent Defendants (2008) 6–8.

NOTES AND QUESTIONS

1. While most errors that produce wrongful convictions are not as egregious as the ones in the Norfolk Four and Krone cases, we now know that the system fails far more often than we once thought. Finding ways to reduce these errors should be part of the national discourse about our criminal justice system.

In a study of over 10,000 cases in which the FBI compared DNA of the suspect with DNA from the crime scene, the DNA tests exonerated the prime suspect in 20% of the cases. In another 20%, the results were inconclusive. Because the inconclusive results must be removed from the sample, the police were wrong in one case in four. The lab records do not indicate whether the 20% of excluded suspects were tried using other evidence. Edward Conners, et al., *Convicted by Juries, Exonerated by Science:*

Case Studies in the Use of DNA Evidence to Establish Innocence After Trial, in National Institute of Justice Report (1996).

The DNA evidence is bound to overstate the error rate in arrests overall. When the identity of the actor is known, and the argument is over whether what he did is a crime, there is no risk of convicting the wrong person and thus no reason to conduct a DNA test. These cases will not, of course, appear in the DNA database, making the error rate in all cases lower than that found in the Justice study. But even if the error rate is only 3%, that means almost half a million innocent defendants are arrested each year. See U.S. Department of Justice, Federal Bureau of Investigation, Crime in the United States, 2004, tbl. 4.1, p. 280 (showing fourteen million non-traffic arrests in 2004).

2. *Is there a reliable estimate of system-wide wrongful convictions?* The short answer is no. By "wrongful convictions," we mean convictions of factually innocent defendants. In his book, excerpted above, Thomas drew on a statistical model and a study of English convictions to produce a rough overall estimate that two percent of convictions are of innocent defendants. Thomas, at 39–40.

Michael Risinger has made a compelling argument that it is a fool's errand to attempt an estimate of a general error rate, both because we lack a methodology and because the error rate will almost certainly vary dramatically by category of crime. See D. Michael Risinger, *Innocents Convicted: An Empirically Justified Factual Wrongful Conviction Rate*, 97 J. Crim. L. Criminology 761 (2007). So, for example, the error rate in armed robbery cases, where identification is a critical issue, will be much higher than in cases of failing to file income tax returns, where it should be almost zero.

But Risinger has developed a methodology for estimating the error rate in rape-murder capital cases. His rigorous methodology produced a minimum error rate of 3.3%. What is your reaction to being told that of 319 capital rape-murder convictions Risinger studied, at least 10 of the men sentenced to die were factually innocent?

George Thomas argues in a forthcoming paper that the general wrongful conviction rate is probably no more than one percent and could be as low as one-eighth of one percent. See George C. Thomas III, *Where Have All the Innocents Gone?*, 60 Ariz. L. Rev. ___ (forthcoming 2018). His estimate is based on the number of applications claiming innocence filed with the North Carolina Innocence Inquiry Commission. If the estimate seems too low based on what you have read so far, consider that 95% of criminal cases are resolved by guilty plea, and the incentive to plead guilty is radically reduced if the defendant knows he is innocent. (The two Norfolk Four defendants who pleaded guilty did it to avoid the death penalty.) Thomas estimates that the rate in cases that are tried is substantially higher, perhaps as high as 4 to 5 percent.

3. The National Registry of Exonerations has over 2000 heart-breaking stories of innocent men and women who have spent years and sometimes decades behind bars. A few have languished on death row. Reading these stories produces disbelief and sorrow. How could the system fail so many so badly?

"There is no worse error in American criminal justice than the wrongful prosecution, conviction, and incarceration of an innocent person, especially in capital cases. . . ." Richard A. Leo, *False Confessions: Causes, Consequences, and Solutions*, in Wrongly Convicted: Perspectives on Failed Justice (Saundra D. Westervelt John A. Humphrey, eds. 2001). Do you have any thoughts about how to avoid these miscarriages of justice? Let's begin with eyewitness identifications.

2. The Problem of Eyewitness Identification

On January 3, 2008, Charles Chatman walked out of a Texas prison a free man. By then he had served twenty-seven years of a ninety-nine year prison sentence for a rape someone else had committed. Eyewitness misidentification was a major factor in Chatman's wrongful conviction. He was exonerated thanks to DNA testing.

Chatman's experience is hardly unique. He was the fifteenth wrongfully convicted prisoner exonerated in Dallas County, Texas in the first seven years of DNA testing. Ralph Blumenthal, *15th Dallas County Inmate Since '01 Is Freed by DNA*, N.Y. Times, Jan. 4, 2008, at A11. And, what is more significant at this point in the casebook is that *eyewitness misidentification is the single most common factor in wrongful convictions throughout the United States.* In a study of 200 DNA exonerations, faulty eyewitness identifications contributed to nearly eighty percent of the improper convictions. Brandon L. Garrett, *Judging Innocence*, 108 Colum. L. Rev. 55, 60 (2008); see also Samuel R. Gross et al., *Exonerations in the United States 1989 Through 2003*, 95 J. Crim. L. & Criminology 523, 542 (2005) (of 340 exonerations between 1980 and 2003, at least one eyewitness misidentified the defendant in sixty-four percent of the trials overall, ninety percent of the wrongful rape convictions, and about half of the homicides). Additional data are set out by Justice Sotomayor in her dissent in Perry v. New Hampshire, later in this chapter.

Although the recent advent of DNA testing has demonstrated that wrongful convictions are more common than previously believed (and, at that, we cannot know how many innocent persons are being convicted because DNA evidence is not left at most crime scenes), social scientists and lawyers have known for a very long time that eyewitness identifications are unreliable.

Why *are* misidentifications such a problem in the criminal justice system? What has the Supreme Court done to reduce the risk of misidentifications? The materials that follow respond to these questions. As you will see, the Supreme Court has done relatively little in the "eyewitness identification" area; however, some state courts and officials—perhaps stung by the high number of DNA exonerations that have occurred—have recently begun to look for means to reform the identification process. And yet, according to one review of appellate court decisions, it appears that "the overwhelming majority of police departments in the cases surveyed followed the same procedures that have contributed to misidentifications and wrongful convictions." Sandra Guerra Thompson, *Judicial Blindness to Eyewitness Misidentification*, 93 Marq. L. Rev. 639, 641 (2009).

In reading the case law in this chapter, you will find it helpful to ask yourself four questions: (1) What constitutional right is implicated?; (2) Did the identification procedure at issue occur before or after formal adversary proceedings commenced?; (3) Was the identification procedure corporeal (*i.e.*, the suspect was personally displayed to the witness) or noncorporeal (*e.g.*, a photograph of the suspect was displayed)?; and (4) Is the prosecutor trying to introduce the witness's *pre*trial identification into evidence at trial, or does she want the witness to conduct an *in*-court identification of the defendant, or both?

a. *Right to Counsel Solution*

UNITED STATES V. WADE

Supreme Court of the United States, 1967.
388 U.S. 218, 87 S.Ct. 1926, 18 L.Ed.2d 1149.

If all stages of the prosecution of a defendant—from arraignment to trial—are important to the conduct of a fair trial, and *Powell v. Alabama,* Chapter 1, tells us that they are, then the key to the case of *United States v. Wade* is the presence or absence of counsel at one of those stages: the pretrial identification. The second question in *Wade* is, assuming an improper and thus tainted pretrial identification, what is the remedy? Is a subsequent courtroom identification during trial so tainted by the one prior that it is also to be excluded? Or, as with the exclusionary rule, are there some cases where the taint of an improper identification before trial can dissipate enough to make an identification during trial admissible?

As you read *Wade*, notice how Justice Brennan describes the difference between eyewitness identifications and the analysis of other types of evidence such as fingerprints, blood samples, hair, clothing, and (these days) DNA. Justice Brennan also spends considerable time discussing the dangers and problems inherent in eyewitness identification. Do you feel the distinction he makes between these categories of evidence is justified?

Compare how Justice Brennan and Justice White view pretrial lineups—the type of identification at issue in *Wade*. Which one do you agree with?

MR. JUSTICE BRENNAN delivered the opinion of the Court [joined by CHIEF JUSTICE WARREN (except as to Part I), JUSTICE BLACK (except as to Parts I and V), JUSTICE DOUGLAS (except as to Part I), and JUSTICES CLARK and FORTAS (except as to Part I)].[1]

The question here is whether courtroom identifications of an accused at trial are to be excluded from evidence because the accused was exhibited to the witnesses before trial at a post-indictment lineup conducted for identification purposes without notice to and in the absence of the accused's appointed counsel.

The federally insured bank in Eustace, Texas, was robbed on September 21, 1964. A man with a small strip of tape on each side of his face entered the bank, pointed a pistol at the female cashier and the vice president, the only persons in the bank at the time, and forced them to fill a pillowcase with the bank's money. The man then drove away with an accomplice who had been waiting in a stolen car outside the bank. On March 23, 1965, an indictment was returned against respondent, Wade, and two others for conspiring to rob the bank, and against Wade and the accomplice for the robbery itself. Wade was arrested on April 2, and counsel was appointed to represent him on April 26. Fifteen days later an FBI agent, without notice to Wade's lawyer, arranged to have the two bank employees observe a lineup made up of Wade and five or six other prisoners and conducted in a courtroom of the local county courthouse. Each person in the line wore strips of tape such as allegedly worn by the robber and upon direction each said something like "put the money in the bag," the words allegedly uttered by the robber. Both bank employees identified Wade in the lineup as the bank robber.

At trial, the two employees, when asked on direct examination if the robber was in the courtroom, pointed to Wade. The prior lineup identification was then elicited from both employees on cross-examination. At the close of testimony, Wade's counsel moved * * * to strike the bank officials' courtroom identifications on the ground that conduct of the lineup, without notice to and in the absence of his appointed counsel, violated his Fifth Amendment privilege against self-incrimination and his Sixth Amendment right to the assistance of counsel. The motion was denied, and Wade was convicted. * * * We granted certiorari, and set

---

1 The Court held in Part I of the opinion, which is omitted, that requiring a person to participate in a lineup does not violate the Fifth Amendment privilege against compulsory self-incrimination, which provision only bars "evidence of a testimonial or communicative nature." The concurring opinion of Justice Clark is omitted, as are the opinions of Justice Black (who concurred in Parts II–IV, but dissented as to Parts I and V), and Justice Fortas (who dissented in part as to Part I).

the case for oral argument with No. 223, *Gilbert v. California*, *post*, and No. 254, *Stovall v. Denno*, [388 U.S. 293, 87 S.Ct. 1967, 18 L.Ed.2d 1199 (1967)], which present similar questions. * * *

II. * * *

* * * [I]n this case it is urged that the assistance of counsel at the lineup was indispensable to protect Wade's most basic right as a criminal defendant—his right to a fair trial at which the witnesses against him might be meaningfully cross-examined. * * *

As early as *Powell v. Alabama* [p. 15], we recognized that the period from arraignment to trial was "perhaps the most critical period of the proceedings * * *," during which the accused "requires the guiding hand of counsel * * *," if the guarantee is not to prove an empty right. * * *

* * * It is central to that principle that in addition to counsel's presence at trial, the accused is guaranteed that he need not stand alone against the State at any stage of the prosecution, formal or informal, in court or out, where counsel's absence might derogate from the accused's right to a fair trial. * * *

In sum, the principle of *Powell v. Alabama* and succeeding cases requires that we scrutinize *any* pretrial confrontation of the accused to determine whether the presence of his counsel is necessary to preserve the defendant's basic right to a fair trial as affected by his right meaningfully to cross-examine the witnesses against him and to have effective assistance of counsel at the trial itself. It calls upon us to analyze whether potential substantial prejudice to defendant's rights inheres in the particular confrontation and the ability of counsel to help avoid that prejudice.

III.

The Government characterizes the lineup as a mere preparatory step in the gathering of the prosecution's evidence, not different—for Sixth Amendment purposes—from various other preparatory steps, such as systematized or scientific analyzing of the accused's fingerprints, blood sample, clothing, hair, and the like. We think there are differences which preclude such stages being characterized as critical stages at which the accused has the right to the presence of his counsel. Knowledge of the techniques of science and technology is sufficiently available, and the variables in techniques few enough, that the accused has the opportunity for a meaningful confrontation of the Government's case at trial through the ordinary processes of cross-examination of the Government's expert witnesses and the presentation of the evidence of his own experts. The denial of a right to have his counsel present at such analyses does not therefore violate the Sixth Amendment; they are not critical stages since there is minimal risk that his counsel's absence at such stages might derogate from his right to a fair trial.

IV.

But the confrontation compelled by the State between the accused and the victim or witnesses to a crime to elicit identification evidence is peculiarly riddled with innumerable dangers and variable factors which might seriously, even crucially, derogate from a fair trial. The vagaries of eyewitness identification are well-known; the annals of criminal law are rife with instances of mistaken identification. Mr. Justice Frankfurter once said: "What is the worth of identification testimony even when uncontradicted? The identification of strangers is proverbially untrustworthy. The hazards of such testimony are established by a formidable number of instances in the records of English and American trials. These instances are recent—not due to the brutalities of ancient criminal procedure." A major factor contributing to the high incidence of miscarriage of justice from mistaken identification has been the degree of suggestion inherent in the manner in which the prosecution presents the suspect to witnesses for pretrial identification. A commentator has observed that "[t]he influence of improper suggestion upon identifying witnesses probably accounts for more miscarriages of justice than any other single factor—perhaps it is responsible for more such errors than all other factors combined." Wall, EYE-WITNESS IDENTIFICATION IN CRIMINAL CASES 26. Suggestion can be created intentionally or unintentionally in many subtle ways. And the dangers for the suspect are particularly grave when the witness' opportunity for observation was insubstantial, and thus his susceptibility to suggestion the greatest.

Moreover, "[i]t is a matter of common experience that, once a witness has picked out the accused at the line-up, he is not likely to go back on his word later on, so that in practice the issue of identity may (in the absence of other relevant evidence) for all practical purposes be determined there and then, before the trial."

The pretrial confrontation for purpose of identification may take the form of a lineup, also known as an "identification parade" or "showup," as in the present case, or presentation of the suspect alone to the witness, as in *Stovall v. Denno*, *supra*. It is obvious that risks of suggestion attend either form of confrontation and increase the dangers inhering in eyewitness identification. But as is the case with secret interrogations, there is serious difficulty in depicting what transpires at lineups and other forms of identification confrontations. "Privacy results in secrecy and this in turn results in a gap in our knowledge as to what in fact goes on * * *." For the same reasons, the defense can seldom reconstruct the manner and mode of lineup identification for judge or jury at trial. Those participating in a lineup with the accused may often be police officers; in any event, the participants' names are rarely recorded or divulged at trial. The impediments to an objective observation are increased when the victim is the witness. Lineups are prevalent in rape and robbery prosecutions and present a particular hazard that a victim's understandable outrage may excite vengeful or spiteful motives. In any event, neither witnesses nor lineup participants are apt to be alert for conditions prejudicial to the suspect. And if they were, it would likely be of scant benefit to the suspect since neither witnesses nor lineup participants are likely to be schooled in the detection of suggestive influences. Improper influences may go undetected by a suspect, guilty or not, who experiences the emotional tension which we might expect in one being confronted with potential accusers. Even when he does observe abuse, if he has a criminal record he may be reluctant to take the stand and open up the admission of prior convictions. Moreover, any protestations by the suspect of the fairness of the lineup made at trial are likely to be in vain; the jury's choice is between the accused's unsupported version and that of the police officers present. In short, the accused's inability effectively to reconstruct at trial any unfairness that occurred at the lineup may deprive him of his only opportunity meaningfully to attack the credibility of the witness' courtroom identification. * * *

The potential for improper influence is illustrated by the circumstances, insofar as they appear, surrounding the prior identifications in the three cases we decide today. In the present case, the testimony of the identifying witnesses elicited on cross-examination revealed that those witnesses were taken to the courthouse and seated in the courtroom to await assembly of the lineup. The courtroom faced on a hallway observable to the witnesses through an open door. The cashier testified that she saw Wade "standing in the hall" within sight of an FBI agent. Five or six other prisoners later appeared in the hall. The vice president testified that he saw a person in the hall in the custody of the agent who "resembled the person that we identified as the one that had entered the bank."

The lineup in *Gilbert*, [388 U.S. 263, 87 S.Ct. 1951, 18 L.Ed.2d 1178 (1967)], was conducted in an auditorium in which some 100 witnesses to several alleged state and federal robberies charged to Gilbert made wholesale identifications of Gilbert as the robber in each other's presence, a procedure said to be fraught with dangers of suggestion. And the vice of suggestion created by the identification in *Stovall* was the presentation to the witness of the suspect alone handcuffed to police officers. It is hard to imagine a situation more clearly conveying the suggestion to the witness that the one presented is believed guilty by the police.

The few cases that have surfaced therefore reveal the existence of a process attended with hazards of serious unfairness to the criminal accused and strongly suggest the plight of the more numerous defendants who are unable to ferret out suggestive influences in the secrecy of the confrontation. We do not assume that these risks are the result of police procedures intentionally designed to prejudice an accused. Rather we assume they derive from the dangers inherent in eyewitness identification and the suggestibility inherent in the context of the pretrial identification. Williams & Hammelmann, in one of the most comprehensive studies of such forms of identification, said, "[T]he fact that the police themselves have, in a given case, little or no doubt that the man put up for identification has committed the offense, and that their chief pre-occupation is with the problem of getting sufficient proof, because he has not 'come clean,' involves a danger that this persuasion may communicate itself even in a doubtful case to the witness in some way * * *." Identification Parades, Part I, [1963] Crim. L. Rev. 479, 483.

Insofar as the accused's conviction may rest on a courtroom identification in fact the fruit of a suspect pretrial identification which the accused is helpless to subject to effective scrutiny at trial, the accused is deprived of that right of cross-examination which is an essential safeguard to his right to confront the witnesses against him. And even though cross-examination is a precious safeguard to a fair trial, it cannot be viewed as an absolute assurance of accuracy and reliability. Thus in the present context, where so many variables and pitfalls exist, the first line of defense must be the prevention of unfairness and the lessening of the hazards of eyewitness identification at the lineup itself. The trial which might determine the accused's fate may well not be that in the courtroom but that at the pretrial confrontation, with the State aligned against the accused, the witness the sole jury, and the accused unprotected against the overreaching, intentional or unintentional, and with little or no effective appeal from the judgment there rendered by the witness—"that's the man."

Since it appears that there is grave potential for prejudice, intentional or not, in the pretrial lineup, which may not be capable of reconstruction at trial, and since presence of counsel itself can often avert prejudice and assure a meaningful confrontation at trial, there can be little doubt that for Wade the post-indictment lineup was a critical stage of the prosecution at which he was "as much entitled to such aid [of counsel] * * * as at the trial itself." Thus both Wade and his counsel should have been notified of the impending lineup, and counsel's presence should have been a requisite to conduct of the lineup, absent an "intelligent waiver." No substantial countervailing policy considerations have been advanced against the requirement of the presence of counsel. Concern is expressed that the requirement will forestall prompt identifications and result in obstruction of the confrontations. As for the first, we note that in the two cases in which the right to counsel is today held to apply, counsel had already been appointed and no argument is made in either case that notice to counsel would have prejudicially delayed the confrontations. Moreover, we leave open the question whether the presence of substitute counsel might not suffice where notification and presence of the suspect's own counsel would result in prejudicial delay. And to refuse to recognize the right to counsel for fear that counsel will obstruct the course of justice is contrary to the basic assumptions upon which this Court has operated in Sixth Amendment cases. We rejected similar logic in *Miranda v. Arizona* concerning presence of counsel during custodial interrogation * * *. In our view counsel can hardly impede legitimate law enforcement; on the contrary, for the reasons expressed, law enforcement may be assisted by preventing the infiltration of taint in the prosecution's identification evidence. That result cannot help the guilty avoid conviction but can only help assure that the right man has been brought to justice.

Legislative or other regulations, such as those of local police departments, which eliminate the risks of abuse and unintentional suggestion at lineup proceedings and the impediments to meaningful confrontation at trial may also remove the basis for regarding the stage as "critical." But neither Congress nor the federal authorities have seen fit to provide a solution. What we hold today "in no way creates a constitutional straitjacket which will handicap sound efforts at reform, nor is it intended to have this effect."

V.

We come now to the question whether the denial of Wade's motion to strike the courtroom identification by the bank witnesses at trial because of the absence of his counsel at the lineup required, as the Court of Appeals held, the grant of a new trial at which such evidence is to be excluded. We do not think this disposition can be justified without first giving the Government the opportunity to establish by clear and convincing evidence that the in-court identifications were based upon observations of the suspect other than the lineup identification. * * *

We think it follows that the proper test to be applied in these situations is that quoted in *Wong Sun v. United States*, [p. 457], " '[W]hether, granting establishment of the primary illegality, the evidence to which instant objection is made has been come at by exploitation of that illegality or instead by means sufficiently distinguishable to be purged of the primary taint.' Maguire, Evidence of Guilt 221 (1959)." Application of this test in the present context requires consideration of various factors; for example, the prior opportunity to observe the alleged criminal act, the existence of any discrepancy between any pre-lineup description and the defendant's actual description, any identification prior to lineup of another person, the identification by picture of the defendant prior to the lineup, failure to identify the defendant on a prior occasion, and the lapse of time between the alleged act and the lineup identification. It is also relevant to consider those facts which, despite the absence of counsel, are disclosed concerning the conduct of the lineup. * * *

On the record now before us we cannot make the determination whether the in-court identifications had an independent origin. * * * We * * * think the appropriate procedure to be followed is to vacate the conviction pending a hearing to determine whether the in-court identifications had an independent source, * * * and for the District Court to reinstate the conviction or order a new trial, as may be proper. * * *

MR. JUSTICE WHITE, whom MR. JUSTICE HARLAN and MR. JUSTICE STEWART join, dissenting [on the Sixth Amendment issue].

The Court has again propounded a broad constitutional rule barring use of a wide spectrum of relevant and probative evidence, solely because a step in its ascertainment or discovery occurs outside the presence of defense counsel. * * *

The Court's opinion is far-reaching. It proceeds first by creating a new *per se* rule of constitutional law: a criminal suspect cannot be subjected to a pretrial identification process in the absence of his counsel without violating the Sixth Amendment. If he is, the State may not buttress a later courtroom identification of the witness by any reference to the previous identification. Furthermore, the courtroom identification is not admissible at all unless the State can establish by clear and convincing proof that the testimony is not the fruit of the earlier identification made in the absence of defendant's counsel—admittedly a heavy burden for the State and probably an impossible one. To all intents and purposes, courtroom identifications are barred if pretrial identifications have occurred without counsel being present.

The rule applies to any lineup, to any other techniques employed to produce an identification and *a fortiori* to a face-to-face encounter between the witness and the suspect alone, regardless of when the identification occurs, in time or place, and whether before or after indictment or information. It matters not how well the witness knows the suspect, whether the witness is the suspect's mother, brother, or long-time associate, and no matter how long or well the witness observed the perpetrator at the scene of the crime. The kidnap victim who has lived for days with his abductor is in the same category as the witness who has had only a fleeting glimpse of the criminal. Neither may identify the suspect without defendant's counsel being present. The same strictures apply regardless of the number of other witnesses who positively identify the defendant and regardless of the corroborative evidence showing that it was the defendant who had committed the crime.

The premise for the Court's rule is not the general unreliability of eyewitness identifications nor the difficulties inherent in observation, recall, and recognition. The Court assumes a narrower evil as the basis for its rule—improper police suggestion which contributes to erroneous identifications. The Court apparently believes that improper police procedures are so widespread that a broad prophylactic rule must be laid down, requiring the presence of counsel at all pretrial identifications, in order to detect recurring instances of police misconduct. I do not share this pervasive distrust of all official investigations. None of the materials the Court relies upon supports it. Certainly, I would bow to solid fact, but the Court quite obviously does not have before it any reliable, comprehensive survey of current police practices on which to base its new rule. Until it does, the Court should avoid excluding relevant evidence from state criminal trials. * * *

I share the Court's view that the criminal trial, at the very least, should aim at truthful factfinding, including accurate eyewitness identifications. I doubt, however, on the basis of our present information, that the tragic mistakes which have occurred in criminal trials are as much the product of improper police conduct as they are the consequence of the difficulties inherent in eyewitness testimony and in resolving evidentiary conflicts by court or jury. I doubt that the Court's new rule will obviate these difficulties, or that the situation will be measurably improved by inserting defense counsel into the investigative processes of police departments everywhere.

But, it may be asked, what possible state interest militates against requiring the presence of defense counsel at lineups? After all, the argument goes, he *may* do some good, he *may* upgrade the quality of identification evidence in state courts and he can scarcely do any harm. Even if true, this is a feeble foundation for fastening an ironclad constitutional rule upon state criminal procedures. Absent some reliably established constitutional violation, the processes by which the States enforce their criminal laws are their own prerogative. * * *

Beyond this, however, requiring counsel at pretrial identifications as an invariable rule trenches on other valid state interests. One of them is its concern with the prompt and efficient enforcement of its criminal laws. Identifications frequently take place after arrest but before an indictment is returned or an information is filed. The police may have arrested a suspect on probable cause but may still have the wrong man. Both the suspect and the State have every interest in a prompt identification at that stage, the suspect in order to secure his immediate release and the State because prompt and early identification enhances *accurate* identification and because it must know whether it is on the right investigative track. Unavoidably, however, the absolute rule requiring the presence of counsel will cause significant delay and it may very well result in no pretrial identification at all. Counsel must be appointed and a time arranged convenient for him and the witnesses. Meanwhile, it may be necessary to file charges against the suspect who may then be released on bail, in the federal system very often on his own recognizance, with neither the State nor the defendant having the benefit of a properly conducted identification procedure.

Nor do I think the witnesses themselves can be ignored. They will now be required to be present at the convenience of counsel rather than their own. Many may be much less willing to participate if the identification stage is transformed into an adversary proceeding not under the control of a judge. Others may fear for their own safety if their identity is known at an early date, especially when there is no way of knowing until the lineup occurs whether or not the police really have the right man.

Finally, I think the Court's new rule is vulnerable in terms of its own unimpeachable purpose of increasing the reliability of identification testimony.

Law enforcement officers have the obligation to convict the guilty and to make sure they do not convict the innocent. They must be dedicated to making the criminal trial a procedure for the ascertainment of the true facts surrounding the commission of the crime. To this extent, our so-called adversary system is not adversary at all; nor should it be. But defense counsel has no comparable obligation to ascertain or present the truth. Our system assigns him a different mission. He must be and is interested in preventing the conviction of the innocent, but, absent a voluntary plea of guilty, we also insist that he defend his client whether he is innocent or guilty. The State has the obligation to present the evidence. Defense counsel need present nothing, even if he knows what the truth is. He need not furnish any witnesses to the police, or reveal any confidences of his client, or furnish any other information to help the prosecution's case. If he can confuse a witness, even a truthful one, or make him appear at a disadvantage, unsure or indecisive, that will be his normal course. Our interest in not convicting the innocent permits counsel to put the State to its proof, to put the State's case in the worst possible light, regardless of what he thinks or knows to be the truth. Undoubtedly there are some limits which defense counsel must observe but more often than not, defense counsel will cross-examine a prosecution witness, and impeach him if he can, even if he thinks the witness is telling the truth, just as he will attempt to destroy a witness who he thinks is lying. In this respect, as part of our modified adversary system and as part of the duty imposed on the most honorable defense counsel, we countenance or require conduct which in many instances has little, if any, relation to the search for truth.

I would not extend this system, at least as it presently operates, to police investigations and would not require counsel's presence at pretrial identification procedures. Counsel's interest is in not having his client placed at the scene of the crime, regardless of his whereabouts. Some counsel may advise their clients to refuse to make any movements or to speak any words in a lineup or even to appear in one. To that extent the impact on truthful factfinding is quite obvious. Others will not only observe what occurs and develop possibilities for later cross-examination but will hover over witnesses and begin their cross-examination then, menacing truthful factfinding as thoroughly as the Court fears the police now do. Certainly there is an implicit invitation to counsel to suggest rules for the lineup and to manage and produce it as best he can. I therefore doubt that the Court's new rule, at least absent some clearly defined limits on counsel's role, will measurably contribute to more reliable pretrial identifications. My fears are that it will have precisely the opposite result. * * *

NOTES AND QUESTIONS

1. *Introducing evidence of the pretrial identification procedure.* In *Wade*, the prosecution did not seek to introduce evidence relating to the lineup. The only issue was the admissibility of the witness's *in*-court identification of Wade. However, in companion case *Gilbert v. California,* cited in *Wade*, the prosecutor elicited testimony at trial of the fact that witnesses had identified the defendant at a post-indictment pretrial lineup at which Gilbert was not represented by counsel. The Court held that

> [t]he State is * * * not entitled to an opportunity to show that that testimony had an independent source. Only a *per se* exclusionary rule as to such testimony can be an effective sanction to assure that law enforcement authorities will respect the accused's constitutional right to the presence of his counsel at the critical lineup.

How would you summarize the "*Wade-Gilbert* rule"? Specifically, under what circumstances does a defendant have a right to counsel at a lineup or other corporeal identification procedure? Does the rule apply to an identification that occurs *before* indictment? Before arrest? And, what are the evidentiary implications if the defendant's counsel right is violated?

2. Reconsider the second and third paragraphs of Justice White's dissent. Has he correctly stated the *Wade* rule, as you understand it from Note 1? Reconsider the fourth paragraph of his dissent. Do you believe that he accurately states the "premise for the Court's rule"?

3. Justice White in his dissent sets out a strong, if perhaps idealistic, view of the dedication and reliability of law enforcement and prosecution authorities. In footnote 5 of his dissent, he included a quote from a previous case on the obligations of a United States Attorney:

> "The United States Attorney is the representative not of an ordinary party to a controversy, but of a sovereignty whose obligation to govern impartially is as compelling as its obligation to govern at all; and whose interest, therefore, in a criminal prosecution is not that it shall win a case, but that justice shall be done. As such, he is in a peculiar and very definite sense the servant of the law, the twofold aim of which is that guilt shall not escape or innocence suffer. He may prosecute with earnestness and vigor—indeed, he should do so. But, while he may strike hard blows, he is not at liberty to strike foul ones. It is as much his duty to refrain from improper methods calculated to produce a wrongful conviction as it is to use every legitimate means to bring about a just one." *Berger v. United States*, 295 U.S. 78, 88, 55 S.Ct. 629, 633, 79 L.Ed. 1314 [1935].

A U.S. Attorney's Office is responsible for prosecuting all federal crimes in its jurisdiction. These are not easy offices to get into. Applicants typically need excellent law school grades and several years of criminal trial experience before they will even be considered. However, remember that the vast majority of crimes in the United States are prosecuted at the county or district level by prosecutors who work for the State. These offices often hire assistant prosecutors straight out of law school. The county or district prosecutor in 47 states is elected and in the other 3 appointed by the governor. Some of these offices—especially in larger jurisdictions—have excellent training programs but most do not, and the hiring criteria can vary widely. Unlike in some other nations, the United States does not have any required apprenticeship or special training for prosecutors.

4. *The problems with eyewitness identifications.* The *Wade* Court noted that "identification evidence is peculiarly riddled with innumerable dangers * * * which might seriously, even crucially, derogate from a fair trial." As two social scientists long ago put it, "people quite often do not see or hear things which are presented clearly to their senses, see or hear things which are not there, do not remember things which have happened to them, and remember things which did not happen." Felice J. Levine & June Louin Tapp, *The Psychology of Criminal Identification: The Gap from Wade to Kirby*, 121 U. Pa. L. Rev. 1079, 1087–88 (1973).

Why and under what circumstances is eyewitness testimony particularly unreliable? Social scientists who have studied the subject provide various answers. (For cites to relevant literature and greater detail on the subject, see 1 Joshua Dressler & Alan C. Michaels, Understanding Criminal Procedure § 26.01 (6th ed. 2013).) First, people tend to see what they expect to see. A hunter looking for a deer in the forest may "see" a deer in the brush that turns out to be a human being. If a witness to a crime has an expectation of what a criminal should look like—the person's age, race, size, gender—she may unconsciously "see" the offender in a way that fits her preconception. Second, there is substantial evidence of unreliability in cross-racial identification cases, *i.e.*, when a person of one racial group attempts to identify a crime perpetrator of a different racial category.

Third, memory decays over time. Worse, memory is an "active, constructive process." Frederic D. Woocher, Note, *Did Your Eyes Deceive You? Expert Psychological Testimony on the Unreliability of Eyewitness Identification*, 29 Stan. L. Rev. 969, 983 (1977). That is, people dislike uncertainty; therefore, when a person experiences a memory gap, the individual unconsciously tries to fill in the memory holes with details that often are inaccurate.

Fourth, post-crime identification police procedures can aggravate the situation. For example, a lineup typically functions as a multiple-choice test in which eyewitness-participants believe—or are led to believe by the police—that "none of the above" is an unacceptable answer. Therefore, witnesses often give the "most correct" answer (pick the person whom they believe most resembles the culprit), rather than indicate that they do not recognize anyone in the lineup. And, once a witness identifies—correctly or incorrectly—someone from a lineup, she becomes psychologically committed to her identification. Her mind may even play tricks on her: when she thinks back to the crime, her "mind's eye" may now "remember" the person she selected from the lineup. It substitutes the lineup image for her initial memory of the culprit.

5. *Remedies.* Jurors tend to place a high value on eyewitness testimony. They do not distinguish between high-risk and low-risk identifications. They tend to overestimate the accuracy of eyewitness testimony. What can be done, therefore, to reduce the inherent risks in eyewitness identification procedures? The *Wade* Court invited legislatures and police departments to reform their procedures and even quoted the following proposal from a scholarly article recommending a model statute to deal with the problem:

> Most, if not all, of the attacks on the lineup process could be averted by a uniform statute modeled upon the best features of the civilian codes. Any proposed statute should provide for the right to counsel during any lineup or during any confrontation. Provision should be made that any

> person, whether a victim or a witness, must give a description of the suspect before he views any arrested person. A written record of this description should be required, and the witness should be made to sign it. This written record would be available for inspection by defense counsel for copying before the trial and for use at the trial in testing the accuracy of the identification made during the lineup and during the trial.
>
> This ideal statute would require at least six persons in addition to the accused in a lineup, and these persons would have to be of approximately the same height, weight, coloration of hair and skin, and bodily types as the suspect. In addition, all of these men should, as nearly as possible, be dressed alike. If distinctive garb was used during the crime, the suspect should not be forced to wear similar clothing in the lineup unless all of the other persons are similarly garbed. A complete written report of the names, addresses, descriptive details of the other persons in the lineup, and of everything which transpired during the identification would be mandatory. This report would include everything stated by the identifying witness during this step, including any reasons given by him as to what features, etc., have sparked his recognition.
>
> This statute should permit voice identification tests by having each person in the lineup repeat identical innocuous phrases, and it would be impermissible to force the use of words allegedly used during a criminal act.
>
> "The statute would enjoin the police from suggesting to any viewer that one or more persons in the lineup had been arrested as a suspect. If more than one witness is to make an identification, each witness should be required to do so separately and should be forbidden to speak to another witness until all of them have completed the process.
>
> The statute could require the use of movie cameras and tape recorders to record the lineup process in those states which are financially able to afford these devices. Finally, the statute should provide that any evidence obtained as the result of a violation of this statute would be inadmissible." Murray, *The Criminal Lineup at Home and Abroad*, 1966 Utah L. Rev. 610, 627–628.

For many years, social scientists have urged changes in police procedures in order to enhance the reliability of the identification process. Until recently, their recommendations were largely ignored. In 2008, however, North Carolina enacted a statute that implemented several reform ideas. Lineups there must be conducted by an independent administrator who does not know which person in the lineup is the suspect (or by a similarly "blind" procedure). The eyewitness must be instructed that the perpetrator might not be in the lineup, that it is as important to exclude innocent persons as it is to identify the perpetrator, and that the investigation will continue whether or not an identification is made. A video recording must be made of the lineup procedure unless it is "not practical." The eyewitness who identifies a person or a photo must be asked to give a statement, in the eyewitness's own words, of his confidence level that the person identified is the perpetrator. The videotape and the eyewitness' statement must be turned over to the defense. Other reform ideas are contained in this comprehensive statute. See George C. Thomas III, *Two Windows Into Innocence*, 7 Ohio State J. Crim. L. 575 (2010).

Other states have sought to reform procedures judicially. See State v. Henderson, 27 A.3d 872 (N.J. 2011) (identifying a wide range of factors, identified in the research, that can led to an unreliable identification and instructing trial judges about when to hold pre-trial hearings into reliability and to make written findings of fact that can be reviewed on appeal); State v. Ledbetter, 275 Conn. 534, 881 A.2d 290 (2005) (ruling that officers administering identification procedures should advise the witness that the perpetrator may or may not be present in the procedure, or else evidence at trial of the identification must be accompanied by a jury instruction stating that "psychological studies have shown" that failure to so admonish eyewitnesses "increases the likelihood that the witness will select one of the individuals in the procedure, even when the perpetrator is not present"); and State v. Guilbert, 49 A.3d 705 (Conn. 2012); Johnson v. State, 526 S.E.2d 549 (Ga. 2000); People v. Lee, 750 N.E.2d 63 (N.Y. 2001); State v. Copeland, 226 S.W.3d 287 (Tenn. 2007) (all holding that expert testimony is generally admissible in criminal trials to demonstrate the potential weaknesses of eyewitness testimony).

6. It has always struck the authors of this book as almost laughable when the prosecutor asks an eyewitness if she can identify the perpetrator in the courtroom. Who else would she identify other than the person sitting next to the defense lawyer? In 2014, the Supreme Judicial Court of Massachusetts put an important limit on this procedure. In Commonwealth v. Crayton, 21 N.E. 3d 157 (Mass. 2014), the court held that an eyewitness who has never made an out-of-court identification of the defendant cannot identify him in court, absent "good reason." One example of a "good reason" is that the victim knew the defendant before the crime occurred.

7. *The role of counsel at the lineup.* Reconsider Justice Brennan's opinion in *Wade.* What does he envision a lawyer doing during the identification process? What is Justice White's understanding in this regard?

What *should* be the role of a lawyer at a lineup? Should she serve simply as a passive observer who can help reconstruct for the judge and jury the events of the lineup, point to alleged abuses, and thereby minimize the incriminating force of the identification? Or should she be permitted to make objections at the time of the lineup and suggest ways to improve the process? If the lawyer's role is passive, is *Wade* an adequate solution to the unreliability problem? If the lawyer's role is active, is Justice White correct in fearing that defense lawyers may make the process less efficient and, ultimately, less accurate?

For a moment, imagine that you are a public defender and are called to the police station to represent a person in a lineup. You look at the lineup and you believe that it is unduly suggestive (perhaps the others in the confrontation do not look like your client). What would you do? Would you complain to the police and urge them to find persons who look more like your client? Would you say nothing? What are the risks of being vocal? Of being passive?

8. As a footnote in *Wade* noted, many other nations surround the lineup with safeguards against prejudice to the suspect. In England the suspect must be allowed the presence of his solicitor or a friend; Germany requires the presence of retained counsel; France forbids the confrontation of the suspect in the absence of his counsel; Spain, Mexico, and Italy provide detailed procedures prescribing the conditions under which confrontation must occur under the supervision of a judicial officer who sees to it that the proceedings are officially recorded to assure adequate scrutiny at trial.

9. *When is the right to counsel triggered?: the Kirby "clarification."* Look again at your answers to the questions asked at the end of Note 1. (You did answer them, right?) Specifically, as you understand the majority opinion in *Wade*, *when* is the right to counsel triggered? Does it apply to an identification that occurs *before* indictment? Before arrest? What is dissenting Justice White's answer?

As it turns out, the answer to the timing question may not have been what some of the *Wade* justices hoped (or feared). In Kirby v. Illinois, 406 U.S. 682, 92 S.Ct. 1877, 32 L.Ed.2d 411 (1972), a case involving a corporeal identification that occurred *after* arrest but *before* indictment or arraignment, a plurality of the Court announced:

> In a line of constitutional cases in this Court stemming back to the Court's landmark opinion in *Powell v. Alabama* [p. 15], it has been firmly established that a person's Sixth and Fourteenth Amendment right to counsel attaches only at or after the time that adversary judicial proceedings have been initiated against him.
>
> This is not to say that a defendant in a criminal case has a constitutional right to counsel only at the trial itself. The *Powell* case makes clear that the right attaches at the time of arraignment, and the Court has recently held that it exists also at the time of a preliminary hearing. But the point is that, while members of the Court have differed as to the existence of the right to counsel in the contexts of some of the above cases, *all* of those cases have involved points of time at or after the initiation of

adversary judicial criminal proceedings—whether by way of formal charge, preliminary hearing, indictment, information, or arraignment. * * *

The initiation of judicial criminal proceedings is far from a mere formalism. It is the starting point of our whole system of adversary criminal justice. For it is only then that the government has committed itself to prosecute, and only then that the adverse positions of government and defendant have solidified. It is then that a defendant finds himself faced with the prosecutorial forces of organized society, and immersed in the intricacies of substantive and procedural criminal law. It is this point, therefore, that marks the commencement of the "criminal prosecutions" to which alone the explicit guarantees of the Sixth Amendment are applicable. * * *

What has been said is not to suggest that there may not be occasions during the course of a criminal investigation when the police do abuse identification procedures. Such abuses are not beyond the reach of the Constitution. As the Court pointed out in *Wade* itself, it is always necessary to "scrutinize *any* pretrial confrontation * * *." The Due Process Clause of the Fifth and Fourteenth Amendments forbids a lineup that is unnecessarily suggestive and conducive to irreparable mistaken identification. When a person has not been formally charged with a criminal offense, [the Due Process Clause rule] strikes the appropriate constitutional balance between the right of a suspect to be protected from prejudicial procedures and the interest of society in the prompt and purposeful investigation of an unsolved crime.

Is *Kirby* consistent with the underlying rationale of *Wade*? Justice White did not think so. He dissented again, in *Kirby*, stating simply that "*United States v. Wade* and *Gilbert v. California* govern this case and compel reversal of the judgment below."

10. What is the practical effect of *Kirby*?

11. *Post-indictment noncorporeal identifications.* In United States v. Ash, 413 U.S. 300, 93 S.Ct. 2568, 37 L.Ed.2d 619 (1973), the Supreme Court held that the *Wade-Gilbert* rule does *not* apply to photographic displays, even if such a procedure occurs after formal criminal proceedings have commenced.

In *Ash*, four witnesses identified Ash from a single black-and-white photograph. Then they were shown five color photographs, one of which included Ash. Three of the witnesses selected Ash, but the other was unable to make any selection. This occurred after Ash had been indicted, and in the absence of defense counsel. In light of *Wade*, can you think of any good reason for the no-right-to-counsel holding in *Ash*?

b. Preventing Unreliable Identifications

PERRY V. NEW HAMPSHIRE

Supreme Court of the United States, 2012.
565 U.S. 228, 132 S.Ct. 716, 181 L.Ed.2d 694.

Here the issue is the admission of a pretrial identification at trial. No courtroom identification took place.

If the police improperly influence an identification, the identification is screened by a judge in a pretrial motion to determine if there is "a very substantial likelihood of irreparable misidentification." But what happens if the improper influence is not the fault of the police? In *Perry v. New Hampshire* the Court holds that in such cases, the question of the identification's reliability is a matter for the jury; no pretrial judicial determination is required. In a quote that brings up shades of the deterrence argument underlying the exclusionary rule for Fourth Amendment violations, the Court identifies the "primary aim of excluding identification evidence obtained under unnecessarily suggestive circumstances" as deterring "law enforcement use of improper lineups, showups, and photo arrays in the first place."

For dissenting Justice Sotomayor, the concern in *Perry* lies not with simply deterring police misconduct, but with avoiding the use of any identification that may have been so suggestive as to be unreliable. Given the role misidentifications play in wrongful convictions and miscarriages of justice, Justice Sotomayor is uncomfortable with leaving such identifications in the hands of fallible and untrained juries, instead of fallible but trained judges.

JUSTICE GINSBURG delivered the opinion of the Court [joined by CHIEF JUSTICE ROBERTS, and JUSTICES SCALIA, KENNEDY, THOMAS, BREYER, ALITO, and KAGAN].

In our system of justice, fair trial for persons charged with criminal offenses is secured by the Sixth Amendment, which guarantees to defendants the right to counsel, compulsory process to obtain defense witnesses, and the opportunity to cross-examine witnesses for the prosecution. Those safeguards apart, admission of evidence in state trials is ordinarily governed by state law, and the reliability of relevant testimony typically falls within the province of the jury to determine. This Court has recognized, in addition, a due process check on the admission of eyewitness identification, applicable when the police have arranged suggestive circumstances leading the witness to identify a particular person as the perpetrator of a crime.

An identification infected by improper police influence, our case law holds, is not automatically excluded. Instead, the trial judge must screen the evidence for reliability pretrial. If there is "a very substantial likelihood of irreparable misidentification," the judge must disallow presentation of the evidence at trial. But if the indicia of reliability are strong enough to outweigh the corrupting effect of the police-arranged suggestive circumstances, the identification evidence ordinarily will be admitted, and the jury will ultimately determine its worth.

We have not extended pretrial screening for reliability to cases in which the suggestive circumstances were not arranged by law enforcement officers. Petitioner requests that we do so because of the grave risk that mistaken identification will yield a miscarriage of justice. Our decisions, however, turn on the presence of state action and aim to deter police from rigging identification procedures, for example, at a lineup, showup, or photograph array. When no improper law enforcement activity is involved, we hold, it suffices to test reliability through the rights and opportunities generally designed for that purpose, notably, the presence of counsel at postindictment lineups, vigorous cross-examination, protective rules of evidence, and jury instructions on both the fallibility of eyewitness identification and the requirement that guilt be proved beyond a reasonable doubt.

I

A

Around 3 a.m. on August 15, 2008, Joffre Ullon called the Nashua, New Hampshire, Police Department and reported that an African-American male was trying to break into cars parked in the lot of Ullon's apartment building. Officer Nicole Clay responded to the call. Upon arriving at the parking lot, Clay heard what "sounded like a metal bat hitting the ground." She then saw petitioner Barion Perry standing between two cars. Perry walked toward Clay, holding two car-stereo amplifiers in his hands. A metal bat lay on the ground behind him. Clay asked Perry where the amplifiers came from. "[I] found them on the ground," Perry responded.

Meanwhile, Ullon's wife, Nubia Blandon, woke her neighbor, Alex Clavijo, and told him she had just seen someone break into his car. Clavijo immediately went downstairs to the parking lot to inspect the car. He first observed that one of the rear windows had been shattered. On further inspection, he discovered that the speakers and amplifiers from his car stereo were missing, as were his bat and wrench. Clavijo then approached Clay and told her about Blandon's alert and his own subsequent observations.

By this time, another officer had arrived at the scene. Clay asked Perry to stay in the parking lot with that officer, while she and Clavijo went to talk to Blandon. Clay and Clavijo then entered the apartment building and took the stairs to the fourth floor, where Blandon's and Clavijo's apartments were located. They met Blandon in the hallway just outside the open door to her apartment.

Asked to describe what she had seen, Blandon stated that, around 2:30 a.m., she saw from her kitchen window a tall, African-American man roaming the parking lot and looking into cars. Eventually, the man circled Clavijo's car, opened the trunk, and removed a large box.

Clay asked Blandon for a more specific description of the man. Blandon pointed to her kitchen window and said the person she saw breaking into Clavijo's car was standing in the parking lot, next to the police officer. Perry's arrest followed this identification.

About a month later, the police showed Blandon a photographic array that included a picture of Perry and asked her to point out the man who had broken into Clavijo's car. Blandon was unable to identify Perry.

B

Perry was charged in New Hampshire state court with one count of theft by unauthorized taking and one count of criminal mischief. Before trial, he moved to suppress Blandon's identification on the ground that admitting it at trial would violate due process. Blandon witnessed what amounted to a one-person showup in the parking lot, Perry asserted, which all but guaranteed that she would identify him as the culprit.

The New Hampshire Superior Court denied the motion. To determine whether due process prohibits the introduction of an out-of-court identification at trial, the Superior Court said, this Court's decisions instruct a two-step inquiry. First, the trial court must decide whether the police used an unnecessarily suggestive identification procedure. If they did, the court must next consider whether the improper identification procedure so tainted the resulting identification as to render it unreliable and therefore inadmissible.

Perry's challenge, the Superior Court concluded, failed at step one: Blandon's identification of Perry on the night of the crime did not result from an unnecessarily suggestive procedure "manufacture[d] * * * by the police." Blandon pointed to Perry "spontaneously," the court noted, "without any inducement from the police." Clay did not ask Blandon whether the man standing in the parking lot was the man Blandon had seen breaking into Clavijo's car. Nor did Clay ask Blandon to move to the window from which she had observed the break-in.

The Superior Court recognized that there were reasons to question the accuracy of Blandon's identification: the parking lot was dark in some locations; Perry was standing next to a police officer; Perry was the only African-American man in the vicinity; and Blandon was unable, later, to pick Perry out of a photographic array. But "[b]ecause the police procedures were not unnecessarily suggestive," the court ruled that the reliability of Blandon's testimony was for the jury to consider.

At the ensuing trial, Blandon and Clay testified to Blandon's out-of-court identification. The jury found Perry guilty of theft and not guilty of criminal mischief.

On appeal, Perry repeated his challenge to the admissibility of Blandon's out-of-court identification. The trial court erred, Perry contended, in requiring an initial showing that the police arranged the suggestive identification procedure. Suggestive circumstances alone, Perry argued, suffice to trigger the court's duty to evaluate the reliability of the resulting identification before allowing presentation of the evidence to the jury.

The New Hampshire Supreme Court rejected Perry's argument and affirmed his conviction. * * *

We granted certiorari to resolve a division of opinion on the question whether the Due Process Clause requires a trial judge to conduct a preliminary assessment of the reliability of an eyewitness identification made under suggestive circumstances not arranged by the police.

II

A

The Constitution, our decisions indicate, protects a defendant against a conviction based on evidence of questionable reliability, not by prohibiting introduction of the evidence, but by affording the defendant means to persuade the jury that the evidence should be discounted as unworthy of credit. Constitutional safeguards available to defendants to counter the State's evidence include the Sixth Amendment rights to counsel; compulsory process; and confrontation plus cross-examination of witnesses. Apart from these guarantees, we have recognized, state and federal statutes and rules ordinarily govern the admissibility of evidence, and juries are assigned the task of determining the reliability of the evidence presented at trial. Only when evidence "is so extremely unfair that its admission violates fundamental conceptions of justice" have we imposed a constraint tied to the Due Process Clause.

Contending that the Due Process Clause is implicated here, Perry relies on a series of decisions involving police-arranged identification procedures. In *Stovall* v. *Denno*, 388 U. S. 293[, 87 S.Ct. 1967, 18 L.Ed.2d 1199] (1967), first of those decisions, a witness identified the defendant as her assailant after police officers brought the defendant to the witness' hospital room. At the time the witness made the identification, the defendant—the only African-American in the room—was handcuffed and surrounded by police officers. Although the police-arranged showup was undeniably suggestive, the Court held that no due process violation occurred. Crucial to the Court's decision was the procedure's necessity: The witness was the only person who could identify or exonerate the defendant; the witness could not leave her hospital room; and it was uncertain whether she would live to identify the defendant in more neutral circumstances.

A year later, in *Simmons* v. *United States*, 390 U. S. 377[, 88 S.Ct. 967, 19 L.Ed.2d 1247] (1968), the Court addressed a due process challenge to police use of a photographic array. When a witness identifies the defendant in a police-organized photo lineup, the Court ruled, the identification should be suppressed only where "the photographic identification procedure was so [unnecessarily] suggestive as to give rise to a very substantial likelihood of irreparable misidentification." Satisfied that the photo array used by Federal Bureau of Investigation agents in *Simmons* was both necessary and unlikely to have led to a mistaken identification, the Court rejected the defendant's due process challenge to admission of the identification. * * *

Synthesizing previous decisions, we set forth in *Neil* v. *Biggers*, 409 U. S. 188[, 93 S.Ct. 375, 34 L.Ed.2d 401] (1972), and reiterated in *Manson* v. *Brathwaite*, 432 U. S. 98[, 97 S.Ct. 2243, 53 L.Ed.2d 140](1977), the approach appropriately used to determine whether the Due Process Clause requires suppression of an eyewitness identification tainted by police arrangement. The Court emphasized, first, that due process concerns arise only when law enforcement officers use an identification procedure that is both suggestive and unnecessary. Even when the police use such a procedure, the Court next said, suppression of the resulting identification is not the inevitable consequence.

A rule requiring automatic exclusion, the Court reasoned, would "g[o] too far," for it would "kee[p] evidence from the jury that is reliable and relevant," and "may result, on occasion, in the guilty going free."

Instead of mandating a *per se* exclusionary rule, the Court held that the Due Process Clause requires courts to assess, on a case-by-case basis, whether improper police conduct created a "substantial likelihood of misidentification." "[R]eliability [of the eyewitness identification] is the linchpin" of that evaluation, the Court stated in *Brathwaite*. Where the "indicators of [a witness'] ability to make an accurate identification" are "outweighed by the corrupting effect" of law enforcement suggestion, the identification should be suppressed. Otherwise, the evidence (if admissible in all other respects) should be submitted to the jury.

Applying this "totality of the circumstances" approach, the Court held in *Biggers* that law enforcement's use of an unnecessarily suggestive showup did not require suppression of the victim's identification of her assailant. Notwithstanding the improper procedure, the victim's identification was reliable: She saw her assailant for a considerable period of time under adequate light, provided police with a detailed description of her attacker long before the showup, and had "no doubt" that the defendant was the person she had seen. Similarly, the Court concluded in *Brathwaite* that police use of an unnecessarily suggestive photo array did not require exclusion of the resulting identification. The witness, an undercover police officer, viewed the defendant in good light for several minutes, provided a thorough description of the suspect, and was certain of his identification. Hence, the "indicators of [the witness'] ability to make an accurate identification [were] hardly outweighed by the corrupting effect of the challenged identification."

B

Perry concedes that, in contrast to every case in the *Stovall* line, law enforcement officials did not arrange the suggestive circumstances surrounding Blandon's identification. He contends, however, that it was mere happenstance that each of the *Stovall* cases involved improper police action. The rationale underlying our decisions, Perry asserts, supports a rule requiring trial judges to prescreen eyewitness evidence for reliability any time an identification is made under suggestive circumstances. We disagree.

Perry's argument depends, in large part, on the Court's statement in *Brathwaite* that "reliability is the linchpin in determining the admissibility of identification testimony." If reliability is the linchpin of admissibility under the Due Process Clause, Perry maintains, it should make no difference whether law enforcement was responsible for creating the suggestive circumstances that marred the identification.

Perry has removed our statement in *Brathwaite* from its mooring, and thereby attributes to the statement a meaning a fair reading of our opinion does not bear. * * * *Brathwaite* Court's reference to reliability appears in a portion of the opinion concerning the appropriate remedy *when the police use an unnecessarily suggestive identification procedure*. * * * The due process check for reliability, *Brathwaite* made plain, comes into play only after the defendant establishes improper police conduct. The very purpose of the check, the Court noted, was to avoid depriving the jury of identification evidence that is reliable, *notwithstanding* improper police conduct.

Perry's contention that improper police action was not essential to the reliability check *Brathwaite* required is echoed by the dissent. Both ignore a key premise of the *Brathwaite* decision: A primary aim of excluding identification evidence obtained under unnecessarily suggestive circumstances, the Court said, is to deter law enforcement use of improper lineups, showups, and photo arrays in the first place. Alerted to the prospect that identification evidence improperly obtained may be excluded, the Court reasoned, police officers will "guard against unnecessarily suggestive procedures." This deterrence rationale is inapposite in cases, like Perry's, in which the police engaged in no improper conduct. * * *

Perry and the dissent place significant weight on *United States* v. *Wade*, [*supra*], describing it as a decision not anchored to improper police conduct. In fact, the risk of police rigging was the very danger to which the Court responded in *Wade* when it recognized a defendant's right to counsel at postindictment, police-organized identification procedures. "[T]he confrontation *compelled by the State* between the accused and the victim or witnesses," the Court began, "is peculiarly riddled with innumerable dangers and variable factors which might seriously, even crucially, derogate from a fair trial." "A major factor contributing to the high incidence of miscarriage of justice from mistaken identification," the Court continued, "has been the degree of suggestion inherent in the manner in which *the prosecution* presents the suspect to witnesses for pretrial identification." To illustrate the improper suggestion it was concerned about, the Court pointed to police-designed lineups where "all in the lineup but the suspect were known to the identifying witness, * * * the other participants in [the] lineup were grossly dissimilar in appearance to the suspect, * * * only the suspect was required to wear distinctive clothing which the culprit allegedly wore, * * * the witness is told by the police that they have caught the culprit after which the defendant is brought before the witness alone or is viewed in jail, * * * the suspect is pointed out before or during a lineup, * * * the participants in the lineup are asked to try on an article of clothing which fits only the suspect." Beyond genuine debate, then, prevention of unfair police practices prompted the Court to extend a defendant's right to counsel to cover postindictment lineups and showups.

Perry's argument, reiterated by the dissent, thus lacks support in the case law he cites. Moreover, his position would open the door to judicial preview, under the banner of due process, of most, if not all, eyewitness identifications. External suggestion is hardly the only factor that casts doubt on the trustworthiness of an eyewitness' testimony. As one of Perry's *amici* points out, many other factors bear on "the likelihood of misidentification"—for example, the passage of time between exposure to and identification of the defendant, whether the witness was under stress when he first encountered the suspect, how much time the witness had to observe the suspect, how far the witness was from the suspect, whether the suspect carried a weapon, and the race of the suspect and the witness. There is no reason why an identification made by an eyewitness with poor vision, for example, or one who harbors a grudge against the defendant, should be regarded as inherently more reliable, less of a "threat to the fairness of trial," than the identification Blandon made in this case. To embrace Perry's view would thus entail a vast enlargement of the reach of due process as a constraint on the admission of evidence.

Perry maintains that the Court can limit the due process check he proposes to identifications made under "suggestive circumstances." Even if we could rationally distinguish suggestiveness from other factors bearing on the reliability of eyewitness evidence, Perry's limitation would still involve trial courts, routinely, in preliminary examinations. Most eyewitness identifications involve some element of suggestion. Indeed, all in-court identifications do. Out-of-court identifications volunteered by witnesses are also likely to involve suggestive circumstances. For example, suppose a witness identifies the defendant to police officers after seeing a photograph of the defendant in the press captioned "theft suspect," or hearing a radio report implicating the defendant in the crime. Or suppose the witness knew that the defendant ran with the wrong crowd and saw him on the day and in the vicinity of the crime. Any of these circumstances might have "suggested" to the witness that the defendant was the person the witness observed committing the crime.

C

In urging a broadly applicable due process check on eyewitness identifications, Perry maintains that eyewitness identifications are a uniquely unreliable form of evidence. See Brief for Petitioner 17–22 (citing studies showing that eyewitness misidentifications are the leading cause of wrongful convictions); Brief for American Psychological Association as *Amicus Curiae* 14–17 (describing research indicating that as many as one in three eyewitness identifications is inaccurate). We do not doubt either the importance or the fallibility of eyewitness identifications. Indeed, in recognizing that defendants have a constitutional right to counsel at postindictment police lineups, we observed [in *Wade*] that "the annals of criminal law are rife with instances of mistaken identification."

We have concluded in other contexts, however, that the potential unreliability of a type of evidence does not alone render its introduction at the defendant's trial fundamentally unfair. We reach a similar conclusion here: The fallibility of eyewitness evidence does not, without the taint of improper state conduct, warrant a due process rule requiring a trial court to screen such evidence for reliability before allowing the jury to assess its creditworthiness.

Our unwillingness to enlarge the domain of due process as Perry and the dissent urge rests, in large part, on our recognition that the jury, not the judge, traditionally determines the reliability of evidence. We also take account of other safeguards built into our adversary system that caution juries against placing undue weight on eyewitness testimony of questionable reliability. Another is the defendant's right to the effective assistance of an attorney, who can expose the flaws in the eyewitness' testimony during cross-examination and focus the jury's attention on the fallibility of such testimony during opening and closing arguments. Eyewitness-specific jury instructions, which many federal and state courts have adopted, likewise warn the jury to take care in appraising identification evidence. The constitutional requirement that the government prove the defendant's guilt beyond a reasonable doubt also impedes convictions based on dubious identification evidence.

State and federal rules of evidence, moreover, permit trial judges to exclude relevant evidence if its probative value is substantially outweighed by its prejudicial impact or potential for misleading the jury. In appropriate cases, some States also permit defendants to present expert testimony on the hazards of eyewitness identification evidence. * * *

Given the safeguards generally applicable in criminal trials, protections availed of by the defense in Perry's case, we hold that the introduction of Blandon's eyewitness testimony, without a preliminary judicial assessment of its reliability, did not render Perry's trial fundamentally unfair.

* * *

For the foregoing reasons, * * * we hold that the Due Process Clause does not require a preliminary judicial inquiry into the reliability of an eyewitness identification when the identification was not procured under unnecessarily suggestive circumstances arranged by law enforcement. Accordingly, the judgment of the New Hampshire Supreme Court is

Affirmed.

[*The concurring opinion of* JUSTICE THOMAS *is omitted.*]

JUSTICE SOTOMAYOR, dissenting.

This Court has long recognized that eyewitness identifications' unique confluence of features—their unreliability, susceptibility to suggestion, powerful impact on the jury, and resistance to the ordinary tests of the adversarial process—can undermine the fairness of a trial. Our cases thus establish a clear rule: The admission at trial of out-of-court eyewitness identifications derived from impermissibly suggestive circumstances that pose a very substantial likelihood of misidentification violates due process. The Court today announces that that rule does not even "com[e] into play" unless the suggestive circumstances are improperly "police-arranged."

Our due process concern, however, arises not from the act of suggestion, but rather from the corrosive effects of suggestion on the reliability of the resulting identification. By rendering protection contingent on improper police arrangement of the suggestive circumstances, the Court effectively grafts a *mens rea* inquiry onto our rule. The Court's holding enshrines a murky distinction—between suggestive confrontations intentionally orchestrated by the police and, as here, those inadvertently caused by police actions—that will sow confusion. It ignores our precedents' acute sensitivity to the hazards of intentional and unintentional suggestion alike and unmoors our rule from the very interest it protects, inviting arbitrary results. And it recasts the driving force of our decisions as an interest in police deterrence, rather than reliability. Because I see no warrant for declining to assess the circumstances of this case under our ordinary approach, I respectfully dissent.

I

The "driving force" behind *United States* v. *Wade*, *Gilbert* v. *California*, 388 U. S. 263 [, 87 S.Ct. 1951, 18 L.Ed.2d 1178] (1967), and *Stovall* v. *Denno*, was "the Court's concern with the problems of eyewitness identification"—specifically, "the concern that the jury not hear eyewitness testimony unless that evidence has aspects of reliability." We have pointed to the " 'formidable' " number of "miscarriage[s] of justice from mistaken identification" in the annals of criminal law. We have warned of the "vagaries" and " 'proverbially untrustworthy' " nature of eyewitness identifications. And we have singled out a "major factor contributing" to that proverbial unreliability: "the suggestibility inherent in the context of the pretrial identification."

Our precedents make no distinction between intentional and unintentional suggestion. To the contrary, they explicitly state that "[s]uggestion can be created intentionally or unintentionally in many subtle ways." Rather than equate suggestive conduct with misconduct, we specifically have disavowed the assumption that suggestive influences may only be "the result of police procedures intentionally designed to prejudice an accused." * * * The implication is that even police acting with the best of intentions can inadvertently signal " 'that's the man.' " * * *

More generally, our precedents focus not on the act of suggestion, but on suggestion's "corrupting effect" on reliability. Eyewitness evidence derived from suggestive circumstances, we have explained, is uniquely resistant to the ordinary tests of the adversary process. An eyewitness who has made an identification often becomes convinced of its accuracy. "*Regardless of how the initial misidentification comes about*, the witness thereafter is apt to retain in his memory the image of the photograph rather than of the person actually seen, reducing the trustworthiness of subsequent * * * courtroom identification." *Simmons v. United States* (emphasis added). Suggestion bolsters that confidence.

At trial, an eyewitness' artificially inflated confidence in an identification's accuracy complicates the jury's task of assessing witness credibility and reliability. It also impairs the defendant's ability to attack the eyewitness' credibility. That in turn jeopardizes the defendant's basic right to subject his accuser to meaningful cross-examination. The end result of suggestion, whether intentional or unintentional, is to fortify testimony bearing directly on guilt that juries find extremely convincing and are hesitant to discredit.

Consistent with our focus on reliability, we have declined to adopt a *per se* rule excluding all suggestive identifications. Instead, "reliability is the linchpin" in deciding admissibility. We have explained that a suggestive identification procedure "does not in itself intrude upon a constitutionally protected interest." "Suggestive confrontations are disapproved because they increase the likelihood of misidentification"—and "[i]t is the likelihood of misidentification which violates a defendant's right to due process."

To protect that evidentiary interest, we have applied a two-step inquiry: First, the defendant has the burden of showing that the eyewitness identification was derived through "impermissibly suggestive" means. Second, if the defendant meets that burden, courts consider whether the identification was reliable under the totality of the circumstances. That step entails considering the witness' opportunity to view the perpetrator, degree of attention, accuracy of description, level of certainty, and the time between the crime and pretrial confrontation, then weighing such factors against the "corrupting effect of the suggestive identification." Most identifications will be admissible. The standard of "fairness as required by the Due Process Clause," however, demands that a subset of the most unreliable identifications—those carrying a " 'very substantial likelihood of * * * misidentification' "—will be excluded.

II

A

The majority today creates a novel and significant limitation on our longstanding rule. * * * Absent "improper police arrangement," "improper police conduct," or "rigging," the majority holds, our two-step inquiry does not even "com[e] into play." I cannot agree.

* * * Those terms connote a degree of intentional orchestration or manipulation. * * * The majority thus appears to graft a *mens rea* requirement onto our existing rule. * * *

I note, however, that the majority leaves what is required by its arrangement-focused inquiry less than clear. In parts, the opinion suggests that the police must arrange an identification "procedure," regardless of whether they "inten[d] the arranged procedure to be suggestive." Elsewhere, it indicates that the police must arrange the "suggestive circumstances" that lead the witness to identify the accused. Still elsewhere it refers to "improper" police conduct, connoting bad faith. Does police "arrangement" relate to the procedure, the suggestiveness, or both? If it relates to the procedure, do suggestive preprocedure encounters no longer raise the same concerns? If the police need not "inten[d] the arranged procedure to be suggestive," what makes the police action "improper"? And does that mean that good-faith, unintentional police suggestiveness in a police-arranged lineup can be "impermissibly suggestive"? * * *

The arrangement-focused inquiry will sow needless confusion. If the police had called Perry and Blandon to the police station for interviews, and Blandon saw Perry being questioned, would that be sufficiently "improper police arrangement"? If Perry had voluntarily come to the police station, would that change the result? Today's opinion renders the applicability of our ordinary inquiry contingent on a murky line-drawing exercise. Whereas our two-step inquiry focuses on overall reliability—and could account for the spontaneity of the witness' identification and degree of police manipulation under the totality of the circumstances—today's opinion forecloses that assessment by establishing a new and inflexible step zero. * * *

C

The majority gives several additional reasons for why applying our due process rule beyond improperly police-arranged circumstances is unwarranted. In my view, none withstands close inspection.

First, the majority insists that our precedents "aim to deter police from rigging identification procedures," so our rule should be limited to applications that advance that "primary aim" and "key premise." That mischaracterizes our cases. We discussed deterrence in *Brathwaite* because Brathwaite challenged our two-step inquiry as *lacking* deterrence value. Brathwaite argued that deterrence demanded a *per se* rule excluding all suggestive identifications. He said that our rule, which probes the reliability of suggestive identifications under the totality of the circumstances, "cannot be expected to have a significant deterrent impact."

We rebutted Brathwaite's criticism in language the majority now wrenches from context: Upon summarizing Brathwaite's argument, we acknowledged "several interests to be considered." * * * First, we noted the "driving force" behind *Wade* and its companion cases—"the concern that the jury not hear eyewitness testimony unless that evidence has aspects of reliability" * * *. We noted a "second factor"—deterrence—conceding that the *per se* rule had "more significant deterrent effect," but noting that our rule "also has an influence on police behavior." Finally, we noted a "third factor"—"the effect on the administration of justice"—describing the *per se* rule as having serious drawbacks on this front. That was no list of "primary aim[s]." Nor was it a ringing endorsement of the primacy of deterrence. We simply underscored, in responding to Brathwaite, that our rule was not without deterrence benefits. To the contrary, we clarified that deterrence was a subsidiary concern to reliability, the "driving force" of our doctrine. It is a stretch to claim that our rule cannot apply wherever "[t]his deterrence rationale is inapposite." * * *

[Second,] the majority emphasizes that we should rely on the jury to determine the reliability of evidence. But our cases are rooted in the assumption that eyewitness identifications upend the ordinary expectation that it is "the province of the jury to weigh the credibility of competing witnesses." As noted, jurors find eyewitness evidence unusually powerful and their ability to assess credibility is hindered by a witness' false confidence in the accuracy of his or her identification. That disability in no way depends on the intent behind the suggestive circumstances. * * *

[Third,] the majority suggests that applying our rule beyond police-arranged suggestive circumstances would entail a heavy practical burden, requiring courts to engage in "preliminary judicial inquiry" into "most, if not all, eyewitness identifications." But that is inaccurate. The burden of showing "impermissibly suggestive" circumstances is the defendant's, so the objection falls to the defendant to raise. And as is implicit in the majority's reassurance that Perry may resort to the rules of evidence in lieu of our due process precedents, trial courts will be entertaining defendants' objections, pretrial or at trial, to unreliable eyewitness evidence in any event. The relevant question, then, is what the standard of admissibility governing such objections should be. I see no reason to water down the standard for an equally suggestive and unreliable identification simply because the suggestive confrontation was unplanned.

It bears reminding, moreover, that we set a high bar for suppression. The vast majority of eyewitnesses proceed to testify before a jury. * * *

Finally, the majority questions how to "rationally distinguish suggestiveness from other factors bearing on the reliability of eyewitness evidence," such as "poor vision" or a prior "grudge," and more broadly, how to distinguish eyewitness evidence from other kinds of arguably unreliable evidence. Our precedents, however, did just that. We emphasized the " 'formidable number of instances in the records of English and American trials' " of "miscarriage[s] of justice from mistaken identification." We then observed that " 'the influence of improper suggestion upon identifying witnesses probably accounts for more miscarriages of justice than any other single factor.' " Moreover, the majority points to no other type of evidence that shares the rare confluence of characteristics that makes eyewitness evidence a unique threat to the fairness of trial. * * *

It would be one thing if the passage of time had cast doubt on the empirical premises of our precedents. But just the opposite has happened. A vast body of scientific literature has reinforced every concern our precedents articulated nearly a half-century ago, though it merits barely a parenthetical mention in the majority opinion. Over the past three decades, more than two thousand studies related to eyewitness identification have been published. One state supreme court recently appointed a special master to conduct an exhaustive survey of the current state of the scientific evidence and concluded that "[t]he research * * * is not only extensive," but "it represents the 'gold standard in terms of the applicability of social science research to law.' " *State* v. *Henderson,* 208 N. J. 208, 283, 27 A. 3d 872, 916 (2011). "Experimental methods and findings have been tested and retested, subjected to scientific scrutiny through peer-reviewed journals, evaluated through the lens of meta-analyses, and replicated at times in real-world settings." *Ibid.;* see also Schmechel, O'Toole, Easterly, & Loftus, Beyond the Ken? Testing Jurors' Understanding of Eyewitness Reliability Evidence, 46 Jurimetrics 177, 180 (2006) (noting "nearly unanimous consensus among researchers about the [eyewitness reliability] field's core findings").

The empirical evidence demonstrates that eyewitness misidentification is " 'the single greatest cause of wrongful convictions in this country.' " Researchers have found that a staggering 76% of the first 250 convictions overturned due to DNA evidence since 1989 involved eyewitness misidentification. Study after study demonstrates that eyewitness recollections are highly susceptible to distortion by postevent information or social cues; that jurors routinely overestimate the accuracy of eyewitness identifications; that jurors place the greatest weight on eyewitness confidence in assessing identifications even though confidence is a poor gauge of accuracy; and that suggestiveness can stem from sources beyond police-orchestrated procedures. The majority today nevertheless adopts an artificially narrow conception of the dangers of suggestive identifications at a time when our concerns should have deepened.

III

There are many reasons why Perry's particular situation might not violate due process. The trial court found that the circumstances surrounding Blandon's identification did not rise to an impermissibly suggestive level. It is not at all clear, moreover, that there was a very substantial likelihood of misidentification, given Blandon's lack of equivocation on the scene, the short time between crime and confrontation, and the "fairly well lit" parking lot. The New Hampshire Supreme Court, however, never made findings on either point and, under the majority's decision today, never will. * * *

Because the New Hampshire Supreme Court truncated its inquiry at the threshold, I would vacate the judgment and remand for a proper analysis. I respectfully dissent.

NOTES AND QUESTIONS

1. Answer these questions posed by Sotomayor in her dissent: "If the police had called Perry and Blandon to the police station for interviews, and Blandon saw Perry being questioned, would that be sufficiently 'improper police arrangement'? If Perry had voluntarily come to the police station, would that change the result?"

2. Suppose we are privileged to peek into the Supreme Court chambers when the justices are discussing *Perry*. Imagine Justice Sotomayor asking Justice Ginsburg,

"What is the harm in giving defendants a chance to demonstrate to a judge that the identification might be unreliable even if the police are not guilty of misconduct?" How do you imagine Ginsburg might respond? Is it fair to say that Justice Ginsburg's majority opinion is more consistent with the narrow holdings in all the eyewitness due process cases and Justice Sotomayor's dissent is more true to the rationale for the due process rule and the social science we discussed earlier?

3. *Problem.* During a murder investigation, the police show witness *R* photographs of six persons. *R* identifies *N* as the murderer, resulting in *N*'s arrest. Months later, as *N*'s trial approaches, the prosecutor meets with *R* to go over her trial testimony. *S*, who had not come forward as a witness, attends the meeting "to provide emotional support for her friend." During the meeting, the prosecutor hands *R* the photo of *N* she had previously identified as the murderer. *S* sees the photo and exclaims, "Oh my God, that's him. That's who I ran up to after the shooting." Would it violate due process to permit evidence at trial of *S*'s identification in the prosecutor's office? See State v. Nolan, 807 N.W.2d 520 (Neb. 2012).

4. For an argument that the Warren Court failed to come to grips with the problem of unreliable eyewitness identifications, in part because of the apparent ease of the right-to-counsel solution, see George C. Thomas III, *The Criminal Procedure Road Not Taken: Due Process and the Protection of Innocence*, 3 Ohio St. J. Crim. L. 169 (2005).

5. *A final thought.* As the *Perry* majority notes, *Neil v. Biggers* held that the identification was reliable despite an "improper procedure" because the rape victim "saw her assailant for a considerable period of time under adequate light, provided police with a detailed description of her attacker long before the showup, and had 'no doubt' that the defendant was the person she had seen."

However, Jennifer Thompson, a rape victim in 1984, was equally sure that she could identify the man who raped her. She had made a conscious decision to study "every single detail on the rapist's face." She gave police a detailed description. She picked a man out of a photo array and later the same man out of a lineup. She said, "I was sure. I knew it." When told that another man had claimed to have raped her, she looked at him and said she had never seen him before and had "no idea who he is." The other man, the one she identified twice, served 11 years in prison before he was exonerated by DNA. The man Thompson had never seen before was the man who had raped her.

> The man I was so sure I had never seen in my life was the man who was inches from my throat, who raped me, who hurt me, who took my spirit away, who robbed me of my soul. And the man I had identified so emphatically on so many occasions was absolutely innocent.

Jennifer Thompson, *I Was Certain But I Was Wrong*, The New York Times, June 18, 2000.

B. IS THE SYSTEM CONTINUING TO FAIL?

1. Overwhelmed Defense Counsel

We saw in Chapter 9 the stresses on indigent defense—far too many cases per defender, inadequate resources for experts and other needed aids for the defense, and marginal quality of some defenders. As a reminder of how indigent defense can become a nightmare, consider the following excerpt.

GERALD B. LEFCOURT—RESPONSIBILITIES OF A CRIMINAL DEFENSE ATTORNEY

30 Loyola of Los Angeles Law Review 59 (1996), 59–63.

Our perspective as criminal defense lawyers is often based on a pivotal experience. Mine was as a law school honors program participant, sent to work with Legal Aid Society lawyers—New York City's public defenders. I was assigned to help a young lawyer handling arraignments. In New York City that meant a daily crush of cases. His job was to seek bail as each defendant entered the system. In disgusting pens holding as many as forty prisoners, I would interview clients. I was the first person many prisoners saw after they had spent up to four days waiting to appear before the court.

The holding pens were filled with huddling defendants, most of whom were standing because there was only one bench. Virtually the entire population of the pens was nonwhite and poor, without the resources or stable families to allow them bail. Most were in shock or panic, yelling questions and begging for help. "What am I charged with?" "When will I ever get out?" "Can you call my mother?" "What if I didn't do it; will they still keep me?" "Will you call my boss because if I don't show up I'll lose my job?"

I came to see that most of them were not really represented at all. Not only would they not make bail, but most would ultimately plead guilty to something, anything, just to move out of the system. I realized that with a lawyer who had a few days to spend with the client instead of a few minutes, a proper fight could be waged, both to get the defendant out on bail and ultimately, to get a favorable disposition. In many cases defendants would not have ended up with criminal records, a millstone that serves to keep the underclasses as underclasses.

I realized that the Legal Aid attorneys, like their counterparts across the country, were not properly trained, had no resources, and were, frankly, overwhelmed. The number of defendants was so great that there was no time for the niceties of an interview long enough to establish any relationship, much less one of trust.

So, there were two systems operating, one for the wealthy who had the resources to seek vindication of their rights and one for the rest of society, left haphazardly to lawyers who could ensure entirely less predictable results.

It was obvious that a system promising the right to counsel was a farce.

NOTES AND QUESTIONS

1. Lefcourt's anecdotal experience is borne out by the data. Researchers McConville and Mirsky concluded in 1990 that in large cities "criminal courts are places of mass processing," which "arraign defendants twenty-four hours a day, seven days a week." On days set for docketing cases, "lower courts commonly docket 100 or more cases a day, while superior courts often docket 60 felony indictments a day. Court business is conducted in a swirl of activity as judges seek to 'move' crowded calendars." Michael McConville Chester L. Mirsky, *Understanding Defense of the Poor in State Courts*, 10 Studies in Law, Politics, and Society 217, 217 (1990).

Any thoughts about why public defense in large cities has become mass processing?

2. Do you think Justice Sutherland, the author of the majority opinion in *Powell v. Alabama,* Chapter 1, would consider the system described by Lefcourt and in Note 1 to constitute the "Assistance of Counsel"? Does this description portend "the guiding hand of counsel at every step in the proceedings"? How is the representation described here better or worse than the representation provided by Mr. Roddy and the local bar in *Powell*?

3. *Is indigent defense really that bad?* In 2009, the National Right to Counsel Committee issued a report entitled Justice Denied: America's Continuing Neglect of our Constitutional Right to Counsel. The report details systemic and endemic failures of indigent defense in this country. It found "overwhelming" evidence that, in most of the country, "quality defense work is simply impossible because of inadequate funding, excessive caseloads, a lack of genuine independence, and insufficient availability of other essential resources."

The report provides twenty-two recommendations for improvement and can be found at https://constitutionproject.org/wp-content/uploads/2012/10/139.pdf. See also Mary Sue Backus & Paul Marcus, *The Right to Counsel in Criminal Cases, A National Crisis*, 57 Hastings L. J. 1031 (2006).

The committee included prosecutors, judges, defense lawyers, and academics. The honorary co-chairs were Walter Mondale, former Democratic candidate for president, and William Sessions, former director of the FBI.

4. *The "best Manner of Trial in the World"?* Matthew Hale, writing in the seventeenth century, called the English trial system the best in the world. Matthew Hale, The History of the Common Law of England 133 (3d ed. 1739) (originally published circa 1686). What we have seen so far in this chapter can certainly lead to doubts about the truth of that claim today. It also raises the question of how much progress we have made in the last century. The book began with cases from the Deep South where the Court was forced to intervene to prevent rank injustices. This chapter demonstrates injustices today that are more subtle, but just as real, and the Supreme Court does not get involved. The Court's unwillingness to take modern cases of injustice stems from the subtlety of the injustices, from the Court's assumption that the right procedure is the best way to protect against wrongful convictions, and from the sheer volume of criminal cases. In effect, the Court has given defendants what at least appears to be a fair procedure without any oversight as to the substantive outcomes. Given the volume of criminal cases, perhaps a procedure that appears fair is the best the Court can do. One might ask, however, whether the turmoil of the mid-twentieth century—when the Court imposed almost all of the Bill of Rights procedure guarantees on the states—accomplished as much as the Court hoped.

2. Unjust Convictions

Until now, the chapter has concentrated on cases involving factually innocent defendants. But protecting innocent defendants is only one goal of the system. There is also the problem of unjust convictions of defendants who might be factually guilty but are treated unfairly. Indeed, while trying to help innocent defendants is surely uncontroversial, the innocence movement has generated criticism for "elevating factual innocence" over other defenses. This could lead jurors to think "that anything short of factual innocence is simply not good enough to justify an acquittal." Margaret Raymond, *The Problem with Innocence*, 49 Clev. St. L. Rev. 449, 457 (2001). Another criticism is that a focus on innocence is a distraction that "may obscure more pervasive flaws in the criminal justice system and have a series of untoward effects on (1) the trial process, (2) legislative reform, and (3) other systemic critiques." Daniel S. Medwed, *Innocentrism*, 2008 U. Ill. L. Rev. 1549, 1555 (articulating, but not embracing, that critique).

Thus, it is perhaps equally important to assess the extent to which the system provides a fair procedure to decide guilt or innocence, irrespective of the defendant's factual innocence. Much of the book has raised, directly or indirectly, questions about fair procedures. For example, one can question the quality of defense representation in a public defense system that, in many parts of the country, is literally overwhelmed with cases. Recall Gerald Lefcourt's reaction to the huddling defendants he encountered in the holding pens in New York City: "I came to see that most of them were not really represented at all." An exhaustive study of New York County in the mid-1980s revealed that private lawyers appointed to represent indigent defendants did not interview their clients in 82% of the non-homicide cases. Even in homicide cases, the lawyer interviewed the client only 26% of the time. Michael McConville Chester Mirsky, *Criminal Defense of the Poor in New York City*, 15 N.Y.U. L. Social Change 581, 758–62 (1986–87).

The Reporters for the National Committee on the Right to Counsel concluded in 2006 that a national crisis exists in indigent defense. Mary Sue Backus Paul Marcus, *The Right to Counsel in Criminal Cases, A National Crisis*, 57 Hastings L. J. 1031, 1045–46 (2006). Even if counsel has sufficient time and provides an adequate defense, the next question is how well the American criminal justice system protects against unjust convictions. Here, we use the term "unjust convictions" to include more than convictions of innocent defendants. It also includes convictions that result from the prosecution taking an unfair advantage of a defendant. While we recognize that "unfair advantage" is a pliable concept, at its core it manifests an important truth. As Stephen B. Bright has put it:

> The Bill of Rights is not a collection of technicalities. It is this nation's most fundamental guarantees of fairness and justice. For 200 years we have revered these rights. This nation is respected and emulated throughout the world because we provide these safeguards of liberty and justice to even the least among us, even those who have offended us most grievously.

Stephen B. Bright, *Death By Lottery—Procedural Bar of Constitutional Claims in Capital Cases Due to Inadequate Representation of Indigent Defendants*, 92 W. Va. L. Rev. 679, 694 (1990).

Here, too, the American system seems to fall short. "Many features of the criminal justice system in the United States are often severely criticized, and fairly so." Backus & Marcus, at 1037. For example, a defendant who did not get access to favorable evidence in the prosecutor's file, to which he was entitled, and who was convicted because he lacked that evidence was also unjustly convicted, again whether or not he was factually guilty.

One procedural defect, according to Professor Shima Baradaran, is the failure of courts to give full effect to the presumption of innocence. See Shima Baradaran, *Restoring the Presumption of Innocence*, 72 Ohio St. L.J. 723 (2011). The United States

Supreme Court has essentially restricted the presumption of innocence to the trial context, where it requires the State to carry the burden of proving the defendant guilty beyond a reasonable doubt. But Professor Baradaran argues that a critically important aspect of the presumption of innocence is in guaranteeing bail to all defendants except those who are unlikely to appear for trial:

> * * * In our modern system of U.S. criminal justice [unlike in Blackstone's day], we proclaim that all are innocent until proven guilty at trial but we allow judges to predict which ones are guilty long before trial. We have adopted practices allowing predictions of guilt and weighing of evidence against defendants before trial since defendants' rights have lacked steady constitutional rooting. * * *
>
> The practical results of the presumption's diminution are apparent and troubling. The number of defendants held pretrial has steadily increased such that the majority of people in our nation's jails have not been convicted of any crime. In the last fourteen years, the United States has gone from releasing 62% of defendants to only 40%, without much complaint, discussion, or even acknowledgement by legal scholars.

Id. at 724–25, 775 (2011). Unsurprisingly, studies show that defendants who are denied bail are less likely to obtain a favorable outcome, at least in part because they are less likely to offer assistance in preparing a defense. Thus, if a defendant was denied bail unjustly, and was convicted because of that denial, it would be fair to conclude that he was unjustly convicted even if he was factually guilty.

And there are other choke points that produce unjust convictions. There is much evidence that some over-zealous prosecutors are parsimonious in complying with the duty to disclose evidence that might help the defense. Jailhouse informants are notorious for telling whatever story will get them a benefit from the State. Attention has recently been given to what some call "junk science"—the use of highly-questionable prosecution experts (as in Ray Krone's case) to "prove" guilt. Fred Zain, when a serologist with the West Virginia Division of Public Safety, apparently testified falsely about scientific results in as many as 182 cases. All of these problems, and more, are discussed in Thomas, Supreme Court on Trial, supra, at 6–44. It is difficult to avoid a conclusion reached by George Thomas and Randy Jonakait, in separate works, that unjust convictions are all too often the result of failures in the American adversarial system. Thomas, at 39; Randolph Jonakait, The American Jury System, 282 (2003).

An indictment of the modern American criminal justice system would thus include failures along the entire temporal dimension of the process—failures in evidence gathering, failures of the defense system, bail denial, over-zealous prosecutors, and failures in the trial process itself. When one adds up the ways American justice seems to fail defendants, one wonders what happened to the criminal trial process that Matthew Hale claimed to be the best in the world.

NOTES AND QUESTIONS

1. You are on a commission to reduce the incidence of unjust convictions in your state. Part of the mandate is that only limited funds are available to spend on improvements to the system. Thus, you cannot recommend large sums be spent to improve indigent defense. What changes would you recommend, knowing that only modest sums of money are available?

2. To keep you from getting too discouraged about the American criminal justice system, please watch "Murder on a Sunday Morning," a documentary about two public defenders in Florida who work tirelessly on behalf of a young black man unjustly tried for murder. We will not spoil the ending for you but if you are not moved by the last few minutes, well, your heart is harder than ours!

CHAPTER 10 SUMMARY

This chapter surveyed the many ways that the criminal justice system can misfire. We saw some of the most famous failures in Chapter 1—the torture that produced "confessions" in *Brown v. Mississippi* and the failure to provide counsel to young men charged with rape in *Powell v. Alabama.* The advent of DNA testing has now uncovered more than 2,000 cases where innocent defendants were convicted of crime and if we expand the category to defendants who are deprived of a fair trial, the number would be in the hundreds of thousands if not millions.

One of the most vexing problems facing the criminal justice system is the unreliability of eyewitness identifications. Many wrongful convictions result from an eyewitness picking an innocent person out of a lineup. But there are other, more subtle errors. Police officers want to be Sherlock Holmes. Once they put together a theory that makes sense, they tend to view all evidence in accord with that theory. Prosecutors fall into the same "tunnel vision" trap. Often, prosecutors who have somewhat exculpatory evidence will refuse to turn it over to the defense because the prosecutor believes him guilty. And defense lawyers can fail along two very different dimensions. First, the sheer volume of cases handled by indigent defenders make it literally impossible to provide an adequate defense in most cases. Second, even if defense lawyers had sufficient time to investigating possible defenses for innocent clients, defense lawyers, like prosecutors, often believe the defendant guilty.

No one knows how often the system misfires. But we do know much more today than we did even a few years ago about the causes of wrongful and unjust convictions. Whether our polity has the political will to remedy some of these causes is yet unknown.

Index